Anonymous

Eucharistic Worship in the English Church

Anonymous

Eucharistic Worship in the English Church

ISBN/EAN: 9783337033880

Printed in Europe, USA, Canada, Australia, Japan

Cover: Foto ©Lupo / pixelio.de

More available books at **www.hansebooks.com**

ON

EUCHARISTIC WORSHIP

IN THE

ENGLISH CHURCH.

BY

AN ENGLISH PRESBYTER.

London:
HAUGHTON AND CO., 10, PATERNOSTER ROW.
1876.

"Now, touching the adoration of the Sacrament, M. Harding is not able to show neither any commandment of Christ, nor any word or example of the Apostles or ancient Fathers, concerning the same. It is a thing very lately devised by Pope Honorius, about the year of our Lord 1226; afterward increased by the now solemn feast of *Corpus Christi* Day, by Pope Urbanus, anno 1264; and last of all confirmed for ever by multitudes of pardons in the Council of Vienna by Pope Clement V., anno 1316. The Church of Asia and Græcia never received it until this day. The matter is great, and cannot be attempted without great danger. To give the honour of God to a creature that is no God, it is manifest idolatry."—BP. JEWEL.

"Adorari ubique Deum, ac presertim in sacris mysteriis oportere dubium non est. Neque ullam esse Ecclesiam arbitror, in qua non adhibeatur solennis quædam ut gratiarum actio, ita etiam et interior et exterior adoratio quum hæc mysteria tremenda, quasi in cœlis potius quam in terris, celebrantur."—BEZA.

"In *adoratione Sacramenti*, ad limen ipsum turpiter impingit. *Sacramenti* ait, id est *Christi Domini in Sacramento, miro, sed vero modo præsentis.* Apage vero. Quis ei hoc dederit? *Sacramenti, id est, Christi in Sacramento.* Imo Christus ipse Sacramenti res, in, et cum Sacramento; extra, et sine Sacramento, ubiubi est, adorandus est. Rex autem Christum in Eucharistia vere *præsentem*, vere et *adorandum* statuit, rem scilicet Sacramenti; at non Sacramentum, *terrenam* scilicet *partem*, ut Irenæus: visibilem, ut Augustinus..... Nec *carnem manducamus, quin adoremus prius*, cum Augustino. Et Sacramentum tamen nulli adoramus..... Fiat, quod fieri voluit Christus cum dixit, *Hoc facite;* nihil reliqui fiet, quod monstret Sacerdos, quod adoret populus, de pyxide."—BP. ANDREWES.

"I may ask any ingenuous man whether he ever heard (I do not say our Church, but) any approved Doctor therein, teach, that we do, or ought to kneel before the Sacrament; that *by it*, or *in it*, we may personally worship Christ, as if He were *really present*." (Bp. Morton's Defence of the Ceremonies, p. 285, London, 1619: "Published by Authority.")

INTRODUCTION.

In sending forth this, the last of this series of papers on the Doctrine of the English Church, I have been influenced not so much by the solicitation of others, as by my own strong conviction that, notwithstanding the recent publication of valuable works on kindred subjects (to which I owe many obligations), some such manual is one of the great wants of our Church at this time.

Those among us who know enough of what is passing in the minds of the younger generation of educated and serious-minded Englishmen to enter somewhat into their peculiar difficulties and trials, can hardly be altogether without a feeling of sympathy with those among them who speak sadly of the want of anything like fixedness and certainty which seems to characterise so much of the religious teaching of our times.

They tell us that they have been brought to witness a review of the so-called Protestantism of our day, which, with its tendencies to various forms of neologian development—unlike the Protestantism of our fathers—is too often willing to break with the past and strike new lights for the future; and they have turned away, they say, in disgust from the miserable march-past of a mere battalion of negations—in undisciplined disorder, yielding little obedience to the hesitating command of that which is merely subjective in religion, and recognising little of authority in the Divine and Scriptural dogmas of our most holy faith—the unchanging faith once for all delivered unto the saints.

There are many such now asking for help in inward conflicts; seeking guidance in the terrible perplexities which surround them, as they weary in the attempt to work out for themselves difficult problems of religion and faith.

To such minds it is no marvel that there is found a speciousness in the claims of Romish teaching: an attractiveness in the dogmas propounded by Romanisers as Catholic truth, which is apt to have a very blinding influence on the examination of controverted questions.

We may be very thankful to be assured that such minds, if they seek the light of God's Spirit in the study of His word, will assuredly be brought to rest in the truth, and to know how that truth is able to commend itself to every man's conscience in the sight of God.

Yet some effort ought assuredly to be made to set before them the true merits of the controversy as between what is truly Scriptural and primitive and catholic on the one side, and what belongs to the addition of human superstition and corruption on the other; and that not with any such *animus* as would seem to regard everyone who needs to be guided out of mists and clouds, and doubts and difficulties, as either something less than human in intelligence, or else something more than human in depravity.

Such an effort this little manual professes to be in one particular branch, and I venture to think the most important branch, of the controversy.

I must add, that I do not pretend to have entered on the inquiry as to the history of Eucharistic worship with anything like an unprejudiced mind.

Indeed, I cannot understand how it is possible for anyone to do this who has been a student of God's word, and has learned with deep and ever-deepening conviction to prize as a whole the doctrinal principles of the English Reformation.

Nevertheless, I trust I have not been so led away by prejudice as wilfully to misrepresent any matter of testimony, or to distort and disguise facts which bear on the subject. And, sensible as I am that the work may be marred by my own incompetence, and not improbably by errors which I shall be thankful to have corrected, no acknowledgment of my own deficiencies must be understood as implying anything like a secret misgiving of the ground I have undertaken to maintain.

I believe that in answer to prayer there has been, and there will yet be, a bringing back of some who have been led astray by the fascinations of novel teaching.

And I pray earnestly that God may graciously shine into the hearts of all who would know His truth, and scatter all mists of darkness which hinder the enjoyment of the true light of the knowledge of the glory of God in the face of Jesus Christ.

N. DIMOCK.

Wymynswold Vicarage,
    Near Canterbury.

SYNOPSIS OF CONTENTS.

THE Vision of Juliana (p. 1 *sqq.*),

Suggesting for consideration three Propositions:—

(1) The introduction of the festival of Corpus Christi did make such a real marked addition to the religion of Western Christendom, as might not unsuitably be symbolised by the passing away of the moon's eclipse. (Pp. 6—10.)

(2) This addition was but a marked and prominent act in a course of progress by which accretions had previously been forming around the religion of earlier times, in relation to the Eucharist. (Pp. 10—13.)

(3) This marked and crowning addition was fitting and appropriate to the previous accretions; so that, if they rested on a true doctrine of the Eucharistic Presence, this did but complete the glory of the Christian Church, and of the religion of Christ. (Pp. 13—15.)

Hence the need of distinguishing the doctrine of the Eucharistic Presence—

Which will not warrant the previous accretions (pp. 14—17), from that which does warrant and demand such a *cultus* (pp. 17—19), and which implies a marvel more wonderful than the Incarnation (pp. 19—28);

And the importance of marking clearly (p. 28 *sqq.*) what is consistent with—

(1) The hypothesis on the one side (pp. 31—33);
(2) That on the other (pp. 33—39).

The side taken by the Church of England. (Pp. 39—44.)

Hasty assumptions that such was not the side of primitive Christianity (pp. 44—57) tested by the following questions :—

(1) If this doctrine of the Real Objective Presence were a part of the faith of the early Church, how comes it to pass that among the accounts of early heresies and their refutations we never meet with a statement of the rejection of this doctrine marked among the heresies; and never find arguments for establishing it among their refutations? (P. 58 *sqq*.)

I. For the doctrine could not have been held by
   a. The Docetæ (p. 58 *sqq*.).
   b. The Eutychians (p. 63 *sqq*.).
   c. Those who denied our Lord's Divinity.

II. And it is really irreconcilable (p. 64) with the language of
   a. Tertullian (pp. 66, 67, 72, 73, 92—96).
   b. Augustine (pp. 68, 69, 72, 73, 76—89).
   c. Procopius (pp. 69, 70, 91, 92).
   d. Ephrem Syrus (pp. 70, 90, 91).
   e. Theodoret (pp. 71, 72, 73, 102—105).
   f. Origen (pp. 96—102).
   g. Chrysostom (pp. 105—108).
   h. The "Opus Imperfectum in Matt." (pp. 108—112).
   i. Jerome (pp. 113—117).
   j. Facundus (pp. 117—122).
   k. Elfric (pp. 122—129).
   l. The Gloss on Gratian (p. 129).
   m. Erigena (pp. 130—132).

(2) How is it that no ancient creed ever expressed this doctrine? (Pp. 133—143).

No satisfactory account can be given for this (pp. 138—141);
Nor for the silence of Holy Scripture (pp. 141—143).

(3) How is it that we have Patristic teaching concerning our Lord's human nature which is irreconcilable with this doctrine? (p. 143 *sqq*.) as, *e.g.*, in

   a. Augustine (pp. 143—145).
   b. Fulgentius (p. 145).
   c. Vigilius Taps. (pp. 145—146).

d. Didymus Alex. (p. 147).
e. Gregory Nys. (pp. 147– 148).

And as clearly stated by

a. Bishop Morton (p. 148).
b. Richard Hooker (pp. 149—153).

(4) How comes it to pass that early Christian Apologists are found ridiculing heathen idolatry in language which might readily have turned against such worship in Christian Churches? (P. 153 *sqq.*)

(5) Did the Corinthian Christians in St. Paul's days believe the doctrine of the Real Objective Presence? (P. 163 *sqq.*)

(6) Did the Apostles understand the words of Institution as teaching the Real Objective Presence? (P. 166 *sqq.*)

(7) For what purpose are we to believe this Presence in the Elements vouchsafed? (p. 170 *sqq.*)

CONCLUSION.—The holding of the Real Objective Presence, rather than its rejection, involves a low view (p. 180 *sqq.*) of Christ's Real Presence (p. 191 *sqq.*) and of Christianity (p. 197 *sqq.*); and cannot be cleared from the charge of idolatry (p. 199 *sqq.*).

APPENDIX.

NOTE A.—On the Testimony of the Fathers on the subject of Eucharistic Worship. (Pp. 203—224.)

NOTE B.—On the Testimony of the Liturgies on the subject of Eucharistic Worship. (Pp. 225—238.)

NOTE C.—On Elevation, and its Relation to Eucharistic Worship. (Pp. 239—253.)

NOTE D.—On Interpretative Dicta of the Fathers. (Pp. 253—266.)

Note E.—On the Patristic Use of the Terms *Figure*, *Type*, and the like, as applied to the Eucharist. (Pp. 266—302.)

Note F.—On the Res Sacramenti of the Eucharist, as in the condition of Death. (Pp. 303—316.)

Note G.—On the Sayings of the Fathers concerning the Sacramental Body of Christ, and concerning His Church and His Poor. (Pp. 317—329.)

Note H.—On the Teaching of the Fathers as to the Res Sacramenti of the Eucharist being the object of Spiritual Senses. (Pp. 329—350.)

EUCHARISTIC WORSHIP IN THE ENGLISH CHURCH.

THE narrative I am going to relate is one which, though cursorily passed over, or but slightly alluded to in many Ecclesiastical histories, seems (if at all reliable) to deserve a more prominent position among the records of the middle ages.

In the thirteenth century there was a certain nun named Juliana, to whom, at the time of her prayers, in ecstasies and visions, was continually shown a moon as with a limb obscured, or as with a dark rent or fissure in it. And afterwards was made known to her by revelation the interpretation of this vision. By it, we are to understand, was signified that there was something yet lacking in the Church on earth; that because of this want there was an obscuring of her glory; and that this eclipse of her light must continue until there should be given to her a special festival to be kept in honour of the Mystery of the Eucharistic Presence.* This led at first to a

* See L'Aroque's History of Eucharist, Walker's translation, pp. 579, 580; Albertinus, De Eucharistiâ, p. 973; and especially Dallæus, De Cultus Rel. Objecto, pp. 282—285, Geneva, 1664. See also

B

local festival in the Diocese of Liége. But after the death of Juliana, the matter was urged on by one of her friends named Eva, who had formerly been among the acquaintances of the ecclesiastic who then sat on the Papal throne. To him were communicated the vision and the revelation. Cardinals were consulted; and at last Eva received from the Pope an assurance that the longing desire of her heart should be granted.

The Pontiff wrote to her out of the fulness of his joy at being thus made an instrument of giving to the Church her full-moon splendour, bidding Eva to rejoice with great joy at the appointment of the festival of Corpus Christi.

"Let thy soul," he said, "therefore magnify the Lord, and let thy spirit rejoice in God thy Saviour; because thine eyes have seen thy salvation, which we have prepared before the face of all people."*

This was in the year 1264. After the death of Urban IV. the new festival was for a time discontinued, but was revived by Clement V. at the Council of Vienne, in 1311.

It will hardly be supposed that such an account as this of the origin of one of the most important festivals of

---

Hospinian, Hist. Sacr., lib. iv. " De Corporis Christi Festo," tom. iii. pp. 326 *sqq.*, Op., Genev. 1681; and Mosheim's Eccles. Hist., edit. Soames, vol. ii. p. 569; Gieseler, Eccles. Hist., vol. iii. pp. 325, 326, edit. Clark; Canon Robertson's Hist. of Ch. Ch., vol. vi. pp. 444, 445, 1874. At whatever date the story arose, it was certainly not the fabrication of Bale. The variations in the narrative are unimportant.

* See Hospinian, Opera, tom. iii. p. 327.

the Romish Church should have been allowed to pass unchallenged. It does not appear to be found in any historical record for nearly a hundred years after the date at which the Festival was appointed.*

* If Gieseler is right, it is first mentioned, and without details, by Johannes Hoesemius, Canon at Liége, about 1848; and the full narrative did not appear before the "Historia Revelationis b. Julianæ" of J. Blærus Diesthemius, in 1496. Afterwards appeared a "Life of Juliana," professedly by a contemporary author. (See Gieseler's Eccles. Hist., vol. iii. p. 326, edit. Clark.)

It may be thought, however, that Hoesemius could hardly have been altogether wrong as to the festival having an origin connected with Liége. There may have been contemporaries of his there, to whose parents the circumstances might have been familiar, not to mention the probability of his having access to some local records.

That Ægidius (closing his history in 1251) makes no mention of the festival could only go to prove that its institution at Liége was somewhat later than the common opinion.

The Bollandists (following Fisen, "De prima origine Festi Corp. Chr.") maintain the integrity of the narrative of Juliana and Eva, and that there is a MS. account by a writer of the same age. They add: "Auctorem hunc Synchronum non longo intervallo (verba sunt Bartholomæi Fisen) secuti sunt Joannes Holsemius Canonicus Leodinensis, Joannes Ultramosanus, et Joannes Warnantius, qui inter res a popularibus suis gestas historiam hanc breviter sed diserte commemorant: scripserunt autem sub annuum MCCCXXX. Ejusdem meminit auctor Magni Chronici Belgici. . . . Sed hi omnes fere de Institutione festi Venerabilis Sacramenti apud Leodienses agunt, absque singulari mentione Julianæ Virginis; ad quam ejus originem primam deduxit Joannes Diesthemius Blærus, Leodii ad S. Jacobi Prior e Benedictinâ familiâ; qui anno MCCCCXCVI. scripsit de ea re commentarium." (Acta Sanctorum, Aprilis Tomus Primus, p. 436, Apr. 5.)

Bishop Wordsworth says of the history of Juliana: "This account of the origin of the festival may be seen in a work, now in the thirteenth edition, by Dom. Giuseppe Riva, Penitentiary of the Cathedral of Milan, A.D. 1862, p. 300." (Tour in Italy, vol. ii. p. 118.)

In the sixteenth century another history is found displacing it,* according to which we are given to understand that a certain priest, having doubts of the truth of transubstantiation, was established in the faith by finding blood issuing from the host, which left an indelible mark in the folds of the corporal. We are told that this blood-stained cloth, having been sent to the Pope, was preserved, and is yet to be seen in the Cathedral of Orvieto† as a witness to the reality of the miracle of Bolsena. Thus, it is said, the Pope was moved to ordain an annual festival in honour of the Sacrament.

This second account, which we may observe has many counterparts ‡ in the records of those dark

* See Onuphrius Panvinius, Annotat. in Platina, Urban IV., pp. 214, 215, edit. Cologne, 1626.

† See Hospinian, Op., tom. iii. p. 326, 1681; Robertson's Hist. of Ch. Ch., vol. vi. p. 441, 1874.

‡ Archbishop Ussher says: "St. Augustine's conclusion may here well take place: 'Let those things be taken away, which are fictions of lying men or wonders wrought by evil spirits. For either there is no truth in these reports, or if there be any strange things done by heretics we ought the more to beware of them; because when the Lord had said that certain deceivers should come, who, by doing some wonders, should seduce, if it were possible, the very elect, He very earnestly commended this unto our consideration, and said Behold, I have told you before;' yea, and added a further charge also, that if these impostors should say unto us of Him, 'Behold, He is in secret closets,' we should not believe it; which, whether it be applicable to them who tell us that Christ is to be found in a pyx, and think they have Him in safe custody under lock and key, I leave to the consideration of others." (Answer to Jesuits' Challenge, Works, edit. Elrington, vol. iii. pp. 78, 79.)

ages,* appears to have been generally preferred to the older narrative.†

But it may be noted that Lambertinus, afterwards Pope Benedict XIV., in his famous work on the Festivals, combines both narratives, regarding both as historical, though without entering into the details of the visions and revelations of Juliana.‡

Now, whatever we may think about these mediæval stories, there are four propositions which I think we may look upon as certain.

(1) The festival of Corpus Christi did originate at this period.

(2) Its introduction did make such a real, marked addition to the religion of Western Christendom, as might not unsuitably be symbolised by the passing away of the moon's·eclipse.

(3) This addition was but a marked and prominent act —perhaps it should be added, a completing and crowning act—in a course of progress and change by which accretions had previously been forming around the religion

---

* See Morton on Eucharist, book iv. ch. ii; Robertson's History of Ch. Ch., vol. vi. p. 441, 1874; Ussher's Works, vol. iii. pp. 75—78.

† Panvinius says: "Quanquam non me lateat, quosdam esse, qui nescio quid de quadam muliere sancta Moniali reclusa nomine Eva fabulentur. Quorum sententiam nihil moror: cum, quod supra dixi, vulgarissimum sit." (In Platina, p. 215, edit. Cologne, 1626.)

‡ See Lambertinus, de D. N. Jes. Chr. Matrisque Ejus Festis, et de Missæ Sacr., Patavii, 1745, Pars Prim. § DXXXII.—DXXXIX. pp. 211—214.

of earlier times, in relation to the Sacrament of the Eucharist.

(4) This marked and crowning addition was so fitting, suitable, and appropriate to the previous accretions, that if only it were granted that *they* formed a true part of the Christian religion, that religion might fairly be viewed as having been maimed and incomplete up to this date. In other words, if the Eucharistic teaching, such as the Church of Rome had before this attained to, were truth, devoid of superstition, then this addition really did, as it were, take away the darkness of an eclipse, which until now had overshadowed the Church of Christ, and kept from her the full measure of her light and glory.

The first of these propositions is a fact of history, about which nothing further need be said. It is acknowledged that there was no festival of Corpus Christi before this.*

Each of the three remaining propositions demands and deserves the earnest attention, and the most careful consideration, of those who would learn lessons from the history of the past to be applied to the questions and to the perils of the present.

I. It is not very material to inquire whether or not the whole ceremonial now connected with the Festival of Corpus Christi formed a part of its original institution.

---

* There may, however, doubtless have been before this some lesser ceremonies and processions, by which the way may have been prepared for the introduction of the new festival. (See Muratori, De Rebus Liturgicis, c. 285, 286.)

It may, perhaps, be that the magnificent pageant followed after some considerable interval of time.* But that it followed naturally and suitably will hardly be disputed by many.

Now let anyone contemplate the religion of Rome as displayed in all the pomp and circumstance of this gorgeous and most attractive spectacle,† and let him compare the glory of this so-called Christian festival with the description of religious feasts among the heathen,‡ especially with the splendour of the ancient festival of Diana;§ and then let him carry back his thoughts

---

* "Diesteim saith that it was Pope John XXII. which introduced this custom [of bearing the host in procession]; but Bossius in his Chronicles, and after him Genebrard, in his Chronology, book iv., place it much later, and say that it began 100 years after the institution of the Holy Day, to be practised at Pavia; from whence it spread itself abroad into all the Western Churches, and especially at Angers, where Berengarius had been Archdeacon." (L'Aroque's History of Eucharist, Walker's translation, p. 581. See also Albertinus, De Eucharistiâ, p. 975.)

Muratori (De Rebus Liturgicis, c. 284, 285) considers that the procession was commenced at Milan in 1336.

Lambertinus, however, seems to favour the opinion that the procession is as old as the festival. (De Festis, par. i. § DXXXIX. pp. 213, 214, edit. 1745.)

† A description of the festival, as seen in the year 1862, will be found in Bp. Wordsworth's "Tour in Italy," vol. ii. pp. 116—132. See also Plate in Elliott's Horæ Apocalypticæ, vol. iii. p. 185, 5th ed.

‡ See Hospinian, Opera, tom. iii. pp. 329, 330, 333, 334, Geneva, 1681, and Prebendary Payne in Gibson's Preservative, vol. x. p. 133, London, 1848; and Dr. Covel's Account of the Greek Church, pp. 100, 101.

§ Polydore Virgil, after describing the various festivities in his day observed in connection with Pentecost and Corpus Christi, adds:

to those earlier times when the remains of the Eucharist were sometimes distributed among school-chil-

" Dii boni, quot in nostra religione ritus habemus ab Ethnicis transpositos, quales procul dubio sunt pompa hæc sacrorum, et omnia alia ad eam rem pertinentia?" (De Invent. Rer., lib. vi. cap. xi., as quoted by Albertinus, De Euch., p. 976.)

In Hospinian (Opera, tom. iii. pp. 328, 329) may be seen the account given by Apuleius of the festival of Diana, compared with the description of the celebration of the festival of *Corpus Christi*.

The very same resemblance is marked by a recent Italian writer, who adds: " Such is Apuleius's description of one of the processions of Paganism. Well, the procession of *Corpus Domini*, which is used in Italy, is it not exactly the same, word for word and point for point?" (The Religion of Rome, by a Roman; London, 1873, p. 271.)

It is added by Hospinian, after giving a similar description of the ceremony of the sacred fire among the Persians: " Manlius, tom. iii. Locorum Comm. fol. 28 refert, Episcopum quendam, statim post suam electionem et confirmationem, in sua diœcesi mandatum edidisse, cujus exordium fuerit, *Sicut Regem Persicum præcedebat equus ignem gestans, qui a Persis pro Deo adorabatur: sic nos præcedet consecrata hostia, quam ut verum Corpus Domini coli et adorari ab omnibus nostris subditis, mandamus.*" (Ibid. pp. 329, 330.)

Concerning the Romish adoration of the host, it has been said: " This adoration is not only in the time of communion, when it is properly the Lord's Supper and Sacrament; but at other times out of it, whenever it is set upon the altar with the candles burning and the incense smoking before it, or hung up in its rich shrine and tabernacle with a canopy of state over it. And not only in the Church which is sanctified, they say, by this Sacrament, as by the presence of God Himself, but when it is carried through the streets in a solemn and pompous procession, as it is before the Pope when he goes abroad, just as the Persian fire was before the Emperor, merely by way of State or for a superstitious end, that he may the better be guarded and defended by the company of his god. In all these times it is to be worshipped and adored by all persons as it passeth by, as if it were the glory of God which passed by. They are, like Moses, to make haste and bow their heads to the earth and worship; but, above all,

dren;* or, in an urgent case, a portion sent by the hand of a boy to be given to a dying penitent;† or still rather, to those earlier days when the profanity of certain neophytes in the Corinthian Church, who discerned not the Lord's Body, was sufficiently rebuked by an inspired Apostle in such words as these: "As often as ye eat this bread and drink this cup, ye do show the Lord's death till He come." Let anyone, I say, compare the two, and say whether there is not here indeed a contrast

---

upon that high day which they have dedicated to this sacrament, as if it were some new deity—the *Festum Dei*, as they call it—the Feast of God; or the *Festum Corporis Christi*, the Feast of the Body of Christ; for to call the Sacrament God is a general expression among them, as when they have received the Sacrament to say, 'I have received my Maker to-day;' and the person who in great churches is to carry the Sacrament to the numerous communicants is called *Bajulus Dei*, the porter or carrier of God; and they also account it, and so always reverence it—as Boileau falsely says the ancients did—as a present *numen* and Deity.'" (Prebendary Payne, in Gibson's Preservative, vol. x. pp. 136, 137, London, 1848.)

On the gradual introduction of Pagan rites, &c., see Hospinian's Works, vol. ii. pp. 110, 116, 129, 146; Maitland's Catacombs, pp. 306—308; Gieseler's Eccles. Hist., vol. iii. pp. 347—349, edit. Clark; Elliott's Horæ Apoc., vol. i. p. 341, 5th edit..; Homilies of Ch. of Eng., p. 177, edit. 1844.

* "Nicephorus Callistus, A.D. 1333, is a witness to the continuance of this custom down to the fourteenth century. He affirms that, when a boy, he had often himself thus partaken of the remains of the consecrated Elements." (Scudamore's Notitia Eucharistica, p. 783.) In 588 an attempt was made by the Council of Macon to introduce this Greek custom into France. (See ibid., pp. 783, 784.)

† See Eusebius, Hist. Eccles., lib. vi. c. 44, Oxford, 1845, p. 219; Bingham, Ant., book xv. cap. iv. sec. 9, London, 1844, vol. v. p. 189; Gibson's Preservative, London, 1848, vol. x. p. 143; Vogan's "True Doctrine," p. 293.

showing such a change in the religion of Europe,* that, if the addition be really an addition of light and glory, it might indeed very fitly be represented by the change from a moon partially overshadowed to a moon shining in its full brightness.

II. But it must not be supposed for a moment that the change in the matter of the Eucharist from the religion of Apostolic and primitive Christianity to that of the later period of the middle age was effected by one step. Such an addition *per saltum* is, indeed, utterly inconceivable. It had taken centuries† to bring the Church up to the point at which the appointment of such a festival as Corpus Christi was possible.‡ But the point

---

*"So great an honour and regard had the primitive Church for the Sacrament, that as they accounted it the highest mystery and solemnest part of their worship, so they would not admit any of the penitents who had been guilty of any great and notorious sin, nor the catechumens, nor the possessed, and *energumeni*, so much as to the sight of it; the ἐποψία, and the participation of this mystery, used always in those times to go together, as Cassander owns, and Albaspinæus proves in his book of the Eucharist. And therefore as it is plainly contrary to the primitive practice to carry the sacrament up and down, and expose it to the eyes of all persons; so the reason of doing it—that it may be worshipped by all, and that those who do not partake of it may yet adore it—was, it is plain, never thought of in the primitive Church, for then they would have seen and worshipped it, though they had not thought fit that they should have partaken of it.' (Prebendary Payne in Gibson's Preservative, vol. x. p. 144, London, 1848.) † See Appendix, Note A.

‡ "It is clear," says Mr. Sadler, "that if all this" [the bringing Christ personally to be worshipped on our altars] " had been in the power of the Church, she could not have been utterly unconscious of it, as assuredly she was for above a thousand years." (The Church and the Age, p. 299.)

had been reached which made this addition but one step —perhaps rather a high step, still but one step—further on in a course of progress which had commenced very early, and had latterly been advancing very rapidly.

Not long before this had been introduced the custom of ringing the sacring bell * at the consecration of the elements, that all assembled might immediately fall down and worship the Saviour now believed to be present in the place of the bread and wine. The host was now to be elevated for purposes of adoration.

It was borne in state with a burning light before it when taken to be administered to the sick. †

Men had come to regard it as Immanuel,—God with man, Christ in the hand of the priest, Christ under the form of bread.

The new uses of the Eucharist had multiplied since the fourth Lateran Council (1215), in which Innocent III. decreed the doctrine of transubstantiation. The adoration of the host had come into prominence since the condemnation of Berengarius. It is acknowledged that the liturgical ceremonies which express it had no place in the earlier part of the century which saw the birth of the doctrine of Paschasius.

There is no trace of it in the ancient liturgies,‡ or in the parts of those liturgies which have any true claim to

---

* See Scudamore's Notitia Eucharistica, p. 618, 2nd edit.
† See Hospinian, Opera, tom. iii. p. 319.
‡ See Appendix, Note B.

be accounted ancient; but step by step, slowly at first but surely, the onward progress was made. Addition followed addition, ceremony followed upon ceremony, novelties afterwards crowded upon novelties,* till at

* Cardinal Allen confesses: "Id scimus, non fuisse in primitiva Ecclesia horum periculorum eam curam aut cogitationem, ut propterea una pars Sacramenti deseretur a populo." (Libri Tres, p. 496, Antwerp, 1576.)

The following passage, read in the light of the truth that the opponents of Berengarius were the real innovators (see "Romish Mass and English Church," pp. 11, 12, 60-67), and that originally the reservation and elevation (whenever it arose) and mission of the consecrated elements were altogether free from anything like the adoration of the host, contains a really interesting account of the onward progress of Eucharistic doctrine in the Church, and of the natural growth by continual accretions round the doctrine of the Corporal Presence.

Cardinal Allen says: "Juvat plurimum intueri, quo modo ab illo tempore, quo hæresis et profanatio hujus Sacramenti per Berengarium et posteriores hæreticos cæpta est, quantoque studio et animi contentione Ecclesia universa se opposuerit, elaboraveritque, ne quicquam summi Sacramenti dignitati ac majestati decederet, quin potius (ut fit) ex contraria hæresi *aliquid etiam venerationis accederet.* Ergo quod antea semper et confectione, et perceptione, et reservatione, et elevatione, et privata portatura, et in alimento vitæ, et in viatico migrationis, et missione ad absentes vel honoris ac pacis communionisque Ecclesiasticæ causa (quomodo olim teste Eusebio, lib. v. cap. 24, deferebatur ad externos Episcopos Romam venientes) vel necessitatis gratia, ut ad ægrotos, summo ac plane divino honore colebatur: idem nunc (rumpantur ut ilia Calvino et Sacramentariis omnibus) circumgestatur in publico, ut olim Arca Testamenti . . . ad pacem et misericordiam procurandam, ad debitum cultum exhibendum, ad protestationem fidei nostræ omniumque Fidelium circa Eucharistiam contra Hæreticos et perfidos Judæos. . . . Haud ita multo post ab Urbano IV. ad *eundem cultum amplificandum* et extinguendam Hæresin instituitur festum Corporis Christi celeberrimum, miris gratiis donatum. Cujus officium S. Thomas (qui et ipse regnans

last Pope Urban crowned the pile by issuing the Bull which orders the perpetual observance of the festival of Corpus Christi.

III. In view, then, of this marked addition to the religion of the West—an addition which, in outward appearance at least, tended so much to assimilate the Rome of mediæval Christianity to the Rome of Pagan idolatry—shall we speak of this annual festival, with its gorgeous apparatus of most imposing ceremonial, as effecting a real inward and essential change in the cultus of Roman Christendom? Shall we regard it as a strange and discordant and unwarrantable, because unfitting and unsuitable, accretion on the religious ideas of the ages preceding? Shall we look upon it as like the growth of a parasite on the branch of another tree of another and quite different kind?

To do this would be to make a great mistake. The inward and essential change had been made long before. What was added now was but a suitable supplement to

---

nunc cum Christo per orbem fidelem colitur) ejusdem Pontificis jussu at Sp. Sancti afflatu conscripsit quo nihil unquam venit in sacrum officium doctius aut sanctius. Tum passim Sancto Sacramento fiunt vota, eriguntur Altaria, applicantur donaria, accenduntur cerei, solvuntur orationum pensa diurna atque nocturna, exhibentur sacræ comœdiæ, instituuntur Collegia, dedicantur libri, et reliqua innumera pietatis officia constituuntur: ut plane videamus *omnem Novi Testamenti religionem Corporis et Sanguinis Christi cultu maxime contineri.*" (Libri Tres, pp. 385—387, Antwerp, 1576; De Euch. Sacr., lib. i. cap. xxx.)

See also Bellarmine, De Sacr. Eucharis., lib. iv. cap. xxx

what had been added already. This is a point which is most important to be insisted upon.

If the cultus and ceremonial which had been established before were right, if they were parts of true Christianity, they must have been so because of the truth of a doctrine concerning the Eucharist; and if only this doctrine were true, nothing could be more fitting and suitable than the solemn, and public, and festive recognition of that doctrine in the annual celebration of the new festival.

If the religion of Rome before this could suitably be compared in any sort to the glory of the moon, then it may be fairly asserted that this addition was really needed to make that glory full.

For let a distinct answer be sought to this question: What could warrant that innovation of ceremonial adoration, connected with that other innovation of elevation following consecration,* which had previously been admitted to form a conspicuous part in the celebration of the Mass? The answer, I think, must be that nothing could warrant it short of an Objective Personal Presence of the Incarnate Godhead in some sort in or under the form or *materies* of the consecrated elements.

Distinctions (if possible) between presence local and supra-local do not really affect the matter. It must be a Presence specially there where the species of bread is seen. However supra-local, it is a Presence *there;*

* See Appendix, Note C.

therefore in some sense certainly a local Presence, however supra-local the manner.

No efforts to draw a distinction between Presence by location and Presence by extension will avail anything at all. It is a Presence in that which is local, even though it be not by location.

Neither is the real point affected by any attempts, possible or impossible, to draw a distinction between "real and essential" Presence and "corporal" Presence. It is the real and essential Presence of the very Body and of the very Person of Christ, however spiritual and incorporeal.

Neither yet is the matter altered by anything which may be said about distinctions between spiritual and material *conceptions* of the Presence. Let the conception of the Presence of Christ *there*, under the forms of bread and wine, be as spiritual, as immaterial, as incorporeal, as supralocal, as it is possible to be, the point to be insisted upon is simply this—that the visible species or substance of the consecrated elements must be regarded either as, in some sort, clothing and hiding the present Saviour, or as forming with the very present Body and Person of Christ one [*] compound, adorable whole; otherwise there would be no warrant for such adoration as

---

[*] So Bellarmine, De Euch., lib. iv. cap. xxix.; De Cont., tom. iii. cc. 920, 923; and Suarez, in Th. Quæst. 79 (quoted by Payne as below), and Henriques and Gregory de Valentia. See Dean Aldrich's "Reply to Two Discourses," p. 42; and Prebendary Payne in Gibson's Preservative, vol. x. p. 122, London, 1848.

formed a part of the religion of the Mass before the festival of Corpus Christi was ever thought of.

No conception of a Presence—if conceivable—of the Body of Christ as crucified and dead, and of the blood of Christ as poured out and shed, would have availed for the purpose. This has been acknowledged.* No conception of spiritual union of the elements with the glorified Body of Christ in heaven would have availed. It is Christ,

---

* See Freeman, Principles of Divine Service, vol. ii. part i. pp. 147, 148. It is however denied by Bellarmine, De Euch., lib. iv. cap. xxix. ; De Cont., tom. iii. cap. 921.

It is truly said, that when Christ's Soul was separated from His Body, His Divinity deserted neither soul nor body. But this must by no means be understood as implying that Christ's lifeless Body was necessarily a proper object towards which adoration might be addressed, though this is maintained by Bellarmine.

The Divine Person of the Son, since the Incarnation, is not to be conceived of as apart from the human soul, which may now be said to be a very part of Himself. And when the human soul had left the Body, the Divine Person was not inhabiting that Body, as when the human soul inhabited and animated it.

And whether in this condition it should be adored is, at least, very questionable. "We might," says Archbishop Wake, "have some cause to doubt whether, since we have received no command concerning it, it were our Saviour's pleasure that His Body should be adored by us in that state ; so that there could be no sin in the not doing it." (See Gibson's Preservative, vol. x. p. 112, London, 1848.)

See Vogan's True Doctrine, pp. 278, 600.

Stillingfleet asks: "Since it doth not follow by virtue of the Hypostatical union, that wherever the Divinity is the human nature of Christ must be there also, how doth it necessarily follow, that wherever the Body of Christ is, the Divinity is so present as to make that Body become an object of Divine adoration? . . . The Scripture is only pretended to speak of the Body of Christ, and not of His Divinity." (Works, vol. vi. p. 76.)

Christ Himself, Christ in His very living Person—body, soul, and divinity—who was adored with adoration addressed to or towards the visible species.

It must be the real Presence of the Divine Person of Christ dwelling in His one human Body—and with that one human Body united—really made to be one with, or to be clothed upon with, the substance or the species of the sacramental elements, which alone can justify that Eucharistic adoration which is the present subject of controversy.

No Presence of virtue or equivalence as distinct from this, and no such notion of Presence as may be reduced to a relation, could possibly meet the requirements of the theory.

Now let us see how this idea of the Presence to be adored in the Eucharist is expressed by a writer who is believed to have influenced largely the novel opinions of a section in our own Church of England :—

" The Eucharist is frequently called the ' Extension of the Incarnation ;' and the expression is significant and appropriate, not simply because the Eucharist is the means of extending the benefits of the Incarnation to all time, but because there is in both cases a real union between the earthly and the heavenly : in the Incarnation between the Eternal Word and man's nature, in the Eucharist between the Person of Christ and the elements of bread and wine : so that it may be said without a metaphor, that there is a renewal or continuation of the Incarnation. What was done in the Incarnation is renewed in the Sacrament; not in the same manner, but in a certain resemblance and proportion." . . . . " In order to this union of the flesh of Christ with ours, He first Incarnates Himself in the hands of the priest; that is, at the moment of Consecration, Christ unites

Himself, Body, Soul, and Divinity, in an ineffable manner, with the elements of bread and wine." .... " Both in the Incarnation and in the Eucharist the mystery is formed by the union of two natures, which remain distinct without mixture or confusion: in the Incarnation, the Divine Word united to the Body, which He took of the Virgin Mary, His Mother; in the Eucharist, the glorified Body of the Lord joined to the earthly substance of bread and wine. But in each case both remain in their own nature; the Divine and Human in the Incarnation, and in the Eucharist the Person of our Lord and the nature of bread and wine. And yet, as the Divine and Human Nature in the Incarnate are called, and are, one Christ; so in the Eucharist the heavenly and the earthly substances, remaining each in its own nature, when united by Consecration are called, and are, the Body of Christ."*

The view expressed here is one which would no doubt be regarded by the writer as separate from what he and others would regard as the distinctively Roman doctrine of the Presence.

This may perhaps be fairly spoken of as the *minimum*,† while the full Romish doctrine of transubstantiation is the *maximum*. The *maximum* doctrine, in destroying the very substances of bread and wine, and leaving only species to deceive the sight and exercise faith in rejecting the evidence of the senses, creating the prodigy of accidents without substances, does indeed add to the marvel of the mystery.

But we may be contented to take the *minimum*—the *minimum* of that which can warrant the adoration of the

---

* Tracts for the Day, pp. 232, 233 : 1868.

† Yet there are some statements in the extract which, in their natural, unmodified sense, would hardly, perhaps, be accepted by some Romish divines.

middle ages. We must regard this with attention. We must compare with it the adorable mystery of the Incarnation.

Why! If only this be true there is nothing but the Incarnation which can be compared to it, and even the Incarnation itself in the blessedness of its glory must pale before it. That tells indeed of a union once effected between the invisible and the visible, the infinite and the finite, the Divine and the Human; yes, between the Divine person and the Human nature of the Lord Jesus Christ. But this tells of union effected every day, and thousands of times in every day, between the same Divine Person and the bread and wine, or the species of bread and wine, on the altar, causing as real a Presence in the hand of the priest as was the Presence of the Holy Child Jesus in the manger of Bethlehem;* and with the further miracle that this union, and this Presence—this Presence of the very Divine Person and Human Body of Christ—is effected without any advent or coming from heaven† to earth, and without any leaving of the throne of His

---

* See Dr. Pusey's "Real Presence the Doctrine of the English Church," p. 329.

† Some, however, if I have been rightly informed, do not hesitate to use popular language suggestive of such a descent. The diversity of view formerly held in the Romish Church is well known. "Quod manifestum arbitratus est Thomas, Christum non per localem motum a Cælo adduci, aliis exagitatum est. Notum est quid senserit Scotistarum Schola, et quantopere reproductionis Thomisticæ commentum derideant." (Præfatio Hist. to "Determinatio Jo. Parisiensis," p. 45, London, 1686.)

glory above, and yet without that human body ceasing to be a human body, with human flesh and bones, and all things appertaining to the perfection and completion of man's nature. And that the union is not a hypostatical one* seems rather to add to than to take from its marvellous character; especially since it is held that as a

* "The human nature itself of Christ, considered alone, and being a mere creature, is not an object of worship, as St. Augustine says, but only as it is hypostatically united to the Divine nature, *i.e.* so intimately and vitally united to it as to make one person with it, with God Himself, one Θεάνθρωπος, and so one object of worship; and if the sacramental symbols or species are to be adored with true *latria*, not *per se*, or upon their own account, but by reason of the intimate union and conjunction which they have with Christ, as they say, not only with Christ's Body, for that alone is not to be worshipped, much less another thing that is united to it; but with Christ's Person, and then there must be as many Persons of Christ as there are consecrated wafers; then these species being thus worshipped upon the same account that Christ's humanity is, as Gregory de Valentia owns they must ('This worship,' says he, 'belongs after a certain manner to the species, as when the Divine λόγος is worshipped in the humanity which he assumed; the Divine worship belongs also to the created humanity.' *Pertinet per accidens suo quodam modo ea veneratio ad species, quemadmodum suo modo, etiam hoc ipso quod adoratur Divinum verbum in humanitate assumpta, pertinet ejusmodi Divinus cultus ad illam humanitatem creatam secundario, neque in hoc est aliqua idololatria*), must be also united to Christ the same way that His humanity is united to His Divinity, so as to become with that one entire object of worship, as the species are, according to them, with Christ in the Eucharist; that is, they must become one *suppositum*, or one person, with Christ. This is so weighty a difficulty, as makes the greatest Atlases of the Roman Church not only sweat, but sink under it. Valentia owns the wonderful conjunction the species have with Christ, but denies their being hypostatically united to Him. But then, how are they to be worshipped? Since it is owned by him and the schoolmen that the very humanity of Christ is to be worshipped

result of the union the present Christ becomes subject in part to the conditions and incapacities which belong to the nature of bread.

only upon the account of its hypostatical union; and though God be very nearly and intimately present in other creatures, yet they are not to be worshipped, notwithstanding that Presence, because they do not make one *suppositum* or *hypostasis* with Him, or are not hypostatically united to Him. Bellarmine being pinched on this side, removes the burden to the other. That is as sore, and can as little bear it. 'Christ,' says he, 'is much otherwise in the Eucharist than God is in other things; for in the Eucharist there is but only one *suppositum*, and that Divine; all other things there present belong to and make one thing with that.' If they do so, then sure they are hypostatically united with Christ, as 'T. G's' learned adversary charges upon Bellarmine from this place; if they make one *suppositum* with him, and but one with him, let it be in what manner it will, they must be hypostatically united to Him. Bellarmine's *Licet non eodem modo*, though not after the same manner, is both unintelligible, and will not at all help the matter; it is only a confession from him, that at the same time that he says they are hypostatically united to Christ and make one *suppositum* with Him, and one object of worship, that he does not know how this can be, and that his thoughts are in a great strait about it, so that he doubts they are not hypostatically united at the same time that he yet says they are so; for this is no way imposed upon him, as 'T. G.' says, notwithstanding his *non eodem modo*. If in the Incarnation of Christ one should say that the Soul and Body of Christ are both united to His Divinity, but that both were not united after the same manner; but the soul in such a manner as being a spirit, and the body in another, yet so, that both made but one *suppositum* with it, and that Divine; and that all His human nature belonged to that, and made one with that, though not after the same manner; would not this be still an owning the hypostatical union between Christ's Divinity and His Soul and Body? And so must the other be between Christ's Divinity and His Body, and the species, if they make one *suppositum*, and are, as they told, to be worshipped as such." (Prebendary Payne's Discourse concerning the Adoration of the Host, in Gibson's Preservative, vol. x. pp. 123—125, London, 1848.)

In the Incarnation we see the Son of God taking upon Him man's nature, so that God and man are one Christ. In the Eucharist we see this same Christ in some sort taking upon Him every day the nature, or the substance, or the form of bread, so that Christ and the consecrated element, or the species of the element, are one host. Moreover, the Incarnation was the union of a Divine Person with the nature of that conscious and intelligent being, which (though fallen indeed) was created in the image of God. But this Eucharistic Presence is the result of a union of Christ with a senseless product of vegetable creation given to be to man for meat.

It detracts nothing from the infinite condescension of the Incarnation of Christ to say that it may not be put on the same footing at all with any kind of impanation of Christ's Body, or Real Presence of Christ in and under the

---

Perrone answering the objection, "Eodem cultu deberemus prosequi creaturas omnes, cum in omnibus Deus sit substantialiter præsens," says : " *Neg.* paritatem. Nam in Eucharistia unum solum est suppositum divinum, Cui tribuimus adorationem ; in creaturis adest quidem Deus substantialiter præsens, sed non est cum illis unum suppositum, neque Deus et creaturæ unum sunt *per hypostasis unitatem.*" (J. Perrone, Prælectiones Theol., vol. iii. p. 203, Paris, 1856.)

Dean Aldrich says: "They" [the Papists] "hold the species united in the Body to make one entire object of adoration; which cannot be without a hypostatical union. Wherefore Bellarmine and Valentia, though they do not use the term " [*hypostatically*], "yet find themselves obliged to say the thing, and explain the union of the species to the Body in the same manner as they do the hypostatical union." (Reply to Two Discourses, p. 42 ; see also p. 47, and especially p. 44 ; see Woodhead's Two Discourses, p. 16.)

form of bread. In the Incarnation the Son of God took upon Him a nature which in us had become sinful, fallen, and lost, but which, spite of all, has Divine affinities. It was the nature of those whom He came to redeem. And it was in order to this redemption that He clothed Himself with it. It is the nature of those whom He would have to be loved, even with the love wherewith He Himself is loved of the Father. It was the nature of those, that great multitude which no man can number, whom He would have to be with Him where He is, who will see Him as He is, and be made like unto Him in His glory. "God was in Christ reconciling the world unto Himself."

Can any of these things be predicated of the union of the Body of Christ, and Christ Himself, with the form or the element of bread? The very asking of such a question has surely a sound too nearly bordering on the profane. It can be justified only by the necessity which arises of showing the contrast between Divine doctrines and human inventions, the wondrous unspeakable love of the one, and the incongruous—may I not say, speaking under the full conviction of its earthly origin?—the monstrous character, which might be likened to some strange and hideous deformity, of the other.

In the Incarnation we behold a Divine Person once for all taking upon Him the form of a servant, and made in the likeness of men. In the Mass we are taught to contemplate this same Divine Person, every day on ten thousand altars, taking upon Him the form of a wafer, and found in the likeness of bread.* And yet, while bowing down before the Presence of Christ with His Body

* So the hymn attributed to Thomas Aquinas: "Visus, tactus, gustus in te fallitur, Sed auditu solo tuto creditur. . . . *In cruce latebat sola Deitas, At hic latet simul et humanitas.* . . . Plagas sicut Thomas, non intueor, Deum tamen meum te confiteor. . . . Jesu, quem velatum nunc aspicio, Oro fiat illud, quod tam sitio. Ut te revelata cernens facie, Visu sim beatus tuæ gloriæ." (See Dallæus, De Cultus Rel. Objecto, p. 287 ; and Prebendary Payne, in Gibson's Preservative, vol. x. p. 135, London, 1848.)

Tertullian speaks very differently: " Non licet, non licet nobis in dubium sensus istos devocare, ne et in Christo de fide eorum deliberetur. . . . Fidelis fuit et visus et auditus in monte : fidelis et gustus vini illius, licet aquæ ante, in nuptiis Galilææ: fidelis et tactus, exinde creduli Thomæ. Recita Joannis testationem: Quod vidimus, inquit, quod audivimus, oculis nostris vidimus, et manus nostræ contrectaverunt, de sermone vitæ. Falsa utique testatio, si oculorum et aurium et manuum sensus natura mentitur." (De Anima, cap. xvii., Op., p. 276, edit. Rigalt, 1689.)

But that which must be especially noticed, in order to see the contrast between the teaching of Tertullian and Aquinas, is this—that Tertullian, after saying " we may not call in question our senses," goes on to give reasons—lest there should be a deceit in various particulars of our Lord's history, which were the objects of the senses. And he concludes this list of particulars with the "taste of the wine which He consecrated to be a memorial of His blood" ["Alium postea vini saporem, quod in Sanguinis sui memoriam consecravit."] (See below, Appendix, Note E, under " pignus et memoria.") If, as in Aquinas's view, the consecration turned the wine into Christ's blood, instead of the *memorial* of His blood, leaving only the *sapor vini*, without the *vinum*, then indeed would there be in the *sapor* that deceit expressed in the words "Visus, tactus, gustus in te fallitur." And thus Tertullian's *reductio ad absurdum* is seen to be brought up just to that point of absurdity at which it meets the conception to which afterwards man's thoughts brought up the faith of the Romish Church.

It has been well said : " Miracles, in the nature and use of them, are not contradictions to sense, but appellations to sense ; and the end

and Blood under the form of bread, we are to believe that Christ's Body remains locally present at God's right hand in heaven, and does not in any way descend, or come from thence to be present in the Eucharist. Not only so, but the very Incarnation and Atonement are in some sort subservient to this daily mystery of the Eucharistic presence, and would indeed be fruitless without it.

of them is by the evidence of our sense to convince our understanding." (Bishop Morley, Treatises, "Against Transubstantiation," p. 9.)

Another has said: "So long as I retain the use of my understanding, I cannot but proceed to the extent which I am now about to mention. Christianity was, by divine appointment, founded on miracles—that is, on events of the truth of which the senses of men were the judges. I should, therefore, beforehand deem it very improbable that the religion so founded on the testimony of the senses would contain anything relating to the objects of the senses which could not be believed, but in contradiction to the senses; because in that case the religion would have the appearance of undermining the ground upon which it had to rest." (Dr. Turton's Reply to Wiseman, p. 300.)

Far more primitive and truly Catholic, and far more consonant with the language of the Fathers than the saying of Aquinas, is the teaching of Zwingle: "Cum ista [Hoc est Corpus meum, &c.] auditus accipit, an non totus consternatur, et admirabundus in hoc unum quod prædicatur intentus est? Cum Deum audit, cum amorem illius, cum Filium pro nobis neci traditum? At cum huc intentus est, an non idem facit quod fides? Fides enim est quæ Deo per Christum nititur. Auditus ergo cum ad idem spectat, jam fidei ancillatur, jam fidem non molestat suis frivolis istis cogitationibus ac studiis. Visus cum panem videt et calicem, quæ vice Christi ut illius bonitatem ingeniumque significent, an non et ille fidei obsequitur? Christum enim velut ante oculos conspicit, quem mens ejus inflammata pulchritudine depetit. Tactus panem in manus sumit, qui jam non panis, sed Christus est significatione. Gustus olfactusque et ipsi huc advocantur, ut odorent quam suavis sit Dominus, quamque beatus sit qui in illo fidit." (Fid. Chr. Exp., Opera, Tig. 1581, tom. ii. fo. 556.)

This is the Presence, then, for which adoration is claimed, and it is readily granted that to the Saviour so present in the elements Divine adoration would undoubtedly be due. Nay, on the theory of such a Presence having been in mercy given, it would not only follow that the Sacrament ought to be adored, but, when the adoration had been given, another consequence would seem to be almost a necessity. On this point, indeed, I would speak perhaps with somewhat more hesitation; yet, it will hardly, I think, be disputed that this further result would follow most naturally. I mean, that this doctrine should be regarded as bringing to our prayers a presence of the Saviour receiving our adoration (in some sense or in some way), objectively nearer and more accessible to us than any we could otherwise have; so that the Sacramental Presence would come to be consistently viewed as a real and material assistance to prayer.*

* In the Romish Church men are certainly taught to regard this presence as having not only an attraction, but a claim and a call altogether beyond that of Christ's spiritual presence.

Thus in "The Roman Missal for the Use of the Laity," 1867, p. 704, we find a prayer (in the "Litany of the Sacred Heart") in which these words occur: "Accept, I beseech Thee, my poor desire to visit Thy divine Majesty in every temple throughout the Christian world, where Thou art present in the blessed Sacrament; thus to invite, by my humble example, all creatures to correspond by frequent visits to the excess of Thy love. But as I cannot effect this, I profoundly adore Thee here really present, and I adore Thee in spirit wherever Thou art in the most holy Sacrament."

See also Papers on the Eucharistic Presence, pp. 587, 588.

The very acknowledgment of such a Presence would seem to require that our Lord's words, "It is expedient for you that I go away," should be understood as supplemented by such words as these: "Yet it is expedient for you also that, though absent in the natural mode of the Presence of My Body, I should still in a supernatural way be present among you, with Body, Soul, and Divinity, under the form of bread, that so you may continually adore Me, and recognise Me there as a present Saviour, ever ready to hear and receive and answer your prayers."

So also in reading the inspired words, "Seeing that we have a great high priest, that is passed into the heavens, Jesus the Son of God," the doctrine of such a Presence would seem to demand of us that we should somehow supply such words as these: "And seeing also that we have Him continually present sacramentally and supralocally on our altars as really here as there; let us not only come boldly to the throne of grace, but let us be diligent also in constantly drawing nigh to the consecrated host, to worship, and offer our prayers to our Lord there present under its form, that so we may obtain mercy, and find grace to help in time of need."

Surely it is scarcely possible unduly to magnify the importance which should belong by right to such a Presence in the scheme of Christian doctrine.

Should, then, the Christian Church keep festival in perpetual memory of the birth of Christ, and a yearly commemoration of Christ's dying on the Cross, and not give a day on which to do honour to the marvel and the mystery of the miracle of the Sacrament of the altar?

Given that Presence,* that adoration is a Christian

* It may be alleged that in the Lutheran scheme of doctrine there is found the Real Objective Presence; but that adoration is rejected on the ground that the Sacrament was not ordained for the purpose of adoration.

But the inconsistency of this has been felt by many, and seems to be virtually acknowledged by some among Lutheran divines.

It is obvious, indeed, to reply that neither have we any sufficient intimation that the Incarnation was for the purpose of adoration. But who will therefore deny adoration to the Incarnate Saviour?

The truth is self-evident, that if a true Presence of Christ (Body, Soul, and Divinity) in the Elements be acknowledged, adoration addressed to Christ as so present must be admissible; and if admissible, it must be due; and if due, it ought to be paid.

We never ask—in the case of the presence of any prince or potentate of this world, in view of the honour or homage suitable to his position—whether the purpose of his presence was to receive this. However alien may be the object of his coming, we inquire only what is due to him, and when in his presence we order ourselves accordingly.

Nor must it be forgotten that the Lutheran teaching as to the Real Presence is teaching uncertain, confused, indistinct—full of strange inconsistencies; and that, as most fully developed in the doctrine of the Ubiquitaries, it makes as real a Presence in any flower of the field as in the consecrated elements. (See Papers on Eucharistic Presence, p. 724.)

Moreover, Lutheran doctrine did not commonly uphold the Presence *extra usum*. And in the use some Lutherans allowed and required the adoration. (See Bellarmine, De Euch., lib. iv. cap. xxix.; De Contro., tom. iii. c. 920.)

Indeed, at one time it appears that Luther taught that the elevation of the Sacrament was useful as a witness to the Real Presence; and that, being elevated, it ought to be adored. (See Consensus Orthodoxus, p. 411, 1605; and Hospinian, Hist. Sacram., part ii. p. 19.)

(See also Chemnitz, as quoted by Dr. Pusey in " Real Presence

duty, and that high festival at least has a suitable and fitting place in the Church's calendar.

But on the other hand, that Presence rejected, Eucharistic adoration with all its attendant ceremonies must fall to the ground.

No doubt there are very many shades of view on the subject of the Eucharist. But one clear, broad line of demarcation must for ever separate them into two distinct classes.

On the one side are those who hold, and on the other side are those who reject, the doctrine of a real Personal Presence of the Man Christ Jesus, in or under the elements or their forms.

Not, of course, that the human nature of Christ is the proper object of adoration.* But since the Incar-

the Doctrine of the English Church," pp. 334, 335; also the words of the Ministers of Zurich, inveighing against the inconsistency of Luther, Ibid. p. 333.)

As to the argument that the Presence may be analogous to the *incognito* of a prince, and therefore adoration should be withheld (see Prebendary Payne, in Gibson's Preservative, vol. x. p. 126, London, 1848), it seems sufficient to reply that when a prince travels *incognito* his desire is that his presence may not generally be known. But all who believe in the Real Presence of Christ in the Eucharist believe that presence to be an object of faith, to be recognised and known of all His faithful people.

"If," says Mr. Vogan, "He is there [in or under the form of the elements He claims as high honour, as absolute adoration there as can be given to Him anywhere else." (True Doctrine, p. 278. See also Papers on Eucharistic Presence, p. 587.)

On Lutheran adoration see Turretin, De Necess. Secess., Disp. iii. § xxiv. pp. 74, 75, Geneva, 1688.)

* "Neque hominem cum verbo adorandum dicimus, sed unum

nation of the Eternal Word, the Divine Person of the Son cannot be adored as apart from the nature which He has assumed.* God and man are now one Christ. And it is the One Christ to whom adoration is to be addressed. Nor, I believe, can our hearts (under ordinary circumstances) rightly address adoration to Him—directed to any circumscribed locality—except as to where His Body is, nor towards any visible object, except as, in some way, inhabited by or identified with His living Body, and that Body animated with His human soul.

And it is not only important that this should be clearly seen in these times, when in the interest of an innovating party special efforts seem to be made to obliterate the true, grand boundaries of Eucharistic doctrine; but it is also most important that we should be led to mark well and carefully what is really consistent with the doctrine

eundemque, ne illud cum verbo aliquam divisiones imaginationem meriti objiciat." (Conc. Ephes., tom. i. c. xii.) "Adoratione vero non seorsim Deum, nec seorsim hominem, sed unum Christum." (Ibid., tom. iv. c. xxvi. See Morton on Eucharist, p. 542.)

"Non est par unio utriusque, nam respectu carnis cum Verbo est unio hypostatica, sed respectu symbolorum et Christi, tantum sacramentalis et relativa, quæ proinde non potest facere unum Suppositum. . . . Supponitur Carnem esse proprium objectum adorationis, quod dici non potest, quando nihil creatum per se est adorabile; Persona proprie adoratur, Causa propter quam adoratur est Divinitas, Caro est illud sine quo non adoratur." (Turretin, De Necess. Secess., Disp. iii. § xii. p. 66, Geneva, 1688.)

* See especially the "Consensus Orthodoxus" of Herdesian, pp. 244—247; and Prebendary Payne in Gibson's Preservative, vol. x. pp. 119, 123, 124, London, 1848.

which stands on the one side, and on the other side, of the one chief separating line of division.

Take the hypothesis on this side, and you may indeed with perfect consistency take a high view of the Eucharistic elements as, in the truest sense, effectual proxies,*

* This is indeed nothing more than the true doctrine of the Reformed Church. And if some writers have, in strong opposition to the Corporal Presence, seemed to fall short of this, or if others have sometimes incautiously expressed themselves as if disallowing it, their language should receive a favourable construction, to bring it into harmony with the more matured and more careful expressions of the truth. (See Papers on the Eucharistic Presence, pp. 397, 410, 722—744; Doctrine of Sacraments in relation to Doctrines of Grace, pp. 69, 70, 102—107.)

Zwingle writes: "Tertia virtus [Sacramentorum]. *Vice* rerum sunt quas significant, unde et nomina earum sortiuntur. . . . Corpus Christi omnia que in illo gesta cum oculis subjici nequeant, panis et vinum *ejus loco* edenda proponuntur. . . . Panis et vinum amicitiæ illius quo Deus humano generi per filium suum reconciliatus est, symbola sunt, quæ non æstimamus pro materiæ pretio, sed juxta significatæ rei magnitudinem, ut jam non sit vulgaris panis, sed sacer: non panis tantum nomen habeat, sed Corporis Christi quoque, *imo sit* Corpus Christi, sed appellatione et significatione, quod recentiores vocant sacramentaliter. . . . Hoc est corpus meum, id est, hoc est sacramentum corporis mei, sive hoc est corpus meum sacramentale sive mysticum, id est, ejus quod vere assumpsi mortique objeci, symbolum, sacramentale et *vicarium*." (Zwingle, Fidei Chr. Expositio, Opera, tom. ii. f. 555, 556, 557, Zurich, 1581.)

Hooker says: "It seemeth therefore much amiss that against them, whom they term Sacramentaries, so many invective discourses are made, all running upon two points, that the Eucharist is not a bare sign or figure only, and that the efficacy of His Body and Blood is not all we receive in this sacrament. For no man having read their books and writings which are thus traduced, can be ignorant that both these assertions they plainly confess to be most true. They do not so interpret the words of Christ as if the name of His Body did impart but the figure of His Body, and to be were only to signify His Blood. They

for all purposes of participation and communion, of those lifegiving things whose names they bear; and by reason of their consecrated relation to things unseen, you may fitly treat them with the reverence due to objects of worship—in the older sense of that word.

It may even be possible to go a step further than this, and to regard the consecrated elements as changed with an inherent change (altogether beyond that change of use taught by our Reformers and our most esteemed Divines since the Reformation); a change by which they become possessed (in some sort) of spiritual efficacy, by the power of the Holy Ghost, or by the presence of lifegiving virtue, for the purposes of Communion. Such a view, indeed, seems to me to go altogether beyond what is warranted by Holy Scripture; and I know no sufficient evidence to justify the assertion of its having formed any part of the primitive faith.* Moreover, it has been felt by those who have held it, to be not the doctrine, and by some to be not consistent with the doctrine, of

grant that these holy mysteries received in due manner do instrumentally both make us partakers of the grace of that Body and Blood which were given for the life of the world, and besides also impart unto us even in true and real though mystical manner the very person of our Lord Himself, whole, perfect, and entire, as hath been shewed." (Hooker, Eccles. Pol., book v. ch. lxvii. § 8, edit. Keble, vol. ii. p. 355.)

* Some such notion, however, has been supposed by some to appear as early as the writings of Justin Martyr and Irenæus. See Bp. Bull's "Corruptions of the Church of Rome," sect. iii. Works, vol. ii. pp. 255, 256, Ox. 1846. But see below, p. 54, 55.

the English Church.* And we may be very thankful to know that our Church has deliberately and carefully eliminated from her formularies whatever might have seemed to lend sanction to such an unscriptural theory.

Yet it may possibly be admitted that some such view might be held by those who stand on this side of the great separating boundary of Eucharistic doctrine. And such a view might justify even a higher degree of reverence for what is outward and visible in the Sacrament.

But adoration, as implying the devotion due to Divinity alone, may not be directed towards the elements. All true adoration must be regarded as a mistake, and a mistake to be carefully shunned by all who would shun the sin of idolatry.

Take the hypothesis on the other side, and to be consistent you must indeed recognise the fitness of Eucharistic adoration addressed to that which is under the forms of bread and wine. But then you must also recognise Christianity as a changeful, growing thing,†

* See Papers on the Eucharistic Presence, pp. 458, 459, and Real Objective Presence, p. 26.

† It has of late been much observed that such phrases as "real presence" are of modern origin.

Examples may, indeed, be alleged of ancient language speaking of Christ as present in the Eucharist; but none, I believe, which can be fairly understood as representing Him present in the elements.

Indeed, when the Fathers do speak of the presence of Christ in the ordinance, I think it will be found that their language rather points to a presence of His person, as distinguished from His Body and Blood—as the *res sacramenti* represented by the elements; and

D

very imperfect in its origin, subsequently by degrees developed, and not reaching maturity for thirteen centuries. You must regard it as at first like the streak of still more to a presence as quite apart from the elements themselves in the sacrament.

He is said, indeed, by one to be present in the Sacrament because it is His body : "In illo Sacramento Christus est, quia corpus est Christi." (De Mysteriis, cap. ix., in Op. Ambrosii, ed. Ben., tom. ii. c. 341.) Compare Florus Magister: " Ubi corpus ejus, ibi Jesus est " (De Expos. Miss. § 67, Op., edit. Migne, c. 60), which perhaps suggested Bp. Andrewes's " Ubi corpus, ubi sanguis, ibi Christus," on which see Vogan's observations, "True Doctrine of Euch.," p. 600.

He is, indeed, in their view, the victim slain (representatively) in the Sacrament. But much rather He is—not in representation only —the Mediator, the Lord of the feast, the Giver of His own sacrificed Body and Blood. (See Papers on Eucharistic Presence, p. 338.)

In the Liturgy of the Apostolic Constitutions the Deacon is directed to say, after the Consecration—Ἔτι καὶ ἔτι δεηθῶμεν τοῦ Θεοῦ διὰ τοῦ Χριστοῦ αὐτοῦ ὑπὲρ τοῦ δώρου τοῦ προσκομισθέντος Κυρίῳ τῷ Θεῷ, ὅπως ἁ ἀγαθὸς Θεὸς προσδέξηται αὐτὸ διὰ τῆς μεσιτείας τοῦ Χριστοῦ αὐτοῦ εἰς τὸ ἐπουράνιον αὐτοῦ θυσιαστήριον, εἰς ὀσμὴν εὐωδίας. (Cotelerius, 1670, tom. i. p. 404. See Romish Mass and English Church, p. 97.)

Ambrose says : " Hunc panem dedit Apostolis ut dividerent populo credentium, hodieque dat nobis eum, quem ipse quotidie sacerdos consecrat suis verbis. Hic panis factus est esca Sanctorum. Possumus et ipsum Dominum accipere, qui suam carnem nobis dedit sicut ipse ait: Ego sum panis vitæ." (Ambrosius, De Benedict. Patriarch., cap. ix. § 38, 39, Opera, ed. Bened., tom. i. c. 524, 525.)

Chrysostom says : Ὁρᾷς αὐτὸν κείμενον· μᾶλλον δὲ καὶ φωνῆς αὐτοῦ ἀκούεις, φθεγγομένου αὐτοῦ διὰ τῶν εὐαγγελιστῶν." (In Matth. Hom. l. al. li., Op., edit. Montfaucon, tom. vii. p. 517.)

Again : Ὁ γὰρ τὸ μεῖζον δοὺς, τουτέσιν ἑαυτὸν παραθεὶς, πολλῷ μᾶλλον οὐκ ἀπαξιώσει καὶ διαδοῦναί σοι τὸ σῶμα. (Ibid. p. 517.)

Again : Ἡ προσφορὰ ἡ αὐτή ἐστι, . . . ἣν ὁ Χριστὸς τοῖς μαθηταῖς ἔδωκε . . . τὸ πᾶν τῆς πίστεώς ἐστιν . . . καὶ τοῦτο τοίνυν σῶμά ἐστι κἀκεῖνο· ὁ δὲ νομίζων τοῦτο ἔλαττον ἐκείνου εἶναι, οὐκ οἶδεν ὅτι

light, as of the new moon in the dark heavens, gradually waxing larger, yet still as partially dark until Pope ὁ Χριστὸς καὶ νῦν πάρεστι, καὶ νῦν ἐνεργεῖ. (Ibid. in 2 Tim. i., Hom. ii., Op., tom. xi. pp. 671, 672.)

Again (alluding to Joseph and Pharaoh's butler): Αὐτὸς ὁ βασιλεὺς εἰς χεῖρα τὴν ὑμετέραν δώσει τὸ ποτήριον τὸ φρικτὸν καὶ πολλῆς γέμον δυνάμεως. (Catech. ad Illumin. i. § i., Op., edit. Montfaucon, tom. ii. p. 226.)

Again: Τράπεζα πάρεστι βασιλίκη, ἄγγελοι διακονούμενοι ἐν τραπέζῃ, αὐτὸς πάρεστι ὁ βασιλεύς. (In Ep. ad Ephes., Hom. iii. § 5, Op., edit. Montfaucon, tom. xi. p. 23.)

Again: Πάρεστι καὶ νῦν ὁ Χριστὸς τὴν τράπεζαν κοσμῶν. (De Prod. Jud., Hom. ii. § 6, Op., edit. Montfaucon, tom. ii. p. 394.)

Again: Ὥσπερ γὰρ ἡ παρουσία αὐτοῦ . . . τοὺς μὴ δέξαμενους αὐτὴν μᾶλλον κατέκρινεν· οὕτω καὶ τὰ μυστήρια μείζονος ἐφόδια κολάσεως γίνεται τοῖς ἀναξίως μετέχουσι. (In 1 Cor., Hom. xxviii. § 1, Op., edit. Montfaucon, tom. x. p. 251).

[The author of the "Opus imperfectum in Matth." says of Christ: "Si sit præsens, non creditur, sed videtur: cum autem absens fuerit, non videtur, sed creditur." (Hom. liii. ex cap. xxv., in Op. Chrysost., edit. Montfaucon, tom. vi. App. p. ccxxi.)]

Proclus says: " Præsepis vice, altare veneremur ; pro infante, panem per infantem benedictum [τὸν διὰ τοῦ βρέφους εὐλογούμενον ἄρτον] complectamur." (Proclus, Orat. xvii. in Biblioth. Max. Patr. Lugd., tom. vi. 1677, p. 609. See Albertinus, De Euch., p. 773.)

Cyril of Alexandria says: Χριστὸς ἡμᾶς σήμερον ἑστιᾶται, Χριστὸς ἡμῖν σήμερον διακονεῖ." (Hom. Div. x., Op., edit. Migne, tom. x. c. 1017).

The venerable Bede says: " Hac ergo frequentia corporalis suæ manifestationis ostendere voluit Dominus, ut diximus, in omni loco se bonorum desideriis *divinitus* esse præsentem. . . . Apparuit in fractione panis his, qui se peregrinum esse putantes ad hospitium vocaverunt: aderit et nobis cum peregrinis et pauperibus, quæcunque possumus, bona libentur impendimus. Aderit et nobis in fractione panis, cum sacramentum corporis ejus, videlicet panis vivi, casta et simplici conscientia sumimus." (Homil. Æstiv. de Tempore Feria Sexta Pasch. Matth. 28, Opera, edit. Cologne, 1688, tom. vii. c. 15.)

Urban gave it its full splendour by appointing the novel festival of Corpus Christi—even as in our own days we have seen a further development of Roman Christianity in the Dedication of the Church by the Pope to the Sacred Heart—in consequence of the mystical visions and supposed revelations made to an ecstatic devotee or a hysterical nun.*

"Jesus, qui altaribus sacrosanctis inter immolandum, utpote proposita consecraturus, adesse non dubitatur." (Hincmar Rem., Ep. ii. Ad Car. Calv. Reg., De Cavendis Vitiis, § xi., Opera, edit. Paris, 1645, tom. ii. p. 88.)

Let the reader be asked to consider whether these passages, fairly interpreted, are suggestive of any other view of Christ's presence in the Eucharist than that which was acknowledged by Zwingle in the words—"Christum credimus vere esse in cœna, imo non credimus esse domini cœnam nisi Christus adsit." (Opera, Tiguri, 1581, tom. ii. fo. 503a.)

It must be remembered, too, that in this matter of Presence, as in other things, the Fathers used much licence of speech.

Damascenus, speaking of the cross, says: "Ἔνθα γὰρ ἦν τὸ σημεῖον, ἐκεῖ καὶ αὐτὸς ἔσται. (De Fid. Orth., lib. iv. c. xii., Op., ed. Lequien, tom. i. p. 265.)

Chrysostom spoke of seeing the King sitting on the throne of His Glory in the Gospel. (In Matth., Hom. ii. § 1, Op., edit. Montfaucon, tom. vii. p. 19.)

Another said: "Sepulchrum Domini quotiescunque ingredimur, toties jacere in sindone cernimus salvatorem involutum." (See Albertinus, De Euch., p. 566.)

Augustine says: "Si bonus es, habes Christum . . . in præsenti per fidem, in præsenti per signum [*i.e.* crucem], in præsenti per baptismatis sacramentum, in præsenti per altaris cibum et potum." (In Joan., Tract. l., Op., edit. Ben. 1680, tom. iii. par. ii. c. 633.)

* "Writing to you on the 17th of June [1875], I gave you a description of the religious revival going forward in honour of the Sacred Heart; the many services already held and to be held throughout the month in at least one hundred different churches in the city; the splendour with which those churches were decorated, and the

And yet further, on this hypothesis, to be consistent, those who are seeking to introduce Eucharistic Adoration among us must not only seek to restore the Eastward

crowds of persons attending them. At the same time I told you that on the 22nd of April the Pope had signed a decree dedicating the Universal Catholic Church to the Sacred Heart; that the dedication was formally made on the 16th June; that on that day, and to that purpose, a special service had been held, with unwonted pomp, in the Church of the Gesu; that the *Te Deum* had been sung in especial honour of the occasion at St. John Lateran, St. Peter's, and at the Gesu; and that the Act of Dedication had been publicly read in those and in all the other principal churches of the city. The 16th of June was chosen for the dedication, as it was the second centenary of the miraculous manifestation said to have been made to Marguerite Marie Alacoque, and the anniversary was celebrated in other places —at Paray le Monial and at Paris, where the foundation-stone of a church dedicated to the Sacred Heart was laid on Montmartre. It was in France this new religion had its origin and has become most extended; and from France innumerable petitions have been laid at the foot of the Papal Throne praying for this very dedication, and for superior authorisation to justify the prayer, 'Dieu de clémence, Dieu protecteur, sauvez Rome et la France, votre Sacré Cœur.' Similar applications were received from other countries, and the reasons for the Pope first limiting the Dedication to Italy are supposed to be that the visible devotions of the French Catholics to the mystical visions of the hysterical nun, Marie Alacoque, had at times taken forms which were rather startling than edifying.

" On the 1st of June the Cardinal Vicar published an *Invito Sacro*, in which he says:—

" ' It is not, therefore, marvellous that this devotion, from Catholic France, where it had its origin, has been propagated and diffused in Italy, in all Europe, and throughout the entire world, and that to-day Bishops and faithful of all nations have turned to the sacred Apostolic See, confidently expressing their desire—namely, that there is no other remedy against the many evils by which the human family is afflicted than to consecrate it wholly to the Holiest Heart of Jesus. For which reason, the Holy Father, in the desire to satisfy in some manner the common desire, has deigned, by decree of the Sacred Congregation

position and the vestments—must not only desire to elevate with sound of sacring bell the host and the chalice; they must also aim at providing in our churches continual access to the Sacramental Presence as a perpetual object to which to address our prayers. It would be uncharitable and cruel to stop short of this. Nay, further; they must seek to restore to us the festival and the ceremonial of Corpus Christi.* Our religion would

of Rites, dated the 22nd of April, to improve the formula of consecration to the Sacred Heart of Jesus, exhorting all the faithful throughout the Catholic world to recite the same, either in congregation or in private, on the 16th of this current June, the 30th anniversary of his assumption of the Supreme Pontificate, and second centenary of the revelation made by the Divine Redeemer to the blessed Marguerite, to propagate the devotion to His Sacred Heart." (Correspondence of the *Times* from Rome.)

* A recent writer of the Church of England (the Rev. F. G. Lee, D.C.L.), is quoted (*Record*, Nov. 29, 1875) as saying: " In countries which are specially and eminently Christian, ... where the Blessed Sacrament of the Altar, God manifest in the Flesh, reposing in the tabernacle, or borne in triumph through aisle, and street, and garden, hallows and feeds the faithful, there the power and influence of the Evil One is circumscribed and weakened."

If such language were according to the mind of the Reformed Church of England, it would seem as if but a few steps further on were needed to bring us to a desire for the restoration of the procession belonging to the discarded Festival.

But very different was the doctrine of such men as Bishop Cosin. "Quinetiam negamus sacramentum, extra usum a Deo institutum, rationem habere sacramenti, in quo Christus reservari aut circumgestari debeat aut possit; quum communicantibus tantum adsit. ... Quod asserunt pontificii,—Christum dare nobis Corpus et Sanguinem suum, ore ac dentibus sumendum et comedendum, ita ut non solum degludiatur ab impiis, verâ fide destitutis, sed etiam a muribus et gliribus,—id vero nos ore, corde, et mente penitus pernegamus." (Cosin, Hist. Trans., cap. iv. § v., Works, A. C. L., vol. iv. p. 49.)

be lacking a suitable recognition of the majesty of this mystery without this.

Before, however, such an attempt is made, is it too much to ask that there may be a reconsideration of this whole subject? Ministers of our own communion may at least be entreated to mark first how clearly and consistently this Reformed Church of England has taken her stand on the other side of the broad line of demarcation.

"Blessed be God," says Archbishop Wake, "our Church is too well persuaded of the unlawfulness of such a worship, ever to require it of us."*

I will not here appeal afresh to the details of the evidence furnished by her Articles and Liturgy,† but I will ask, What else can be the meaning of the rejection of elevation, reservation, and ostension? How else can we possibly account for the reason given to justify kneeling reception? Has she not plainly declared "that thereby no adoration is intended, or ought to be done,‡

Again: " Cum poculum nonnisi sacramentali metonymia possit esse illud testamentum, planum fit, nec panem aliter esse posse Corpus Christi." (Cosin, Hist. Transub., cap. v. § iv., Works, A. C. L., vol. iv. p. 58.)

* See Gibson's Preservative, vol. x. p. 113, London, 1848.

† See Papers on the Eucharistic Presence, Nos. vii. and viii.

‡ "We kneel, and the Papists kneel; but we declare when we kneel, we intend no adoration to the Elements; but the Papists cannot deny that they do give proper adoration to that which is before them; which we say is Bread, and they say, the Body of Christ under the species of Bread; and yet not merely to the invisible Body

either unto the Sacramental Bread or Wine there bodily received, or unto any Corporal Presence of Christ's natural Flesh and Blood?" And has she not added this further reason against such adoration: "The Sacramental Bread and Wine remain still in their very natural substances, and therefore may not be adored;* (for

of Christ, but taking the species of Bread as united to that Body of Christ, and so directing their worship to these two together as the proper objects of Divine adoration. And to make this evident to you, their adoration is performed at the elevation of the Host; and at the carrying it about in Processions, and at the exposing it on their Altars; and not merely in the participation of it. Whence it is observable, that the Church of Rome does not strictly require kneeling at the participation, which it would do if it looked on the kneeling at receiving as a proper act of Adoration. The Rubricks of the Mass do not, that I can find, require the Priest to kneel in the act of receiving; and the Pope, when he celebrates, receives sitting. Espencæus saith, in the Church of Lyons, many of the people did not receive kneeling; and upon complaint made about it, they were by the advice of Two Cardinals left to their old custom. And I wonder your Brethren have not taken notice of the difference of kneeling at the elevation of the Host, and in the act of receiving it; the one was required by the Constitution of Honorius, and was intended for an act of Adoration to the Host: The other was derived from the Ancient Church, which although it did not always use the same posture of Adoration that we do; yet it is sufficient for our purpose, if they received the Sacrament in the same posture in which they worshipped God. And this I could easily prove, if this were a place or season for it." (Stillingfleet, Conferences concerning the Idolatry of the Church of Rome, Works, vol. vi. p. 14.)

* "It is evident," says Dean Aldrich, "that when we say Christ is present, or adorable in the Sacrament, we do not mean in the elements, but in the celebration. We affirm His natural body to be locally in heaven and not here; and that we, who are here and not in heaven, ought to worship it as locally present in heaven, while we celebrate the Holy Sacrament upon earth." (Reply to Two Discourses, p. 17.)

that were idolatry to be abhorred of all faithful Christians) ?"
Above all, has she not added this declaration also: "The natural Body and Blood of our Saviour Christ are in heaven, and not here; it being against the truth of Christ's * natural Body to be at one time in more places than one ? " †

* Christ's natural body is distinguished from His mystical body (the Church), and His sacramental body (*i.e.* the sacrament of His body), and is not distinguished at all from any spiritual body of Christ. Indeed, it has been very truly observed by Mr. Milton : " His natural and His spiritual body is one and the same—natural in the truth of our nature, spiritual in its risen and glorified condition." The term ψυχικὸν (1 Cor. xv. 44) is not now applicable to our Lord's body, because it is the body of the resurrection. And of that natural glorified spiritual body the ' Declaration ' asserts that ' it is in heaven and not here.'" (See Milton, Eucharist Illustrated, p. 77.)

† " The Rubric saith expressly,*That it is against the truth of Christ's natural body to be at one time in more places than one. It doth not say, against the corporeal presence of His natural body, but the truth of it.* From whence it follows, that our *Church* believes the *true natural body of Christ,* which was born of the Virgin, suffered on the cross, and ascended into heaven, *can be but in one place,* which is declared in the foregoing words : *And the natural body and blood of our Saviour Christ are in heaven and not here; i.e.* in heaven exclusively from being in the *Sacrament.* Which are not true, if the same *natural body* of *Christ* could be at the *same time* in *heaven* and in the *Host.*" (Stillingfleet, Works, vol. vi. p. 19.)

" If any do seem to speak of the presence of *the very same Body which is in heaven,* I desire them, in the *first place,* to reconcile that *doctrine with* this *dogmatical assertion* at the end of this *rubrick ; that it is against the truth of Christ's natural body* (not against the corporal presence of it), *to be at one time in more places than one.* Let men imagine what *kind* of *presence* they please of the *same body,* I only desire to know, *whether to be in heaven, and to be in the Sacrament,* be to be in the *same or distinct places ?* If the *places be distinct,*

Have we not here a rejection, not only of the adoration, but of the Presence which some are so earnestly contending for? And have we not also here a recognition of the truth that the question of adoration should be determined by the question of the Presence? *

as no doubt *heaven* and *earth* are, then our *Church* declares, *That it is contrary to the truth of Christ's natural body to be in more places than one at one time.*" (Stillingfleet, Works, vol. vi., pp. 22, 23.)

" The sense of the *rubrick* lies in these two propositions: 1. That it is *idolatry* to give *adoration* to the *elements remaining in their natural substances.* 2. That it is absurd to believe *Christ's natural body to to be present, because then it must be in more places than one, which is repugnant to the truth of a body.* These things, to my apprehension, are the plain and natural sense of this *rubrick.*" (Ibid., p. 16.)

* On the change of the term " corporal presence " to " real and essential presence," at the last review, see Papers on the Eucharistic Presence, pp. 467—474, 578—586; Real Objective Presence, pp. 40—43.

The change of *expression* was desirable, because there is, in the teaching of Reformed theology, a real and essential presence to the soul, as distinguished from a corporal presence, which is a presence to the body. (See Real Presence of Laudian Theology, p. 62.)

Archbishop Tennison says of the presence: " Real it is, if it be present in its real effects, and they are the essence of it, so far as a communicant doth receive it." (Discourse of Idolatry, London, 1678, p. 181.)

But the structure of the rubric itself renders a purpose of changing the *doctrinal statement* inconceivable.

Let it be carefully considered what such a change would amount to. It would be a designed rejection of the previous statement, admitting its contradictory.

But the contradictory of the previous statement would be that adoration may be done to a *real and essential* presence there being of Christ's natural flesh and blood—the amended statement still declaring that no adoration ought to be done to any *corporal* presence of Christ's natural flesh and blood.

The effect of the change of statement would obviously be to make

Surely, herein she has learned a lesson from the words of Cranmer, words never to be forgotten—those words of prophetic warning against the roots of error in the doctrine of Transubstantiation and the Real Presence; "which roots," he says, "if they be suffered to grow in the Lord's vineyard, they will overspread all the ground again with the old errors and superstitions." *

a distinction between a real and essential presence (not to the soul but upon the table), and a corporal presence there; allowing adoration to the one, and refusing it to the other.

But the whole argument of the rubric will be found to apply as much to the exclusion of adoration to the one as to the other. If the rubric allows adoration to a real and essential presence in the elements, then the order of kneeling is certainly not well meant for a signification of our humble and grateful acknowledgment of the benefits of Christ given in the Lord's Supper to all worthy receivers: and further, not only is it foolish to argue from the statement of Christ's natural body and blood being in heaven, but it is actually untrue to declare that they are in heaven and *not here.* And then, further still, it cannot be maintained that it is against the truth of Christ's natural body to be at one time in more places than one.

On the hypothesis of the doctrinal statement being thus changed to admit of the teaching of the adorable presence of Christ's Body really and essentially present after the manner of a spirit in the elements, it will be found that there is a cause for the statement appended to the statement, which alleged cause is not only inapplicable to the statement, but is actually destructive of it.

But further: looking at the object of the rubric, it cannot be denied that, upon the supposition of such an intentional change of the doctrinal statement, the whole rubric would have been a miserable delusion, an attempt to put to rest men's suspicions by a declaration, which declaration in its changed form (with the change so understood), instead of removing suspicions, would not merely have aggravated them, but have raised the fiercest opposition. Such an attempt at public deception is not only incredible, it would have been worthy of infamy.

* Preface to Answer to Gardiner, ed. 1550.

Now, before we consent to be guided by a theology which has already bidden us regard Cranmer as a heretic,* which in consistency must teach us not only to condemn our Reformers and our great Church of England divines, but also step by step to undo the work and undermine the teaching of our Reformation, till we have restored to us the festival of Corpus Christi, let the question of Eucharistic Presence be carefully and thoroughly investigated.

I can scarcely think it too much to say that the views of a considerable number of the younger generation of

---

* Thus Dr. Pusey speaks of " the meaning of the Zwinglian school, into which Cranmer afterwards unhappily fell" (Real Presence the Doct. of the Eng. Ch., p. 159), and this, in the context immediately preceding, is called " the Zwinglian heresy."

So Dr. Neale, in his Preface to the " Tetralogia Liturgica," uses the term " hæretici " to signify the " Reformed," and " hæresis Zwingliana" to express their views. (See pp. xii. and xvii.)

Nor is there in this anything to be complained of. Rather it is desirable that it should be clearly seen that from the standpoint of those who hold the Real Objective Presence in the elements, those who reject that doctrine ought, in charity as well as in truth, to be thus denominated. See Essays on the Reformation (Vivish, Maidstone), pp. 18—25.

The doctrine, when held in its distinctness, must in consistency have its claim admitted to be regarded as an article of the faith. And when it has been marked as " of the faith," its repudiation must also be marked as *heretical.*

See Dr. Pusey, as quoted in Dr. Harrison's " Challenge Answered," vol. ii. p. 341; see also Papers on Eucharistic Presence, p. 687.

" If your assertion is correct," wrote Bp. Shuttleworth, in 1841, to one now a Romish priest, " our Canons are heretical, the Prayer-book is heretical, St. Paul is heretical." (Last Three Sermons, Rivington, p. 94.)

our clergy have been largely influenced—not to say grievously warped—by assuming that what is now called the doctrine of the Real Objective Presence has certainly been the teaching of the Catholic Church of Christ in all ages, and that the testimony of all the early Fathers is found clearly to support it. Indeed, I quite believe that a very considerable number of persons are even still persuaded that in shielding the Eucharistic doctrine of the extreme Ritualists, they are only defending the position of a continuous succession of our most honoured Church of England divines. And though *this* error is by degrees giving way, the result in too many cases, I fear, is simply that men fall back on the assumption that, at any rate, it is the doctrine of Christian antiquity; and therefore the Church of England, seeing she professes to seek the old paths, ought certainly to teach it.

Such an assumption, indeed, might seem unaccountable but for the confidence of assertion which may sometimes seem to support it, and the facility with which passages—numbers of them—may be quoted, in which language is found, such as might safely enough be used before the idea of the Corporal Presence was ever dreamt of, but which, if employed after the birth of the Paschasian doctrine, might (it is readily granted) fairly have been regarded as tending rather to support it.

It is, perhaps, scarcely to be wondered at, if controversialists have learned so to marshal these passages in order as to produce a really imposing effect. But it is to be regretted that they have also too often written as if they expected that, without further examination, all opposition must give way before them, and (except in cases of invincible prejudice) the question must be regarded as settled, and the victory won *—ignoring

* This assumption is very observable in the works of some Roman Catholic divines. But some striking examples of it might be cited from publications of our own day, not written by Romanists.

It is curious to observe how Dr. Neale writes, as if in the seventeenth century Arnauld had, in this controversy, won, with a master's hand, an easy victory over all opponents, and reduced to silence all enemies of the Romish doctrine.

He says: "Nicole and Arnauld laboured at their 'Perpetuity of the faith of the Church concerning the Doctrine of the Holy Eucharist,' in which the ablest of the Calvinist authors, Claude, Aubertin, and Blondel, were so thoroughly crushed and overwhelmed, that they never ventured to make head on that subject again." (Jansenist Church, Introduction, pp. 32, 33.) Did any divine of the Church of England ever express himself thus on this controversy before?

Dr. Neale cannot possibly have meant to convey such an impression. Yet his words might not very unnaturally (I think) lead the reader to suppose that no attempt even was ever made to answer "La Perpetuité de la Foi;" that the three champions of the Reformed faith looked on and saw a death-blow given to their belief; that they recognised in the work of their opponents a confutation of their writings which they all felt to be unanswerable, or which, at any rate, they knew they had no power to reply to.

It is, indeed, quite true that Aubertin (Albertinus) wrote no reply. He had been dead some years; so also had Blondel.

But it is well known with what vigour the controversy was carried on by Claude, whose ability has won the admiration of Romanists. See Walchii Bibliotheca Theol., tom. ii. pp. 232—236, 321, 322, and Chalmers's Biographical Dictionary, art. Arnauld and Claude. See also Claude's Catholic Doctrine of the Eucharist, Pref., p. 1, Eng. trans. (London, 1684).

Claude's power was signally displayed in replying to the tracts

the fact that side by side sometimes with such sayings of the Fathers may be found interpretative named by Dr. Neale. And that he suffered Nicole and Arnauld in their work " La Response aux Passages Difficiles des Pères," published in 1672, to have the last word, was certainly not because he yielded the victory. See Walch, p. 233. In the following year he published his " Defence of the Reformation." See Walch, p. 321.

Claude himself had been dead nearly twenty years, when, in 1704, the collected pieces of Arnauld and Nicole, in four volumes, were published under the title, "La Perpetuité de la Foi," &c. See Deylingius, Obs. Sac., par. iv. p. 161.

Moreover it was as *his* contribution to this controversy, and especially as an antidote to the great fallacies which he saw running through the argument of Arnauld, that our own Bishop Cosin was induced to publish, in 1675, his valuable " History of Transubstantiation " (which he had written previously), in defence of the "Real Presence" of Protestants (Continental as well as English, Reformed not less than Lutheran), *i.e.* of the primitive doctrine of the Eucharist, against the corruptions of the Romish doctrine. (See Durel's " Præfatio," in Cosin's Works, A. C. L., vol. iv. pp. 7, 8. See also Cosin's Letter to Blondel, Ib., pp. 482, 483.)

The great fallacy which Cosin observed in the argument of Arnauld, was the same which had appeared before in the book by which La Milletière had, in his own judgment, triumphed so gloriously over Albertinus or Aubertin. (See Bramhall's Works, A. C. L., vol. i. CXLI. CXLII.)

Archbishop Bramhall (then Bishop of Derry) then wrote to him in reply : " Having viewed all your strength with a single eye, I find not one of your arguments that comes home to Transubstantiation, but only to a true Real Presence, which no genuine son of the Church of England did ever deny, no, nor your adversary [Aubertin] himself." (Works, A. C. L., vol. i. p. 8.)

With reference to the controversy of the Jansenists, our Archbishop Wake wrote : " The first attempt they [the Jansenists] made was a little piece that has since given occasion to a very long controversy between *Monsieur Arnauld* and *Monsieur Claude, of the Perpetuity of the Faith as to the real Presence of Christ in the Holy Eucharist.* A tract, which if we regard only the neatness and subtilty of the composure, it must be avowed scarce anything ever appeared more

dicta* before which the army with banners is seen†
worthy that applause it met with in the world. . . . But the *sophistry* of this *method* has been sufficiently exposed in the volumes composed on this occasion. . . . . In effect the design of this first method amounted to this much; that *Transubstantiation* . . . . was visibly once the common doctrine of the Church: and 'tis impossible it should have been so then, had it ever been otherwise before. And this to be believed in the strength of a sophistical argument, notwithstanding all the evident instances of *matter of fact* which Monsieur d'Aubertine and others have at large collected to the contrary." (Defence of the Exposition of the Doct. of the Ch. of E., 1686, Pref., pp. ii. iii.)

* See Appendix, Note D.

† It should be noted that not only have we *interpretative dicta* in the writings of the Fathers, but also illustrations of their language as applied to the elements drawn from their mode of speaking of other things.

Thus Chrysostom affirms not only that the table on which he consecrated was the same as that which Christ used, but that his church was that very same upper chamber where Christ and His disciples were when He instituted the Lord's Supper. (See Harrison's "Dr. Pusey's Challenge Answered," vol. ii. p. 186.) Not only so, but the hand from which the elements are received is to be regarded as the hand not of the minister, but of Christ Himself (Ibid., p. 181); though elsewhere he says "as from the tongs of the seraphim." (See Albertinus, De Euch., p. 578.)

Moreover, he teaches Christians to believe that it is the very same Supper in which Christ reclined. (In Matt., Hom. 1. al. li., Op., ed. Montfaucon, tom. vii. p. 517, and in ii. Ep. ad Tim. cap. i., Hom. ii., Op., tom. xi. p. 671.) All which is obviously untrue (as St. Augustine teaches: see Albertinus, De Euch., p. 731) except to faith, to which "præterita sunt præsentia."

St. Augustine says: "Judex fuerat in præcone. Quia et quando judex loquitur per præconem, exceptor non facit, Præco dixit; sed, Judex dixit." (In Joan. Evang. cap. x., Tract. xlv., Op., edit. Ben. 1680, tom. iii. par. ii. c. 398.)

ʽΑ μὴ δι' ὅλων ἐστὶν ὅπερ λέγεται, ἐκ καταχρήσεως ἔχει τὴν κλῆσιν. (Gregory Nys., De Opificio Hominis, c. xv., Op., edit. Migne, tom. i. c. 176.)

so to melt away that its thinned ranks cease to be formidable.*

What we have to ask is, that thoughtful men, not trusting to the guidance of books written in the interests

---

* As to that other class of extracts, in which the *change* of the Elements is spoken of, Bishop Cosin writes : " Hic mire gloriantur transubstantiatores, habere se consensum totius antiquitatis. Resp. At respondendum est, a non distributo ad distributum non valere consequentiam. ... Quoniam igitur vulgaris panis per benedictionem convertitur in panem qui, a communi usu exemptus, in hunc usum sacrum ex instituto divino adhibitur, ut sit symbolum sacramentale, per quod representetur Corpus Christi, in quo plenitudo Deitatis habitat corporaliter; atque adeo, in alium ac nobiliorem statum translatus, fiat quiddam amplius quam quod erat antea ; inde veterum nonnulli panem mutatum et transmutatum esse dixerunt. Et est sane illa mutatio vere magna, eaque non naturalis, sed supernaturalis. ... Quid, quod ipsi etiam patres has easdem μεταβολῆς, μεταποιήσεως, et μεταστοιχώσεως voces usurpant, quum de rebus aliis loquuntur, quæ substantiam suam minime vel amittunt vel mutant? Sunt enim voces istæ tam amplæ significationis, ut quamvis aliquoties denotent mutationem substantialem, plerumque tamen nonnisi moralem, aut mutationem qualitatum, conditionis, muneris, status, et id genus alias indicent." (Works, A. C. L., vol. iv. pp. 99, 100.)

Some examples may be seen in the notes to Cosin, p. 101.

Others will be found in Dr. Pusey's " Real Presence from the Fathers," Note Q, pp. 162 *sqq.*

The reader may also be referred to Albertinus, De Eucharistia, (1) for the term μεταποιεῖσθαι, p. 487 ; (2) for the term μεταστοιχειοῦν, p. 488 ; (3) for the term μεταρυθμίζειν, p. 574; (4) for the term μεταβάλλειν, p. 424; (5) for the term μετασκευάζειν, p. 489.

Let it suffice here to give one example of each :—

(1) Gregory Nys. says of the shining of the face of Moses : Οὕτω γίνεται τοῦ Μωυσέως ἡ ἐπὶ τὸ ἐνδοξότερον μεταποίησις τοιαύτη καὶ τοσαύτη, ὡς ἀχώρητον εἶναι τῷ κάτω ὀφθαλμῷ τὴν τῆς δόξης ἐκείνης ἐμφάνειαν. (De Vita Moysis, Mystica Interpretatio, Opera, tom. i. c. 397, edit. Migne.)

of a party, will calmly, and not superficially, examine this subject for themselves.

There is, indeed, abundant evidence to show that Christians of old time did not regard the sacramental elements as *bare* signs; that they did think of it as a

(2) Cyril Alex. says of Baptism: "Ὅνπερ γὰρ τρόπον τὸ ἐν τοῖς λέβησιν ἐκχεόμενον ὕδωρ ταῖς τοῦ πυρὸς ὁμιλῆσαν ἀκμαῖς τὴν ἐξ αὑτοῦ δύναμιν ἀναμάττεται, οὕτω διὰ τῆς τοῦ Πνεύματος ἐνεργείας τὸ αἰσθητὸν ὕδωρ πρὸς θείαν τινὰ καὶ ἄρρητον ἀναστοιχειοῦται [al. μεταστοιχειοῦται] δύναμιν, ἁγιάζει τε λοιπὸν τοὺς ἐν οἷς ἂν γένοιτο. (In Joan. Evang., Lib. ii. in Ch. iii. v. 5, 147, Opera, tom. vi. c. 245, edit. Migne.)

(3) Gregory Nys. says Baptism is received ἐπὶ ἀνακαινισμῷ καὶ τῇ μεταβολῇ τῆς φύσεως ἡμῶν. (Orat. Catech. c. xl., Opera, tom. ii. c. 101, edit. Migne.)

(4) Clemens Alex. says: Διδάχη μεταρρυθμίζει τὸν ἄνθρωπον. (Stromat., lib. iv. § xxiii. Op., tom. i. p. 631, edit. Potter, Venice, 1757).

(5) Clemens Alex. says: Μετασκεύασε τὰς γυναῖκας εἰς πόρνας ὁ προαγωγὸς οὗτος δράκων. (Pædagogus, lib. iii. cap. ii., Op., tom. i. p. 253, edit. Potter, Venice, 1757.)

Bishop Cosin adds: "Talem omnino permutationem, sacramentis omnibus communem, hic fieri intellexerunt [Patres] quâ externa symbola in res ipsas divinas conversa esse non aliam ob causam dicuntur, quam quia vere et efficaciter illas repræsentant, et fideles vere illarum participes fiunt, dum ea ore percipiunt; eamque, ex Spiritûs S. virtute, et Christi Domini instituto, prærogativam divinam acquirunt, quam ex naturâ suâ non habent" (p. 95). See Waterland's Works, vol. iv. p. 598, edit. Oxford, 1843, and Morton on Eucharist, p. 494, edit. 1635.

Very hyperbolical language is used sometimes by the Fathers, of the change of the water of Baptism. In some Eastern offices are found not only prayers for this change in very remarkable language, but prayers also for the return of the water afterwards to its natural condition. (See Neale's Hist. of Holy Eastern Church, Introduction. pp. 970—977.)

part of Christian duty to receive them as made to them the Communion of the Body and Blood of Christ. And it is readily granted that the Fathers have many times spoken of the Eucharist in highly rhetorical language— in language sometimes which, literally understood, would seem to suggest such materialistic views as are repudiated even by Romanists.* Nay, more: it will be found, if I mistake not, that at an early date a super-

* Such, I mean, as (unexplained) might, at first sight, seem to imply a notion approaching to that conveyed in the literal meaning of the following words as understood in their gross and carnal sense : " Corpus Domini Jesu Christi, quod accepimus, et sanctus sanguis Ejus, quem potavimus adhæreat visceribus nostris." (Mozarabic L. in Neale's Tetralogia Liturgica, pp. 195, 196.)

Bishop Morton says: "Sometimes the Fathers are found, in this Sacrament, to speak ἀκριβῶς, that is *exactly* and precisely, and sometime ἀκυρῶς, and οἰκονομικῶς, *improperly*. When they speak of a Corporal Conjunction with Christ's Body, *exactly* and simply so taken, so often they appear to deny it absolutely from point to point. As (1) by their *No bodily touch of Christ after His resurrection*. So Ambrose [*Serm.* 58: " Non super terram, nec in terra, nec secundum carnem, debemus quærere Salvatorem"]. (2) *No meat for teeth.* So *Augustine* [*Serm.* 33 *de v. Dom.*: "Non dentis cibus"]. (3) *Not to be devoured with throat.* So *Attalas* the Martyr. (4) *Not for the belly.* So *Cyprian* [*Pseudo-Cyprian, De Cœna Dom.*: "Non ventris cibus"]. (5) *Not for bodily Conjunction of Persons, nor for union of substances.* So also the same Father [*Pseudo-Cyprian, De Cœna Dom.*]. (6) *Not to be cast into the draught.* So *Cyril of Hierusalem* [οὐκ εἰς κοιλίαν, οὐκ εἰς ἀφεδρῶνα, Myst. 5]. Whereunto you may add, as the complexion and comprehension of all the rest, that of Chrysostom concerning this Sacrament, οὐδεν σαρκικὸν ἔχοντα, οὐδε ἀκολουθίαν φυσικὴν, that is, *Having no fleshly thing, nor yet that hath any natural consequence* thereof, namely, of fleshly *union*. In which you have all as flat negatives to your Romish Corporal Union, by your Bodily Touch, whether by hand, mouth, or belly, as the ancient Fathers could have given, if they had

stitious * regard for the elements was found adhering to the earlier and Scriptural view which looked upon them

concluded their judgments in a synod. . . . First then the Fathers, in their symbolical language, have called Bread the Body of Christ, only *sacramentally*, because it is a Sacrament and Sign of Christ's Body: which was the conclusion of our Second Book. II. They have not spared to call the change of bread into our bodies, a change of Christ's Body into ours, in a like Sacramental signification, as hath been shown in the Third Book. III. Upon the same sacramental and analogical reason, they have used to say that we see, touch, taste, and eat Christ's Body, albeit improperly, as hath been plentifully declared, and confessed in this Fifth Book. IV. (Because eating produceth a nourishing and augmentation of the body of the eater, by the thing eaten) they have attributed like phrases of our Bodily nourishment and augmentation by Christ's Body; which you yourselves have confessed to be most improperly spoken; in the same book. V. Almost all the former unions corporal of our bodies with Christ, have been ascribed by the same Fathers unto the Sacrament of Baptism; wherein there cannot properly be any corporal touch, or conjunction at all." (Bp. Morton on Eucharist, book v. ch. ix. § 3, 4, pp. 370, 371, London, 1635.)

" His Body and Blood are considered as intermingled with ours, when the symbols of them really and strictly are so: for the benefit is completely the same." (Waterland, Works, vol. iv. p. 594, Oxford, 1843. See his Notes, pp. 594, 595.)

The subject is very fully and ably argued in Chamier, Panstratia Catholica, De Euch., lib. xi. c. viii. ix. t. ii. pp. 304-316, ed. 1627.

Hooker says: "Christ is both as God and man that true vine whereof we both spiritually and corporally are branches. The mixture of His bodily substance with ours is a thing which the ancient Fathers disclaim. Yet the mixture of His flesh with ours they speak of, to signify what our very bodies through mystical conjunction receive from that vital efficacy which we know to be His; and from bodily mixtures they borrow divers similitudes rather to declare the truth, than the manner of coherence between His sacred Body and the sanctified bodies of Saints." (Eccles. Pol., book v. ch. lvi. § 10, edit. Keble, vol. ii. p. 252. See notes there.) See also Papers on the Eucharistic Presence, p. 141.

* I may mention, as an example of this superstitious regard, the

53

as effectual signs indeed, but still as signs, and figures, and symbols of the crucified Body and the outpoured

wearing of the Sacrament as a preservative against perils by land or by sea (see Arcudius, De Concordia, lib. iii. cap. lix. p. 399); also the practice, obtaining in different parts of the world—Africa and France, as well as apparently the East—of giving the consecrated bread to the dead, which was censured by St. Chrysostom and condemned in the Councils of Carthage III., Auxerre, and in Trullo. (See Bingham, Antiquities of Chr. Ch., book xxiii. sect. xiv. vol. vii. pp. 432, 433, 1844.)

So St. Basil is reported, after receiving one part of the Sacrament, to have waved another part over the altar, and to have desired that another part should be buried with him. (See Taylor's True Doctrine of Euch., p. 221.)

Gregory the Great tells of a young man dying without receiving the Sacrament (Dial., lib. ii. cap. xxiv., Op., edit. Benedict., tom. ii. c. 255), whom the grave would not retain till the Lord's Body was laid on his breast. But such customs are now spoken of by Romish divines as "cum institutione et majestate Eucharistiæ parum conformes." (Muratori, De Rebus Liturgicis, c. 283.)

Later than this we have examples of the consecrated wine being mixed with ink for solemn uses, as when, in 870, the Bishops at the Fourth Council of Constantinople subscribed the deposition of Photius. See Taylor's True Doctrine of Euch., p. 223, and Hospinian's Works, vol. iii. pp. 244, 245, and Carranza, tom. ii. p. 493.

The Scriptural word "mystery," though at first (we may believe) adopted to signify Christian Sacraments, with no such view (see Harrison's "Dr. Pusey's Challenge Answered," pp. 241—246), seems, in the progress of this superstitious growth, to have assimilated to itself the ideas which belonged to the "mysteries" of the heathen. And, as a consequence of that assimilation, the Eucharist seems to have acquired that character of concealment, and made that demand of secrecy in respect of the uninitiated, which clung to it for centuries. (See Albertinus, De Euch., p. 703 *sqq*.)

Indeed, it is very observable, and very suggestive as to the causes at work in the corruption of Christian truth, that Tertullian (and the practice of secrecy seems to be not much older than his time) urges the example of the Eleusinian mysteries as a reason for the

Blood of Christ; that upon this followed afterwards a conception of the consecrated elements * as united by silence of Christians. He writes: "Vel ex forma omnibus mysteriis silentii fides debeatur. Samothracia et Eleusinia reticentur, quanto magis talia, quæ prodita interim etiam humanam animadversionem provocabunt, dum divina servatur? Si ergo non ipsi proditores sui, sequitur ut extranei : et unde extraneis notitia? Cum semper etiam piæ initiationes arceant profanos, et arbitris caveant." (Tertul. Apologeticus, cap. vii., Opera, p. 8, edit. Rigalt., Paris, 1689.)

* I submit for consideration (not without diffidence) whether this doctrine of adoption, or spiritual union, or augmentation, or something like it, or approaching towards it, was not the most natural first step in the falling away from the primitive doctrine of the Eucharist; and whether it did not prevail to a wider extent than has generally been supposed; and whether it does not afford the most natural interpretation of some of those passages, to be found especially in the writings of the later Eastern Fathers, which seem, at first sight, to embody some sort of materialistic notion.

Possibly, also, some sort of approaches to this doctrine may have found place at an earlier period than has been usually thought. Such a view may, no doubt, take the form of an impanation and invination of the Second or Third Person of the Holy Trinity. (See Vogan's True Doctrine, p. 325.) And I conceive that it probably did amount to this, as the doctrine of Transubstantiation was nearly approached. But it is also quite possible, I think, that some such view may have been held without a conception of anything amounting to this, or anything like this.

It must, however, be remembered, in interpreting the language of the Fathers which seems to imply an inherent Divine efficacy imparted to the Eucharistic symbols, that the same sort of language is freely used also concerning the water of Baptism. And whatever abatement is required by the analogy of faith in the sense given to such language in the case of the one Sacrament, may not unfairly be applied to the similar case of the other. (See Goode on Eucharist, i. pp. 403—409, 411.)

It is well known also that similar language is used of the *Chrism*. Indeed, the change in the Eucharistic elements is paralleled by the change in the ointment. (See Goode, pp. 410, 414; see also Harrison's "Dr. Pusey's Challenge Answered," pp. 277—279.)

the Spirit to the Body of Christ; so that they might be more fitly called the Body and Blood of Christ than symbols of that Body. But it is not, I believe, till the ninth century * that we have any trace of the doctrine

* The doctrine of Paschasius was indeed a startling innovation, and took long to establish itself as the belief of the Western Church. (See Romish Mass and English Church, pp. 11, 12, 65—67.) Moreover, in his own day, and in his own teaching, it had scarcely hardened into that distinctness of shape which it afterwards assumed.

But it would scarcely have been possible for it to obtain a footing at all, if there had been before his time no falling away from the doctrine of St. Augustine. Doubtless, that Father's vast authority in the West had done much in the way of restraining tendencies to superstition and quasi-materialistic conceptions of Eucharistic doctrine. Yet, if I mistake not, the Churches of the Roman Communion had—to some extent—been brought up to the point at which the step to Paschasian doctrine was possible, by gradual approaches (made, perhaps, in the mist of the vaguest theories) towards some such doctrine of spiritual incorporation of the elements into the Body of Christ as had been propounded by Damascenus, and had to a great extent taken hold of the mind of the Eastern Church. (See Romish Mass and English Church, p. 62.)

When, by another step downwards, men came to believe that the consecrated bread was called Christ's Body—not because of its being an effectual proxy, nor yet because of its being spiritually united or incorporated into Christ's Body, but because the bread was substantially changed into flesh, their faith was at first truly and naturally expressed in the language of Berengar's confession: "Verum corpus et sanguinem domini nostri Jesu Christi esse: et sensualiter non solum sacramentum, sed in veritate manibus sacerdotum tractari frangi, et fidelium dentibus atteri." (See Anselm, Epist. cvii., Op. p. 453, Paris, 1721, who leads the way to scholastic distinctions.)

It was not till after this, when the new doctrine had been scientifically dissected by the skilful hands of Scholastic divines, and put under the microscope of Angelical doctors, that the distinction came out clearly between the substance of Christ's Body, which is eaten, but not divided by the teeth, and the accidents of bread and wine, which

which, on the supposition of its being true, would justify

alone are the subjects of lesion and mastication, and which alone can have to do with nourishing or entering into the substance of our bodies. Then it became necessary to gloss the words approved by Pope Nicholas and the Sacred Synod, and published as the faith of the Church through the cities of Italy, Germany, and France. Then the so-called Catholic faith was defended by the note, "Nisi sane intelligas verba Berengarii, in majorem incides hæresin quam ipse fuerit: et ideo omnia referas ad species ipsas. Nam de Christi corpore partes non facimus." (In Gratian, De Cons., Dist. ii., can. xli.)

The dominant party in the time of Berengarius had known nothing of the need of this caution. They had proclaimed aloud, and published abroad, as containing the faith which was to confound heresy, language which spoke naturally of the substance, but which, if understood of the substance, was more heretical than Berengarius, from the standpoint of later developments.

In truth, however, this later development, with all its subtilties and niceties of distinction, fell into a pit, from which the grossness of the doctrine, as put into the mouth of Berengar, was free. For the doctrine had been built up on the literal interpretation of figurative and sacramental sayings, both in the New Testament and the Fathers.

The Fathers had spoken sacramentally of eating Christ's Body. Therefore, because such language must not be figuratively understood, Christ's Body must be really eaten with the mouth.

But then the ancient Fathers spoke also of Christ's Body as being torn with our teeth and as nourishing our bodies. To understand this literally would be heresy, according to the Scholastic divines. Yet the whole theology of which this is the crowning arch, rests only for its foundation on the assumption that such sayings concerning eating *must* be literally understood.

This is admirably enforced by Bp. Bilson in his "True Difference," pp. 769—772.

I give the following brief extract:—"*Theophilus the Christian.*—How think you? Must this [the language of the Fathers asserting nourishment by the Body of Christ] be referred to the natural and true Body and Blood of Christ, or else to the signs bearing those names when once they be sanctified? *Philander the Jesuit.*—No doubt to

and require the Eucharistic adoration which is now in question.*

It would, however, be travelling beyond the purpose of the present paper to enter more particularly into the discussion of Patristic teaching, and the gradual development of the doctrine of the Presence.

I must content myself with asking a few questions, the answers to which (though pointing only to a portion of the evidence on the subject), I cannot but think, would suffice to justify our Church in rejecting Eucharistic adoration (as now taught), and rejecting it

---

the signs. *Theoph.*—And were it not open madness to avouch it to be really true of the things themselves whose signs those are? *Philand.*—It were. *Theoph.*—Why, then, since corporal eating serveth only for corporal nourishing, and hath a continual and natural coherence with it, do you confess the truth in the latter and not as well in the former part of the action? Why do you not expound them both alike? *Philand.*—To say the immortal flesh of Christ is converted and turned into the quantity and substance of our mortal flesh is an horrible heresy. *Theoph.*—And to say that His flesh is eaten with our mouths and jaws, and lieth in our stomachs, is the very pathway and right introduction to that heresy, or at least to as brutish and gross an error as that is. *Philand.*—The Fathers affirm that His Body is eaten with our mouths. *Theoph.*—And so they affirm that His Body and Blood do increase and augment the substance of our mortal and sinful bodies." (True Difference, pp. 770, 771, Oxford, 1585.)

* Even as regards Paschasius himself it may perhaps fairly be doubted whether adoration, apart from partaking, could consistently be connected with his doctrine, if his teaching were consistent with itself. (See Soames's Latin Church during Anglo-Saxon Times, pp. 407, 408.) Nor, as a matter of fact, have we any sufficient reason to believe that Eucharistic adoration followed at all closely on the acceptance of his view. (See below, Appendix, Notes A, B, & C.)

on the ground that the Body of Christ is in heaven, and not here.

In these questions I designedly aim at meeting opponents on their own ground.

(1) The first question is : If this doctrine of the Presence were indeed a part of the faith of the early Church, how comes it to pass that among the accounts of early heresies and their refutations, we never meet with a statement of the rejection of this doctrine marked among the heresies, and never find arguments for establishing this doctrine among their refutations?

It must be obvious that if this doctrine were regarded as true its importance must have been regarded as great.

Yet it can hardly be maintained that some at least, among the early Christians, did not hold, and teach, the doctrine of the Real Absence of our Lord's Body and Blood in respect of the Eucharistic elements.

How, then, on the hypothesis of our new teachers, is it to be accounted for that none of them at the time seem to have been charged on this account with heresy, or false doctrine?

Thus, for example, the Docetæ, and kindred sects in the early Church,* could not possibly have held any such Real Presence of Christ's Body † in the Eucharistic elements.

---

* See Hagenbach's History of Doctrines, vol. i. p. 48, edit. Clark.

† Tertullian indeed says: " Aut si propterea panem corpus sibi finxit quia corporis carebat veritate; ergo panem debuit tradere pro nobis.

And there *is* found, indeed, one single and noteworthy statement,* pointing to the defect of their faith as it

Faciebat ad vanitatem Marcionis ut panis crucifigeretur." (Advers. Marci., lib. iv. § xl. p. 458, edit. Rigaltius, 1689.)

And these words suggest the thought that Marcion held the Bread of the Eucharist to be Christ's Body, or rather to be to Christ instead of a real Body. If such were the opinion of the Phantasiasts generally, it might perhaps deduct something from the force of the argument in the text, so far as it is concerned with this form of heresy. This, however, does not appear to be the case. (See Albertinus, De Eucharistia, pp. 300 and 328.)

In any case the argument from the use made of the Eucharistic doctrine by the opponents of the heresy remains in full force.

* It is a passage in the Epistle to the Smyrnæans attributed to Ignatius, in which certain heretics are denounced "who abstain from the Eucharist and prayer, because they confess not that the Eucharist is the Flesh of our Saviour Jesus Christ, which suffered for our sins." But the heretics alluded to would appear to be the Phantasiasts, who denied a true Body to our Lord, and therefore could not hold any *communion or partaking* of His flesh and blood in the Eucharist.

And that the denial of *this*—not of the Real Presence in the elements—is the error attributed to them in this Epistle—may be confirmed by observing that the words (with a slight change) are adopted by Theodoret in his controversy with the Eutychians, where he certainly does not employ them to establish such a Real Presence. (See Appendix, Note E, and Cosin's Hist. Transubst., cap. vi. § xi. p. 107, A. C. L. See also Albertinus, De Eucharistia, pp. 286, 287; and Waterland's Works, vol. iv. pp. 580, 581; and Harrison's Reply to Dr. Pusey's Challenge, pp. 587, 588; but especially Jacobson's Patres Apost., tom. ii. pp. 429, 430, Oxon. 1840.)

As to the charge against the Messalians, see Hospinian, Works, tom. iii. p. 149.

The Ebionites are condemned by Irenæus for using water only in the Eucharist, " not receiving God to their commixture." (Cont. Hær., lib. v. cap. i., Op., edit. Migne, c. 1123.)

Irenæus dwells also on the difficulty which they, who do not believe Christ to be the very Word of God, through whom all things were made, must experience in receiving the truth that the bread over

affected the matter of the Eucharist. But the words of the writer, if I mistake not, may very well be understood* as implying such a Real Presence only as need be, and ought to be, no matter of controversy. And with this solitary † exception (an exception which may be said to make the rule only more remarkable) the want of faith in the Eucharistic Presence is never, I think, laid to their charge among the accusations of their opponents.

And this is all the more observable because an argument from the Eucharist *is* used against such views. The argument is that the Eucharist is a figure of Christ's Body, and that a figure implies the truth and reality of the Body which it figures‡—an argument strangely expressed, surely, on the hypothesis of the Presence of Christ's Body under the form of the elements.

The argument § sometimes takes the form of this

which thanks have been given is the Lord's Body. (Hæres. iv. 18, § 4, Op., edit. Migne, c. 1027.)

* So it is said by the writer of the treatise "De Mysteriis:" "Vera utique caro Christi, quæ crucifixa est, quæ sepulta est; vere ergo carnis illius sacramentum est." (De Mysteriis, cap. ix. § 53, Ambrosii, Op., tom. ii. c. 339, edit. Benedict. Paris, 1690.)

It was doubtless just the denial of this which St. Ignatius is condemning.

In the next sentence it is declared "post consecrationem *Corpus significatur.*"

† If it should appear that other instances are to be found, they will at least, I venture to think, be so few or obscure, as not very materially to affect the argument.

‡ See Tertullian adv. Marcionem, lib. iv. ch. xl., and lib. v. ch. viii., Opera, edit. Rigaltius, 1689, pp. 457, 458, 470.

§ See Albertinus, De Eucharistiâ, p. 287; Goode on Eucharist, i. p. 264.

question :—If Christ had not a real Body, of what are the elements the representative signs or symbols ? *—a form

* It may be observed, that in respect of the use of this argument, and its applicability, the cases of the Phantasiasts and of the Eutychians stand on the same footing. Of the following examples those first cited were written with reference to the one, the remainder are applied to the other.

(1) " Figura autem non fuisset, nisi veritatis esset corpus. Ceterum, vacua res, quod est phantasma, figuram capere non potest." (Tertullian, Adv. Marcion., lib. iv. cap. xl. p. 458, edit. Rigaltius, 1689.)

(2) " Panis et calicis sacramento jam in Evangelio probavimus corporis et sanguinis Dominici veritatem, adversus phantasma Marcionis." (Ibid., lib. v. cap. iii. p. 470.)

(3) Εἰ δ', ὡς οὗτοι φασὶν, ἄσαρκος καὶ ἄναιμος ἦν· ποίας σαρκὸς ἢ τίνος σώματος, ἢ ποίου αἵματος εἰκόνας διδοὺς, ἄρτον τε καὶ ποτήριον, ἐνετέλλετο τοῖς μαθηταῖς διὰ τούτων τὴν ἀνάμνησιν αὑτοῦ ποιεῖσθαι; ὧν καὶ ὁ Ἀπόστολός ἐστι· μαρτυρῶν γὰρ τούτοις φησὶ τόν τε ἄρτον καὶ τὸ ποτήριον τῆς εὐλογίας κοινωνίαν αἵματός τε εἶναι καὶ σάρκος. (Adamantius, in Op. Originis, tom. i. c. 1840, edit. Migne.)

(4) So Ephrem Syrus speaks of the truth of Christ's Body as " written on bread," and " marked on wine." (See Pusey's " Real Presence from the Fathers," p. 77.)

And the following words enforce more clearly his argument against the Docetæ :—

(5) " If the Lord put on a Body in appearance, it were right that they should break a shadow ; and if He shewed the likeness of blood, let them put into the cup the shadow of wine. But if they break true bread, which they truly touch, and it is not in appearance, the sinful woman who apprehended our Lord touched a true Body. Do thou bless Him who bade Thomas touch a Body, not a shadow." (Ibid., p. 79.)

(6) Δι' οὗ σώματος ἀρχιερεὺς καὶ ἀπόστολος γέγονε καὶ ἐχρημάτισε· δι' οὗ παρέδωκεν ἡμῖν μυστηρίου, λέγων, τοῦτό ἐστὶ μου τὸ σῶμα τὸ ὑπὲρ ὑμῶν, καὶ τὸ αἷμα τῆς καινῆς διαθήκης· οὐ τῆς παλαιᾶς· τὸ ὑπὲρ ὑμῶν ἐκχυνόμενον· θεότης δὲ οὔτε σῶμα οὔτε αἷμα ἔχει.

of which it may be said that it is perfectly consistent with the theory of the Real Absence from the elements,

(Athanasius, Orat. de Fide, Fragment cited by Theodoret., Dial. ii. *Inconfusus*, Opera, tom. iv. p. 138, edit. Schulze, 1772, in support of his argument against the Eutychians. See Athan., Opera, edit. Bened., 1777, tom. i. par. ii., p. 1019.)

(7) Εἰ τοίνυν τοῦ ὄντως σώματος ἀντιτυπά ἐστι τὰ θεῖα μύστηρια, σῶμα ἄρα ἐστὶ καὶ νῦν τοῦ Δεσπότου τὸ σῶμα, οὐκ εἰς θεότητος φύσιν μεταβληθὲν. (Theodoret., Dial. ii. *Inconfusus*, Opera, tom. iv. p. 125, edit. Schulze.)

(8) Εἰ δὲ ἡ σὰρξ εἰς θεότητος μετεβλήθη φύσιν, οὗ δὴ χάριν μεταλαμβάνουσίν τῶν ἀντιτύπων τοῦ σώματος; περιττὸς γὰρ ὁ τύπος ἀνῃρημένης τῆς ἀληθείας. (Ibid. Demonstratio—Quod unio sit inconfusa, Opera, tom. iv. p. 269, edit. Schulze.)

(9) Τίνος ἡγῇ σύμβολόν τε καὶ τύπον τὴν παναγίαν τρόφην; τῆς θεότητος τοῦ Δεσπότου Χριστοῦ, ἢ τοῦ σώματος καὶ τοῦ αἵματος; (Ibid., Dial. i. *Immutabilis*, tom. iv. pp. 26, 27.)

(10) Ὁ Κύριος τὸ σύμβολον λαβών, οὐκ εἶπε, τοῦτο ἐστιν ἡ θεότης μου· ἀλλὰ τοῦτό ἐστι τὸ σῶμά μου. (Ibid. p. 27.)

Compare Cyril Alex.: Εἰ Θεοῦ αἷμα τὸ πόμα, οὐκ ἄρα Θεὸς γυμνὸς, ... ἀλλ' ἐνανθρωπήσας Θεὸς Λόγος. (Homil. Div. x., Opera, edit. Migne, tom. x. c. 1028-9.)

It is impossible not to observe on these extracts how they imply the existence of the elements after consecration: indeed, the very argument actually requires the substantial reality of the bread and wine. If, according to the Romish doctrine, the substance of bread and wine were gone—their *species* only remaining—they might very fitly represent a Body having the *species* of a body only without the substance, such as the Phantasiasts imagined—a *vacua res, quod est phantasma*. But the argument of these writers proceeds from the reality of the signs in the Eucharist to the reality of that which is signified and represented by them. (See especially the quotations from Tertullian and Ephrem Syrus.)

And this being so, the bread and wine, according to the teaching of even Romish divines, can only be the Body and Blood of Christ typically and figuratively. (See Romish Mass and English Church, pp. 89, 90.)

but that it would hardly have been naturally assumed upon the theory of a Real Presence in them.

The same may be said of the Eutychians, or those who held in their extreme form the doctrine by some attributed to Eutyches.* No other view than that of the Real Absence would seem to square well with their teaching concerning the nature of Christ; yet they do not seem to have ever been accused of heresy on the subject of the Eucharist.†

Again, how is it possible that those who refused to recognise Christ Himself as Divine should have paid Divine adoration to the consecrated antitypes of Christ's Body? And, if Christians generally *did* do this, how is it possible that the difference of practice should have been otherwise than marked and observable? And is it likely that such a conspicuous matter of dissent from the

---

* "Lectores autem hîc rogo, ut mecum expendant quiddam ad Eutychianorum contrà quos Leo disputat, Hæresin spectans, consideratione dignissimum. Hæretici enim illi, ex quorum sententia, ut notat Leo, *Verbi incarnatio non unitio est divinæ humanæque naturæ, sed hoc ipso concurso, quod geminum est, factum est singulare*, credere nullomodo poterant, panem et vinum in corpus et sanguinem Christi in Eucharistiâ substantialiter mutari, aut corpus et sanguiuem Christi sub eorum accidentibus delitescere. Nihilominùs veteres eorum hæresin describentes, nunquàm eos incusant negatæ transubstantiationis aut præsentiæ realis: quod procul dubio non omisissent, si hactenus quoque tam sacrilegè errassent. Apertum ergò indicium est transubstantiationem ac præsentiam realem, tunc non magis ab Ecclesia quàm ab ipsis Eutychianis fuisse creditas." (Albertinus, De Eucharistiâ, p. 840.)

† See Albertinus, De Eucharistiâ, p. 840; Hospiniani Opera, tom. iv. p. 149.

universal rule of the Christian Church should not have been urged by the orthodox as clear evidence of heresy? Yet, when were *these* heretics ever assailed by any such argument as this?

So, also,* when human ingenuity has done its best to avoid the conclusion, it is impossible to deny that statements occur in individual writers which can never be

* We learn from the writings of Cyril Alex. (Adver. Nestorium, lib. v. cap. vi., Op., edit. Migne, tom. ix. c. 202) that Nestorius, expounding the words of the Apostle "as oft as ye eat this bread," added, by way of interpretation, the words οὗ ἔστι τὸ σῶμα ἀντίτυπον. On which Albertinus writes: "Cum dicat, *Corpus Domini* esse *panis illius antitypum*, hoc est, rem seu veritatem ab illo pane tanquam a typo suo figuratam, *typusque* (ut notat Cyrillus) *non sit veritas* quam figurat, *sed illius simulachrum;* per panem illum non potest intelligere proprium Domini corpus." (De Euch., p. 773.) Was Nestorius for *this* ever accused of heresy? It is confessed that between the Nestorians and the orthodox there was agreement on the doctrine of the Eucharist. (See Albertinus, pp. 758, 772, 773, 777. See, however, Renaudot, Lit. Orient. C., tom. ii. p. 507, and Crakanthorp, Def. Eccles. Angl., p. 516, A. C. L.)

The rendering given by Aubertin here to ἀντίτυπον is, no doubt, unusual. Bellarmine says: "Vox *antitypon* nunquam accipitur pro exemplari." (De Euch., lib. ii. cap. xv., Op., tom. iii. c. 600, edit. 1601.)

Yet Suicer gives an example of this sense from Synesius (Ep. ad Theoph.), and it seems almost necessary thus to understand Nestorius. The Latin version of Agellius is "Cujus est ipsum corpus antitypum."

Cyril, in reply, while arguing from the fact that the Eucharist is, and is called, the Lord's Body, not His Divinity, takes no exception to these words of Nestorius. Yet he could hardly have failed to do so if he had believed that the Eucharist was named the Lord's Body because of its being so ἁπλῶς.

The language of Nestorius is certainly most extraordinary language to use on the theory of the Real Objective Presence in the bread. And the argument of Albertinus seems to have very great weight.

understood naturally as implying less than the denial of the doctrine of the Real Presence in the Elements. And yet for this teaching the writers pass uncondemned and unaccused.*

* There is a fragment of Irenæus, in which he tells of the slaves of certain catechumens, who being put to torture by their Greek captors to compel them to reveal Christian secrets, declared that the Divine Communion was the Body and Blood of Christ (τὴν θείαν μετάληψιν αἷμα καὶ σῶμα εἶναι Χριστοῦ). And Irenæus gives us to understand that they said this in consequence of what they had heard from their masters, thinking themselves that the Communion was in reality Blood and Flesh (αὐτοὶ νομίσαντες τῷ ὄντι αἷμα καὶ σάρκα εἶναι).

Did Irenæus consider this report a true one? His faith was very different from that of teachers of the Real Objective Presence, if he did not. But he could hardly have written concerning these slaves as he does, if he did. He accounts for their report by saying *they thought* that the Communion was in reality flesh and blood.

But Irenæus goes on to say that other Greeks being informed of this, two martyrs were compelled by torture to make confession [ὁμολογῆσαι διὰ βασάνων ἠνάγκαζον.] And what was the confession they made? Blandina, we are told, spoke out plainly, and to the point, saying: "How could these things be endured by those, who for religious exercise did not even allow themselves lawful meats?" (Οἷς εὐστόχως Βλανδίνα ἐπαρρησιάσατο, Πῶς ἄν, εἰποῦσα, τούτων ἀνάσχοιντο οἱ μηδὲ τῶν ἐφειμένων κρεῶν δι' ἄσκησιν ἀπολαύοντες;)

The fragment will be found in Migne's edition of Irenæus, c. 1236.

Was Irenæus of old time accounted a heretic for this? Or was Blandina's confession ever condemned as containing either false doctrine or misrepresentation? Yet are they not both found virtually denying what is now regarded as the Catholic faith of the Eucharist?

There is not a word to suggest or support the notion that in their view the slaves were only wrong in their conception of the *mode* of partaking; nothing whatever to make us suppose that Blandina meant to express, or that Irenæus would have thought her right in expressing, "Though it really is flesh and blood, yet it has no appearance of flesh and blood, but is received under the forms of bread and wine."

Yet, except on this supposition, it is absolutely impossible to escape

F

Thus, for example, take the words of Tertullian, written very early in the third century: "Acceptum panem, et

the conclusion that in Irenæus's view the Communion is *not* in reality the flesh and blood of Christ, and that, therefore, he must have understood John vi. 53 as a figure, and could not have understood the words of institution in any other than a tropical sense.

With this language of Irenæus may be compared that of Tertullian : ' Quia durum et intolerabilem existimaverunt sermonem ejus, quasi *vere* carnem suam illis edendam determinasset, ut in spiritum disponeret statum salutis, præmisit : *Spiritus est qui vivificat.* Adque ita subjunxit, *Caro nihil prodest,* ad vivificandum scilicet. . . . . Itaque sermonem constituens vivificatorem, quia spiritus et vita sermo, eumdem etiam carnem suam dixit, quia et sermo caro erat factus, proinde in causam vitæ appetendus, et devorandus auditu, et ruminandus intellectu, et fide digerendus. Nam et paulo ante carnem suam panem quoque cælestem pronunciarat: urgens usquequaque per allegoriam necessariorum pabulorum, memoriam Patrum qui panes et carnes Ægyptiorum præverterant divinæ vocationi." (De Resurrectione, cap. xxxvii., Opera, edit. Rigaltius, 1689, p. 347.)

Here we have not only support for St. Augustine's interpretation of John vi. 53, but the clearest implication that *they* quite misunderstood Christ's words who supposed that His flesh was to be eaten *really* (verè).

Is not Tertullian here standing by the side of Irenæus in regarding as a gross misrepresentation of the Christian belief just that which is now so loudly proclaimed as the ancient and unchanging faith of the Catholic Church concerning the Eucharist?

And, again, there is here not a word to indicate a solution of that which seemed hard in our Lord's discourse, by having recourse to a distinction in *modes* of eating. Nay, more. There is that which is subversive of such a theory. For the solution which Tertullian does give is one which, had he recognised *that*, he never could have admitted. But all is in accord with the teaching of Tertullian elsewhere as to the figurative sense of the words of institution. (See below, pp. 72, 92, 94.)

To the same effect is the clear teaching of Origen : " Si secundum literam sequaris hoc ipsum quod dictum est ' Nisi manducaveritis carnem meam, et biberitis sanguinem meum,' occidit hæc litera." (In Levit., Hom. vii., Op., ed. Migne, tom. ii. c. 487.)

So also we find Cyril of Jerusalem speaking of the Capernaites :

distributum discipulis, corpus illum suum fecit,* Hoc est corpus meum dicendo, id est figura corporis mei." (Adv. Marc., lib. iv. ch. xl., Op., pp. 457, 458, ed. Rigalt., 1689.)

Εκεῖνοι μὴ ἀκηκοότες πνευματικῶς τῶν λεγομένων, σκανδαλισθέντες ἀπῆλθον εἰς τὰ ὀπίσω, νομίζοντες ὅτι ἐπὶ σαρκοφαγίαν αὐτοὺς προτρεπέται. (Mystag. iv., sect. iv. p. 321, edit. Bened.), where what Cyril says they thought 'is, according to Romish teaching, what they ought to have understood, and what necessarily results from the literal sense of John vi. 53, and of the words of institution. And, again, there is no hint of a supernatural mode of σαρκοφαγία. To understand spiritually, in Cyril's teaching, excludes all real eating of flesh. (See Waterland's Works, vol. iv. p. 595, edit. 1843.)

So it is said by St. Athanasius: Διὰ τοῦτο τῆς εἰς οὐρανοὺς ἀναβάσεως ἐμνημόνευσε τοῦ υἱοῦ τοῦ ἀνθρώπου, ἵνα τῆς σωματικῆς ἐννοίας αὐτοὺς ἀφελκύσῃ, καὶ λοιπὸν τὴν εἰρημένην σάρκα βρῶσιν ἄνωθεν οὐράνιον, καὶ πνευματικὴν τροφὴν παρ' αὐτοῦ διδομένην μάθωσιν· ἃ γὰρ λελάληκα, φησὶν, ὑμῖν, πνεῦμά ἐστι καὶ ζωή· ἴσον τῷ εἰπεῖν, τὸ μὲν δεικνύμενον καὶ διδόμενον ὑπὲρ τῆς τοῦ κόσμου σωτηρίας, ἐστὶν ἡ σὰρξ ἣν ἐγὼ φορῶ· ἀλλ' αὕτη ὑμῖν καὶ τὸ ταύτης αἷμα παρ' ἐμοῦ πνευματικῶς δοθήσεται τροφὴ, ὥστε πνευματικῶς ἐν ἑκάστῳ ταύτην ἀναδίδοσθαι, καὶ γίνεσθαι πᾶσι φυλακτήριον εἰς ἀνάστασιν ζωῆς αἰωνίου. (Athanas. Ep. 4, ad Serap. § 19, Op., ed. Ben., tom. i. pt. 2, p. 568. See Theod. Heracl. in Corderius, Cat. in Joan., pp. 193, 197.)

So also writes Eusebius: Ἀλλ' εὖ ἴστε, ὅτι τὰ ῥήματά μου ἃ λελάληκα ὑμῖν, πνεῦμά ἐστι καὶ ζωή ἐστι· ὥστε αὐτὰ εἶναι τὰ ῥήματα καὶ τοὺς λόγους αὐτοῦ, τὴν σάρκα καὶ τὸ αἷμα, ὧν ὁ μετέχων ἀεὶ, ὡσανεὶ ἄρτῳ οὐρανίῳ τρεφόμενος, τῆς οὐρανίου μεθέξει ζωῆς. (Eusebius Cæsar. Contra Marcell. de Eccl. Theol., lib. iii. c. 12, ad fin. Demonst. Evangel., p. 180, edit. Paris, 1628.)

Compare the following: "Quando dicit, qui non comederit carnem meam, et biberit sanguinem meum, licet et in mysterio possit intelligi, tamen verius corpus Christi et sanguis ejus sermo Scripturarum est, doctrina divina est." (Breviar. in Psalm., Ps. 147, in Opera Hieron., ed. Vallars., tom. vii., Appendix, pp. 530, 531.)

* Muratori indeed says that one thing only is clear in the words of

By the side of this I will set for the sake of comparison the saying of St. Augustine: "Non enim Dominus Tertullian, which is "Panem ex verbis Domini fieri Corpus Christi." (Liturgia Romana Vetus, pp. 186, 187, Venice, 1748.)

But for those who can see a clear and natural meaning in the very plain declarations of Tertullian, it must be obvious that we have here his own interpretation of the phrase "making the Body of Christ."

And the words of Tertullian may very well be regarded as giving the true explanation of the language of subsequent Fathers, who speak of *making* the Body of Christ. Christ, according to Tertullian, made the bread His Body, by appointing it by His word to be an effectual sign or figure of His Body.

In the same way Christ's ministers, obeying His command, in doing as He did, when they consecrate the bread by His word and by prayer, are setting apart the element for Christ's use in the Sacrament, that it may represent and be the Communion of His Body, and may thus be said also to *make* the Body of Christ.

Bp. Cosin writes (Hist. Trans. cap. vi. § vi., vol. iv. pp. 98, 99, A. C. L.): "Ad secundam classem ea pertinent testimonia, quibus προεστῶτες, et presbyteri, Christi Corpus ore sacro conficere dicuntur: quemadmodum loquitur Hieronymus epistola ad Heliodorum; et, præter alios, S. Ambrosius de iis qui mysteriis initiantur. Resp. Nempe, ad presbyterorum preces et benedictiones, panis communis factus est panis sacramentalis; qui, quando frangitur et manducatur, κοινωνία Corporis Christi est, adeoque sacramentaliter Corpus Christi recte dicitur: nam non solum Corpus Domini repræsentat, sed (ut sæpius jam dictum est) eo percepto vere quoque Corporis Ejus participes efficimur. Ita enim Hieronymus ad Evagrium: 'Ad presbyterorum preces Christi Corpus Sanguisque conficitur'; id est, materia talis facta est, ut sumpta sit communio Corporis et Sanguinis Domini; qualis non esset, nisi preces istæ præcessissent. Græci dicunt κατασκευάζειν et ἱερουργεῖν τὸ Σῶμα Κυρίου. Bene vero hic ait Chrysostomus: 'Non sunt opera humanæ facultatis, quæ proponuntur. Qui olim hæc in illâ cœnâ fecit, idem et nunc ea operatur: nos autem (ὑπηρετῶν) ministrorum tantum ordinem tenemus. Ipse vero est, qui ea sanctificat (καὶ μετασκευαζων) et transmutat."

The words of St. Jerome may be specially observed: "De quo [fru-

dubitavit dicere, Hoc est Corpus meum: cum signum daret corporis sui;"* and that of the commentary attributed to Procopius of Gaza,† (following Eusebius ‡

mento et vino] conficitur panis Domini, et sanguinis ejus impletur typus." (In Jerem. lib. vi. cap. xxxi., Op., ed. Vallarsius, tom. iv. c. 1063.)

Here the word *conficitur* is spoken not of the "*Corpus Christi*" but of the "*panis Domini;*" and the saying concerning the one element is paralleled by the declaration concerning the other, "sanguinis Ejus impletur *typus.*"

Moreover both these assertions are made to stand as on a level with what immediately follows concerning *oil* "et benedictio sanctificationis ostenditur." (See below, Appendix, Note E, under τύπος.)

See also Dr. Harrison in "The Fathers *versus* Dr. Pusey," pp. 151 —153, and "Answer to Dr. Pusey's Challenge," pp. 598, 599.

Doubtless, however, in the progress of superstition towards the Paschasian doctrine, the expression *conficere Corpus Christi* gathered around it by degrees a more sacerdotal and mysterious sense than this.

* Contra Adimant., cap. xii. § 3, tom. viii. c. 124, edit. Benedict., Paris, 1688.

† "Indicatur et lætitia, quæ capitur ex mystico vino, quod propinans suis discipulis profatur: 'Accipite, bibete, hic est sanguis, qui pro vobis effunditur in remissionem peccatorum.' Simul quoque per illa verba docet, quod valde benevole respiciat omnes, quotquot in ipsum credunt. Proprium enim est quodammodo vini; ut blande ab hominibus aspiciatur. Ver. 12, *Albi dentes ejus,* etc. Lac fortassis nobis demonstrat sinceritatem et puritatem mystici alimenti. Dedit enim sui corporis imaginem vel effigiem aut typum discipulis, haud amplius admittens et acceptans legis cruenta sacrificia." (Procopii Gazæi, Comment. in Gen., cap. xlix., Opera, edit. Migne, tom. i. p. 502.) See Albertinus, De Eucharistia, p. 856, who (see margin) quotes the Greek from a MS. used by Coffetel, παρέδωκε γὰρ εἰκόνα τοῦ ἰδίου σώματος μαθηταῖς.

‡ Αὐτὸς τὰ σύμβολα τῆς ἐνθέου οἰκονομίας τοῖς αὐτοῦ παρεδίδου μαθηταῖς, τὴν εἰκόνα τοῦ ἰδίου σώματος ποιεῖσθαι παρακελευόμενος. Ἐπειδὴ γὰρ οὐκέτι τὰς δι' αἱμάτων θυσίας, οὐδὲ τὰς παρὰ Μωσεῖ ἐν διαφόρων ζώων σφαγαῖς νενομοθετημένας προσίετο, ἄρτῳ δὲ χρῆσθαι

of Cæsarea), "Dedit proprii Corporis imaginem discipulis." *

And I will add the parallel language of Ephrem Syrus, or of one in his name, " Attende, quomodo panem benedixit ac fregit in figuram (ἐν τυπῷ) immaculati Corporis Sui, calicemque in figuram Sanguinis Sui benedixit, deditque discipulis suis ; "† and that of

συμβόλῳ τοῦ ἰδίου σώματος παρεδίδου, εἰκότως κ.τ.λ. (Euseb. Cæsar. Demonst. Evang., lib. viii., A Genesi, p. 380, ed. Paris, 1628.)

* So St. Jerome: "Dominus mysterium corporis et sanguinis sui tradidit discipulis" (In Ezekiel xli. tom. v. c. 498, edit. Vallarsius), where no doubt *mysterium* is equivalent to *signum* or *figura*. So St. Augustine : "Idem in mysterio cibus et potus illorum qui noster" (in Ps. lxxvii.), *i.e.* in signification ; as he says, "*Petra erat Christus in signo*" (In Joan., Tract 26). See Albertinus, De Eucharistia, p. 4. See also below, p. 120.

So also the Commentary on St. Mark which is found among the Works of St. Jerome (Op., tom. xi. par. iii. c. 118, edit. Vallarsius) says : " Benedicens fregit, *transfigurans* corpus suum in panem, quod est Ecclesia præsens, quæ accipitur in fide, benedicitur in numero, frangitur in passionibus, datur in exemplis, sumitur in doctrinis ;" where the same word is used which St. Augustine uses in interpreting the words to Saul, " Why persecutest thou Me?"—" Caput pro membris clamabat, et membra in se caput *transfigurabat*." (In Ps. xxx. Enarr. ii., Opera, edit. Benedict., Paris, 1681, tom. iv. par. i. c. 147. See Dr. Harrison's "The Fathers *versus* Dr. Pusey," p. 4.)

† Quoted from his *Sermo* (not found in the Syriac): "De eis, qui Filii Dei Naturam scrutantur," Opera, tom. i. p. 497, edit. Venice,1755. See App., Note E. In the edition of Rome, 1732, the same *Sermo* will be found in vol. iii. p. 418. For an answer to the Romish evasions of Ephrem's teaching see Albertinus, De Eucharistiâ, pp. 450, 452.

Other language of Ephrem has been cited as strongly supporting Lutheran views, which again has been skilfully twisted into an assertion of transubstantiation. (See Antirrheticon adv. Kohlium, appended to vol. ii. of his works, Venice, 1756, pp. 1, 2.)

In truth the words alleged, though admitting, no doubt, a Lutheran

Theodoret, who says, " Christ took the Symbol and said, 'This is My Body.' " *

Now the common answer † of Romanists to the argument derived from the frequent use of such words as ‡ *symbols, signs, types, antitypes, figures, images,* when applied to the Eucharist, is that these words do not imply that the elements (or elemental forms) are *only* signs, or that the things signified may not be really present as well as the signs.§

sense, may very well be understood as equivalent to the statement of Irenæus that the Eucharist consists of two things—an earthly and a heavenly (concerning which see Albertinus, De Euch., p. 306)—which by no means necessarily implies any real local *inexistentia* of the one in the other. See Cosin's Works, vol. iv. A. C. L. p. 48; and Papers on Eucharistic Presence, pp. 484, 485.

* Λαβὼν τὸ σύμβολον ἔφη, τοῦτό ἐστι τὸ σῶμά μου. (Epist. cxxx. Op., edit. Schulze, tom. iv. p. 1218.)

So again: Τὸ σύμβολον κλάσας καὶ διανείμας, ἐπήγαγε· τοῦτο μοῦ ἐστὶ τὸ σῶμα. (Epist. cxlv., Op., edit. Schulze, tom. iv. p. 1251. See below, App., Note E. under Σύμβολον.

† Some divines, however, in some cases, explain that the Body of Christ in its glorified condition, though under the forms of bread and wine, is to be understood as being the symbol and antitype of the same Body in its crucified condition: as a king, acting in a play a representation of a battle which he had fought, might be said to be a symbol or representation of himself in another condition. (See Bellarmine, De Sacr. Euch., lib. ii. cap. xv., Opera, tom. iii. c. 601, 602, 1001; and Bibliotheca Maxima, Lugd. 1677, tom. viii. p. 703, margin, and Goar, Euchologium, p. 158. See also Albertinus, De Eucharistia, pp. 320, 329, 471.)

It is scarcely needful to add, that such a notion is altogether alien to the teaching of Christian antiquity. (See Albertinus, pp. 451, 620, and Claude's Answer to Arnauld, part ii. p. 243, London, 1684.)

‡ See Appendix, Note E.
§ See Arcudius, De Concordia, p. 301.

But I would ask whether such an explanation can possibly break the force of the argument derived from these sayings* of Tertullian, and Ephrem, and St.

* These sayings, and others like them, should be well weighed in view of the teaching that the two dicta "The Word was made flesh," and "This is My Body" must be understood to be both equally literal. Dr. Harrison says: "No orthodox Father ever said of the phrase 'The Word was made flesh,' 'that is, a figure of the flesh.' But Tertullian has said of the phrase 'This is My Body,' 'that is, a figure of My Body.' ... No orthodox Father ever affirmed 'that St. John did not hesitate to say, *The Word was made flesh*, when he meant a sign of his flesh.' But Augustine has said, 'The Lord did not hesitate to say *This is My Body*, when He gave a sign of His Body.'" ("Dr. Pusey's Challenge Answered," pp. 398, 399.)

It is much more in accordance with the teaching of the Fathers to put together as parallel the two sayings, "I am the true Vine," and "This [wine] is My Blood." (See Ibid., pp. 495—498.)

Clemens Alexandrinus says: Τὸν κόσμον ὅλον, αἵματι πληρώσας, ἀμπέλου ποτὸν ἀληθείας, τὸ κρᾶμα τοῦ νόμου τοῦ παλαιοῦ καὶ τοῦ Λόγου τοῦ νέου . . . παρασχών· μυστικὸν ἄρα σύμβολον ἡ γραφὴ αἵματος ἁγίου, οἶνον ὠνόμασεν. (Pæd., lib. ii. cap. ii., Op., edit. Potter, tom. i. p. 184.)

Again: Καὶ εὐλόγησε γε τὸν οἶνον, εἰπὼν, Λάβετε, πίετε· τοῦτό μου ἐστὶν τὸ αἷμα, αἷμα τῆς ἀμπέλου· τὸν Λόγον, τὸν περὶ πολλῶν ἐκχεόμενον εἰς ἄφεσιν ἁμαρτιῶν, εὐφροσύνης ἅγιον ἀλληγορεῖ νάμα. (Ibid., p. 186.)

And again: Φέρει . . . οἶνον ἡ ἄμπελος, ὡς αἷμα ὁ λόγος. (Ibid., lib. i. cap. v. p. 107.)

So Tertullian, explaining Genesis xlix. 11: "Stolam et amictum carnem demonstrans, et vinum sanguinem. Ita et nunc sanguinem suum in vino consecravit, qui tunc vinum in sanguine figuravit." (Advers. Marcion, lib. iv. § xl., Opera, edit. Rigaltius, 1689, p. 458.)

Cyprian says: "Cum dicat Christus *Ego sum vitis vera*. sanguis Christi non aqua est utique, sed vinum." (Cyprian, Epist. ad Cæcilium, Op., edit. Baluzius, p. 226.)

Origen says: "Hic sanguis qui nominatur uvæ, illius uvæ est quæ

Augustine? It is a question which appeals very simply to candour and common sense. Let the passages be read carefully in view of such an interpretation.

nascitur ex illa vite, de qua Salvator dicit 'Ego sum vitis vera.'" (In Num., Hom. xvi., Op., edit. Migne, tom. ii. c. 702.)

Again: "Tu es verus populus Israel, qui scis sanguinem bibere, et nosti carnem Verbi Dei comedere, et sanguinem bibere, et uvæ sanguinem illius quæ est ex vera vite et illis palmitibus quos Pater purgat, haurire." (Ibid., c. 702.)

Again: "Potus iste generatio vitis veræ quæ dicit: ego sum vitis vera. Et est sanguis uvæ illius, quæ missa in torcular passionis protulit potum hunc. Sic et panis est verbum Christi factum de tritico illo quod cadens in terram multum reddidit fructum." (Origen in Matth., Vet. Interpr., § 85, Op., edit. Migne, tom. iii. c. 1734.)

And yet again, in a very important passage, which must be given at length: "Si ergo et nos volumus panem benedictionis accipere ab Jesu qui consuetus est eum dare, eamus in civitatem in domum cujusdam, ubi facit Jesus pascha cum discipulis suis præparantibus ipsum notis ipsius, et ascendamus ad superiorem partem domus magnam, et stratam et præparatam, ubi accipiens a Patre calicem, et gratias agens, dat eis qui cum ipso ascenderint, dicens: *Bibite, quia hic est sanguis meus novi testamenti*, qui et bibitur et effunditur: bibitur quidem a discipulis, effunditur autem in remissionem peccatorum commissorum ab eis a quibus bibitur et effunditur. Si autem quæris quomodo etiam effunditur, discute cum hoc verbo etiam quod scriptum est: *Quoniam charitas Dei effusa est in cordibus nostris.* Si autem sanguis testamenti infusus est in corda nostra in remissionem peccatorum nostrorum, effuso eo potabili sanguine in corda nostra, remittuntur et delentur omnia quæ gessimus ante peccata. Ipse autem qui accepto calice dicit: *Bibite ex hoc omnes*, nobis bibentibus non discedit a nobis, sed bibit eum nobiscum cum sit in singulis ipse: quoniam non possumus soli et sine eo vel manducare de pane illo, vel bibere de generatione illius vitis veræ. Nec mireris quoniam ipse est et panis, et manducat nobiscum panem, ipse est et potus generationis de vite, et bibit nobiscum. Omnipotens est enim Verbum Dei, et diversis appellationibus nuncupatur, et innumerabilis est ipse secundum multitudinem virtutum, cum sit omnis virtus unus et ipse." (In Matth., Interp. Vet., § 86, p. 899, Op., ed. Migne, tom. iii. c. 1736.)

Now, let it be observed, I am not for a moment supposing that these writers held or taught that in the Holy

Cyril of Jerusalem says: Ἑκάστῳ δὲ πυικίλος ὁ Σωτὴρ γίνεται πρὸς τὸ συμφέρον. τοῖς μὲν γὰρ εὐφροσύνης χρείαν ἔχουσιν ἄμπελος γίνεται. (Catech. x. § v., Op., edit. Toutte'e, p. 138.)

Compare Didymus: Ἐξ ἀμπέλου οἶνον εὐφραίνοντα καρδίαν ἀνθρώπου λαμβάνων. (In Corderius, Cat. in Joan. vi. vs. 59, 60, p. 169, Antwerp, 1630.)

Theodoret says, speaking of Jacob's prophecy concerning Judah: Οἶσθ' ὅτι ἄμπελον ὁ Κύριος ἑαυτὸν προσηγόρευσεν;... Ὁ δὲ τῆς ἀμπέλου καρπὸς πιεθεὶς ποίαν ἔχει προσηγορίαν;... Αἷμα ἄρα σταφυλῆς τὸ τοῦ Σωτῆρος προσηγόρευσεν αἷμα. εἰ γὰρ ἄμπελος ὁ Δεσπότης ὠνόμασται, ὁ δὲ τῆς ἀμπέλου καρπὸς οἶνος προσαγορεύεται, αἵματος δὲ καὶ ὕδατος ἐκ τῆς τοῦ Δεσπότου πλευρᾶς κρουνοὶ προχεθέντες διὰ τοῦ λοιποῦ σώματος ἐπὶ τὰ κάτω διῆλθον, εἰκότως ἄρα καὶ προσφόρως προεῖπεν ὁ πατριάρχης, Πλυνεῖ ἐν οἴνῳ τὴν στολὴν αὐτοῦ, καὶ ἐν αἵματι σταφυλῆς τὴν περιβολὴν αὐτοῦ. ὥσπερ γὰρ ἡμεῖς τὸν μυστικὸν τῆς ἀμπέλου καρπὸν μετὰ τὸν ἁγιασμὸν αἷμα δεσποτικὸν ὀνομάζομεν· οὕτω τῆς ἀληθινῆς ἀμπέλου τὸ αἷμα σταφυλῆς ὠνόμασεν αἷμα. (Dial. i., Immutabilis, Op., edit. Schulze, tom. iv. p. 25.)

Again: Ἐν δὲ γε τῇ τῶν μυστηρίων παραδόσει, σῶμα τὸν ἄρτον ἐκάλεσε καὶ αἷμα τὸ κρᾶμα... Ὁ δὲ γε Σωτὴρ ὁ ἡμέτερος ἐνήλλαξε τὰ ὀνόματα· καὶ τῷ μὲν σώματι τὸ τοῦ συμβόλου τέθεικεν ὄνομα τῷ δὲ συμβόλῳ τὸ τοῦ σώματος, οὕτως ἄμπελον ἑαυτὸν ὀναμάσας, αἷμα τὸ σύμβολον προσηγόρευσεν. (Ibid., p. 26.)

Ambrose says: "Bibe Christum, quia vitis est... bibe Christum, ut bibas sanguinem quo redemptus es." (In Ps. i. § 33, Op., edit. Ben., tom. i. c. 754.)

So the author of the "Interpretationes ex Vet. Test." found among the writings of Athanasius, explaining Gen. xlix. 11, says: Τὰ κατὰ τοῦ πάθους τοῦ Χριστοῦ λέγει, καὶ τὸ μὲν σῶμα στολὴν ὀνομάζει· τὸ δὲ αἷμα οἶνον· ἐπειδὴ καὶ τὸν μυστικὸν οἶνον αἷμα κέκληκεν ὁ Δεσπότης. (Op. Athanas., edit. Benedict. 1777, tom. ii. p. 269.)

On which Albertinus remarks: "Patriarcha autem Jacobus sanguinem illius olim figurate tantummodo vini et sanguinis uvæ

Sacrament of Christ's Body and Blood there is the giving of nothing but *bare, ineffectual* signs and *hollow, empty* figures.

But, I ask, if St. Augustine had believed that the very Body of Christ was present under the form or sign of

nominibus decoraverat. Intelligit ergo Dominum similiter quoque figurata attributione sanguinis sui titulo et nomenclatura vinum honorasse, ac utrobique esse nominum permutationem absque ulla substantiali rerum iis affectarum mutatione et conversione." (De Eucharistia, p. 407.)

Gaudentius says: " Quod accepis, Corpus est illius panis cœlestis, et Sanguis est illius sacræ vitis." (Gaudentius, Brin., serm. ji., Op., edit. Galeardus, p. 37.)

Again: " Recte etiam vini specie sanguis ejus exprimitur, quia cum ipse in Evangelio dicit: Ego sum vitis vera, satis declarat sanguinem suum esse omne vinum quod in figura passionis ejus offertur." (Ibid., p. 33.)

Hesychius of Jerusalem writes: "Vinea autem, Evangelica sine aliqua dubietate prædicatio est: Christus enim ei occasionem et materiam dedit, qui dixit: *Ego sum vitis,* . . . . Quæ est sanctificationis uva: sciunt qui imbuti sunt Christi mysterium." (In Levit., lib. vii. cap. xxv., in Bibli. Max. Patr., Lugd. 1677, tom. xii. p. 162a.)

Isidore says: "Vinum autem sanguis ejus est, et hoc est, quod scriptum est: *Ego sum vitis vera.*" (Isidorus Hisp., De Eccles. Officiis, lib. i. cap. xviii., Op., edit. Migne, tom. v. c. 755.)

Etherius and Beatus say: "Vinum autem sanguis ejus est. Et hoc est, quod scriptum est: *Ego sum vitis.*" (Etherius et Beatus, Contra Elipandum, in Bib. Max. Patr., Lugd. 1677, tom. xiii. p. 372.)

Rabanus Maurus says: " Ergo panem infermentatum, et vinum aqua mistum in sacramentum corporis et sanguinis Christi sanctificari oportet, quia ipsas res de se Dominum testificari Evangelium narrat. Ait enim ipse Dominus: *Ego sum panis vivus* . . . et item: *Ego sum,* inquit, *vitis vera.*" (Rabanus Maurus, De Clericorum Institut., lib. i. cap. xxxi., Opera, edit. Migne, tom. i. c. 318.)

Again: "Istudque vinum lætificat cor hominis, quod ex verû vite processit." (Ibid., c. 318.) See Cyril Alex. Hom. Div. x., Op., ed. Migne, tom. x. c. 1020, 1021. See also below, p. 92.

the bread, could he naturally have said, "The Lord did not hesitate to say, 'This is My Body,' when He gave a sign of His Body?"

Does not the saying become literally nonsense on such a suggestion? What room was there for doubting or hesitation if the thing given in the hand was indeed the very Body of Christ? And to what purpose are the explanatory words, "when He gave a sign of His Body," as connected with the saying, "This is My Body," if under the sign was the present Body itself? *

* The following observations of Albertinus on this passage from St. Augustine are of great weight: "Palmarium sane in rem nostram testimonium, et in quo tria sunt consideratione dignissima. Primo enim Augustinus ait, illud quod Dominus dabat cum diceret, *Accipite, edite, hoc est corpus meum*, signum corporis ipsius fuisse. Unde sic argumentamur; *Nulla res alicujus, ipsa est cujus est*, ut observant Tertullianus et Athanasius jam supra citati. At id quod Dominus dabat cum diceret, *Accipite, edite, hoc est corpus meum*, erat, juxta Augustinum res alicujus, videlicet, signum corporis ipsius : Ergo non erat ipsummet corpus. Secundo clarissime innuit hujusce propositionis *hoc est corpus meum*, sensum ejusmodi esse, *hoc est signum corporis mei;* adeoque, aut verbum *est* in ea poni pro significare, aut *corpus* pro signo corporis per metonymiam subjecti pro adjuncto: quemadmodum sanguis dicitur esse anima, hoc est, animæ signum. Denique idem confirmat, cum ait : *Non dubitavit Dominus dicere, hoc est corpus meum, etc.* Hac enim loquendi forma indicat, Dominum, sensu, licet vero, non tanem proprio, sed figurato corpus suum id quod dabat appellasse : quemadmodum et Fulgentius quando similiter ait: *cum electionis vas dicat, quia Christus caput est corporis Ecclesiæ, ipsum tamen corpus Christi non dubitat Christum veraciter appellare*. Nam ea observatio locum nunquam habet in propriis locutionibus. Nemo est qui dixerit : non dubitavit Dominus dicere, hoc est aurum, si vere aurum daret, hoc est aqua, si vere aqua foret, etc. Ea tantum adhibetur, quando quis aliquid, licet non proprie sit id, quod ipsum dicit esse, sic nihilominus appellare non refugit. In

The strength of the argument might yet be added to by observing the occasion on which St. Augustine introduces this observation: for it is to fortify his position that when one thing (*sanguis*) is said to be another thing (*anima*) the saying may be interpreted as figurative * ("possum interpretari præceptum illud in signo esse positum"); and that, only a little further on, he further fortifies the same position by quoting the words, "That Rock was Christ," carefully noting that the Apostle does not say *signified* Christ, but *was* Christ; † and yet further,

hoc igitur illustri Augustini loco quot pene verba sunt tot utique sunt fulmina contra Adversariorum sententiam. . . . Fatetur Milleterius *eorum nonnullos ad hunc locum contremiscere, violentisque interpretationibus Augustini verba torquere.* Utinam sic semper verum diceret!" (Albertinus, De Eucharistiâ, p. 624.)

* The learned Pichellerus says of this passage: "Ipse autem Augustinus quo sensu verbum substantivum, *est*, in dicto, *Hoc est corpus meum* intelligeret, satis etiam aperte declarat, quum veteris testamenti locum explicaturus, qui sanguinem ait esse animam . . . ejus loci intelligentiam hujus intelligentia metitur, et ad hanc reducit: nempe quemadmodum hic *panis est corpus in signo*, ita et illic sanguis sit anima in signo. . . . Unde apparet eam hujus loci Matthœi interpretationem fuisse ætate Augustini *vulgarem, publicoque consensu receptam.*" (Opuscula, p. 23.)

Such a testimony from a truly Catholic Romanist, and really great theologian, not only to the one natural and genuine sense of St. Augustine's words, but also to the evidence they afford of the then received interpretation of the words of institution, presents a striking contrast indeed to the violence which is offered to St. Augustine's language in the various strange and conflicting explanations which have been devised by those who would force everything into harmony with the Romish doctrine.

† St. Augustine often refers to this saying, setting it beside such sayings as "the good seed are the children of the kingdom"—using it as an illustration of the truth that Scripture is wont to call things

by marking how, when magnifying the mercy of Christ towards Judas, he * speaks of His admitting him to that feast in which He commended and delivered to His disciples, not His Body and Blood, but *a figure* † of His

signifying as if they were the things signified, and declaring that to understand it in its proper signification would be blasphemy. (See quotations in Dr. Harrison's "Dr. Pusey's Challenge Answered," vol. ii. pp. 152, 155, 162, 168.)

But especially to be observed in connexion with the doctrine of the Eucharist is his saying. " Fide manente, signa variata. Ibi petra Christus, nobis Christus quod in altari Dei ponitur." (In Johan. Evangel. cap. x. Tract. xlv., Op., edit. Ben., 1680, tom. iii. par. ii. c. 598.)

* Isidore Hispal. makes this language of Augustine his own: " Alii Absalom Judam traditorem intelligunt, quem tanta et tam admiranda patientiâ Christus pertulit, tanquam bonum, cum ejus cogitationes non ignoraret, cum adhibuit convivio in quo corporis et sanguinis sui *figuram* discipulis commendavit et tradidit." (Quæst. in Vet. Test. in Reg. ii. cap. iii., Opera, edit. Migne, tom. v. c. 412, 413.)

And our Venerable Bede uses similar language: " Nec a sacratissima cœnâ in quâ *figuram* sacrosancti corporis sanguinisque suis Discipulis tradidit ipsum [Judam] exclusit." (In Psalm iii., Op., tom. viii. c. 323, 324, ed. Col., 1612.)

† On this passage Albertinus says: "Primo sic argumentamur: *Figura non est veritas, sed imitatio veritatis.* Verba sunt Gaudentii. [See below, Appendix, Note E, at end, under *Figura.*] At quod Dominus in Eucharistiæ suæ convivio Discipulis suis dabat, erat juxta Augustinum figura corporis et sanguinis ipsius: non igitur erat veritas corporis et sanguinis. Secundo, unde colligit Augustinus, Dominum in Eucharistiæ convivio corporis et sanguinis sui figuram Discipulis commendavisse et tradidisse? Procul dubio ex his verbis institutionis, *Accipite, edite, hoc est corpus meum, hoc est sanguis meus.* Ergo, inquam, juxta Augustinum sensus horum verborum est, *hoc est figura corporis mei, hoc est figura sanguinis mei*, plane ad mentem nostram. Neque enim ex his verbis ullo modo deduci potest, Dominum figuram corporis et sanguinis sui tradidisse, nisi in hunc modum exponantur." (De Eucharistia, p. 620.)

Body and Blood ("adhibuit ad convivium, in quo Corporis et Sanguinis Sui figuram discipulis commendavit et tradidit").*

I can scarcely suppose that there remains room for doubt as to the sense in which St. Augustine understood the words of our Lord, "This is My Body." In his view it is to be figuratively interpreted.

But we may yet further fortify our conclusion by observing that we have also an interpretation from the same Father of the words, "Except ye eat the flesh of the Son of Man, and drink His Blood, ye have no life in you." His sense of these words is not doubtfully expressed.† He will allow them no other than a figurative meaning.‡

---

* Ennar. in Ps. iii., § 1, tom. iv. par. 1, col. 7, edit. Benedict., Paris, 1688.

† Clemens Alexandrinus had written before : Καὶ ὁ Κύριος ἐν τῷ κατὰ Ἰωάννην Εὐαγγελίῳ, ἑτέρως ἐξήνεγκεν διὰ συμβόλων. Φάγεσθε μου τὰς σαρκὰς, εἰπὼν, καὶ πίεσθέ μου τὸ αἷμα· ἐναργὲς τῆς πίστεως καὶ τῆς ἐπαγγελίας τὸ πότιμον ἀλληγορῶν. (Pædagogus, lib. i. cap. vi., Opera, edit. Potter, Venice, 1757, tom. i. p. 121.)

And so the writer of a tractate on the Passover, under the name of Athanasius, says : " Comedere hujus agni carnes jubemur, quia liberandus est populus, sicuti Christus ait: *Nisi quis comederit carnem meam* non habet vitam manentem. Caro autem Christi verbum est Dei, qui [quia ?] *Verbum caro factum est, et habitavit in nobis ;* sic istas carnes assatas comedere mandamur, crudas elixasque prohibemur. Cocta enim Christi verba non cruda, probata in multo tentationum ardore, nec mollia, nec fluxa, nec labi facilia." (Opera Athanasii, edit. Benedict., 1777, tom. ii. p. 669. See above, pp. 66, 67, and below, p. 82, 100.)

‡ It is quite true, indeed, that many Romish divines of high esteem in former days—including two popes, four cardinals, two archbishops, five bishops, together with very many doctors and professors (see

And to allow *these words* none but a figurative sense is to necessitate a figurative interpretation of the words Albertinus, De Euch., lib. i. cap. xxx. pp. 209 *sqq.*; and Wake in Gibson's Preservative, vol. x. p. 40; also Turton's Reply to Wiseman, pp. 103, 104)—have held that the declarations in the latter part of the sixth chapter of St. John are to be understood of eating spiritually, not literally, and that they have a meaning apart from or beyond Eucharistic participation.

Thomas Aquinas seems to have preferred this interpretation; and the Council of Trent appears to have designedly left the matter undetermined. (See Albertinus, p. 210.)

The question whether or not this position can be consistently maintained by those who require the words of institution to be understood *proprie* is not material to the argument in the text. The answer, however, would probably be a decided negative from such men as Cardinal Wiseman (see Turton's Reply to Wiseman, p. 97, and Dr. Harrison's Answer to Pusey, vol. ii. p. 318), and, I believe, generally from those who now maintain the doctrine of the Real Objective Presence.

But it is important to observe that it is quite another, and an entirely distinct question, whether those who insist on understanding literally (without any figure) the words " Take, eat; this is My Body," could consistently say (or assent to the saying) concerning the words, "Except ye eat the flesh," &c., that *facinus vel flagitium videtur jubere: figura est ergo.*

Certainly this declaration involves the injunction of no greater *flagitium* than the literal obedience to the words of institution literally understood.

And if it could be urged that the *flagitious* character of the act is removed by the supernatural mode in which the Body is presented to be eaten in the Eucharist (see Estius, quoted in Turton, p. 95; see also p. 99), then it would be easy to answer, that Augustine's words know nothing of any new mode of giving to be eaten. He does not say, " It must, therefore, be understood of some ineffable way in which the flesh of Christ is given to be literally eaten in another form than that of flesh." Neither does he say, " Therefore the words must *either* be a figure, *or* be understood of that Divine way in which Christ's flesh is made present to be literally eaten in the Eucharist." But he says distinctly, " Figura est ergo."

of Institution. He says, "Facinus vel flagitium videtur jubere: figura est ergo, præcipiens passioni Dominicæ

With him this is the only alternative. The words must contain either *facinus* or *figura*. And when the *facinus* is rejected, the figurative sense is the only admissible sense of our Lord's declaration.

Could it, we may ask, have been thus, if in his days the Christian Church had been familiar with the idea of any such second mode of really and literally eating Christ's flesh in the Eucharist without *flagitium?* Nay, could it have been thus if St. Augustine's own mind had ever conceived the idea of any such *oral manducation* in the Eucharist of the very Body of Christ really present in, or under the form of, the bread?

Moreover, when elsewhere Augustine *does* speak of the *mode* of the impartation of Christ's gift, he does not make it to be by any spiritualizing of His flesh, but by the spirituality of the recipient's participation. (See Goode on Eucharist, i. pp. 338, 339.)

No doubt passages may be easily quoted from St. Augustine which, literally understood, would be inconsistent with what he says here, and would, in their naked literality, involve the very same *facinus* as the words which he is here expounding. (See Paschasius, Epist. ad Frudegard., Opera, Paris, 1618, c. 1620.)

But surely what he says here of our Lord's words ought to avail for the explaining of similar utterances of his own. And even if this were otherwise, his own *Interpretative Dicta* (see below, Appendix, Note D) would certainly suffice to remove from them all ambiguity.

And all will then, I believe, be found to be in perfect harmony with (and will indeed be confirmed and illustrated by) his teaching elsewhere as to the distinction between eating and drinking the Body and Blood of Christ *sacramentally*, or *sacramento tenus*, only (which is common to the faithful and the unbelieving), and the eating and drinking *re verâ*, which belongs to the truly faithful only. (See Papers on Eucharistic Presence, pp. 657—660, 677—681, 753—759.)

It may be well also to observe how Fulgentius supports from St. Augustine his own position that the requirement of our Lord in John vi. is met by the reception of Baptism as well as the Eucharist: " Nullus debet moveri fidelium in illis, qui etsi legitimè sana mente baptizantur, præveniente velocius morte, carnem Domini manducare, et sanguinem bibere non sinuntur: propter illam videlicet sententiam

communicandum, et suaviter atque utiliter recondendum in memoriâ, quod pro nobis Caro ejus crucifixa et vulnerata sit."* (De Doctrina Christiana, lib. iii. cap. xvi.,

Salvatoris qua dixit: *Nisi manducaveritis carnem filii hominis, et biberitis ejus sanguinem, non habebitis vitam in vobis.* Quod quisquis non solum secundum *veritatis mysteria,* sed secundum *mysterii veritatem* considerare poterit, in ipso lavacro sanctæ regenerationis hoc fieri providebit. Quid enim agitur sacramento sancti baptismatis, nisi ut credentes membra Domini nostri Jesu Christi fiant, et ad compagem corporis ejus Ecclesiastica unitate pertineant? Ipsis enim dicit B. Apostolus, *Vos estis Corpus Christi, membra de membro.* Quos ostendit non solum ipsius sacrificii participes, sed *ipsum sanctum sacrificium* esse.... Qui ergo membrum corporis Christi fit, quomodo non accipit quod ipse fit, quando utique illius fit verum corporis membrum, *cujus corporis* est in sacrificio *sacramentum?* Hoc ergo fit ille regeneratione sancti baptismatis, quod est de sacrificio sumpturus altaris. Quod etiam *sanctos Patres indubitanter credidisse ac docuisse* cognoscimus. Beatus quoque Augustinus de hac re sermonem fecit admodum luculentum." (De Baptismo Æthiopis, cap. xi., in Heptas Presul. Christ., edit. Raynaudus, Paris, 1661, pp. 611, 612.) The extract which Fulgentius gives from St. Augustine will be found among the *Interpretative Dicta* below, in Appendix, Note D.

Fulgentius concludes: " Sacramenti quippe illius participatione ac beneficio non privatur, quando ipse *hoc quod illud sacramentum significat,* invenitur." (P. 612.)

So Cyril Alex. says of the Ethiopian eunuch: Μέτοχος ἤδη τοῦ νοητοῦ προβάτου διὰ τῆς ἐρεύνης ἀνεδείκνυετο. Ἠξίου γὰρ εὐθὺς καὶ βεβαπτίσθαι. (Glaph. in Exod., lib. iii. § 2, Op., ed. Migne, tom. ii. c. 425.)

And again he speaks of the Gentiles becoming Μέτοχα τῆς ἁγίας αὐτοῦ σαρκός ... διὰ τοῦ ἁγίου δηλονότι βαπτίσματος. (In Johan. lib. vi. In cap. ix. vs. 6, 7, Op., tom. vi. c. 964.)

* This passage of St. Augustine is quoted by Bertram in support of his views; by Rabanus Maurus also, as a key to determine whether a passage of Scripture is to be literally or figuratively understood; by Frudegard also, as an argument against Paschasius.

Of the attempt of Paschasius to answer the argument derived from

Opera, tom. iii. par. i. c. 52, edit. Benedict., Paris, 1680.)

The authority of St. Augustine became so great in the Western Church, that his words are frequently adopted by subsequent writers, and his language incorporated in their own discourses or treatises. And so it has come to pass that these words of his, requiring a figurative interpretation of our Lord's saying in the sixth chapter of St. John, were made his own by Fulbert, Bishop of Chartres (who was also the instructor of Berengarius), in the early part of the eleventh century. And when, in 1608, De Villiers edited the works of Fulbert (which had never been printed before), he showed how this saying was naturally regarded, in the view of such as himself, by actually inserting before it the words " dicet hæreticus " (apparently adding also a *tantum*), thus making it appear that the words did not represent at all the mind of Fulbert, but were marked by him for reprobation as the teaching of false doctrine.* He was, in fact, making Fulbert put the words of St. Augustine into the mouth of the heretic.

Whether or not the blame of this rests with him chiefly

---

this passage, Dr. Harrison says that it " probably has never been repeated, and is beneath notice." (Dr. Pusey's Challenge Answered, p. 187 ; see also pp. 201, 206.)

* On the views of Fulbert see " Romish Mass and English Church," p. 62, and Albertinus, De Eucharistia, pp. 944 *seq.*, especially p. 946. See also Du Pin, Eccles. Hist., Eng. transl., London, 1699, p. 2. See also Appendix, Note E.

or with him only, we need hardly inquire. It is really immaterial for our purpose whether he did it altogether *proprio motu*, or whether he did it with the support of any authority of any sort whatsoever.

What *does* concern us to mark is this : the words were certainly not in the MS. of Petavius which he was using. In inserting them he was inserting, as if the language of Fulbert, words which very few indeed, I think, will now believe that Fulbert could have written,* and words

---

* It is not improbable that, when Berengarius wrote of "the doctrine of the Eucharist which is in the writings of Bishop Fulbert of glorious memory, and which some esteem to be of this bishop, *but it is of St. Augustine*" (Spic. D'Ach., tom. ii. p. 510. See L'Aroque, Hist. of Euch., p. 451, Eng. tr. 1684), he may have been referring to this place.

But if not, his words concerning Fulbert (his former teacher) make it in the highest degree improbable that Fulbert's views on the Eucharist should have been in pronounced opposition to those of St. Augustine.

And even apart from this, who could believe that Fulbert would thus have set himself in a position of antagonism to the authority of such a Master in Israel?

Supposing it were possible that Fulbert were anxious to utter a word of warning against an exclusively figurative interpretation of our Lord's words, it is incredible that he should have chosen to do this by putting a *dicet hæreticus* (even with the insertion of a *tantum*) before the *ipsissima verba* of one whom both parties in the Eucharistic controversy were most anxious to claim as their own, and by whose language, on either side, men desired their cause to be supported.

Very differently did Rupertus Tuitiensis, when really opposing the sense of St. Augustine, deal with his name and his teaching. (See his Comment. in Joan., lib. vi., Opera, edit. Migne, tom. iii. c. 461—463, 469.)

And very differently had Paschasius dealt with this quotation from St. Augustine. (Opera, Paris, 1618, c. 1620.)

which declared the *dictum* of St. Augustine to be the language of heresy.

It would appear probable, however, that subsequently,* after the printing of the sheets, it was pointed

But even if, against all credibility, it could be proved that Fulbert had actually written the words, it would only go to show the contrast between the Eucharistic views of St. Augustine and those of some in an earlier age than that in which, beyond all reasonable question, the words were interpolated.

* It seems difficult, on any other hypothesis, to account for the fact that what De Villiers had to observe on the text is found, not as a note, but among the *errata;* especially since he inserted a conspicuous notice immediately after the prefatory Epistle, which naturally leads to the conclusion that none but typographical errors were to be looked for under this head.

The notice runs thus: " Lectores admonitos velim, si forte quosdam errores invenerint, ad errata recurrant. Etiamsi Argus esses, Lector, in eo munere, tamen aliquis error semper irrepit in Tipog."

Notwithstanding De Villiers's "erratum," the error was not corrected in the "Bibliotheca Magna" (Colon., 1618), nor again in Despont's "Bibliotheca Maxima" (Lugd., 1677); but the words "dicet hæreticus" were allowed to reappear in the text, with the marginal note " Interpretatio est mystica, et nota hæc duo verba *dicet hæreticus* non haberi in MS. D. Petavii." (See Bibl. Max., tom. xviii. p. 47); so also in Migne's Patrologia, tom. cxli. c. 334.

In the original edition of 1608 the words on the subject found in the *errata* are these: " Fol. 168. Adverte ista verba figura ergo est, additum est, *dicet hæreticus*, nam non habentur hæc duo verba in Manuscript. D. Petavii, ne quis tamen fallatur cum leget ista, figura ergo est, interpretatio est mystica." In the title-page De Villiers professes to edit Fulbert's "Opera Varia" " ex MS. Cod. Biblioth. Reg. Colleg. Navarræ, et Clarissimor. virorum D. Petavii Senat. Reg. et N. Fabri."

In the prefatory Epistle he says: " Nactus . . . manuscriptum ex Bibliotheca Collegii Reg. Navarræ, in quo multa vetustate exesa fermò videbantur, hæc describenda curavi, meoque labore id assecutus

out to De Villiers that the saying was found in the writings of the great Bishop of Hippo ; for he did his

sum, ut tam præclarum virtutis lumen sub modio non delitescat. Hoc unum tamen silentio non involvam, me a doctissimo Petavio Senatore Regio æquissimo, et Nicolao Fabro viro clarissimo accepisse . . . quædam, ex ipsorumque Bibliothecis desumpta huic auctori inseruisse, quæ in nostro M.Sc. non exstabant."

From this the most natural inference is that the other two MSS. supplied him with additional and separate materials, which he used only when his own MS. failed him.

Moreover, the interpolated passage occurs in what is evidently but a very imperfect fragment, made up of fragmentary quotations; so that the conclusion becomes almost inevitable that he had here only the MS. of Petavius to use, and that as the words "dicet hæreticus" were not in that MS., he did not find them in any MS.

The interpolation was detected by Archbishop Ussher (then Bishop of Meath), who, writing in 1625, says: "He that put in those words 'dicet hæreticus' thought he had notably met with the heretics of this time, but was not aware that thereby he made St. Augustine a heretic for company. For the heretic, that speaketh thus, is even St. Augustine himself: whose very words these are, in his third book De Doctrina Christiana, the sixteenth chapter. Which some belike having put the publisher in mind of, he was glad to put this among his errata, and to confess that these two words were not to be found in the manuscript copy which he had from Petavius; but telleth us not what we are to think of him, that, for the countenancing of the popish cause, ventured so shamefully to abuse St. Augustine." (Answer to Jesuits' Challenge, Introductory Ch., Works, edit. Elrington, vol. iii. p. 22.)

Subsequently, the falsification was exposed in France, by Aubertin, from information which he had derived from very good authority. The French edition of his work on the Eucharist appeared in 1633. The following is from the Latin edition of 1654: "Nescio quis Carolus Villerius qui ex duobus manuscriptis Bibliothecarum Navarrenæ et Petavianæ Fulberti Carnotensis opera Lutetiæ edidit, cum in eis hunc Augustini locum citatum reperisset, post hæc verba, *figura ergo est*, summa impudentiâ ac fœdissima impostura in æternum exprobanda, contra manuscriptorum illorum fidem (quod a Clariss.

best then to undo what he had done; and accordingly he included in the list of "Errata" the words that had been interpolated (as if they had crept in by a misprint), adding the note, "Interpretatio est mystica."*

des Cordes qui Petavianum codicem præbendam impetraverat, didici) addere ausus est, *dicet Hæreticus.*" (De Eucharistia, p. 667.)

Cave says: "Qualem in operibus istis edendis fidem præstiterit Doctor ille Parisiensis, vel unico hoc exemplo abunde patet: Fulbertus, p. 168, verba isthæc ex S. Augustino describit. *Nisi manducaveritis,* &c. Hic loci misellus editor, refutandis hæresibus hujus temporis (uti in editionis fronte gloriatur) intentus, post voces istas *figura ergo est,* glossam istam, *dicit Hæreticus,* inseruerat. Tandem post emissum prælo librum, integram periodum in S. Augustin, Operibus legi, et exinde a Fulberto descriptam esse admonitus, binas istas voces, *dicit Hæreticus,* inter errata typographica retulit, eas præter Codicis, quo usus est, MS. fidem, additas esse confessus." (Historia Literaria, p. 418, Geneva, 1694.)

Even supposing that there were found any manuscript support for the words it will hardly be questioned that the insertion must originally have been fraudulently made. Indeed the statement of De Villiers himself virtually contains the acknowledgment that the words are not the words of Fulbert.

Schröckh says that De Villiers, full of wretched apprehension that the words *figura ergo est* might be damaging to the doctrine of the Church, inserted *dicet hæreticus,* and that this shameless falsification has drawn on him the lasting suspicion that he may probably have altered by his own authority other passages of his edition. (Schröckh. Christliche Kirchengesch., vol. xxiii. p. 506, as referred to by Canon Robertson, Hist. of Ch. Ch., vol. iii. p. 344.)

The fact of the falsification of Fulbert by some one can scarcely be regarded as doubtful. The object of the falsification is equally clear. And the witness to the change of Eucharistic doctrine between the time of St. Augustine and the date at which the falsification was made is surely decisive.

* See Canon Robertson in History of Christian Ch., vol. iii. p. 344 edit. 1874, to whom I am indebted for first directing my attention to what I am now (after correspondence with him) fully satisfied must, almost without a doubt, be the true history of this remarkable interpolation.

This incident is not uninstructive. Over and beyond its bearing on St. Augustine's view of the words of Institution, it suggests matter of inquiry. It is scarcely possible not to ask the question,—Is it thus that the language of the Fathers, when too plainly clashing with the Romish Real Presence, is first, if possible, to be marked as heretical, and denounced as if by the voices of the Fathers themselves, and then, failing this, to have its doctrinal import over-ridden *ad libitum* by simply ridiculous glosses?

In the title-page De Villiers commends the writings which he edits as availing for the confutation of the heresies of his day.*

Is it by such processes as these that the works of Christian Bishops of former days are to be made to condemn with one crushing anathema the doctrines of the Reformation and of Christian antiquity together?

Are the writings of the Fathers thus, at all hazards, to be made to speak the language of Rome?

No doubt there are many Romish divines who would abhor † all such methods of tampering with the texts of

---

* The words are, "Quæ tam ad Refutandas hæreses hujus temporis quam ad Gallorum Hist. pertinent."

† Baronius, tom. v. p. 455 (quoted by James, Corruptions of Sc., p. 73, London, 1843), says: "Vehementius commoveor in eos, qui mendaciis labefactant, quam se putant suffulsisse Dei Ecclesiam, columnam et firmamentum veritatis."

Du Pin has noticed that there was "a great deal of remissness" in the edition of De Villiers. (See Eccles. Hist., English trans., London, 1699, vol. ix. p. 6.)

ancient authors. Doubtless, too, it may be pleaded, in extenuation of the act, that those who were parties to it did what they did with a view to the maintenance of what they believed to be the truth. But is it possible to avoid a suspicion arising—apart from all other evidence —of something really rotten at the bottom of a system which has too often been propped up by suchlike pious* frauds?

The most important inquiry, however, for our present purpose is this:—How comes it to pass that a saying which, at first sight, was so clearly heretical that the works of Fulbert ought (in the view of some) to be thus tampered with, lest he should seem to sanction it, was never seen to have anything in it of an heretical sound in the days of St. Augustine, who wrote it? †

* See Romish Mass and English Church, pp. 63, 64. See also James's " Corruptions of Scripture, Councils," &c., pp. 75 *sqq.*, London, 1843.

† It may be noted also, as a very obvious argument to show that St. Augustine held no such doctrine of Real Objective Presence of Christ's Body and Blood in the Eucharist as is now taught, that he doubted whether the glorified body of Christ has any real blood.

Mr. Patrick says: " The very reading of that 146th epistle of St. Austin, wherein he plainly, in his answer to that question, betrays his doubting of it, as well as in other of his works; his distinguishing betwixt Christ's having a true body after His resurrection, and His having flesh and blood; the testimonies there of other of the ancients, especially of Origen and his followers, that seem plainly to make both the glorified body of Christ, and also of believers, to be of another composition than that of proper flesh and blood; these, I say, are a demonstration that the ancient Fathers did not believe any presence of true flesh and blood to be now in the Eucharist. . . .

" Why St. Austin should ever at all doubt or hesitate about this

But to pass now from St. Augustine, let it be observed how in the teaching of Ephrem of Edessa, or of another in his name, not only what Christ broke was bread, what He gave was bread also. Not only so, but what was thus broken and given was for a figure of Christ's Body. Would anyone have ever thought of writing thus, unless, like St. Augustine, he had supposed that the words of institution were to be figuratively understood? Who would have ventured thus to express himself, who regarded the words "This is My Body," as requiring of us the belief that that which is given is Christ's very natural Body really present in the hand, either in the

matter of Christ's blood after His resurrection is inconceivable, if he, with the rest of the Fathers, had such a constant belief of its presence in the Eucharist as the Romanists affirm." (Patrick, in Gibson's Preservative, vol. ix. pp. 187, 188, London, 1848.)

See much more on this subject in Allix's anonymous "Dissertatio de Sanguine D. N. Jesu Christi ad Epistolam cxlvi. S. Augustini, quâ num adhuc existat, inquiritur," of which a copy is to be found in the Lambeth Palace Library.

And a scarcely less cogent argument may be drawn from his comparison of the caution to be used in receiving the word of God with that manifested in receiving the sacrament of Christ's Body.

Albertinus writes: "Annon apud omnes in confesso est Christum in verbo quod prædicatur non aliter quam in signo aut significative esse? Augustinus tamen, aut quicumque alius sit sub ejus nomine, in receptione prædicationis et in susceptione Eucharistiæ eamdem omnino cautionem vult adhiberi: *quanta sollicitudine observamus,* inquit, *quando nobis Corpus Christi ministratur, ut nihil ex ipso de nostris manibus in terram cadat, tanta sollicitudine observemus, ne verbum Dei quod nobis erogatur, dum aliquid aut cogitamus aut loquimur, de corde nostro pereat.*" (Albertinus, De Eucharistiâ, p. 432.) See Origen, as quoted below, p. 97.

place of the bread, or contained within the bread, concealed under its form?

And the same must be said of the words of Eusebius of Cæsarea, and of Procopius* of Gaza. What is to account for their saying that Christ gave His disciples an image (εἰκόνα) of His own Body, if their meaning was that what He gave in the hand was that very Body itself? The second Nicene Council declared plainly that if the Eucharist were an image (εἴκων) of Christ's Body it could not possibly be the Divine Body itself.† What,

* Coffetel would make it appear that Procopius meant "Dominum in Eucharistia non instituisse sacrificium qualia erant sub legem in umbra et figura, sed sacrificium has figuras adimplens, et rerum (hoc est corporis et sanguinis Christi) imaginem seu substantiam ipsam contiuens."

Albertinus answers: "Verum, illam *imaginis* acceptionem hic locum non habere, manifestum ex Eusebio unde hæc omnia Procopius mutuatus est. Eusebius enim indiscriminatim ait, tum Dominum *divinæ œconomiæ symbola* tradidisse, ac *pane* velut *corporis proprii symbolo uti* jussisse, tum *proprii corporis imaginem efficere* mandasse." (De Eucharistia, pp. 857, 858.)

† Εἰ εἰκὼν τοῦ σώματος ἔστιν, οὐκ ἐνδέχεται εἶναι ἄυτο τὸ θεῖον σῶμα. (Labbæus, tom. vii. c. 449.) This was said as in condemnation of the Council of Constantinople, which had spoken of the Eucharist as being (in some sense) both. (Mansi, tom. xiii. c. 265.)

So again: Ἄλλο γὰρ ἐστὶν εἰκὼν, καὶ ἄλλο τὸ πρωτότυπον, καὶ τὰ ἰδιώματα τοῦ πρωτοτύπου οὐδαμῶς τις τῶν εὖ φρονούντων ἐν τῇ εἰκονι ἐπιζητεῖ, ἐν γὰρ τῇ εἰκόνι ἄλλο οὐδὲν ὁ ἀληθής λόγος γινώσκει, ἢ κατὰ τὸ ὄνομα κοινωνεῖν, οὗτινός ἐστιν εἰκὼν, καὶ οὐ κατὰ τὴν οὐσίαν. (Labbæus, tom. vii. c. 441. See also c. 445. Mansi, tom. xiii. c. 257.)

See "Romish Mass and English Church," pp. 62, 63. See also below, Appendix, Note A, *sub fin*.

So also Nicephorus of Constantinople says: "Quod est alicujus imago, hoc corpus ejus esse non potest." (De Cherubim, cap. vi., in Bibl. Max. Patr., Lugd. 1677, tom. xiv. p. 94.)

then, could have induced these writers to reduce the gift to an image (εἴκων), if they believed that what the Disciples received in their hands was αὖτο τὸ Θεῖον σῶμα? Must we not be driven to the conclusion that they spoke of the gift of the image for just the same reason that St. Augustine spoke (in the passage just quoted) of Christ's giving to His Disciples, not His Body, but a figure of His Body? And must not that reason be this, that they and he alike understood the words which our Lord spake as figurative words?

So, again, how could Tertullian have *explained* our Lord's saying, "This is My Body," by saying, "Id est, figura* corporis Mei," if he had supposed that under the figure of the Body, the Body itself was present? †

---

* Compare Clemens Alexandrinus, Pædagogus, lib. ii. cap. ii.: Μυστικὸν ἄρα σύμβολον ἡ γραφὴ αἵματος ἁγίου, οἶνον ὠνόμασεν. (Op., tom. i. p. 184, edit. Venice, 1757.) Καὶ εὐλόγησε γε τὸν οἶνον, εἰπών, Λάβετε, πίετε· τοῦτό μου ἐστὶν τὸ αἷμα, αἷμα τῆς ἀμπέλου τὸν Λόγον, τὸν περὶ πολλῶν ἐκχεόμενον εἰς ἄφεσιν ἁμαρτιῶν εὐφροσύνης ἅγιον ἀλληγορεῖ νάμα. (Ibid. p. 186.) On which Bp. Potter observes: "Clementi idem est, *sanguis* Christi, et *sanguis vitis*. Adjicit præterea Christum (εὐφροσύνης νᾶμα) *lætitiæ laticem*, seu vinum lætitiæ effectorem (ἀλληγορεῖν) *allegorice vocare* Logon, hoc est semetipsum, *qui*, hoc est, cujus sanguis, *pro multis effusus est*. Quod si Clementi idem liquor sit *sanguis Christi* et *sanguis vitis*, vino præterea sanguinem Christi per allegoriam significante, apparet eum de Sacramento Eucharistiæ idem sensisse, quod Tertullianus." (P. 186.)

† "Contra hanc detestandam hæresim disputans Tertullianus, atque argumentum petens a Sacramento Eucharistiæ, Christum non phantasticum, sive imaginarium, sed verum et naturale Corpus habuisse, ad hunc modum probat. Figura corporis corpus naturale arguit; spectri enim seu phantasmatis nulla est figura. At (inquit)

To say that Tertullian meant that *in the Old Testament* bread was a figure of the Body of Christ, is to say that Tertullian did not know what he was speaking about. Muratori* indeed says, that this is the only way in which Tertullian's words (which are *tenebrosa*) can be explained. And I suppose it is the only way in which they can be understood on the theory of Romish theology.† But

Christus ' acceptum panem, et distributum discipulis, Corpus Suum illum fecit dicendo, Hoc est Corpus Meum, id est, figura Corporis Mei: figura vero non fuisset, nisi veritatis fuisset Corpus. Res enim vacua, ut est phantasma, figuram capere non potest.' Hujus argumenti pars quæque vera est, et necessariam rationis consecutionem continet. Primo enim oportet panem manere panem; alioqui, retorto argumento, dixisset Marcion non esse panem; sed mera panis accidentia, quæ panis esse videbantur: (sicut respondent transubstantiatores). Secundo, Corpus Christi exponitur per veri illius Corporis figuram, quæ pani attribuitur. Est enim panis aptus repræsentare Corpus Domini, propter alendi vim, quæ illi terrena inest, huic cœlestis. Tertio denique veritas Corporis eo probatur, quod verâ et substantiali figurâ repræsentetur; quum, sublatâ (prout pontificii volunt) panis substantiâ, ipsa quoque Corporis Christi veritas in sacramento destruitur." (Cosin's Works, A. C. L., vol. iv. p. 61.)

* Liturgia Vetus Romana, p. 187, Venice, 1748.

† " Nonnulli Tertullianum a nostris partibus stare pene confitentur. Sic enim Gardinerus Wintoniensis sub ementito Marci Antonii Constantii nomine: *Tertullianus eam verborum Christi interpretationem explicavit, quam ante eum nemo, nec post eum quisquam Catholicus, tanquam ex ore Christi.* . . . Hardingus similiter: *Tertulliani interpretatio non nihil revera a recto verborum* Christi sensu (hoc est, a sententia Adversariorum) *deflectit.* Et rursum: *Non tam spectavit Tertullianus accuratum verborum sensum, quam in eo elaboravit ut institutum suum evinceret.* Idem quoque innuere videtur Rhenanus, quando in admonitione de Tertulliani dogmatis, simpliciter notat, *errorem putantium corpus Christi in Eucharistia tantum esse sub*

certainly there is another very natural and simple way in which his words may be understood. Tertullian is dealing with—not Old Testament types but—the very words of Christ: "This is My Body;" and it is those very words which he is explaining* when he adds, "Id est, figura corporis Mei." Surely there is no difficulty in the interpretation of these words, which in themselves are certainly not "tenebrosa." They have one obvious meaning—a meaning which is confirmed by the assertion which follows, that in the Old Testament bread was a figure of the Body of Christ—and that meaning† is ob-

---

figura, jam olim condemnatum fuisse in Synodo Vercellensi sub Leone Pontifice Romano, ut scribit Lanfrancus; absque ulla alia Tertulliani excusatione. Alii vero ex Adversariis, aut quia sint minus æquiores, aut quia se subtiliores existiment, supracitata Tertulliani verba nobis ullo pacto favere negant. Locum tamen integrum, Licet *radio solis scriptum;* ut alicubi loquitur Tertullianus, *obscurum,* imo *obscurissimum* esse præfantur. Id autem eos causari, non ex intimo animi sensu, sed præ solutionis idoneæ diffidentia, satis indicat Justinianus, qui postquam præmonuisset *perobscurum esse locum,* illico subjungit, *in quo Haeretici triumphant, Catholici miris torquentur modis.* Sed quantum illo torqueantur, ac vicissim quam illum torqueant ut fulgentem ejus lucem obnubilent et obscurent, clarius adhuc patebit ex variis quas undique conquirunt responsionibus, earumque discussione." (Albertinus, De Eucharistia, pp. 327, 328.) See Gardiner's "Confutatio Cavillationum," Paris, 1552, fol. 113, and Morton on Eucharist, pp. 212, 501, 502.

* If there were any doubt of this, it would surely be removed by the words of Tertullian himself, who in the next book (cap. 8), alluding to his argument here, says: " Panis et Calicis sacramento jam in Evangelio probavimus corporis et sanguinis Dominici veritatem adversus Phantasma Marcionis." (See Albertinus, p. 332.)

† Two other sayings of Tertullian may be read in the same connection : (1) . . . "Vini saporem, quod in sanguinis sui memoriam

viously destructive of the Real Presence.*

Indeed, I see not how the conclusion is to be avoided, that, like St. Augustine, Tertullian also understood that when our Lord said "This is My Body," what He meant and what He gave was a figure of His Body.

But it may be alleged that Tertullian was a heretic. Indeed, it *is* alleged by Harding, and implied by others,† that here Tertullian has fallen into error in interpreting the words of Christ. It is true, indeed, that after writing a treatise to preserve Christians from the allurements of a novel teaching, Tertullian himself lapsed into the errors of Montanism.

The question, however, with which we are concerned is this :—Did any Christian writer of old time bring *this* as a charge against the faith of Tertullian, or Ephrem, or Eusebius, or of St. Augustine or others, that he or they taught concerning the Eucharist, that in it was not Christ's true Body, but a figure which Christ called His Body ? ‡ If not, it must be acknowledged that sayings

consecravit." (De Anima, cap. xvii., Op., p. 276, edit. Rigalt., 1689);
(2) . . . " Panem, quo ipsum corpus suum repræsentat." (Adv. Marcion., lib. i. cap. xiv. p. 372.)

And on the sense of "*repræsento*" see Albertinus, De Eucharistiâ, pp. 321—323, 587, 590; Claude's Catholic Doctrine of Euch. (Lond. 1684), part i. pp. 184, 185, 342, 343, part ii. pp. 29, 242, 243 ; Goode on Eucharist, i. p. 261; Pusey's Real Presence from Fathers, pp. 82, 83; Dr. Harrison's "Dr. Pusey's Challenge Answered," vol. i. pp. 487—490; vol. ii. pp. 131, 240.

* See Albertinus, De Eucharistia, p. 331.
† Ibid, p. 328.
‡ See Ussher's Works, vol. ii. p. 211, edit. Elrington.

which, at least, could only naturally be understood as teaching this, were allowed in the earlier days of Christianity to pass unchallenged for their orthodoxy, unquestioned as to the soundness of their doctrine.

In such sayings was no note of discord that jarred upon the unity of the faith once delivered to the saints, or that broke the harmony of the truth as then received by the Church of Christ.

So, again, in the works of Origen are many passages which, taken together at least, leave an indelible impression of teaching on the subject which would now be accounted as the doctrine of Sacramentaries.

Take, for example, what he says of "the consecrated bread" and "the Lord's Bread,"—"of the typical and symbolical Body" (περὶ τοῦ τυπικοῦ καὶ συμβολικοῦ σώματος), as clearly distinct (with all the distinction between one thing and another thing) from the Word made flesh, the living Bread which can only be eaten unto eternal life;* his discussion concerning our Lord's say-

* The entire passage should be carefully read in order to appreciate its bearing on the controversy:—

"Dixerit autem aliquis qui in hunc inciderit locum, quemadmodum *Non quod intrat in os coinquinat hominem;* etiamsi existimetur a Judæis impurum; ita quod ingreditur in os non sanctificare hominem, etiamsi a simplicioribus existimetur sanctificare, *id quod Domini panis appellatur* (ὁ ὀνομαζόμενος ἄρτος τοῦ Κυρίου). Et sermo quidem ille minime, opinor, aspernandus est, proptereaque perspicua indigens explicatione, quæ mihi ita se habere videtur. Quemadmodum non cibus, sed conscientia ejus qui cum dubitatione comedit, comedentem coinquinat. Nam qui dubitat, si manducaverit, damnatus est, quia non ex fide; et quemadmodum inquinato et incredulo nihil purum

ing, "Not that which goeth into the mouth defileth a man," in its bearing on the Eucharist.* I suppose, if

est, non quidem per se, sed propter illius contaminationem et incredulitatem; ita id quod sanctificatum est per verbum Dei et orationem, *non ex se utentem sanctificat;* nam si id ita esset, sanctificaret et illum qui indigne Domino comedit, nec ullus propter cibum hunc infirmus factus fuisset, aut imbecilis, aut mortuus: tale enim quidpiam Paulus docuit his verbis: Ideo inter vos multi infirmi, et imbeciles, et dormiunt multi. Ac proinde in *pane Domini* utilitas est ei qui utitur, cum intemerata mente, et pura conscientia panis fit particeps. Sic autem neque bono aliquo privamur, ex eo quod non comedamus *de pane* per verbum Dei et orationem *consecrato,* nempe propter ipsam ab esu abstinentiam; neque ex eo quod comedamus, bono aliquod abundamus: nam causa privationis, malitia est, et peccata; et abundantiæ causa, justitia est et recte facta: ut tale sit id quod a Paulo dicitur his verbis. Neque enim si manducaverimus, abundabimus, neque si non manducaverimus, deficiemus. Quod si vero id omne quod intrat in os, in ventrum vadit, et in secessum emittitur; et *cibus ipse* per verbum Dei et orationem *consecratus,* secundum illud quidem ipsum *quod materia constat* (κατ' αὐτό μὲν τὸ ὑλικὸν), in ventrem abit, et in secessum ejicitur; secundum orationem autem quæ illi accessit, juxta proportionem fidei, utilis fit, efficitque ut perspicax fiat animus, spectans ad id quod prodest; nec panis materia, sed super eum prolata oratio, ea est quæ illum juvat, qui non indigne Deo hunc comedit. *Et hæc quidem de typico et symbolico corpore.* Multa autem de ipso verbo (περὶ αὐτοῦ τοῦ λόγου) dici queant, quod caro factum est, verusque cibus (ὅς γέγονε σάρξ, καὶ ἀληθινὴ βρῶσις), quem qui comederit, omnino in æternum vivet, cum nullus malus eum possit comedere." (Com. in Matt., pp. 253, 254, edit. Huetius, 1685. See also pp. 177—179, Origeniana.)

* Origen writes: "Nostis qui divinis mysteriis interesse consuestis, quomodo cum suscipitis corpus Domini, cum omni cautela et veneratione servatis, ne ex eo parum quid decidat ne *consecrati muneris* aliquid dilabatur. Reos enim vos credits, et recte creditis, si quid inde per negligentiam decidat. Quod si circa corpus ejus conservandum tanta utimini cautela, et merito utimini; quomodo putatis minoris esse piaculi verbum Dei neglexisse quam corpus

anything beyond the sayings of Origen himself were needed to show clearly the contrariety between the natural meaning of his words and the Romish doctrine of the Real Presence, it would be found* in the various tortures with which they have been racked by Romish divines, in order to extract from them an unnatural sense. Insomuch that, besides a vain attempt to get them removed from the genuine writings of Origen, Cardinal Du Perron,† after all, would fain shield the Romish doctrine by pleading the worthlessness of Origen's testimony, because, forsooth, "he is accused of various heresies by Epiphanius, Theophilus, Jerome, Cyril, and others." ‡

It is most true that Origen was so charged; that

ejus?" (In Exod., Hom. xiii. 176, Opera, edit. Migne, tom. ii. c. 391.)

The question would surely be something monstrous on the supposition that the "*corpus Domini*" was to be understood *proprie*, and as involving the real presence of the living Christ, Body, Soul, and Divinity.

But it is fitting and forcible if the "corpus Domini" is understood of the "consecratum munus," which sacramentally bears that name, *i.e.* of the "typical and symbolical body" which Origen distinguishes. (See above, p. 90.)

* See Albertinus, De Eucharistiâ, pp. 349 *sqq*.

† "Accipio quod concedit Perronius Originem ... negare panem Eucharistiæ esse vere et proprie corpus Christi. Inde enim liquido patet quam inepte contra nos urgeat loca illa veterum Scriptorum, ipsius quoque Origenis, ubi sacramentum Eucharistiæ corpus Christi indigetant, cum Origenes qui illud sæpe sic appellat, nihilominus neget esse vere et substantialiter Christi corpus." (Albertinus, De Eucharistiâ, p. 354.)

‡ See Albertinus, De Eucharistia, p. 354.

his bitter opponents were unceasing and untiring in seeking and finding matter of accusation against him.

They spared him not when they lighted on anything which sounded like heresy in his writings; and they had a very keen scent in the hunt after whatsoever might savour of heterodox opinions.

Now, the important question is,*—Did they ever charge Origen with false doctrine for his teaching here or elsewhere concerning the Eucharist? If not, what Perronius alleges of his heresies and his enemies only shows that in those days men viewed his writings from the stand-

* With reference to what Theophilus of Alexandria had said respecting Origen's views concerning the sanctification of things inanimate, Albertinus says :—

"Neque enim illum [Origenem] accusat [Theophilus], aut quivis alius totius antiquitatis eum unquam incusavit quod de sacramentis male senserit, quod impie negaverit panem et vinum Eucharistiæ esse proprie corpus et sanguinem Christi, quod falso affirmaverit verum Domini corpus ab indignis edi non posse, et similia; indicio manifesto illum hac in parte orthodoxum ab omnibus, etiam inimicissimis, fuisse judicatum; sed arguit incogitantiæ et inadvertentiæ; quod asserens Spiritum Sanctum in res inanimas non operari, communes hypotheses imprudens everteret, propriamque fidem de baptismi et Eucharistiæ sanctitate et virtute labefactaret et destrueret." (Albertinus, De Eucharistia, p. 358.)

The statement of Theophilus was as follows :—

"Quod asserens [Origenes] non recogitat aquas in Baptismate mysticas adventu Sancti Spiritus consecrari; panemque Dominicum, quo Salvatoris corpus ostenditur, et quem frangimus in sanctificationem nostri; et sacrum calicem (quæ in mensa Ecclesiæ collocantur), et utique inanima sunt, per invocationem et adventum Sancti Spiritus sanctificari." (Theophili Alex., Paschalis ii., in Oper. Hieron., Epist. xcviii. § 13, tom. i. c. 595, edit. Vallarsius, Venice, 1766.)

point of a faith concerning the Sacrament which is not that of modern Romanists and Romanisers.

Another passage from Origen ought not to be passed over in this connection.*

* It should also be noted that Origen understood John vi. 53 in the same figurative sense as Irenæus, Tertullian, and St. Augustine. (See above, pp. 65, 66, 79, 80.) He says:—
"Dominus et Salvator noster dicit: 'Nisi manducaveritis carnem meam, et biberitis sanguinem meum, non habebitis vitam in vobis ipsis. Caro mea vere est cibus, et sanguis meus vere est potus.' . . . Hæc qui audire nescit, detorqueat fortassis, et avertat auditum secundum illos, qui dicebant: 'Quomodo dabit nobis Hic carnem suam manducare? Quis potest audire Eum? Et dicesserunt ab Eo.' Sed vos si filii estis Ecclesiæ, si evangelicis imbuti mysteriis, si Verbum caro factum habitat in vobis, agnoscite quæ dicimus, quia Domini sunt, ne forte qui ignorat ignoretur. Agnoscite quia *figuræ* sunt, quæ in divinis voluminibus scripta sunt, et ideo tanquam spiritales et non tanquam carnales examinate, et intelligite quæ dicuntur. Si enim quasi carnales ista suscipitis, lædunt vos, et non alunt. Est enim et in evangeliis litera quæ occidit, non solum in Veteri Testamento occidens litera deprehenditur. Est et in Novo Testamento litera, quæ occidat eum, qui non spiritaliter quæ dicuntur adverterit. Si enim secundum literam sequaris hoc ipsum quod dictum est 'Nisi manducaveritis carnem meam, et biberitis sanguinem meum' occidit hæc litera." (In Levit., Hom. vii. 225, Opera, edit. Migne, tom. ii. c. 486, 487.)

And as with St. Augustine so with Origen; there is not a word to indicate the notion of any other than the one natural mode of eating with the bodily mouth. (See above, p. 80.)

The letter of this saying (according to Origen) killeth, therefore it is to be recognised as *a figure*.

To say: "Id unum significat hoc loco Origenes carnem Christi non manducari more aliorum ciborum circa externum symbolum" (Delarue *in loc.*) is to follow a method of shielding Romish doctrine from the wounding power of the one natural sense of such sayings, by confidently asserting only that their meaning is something which it is absurd to suppose that the Fathers ever meant, and has relation to

It is as follows: "Non enim panem illum visibilem quem tenebat in manibus, corpus suum dicebat Deus verbum, sed verbum in cujus mysterio fuerat panis ille frangendus. Nec potum illum visibilem sanguinem suum dicebat, sed verbum in cujus mysterio potus ille fuerat effundendus. Nam corpus Dei Verbi, aut sanguis, quid aliud esse potest, nisi verbum quod nutrit, et verbum quod lætificat cor?"* Now, I think it needless to examine the proof of human ingenuity displayed in the interpretation which has been given to this passage, to bring it into harmony with Romish doctrine. The honour of discovering such a sense is given by the Benedictine editor to M. Robbe, in the following words: "Suam hic laudem fas sit tribuere clarissimo viro D. Robbe, hujusce operis censori regio, qui *mihi hærenti et*

conceptions which have been the unnatural birth of scholastic subtilties and pseudo-philosophical distinctions—the strange product of human thoughts elaborating with marvellous skill a consummate system of superstition—and all called forth to meet the necessary demands made by the formation, expansion, and crystallisation of Romish mediæval theology.

Albertinus says: "Eum [Origenem] denuo per exclusionem manducationis carnis Christi juxta literam, quamlibet illius, seu cum sui læsione, sive absque læsione, seu integræ, seu per particulas sumptæ manducationem (ut ita dicam) literalem et corporalem similiter explodere, evidenter ex eo patet, quod huic quam rejicit manducationi juxta literam intellectæ, aliam quadantenus literalem et corporalem, qualem fingit Adversarius, minime opponat, sed alteram diversi plane generis, manducationem scilicet spiritualem et mysticam." (De Eucharistia, p. 360.)

* In Matth. Comment. Series, § 85, p. 898, edit. Bened., tom. iii. c. 1734-5, edit. Migne.

incerto genuinum hunc verumque intricatæ hujus allegoriæ sensum docte solus inter plurimos aperuit."

It is sufficient for my purpose to accept the concession made by the same editor in the words, " Videntur [hæc verba] prima fronte *parum Catholice* de Eucharistia sonare."

Their obvious sense is quite sufficient to account for the fact that they were omitted in all editions of Origen's works previous to the Benedictine. In the Benedictine edition they are restored, because found in two ancient MSS. ; in one of which, however, a pen had been drawn through them [*stylo expuncta sunt*]. "It is well," says Dean Goode, "to notice these proofs of the way in which the writings of the Fathers have been tampered with by the Romanists." (On Euch., p. 324.)

Yet these words, which were thus evidently seen by others as well as by ourselves, to bear a natural meaning contradictory of the Real Presence, were never alleged by Origen's adversaries as evidence of a tendency to unsound doctrine on the subject of the Eucharist.

So again it is said by Theodoret, that Christ gave to the symbols the name of His Body, which he could hardly have done* if he had supposed that Christ's Word

---

* " The Fathers, knowing that the Eucharist was not in a proper sense Christ's Body, give us several reasons why it is *called* His Body. But nobody uses to give a reason why he *calls* a thing by its proper name.

" One reason they give is from its likeness and resemblance, either in respect of what it consists of, or from the likeness of its effects. . . .

made His Body to be present under the form of the symbols.

He says, that Christ called the elements His Body and Blood, and honoured them with this appellation;*

"Another reason why they call the Eucharist Christ's Body is because it supplies the place, is instead of it, is its representative, its pledge, and pawn.

"Tertullian: 'His Body is reputed to be in the bread: This is My Body.'

"St. Austin: 'See how the signs are varied, faith remaining the same. There (in the wilderness) the rock was Christ; to us, that which is placed on God's altar is Christ.'

"Again elsewhere, more fully: 'All things intended to signify, seem in a sort to sustain the persons of those things which they signify, as the Apostle says, The Rock was Christ, because that rock of which this is spoken did signify Christ.'

"Cyril of Jerusalem says: 'Wherefore with all assurance let us receive it (viz. the bread and wine) as the Body and Blood of Christ, for in the type of bread His Body is given thee, and in the type of wine His Blood.'

"Proclus of Constantinople: 'Instead of the manger let us venerate the altar; instead of the Infant let us embrace the bread that is blessed by the Infant (viz. Christ).'

"Victor Antiochen: 'When the Lord said, This is My Body, this is My Blood, it was fit that they who set forth the bread should, after giving of thanks, reckon it to be His Body, and partake of it, and account the cup to be instead of His Blood.'

"The author of the commentaries attributed to St. Jerome: 'Christ left to us His last remembrance, just as if a person, taking a journey from home, should leave some pledge to one whom he loves, that as oft as he looked upon it, he might call to mind his kindnesses and friendships.'

"So also Amalarius: 'Christ bowing His head gave up the ghost. The priest bows himself, and commends to God the Father this which is offered as a sacrifice in the place of Christ.'" (Patrick in Gibson's Preservative, vol. ix. pp. 142—144, London, 1848.)

* Compare Cyprian: " Quando Dominus corpus suum panem *vocat* de multorum granorum adunatione congestum, populum nostrum

and illustrates the language by our Lord's discourse in which He names Himself the vine.*

Surely, this is not the language of one holding the doctrine of the Real Objective Presence.

Surely, these are forms of expression which no one would ever think of using on the hypothesis, either of the elements on consecration actually becoming ἁπλῶς what they are named, or of their receiving within them the Real Presence of those things by whose names they are honoured.

We cannot be surprised if modern Romanists have been found to regard Theodoret as unsound on the subject of the Eucharist.† It seems as clear as the day that Transubstantiation, at any rate, had not been dreamt of

quem portabat indicat adunatum; et quando sanguinem suum vinum *appellat* de botris atque acinis plurimis expressum atque in unum coactum, gregem item nostrum significat commixtione adunatæ multitudinis copulatum." (Epist. lxxvi. ad Magnum, Opera, c. 318, edit. Baluzius, Venice, 1728.)

Again: "Invenimus . . . vinum fuisse quod sanguinem suum *dixit.*" (Epist. lxiii. ad Cæcilium, Op., c. 228.)

And let it be observed that Cyprian uses language which points quite as much to a Real Presence in the Sacrament of the faithful people, as of Christ: " Quia nos omnes portabat Christus, qui et peccata nostra portabat, videmus in aqua populum intelligi, in vino vero ostendi sanguinem Christi. Quando autem in calice vino aqua miscetur, Christi populus adunatur, et credentium plebs ei in quem credidit copulatur et conjungitur. . . . Si vinum tantum quis offerat, sanguis Christi incipit esse sine nobis. Si vero aqua sit sola, plebs incipit esse sine Christo." (Epistola lxiii., ad Cæcilium, Opera, c. 229, 230.)

* See above, p. 74. St. Augustine, as is well known, abounds in similar teaching.

† See Albertinus, De Eucharistiâ, pp. 421, 774; Edgar's Variations of Popery, p. 363, 2nd edit.

in his time. Nor can his words, taken in their natural sense, be reconciled with any other theory of a presence in or under the elements.*

But, though his faith on other points was sometimes suspected, we ask confidently, was he ever regarded as unsound on *this* point by Christians of old time? Very similar to the language of Theodoret is that of St. Chrysostom (for there is no good reason to doubt that it is his†) in the Epistle to Cæsarius, which, as first alleged by Peter Martyr from a Florentine MS., was repelled by Cardinal Du Perron‡ and others as a Protestant forgery.

* " Theodoretus ipsemet de imaginibus loquens: *imago figuras, sed non res habet*. Et rursum: *inanimæ imagines non habent substantiam rerum quarum imagines sunt*. Symbolum autem et imaginem hîc illi idem esse, aperte patet ex dialogo secundo, ubi postquam dixisset, *mystica symbola corporis ac sanguinis veri symbola esse*, atque, in hoc habuisset Eranisten assentientem, confessioni ejus applaudit, et ait: Optime. Oportet enim imaginis esse Archetypum, et pictores naturam imitantur, et eorum quæ videntur imagines pingunt." (Albertinus, De Eucharistia, p. 776.)

† To suppose with Gardiner and Turrian, Vasquez and De Valentia, that the Epistle was written by John of Constantinople in the sixth century, would only be to add force to the argument. On that hypothesis it would show that more than a century later this saying had nothing in it which was contrary to the then received faith concerning the Eucharist. (See Wake's Defence of the Exposition, pp. 142, 143, London, 1686.)

For a vindication of the authenticity of the Epistle see Deylingius, Obs. Sacr., Lips. 1757, par. iv. pp. 366, 367. See also pp. 362—366.

‡ It is of this Cardinal du Perron that Abp. Wake writes: " It will more be wondered that a person so eminent amongst them as Cardinal du Perron, and that has written so much in defence of Transubstantiation, should nevertheless all the while himself believe nothing of it; and yet this we are assured he freely confessed to some of his friends not long before his death; that he thought the doctrine to be

In it it is declared that after consecration, the bread, though bread by nature still, "is esteemed worthy to be called the Lord's Body."*

When Bigotius, having obtained a copy of this Epistle from Florence,† in the year 1680 printed it in his edition of Palladius, this part was interdicted by the Doctors of the Sorbonne,‡ and the printed leaves were actually

monstrous; that he had done his endeavour to colour it over the best he could in his books; but that, in short, he had undertaken an ill cause, and which was not to be maintained." (Preface to Discourse of the Holy Eucharist, pp. x. xi., London, 1687. See his quotation from Drelincourt, pp. xi. xii.)

* "Sicut enim antequam sanctificetur panis panem nominamus, divinâ autem illum sanctificante gratiâ, mediante sacerdote, liberatus est quidem appellatione panis, dignus autem habitus Dominici corporis appellatione, etiamsi natura panis in ipso permansit, et non duo corpora sed unum corpus Filii prædicamus; sic et," &c. (Op., edit. Montfaucon, tom. iii. p. 744.)

† An imperfect and incorrect version of the Epistle had been published the year before Wake's publication (*i.e.* in 1685) by Steph. le Moyne, among his "Varia Sacra." (See Wake's Defence of Exposition, p. 145, London, 1686, and Routh's Opuscula, tom. ii. pp. 124, 125.) After Wake's publication an edition was published at Rotterdam by J. Basnage in 1687; and in 1689, another by Harduin. (See Chrysostomi Opera, edit. Montfaucon, tom. iii. 736.)

‡ Abp. Wake says: "I speak no more than what he [Bigotius] himself declared to his friends, insomuch that he resolved to reserve privately some few copies, for fear the rest should run that risk, which indeed they accordingly did. For being now quite finished, and just ready to come abroad, some of the doctors of the Sorbonne ... caused it to be suppressed, and the printed leaves cut out of the book, without anything to supply the place of them; and of this the edition of Palladius of that year remains a standing monument. ... As to the authority of the piece, I shall need say no more than what Monsieur Bigot has already done to prove it to be genuine. So many ancient authors have cited it as St. Chrysostom's Epistle to

cut out of the book before it was allowed to be published.*

Dr. Wake, however, afterwards Archbishop of Canterbury, obtained a copy† of these leaves thus cut out, and published the contents in an appendix to his "Defence of the Exposition of the Doctrine of the Church of England." And the Epistle is now printed in the Bene-Cæsarius; such fragments of it remain in the most ancient writers as authentic, that he who after all these shall call this piece in question may with the same reasonableness doubt of all the rest of his works, which, perhaps upon less grounds, are on all sides allowed as true and undoubted." (Defence of Exposition, pp. 144, 145, London, 1686. See also Wake's Preface to Discourse of the Holy Eucharist, p. xiv. London, 1687.)

* It seems to have been judged necessary that the work should not be published in this maimed condition without some change to give it the appearance of completeness.

A new title-page was provided, and much ingenuity appears to have been displayed in substitutions and other alterations, especially in a curious arrangement of the pagination, to give an appearance of errors caused by the carelessness of the printer.

These contrivances, as detected by Mr. Mendham in a copy in his possession, are explained in detail in a note given at the end of his Preface to "An Index of Prohibited Books by command of Pope Gregory XVI." (1840.)

Mr. Mendham adds: "It is seldom that fraud presents us with so many subsidiary points of detection, so minute, so accidental, and yet so decisive." (P. xxxiv.)

I may add that there is a copy in the library of Lambeth Palace, an examination of which will satisfy those who need to be satisfied of the accuracy of Mr. Mendham's observations.

For an example of a somewhat similar treatment of a passage from St. Cyprian, bearing on the Pope's supremacy, see Mendham's Memoirs of the Council of Trent, pp. 277—279.)

† The late Dean Goode had a copy of the mutilated edition, and he says such copies are not rare. (See his "Rule of Faith," vol. i. p. 192.) Abp. Wake said of the original leaves in his possession, that they "may at any time be seen." (See "Defence of Exposition," p. 128.)

dictine edition of St. Chrysostom's works, though regarded by Montfaucon as spurious.*

It is certainly no modern writing, for even Montfaucon acknowledges that it is quoted by Joannes Damascenus, Anastatius the Presbyter, Nicephorus, and others.

Why, then, was this language (whether St. Chrysostom's or not), which has such a Protestant sound, and which Romanists would so gladly have repudiated or suppressed (whatever they may be obliged to make of it now),—why, we ask, was it never charged with heresy in earlier days, if the faith of those days was the same as the so-called Catholic faith concerning the Eucharist now?

So, again, very plain and unmistakeable is the language in one of the homilies contained in the imperfect work on St. Matthew's Gospel which is found among the works of St. Chrysostom. There the writer, contrasting the vessels of our human bodies (the habitation of Deity) with the sacred vessels used for the Eucharist, says of *them*,† "in quibus non est verum corpus Christi, sed mysterium corporis ejus continetur."‡

* See Chrysostomi Opera, tom. iii. pp. 736 *sqq.*, edit. Montfaucon, Paris, 1721.

† Chrysostomi Opera, tom. vi., Appendix, p. lxiii., edit. Montfaucon, 1724.

‡ Hincmar of Rheims seems to draw a similar, though less strongly-marked distinction between the *mystery* of Christ's Body, and the *Body Itself.* He says : " Nec dubitari licet, ubi corporis et sanguinis Dominici *mysteria* geruntur, supernorum civium adesse conventus, qui monumentum quo *corpus ipsum* venerabile positum fuerat, et unde resurgendo abscesserat, tam sedulis servant excubiis." (Opera, tom. ii. p. 78, edit. Sismondi, 1645.)

This declaration is, indeed, *so* plain, that we do not wonder to read in the margin* of one edition after another, "hæc in quibusdam exemplaribus desunt." †

* There is something so unsatisfactory in the transmission of such marginal notes from one edition to another (see above, p. 85), that it is matter for regret, if not for surprise, that this note should have been permitted to reappear in the margin of Montfaucon's Benedictine edition, and that without any other words of explanation or information on the subject.

If, as some seem to have thought, the note can only be truly understood to mean, that after one edition had been correctly printed at Paris, other early editions were expurgated of (so-called) Protestant heresy by requiring these words to be left out in the printing; then it would surely have been better to omit a comment, which must be worthless except to mislead.

But if, on the other hand, any MSS. had been collated by the editor in which the words were not found, why are we not informed where these MSS. are to be seen, and what is their probable age, and whether in the place of the omission there is any sign of erasure ?

† "One may trust an adversary as to his opinion of what makes against him; these words were looked upon as so considerable an objection, that an attempt to corrupt them was practised long ago. The learned Archbishop Ussher (in the Preface of his Answer to the Jesuits' Challenge) has observed, ' that those words (*in quibus non est verum corpus Christi, sed mysterium corporis ejus continetur*) were left out wholly in an edition at Antwerp, 1537, and at Paris, 1543, and in another at Paris, *apud Audoenum Parvum*, 1557.' Dr. James (in his ' Corruption of True Fathers,' p. 53) says: 'Those words are found in all the ancient copies at Oxford, as Archbishop Ussher says they were extant in the ancienter editions, as in 1487. And I myself have seen one Paris edition, even in the year 1536 (*apud Claud. Chevallonium*), where those words are extant. So that I conclude that the Antwerp edition first mentioned (*apud Joan. Steelsium*, 1537), was the first that made the alteration. But then I further observe, that in the large Paris edition in Latin of St. Chrysostom, 1588, which I have by me, those words are inserted, indeed, in the text, but enclosed within two brackets, with this note in the margin, *Hæc in quibusdam exemplaribus desunt*, which is very fine work, when they themselves had omitted them in the forenamed prints.'

The marginal note of Albertinus is, "In quibusdam exemplaribus non sine fraudis suspicione abrasa sunt."* The words are acknowledged by the Benedictine editor to be "prave dicta;"† though of their genuineness there can now be scarcely a reasonable doubt.‡

"They have played the same prank with the same author in another of his homilies (viz. Hom. 19), whose words were not favourable to the Real Presence of Christ's Body in the Eucharist. The words are these:—

"'Perhaps thou wilt object, how can I say that he is not a Christian, whom I see confessing Christ, having an altar, offering the sacrifice of bread and wine, baptizing,' &c.

"In the Paris edition *apud Audoenum Parvum*, an. 1557, as Dr. James notes, those words *Sacrificium panis et vini* are changed into these, *Sacrificium corporis et sanguinis Christi*. The Paris edition of 1588 (before mentioned), though it had more conscience than to insert this change into the text, yet so far complied with the cheat as to put in the margin (alias, *Sacrificium corporis et sanguinis Christi*).

"If this trade had gone on successfully, they might have had in time a consent of Fathers on their side; but it can never be without it." (Patrick, View of the Doctrines and Practices of the Ancient Church relating to the Eucharist, ch. ix. 5th position, in Gibson's Preservative, vol. ix. pp. 186, 187, London, 1848.) See James's "Corruptions of Scripture, Councils," &c. pp. 122—124, London, 1843. See also Ussher's Works, edit. Elrington, vol. iii. p. 21.

* Albertinus, De Eucharistiâ, p. 561: see Goode on Eucharist, i. p. 272; and Papers on the Eucharistic Presence, p. 52.

† Chrysost. Opera, tom. vi., Appendix, p. x., edit. Montfaucon, 1724.

‡ "The same words are found in all our ancient copies, so as Peter Martyr hath alleged them. Bellarmine having nothing to say hereunto, would have us to think that these words are inserted by some of Berengarius' disciples. And to prove this, he refers us to a place in Sixtus Senensis . . . . which proves this book to be corrupted in many places. But to grant so much, and to deal liberally with the cardinal; yet, from thence shall we infer, that Chrysostom in this place is corrupted by heretics?" (James's "Corruptions of Scripture, Councils, Fathers," p. 123.)

111

But we *do* wonder, that it should have remained for after ages to discover so grievous an error, and to

It is scarcely correct to say that Sixtus Senensis himself proves this book to be corrupted. He does but profess to be reporting the arguments of others (p. 266), on which (p. 267) he declines to express an opinion.

Sixtus Senesis himself quotes the words as the words of the author of the " Opus Imperfectum " in Bibl. Sanc., lib. vi. Annot. xxi. p. 439, edit. Col. 1586, though doubtless as containing one of those errors he speaks of when he says (liber iv. p. 267) : " Ipsum opus disertum et doctum esse, et dignum quod assidue legatur, si tamen prius diligentissime expurgatum fuerit ab iis erroribus, quos in sexto libro in censuris super Matthæi expositoribus annotavimus."

I am indebted to the kindness of the Rev. H. O. Coxe, Bodley's Librarian, for the information that there are in Oxford twelve MSS. copies of this " Opus Imperfectum." Two of these are of the fifteenth century, the rest of the fourteenth. The following is a list : (1) Laud MS. No. 444; (2) Bodleian, No. 709 ; (3) Do. No. 811; (4) Balliol, No. 58 ; (5) Merton, No. 10 ; (6) Do. No. 11 ; (7) Do. No. 38 ; (8) Exeter, No. 6 ; (9) Oriel, No. 52 ; (10) New Coll. No. 50 ; (11) Do. No. 51 ; (12) Do. No. 52.

All these MSS. have recently been examined with reference to this point. The result of the examination is that the words are found in them all, without exception ; and the variations of reading are quite unimportant.

What Sixtus Senensis says of alleged omissions in certain MSS. has especial reference to passages having too clearly a sound of Arianism. And the history of such omissions is thus given by the Benedictine editor (Diatriba ad Op. Imperf. § vi. p. 7) : " Multi in tot loca Arianismum præ se ferentia incidentes, ea vel quibusdam mutatis in Catholicam sententiam reducere conati sunt, vel penitus sustulerunt ; alii postea qui in hæc truncata ac mutata exemplaria inciderunt, ea quæ sublata fuerant in margine scripserunt."

What more likely than that the same unscrupulous purpose of reducing the work to orthodoxy anyhow, which caused the removal of what might give support to Arianism, should also have omitted a passage which might give such support to the followers of Berengarius?

The editor (p. 9) asks also of a passage altogether omitted by

eliminate such false teaching, if indeed it was a part of the primitive faith to believe that in the vessels of the Eucharist were really present, not merely the sacrament or mystery of Christ's Body, but Christ's very Body itself, with His soul and Divinity; seeing it is certain that (notwithstanding its alleged heretical pravity) this work was of old time attributed to St. Chrysostom,* and in the ninth century was quoted as his by no less an authority than Pope Nicholas I.†

Mahusius: "Invectum autem fuisse in textum Scriptoris, quis crediderit unquam?" And may not the very same question be asked (and perhaps with still more force) of the passage which speaks of *non verum corpus, sed mysterium corporis?* Its occasional omission (the passage being genuine) is intelligible, accountable, and even, it may be said, natural. Its general insertion (supposing the passage to be not genuine) seems unintelligible and incredible.

I will add that there is a passage from the last Homily of this same work, of such similar construction to the passage in question with its context, yet with nothing at all like imitation, that I think it may very well be put in as evidence, tending to show that both came from the same pen. It is as follows: " Si enim hæc corpori, corporibus non præstare tantæ impietatis est, quæ et si accipiunt ea, non possunt vivere semper: putas quantæ impietatis est, hæc omnia spiritualiter animabus periclitantibus non ministrare, quæ poterant vivere in æternum, si hæc eis ministrata fuissent." (Hom. liv. p. 228.)

The passage to be compared runs thus : " Si ergo hæc vasa sanctificata ad privatos usus transferre sic periculosum est [in quibus non est verum corpus Christi, sed mysterium corporis ejus continetur]: quanto magis vasa corporis nostri, quæ sibi Deus ad habitaculum præparavit, non debemus locum dare diabolo agendi in eis quod vult?" (Hom. xi. p. 63.)

* See Chrysos. Opera, tom. vi., pp., p. vi., edit. Montfaucon.

† The Arian (if he were such) desiring his writings to pass under the name of St. Chrysostom, would have been very little likely to give expression to language concerning the Eucharist which he would have supposed to run counter to the universal creed of the Church.

113*

Indeed, after all, I do not know that the assertion of this writer can be said to go much further than the state-

If, in the genuine writings of St. Chrysostom, no passage can be found speaking so distinctly to the point, there are certainly many sayings which can hardly without violence be made at all to harmonise with the doctrine of a Presence in the elements.

Several passages will be found quoted below, in Appendix. Let it suffice here to refer to one or two of his sayings.

In his "Commentary on the Galatians," Chrysostom says: Τῷ δὲ τῆς σαρκὸς ὀνόματι πάλιν καὶ τὰ μυστήρια καλεῖν εἴωθεν ἡ γραφή, καὶ τὴν ἐκκλησίαν ἅπασαν, σῶμα λέγουσα εἶναι τοῦ Χριστοῦ. (Com. in Gal. v. 17, Opera, tom. x. p. 720, edit. Montfaucon.) On which it has been very truly observed: "The phrase, 'accustomed to call by the name,' shows at once what is meant; as does also the coupling of the 'mysteries' with 'the whole Church' as bearing the *name*. Indeed, Chrysostom's argument is destroyed, if you suppose the 'mysteries' to *be* really the Body of Christ." (Goode on Eucharist, i. pp. 271, 2/2.)

Again, Chrysostom asks: Εἰ γὰρ μὴ ἀπέθανεν ὁ Ἰησοῦς, τίνος σύμβολα τὰ τελούμενα; (In Matt. Hom. 82, § 1, Op., tom. vii. p. 783, edit. Montfaucon)—a question which, in its natural meaning, surely implies that the consecrated elements do not contain the presence of Christ's Body glorified, but are symbols of Christ's Body as dead, and of His Blood as poured out, which is perfectly in accordance with his habitual teaching. (See Appendix, Note F.)

So again Chrysostom says: Σῶμα καὶ αἷμα μυστικὸν οὐκ ἄν ποτε γένοιτο τῆς τοῦ πνεύματος χάριτος χωρίς (Hom. De Resurr., Op., edit. Montfaucon, tom. ii. p. 436)—which can only, I believe, be understood of the sacramental as distinct from the true natural Body of Christ.

Albertinus says: "Per corpus et sanguinem Christi mysticum de quibus loquitur, non intelligit proprium Domini corpus et sanguinem. Nec enim, aut à Chrysostomo, aut ab ullo alio veterum corporis et sanguinis mystici nomenclatura unquam illis tribuitur. Imo contra, Eusebius Cæsariensis ea diserte distinguit à corpore et sanguine mystico, quæcumque illa sint: *Dominus*, inquit, *non de carne quam assumpsit loquebatur, sed de corpore et sanguine mystico ;* per corpus et sanguinem mysticum Domini sermones ibi designans. Quod et non

I

ment of St. Jerome, that the sacred chalices are to be treated with the same veneration (*eadem majestate veneranda*) as the Body and Blood of our Lord.*

obscurè fatentur Adversarii ipsi quando ad hæc Olympiodori in Ecclesiastem verba, *mysticam corporis Christi participationem*, hæc alia ad marginem notant, *nedum mysticè, sed verè et realiter ipsum Christi corpus in Eucharistia participamus*. Hac enim appellatione veteres tantum insigniunt, aut morale ejus corpus et sanguinem, videlicet, Ecclesiam, aut sermones ipsius, aut sacramentale corpus et sanguinem, seu sacramentum corporis ejus et sanguinis, hoc est, panem et vinum, quæ interdùm vocant corpus et sanguinem Christi, quia (ut notat Facundus) *in se mysterium corporis ejus sanguinisque contineant*." (Albertinus, De Eucharistiâ, pp. 531, 532.)

So, again, Chrysostom writes: "Ὥσπερ γὰρ ἡ παρουσία αὐτοῦ ἡ τὰ μεγάλα ἐκεῖνα καὶ ἀπόρρητα κομίσασα ἡμῖν ἀγαθά τοὺς μὴ δεξαμένους αὐτὴν μᾶλλον κατέκρινεν. Οὕτω καὶ τὰ μυστήρια μείζονος ἐφόδια κολάσεως γίνεται τοῖς αναξίως μετέχουσι. (Hom. xxviii. § 1, in 1 Cor., Op., ed. Montfaucon, tom. x. p. 251.) On which passage Albertinus has well observed: "Christi præsentiam, seu, quod idem est, Christum præsentem Eucharistiæ sacramento relative opponit, atque ex illius effectis per accidens, ad Eucharistiæ tanquam similis effecta (*sacramenta* enim, ut Augustinus observat, Eucharistiam etiam ipsam in exemplum adducens, *similitudinem habent earum rerum quarum sacramenta sunt*) argumentum ducit. Non igitur existimavit Sacramentum Eucharistiæ esse Christum ipsum substantialiter præsentem." (Albertinus, De Eucharistiâ, p. 530.)

* " Mirati sumus in opere tuo utilitatem omnium ecclesiarum ut discant qui ignorant, eruditi testimoniis Scripturarum, qua debeant veneratione sancta suscipere et altaris Christi ministerio deservire; sacrosque calices, et sancta velamina, et cætera quæ ad cultum Dominicæ pertinent Passionis, non quasi inania et sensu carentia sanctimoniam non habere; sed ex consortio corporis et sanguinis Domini eadem qua Corpus ejus et Sanguis majestate veneranda."
(Epistola cxiv. ad Theoph. Alex., Opera Hieron., tom. i. c. 759, edit. Vallarsius, Venice, 1766.)

This is written with reference to the views of Origen as to the operation of the Holy Ghost on things inanimate, concerning which

Surely the man who could write this was not accustomed to see Divine adoration addressed to the consecrated host.

see Albertinus, De Eucharistia, pp. 357, 358. See also above, p. 99. For an answer to Romish evasions of the argument from this passage see Albertinus, De Eucharistia, p. 585.
It is misquoted by Gregory de Valentia, as if the words were "*magna* veneratione coluntur." (De Chr. Præsentia in Euch., lib. i. cap. vi. "Sexto"; De Rebus Contr., Paris, 1610, p. 492.) And Coster (as quoted by Albertinus, p. 585) appears also to have misrepresented Jerome as saying only "summa majestate veneranda."
One would hardly, perhaps, have thought it possible that this very passage from St. Jerome should have been quoted by a Romish divine of authority in support of the adoration of the host, yet the following are the observations of Muratori after making this quotation, in his chapter entitled "Adoratio Eucharistiæ a Liturgiis et Patribus confirmata:"—"Non ait Hieronymus adoranda, sed veneranda, sive veneratione digna. An figuram tantummodo corporis Domini in Eucharistia crederet, qui scribit, participes fuisse sacros calices venerationis debitæ Christo Domino, quod ex ejus corporis et sanguinis consortio sive contactu sanctificati forent, cuicumque æquo et perspicaci lectori dijudicandum relinquo." (De Rebus Liturgicis, cap. xix.; ed. Migne, c. 1012; Lit. Rom., c. 234.)
A little before Muratori had spoken of the "veneratio et latriæ cultus" which "etiam extendebatur ad sacra vasa tremendi sacrificii; qui cultus tamen non in materie sistebat, sed ad ipsum adorandum Dominum ferebatur." (Lit. Rom., c. 234.)
Now the language of Jerome leads to no question as to whether the veneration due—whatever it be—rests with the vessels or goes beyond them. But does Muratori really mean us to understand Jerome as teaching that the *cultus latriæ* was due to the vessels? If so, then the *cultus latriæ* has a new sense, in which, we are willing to allow, it is due to the sacramental Body of Christ.
But if so, what does Muratori mean by his careful distinction between adoration and veneration—"Non ait adoranda, sed veneranda"? Are we not to gather from this that to the vessels is due, according to Muratori, not adoration, but only reverence? And if so, how are we to escape from the conclusion that, in the teaching of Jerome, to the

That sacramental Body and Blood to which is due no higher adoration than that which should be given to the vessels of ministration, is surely not the true Body and Blood of Christ, with His soul and divinity, but the sacrament or mystery of them.*

We may very possibly be disposed, some of us, to think that there are evidences in the writings of the Fathers of a somewhat excessive reverence shown to these vessels. But we should be wronging the ancient Fathers indeed if we were to suppose that they did not know how to draw the line clearly and broadly between the veneration due to such instruments as these, sacred for most sacred uses, and the worship due to Him to whom there is a name

---

Sacramental Body and Blood of Christ is due also, not adoration, but only reverence, seeing the vessels are "eadem majestate veneranda," and that, therefore, the sacramental symbols are not to be "participes venerationis debitæ Christo Domino" (of which Jerome has said nothing); and, therefore, that the sacramental Body and Blood are not the true Body and Blood of Christ, but the sacrament or mystery of them, bearing their names?

* With reference to the saying of Jovinianus, "Dominus in typo sanguinis sui non obtulit aquam, sed vinum," Perronius pleads that these are the words of a heretic; to which Albertinus forcibly answers: "Verum, id nihili est. Nam si verba hæc tanquam Joviniani simpliciter considerentur, sic multiplicatur nobis numerus testium, hæreticis et Orthodoxis in hac quæstione nobiscum consentientibus. Sed addo censeri debere, non Joviniani modo, sed etiam Hieronymi, quandoquidem Jovinianus non ibi loquitur ex propria hypothesi a qua Hieronymus disserentiret, verum ex fide communi de Eucharistia, in qua illi omnino cum Hieronymo conveniebat. Unde et Hieronymus né minimam quidem illius carpendi occasionem prætermittens, in his verbis nihil arguit tanquam falsum aut hæreticum.' (Albertinus, De Eucharistia, p. 579.)

given above every name, The Exalted Saviour, Head over all, King of Kings, and Lord of Lords.

Moreover there is a well-known saying of Facundus Hermianensis, in his work in defence of the three Chapters, which, if possible, speaks with even more distinctness to the same point: " Sacramentum corporis et sanguinis ejus, quod est in pane et poculo consecrato, corpus ejus et sanguinem dicimus; non quod proprie corpus ejus sit panis, et poculum sanguis; sed quod in se mysterium* corporis ejus sanguinisque contineant.

* It is a necessity with Romish theologians to reduce the language of Facundus into conformity with the doctrine of Rome. The process by which this result is attained is very observable.

(1) The terms used by Facundus, *sacramentum, panis, poculum*, are equivalent to *symbola* and *signa*; and the *symbola* and *signa* are to be understood of *accidents* of bread and wine, without any substance. Muratori says: "Panis et vinum in Eucharistia symbola sunt et signa, quæ per verba consecrationis divinitus sanctificata, veram carnem et sanguinem Christi continent. Neque per consecrationem desinunt esse symbola ac signa, quamquam panis et vini substantia convertatur in Corpus et Sanguinem Domini." (De Rebus Liturgicis, c. 107, Venice, 1748. See also note of Sirmondus *in loc.*)

(2) There being thus nothing left but the *accidents* or *species* of the elements (though Facundus speaks quite plainly, not of *species*, but of bread and wine), the assertion of Facundus that the bread and wine are not *properly* the Body and Blood of Christ may be regarded as quite true from the Roman standpoint, because no one supposes that the *species* or *accidents* are properly Christ's Body and Blood. " Pete nunc," says Muratori, "an *proprie panis* sacratus (hoc est species panis) *sit Corpus Domini, et poculum sit Sanguis ejus*. Negat hoc Facundus, neque immerito. Quamquam enim symbola vere contineant Corpus et Sanguinem, non ipsa tamen sunt ipsum Corpus et Sanguis." (Ibid, c. 107.)

But where is there anything in the words of Facundus to justify the gloss, " hoc est species panis " on the word " panis sacratus "?

Hinc et ipse Dominus benedictum panem et calicem quod discipulis tradidit, corpus et sanguinem suum vocavit." (Pro Defens. Tri. Cap., l. ix. c. v., ed. Migne, c. 762, 763.)

(3) There remains to be explained away the comparison with baptism: " The sacrament of adoption may be called Adoption, as the sacrament of the Body and Blood are called the Body and Blood of Christ."

Does the element of baptism thus lose its substance? Under the *species* and *accidents* of the *symbolum* is there left only the substance of " *adoptio* " ?

By turning quite aside from the real point which has to be touched, Muratori would make it appear that the comparison does but tend to support the Romish interpretation.

He says: " Resultat hæc eadem veritas e comparatione baptismi, qua utitur idem Facundus. Quamvis baptismus tantummodo sit *sacramentum*, hoc est visibile signum *adoptionis*, et non sit ipsa *adoptio*: attamen *baptismus potest adoptio nuncupari*. Porro nulla dubitatio est, quin homines, baptismum recipientes, veram et non figuratam adoptionem filiorum Dei accipiant." (Ibid. c. 108.)

True it is, indeed, that in baptism believers receive the true, and not merely figurative, adoption of sons; and equally true it is that the faithful do indeed by faith receive in the Lord's Supper the true, and not the mere figurative, Body and Blood of Christ.

But this is altogether beside the point. The point in discussion is the doctrine of the Real Presence of Christ's Body and Blood, not to the faith of the receiver, and not in the ministration of the ordinance, but in the consecrated elements or their forms.

And the important question to be asked in reference to this point, and in view of the teaching of Facundus, is this:—Is the adoption, which comes of the washing of the Blood of Christ, really present under the form of water, or contained in the element of water, in the sacrament of baptism?

If not, then certainly does the outward sign, in the sacrament of baptism, avail to convey its gift, without containing that gift within itself. And baptism (according to Facundus) is called by the name of its gift without having any real objective presence of its " res sacramenti " in or under its symbol.

And it is not immaterial to observe for what purpose these words were written. They are intended to justify

And then, as certainly, may the sacrament of the Lord's Supper avail to the giving and receiving, after a heavenly and spiritual manner, the Body and Blood of Christ, without having these gifts contained in its symbols. And its outward signs may be called, and, according to Facundus, are called, the Body and Blood of Christ [" Corpus ejus et Sanguinem *dicimus*," for which Muratori misquotes "*sumimus*," c. 106], and may be said to contain their *mystery*, without having any real objective presence of Christ or of His Body and Blood under the form of bread and wine.

So St. Chrysostom: Ἐπεὶ οὖν ὁ λόγος φησί· τοῦτό ἐστὶ τὸ Σῶμά Μου· καὶ πειθώμεθα, καὶ πιστεύωμεν, καὶ νοητοῖς αὐτὸ βλέπωμεν ὀφθαλμοῖς, οὐδὲν γὰρ αἰσθητὸν παρέδωκεν ἡμῖν ὁ Χριστός, ἀλλ' αἰσθητοῖς μὲν πράγμασι, πάντα δὲ νοητά. οὕτω γὰρ καὶ ἐν τῷ βαπτίσματι δι' αἰσθητοῦ μὲν πράγματος γίνεται τοῦ ὕδατος τὸ δῶρον, νοητὸν δὲ τὸ ἀποτελούμενον, ἡ γέννησις. (In Matthæum, Hom. lxxxii. al. lxxxiii., Opera, tom. vii. p. 787, edit. Montfaucon, 1727.)

The argument of Facundus would be a worthless one if the sacrament of the Eucharist had any truer or higher claim to be called by the name of its *res sacramenti* than the sacrament of Baptism has to be called by the name of its gift. His reasoning could be nothing but a fallacy unless the sacrament of Baptism had quite as true a real presence of " adoption" under the form of water as the sacrament of the Eucharist has of the Body and Blood of Christ under the form of bread and wine.

But special attention should be directed to the words of Facundus following: "Hinc et ipse Dominus benedictum panem et calicem quem discipulis tradidit, Corpus et Sanguinem suum vocavit." He regards what he has said before as the true explanation of our Lord's words, calling the bread and wine His Body and Blood. But in the Romish interpretation there is nothing in those words that needs to be explained; they are *proprie dicta;* and all explanations of them on the principle of that sacramental language which gives to the *signs* the name of the *things signified and exhibited* are inadmissible.

Let any one carefully read through the whole extract from Facundus, and judge for himself whether they were so understood by

the language which speaks of our Lord Himself as "receiving the adoption of sons."

him, and whether he supposed that they would be so understood by the Christian Church in his time.

In answer to the argument made by La Milletière, from Facundus's use of the word *mysterium*, Albertinus says: "Per *mysterium* sacramentum intelligit, prout ipse Milleterius alibi affirmat, Græcos et Latinos per hæc duo verba rem eandem designasse; ac dicit, panem et vinum *in se continere*, non Corpus et Sanguinem Christi, sed *mysterium* seu sacramentum *corporis et sanguinis*: quomodo Eusebius ait prophetiam Jacobi *continere novi testamenti sacramenta* [τῆς καινῆς διαθήκης τὰ μυστήρια περιέχειν : Dem. Ev. lib. viii.] ... Bertramus: *Mysterium quod supra mensam positum est mysterium continere populi credentis*, hoc est, esse ipsius signum." (De Eucharistiâ, p. 890. See also p. 4, on the sense of *mysterium*.)

The distinction of Facundus between what is "proprie corpus" and that which "continet mysterium corporis" may be compared with the distinction drawn in the imperfect work on St. Matthew, in the words spoken of the sacred vessels, "in quibus non est verum Corpus Christi, sed mysterium corporis ejus continetur." (See above, p. 108. See also Hincmar, as quoted above, p. 108.)

It should be added that Christian antiquity in its teaching concerning sacraments in general recognises no such distinction between Baptism and the Eucharist as would give a real presence to the one which does not belong to the other.

Isidore Hispalensis says : " Sacramentum est in aliqua celebratione cum res gesta ita fit ut aliquid significare intelligatur, quod sancte accipiendum est. Sunt autem sacramenta baptismus et chrisma, Corpus et Sanguis. Quæ ob id sacramenta dicuntur, quia sub tegumento corporalium rerum virtus divina secretius salutem eorumdem sacramentorum operatur, unde et a *secretis* virtutibus, vel a *sacris* sacramenta dicuntur. . . Græce mysterium dicitur quod secretam et reconditam habeat dispositionem." (Etymol., lib. vi. cap. xix., Opera, edit. Migne, tom. iii. c. 255, 256.

St. Augustine had said: "Sacramentum est in aliqua celebratione, cum rei gestæ commemoratio ita fit, ut aliquid etiam significari intelligatur, quod sancte accipiendum est. (Ep. lv. ad Januarium, Opera, tom. ii. c. 128, edit. Benedict. 1679.) "Tenere te volo, quod est

He says: "Nam sacramentum adoptionis suscipere dignatus est Christus, et quando circumcisus est, et quando baptizatus est; et potest sacramentum adoptionis adoptio nuncupari."

His argument is this: the sacrament of adoption may be called adoption in the same way as the Sacrament of Christ's Body and Blood is spoken of as His Body and Blood, and as the consecrated elements were so called by Christ Himself—though they are not properly so, but only contain the mystery or sacrament of them. Therefore he goes on to say: "Quocirca sicut Christi fideles sacramentum corporis et sanguinis ejus accipientes, corpus et sanguinem Christi recte dicuntur accipere, sic et ipse Christus, sacramentum adoptionis filiorum cum suscepisset, potuit recte dici adoptionem filiorum suscepisse."

Now whatever senses may be put upon the words of Facundus by modern Romanists, shall we think that Christians of old time did not understand them in their natural and obvious sense? And can we really doubt what is the natural meaning of this language? And was then, we ask, Facundus for the use of such language

hujus disputationis caput, Dominum nostrum Jesum Christum, sicut ipse in Evangelio loquitur, leni jugo suo nos subdidisse et sarcinæ levi: unde sacramentis numero paucissimis, observatione facillimis, *significatione* præstantissimis, societatem novi populi colligavit, sicuti est baptismus Trinitatis nomine consecratus, communicatio corporis et sanguinis ipsius, et si quid aliud in Scripturis canonicis commendatur, exceptis iis," &c. (Ep. liv. ad Januarium, Op., tom ii. c. 124.)

ever regarded in his own day as having on him the taint of heresy?

Nay, rather, does not his very argument imply that he looked to find the obvious sense of his words universally accepted without questioning, and recognised at once as the well-understood explanation of sacramental language as received and used by all?

And it should be observed in passing, that this is no more than is not only implied in very much of the language of the ancient Fathers, but is not obscurely stated in what some of them have taught us concerning the Sacraments in general.

To us it is a matter of special interest to observe, that spite of the growth of superstition in times of mediæval darkness, teaching such as this lived on in England, and lifted up its head as the belief of the Anglo-Saxon Church, for more than four hundred years later.

The Homilies of Elfric are well known.* They have often been alleged as evidence against the doctrine of Rome.†

But besides these, we have in Latin and in Saxon a

---

* Cave writes: " Vir certe erat Ælfricus noster supra communem sui sæculi sortem in Theologicis, presertim vero in Grammaticis (*Grammaticus* inde dictus) eruditus: tantam exinde apud populares suos famam adeptus, ut Sermones ab eo scripti, vel Saxonice versi in Ecclesiis publice legi juberentur, atque ex ipsius Epistolis haud paucæ in vetustum Ecclesiæ Anglicanæ Synodicon cooptarentur." (Historia Literaria, pp. 412, 413, Geneva, 1694.)

† See Papers on the Eucharistic Presence, pp. 651, 652.

letter of Elfric to the Archbishop of York, named Wulstan,* written probably about the close of the tenth or the beginning of the eleventh century.

In this letter there occurs language just parallel with the language of Facundus. It distinctly denies that the Sacramental Body and Blood are really the Body and Blood of Christ which were crucified and shed. It is Christ's Body as the manna in the wilderness was His Body. It is Christ's Blood as the water which flowed from the rock was His Blood: †—

"Non ‡ sit tamen hoc sacrificium Corpus ejus in quo passus est pro nobis, nec sanguis ejus quem pro nobis effudit: sed spiritualiter Corpus ejus efficitur et sanguis: sicut manna quod de cœlo pluit, et aqua quæ de petra fluxit."

* There were two Archbishops of York of the same name. The former died in 956, the latter in 1023. Mr. Soames says, "To this latter only could Elfric have written." (Anglo-Saxon Church, p. 221.)

† As to the teaching of this extract, "much of it," says Mr. Soames, "is to be found in the Epistle to Wulfsine, or *Elfric's Canons*; many things also are in the famous Paschal homily (styled in two MSS. in the Public Library at Cambridge, Sermo de Sacrificio in Die Paschæ), but upon the whole, the doctrine is brought out more forcibly in this Epistle to Wulfstan, than in either of the other pieces. This may appear an additional reason for believing that the Epistle to Wulfstan has been rightly considered as posterior to the other two pieces. That it is by the same author, and not by Elfric Bata, or some other writer, may fairly be presumed from the identity of doctrine, and even of language, running through all the three." (Anglo-Saxon Church, p. 324.)

‡ Perhaps the true reading may be *fit*. See Routh's Opuscula, vol. ii. pp. 181, 168.

Certainly the Rock and the Manna were not Christ personally. Nor was it ever heard of that men should think of worshipping Christ under their forms.

These words of Elfric, however, had been completely erased from the Latin copy of the letter which remains to us.* This Latin MS. is yet to be seen in the library of Corpus Christi College, Cambridge.† The omitted words were brought to light by the discovery of a Saxon MS. in the library of the cathedral at Exeter.

* See James, Corruptions of Sc., Councils, and Fathers, pp. 125,126, London, 1843. The MS. now in the library of Corpus Christi College, Cambridge, is probably the same mentioned by Foxe as in the library of Worcester. See Acts and Monuments, vol. v. p. 279, London, 1838.

† In Archbishop Parker's " Testimonie of Antiquitie," published by John Day, there is this note on the omitted piece : " ( ) The words inclosed between the ii. half circles, some had rased out of Worcester booke, but they are restored agayne out of a booke of Exeter Church." (See Thompson's Edition, Lumley, Chancery-lane, p. 76.)

Dr. Routh says: " Hodie superest . . . . hic liber Vigorniensis sæculo undecimo scriptus, inter codices Parkeranos, numero cclxv. signatus, ad quem hoc extat in *Catalogo* eorundem librorum Nasmithano, p. 311: '*Non fit—de petra fluxit*. Ultimum hunc locum a papista quodam olim abrasum e veteri libro Exoniensis bibliothecæ fuisse restitutum testatur in margine quidam neotericus.' Manu, ut videtur, Joscelini . . . . notam ad marginem scriptam fuisse, ait Humphredus Wanleius in vol. ii. *Thesauri Hickesiani*, pag. 109. addens, codicem Exoniensem nunc esse bibliothecæ Collegii Corporis Christi." (Opuscula, vol. ii. p. 181.)

This Jocelyn is by some supposed to have written the Preface to the " Testimonie of Antiquitie." He was Chaplain of Archbishop Parker. Strype attributed it to Parker himself. See Thompson's " Select Monuments," Introduction, pp. iii. and v., and Routh's Opuscula, vol. ii. p. 179.

There are also other MSS.* in Saxon, now known, of the same Epistle.

But if the Cambridge MS. alone remained, we should never have known what had been erased, or why the erasure had been made.

But it would be idle for us to pretend now that we cannot tell what led to the expunging of these words of Elfric.† Their repugnance to the doctrine afterwards upheld by Lanfranc was too plain and unmistakable. In the view of Lanfranc's disciples, it is clear such teaching must have been heresy. But then, we ask, was it counted heresy in England before? And in answer we appeal to the fact that the Homilies of Elfric (probably the same Elfric) ‡ had been submitted to Sigeric, Archbishop of Canterbury, and highly approved by him.

Nay, they were authorised by him for use in the pulpits of England.§ And, indeed, there is at least some ground

* There are two in the Bodleian Library, from one of which is printed the transcript given in Soames's Anglo-Saxon Church, p. 308 sqq. See note 3, p. 310.

† See Ussher's Works, vol. ii. p. 210, edit. Elrington.

‡ See Soames's Anglo-Saxon Church, p. 324. The argument, however, would not be weakened if it were another Elfric.

§ Lingard has said: "Ælfric may be a faithful expositor of the opinion of Bertram, but it remains to be shown that he is a faithful expositor of the faith of the Anglo-Saxon Chiistians." (Hist. and Antiq. ii. 460.)

In reply, Mr. Soames writes: "The authority of English theologians anterior to Elfric is not set aside, but habitually produced in confirmation of his views. His greater precision of language, and fulness of detail, no doubt came from the foreigner Bertram, or Ratramn.

for believing that this same Elfric was himself subsequently an Archbishop of the Anglo-Saxon Church. And these Homilies, though by no means free from the superstitions of the times, have, on the subject of the Eucharist, borrowed matter largely from the Book of Bertram or Ratramn, the great opponent of Paschasius, and teach doctrine, though not perhaps quite so distinct,*

But that writer's language was caused by the language of another foreigner, namely, Radbert. .... That Elfric was 'a faithful expositor of the faith of the Anglo-Saxon Christians' is shown sufficiently by the approbation of Sigeric, Archbishop of Canterbury." (Latin Church during Anglo-Saxon Times, p. 424.) When Elfric sent his Homilies to the Archbishop for inspection, he especially called attention to the great care taken for avoiding heresy and error: "Ne inveniremur aliquâ hæresi seducti, seu fallaciâ fuscati." (See Soames's Anglo-Saxon Church, pp. 219, 220. See also Soames's Latin Church during Anglo-Saxon Times, pp. 429, 431; and Soames's Bampton Lectures, Sermon vii.) He asks also for the corrections of the Archbishop: "Ut digneris corrigere, per tuam industriam, si aliquos nævos malignæ hæresis, aut nebulosæ fallaciæ, in nostrâ interpretatione reperies; et adscribatur dehinc hic codicillus tuæ auctoritati, non utilitati nostræ despicabilis personæ." (Hickes as quoted in Soames, Anglo-Saxon Church, p. 220.)

See also Hook's Lives of the Archbishops, vol. i. pp. 436, 438—440, 442, 443. Dr. Hook thinks that this Elfric was Archbishop of Canterbury. Mr. Thorpe considers that "with better foundation we may assume him to have been Ælfric, Archbishop of York." (Preface to Homilies, Ælfric Society, vol. i., Pref. p. v.)

* On the doctrine of the Homilies Dr. Routh writes : " Joannes Lingardus, doctus in primis et disertus scriptor, id nuper conatus est ostendere, quod et alii ante eum communionis Romanæ asseclæ aggressi fuerant, constare posse, imo bene congruere, hæc Ælfrici verba, nam tacet Epistolas illas supra allatas vir clarus, cum dogmate transubstantiationis Eucharisticæ, quod apud Romanistas receptum est. Vide *Antiquitates ejus Anglo-Saxonicæ Ecclesiæ*, in Notis, pp. 497—506, edit. secundæ. Etenim commentatum esse de hoc mys-

yet similar to that which is so very distinctly stated in terio Ælfricum duce atque magistro celebri illo Bertramo, seu Ratramno, ait ibi Lingardus; neque hoc quidem a vero distat; cum plurima ad verbum ex illo sumpserit Ælfricus. Sed interea hunc ipsum Ratramnum, postquam libellus ejus de Eucharistia a Boilavio doctore Sorbonico in linguam Gallicam exeunte sæculo decimo septimo conversus fuerat, plus Calvinistam fuisse, quam Calvinum ipsum (*Rhatram est plus Calviniste, que Calvin même*) pronunciavit eruditissimus ille Longueruæus." (Opuscula, vol. ii. p. 185.)

Dr. Rock contends ("Church of our Fathers," vol. i. p. 24) that the expressions of Ælfric which are laid hold of by Protestant writers mean "that Christ's true, real, very Body, given them in the housel or sacrament of the altar, was not there in the same state in which it existed on earth before His death; like what human flesh and blood are now; but as Christ's Body at present exists in heaven, in a glorified state."

Yet in the same page Dr. Rock himself quotes the words: " He changed, through invisible might, the bread to His own Body, and the wine to His Blood—as He had done before in the wilderness— before He was born as man, when He changed the heavenly meat to His Flesh, and the flowing water, from the stone, to His own Blood."

Surely Dr. Rock will not maintain that the manna was transubstantiated into Christ's glorified Body before the Incarnation, nor that Christ's Blood, as it is now in heaven, was, before His birth, made to be really present in the water from the rock in the wilderness.

From the standpoint of the Augmentation doctrine, Rupertus Tuitiensis says : " Hoc loco silendum non est, male quosdam ignotos, sed absconditi nominis homines opinari, suis quoque defendere dictis et scriptis, panem verum et potum quem in sancto altari sumimus nihilominus patres illos manducasse tunc temporis et bibisse, et nihilo magis hoc esse verum corpus et sanguinem Christi, quam fuit illud manna quod ille populus comedit." (Comment. in Joan., lib. vi., Opera, edit. Migne, tom. iii. c. 460.)

It is plain from what follows (see especially c. 463 and 469) that those whom Rupert condemns relied on the support of St. Augustine's teaching. And it is scarcely possible to doubt that the doctrine which Rupert so strongly opposed was indeed the doctrine not only of the Anglo-Saxon Church, but of St. Augustine. See Ussher's Works, vol. ii. pp. 210—212, edit. Elrington.

this letter to Wulstan, from which other hands have desired to obliterate it as heretical.*

How, then, is it possible for us to believe that the doctrine of the Eucharist which was afterwards brought

> Dr. Rock, however, further argues that the Anglo-Saxons must have believed transubstantiation from the superstitious custom of putting the Eucharist with the relics, or, failing relics, as a substitute for them, within the altar of a newly consecrated church (p. 41).
> He says that thus "the Anglo-Saxons proclaimed the Eucharist to be, with regard to Christ, what saints' relics were to those saints; but saints' relics are their bodies." (P. 43.)
> On which it may be sufficient to observe that the relics are the *dead* bodies of the saints. But in the faith of the Romish Church the Eucharist is the *living and glorified* Body of Christ, with soul and Divinity. And there is surely something strangely incongruous in the idea of laying up *this*, instead of relics, or by the side of relics, to serve for a Church's consecration. Surely the custom might have arisen far more naturally from a view of the Eucharist as symbolically and virtually the *dead* Body of Christ.
> * The Homilies were in Saxon, "a language," Mr. Soames observes, "with which Anglo-Normans, of any distinction, were unacquainted. Hence, after a few years, no cultivated mind was ever likely to be awakened by hearing any of his homilies. Books were few; and such as Elfric left might shortly be rendered useless by refraining from translating them into Latin. They were actually classed among old and useless books by the Monks of Glastonbury, in cataloguing their library, so early as the thirteenth century. . . . . Such was the policy pursued; and being favoured by a prevailing disregard for Anglo-Saxon literature, even by general ignorance of the character in which it was preserved, Elfric's memory became all but wholly lost." (Anglo-Saxon Church, pp. 230, 231.)
> We may probably have here the true way of accounting for the fact, that the same pains which was bestowed on expurgating the Latin MS. of Elfric's Epistle, was not applied also to the Saxon MSS., which still retain the obnoxious passage. See Foxe's Acts and Monuments, vol. v. pp. 278, 279, London, 1838.

in from Rome, was in agreement with the ancient doctrine of the Anglo-Saxon Church?

But the saying of Facundus may be nearly matched by another which few perhaps will like to brand as heretical, and to which I would direct attention for a moment, not so much (let this be well observed) to add anything to my argument, as to illustrate it.

It is an old *dictum* (following the teaching of the Fathers)—perhaps it might be regarded as a kind of *cento* of more ancient *dicta*—which by some strange coincidence has been suffered to hold its place, not indeed as a part of the Canon Law, but among the unauthoritative glosses appended to the "Decretum" of Gratian.*

In whatever sense it may be *intended* to be understood, its natural meaning is too obvious to need any comment. Let it speak for itself.

It is as follows: "Id est, cœleste sacramentum, quod vere repræsentat Christi carnem, dicitur Corpus Christi, sed improprie. Unde dicitur suo modo, sed non rei veritate, sed significati mysterio, ut sit sensus, vocatur Christi Corpus, id est, significat."†

* Decret., Pars iii., De Consecra. Dist. ii. can. xlvii. p. 1278 edit. Venice, 1567.

† This is a gloss on the words quoted as from Prosper's "Book of Sentences from Augustine:" "Sicut ergo cœlestis panis *qui Christi caro est*, suo modo vocatur Corpus Christi, cum re vera sit sacramentum corporis Christi," &c., where the words in italics are (with reason, it can hardly be doubted) supposed to be interpolated or corrupted. See Goode on Eucharist, i. p. 263.

But, not to cite other examples, let me just observe, that though, when Berengarius was condemned, the book attributed to Johannes Scotus Erigena* was denounced

The words of the gloss can only be reconciled with Romish doctrine by taking " cœleste sacramentum" as equivalent to "accidentia panis." (See Albertinus, De Euch., p. 407.)

It may doubtless be pleaded that this is indeed to be regarded as the true interpretation of the gloss, and then it affords (in connection with the entire text of the canon which it explains, and with its other glosses) most startling evidence of the strange violence which has to be put upon ancient language in order to bring it into forced conformity with Roman doctrine.

Whatever may have been the intention of the glossator, it is impossible to believe that the language of the Fathers, which he has more or less nearly followed, was intended by them to be understood in any such tortured sense as would shield instead of condemning the Real Presence in the Romish sense. (See Albertinus, De Eucharistia, p. 621.)

It would not be difficult, I think, to show that every statement made is supported by the language and teaching of Christian antiquity.

Let it, however, be interpreted of the accidents only. (See Anselm, Epist. cvi., Op., pp. 452, 453, Paris, 1721.) Even so it must clearly be understood to mean that *that* (that same, whatever it be) which is called the Body of Christ is called so by reason of its being so in figure, and not in reality; whereas the whole strength of the position of our opponents seems to lie in the assumption that (as regards the words "Hoc est corpus meum") that which is called the Body of Christ must be so called by reason of its being so in reality, and not in figure.

* The book attributed to Scotus has sometimes been supposed to be the work of Ratramnus or Bertram; but even if Scotus did not write a separate treatise on the Lord's Supper, there can be little doubt that his views on the subject were decidedly anti-Paschasian. (See Canon Robertson's History of the Christian Church, vol. iii. p. 348, 349, 1874). Indeed, there is reason to think that he allowed his tendencies toward rationalistic philosophy to draw him far in the direction of Pantheism. (Ibid., pp. 358, 359.)

by wild acclamation,* yet albeit censured for his views of predestination, &c., this remarkable writer seems never before to have been condemned for his teaching on the Lord's Supper.† In other words, his book on the Sacrament appears to have been uncensured for about two hundred years, till the days of Lanfranc, of whom we are

* See Milman's Latin Christianity, vol. iii. p. 393, 394, Lond. 1867.
† So also as to Bertram's book:—" Hunc autem Bertramum Joannes Trithemius Abbas Spanheimensis, vir tempore suo doctissimus, in Catalogo Scriptorum Ecclesiasticorum recenset, illumque in divinis Scripturis valde peritum, et in literis secularium disciplinarum egregie doctum, ingenioque subtilem et clarum eloquio, nec minus vita quam doctrina insignem fuisse testatur. Ac tantum abest, ut ob scriptum hoc de corpore et sanguine Christi opusculum, hæreseos macula illum aspergat, ut potius commendabile illud esse opus inter cætera prædicet. Ita vero viri graves et eruditi, nullisque animi morbis ac perturbationibus obnoxii, tam singulare de Bertramo ferentes judicium, Jesuitas, qui hodie odiosum hæreseos crimen illi objiciunt, præcipiti potius ac temerario raptari affectu, quam recto animi judicio duci abunde coarguunt." (Hospinian, Op., tom. iii. p. 269.)

Paschasius's doctrine "received no synodical confirmation until the eleventh century, when it obtained an indirect one at the Council of Vercelli, by the condemnation of Erigena." (See Soames's Latin Church during Anglo-Saxon Times, p. 433.)

By the acknowledgment of Paschasius himself, many doubted in his time of the doctrine which he maintained. (See " Romish Mass and English Church," p. 65.)

But how could any doubt if Divine adoration in his time were habitually given to Christ as present in the Elements?

Or, even supposing any *could* doubt, why were not their doubts met at once by an appeal to the *fact* of adoration? Anyhow, why was not this argument—which, if the fact were so, would have been so obvious—brought against those who maintained the views of Bertram and Scotus: " Why! if such views are true, the whole Christian Church has been from the beginning an idolatrous Church, worshipping as Christ that which is but an effectual symbol of His Body "?

told that * he first leavened the Church of England with the corrupt doctrine of the Carnal Presence.

I say, then, that some answer is needed to the question— How is it to be accounted for, on the hypothesis of the Real Presence forming a part of the ancient faith, that views and statements which seem to be a clear denial of it were allowed for so many centuries to pass uncondemned,† and that the rejection of the doctrine is

* See Ussher's Works, vol. iii. pp. 84, 85, edit. Elrington.

† "The Fathers speak of Christ's Body and Blood in the Eucharist with such terms of restriction and diminution which plainly tell us that they understood it not of His substantial and natural Body, but in a figurative sense. Thus:—

"Origen says: 'That bread in the Eucharist is made by prayer a certain holy body.'

"And St. Austin: 'Christ took in His hands what the faithful understand, and after a sort, carried Himself when He said, This is My Body.'

"Bede, upon the same Psalm, has the same term of restriction: 'Christ, after a sort, was carried in His own hands.'

"St. Austin elsewhere: 'In a certain sense, the sacrament of the Body of Christ is Christ's Body, and the sacrament of the Blood of Christ is Christ's Blood.' Just as at Easter, we say, 'This day Christ rose,' because it is a memorial of it.

"St. Chrysostom says of the consecrated bread: 'That it has no longer the name of bread (though the nature of it remains), but is counted worthy to be called the Lord's Body.'

"Theodoret, in like manner: 'He honoured the visible symbols with the appellation of His Body and Blood.'

"Facundus Hermian. is most express: 'We call,' says he, 'the sacrament of His Body and Blood, which is in the consecrated bread and cup, His Body and Blood; not that properly the bread is His Body, and the cup His Blood,' &c.

"So also is St. Chrysostom in another place, where he shows that the word flesh is not always taken for the $\phi\acute{v}\sigma\iota\varsigma$ $\sigma\acute{\omega}\mu\alpha\tau\sigma\varsigma$, the nature and substance of the Body (which is the only proper sense); and he gives

nowhere found marked among the heresies to be shunned by faithful Christian men? *

(2) Closely connected with this is another question. If a doctrine so wonderful, so important, so full of blessing, were from the beginning an essential part of the Christian faith, how is it that no creed of the Christian Church ever expressed it before the Council of Trent and the Creed of Pope Pius IV.?

In the thirteenth century this question was answered

other instances which are improper, as, that flesh signifies a depraved will; and adds two other improper senses, in these words : ' By the name of flesh the Scripture is wont also to call the mysteries.' He adds, also, that it calls the Church so when it calls it the Body of Christ.

" 'The very phrase of being *wont to call* shows that of which it is affirmed to be improperly so called, as the phrase of ' being thought worthy of the name' (as we heard before), argues the name not properly to agree to it." (Patrick in Gibson's Preservative, vol. ix. pp. 141, 142, London, 1848.)

* I have not quoted the very remarkable saying of Maximus, the Scholiast on the Pseudo-Dionysius Areop.: σύμβολα ταῦτα καὶ οὐκ ἀλήθεια (Eccles. Hierarch., cap. iii. Schol. iii. § 1, Op., tom. i. p. 306, edit. Corderius, Antwerp, 1634), because (though often quoted in the Eucharistic controversy) it may be urged that these words have not special and immediate reference to the consecrated elements.

It would not be easy, however, to exclude these from the natural import of his language.

Indeed, shortly afterwards, we find the Scholiast interpreting the word συμβόλων by the words τοῦ σώματος καὶ αἵματος. (Ibid. § 9, p. 311.)

And yet a little further on he says: Τουτέστι τὸν ἄρτον καὶ τὸ ποτήριον εὐλογῶν τῶν ἁγίων δώρων. Σημείωσαι δὲ, ὅτι πανταχοῦ συμβολικὴν λέγει τὴν θείαν ἱερουργίαν, καὶ τὰ ἅγια δῶρα, σύμβολα τῶν ἄνω καὶ ἀληθινωτέρων. (Ibid., § 12, p. 313.)

by declaring that in the primitive Church Transubstantiation was received universally without doubting, and no heresy required to be checked by any such article in a creed; and that it might moreover be said to be contained in the Apostles' Creed under the words, "The Communion of Saints;"*—assertions which certainly need something better than assertion to rest upon.

The difficulty involved in the answer to the question cannot but be felt, and accordingly a new attempt has recently been made to meet it,—with no lack of ingenuity, and certainly with boldness and confidence enough; with what success I must leave wise men to judge. Thus

---

* "Alanus quidem libro contra Waldenses et Albigenses cap. 79, quærens, Utrum sit articulus fidei panem transubstantiari in Corpus Christi, cùm de hoc non fiat mentio in aliquo Symbolo? ... Non enim in Symbolo Apostolico; scilicet credo in Deum, vel in Nicæno, credo in unum, etc., vel in Symbolo Athanasii, Quicumque vult, etc. Cùm in his Symbolis de omnibus articulis fidei Christianæ fiat mentio, cur non fit mentio de illo ineffabili Sacramento, cui magis videtur obviare humana ratio. Ad hoc dicunt quidam, quòd in Primitiva Ecclesia ita omnibus patebat transubstantiari panem in Corpus Christi, quod nulli dubium erat, cùm Christus hoc esset in Evangelio testatus. Nec super hoc in primitiva Ecclesia ulla Hæresis pullulavit, ad quam reprimendam opus esset mentionem fieri de hoc in aliquo Symboli articulo. ... Dici tamen potest, quòd in Apostolico Symbolo fiat mentio de Eucharistia cùm dicitur, Sanctorum Communionem. In hoc enim spiritualiter communicant Sancti, dum recipiunt Corpus Christi, non solùm sacramentaliter, sed etiam spiritualiter." (Determinatio Fr. Joannis Parisiensis, London, 1686, Præfatio Historica, p. 49.)

The writer whom Allix here quotes is Alanus Magnus, who died A.D. 1294.

writes on the subject one of the writers of "Tracts for the Day:"—

"It has been observed, sometimes with surprise, or by way of objection, that the doctrine of the Eucharist has no place among the articles of faith in the Creed. That, however, can scarcely be admitted, seeing the doctrine of the Incarnation is distinctly asserted in the shortest of our Creeds, and set forth with elaborate definition in the Nicene and Athanasian, as the fundamental truth of Christianity. . . . .

"Admit the Incarnation, and it necessarily follows that the Sacraments, and every means by which the Pure Humanity of the Word is brought into contact with our fallen nature, must be received as essential parts of one dispensation. . . .

"No need, therefore, to particularise the Real Presence in the Eucharist as an article of faith; for everyone who admits that the restoration of Human Nature was the end of the Incarnation, must see that the Real Presence of Christ's Body and Blood, as well as the necessity of receiving them, is involved in that doctrine, since nothing else can make us the better for the Son of God having assumed our nature—nothing but that which unites us to Him, in whom is the fulness of grace and blessing. To say that 'for us men and for our salvation He came down from heaven and was incarnate by the Holy Ghost,' enforces the additional confession that for your salvation and for mine He incarnates

Himself, so to say, in the bread and wine of the Holy Eucharist, that He may give us to eat of that Flesh which is the life of the world, and to drink of that Blood which cleanseth from all sin.

"The Eucharist is the complement and extension of the Incarnation. The one would be fruitless without the other. Faith must embrace both alike."*

Now I submit for consideration whether it is not altogether a mistake, and a serious and misleading mistake, to connect the doctrine of the Eucharist so exclusively and immediately with the doctrine of the Incarnation. It is not the flesh of the Incarnation simply as such; it is not the Body of Christ simply as such; neither is it the flesh of Christ as glorified in heaven, according to the teachings of our Lord, which profiteth for the true hunger of men's souls. So far, even the flesh of the Son of God availeth not for the salvation of sinners, nor to be meat indeed for man's spirit: else what need that the Son of Man should be lifted up, to give life to the perishing?

It is the Flesh of Christ as given for the life of the world, as indwelt by the Divine Power, which after death would raise Him from the dead; it is the Blood of Christ as in sacrificial death poured out; it is the Blood of Atonement as such, the Blood of Redemption for souls, the Blood of the Son of God shed for the remission of

---

* Tracts for the Day, pp. 259, 260, 1868.

sins,—this it is * which the faith of the sinner is to look to, and which the faith of the believer has to feed on. And this it is which is, † according to Christ's own words of institution, the true "res sacramenti" in the Eucharist.‡

Upon the spiritual participation of this, indeed, follows immediately the spiritual union with our glorified Lord. But yet the Exalted Saviour is not in Holy Scripture set before us as directly the food of our souls. The interpretation of, "He that eateth Me, even he shall live

* "Non ullum sub elementis cœnæ realiter delitescens corpus, aut sub vino sanguis, sed unicum duntaxat illud Christi corpus pro nobis semel in mortem oblatum, et ejus sanguis effusus, sunt verus animæ nostræ cibus et potus; quibus anima nostra spiritualiter esuriens, spiritualiter pascitur, dum sacrificium illud corporis et sanguinis Christi vera et viva fide per Spiritum sanctum apprehendit. Quod eximium salutis beneficium in cœna Dominica fidelibus, ex Christi instituto, ad summam illorum consolationem, adversus omnes dubitationes machinationesque Satanicas obsignatur. Huc illud pertinet, quòd postquam docuit Christus, se esse panem illum verum, addit: Panis quem ego dabo (videlicet in mortem) pro mundi vita. His verbis significans, se eatenus tantum esse animæ nostræ cibum, quatenus pro nobis in mortem oblatus est semel. Hoc eximium salutis nostræ in Christo mysterium planè obscuratur per vestram doctrinam, per quam homines à carne pro nobis in mortem data, ad imaginarium quendam sub pane delitescentem Christum abducuntur. Quæ vestra doctrina infinitis præterea absurdis referta est." (Micronius in "Utenovii Simplex et Fidelis Narratio," 1560, pp. 174, 175.)

† I am not meaning to condemn those writers who speak of the "*res sacramenti*" as the living Christ with the fruits of His Sacrifice; but I conceive that this language is less strictly accurate than that which speaks of the "*res sacramenti*" as the Body and Blood of Christ separate in death. (See Vogan's True Doctrine, pp. 277, 278.)

‡ See Appendix, Note F.

by Me" (John vi. 57), must be governed by ver. 51: "I am the living bread which came down from heaven: if any man eat of this bread, he shall live for ever: and the bread that I will give is My flesh, which I will give for the life of the world." *

If I mistake not, this consideration will be found very materially to affect the whole question of the Eucharistic Presence, and of Eucharistic Adoration.

But to pass this by now,—According to the teaching which has just been quoted it is an error to suppose that the teaching of the Real Objective Presence is not contained in the Creed. The doctrine is there, because the doctrine of the Incarnation is there.

I cannot but think, if we were to take St. Augustine for our guide,† we should much rather learn that the Real

---

* See Real Presence of Laudian Theology, p. 53.

† "Dominus consolans nos qui ipsum jam in cœlo sedentem manu contrectare non possumus, sed fide contingere, ait illi. Quia vidisti, credidisti, beati qui non vident et credunt." (Aug. in Epist. Johan., cap. i. Tractatus i. § 3, Op., tom. iii. par. 2, col. 828, edit. Benedict., Paris, 1680.)

"Ipse Christus homo et Deus. Ergo et ibat per id quod homo erat, et manebat per id quod Deus erat.: ibat per id quod uno loco erat, manebat per id quod ubique erat." (Ibid., In Johan. Evang., cap. 14, Tract. lxxviii. § 1, c. 698.)

"Deus hoc facit. Homo enim secundum corpus in loco est, et de loco migrat, et cum ad locum venerit, in eo loco unde venit, non erit: Deus autem implet omnia, et ubique totus est.: non secundum spatia tenetur locis. Erat autem Dominus Christus secundum visibilem carnem in terra, secundum invisibilem majestatem in cœlo et in terra." (Ibid., c. 7, Tractat. xxxii. § 9, c. 524.)

"Respondent, Quomodo tenebo absentem? Quomodo in cœlum manum mittam, ut ibi sedentem teneam? Fidem mitte, et tenuisti.

Objective Absence is there, because the words "He ascended into heaven" are there. But not to insist on this * (though the teaching of Augustine on this subject

Parentes tui tenuerunt carne, tu tene corde : quoniam Christus absens etiam præsens est. Nisi præsens esset, a nobis teneri non posset. Sed quoniam verum est quod ait, Ecce ego vobiscum sum usque ad consummationem sæculi : et abiit, et hic est; et rediit, et nos non deserit: corpus enim suum intulit cœlo, majestatem non abstulit mundo." (Ibid., cap. 12, Tract. 1. § 4, c. 630, 631.)

"Ecce ipse est Jesus: adscendit ante vos, sic veniet quemadmodum eum videtis euntem in cœlum : tollitur quidem corpus ab oculis vestris, sed non separatur Deus a cordibus vestris: *videte adscendentem, credite in* ABSENTEM, sperate venientem; sed tamen per misericordiam occultam etiam sentite præsentem." (Enarr. in Psalm. xlvi. § 7, Op., tom. iv. par. i. c. 411, edit. Benedict., Paris, 1681.)

"Si bonus es, si ad corpus pertines, quod significat Petrus; habes Christum et in præsenti et in futuro: in præsenti *per fidem*, in præsenti *per signum*, in præsenti *per baptismatis sacramentum*, in præsenti *per altaris cibum et potum*. . . . Secundum majestatem suam, secundum providentiam, secundum ineffabilem et invisibilem gratiam, impletur quod ab eo dictum est, Ecce ego vobiscum sum usque in consummationem sæculi. Secundum carnem vero quam Verbum assumsit, secundum id quod de virgine natus est, secundum id quod a Judæis prehensus est, quod ligno crucifixus, quod de cruce depositus, quod linteis involutus, quod in sepulcro conditus, quod in resurrectione manifestatus, *non semper habebitis vobiscum*. Quare? Quoniam conversatus est secundum corporis præsentiam quadraginta diebus cum discipulis suis, et eis deducentibus videndo non sequendo, *adscendit in cœlum, et non est hic*." (In Johan. Evang., cap. 12, Tract. l., § 12, 13, Op., tom. iii. par. ii. c. 633, 634, edit. Bened. Paris, 1680.)

"Illi enim putabant eum erogaturum corpus suum, ille autem dixit se adscensurum in cœlum, utique integrum. *Cum videritis filium hominis adscendentem ubi erat prius;* certe vel tunc videbitis, quia non eo modo quo putatis erogat corpus suum ; certe vel tunc intelligetis, quia gratia ejus non consumitur morsibus." (In Johann. Evang., cap. 6, Tractat. xxvii. § 3, Op., tom. iii. par. ii. c. 502, edit. Benedict., Paris, 1680.)

* Thorndike writes: "If in the proper dimensions thereof [*i.e.* of

seems to be the only Scriptural teaching), let me ask—
Might it not quite as forcibly and quite as conclusively

Christ's body] He 'parted from' His disciples, and 'went,' was
'carried,' or lifted and 'taken up into heaven;' ... if 'the heavens
must receive Him till' that time; ... if 'to that purpose He leave
the world'...'*no more*' to be '*in*' it ... so that we shall have Him
no more with us,... it behoveth us to understand how we are
informed, *that the promise of His Body and Blood* IN THE EUCHARIST
imports an EXCEPTION *to so many declarations, before we believe it.*
Indeed, there is no place of God's right hand, by sitting down at
which we may say that our Lord's Body becomes confined to the said
place; but seeing the flesh of Christ is taken up into heaven to sit
down at God's right hand (though, by His sitting down at God's
right hand we understand the man Christ to be put into the exercise
of that Divine power and command which His Mediator's office
requires), yet His *Body we must understand* to be *confined to that place*,
where the majesty of God appears to those that attend upon His
throne. Neither shall the appearing of Christ to St. Paul (Acts
xxiii. 11) be any exception to this appointment. He that would
insist, indeed, that the Body of Christ stood over Paul in the castle
where then he lodged, *must say* that it *left heaven* for that purpose."
(Works, A.C.L., vol. iv. part i. pp. 47, 48.)

With this compare the following from Beza: "Qui Christum negat
secundum carnem venisse eo quo veniebat, et abiisse unde abibat, ac
proinde non vere abfuisse et adfuisse certis locis, historia Evangelica
refellitur.... Qui denique proprietatem verborum in ascensionis
historia servari posse putant cum reali, sive per Consubstantiationem,
sive per Transubstantiationem, præsentia, duo contradictoria simul
ponunt: cui contradictioni neque in natura, neque in fidei mysteriis
locum esse suo loco demonstrabimus. Valet igitur hæc collectio, et
est inexpugnabilis. Christus secundum carnem proprie discessit a
nobis supra cœlos, non prius inde rediturus quam iterum veniat judicaturus vivos et mortuos. Ergo neque panis qui est in terris, est
proprie caro ipsa Christi, neque caro Christi est proprie In, vel Sub,
vel Cum pane." (Tract. Theol., vol. iii. p. 362, Geneva, 1582.)

Compare also especially the following: "Putavimus verum corpus,
id est, *suis dimensionibus* constans, Christo abs te tribui cum scripturis.... Putas corpus Christi esse in pane definitive, esse ubique

be argued that the doctrine of Papal Infallibility is contained in the Apostles' Creed, because the article of Christ's ascending into heaven is there?

If it be said that in the view of some, the doctrine of the Real Objective Presence is but a needful consequence of the Incarnation, it is easy to reply that in the view of others, the belief in the Infallibility of the Pope is also a necessary consequence of the ascension of our Lord.*

But as there are those who, believing in Christ's Ascension, regard the position of one claiming to be His Vicar on earth as the claim of Antichrist to sit in Christ's place in the temple of God, so also there are those who, devoutly believing in the Incarnation and Atonement of Christ, regard the doctrine of the Real Presence in the elements as tending to fill up the winecup of the abominations of Babylon, turning the mystery of godliness into the mystery of iniquity.

Let me observe before passing on, that not only, on

---

repletivè supernaturaliter. Nos hanc philosophiam et hæc portenta prorsus libenter tibi relinquimus; et quoniam scimus verum Christi Corpus, ac proinde finitum et circumscriptum cœlos transcendisse, ibique Petrum testari oportere ut eum capiant cœli, ideo etsi non investigamus curiose an sit supra cœlos locus, neque quo modo illic capiatur, neque enim negamus quin nihilominus tam vere noster fiat, et vitam nobis inspiret, quam promittit verbo, et sacramentis figurat, imo enim efficacius multo quam si naturaliter conjungeretur; tamen cum quod ad humanitatem attinet non alibi quam in cœlis esse, et spiritualiter ibi quærendum credimus." (Beza, Tract. Theol., vol. i. p. 244, 245.)

* See, *e.g.*, Laud's Conference with Fisher, pp. 320, 321, Oxford, 1839.

the theory of the Real Objective doctrine, ought an article to have been added to the Apostles' Creed, but that, on the same theory, I cannot see how we are to acquit St. Paul of making a grievous omission in his brief summary of the chief doctrines of Christianity; for he certainly ought to have written, " Without controversy great is the mystery of godliness; not only was God manifested in the flesh, justified in the spirit, seen of angels, preached unto the Gentiles, believed on in the world, received up into glory; but He is also continually incarnating Himself afresh in the hands of His priests, in the mystery of the Eucharist."[1]

And if it is unaccountable, on this theory, that the Apostle should thus have stopped short and made no mention of the perpetual extension of the Incarnation, is it not still more unaccountable that not one of the sacred writers should ever have alluded to it?

And still further, on the same theory, ought we not to look for and to find this doctrine standing out with a noticeable clearness and prominence in the writings of the first ages of the Christian Church?

But what is the fact, even as regards such questionable evidence as is adduced in its support?

The scarcity of early evidence in support of the Papal supremacy is acknowledged. But "in truth," says Dr. Newman in his Essay on the Development of Christian Doctrine, "scanty as the Ante-Nicene notices may be of the Papal Supremacy, they are both more numerous and more definite than the adducible testimonies in favour of the Real Presence."*

(3) Another very important question to be asked is this: If this doctrine of the Adoration and of the Presence were indeed the doctrine of the Fathers, how comes it to pass that we find one and another among those Fathers continually teaching, concerning our Lord's human nature and concerning our Lord's human Body, that which, to ordinary minds and understandings at least, can never be made to seem consistent with it? Take one or two examples from St. Augustine.† He

* See Charge of Bishop of Llandaff, 1866, p. 119.
† Bellarmine (De Euch., lib. iii. cap. iii., De Contr., tom. iii. c. 665) argues from St. Augustine's question concerning the martyrs: *Utrum ipsi per seipsos adsint uno tempore tam diversis locis?* (*Cura pro mortuis*, c. 16.) So Woodhead (Two Discourses, p. 22).

Dean Aldrich replies: "Would not any man imagine now, who knows what point [the author drives at, that he would have S. Austin say a Martyr's *Body* might be in two places at once? and would he not wonder that S. Austin should be quoted for this purpose, who is elsewhere so express and peremptory that the Natural *Body* of Christ himself cannot be in two places at once? But the author is wary; for he knew very well that by *ipsi per seipsos* S. Austin meant, as he explains himself, *ipsorum animæ in figura corporis sui*." (Reply to Two Discourses, pp. 28, 29.)

Another ancient writer, touching on the same subject, wrote: " Quomodo, dic mihi, beati Petri vel Pauli anima una possit eodem momento in memoria sive monumento ejus apparere in mille ejus templis per totum orbem? Id enim nec unus Angelus queat unquam præstare. Solius siquidem Dei est duobus in locis et toto in mundo eodem momento reperiri." (Quæstiones ad Antiochum, in Op. Athanasii, edit. Benedict. 1777, tom. ii. p. 222.)

On the subject of the superstition to which the question of St. Augustine refers, see Maitland's Catacombs, pp. 306—308.

argues against the follies of the Manichæan heretics, who spoke of the presence of Christ 'in the herbs of the field, in the sun and in the moon. He asks whether there is one Christ here, another there, and another who was crucified under Pontius Pilate; and he adds: "Secundum præsentiam quippe spiritalem nullomodo illa pati posset: secundum præsentiam vero corporalem simul et in sole et in luna, et in cruce esse non posset."*

Again, he writes: " Sursum est Dominus, sed etiam hic est veritas Dominus. Corpus enim Domini in quo resurrexit uno loco esse oportet; veritas ejus ubique diffusa est,"†—a passage so damaging to the mediæval view of the Eucharistic Presence, that it is no wonder it was afterwards corrupted, and for the words "uno loco esse oportet" was written and printed "uno loco esse potest."‡

* Contra Faustum, lib. xx. cap. xi., Op., edit. Benedict., Paris, 1688, tom. viii. c. 341.

For the explanations and evasions of Romanists, see Albertinus, De Eucharistiâ, p. 733.

† In Joan. Evang., cap. vii., Tract xxx. § 1, Op., tom. iii. par. ii. c. 517.

‡ See Albertinus, De Eucharistia, p. 735; Goode on Eucharist, i. p. 311; Aldrich's Reply to Two Discourses, p. 28.

The Benedictine editors state that the passage is quoted with "oportet" by Ivo, Gratian, Lombard, and Aquinas.

I may add that it is quoted with "oportet" by Berengarius (De Sacrâ Cœnâ, adv. Laufrancum, p. 266, edit. Vischer, Berlin, 1834), whose adversaries would certainly not have failed to bring this up against him as a falsification made to prop up his heresy, if the received reading had been "potest" in those days.

The true reading of St. Augustine being thus restored, there can

Again, he writes: "Spatia locorum tolle corporibus, nusquam erunt; et quia nusquam erunt, nec erunt."*

And yet again: "Cavendum est, ne ita divinitatem adstruamus hominis, ut veritatem corporis auferamus. . . . Una enim persona Deus et homo est, et utrumque est unus Christus Jesus; ubique per id quod Deus est, in cœlo autem per id quod homo."†

So Fulgentius declares: "Unus idemque homo, localis ex homine, qui est Deus immensus ex Patre."‡

And Vigilius of Thapsus: "Si verbi et carnis una natura est, quomodo, cum Verbum ubique est, non ubique inveniatur et caro? Nam quando in terra fuit, non erat utique in Cœlo: et nunc quia in Cœlo est non est utique in terra. . . . Diversum est autem et longe dissimile circumscribi loco et ubique esse: et quia Verbum ubique est, caro autem Ejus ubique non est, apparet unum eundemque Christum utriusque esse naturæ: et esse

be little doubt that in the corresponding passage of Fulgentius (Ad Trasim. Reg., lib. ii. cap. xviii.), printed thus: "quod si verum est corpus Christi, loco *potest* utique contineri," the word "oportet" should be read instead of "*potest*;" as has been observed by Albertinus, De Eucharistia, p. 883.

Indeed the whole argument of Fulgentius aims at a point which is hit by "oportet," but is untouched by "potest."

* Liber ad Dardanum, seu Epist. clxxxvii., cap. vi. § 18, Op., tom. ii. c. 683, edit. Benedict., Paris, 1679.
For an answer to Bellarmine's evasion, see Albertinus, De Eucharistiâ, pp. 738 *sqq*.

† Liber ad Dardanum, seu Epist. clxxxvii., cap. iii. § 10, Op., tom. ii. c. 681.

‡ Ad Trasimundum Regem, lib. ii. cap. xvii. In "Heptas Presulum," Paris, 1661, p. 464.

quidem ubique secundum naturam divinitatis suæ, et loco contineri secundum naturam humanitatis suæ. .... Igitur unus Dei Filius .... circumscribitur loco per naturam carnis suæ, et loco non capitur per naturam divinitatis suæ ... mortuus est natura carnis suæ, et non est mortuus natura divinitatis suæ. Hæc est fides et confessio Catholica, quam Apostoli tradiderunt, Martyres roboraverunt, et fideles nunc usque custodiunt."*

It is to be observed that in all these passages, asserting so distinctly the local circumscription of Christ's human Body (and such passages might easily be multiplied from Greek as well as Latin Fathers), there is nothing to indicate a distinction between presence visible and invisible, palpable and impalpable, as if it were meant to limit only the visible and sensible presence of Christ's Body, and to assign to that Body the power of being present invisibly in many places at the same time. Indeed, there is not wanting evidence that the Fathers were strangers to such conceptions of the invisible and impalpable presence of the human Body of Christ.†

---

* Contra Eutychetem, lib. iv. cap. xiv. xv., edit. Chiffletius, 1664, pp. 44, 45.

† "Veteres unanimiter affirmant, *id quod invisibile est corpus* (solidum saltem) *nullo modo esse.* Tertullianus: *Corpus hominis non aliud intelligam quam, &c., quod videtur, quod tenetur* [De Resur. c. 35]. Methodius: *Deus incorporeus est et propterea invisibilis* [Ap. Phot. Cod. 234]. Eustatius Antiochenus: *Si invisibilis erat procul dubio incorporeus erat* [De Engast.] Titus Bostrensis: *Omne quod sub aspectum cadit, cum sit corpus, naturâ oppositum est in-*

"For things which are invisible," says Didymus Alexandrinus, "this follows as a consequence, that they have no body."* And Gregory of Nyssa not less conclusively declares, or rather assumes it as unquestionable: Οὐκ ἔστι σῶμα, ᾧ τὸ χρῶμα, καὶ τὸ σχῆμα, καὶ ἡ ἀντιτυπία, καὶ ἡ διάστασις, καὶ τὸ βάρος, καὶ τὰ λοιπὰ τῶν ἰδιωμάτων

aspectabili et incorporeo. . . . [Contra Manich., lib. 2]. Gregorius Nazianzenus: *Si Deus corpus est, qualenam corpus, et quomodo, &c., intangibile et invisibile? Non enim hæc est natura corporum, aut id corpus est. Minime* [Orat. 34]. . . . Denique Damascenus: *Quomodo corpus est id quod est invisibile?* [De Fid. Orth., lib. i. cap. 4].
. . . Veteres quidem nunnunquam dixerunt *Corpus Christi in pane esse intelligendum*, quemadmodum aiunt *Christum in petra fuisse intellectum*, ad designandum concipi debere velut ab iis significatum." (Albertinus, De Eucharistia, p. 5. See also pp. 389, 621.)

Another has said of Christ: "Si sit præsens, non creditur sed videtur: cum autem absens fuerit, non videtur sed creditur." (Opus Imp. in Matt. in Op. Chrysost., edit. Montfaucon, tom. vi., App. p. ccxxi.)

* Ἐπεὶ ἀόρατος ὁ Θεός, ἀκολουθεῖ δὲ τῶν ἀοράτων τὸ ἀσώματον· ἀσώματος ἄρα ὁ Θεὸς ὤν, ἀόρατός ἐστιν. (Didymus Alex., Fragmenta in Joannem, cap. iv. v. 24, *Spiritus est Deus;* Opera, edit. Migne, Patrologiæ, tom. xxxix. c. 1645. See Albertinus, De Eucharistia, pp. 5, 640.)

So Eustathius Antiochenus says (of the ghost of Saul): Εἰ μὲν ἀόρατος ἦν, ἀναμφιλόγως ἀσώματος ἦν "absque dubio et corporis expers erat." (De Engasthrimytho Diss. in Bibliotheca Max. Patr., tom. xxvii. p. 46. See Albertinus, De Eucharistia, p. 389.)

So Methodius had written: Ἀσώματος ὤν, διὸ καὶ ἀόρατος. "Eo invisibilis, quod incorporeus existat." (De Resurrectione, in Bibl. Max. Patr., tom. iii. p. 712. See Albertinus, p. 389.)

And so also Titus Bostrensis: "Omne enim, quod sub aspectum cadit, cum sit corpus, natura oppositum est inaspectabili et incorporeo, cujus opus esse potest, et quidem opus valde mirabile, similitudinem vero naturæ nullam habere potest." (Contra Manichæos, lib. ii., in Bibliotheca Max. Patr., Lugd. 1677, tom. iv. p. 465.)

οὐ πρόσεστιν.* And to the same effect St. Augustine: "Nisi corporaliter abiret a nobis, semper ejus corpus carnaliter videremus."†

"If," says Bishop Morton, "St. Gregory, once Bishop of Rome, had believed that Christ's Body is whole in every least indivisible part of the Host, he would never have condemned the Eutychian heretic for believing the Body of Christ to have been brought into such a subtilty that it cannot be felt. But a greater subtilty there cannot be, than for a divisible body to be enclosed in every least indivisible point. Show us this doctrine taught by any Catholic doctor in the Church, within the compass of twelve hundred years after Christ, and then shall we conceive better of your cause."‡

In view of the teaching of the Fathers concerning the human nature of Christ,§ I know not what more can be

---

* De Hominis Opificio, cap. xxiv., Opera, edit. Migne, tom. i. col. 213. See the whole context. See also Albertinus, De Eucharistiâ, p. 479.

† Sermo cxliii. § 4, Opera, edit. Benedict., 1683, tom. v. par. i. col. 692.

‡ On the Eucharist, book iv. ch. viii. § vi. p. 274, ed. 1635.

§ The following quotations are but a selection. Yet as samples they seem abundantly sufficient to bear witness to the general testimony of the Fathers to these two truths: (1) that our Lord's human Body is to be regarded as having still that local and circumscribed nature which causes that since His Ascension into heaven it is no longer present upon earth; (2) that the enduring Presence of Christ with His Church is therefore a Spiritual Presence—a Presence of Deity, of Divine power and grace and blessing—as distinguished from any Presence of His flesh, or of His natural human Body in the world.

needed to justify the language of Hooker : "The substance of the Body of Christ hath no presence, neither can have,

And it is to be observed how this consentient testimony is borne by one after another, from East and from West, without a hint as to these truths admitting any sacramental exceptions to meet the requirements of faith in the words " Hoc est corpus meum."

" Unigenitus Dei est, Deus Verbum, et sapientia, et justitia, et veritas, qui non est corporeo ambitu circumclusus. Secundum hanc Divinitatis suæ naturam non peregrinatur, sed peregrinatur secundum dispensationem corporis quod suscepit." (Origen, Vet. Int. Comm. in Matth., § 65, Op., edit. Migne, tom. iii. c. 1703.)

" Considera quoniam non videtur redditio sermonis ita conscripta : Sicut homo perigrinans, sic et Jesus, aut ita : sic et Filius hominis : quoniam ipse est qui in parabola proponitur peregrinans quasi homo. Nec enim est homo, qui est ubicunque duo vel tres in nomine ejus fuerint congregati. Neque homo nobiscum est omnibus diebus usque ad consummationem sæculi. Nec congregatis ubique fidelibus *homo* est præsens, sed *virtus divina* quæ erat in Jesu." (Origen, Vet. Int. Comm. in Matth., § 65, Op., edit. Migne, tom. iii. c. 1704.)

[In the previous column it is said: " Si enim *virtus* Jesu congregatur cum his qui congregantur in nomine ejus, non peregrinatur a suis, sed semper præsto est eis."]

" Secundum præsentiam majestatis semper habemus Christum: secundum præsentiam carnis, recte dictum est discipulis, me autem non semper habebitis. Habuit enim illum Ecclesia secundum præsentiam carnis paucis diebus : modo fide tenet, oculis non videt." (Augustin. In Joan. Evang., Tract. l. § 13, Op., ed. Bened., Paris, 1680, tom. iii. par. ii. c. 634.)

" Relicturus eos præsentia corporali, cum omnibus autem suis usque in consummationem seculi futurus præsentia spiritali." (Ibid., In Joan., Tract. xcii. § 1, Op., tom. iii. par. ii. c. 723.)

" Quos in se credentes servare jam ceperat præsentia corporali, et quos relicturus fuerat absentia corporali, ut eos cum Patre servaret præsentia spiritali." (Ibid., Tract. cvi. § 2, c. 705.)

[Let it be observed that Augustine writes as one who knows nothing of anything intermediate between bodily absence and bodily presence. With bodily absence consists, in his view, a Spiritual Presence, but there is nothing to indicate that there is in his mind

but only local. It was not, therefore, everywhere seen, nor did it everywhere suffer death; everywhere it could

room for a conception of a Presence of Christ's Body invisibly and after the manner of spirits.]

Ἆρ' οὖν ἀπενοσφίζετο τῶν μαθητῶν ὁ Σωτὴρ ἀναφοιτήσας πρὸς τὸν Πατέρα, καὶ συνῆν αὐτοῖς τῇ τοῦ Πνεύματος ἐνεργείᾳ τε καὶ δυνάμει, καὶ χάριτι; Πῶς, ἢ κατὰ τίνα τρόπον; Οὐ γὰρ ψεύδεται λέγων· ἰδοὺ ἐγὼ μεθ' ὑμῶν εἰμι πάσας τὰς ἡμέρας καὶ ἕως τῆς συντελείας του αἰῶνος, πλὴν ὅσον εἰς σάρκα καὶ τὴν μετὰ σώματος παρουσίαν, οὐδαμόθεν ἀμφίβαλον. (Cyrill. Alex., Com. in Joan., lib. x. in c. xvi. 5, 6, Op., edit. Migne, tom. vii. c. 429.)

Εἰ γὰρ καὶ ἀποδημεῖ σαρκί, παραστήσας ἑαυτὸν ὑπὲρ ἡμῶν τῷ Πατρὶ, καὶ καθίσας ἐκ δεξιῶν τοῦ γεννήσαντος, ἀλλ' ἐναυλίζεται τοῖς ἀξίοις διὰ τοῦ Πνεύματος, καὶ συνέστι τοῖς ἁγίοις διὰ παντός. (Ibid., lib. x. in c. xvi. 16, Op., tom. vii. c. 453, 456.)

Ἔστι τοίνυν τὸ Θεῖον ἀσώματον, ἄποσόν τε καὶ ἀμέγαθες, καὶ οὐκ ἐν εἴδει περιγράπτῳ ... τὸ γὰρ ὅλως ἐν σχήματι, πάντως ποῦ καὶ ἐν ποσῷ, καὶ ἐν τόπῳ. Τὸ δὲ ἐν τόπῳ νοούμενον οὐκ ἔξω περιγραφῆς. Ταῦτα δὲ σωμάτων μὲν ἴδια, τῆς δὲ ἀσωμάτου φύσεως ἀλλότρια παντελῶς. (Cyrill. Alexandr. adv. Anthopomorph., cap. i. 366, Opera, edit. Migne, tom. ix. c. 1077.)

"Cum ergo caro Christi localis absque dubitatione monstraretur, Divinitas tamen ejus ubique semper esse, Paulo testante, cognoscitur, &c. (Fulgentius ad Trasimundum Regem, lib. ii. cap. xviii., in Heptas Presul. Christ., edit. Raynaudus, Paris, 1661, p. 465.)

"Unus idemque secundum humanam substantiam, absens cœlo, cum esset in terra, et derelinquens terram, cum ascendisset in cœlum. ... Quomodo autem ascendit in cœlum, nisi quia localis et verus et homo? Aut quomodo adest fidelibus suis, nisi quia idem immensus et verus est Deus? ... ait *Nemo ascendit in cœlum, nisi qui de cœlo descendit, filius hominis qui est in cœlo:* non quia humana Christi substantia fuisset ubique diffusa, sed quoniam unus idem que Dei filius atque hominis filius, ... licet secundum veram humanitatem suam localiter tunc esset in terra, secundum divinitatem tamen (quæ loco nullatenus continetur) cœlum totus impleret et terram." (Ibid., cap. xvii. pp. 464, 465.)

not be entombed; it is not everywhere now being exalted
into heaven. There is no proof in the world strong

"Quod aliquo circumscribitur fine, necesse est, ut loco teneatur,
aut tempore." Fulgentius, *op. cit.*, cap. vii. p. 459.)
" Certum est omne locale in loco esse." (Ibid., cap. vii. p. 459.)
"Corpora quæ sine loco esse non possunt." (Ibid., Contra Sermonem Fastidiosi, cap. iv. p. 598.)
" Non ergo, inquam, unius naturæ est, præsepis gremio contineri, et astrorum indiciis prodi; hominibus subjici, et ab Angelis ministrari; do loco ad locum fugere, et ubique sui præsentiam exhibere; terrena incolere, et cœlestia non deserere." (Vigilius Tapsensis, Contra Arium, Sabellium, et Photinum, lib. ii. cap. xlix., Opera, edit. Chifflet. 1664, p. 186.)
" Quomodo ait, *Vado ad Patrem*, cum quo et semper erat, et a quo nunquam recesserat? (Ejus est enim ire et venire, qui aliquibus locorum terminis circumscribitur; ut eum in quo erat deserens locum, ad alium ubi non erat veniat;) nisi quia utique de illo quem adsumpserat homine loquebatur, quod ipse erat iturus ad Patrem, a quo et venturus est judicare vivos et mortuos? Cæterum ubi divinitas, quæ, ut diximus, universa implens, nullis locorum spatiis terminatur, sicut nihil est unde discedat, ita nihil est ubi veniat." (Ibid., cap. xviii. p. 159.)
" Verbi natura non est mutata, nec confusa in carne; et rursus carnis natura non est mutata, nec confusa in Verbo." (Ibid., Contra Eutychet., lib. iv. cap. xix. p. 50.)
" Christus in cœlum ascendens discessit quidem carne, sed præsens est majestate." (Isidorus Hispalensis, Sent., lib. i. cap. xiv., Op., ed. Migne, tom. vi. c. 568.)
" Quia enim ipse Deus et homo est, assumptus est in cœlum humanitate quam de terrâ susceperat, manet cum Sanctis in terra divinitate quæ terram pariter implet et cœlum." (Ven. Beda, Hom. Æstiv. de tempore Fer. 6 Pasch., Op., tom. vii. c. 14, Cologne, 1688.)
" Qui tunc corporali præsentiâ fuit in mundo, nunc divinâ præsentiâ præsens est ubique in mundo." (Ibid., In Joan., c. 9, Op., tom. v. c. 537.)
" Non semper in terris corporaliter mansurus, sed per humanitatem quam assumpsi jam sum ascensurus in cœlum." (Ibid., Hom. Æstiv. de temp. Domin. Jubilate, Op., tom. vii. c. 16.)

enough to enforce that Christ had a true Body but the true and natural properties of His Body. Amongst which properties, definite or local presence is chief. . . . If His majestical Body have now any such new property, by force whereof it may everywhere really ever *in substance* present itself, or may at once be in many places, then

" Post resurrectionem ascendens in cœlum eos corporaliter deseruit, quibus tamen divinœ præsentia majestatis numquam abfuit." (Ven. Beda, Hom. Æst. de temp. In Fest. Pentecostes, Op., tom. vii. c. 39.)

" Habemus paracletum Dominum nostrum Jesum Christum, quem etsi corporaliter videre nequimus, ea tamen quæ in corpore gessit et docuit in Evangeliis Scripta tenemus." (Ibid., In Fest. Pentecostes, Op., tom. vii. c. 39.)

"Naturale est illi venire in hoc mundo solus minoratus paulo minus ab Angelis. Naturale est illi ubique esse cum Patre. Naturale est illi localis esse solus filius." (Etherius et Beatus, Contra Elipandum, lib. i., In Biblioth. Max. Patr., Lugd. 1677, tom. xiii. p. 368.)

Οὐδεὶς τῶν εὖ φρονούντων περίγραπτην λέγων τὴν ἀνθρωπείαν φύσιν, ταύτῃ συμπεριγράφει τὴν ἀπερίγραπτον οὖσαν. καὶ γὰρ ὁ Κύριος, καθὸ τέλειος ἄνθρωπος ἦν, ὧν ἐν τῇ Γαλιλαίᾳ, οὐκ ἦν ἐν τῇ Ἰουδαίᾳ· καὶ τοῦτο αὐτὸς πιστοῦται λέγων· ἄγωμεν εἰς τὴν Ἰουδαιάν πάλιν· καὶ περὶ τοῦ Λαζαροῦ διαλεγόμενος τοῖς αὐτοῦ φοιτηταῖς, οὕτως ἔφη· χαίρω δι᾽ ὑμᾶς, ὅτι οὐκ ἤμην ἐκεῖ· καθὸ δὲ Θεός ἐστιν, ἐν παντὶ τόπῳ τῆς δεσμωτείας αὐτοῦ πάρεστι, μενών παντάπασιν ἀπερίγραπτος. (Second Nicene Council, in Labbæus, tom. vii. c. 450. Mansi, tom. xiii. c. 253.)

" Tamdiu conversatus est cum discipulis quousque vidit eos non indigere præsentiâ corporalis instructionis, et post recessit ab eis corporaliter, quos tamen spiritualiter numquam deseruit." (Christian Druthmar, Expositio in Matt. Evang., cap. lvi. fo. lxxx. edit. Strasburg, 1514.)

" De præsentia corporis loquebatur: quia recessurus erat ab eis. Nam præsentia divinitatis adest omnibus electis suis, sicut ipse post resurrectionem suis discipulis dixit, Ecce ego vobiscum sum usque ad consummationem sæculi." (Ibid., fo. lxxxiii., Expositio in Passionem Dominicam.)

hath the majesty of His estate extinguished the verity of His nature."*

(4) Another question to which I desire specially to direct attention is this :—If this doctrine of the Eucharistic Presence and of Eucharistic Adoration were the doctrine of the Primitive Church, how then does it come to pass that we find our early Christian apologists ridiculing the idolatry of the heathen in language which might so readily have been turned against themselves, and against the worship to be seen in Christian churches ? Take an example from Arnobius. He deals with the heathen's plea, that they do not worship images, but only adore divinities present in the images after consecration. He asks : "In simulachris Dii habitant: singuline in singulis totis, an partiliter atque in membra divisi ?" And mark what follows : " Neque unus Deus in compluribus potis est uno tempore inesse simulachris, neque rursus in partes sectione interveniente divisus. Constituamus enim decem millia simulachrorum toto esse in orbe Vulcani : numquid esse, ut dixi, decem omnibus in millibus potis est unus uno in tempore ? Non opinor. Qua causa ? Quia quæ sunt priva singulariaque natura, multa fieri nequeunt simplicitatis suæ integritate servata : et hoc amplius nequeunt, si hominum formas Dii habent, opinatio ut vestra declarat. Neque enim manus a capite separata, aut pes divisus a corpore, summam possunt præstare totius : aut dicendum est portiones idem posse

* Eccles. Pol., book v. ch. iv. § vi., Keble's edit. vol. ii. pp. 241, 242.

quod totum, cum consistere nequeat, nisi fuerit partium congregatione conflatum. Si autem in cunctis idem esse dicetur, perit omnis ratio atque integritas veritati, si hoc fuerit sumptum, posse unum in omnibus uno tempore permanere: aut Deorum est unusquisque dicendus ita ipsum semet ab ipso sese dividere, ut et ipse sit et alter, non aliquo discrimine separatus, sed ipse idem et alius. Quod quoniam recusat, et respuit, aspernaturque natura, aut innumeros dicendum est, confitendumque esse Vulcanos, si in cunctis volumus eum degere, atque inesse simulachris : aut erit in nullo, quia esse divisus natura prohibetur in plurimis."*

This passage has been selected from other similar ones† to be found in the writings of early apologists,‡

* Adversus Gentes, lib. vi. pp. 204, 205, edit. Ludg. Bat. 1651.
† See Albertinus, De Eucharistiâ, lib. i. cap. xxvii. xxviii. p. 182, 104, and lib. ii. cap. iii. pp. 381, 382.
‡ " The truth is, of all idols that ever were worshipped by Pagans, there is none so open and exposed to all the reproaches and censures of holy men in Scripture, as is this which Roman Catholics adore solemnly at every Mass; and if this which they thus adore were truly Christ, one might safely aver (what even to think were blasphemy) that neither Prophets nor holy Fathers, in their speeches against heathenish gods, either considered well what they said, or ever thought well of their Saviour.

" To begin with their original, when the Prophet Isaiah inveighs against them who worship gods made by a carpenter of a tree which the worshippers had planted, and after hewn into pieces, whereof one was to heat an oven and the others to make a god, c. 43, v. 14, 15, 17, Can any rational man think that the Holy Ghost did foresee that all true worshippers in the times of the Messias were to adore a God every morning made of, and every morning inclosed within somewhat of that wheat that first countrymen had sown, and bakers baked into

because it presents some points of singular and most wafers of which afterwards an apothecary was to take some to wrap pills in, and a Priest all the rest to consecrate into a God ? And if the taking that for a God which before the consecration was but a stock is a Pagan blindness fit for a Prophet to wonder at, v. 18, is the adoring that for a Saviour which, immediately before the uttering of some few words, was a thin wafer, such clear understanding as may become a Catholic? Here, saith honest Minutius, Pagans melt brass, they cast it, they set it up, they fasten it; 'tis yet no God: they polish it, they adorn it; neither is it yet a God. But see now, they consecrate it, and pray to it, then as soon as men will have it to be a God, it is a God. Was this wise man blind, not to see that Pagans might return the same raillery? Christians sow wheat, they cut, gather, and thresh it; 'tis no Christ yet. They grind it, they sift it, they bake it; 'tis but a wafer; they set it upon an Altar, they elevate it, and cross it several times; no wonder yet: at last they speak five words upon it, presently ten Miracles break forth, and among an hundred wafers, which are all like one to another, that which they are pleased to think upon is their Saviour.

" Where was the wit and judgment of holy Fathers, St. Chrysostom, Arnobius, Tertullian (if they had then Rome's Mass worship), when they charged Pagans with flat madness for lodging their Gods in Images, and for dreaming of Consecrations, which might turn the fate of vile materials into Gods, or shut these venerable Gods in vile vessels; not perceiving in the meanwhile, that if Christians did then what Roman Catholics do now, both ancient Christians and new Catholics fall visibly to worse follies? For the blindest Pagans never dreamed in the consecrating of their Idols, to turn effectually the substance of brass, stone, or timber, into the very nature of their Gods; as these, who think and talk always of converting the whole substance of Wafers into the whole Body of Christ. Pagans could change, by their Idol worship, the glory of the incorruptible God into Images, Rom. i. 23, made of vile materials; but they did not intend, by any help of miracles, to change this vile material into any God. This extraordinary attempt was never owned, as I can remember, during the times of Pagan Rome. And Pagans did acknowledge their wood and stones, even after they had consecrated them into their Gods, to be no more than Seats and Domicils made of wood and stone, where their Gods did love to appear; and where their assisting power,

striking adaptation to the Eucharistic controversy.* It is curious to compare some parts of it with some parts of the chapters of Bellarmine, in which he sets himself to prove—"Posse unum corpus simul esse in pluribus locis,"† and to refute the objections of those who see a contradiction in this.

Can the real objective Presence of Christ's Body at one time to be adored on ten thousand altars be maintained at all, without its being open to the same objections as the presence of Vulcan to be adored in ten thousand of his images?

Can it be conceived without causing that, in the view of Arnobius, "perit omnis ratio atque integritas veritati?"

Can such a presence be really distinguished, in any essential particular, from that which Arnobius declares to be "quod recusat, et respuit, aspernaturque natura?" which they did call Numen, was wont to work." (Dean Brevint, Depth and Mystery of R. Mass, pp. 94—97, Oxford, 1673.)

* Tatian and Minutius Felix ridicule as absurd the practice of the Heathen in adoring and worshipping that which they immolate and sacrifice. Dallæus well says: "Atqui hoc ipsum faciunt Latini. Eucharistiam eandem et adorant et immolant; et quam religiosissime divinissimo latriæ cultu adorarunt, eam statim immolant; neque ullum Deo a se offerri sacrificium melius aut magis legitimum arbitrantur." (De Rel. Cultus Objecto, p. 327, lib. ii. cap. xxvi.)

Minutius Felix ridicules the Egyptian custom of feeding that which is worshipped. Dallæus says: "Sed, si hoc absurdum est, illud profecto longe etiam absurdius videtur, ut Eucharistiam adores, qua pasceris. Ergo si eam adorasset Octavius, cavisset ab hoc joco; neque Ægyptiis dixisset, *Nonne quem pascitis adoratis?*" (Ibid., p. 327.

† De Sacramento Eucharistiæ, lib. iii. cap. iii. iv.; see also cap. v. vi. vii.

And could Arnobius have written thus if this view of the Eucharistic Presence, and this teaching of Eucharistic adoration, had been a part of the faith and the worship of the Christian Church in his day? Could he have thus laid himself open to the stinging retorts of the heathen? And would the advocates of Pagan idolatry have spared their lashes in reply? And it will not be altogether out of place to mark here how Julian the Apostate—who knew well what the religion of Christians was, and what the mystery of the Eucharist was—is found ridiculing Christians for the worship of Christ*—the man Christ Jesus, and regarding Him as God. Nay, more, he upbraids them for their προσκύνησις of the Cross.† Is it conceivable that he

* See Cyril. Alex., Op., tom. ix. c. 743, 810, 887, 902, 910, 911, 946, 951, 1003, 1014, edit. Migne. See also Faber's Difficulties of Romanism, pp. 415—417, 2nd edit.

† Εἶτα, ὦ δυστυχεῖς ἄνθρωποι, σωζομένου τοῦ παρ' ὑμῖν ὅπλου Διοπετοῦς, ὃ κατέπεμψεν ὁ μέγας Ζεὺς, ἤτοι πατὴρ Ἄρης, ἐνέχυρον διδοὺς, οὐ λόγον, ἔργον δὲ, ὅτι τῆς πόλεως ἡμῶν εἰς τὸ διηνεκὲς προασπίσει, προσκυνεῖν ἀφέντες καὶ σέβεσθαι, τὸ τοῦ σταυροῦ προσκυνεῖτε ξύλον, εἰκόνας αὐτοῦ σκιαγραφοῦντες ἐν τῷ μετώπῳ καὶ πρὸ τῶν οἰκημάτων ἐγγράφοντες; Ἆρα ἀξίως ἄν τις συνετωτέρους ὑμῶν μισήσειεν, ἢ τοὺς ἀφρονεστέρους ἐλεήσειεν, οἱ κατακολουθοῦντες ὑμῖν, εἰς τοῦτο ἦλθον ὀλέθρου, ὥστε τοὺς αἰωνίους ἀφέντες θεοὺς, ἐπὶ τὸν Ἰουδαίων μεταβῆναι νεκρόν; (In Cyrill. Alex. Contra Julian., lib. vi. 194, Opera, edit. Migne, tom. ix. c. 796, 797.)

The answer of Cyril to the charge concerning the cross is: Ἡμεῖς ... παντὸς ἀγαθοῦ καὶ ἁπάσης ἀρετῆς εἰς ἀνάμνησιν, τὸ τοῦ τιμίου σταυροῦ ποιούμεθα ξύλον. (c. 797.)

If in Julian's time Eucharistic worship had been seen in the Christian Church, such as is now seen in the Church of Rome (or anything

would have had no word of contumely for the worshipping of bread, if in his time the Christian Church had practised the adoration of the host?

We know how, in later times, that worship was derided by the Jews.*

We know, also, how, after the birth of transubstantiation, Averroes regarded the matter.† In the earlier

like it), is it possible that he could have written thus of the reverent and loving honour given by Christians to the Cross as the memorial of their Lord's passion, and have said not a word concerning the Divine adoration paid to the Sacramental bread and wine (or to that which is really present in them), symbolising and showing forth the Lord's death?

We possess, indeed, but a portion of what Julian wrote against Christianity, but we have here just the part in which the notice of Eucharistic adoration certainly should have come, if he had had anything to say in ridicule of it.

* Lyranus represents the Jews as saying of Christians: " Sunt Idololatræ pessimi adorantes Jesum hominem tanquam Deum, et quod pejus est Hostiam de frumento ab iis formatam et coctam adorant sicut Deum, quod est derisibile, et postea comedunt, quod est horribile " (Tractatus contra Judæos). Again in another tractate he is quoted as saying of the Jews: " In ipso Sacramento Eucharistiæ reputant nos pessimos Idololatras, sicut per experientiam cognoverunt illi qui frequenter de istis cum illis contulerunt, et ideo a fide Catholica pro talibus avertuntur, et plures jam baptizati ad vomitum revertuntur." See Allix, in Historical Preface to "Determinatio J. Parisiensis," 1686, p. 46.

No mention is made, if Allix is right, of any such charge brought by Jews against Christians before the time of Thomas Aquinas.

† "Those witty adversaries, Celsus, and Porphyry, and Julian, would have thrown all that the Christians had said against the heathen idols back upon themselves, and have improved them with as great advantage, and retorted them with as much force, had the Christians in those times worshipped the host, or the sacramental elements, as the Papists do now; and it is more than a presumption, no less than

ages of Christianity, who, among the enemies of Christianity, spake as he spake? Why did they not? Is there any other plausible reason to be given but this—that hitherto it was a thing unknown among Christians?

But I must not pass on to my next question without reverting for a moment to the passage just cited from Arnobius, for the purpose of directing special attention to it in its bearing on a particular phase of the Eucharistic controversy with which we are now familiar.

Is it possible that Arnobius could have written thus if in his day the Church of Christ had been taught to believe that indeed the Body of Christ was present naturally, and locally, only in heaven, but that in another ineffable way, divinely, supernaturally, and supra-

a demonstration, that the Christians did not, because none of these things that were so obnoxious and so obvious were ever in the least mentioned by the heathens, or made matter of reflection upon them, when they picked up all other things, let them be true or false, that they could make any use of to object against them. But the primitive Christians gave them no such occasion, which was the only reason they did not take it. As soon as the Church of Rome did so, by setting up the worship of the host, Averroes, the Arabian philosopher, in the thirteenth century, gave this character of Christians, that he had found 'no sect more foolish, or worse than they,' in all his travels and observations, upon this very account, 'for they eat the God whom they worship;' and a later historian and traveller tells us that it is a common reproach in the mouths of the Turks and Mahommetans to call the Christians devourers of their God; and a Jew, in a book printed at Amsterdam in the year 1662, among other questions put to Christians, asks this shrewd one: 'If the host be a God, why does it corrupt and grow covered with mould? And why is it gnawn by mice or other animals?'" (Prebendary Payne in Gibson's Preservative, vol. x. p. 156, London, 1848.)

locally, the same Body was present in the sacramental elements on ten thousand altars on earth?* Why!

* Bp. Jeremy Taylor argues against the Romish doctrine, as Arnobius against the worship of the heathen. He says : "It will also be an infinite impossible contradiction which follows the being of a body in two places at once, upon this account: for it will infer that the same body is at the same time, in the same respect, in order to the same place, both actually and potentially, that is possessed and not possessed of it, and may go to that place where it is already." (Works, vol. vi. p. 112, edit. Eden, " Real Presence," sect. xi. § 22.)

And with reference to the evasion of " presence by another mode" he writes : " But now a fourth word must be invented, and that is *sacramentaliter*, Christ's Body is sacramentally in more places than one ; which is very true, that is, the sacrament of Christ's Body is; and so is His Body figuratively, tropically, representatively in being, and really in effect and blessing ; but this is not a natural, real being in a place, but a relation to a person." (Works, vol. vi. p. 109, "Real Presence," sect. xi. § 17.)

Again: " Aquinas hath yet another device to make all whole, saying that one body cannot be in divers places *localiter*, but *sacramentaliter*, not locally but sacramentally. But first I wish the words were sense, and that I could tell the meaning of being in a place locally and not locally, unless a thing can be in a place and not in a place, that is, so to be in that it is also out; but so long as it is a distinction it is no matter, it will amuse and make way to escape, if it will do nothing else. But if by being sacramentally in many places is meant figuratively (as before I explicated it), then I grant Aquinas's affirmative ; Christ's Body is in many places sacramentally, that is, it is represented upon all the holy tables or altars in the Christian Church. But if by sacramentally he means naturally and properly, then he contradicts himself, for that is it he must mean by *localiter* if he means anything at all. But it matters not what he means, for it is sufficient to me that he only says it and proves it not; and that it is not sense ; and lastly, that Bellarmine confutes it as not being home enough to his purpose, but a direct destruction of the fancy of Transubstantiation." (Works, vol. vi. pp. 111, 112, edit. Eden, " Real Presence," sect. xi. § 21.)

Turretin writes: " Nec rectius distingui volunt inter *præsentiam*

if Christians believed this, why should not heathens believe the same of their divinities? How could then

finitam, creatam, definitivam, et *præsentiam divinam* ILLOCALEM, *increatam, infinitam;* Illâ Christum esse in cœlo, Istâ vero in Cœna. Quia supponitur semper πρῶτον ψεῦδος dari duplex præsentiæ genus respectu Corporis Christi, quod tanquam impossibile et naturæ Corporis contrarium admitti nequit." (Turretin, Instit. Theol. Elenct. iii. p. 570, Genev. 1686. See also p. 580, and Papers on the Doctrine of the English Church, pp. 18—20.)

So also Ursinus: " Distinctio ista *localis* et *illocalis* præsentiæ rei corporeæ secundum substantiam, est commentitia, nusquam tradita aut fundata in verbo Dei. Ubicunque enim res corporea, sua substantia præsens est, ibi localiter et circumscripte præsens est. Neque testimonium ullum Scripturæ proferri potest, de Corpore Christi illocaliter usquam existente; plurima autem, quæ contrarium docent." (Ursinus, Opera, vol. ii. c. 1340, edit. Reuter, Heidelberg, 1612.)

So Beza, Adversus Heshusium: " HES. Negamus etiam localem inclusionem. THEOPHILUS. Et nos pernegamus. HES. Sed dicimus Christi Corpus nihilominus esse in pane. THEOPHILUS. Id est, dicitis Christum esse in loco, sed non *localiter*, sive non eo modo quo naturalia corpora in suis locis versantur. HES. Recte. THEOPHILUS. Imo insane. Sic enim tribuisti Christo σῶμα ἀσώματον." (Tract. Theol., vol. i. p. 264, Geneva, 1582.)

"Cum statuant vere adesse, et corporaliter et carnaliter, ut dicunt, sed non *localiter*, quis non videat ista conficta esse ad eludenda argumenta?" (Peter Martyr, Loci Communes, vol. i. pp. 1567, 1568. Basle, 1580.)

See also especially Sadeel, Works, p. 435; Offic. Sanctand., 1593.

Se also Du Moulin's " Buckler of the Faith," pp. 463, 465, London, 1623.

Dean Aldrich says: " The difference between us and the Papists is plain. They (however they express themselves) understand a *local* presence, which we deny, and therefore reject their expression. We (whatever term we use) mean only a *spiritual* and *virtual* presence, and explain the term we make use of to that effect." (Reply to Two Discourses, p. 17.)

the Christian apologist have ridiculed as inconceivable the presence of Vulcan, which the Pagan worshipper believed to be in ten thousand temples, if the absurdity he characterised as against nature and reason and truth could be turned at once into a credible matter of faith, by the simple reply that this was to be understood of a presence supra-local, ineffable, and divine?

Allow the possibility of the two modes of presence, one local and one supra-local, which are now so earnestly contended for as essential to the orthodox doctrine of the Eucharist, and the argument of Arnobius is utterly futile. Nay, more; he has brought contempt on himself and the Christian Church for counting and treating as folly—yea, as the folly of follies—just that very particular in the worship of idols which has (may I not say?) a singularly exact counterpart in the so-called Catholic doctrine of the Mass.

So Crakanthorp had said : " Quamvis Christi Corpus sit in hostiâ solùm *Sacramentaliter* et non localiter, tamen in illo loco qui hostias continet, gratiâ hostiæ, est etiam *localiter*, et *circumscriptivè*, ut rectè agnoscit tuus Cardinalis, nam locus qui continet et circumscribit hostiam, etiam gratiâ hostiæ, continet et circumscribit Corpus Christi quod est sub hostiâ." (Defensio Eccles. Anglican., p. 286, edit. Anglo-Cath. Libr.)

So also Forbes of Corse : " Nos præsentiam illam, quam tuentur Transubstantiarii et Consubstantiarii, vocamus *localem ;* eodem sensu, quo explicat Bonaventura. Quamvis distinctionem istam repudiemus ; nam ubicunque est aliquod Corpus corporaliter, et quidem cum tota sua quantitate dimensiva, ibi est dimensivè, et secundum commensurationem corpori debitam." (J. Forbes of Corse, Works, vol. ii. p. 503*a*, Amsterdam, 1702.)

Need I add that the same remark applies to the argument of St. Augustine against the Manichees, in the words just cited—"Secundum præsentiam corporalem simul et in sole et in luna, et in cruce esse non potest"? He does not say "esse non potest naturaliter et localiter." He declares an impossibility in the nature of things, and his whole argument depends on that impossibility being complete and absolute. To suppose that Augustine's mind was familiar with the conception of Christ's Body being present in more places than one in some other ineffable manner, because the whole Christian Church believed it to be so in the Eucharist; to conceive that his words "esse non potest" might well admit a gloss "esse tamen potest supernaturaliter et supralocaliter;" to imagine that his "uno loco esse oportet" must admit of those divinely ineffable exceptions, which subsequently demanded the change into "uno loco esse potest,"—is to suppose that St. Augustine was capable of arguing against heretics from a major premiss which was the contradictory of a proposition affirmed by the universal creed of Christendom, and was willing to expose that creed to the scorn and contumely of its enemies, in words returning as the mere reverberation of his own arguments—arguments from intuitive axioms of reason—with which he had assailed the insane dreams of bewildered fanatics.

(5) Another and a still more important question to be asked is this,—Did the Corinthian Christians in

St. Paul's days* believe this Real Objective Presence of

* From 1 Cor. x. 18—22 it would not be safe to argue that the Communion the Apostle speaks of could not possibly be a real and literal eating of the Body of Christ; because the Apostle's argument would hold good though there might be a great disparity between the κοινωνία τοῦ σώματος τοῦ Χριστοῦ and the κοινωνία τῶν δαιμονίων. There might be a partaking of the Lord's table, altogether different not only in degree and in kind but also in mode, from the partaking of the table of devils; and, no doubt, some of the Fathers do insist on the fact that an idol is nothing, and its sacrifices are void (see Theodoret, edit. Schulze, tom. iii. p. 229; Chrysostom, edit. Montfaucon, tom. x. p. 214), while the communion of Christians is a real communion with Christ, and a partaking of His Body. Yet it is observable that some of the Fathers seem rather to point to a parity in the mode of κοινωνία on the one side and on the other, as far as regards the instrumental mediation of what is eaten, in such a way as would hardly have been possible if, on the one side, they had regarded the κοινωνία as depending upon the Real Presence of Christ's Body in or under the form of the bread.

Cyril of Jerusalem says: Ὥσπερ ὁ ἄρτος καὶ ὁ οἶνος τῆς εὐχαριστίας, πρὸ τῆς ἁγίας ἐπικλήσεως τῆς προσκυνητῆς τριάδος, ἄρτος ἦν καὶ οἶνος λιτός· ἐπικλήσεως δὲ γενομένης, ὁ μὲν ἄρτος γίνεται σῶμα Χριστοῦ, ὁ δὲ οἶνος αἷμα Χριστοῦ· τὸν αὐτὸν δὴ τρόπον τὰ τοιαῦτα βρώματα τῆς πομπῆς τοῦ Σατανᾶ, τῇ ἰδίᾳ φύσει λιτὰ ὄντα, τῇ ἐπικλήσει τῶν δαιμόνων βέβηλα γίνεται. (Cyril. Hieros. Catech. Myst. I. § vii., Opera, ed. Bened., p. 308.)

Primasius says: "Panis quem frangimus nonne participatio Corporis Domini est? Sic et idolorum panis dæmonum participatio est." (In 1 Cor. x., In Bibli. Max. Patr., Lugd. 1677, tom. x. p. 188.)

Rabanus Maurus says: "Sicut nos . . . participes sumus Corporis Domini ita et qui edunt hostias participes sunt altaris erroris. (Enar. in Ep. Pauli, lib. x. In Ep. 1 ad Cor. x., Op., ed. Migne, tom. vi. c. 94.)

Œcumenius says: Εἰ γὰρ οἱ τῆς μυστικῆς μετέχοντες τραπέζης κοινωνοῦσι Χριστῷ, οἱ Δαιμόνων μετέχοντες τραπέζης δηλονότι Δαίμοσι κοινωνοῦσιν. (In 1 Cor. x., Opera, Paris, 1631, tom. i. p. 516.) See Waterland's Works, vol. iv. pp. 630—638, 87, 88, and especially Sedulius in 1 Cor. x. in Bibl. Max. tom. vi. p. 544.

Christ—the proper object of adoration—under the form of bread and wine in the Sacrament of the Lord's Supper ? If they did not believe it, then ought not the Apostle to have clearly and plainly supplied this deficiency of their faith in this most important particular, when he heard how they came together to the Eucharist each one as to his own supper ?

If they did believe it, why did not the Apostle in his warning words on the subject appeal to this faith, and to their knowledge of this truth? Why did he not rebuke them for not prostrating themselves in humblest adoration?

Or, at least, when blaming them for not discerning the Lord's Body, why did he not remind them, that what they held in their hands and ate with their mouths was but the veil under which Christ Himself was really present,—Body, Soul, and Divinity; that therefore they might most fitly, all with one accord, fall down and worship before the consecrated elements and say, each one, "My Lord and my God?" Why did the Apostle, instead of saying this, say "Let a man examine himself, and so let him eat of that bread and drink of that cup"?

Let any one with an honest heart and unbiassed mind, or at least with a true desire to form a right judgment, read the whole passage in the Epistle, and say— Was this an adequate way of dealing with the sin of the Corinthians, if indeed the Apostle had believed that doctrine of Presence which lies at the foundation of

Eucharistic adoration as directed to, or towards, the consecrated elements ? *

(6) But the most important question remains. Let it be most carefully considered by all who would be guided aright in this most important controversy.

The question is this :—In what sense, and with what limitations, would the Apostles naturally† have understood

---

* Dr. Turton says : " We know that there is nothing, however sacred and momentous, which is not liable to be perverted from its original design ; and we may generally perceive in what way a perversion is the most likely to ensue. Let us, in this point of view, consider the Eucharist, assuming that from the period of its institution a transubstantiation of its elements was understood to take place, so that our Lord became corporally present—present in His entire human and divine nature. The consciousness of a Deity leads men to adoration—to acts of worship; and in a case like this may easily lead to superstitious rites and gross idolatry. Such is the danger to be apprehended on this assumption. . . . . Let us now, in the same point of view, consider the Eucharist according to the Protestant interpretation, as exhibiting the symbols of our Lord's Body and Blood. If, along with this doctrine, the notion of the Lord's Table—the Lord's Supper—be taken into account, we can imagine that the rite may insensibly acquire too much of an appearance of a social repast, and thus at length the religious character of the meeting be nearly lost in the convivial. On this side the danger lies in the profanation of sacred things. . . . . Idolatry, then, results from the perversion of the Roman Catholic system; and profaneness from that of the Protestant system ; and so obviously do these consequences follow, that no reasonable person, I am persuaded, would hesitate to declare the causes when the consequences were laid before him. Now, profaneness was the sin of the Corinthians in this matter. Here, therefore, we have what I take to be a clear proof that they had never heard of the doctrine of Transubstantiation." (Turton's Reply to Wiseman, pp. 320, 321.)

† In the "Fortalitium Fidei" we find among the objections answered, the view of Jews of that day as to the interpretation of the

the words of their Divine Master when, instituting the words of Institution. It is one which certainly lends little support to the Real Objective Presence. And it is observable that for answer the author appeals first to the tradition of the Church.

The following quotation (notwithstanding the curious addition of a somewhat incongruous notion) is deserving of very careful attention: "Dicunt enim Judæi, Vos Christiani dicitis in illo Sacramento esse realiter Corpus et Sanguinem Christi, hoc est impossibile, quia cùm dixit vester Christus demonstrato pane, hoc est Corpus meum, significativè locutus est et non realiter, ac si diceret, hoc est signum vel figura corporis mei, secundùm quem modum Paulus dixit, 1 Corinth. 10, Petra autem erat Christus, id est Christi figura; et patet clarissimè, quòd ista fuerat intentio Christi vestri, quia cum de sui Corporis comestione et sanguinis potatione loqueretur, ut discipulorum scandalum quod obortum fuerat sopiretur, quasi seipsum exponens dicit, Verba quæ locutus sum vobis spiritus et vita sunt, quasi ea quæ dixerat non ad literam, sed secundùm spiritualem sensum intelligenda essent.

"Et cùm Christus dixit hoc est Corpus meum, tenens panem in manibus, intellexit, quòd ille panis erat Corpus suum in potentia propinqua, scilicet postquam comedisset illud, quia tunc converteretur in Corpus suum, sive in carnem suum; et similiter de vino. Et isto modo nos Judei facimus illa die Azymorum, quia accipimus panem azymum in memoriam illius temporis quando educti sunt patres nostri de terrâ Ægypti, et non sunt permissi ibidem permanere per tantum tempus quod possit panis fermentari, qui pascatus erat, et dicimus iste est panis quem comederunt patres nostri, licèt illé panis præsens non sit, cùm fuerit præteritus; et sic ut iste panis non est ille, sic iste panis de quo fit istud sacrificium in altari. Dicere sufficeret Christianis, quòd esset in memoriam illius panis Christi, licèt iste panis non sit ille. Et quoniam est impossibile, quòd servaretur unum frustum carnis ad sui memoriam, mandavit quod fieret ille panis et illud vinum qui erat caro et sanguis in potentia propinqua ad exeundum in actu, sicut nos Judæi facimus in Pascate de azymo pane sicut dictum est. Cùm ergo Christus vester in mensa accepit panem et calicem et dedit discipulis suis, non mandavit eis credere panem et vinum in Corpus suum transmutari. Sed quòd quotiescumque hoc facerent in memoriam suam, facerent scilicet in memoriam illius panis præteriti, et nunc si vos Christiani intelligeretis

Sacrament of His Supper, He said to them,* " Take, eat: this is My Body?"

This is a question the importance of which in these days seems to have been strangely overlooked,—seeing it will hardly be disputed that the meaning which the words bore for them, they ought also to bear for us.

It has been argued, indeed, that philosophy does not know enough about the nature of bodies† to be justified in

---

nullum sequeretur impossibile, sed dicere oppositum sicut asseritis, dicitis rem impossibilem et contra mentem Christi vestri ut patuit.

" Respondetur quod traditio Ecclesiæ Catholicæ de hoc sacramento vera est, sc. quod in hoc sacramento est realiter et non significative verum corpus et verus sanguis Christi : sicut declaratum fuit supra." (Fortalitium Fidei, lib. iii. Consideratio vi. fol. cxxxi., Nurnberg, Ant. Koberger, 1494.)

The author of this work is said to have been Alphonso de Spina. It first appeared in 1487. See Walchii Biblioth. Theol., tom. i. pp. 610, 611.

* It was urged by some of the Reformers, in support of a figurative interpretation of the words of Institution, that the Hebrew language has no word meaning *to represent*.

It has been alleged in reply that this is not the case with the Syriac.

Admitting this, Dr. Turton says: "I may, however, observe that the peculiarity in question is allowed to belong to the Hebrew language; that that language—by itself and by its representative, the Septuagint—had great effect upon the language of the New Testament; that in deciding the meaning of the words of Institution, the idiom of the Hebrew and the Septuagint cannot but, as in other cases, be taken into account; and that the idiom, prevailing in those ancient authorities, tends strongly to confirm the figurative interpretation which is contended for by Protestant communities." (Reply to Wiseman, p. 310.)

† See, *e.g.*, Leibnitz, System of Theology, pp. 99, 100, edit. Russell (London, Burns and Lambert), 1850.

asserting the impossibility of the same body being, at the same time, in more places than one.

But then, it is material to observe that the philosopher himself judged otherwise, by his own acknowledgment,* till in the upper forms of this School of Philosophy he reached by attainment to this capacity of doubt. And the important question we have to ask is this,—Does the word of God adapt its language to the level attained by these high flights of scientific speculation?

It is reported to have been said by no mean authority, that no man was ever a great metaphysician without doubting at some time the existence of matter. We know what subtle powers of metaphysical skill have been displayed by an eminent Irish prelate in maintaining the position, that to believe the existence of matter at all, is to believe a delusion which lends support to superstition, Socinianism, and idolatry.†

Let metaphysicians deal with such questions as they may; it is enough for us to know that the Bible addresses itself to the ordinary apprehensions of ordinary men, who do not question either the existence or the laws of matter, and do not doubt the reality or the properties of a human body.

I ask, then, were these twelve men versed in the subtilties of such transcendental philosophies as these? And

---

* Leibnitz, System of Theology, p. 112, edit. Russell (London, Burns and Lambert), 1850.

† See Bp. Berkeley's Works, 1820, vol. i. pp. 71, 72.

not to touch here on the interpretative power of the leading preparation of the Passover feast, I ask,—Will it be contended that these plain, unlearned men would naturally understand from their Lord's words that what each now held in his hand was to be to him that which he was to address as his Master, or to adore as having under its form the very presence of His Lord?*

What! Christ whole and entire in each piece of that broken bread, just now in the hands of Christ Himself, and now in the hands of the Twelve,—while yet Christ, in His own proper form, is there before their eyes! †

---

* "In the institution of the Eucharist there was no appearance of change; there was nothing to suggest the idea of power. The notion of a miracle—to them, at that time—must have been as remote as possible from their thoughts. A miracle attested by no change must not only have been contrary to all their experience, but to all their perceptions of the reasons for which miracles were wrought. . . . Our Lord spoke to them, as He had been in the habit of speaking, in figurative language; and no evidence, I will venture to say, has yet been produced, in proof that they took His words in a literal sense." (Dr. Turton's Reply to Wiseman, pp. 295—297.)

† The following is from a sermon, "The Sacrament of the Lord's Supper," by the Rev. Claude Bosanquet (Wiginton, Folkestone), pp. 5, 6 :—

"There He was in flesh and blood before them, when He took the Bread and Wine and pronounced the words of institution, and it is impossible to believe that the Apostles thought they were receiving His very Body and Blood. Then again you know that one of the earliest precepts was that the blood was not to be eaten. Thus we read in the 9th chapter of Genesis and the 4th verse—'But flesh with the life thereof, which is the blood thereof, shall ye not eat;' a precept you see given even before the law of Moses. Great wrath was against the children of Israel for eating with the blood in the time of Saul. Had they believed that this, that they were eating and

Well indeed we may believe that the Apostles may have been filled with admiring, adoring wonder, believing their Lord's words, and remembering how He had said, "Whoso eateth My flesh and drinketh My blood, hath eternal life; and I will raise him up at the last day."

Hooker has well said: "When they saw their Lord and Master, with hands and eyes lifted up to heaven, first bless and consecrate for the endless food of all generations till the world's end the chosen elements of bread and wine, which elements, made for ever the instruments of drinking, were literal flesh and blood, we may feel sure that, with their Jewish prejudices, they would have remonstrated on the spot. When Peter saw the vision of the sheet let down from heaven, 'wherein were all manner of four-footed beasts of the earth, and wild beasts, and creeping things, and fowls of the air,' and the voice said to him—'Arise, Peter, kill and eat,' he at once replied—'Not so, Lord; for I have never eaten anything that is common or unclean.' Then how much more certainly would he have remonstrated with his Lord now; for at this very Supper where the Saviour came to Simon Peter with the bason and the towel, Peter said to Him—'Dost thou wash my feet?' 'Thou shalt never wash my feet.' And so also it would have been exceedingly difficult to persuade the Jews, when they had embraced Christianity, to receive the Sacrament, if this were a true view with respect to it. But we never hear of any single objection; we never find that anyone had the least difficulty about it; on the contrary, there can be no doubt that the Lord's Supper was at first commemorated at every evening meal in every Christian household. Yet the disciples still believed the precept against blood to be binding; for when there arose the dispute with the Gentile Christians, which led to the Council of Jerusalem, in their letter to the churches, they enjoined that there should be the abstaining from blood."

This argument tells not only against transubstantiation, but against any Real Objective Presence of Christ's Flesh and Blood in or under the form of the consecrated elements.

life by virtue of His divine benediction, they being the first that were commanded to receive from Him, the first which were warranted by His promise that not only unto them at the present time, but to whomsoever they and their successors after them did duly administer the same, those mysteries should serve as conducts of life, and conveyances of His Body and Blood unto them, was it possible that they should hear that voice, 'Take, eat: this is My body; drink ye all of this: this is My blood;' possible that doing what was required and believing what was promised, the same should have present effect in them, and not fill them with a kind of fearful admiration at the heaven which they saw in themselves?"*

But who will persuade us to believe that the natural sense of the words as heard by the Apostles from the lips of their Lord must have been that which conveyed to them the idea of the Real Objective Presence of that same Lord in the very elements which they received from His hand?†

---

* Eccles. Pol., book v. ch. lxvii. § 4, vol. ii. p. 351, edit. Keble.

† " Literalis illa verborum cœnæ Domini expositio arguit, Christum Dominum omnem corporis sanguinisque sui substantiam Apostolis suis, ore carnali manducandam tradidisse. Si autem Christus Dominus corpus sanguinemque suum ita ipsis comedendum bibendumque tradidisset, nullum proculdubio corpus frangendum sanguinemque effundendum habuisset. Igitur ea carnalis imaginatio, tanquam absurda (ne dicam impia) protinus est rejicienda. Si verba illa cœnæ, Hoc est corpus meum quod pro vobis frangitur, hoc est sanguis, etc. debeant juxta literam, ut sonant, exponi: consequetur, corpus Christi Domini adhuc frangi, et sanguinem suum effundi oportere. Ergo omnis ejus-

Lutheran divines, indeed, have much insisted on it, that this language must necessarily be understood " ut verba sonant."

But, not to dwell on the variety of opinion which results from viewing the words through this rule of interpretation, will anyone maintain that the intuitions of common sense, when they would naturally modify, may not legitimately make limitations for the sense of the plainest expressions ? *

The facts of the case, not less than the sound of the words, will be found in the ordinary use of discourse to be an essential element in the interpretation of language.†

modi carnalis imaginatio, tanquam absurda, est explodenda." (Utenoius, " Simplex et Fidelis Narratio de instituta et demum dissipata Belgarum, aliorumque peregrinarum in Anglia Ecclesia," 1560, p. 272.)

* Alias propositiones fides Ecclesiæ et doctrina animo præconcepta vetabat sumi ut sonant." (Toutte'e in Cyril. Jerus., Dissert. iii. cap. ix. c. ccx., Paris, 1720.)

† The author of the " Fortalitium Fidei " (see above, p. 168), after replying to the argument of the Jews, who in his day maintained that the words of Institution must have been intended to be understood figuratively, takes notice of certain heretics, of whom he says: " Similes Judeis predictis voluerunt dicere quod ista locutio: *hoc est corpus meum:* fuit figurativa—sicut illa Johannes xv., *Ego sum vitis vera.*" (Lib. iii. Consid. vi. fol. cxxxi., Nurnberg, 1494.) In this matter, at any rate, these heretics appear to have followed in the track of the ancient Fathers. (See above, p. 72, *sqq.*)

The author's attempt at a confutation of their heresy is very remarkable. His words are: " Istud est omnino contra intentionem Salvatoris, quia ut ait Augustinus in libro lxxxiii. questionum, questione lxvii. solet circumstantia scripturarum illuminare scripturam. Nam ex

We remember the words which David said, when at the hasty utterance of a wish, his three mighty men brought water from the well of Bethlehem, cutting their way through the hosts of the enemy, to quench their master's thirst. He said, "Be it far from me, O Lord,

precedentibus vel ex sequentibus potest colligi an loquatur figurative: an non. Nam cum Christus dicit, Ego sum vitis vera, statim subjunxit, et vos palmites. Sed constat quod discipuli non erant palmites naturales sed tamen figuraliter, igitur loquebatur figurative. Sed cum dicit Luc. xxi. hoc est corpus meum, statim subjunxit, quod pro vobis tradetur. Sed ista traditio non erat figurativa sed realis et vera, igitur realiter et vere dictum est, hoc est corpus meum."

Now, as the writer says, "Constat quod discipuli non erant palmites naturaliter," and regards this fact as governing the interpretation of our Lord's words, why might it not be said also, "Constat quod hoc non est corpus naturaliter?" and should not this fact also be regarded as governing the interpretation of the words of Institution?

But not to press this, let it be observed that the words by which he would govern the interpretation of the words of Institution are "quod pro vobis tradetur" ($\tau\grave{o}\ \acute{v}\pi\grave{\epsilon}\rho\ \acute{v}\mu\hat{\omega}\nu\ \delta\iota\delta\acute{o}\mu\epsilon\nu o\nu$). His argument is that the reality of the *traditio* spoken of, which is not figurative, requires that we understand the words "hoc est corpus meum" as not figurative.

But the question is not whether the Lord had a real Body, nor whether that Body was really delivered over to be put to death. The question is whether that Body is really or figuratively *in the elements* of the Lord's Supper, and whether *in that Supper* the delivery of that sacred Body to be crucified and slain be figurative or real. If the death be real and not figurative, then, in the words of Bellarmine, the Eucharist must be sacrilege, not sacrifice. (See "Romish Mass and English Church," p. 19.) If it be figurative and not real, then, according to the author's own reasoning, must the words "hoc est corpus meum" be understood figuratively, and not literally.

that I should do this : is* not this the blood of the men that went in jeopardy of their lives ? "

What should we think of an expositor who should tell us that these words are far too distinct to have their literal meaning evaded; that they must clearly be accepted strictly κατὰ τὸ ῥητόν, unless we would question David's sincerity and truth; that therefore we must certainly either suppose that, the appearance of water remaining, its substance was turned into blood, or else that the blood of those living men was in an ineffable way at that moment made to be really, though invisibly and supralocally, present in the water which David would not drink, but "poured it out to the Lord," because it was blood ?

But, not to multiply examples, it may suffice to quote in evidence the words of our Lord Himself to His beloved disciple, "Behold thy mother," and to His Blessed Virgin Mother "Woman, behold thy son "— words which have never yet, I suppose, been interpreted " ut verba sonant."

(7) These questions may suffice† to put unprejudiced minds on a track which will lead them clear away from

---

* Or, "shall I drink the blood?" See note in Speaker's Commentary, 2 Sam. xxiii. 17, and compare 1 Chron. xi. 19. The LXX. have εἰ αἷμα τῶν ἀνδρῶν τῶν πορευθέντων ἐν ταῖς ψυχαῖς αὐτῶν πίομαι in 2 Sam., and εἰ αἷμα ἀνδρῶν τούτων πίομαι ἐν ψυχαῖς αὐτῶν in 1 Chron.

† See Appendix, Note G.

the mazes which surround the pseudo-Catholic doctrine of the Real Presence.

Yet, before dismissing the subject, there is just one other inquiry which may well and suitably be made. It concerns the end and object of this Presence in the view of those who maintain it.

The Presence, in itself such a marvel of marvels, becomes a stupendous prodigy indeed, unless there be something like an adequate cause for such a miraculous interposition.*

For what purpose then, let it be asked, are we to believe that this Presence in the elements is vouchsafed?

If we look to the teaching of Scripture we find no other purpose for which the Sacrament was ordained, than for the remembrance of Christ's death, and for our partaking or communion in His sacrifice. Shall we say, then, that the end of this Presence is for the purposes of communion? But the Lutherans, who answer "Yes," when further questioned acknowledge that it subserves

---

* "Sumus enim (Deo gratia) ab omni profanationis sacramentorum culpa liberi, atque de cœna Dominica quam honorificentissime sentimus. Agnoscimus enim, primarium mysterium esse, salutarem corporis et sanguinis Christi communionem, qua in re nos inter nos convenire puto. Superest quæstio, num ad salutarem hanc communionem necessaria, aut ulla ex parte utilis sit, carnalis substantiæ corporis et sanguinis ejus sub et in pane ac vino præsentia quod nos negamus, indicantes ejusmodi præsentiam inutilem esse atque impossibilem, et cum infinitis propemodum Scripturæ locis manifestissimè pugnare." (Utenovii "Simplex et Fidelis Narratio," 1560, p. 174, relating the words of Micronius.)

the purpose of communion only by strengthening faith. How could they do otherwise without denying the " Crede et manducasti " of St. Augustine? And of the Papists some answer " No." Bellarmine, at least, distinctly confesses that for sacramental purposes the Real Presence is needless.* And this is, indeed, the only consistent answer which can be given, for none deny a real partaking of Christ in the Sacrament of Baptism, and none claim for Baptism any such Real Presence.†

* See " Romish Mass and English Church," p. 80.
† " Which both [*i.e.* Consubstantiation and Transubstantiation] to our mystical communion with Christ are so unnecessary, that the Fathers who plainly hold but this mystical communion cannot easily be thought to have meant any other change of sacramental elements than that which the same spiritual communion did require them to hold." (Hooker, Eccl. Pol., book v. ch. lxvii. § 11, vol. ii. pp. 358, 359, edit. Keble.)
And is not St. Paul, in 1 Cor. x. 16, in fact, interpreting to us the words of institution? " If," says Hooker, " we doubt what those admirable words may import, let him be our teacher for the meaning of Christ to whom Christ was Himself a schoolmaster, let our Lord's Apostle be His interpreter, content we ourselves with his explication, My Body, *the communion of My Body;* My Blood, *the communion of My Blood.* . . . The bread and cup are His Body and Blood, because they are causes instrumental upon the receipt whereof the *participation* of His Body and Blood ensueth." (Eccl. Pol., book v. ch. lxvii. § 5, vol. ii. p. 352, edit. Keble.)
So Cranmer had written : " St. Paul is not afraid for our better understanding of Christ's words, somewhat to alter the same, lest we might stand stiffly in letters and syllables, and err in mistaking the sense and meaning. . . . . Christ said, *His Body,* and St. Paul said, *the communion of His Body,* meaning, nevertheless, both one thing, that they which eat the Bread worthily do eat spiritually Christ's very Body." (See Aldrich's " Reply to Two Discourses," p. 51.)
And Bishop Cosin follows in the same track: " Ipsa sane insti-

Is it, then, for the purposes of sacrifice that the Church may ever have that which she may offer as a continual sin-offering, to make propitiation for iniquity? The Church of Rome answers "Yes." But it is an answer which can hardly commend itself to those who have been taught by the Word of God that Christ "by one offering hath perfected for ever them that are sanctified," and that therefore "there is no more offering for sin."*

It remains, therefore, that we ask,—Is it then for purposes of adoration? Nay. But, while we readily admit that adoration would be needed for such a presence, we can hardly believe that such a presence is needed for adoration. Surely we can adore Christ in spirit and in truth without directing our adoration to visible signs—without having our eyes directed to elevated elements or a conspicuous monstrance—without our being taught "Behold here is Christ, or there." And if so, there is here no "dignus vindice nodus"—no adequate cause for such a marvel of miracles: not to say that if this were the object of the Presence, Christianity must be a religion of

---

tutionis verba, panem esse, quicum exhibetur Corpus Domini (estque eadem ratio, si vinum et Sanguinem attendamus), manifeste eis ostendunt, qui veritati cedere, quam contentioni indulgere, malunt; nempe Christi verba sunt (postquam panem accepisset, benedixisset, fregisset): 'Hoc est Corpus meum;' verba vero Apostoli (quo nemo melius mentem Christi explicare potuit): 'Panis quem frangimus est κοινωνία Corporis Christi,' id est, exhibitio Corporis Christi, quâ fideles ejusdem Corporis participes fiunt." (Cosin's Works, A.C.L., vol. iv. p. 57.)

* See "Romish Mass and English Church," p. 40 *sqq*.

development indeed. What! This adoration the end of the Sacramental Presence, and this adoration a thing unknown for centuries! This the true purpose of Christ's holy ordinance, which can historically be regarded as nothing but an afterthought, coming in in dark ages of superstition, and culminating (attaining its full-moon glory) in the pageantry of a festival, of which even some Romish divines have spoken as men speak of that of which they are almost ashamed!*

Let me, in conclusion, be permitted to add a few words by way of correcting serious misapprehension.

* "Consuetudo vero qua panis Eucharistiæ in publica pompa conspicuus circumfertur, ac passim omnium hominum oculis ingeritur præter Veterum morem et mentem, haud ita longo tempore inducta et recepta videtur; illi enim hoc mysterium in tanta religione et veneratione habuerunt, ut non modo ad ejus perceptionem, sed ne inspectionem quidem admitterent nisi fideles, quos Christi membra et tanti mysterii participatione dignos esse existimarent. . . . . Quare videtur hic circumgestationis usus, citra grave ecclesiæ damnum, imo cum ipsius lucro (si modo id prudenter fiat) omitti posse, cum et recens sit, et diù sine ea circumgestatione, sacramento suus honos constiterit, et hodie constare possit. Deinde cum hodie plerumque non devotioni populi, sed pompæ magis et ostentationi serviat." (Cassander, Consultatio, De Circumgestatione, Op., p. 984, Paris, 1616. See also Krantz, as quoted in Bingham, Antiq. of Chr. Church, book xv. c. v. § 5, pp. 257, 258, ed. 1844.)

"Queen *Catharine de Medicis* wrote unto the Pope in the year 1561 . . . to demand of him that the Holy Day of the Body of Jesus Christ, which had been newly invented, might be abolished, because t was the occasion of many scandals, and that it was in no way necessary; for (said she) this mystery was instituted for a spiritual worship and adoration, and not for pomp and pageantry." (L'Aroque, History of Eucharist, Walker's translation, p. 582, from Thuan. Hist., l. 28.)

It is for no low view of the Eucharistic mystery that I am contending.

The giving of an effectual* sign is itself a sign—and an effectual sign—significant of the real donation of the thing signified.† In other words, the formal act of the

---

* Sayings may be quoted from later Fathers, emphasising the fact that Christ did not say, " This is a type or figure of My Body," but "This is My Body."

Such sayings of course must not be made to contradict the habitual use of such terms as figure, type, &c., to represent the consecrated elements. (See below, Appendix, Note E.)

And the harmonising of the two classes of sayings presents no great difficulty. (See especially Spinkes's Answer to Essay for Catholic Communion, pp. 134, 135.)

The giving of an effectual sign is the donation of the thing signified, and must not be reduced to the tradition of a mere figure or type, when, for the sake of the real donation, it bears the name not of the *sacramentum*, but of the very *res sacramenti*. See above, p. 74; see also p. 31. Also, " The Sacraments and the Doctrines of Grace," pp. 70, 104 *sqq.*, 125 *sqq.*

† " Dulcissimus Salvator noster omnia ejus beneficia consolatione plenissima animæ digne communicanti obsignare voluit. Perinde igitur ac si Rex, fideli subdito castellum donans, diploma sigillo munitum porrigeret, dicens. En, tibi accipe quod do, est autem tale aut tale castellum. Quamvis enim dicere potuisset hoc, quod tibi porrigo, diploma, talis castelli donationem significat, multo tamen signantius, et ad cor lætitia perfundendum penetratius dicitur, Est tale castellum. Sic enim Rex demonstrat ex hoc sigillo illum in actualem castelli possessionem mittere. Eodem plane modo Dominus noster Jesus Christus, quamvis dicere potuisset, Hoc significat corpus meum, vel, Hoc est corporis mei Sacramentum, maluit tanem dicere, *Hoc est Corpus meum*, ut cor fidele gaudio (ut ita dicam) magis cordiali impleret, nos certificans, se dum panem donat, seipsum etiam donare, et exhibere; nosque in actualem gratiarum et beneficiorum sanguine suo nobis partorum possessionem introducere." (Mason's Vindiciæ Eccles. Angl., pp. 612, 613, London, 1625.)

delivering over as a gift of that which in itself is of trifling worth, but is delivered as a sign of some precious thing, whose name in the delivery it bears, that solemn act, I say, is itself a sign. It signifies effectually the actual giving of that precious gift, whose name is thus borne by its proxy in the transaction, and which thus has made its very symbol to be honoured in the delivery.

For such purposes of conveyance it needs not that the sign should be changed into the thing signified, nor that the thing given, or its virtue, should be contained in the sign. But the sign *is*, in effectual representation, that very thing which it is called, for all the purposes of donation.

And never let it be forgotten that in the case of the Eucharist, this giving is the donation of things—Christ's crucified Body and the shed Blood given for our Redemption—things which, though absent from the body, are present to the spirit—very present indeed to the faith* which verily and indeed receives and feeds on them. To bid us, indeed, believe contradictions—contradictions in terms and contradictions to common sense—because the Eucharist is acknowledged to be an ineffable mystery—this is to construct an argument by playing upon words.† But there is an error on the other side, against which we may well be cautioned in the words of

---

* See Appendix, Note H.

† See Aldrich's "Reply to Two Discourses," pp. 20 and 21; also Papers on the Eucharistic Presence, p. 524.

Hooker: "We all admire and honour the holy Sacraments, not respecting so much the service which we do unto God in receiving them, as the dignity of that sacred and secret gift which we thereby receive from God."* It is the real sacramental union† in the faithful use of

* Eccles. Pol., book v. ch. 1. § 2, vol. ii. p. 219, edit. Keble.
† It will be found, I believe—
(1) That English divines, as well as foreign Reformed theologians, taught very plainly the doctrine of Sacramental Union.
(2) That the Sacramental Union which they maintain is (*a*) not "the co-existence of the two substances—that of the Bread and that of the Body," but (*b*) the relation (according to Christ's ordinance) of the *sacramentum* to the *res sacramenti*, by virtue of which the giving (by the minister) and the taking and eating (by the body) of the one is accompanied by and in union with the giving (by Christ) and the taking and eating (by the soul) of the other.

As the matter is important, I will fortify my assertion by the following quotations:—

"This sacramental union (1) is not natural according to place; for there is no mutation of the sign into the thing signed; neither is the thing signed either included in or fastened upon the sign. But (2) it is respective, because there is a certain agreement and proportion of the external things with the internal, and of the actions of one with the actions of the other. . . . This mutual and, as I may say, sacramental relation is the cause of so many figurative speeches and metonymies which are used." (Perkins, Works, vol. i. p. 72, Cambridge, 1616.)

"The bread may truly be termed the Body of Christ, because of a relative, pactional, and sacramental union, and donation of the things signified, together with the signs worthily received. . . The object, or thing carnally and bodily received, is the elemental creature. The object and thing received spiritually and internally is the Body and Blood of Christ crucified upon the cross. The donor and distributor of this inward gift is the Blessed Trinity, the Son of God Himself, and, by appropriation, the Holy Ghost. The eating and drinking of it is by faith." (White's Reply to Fisher, pp. 405, 406, London, 1624.)

the ordinance which constitutes the true dignity of this holy mystery.

"By the sacramental union of the Body and Blood of Christ with the consecrated elements of bread and wine, it cometh to pass that the sacramental bread is Christ's Body, and the sacramental wine His Blood." "There resulteth a twofold presence of the Body and Blood of Christ in this sacrament. The first is in respect of the consecrated elements of bread and wine, to which the Body and Blood of Christ are present sacramentally. That is, as they are signs, and have a reference and relation to the things signed and signified by them, which relation dependeth upon the institution and ordination of Christ. This presence doth consist in this, that so often as the bread and wine in the Holy Sacrament are offered to any communicant, at the same instant the Body and Blood of Christ do also present themselves truly to the soul of that person. . . . The Real Presence of Christ's most blessed Body and Blood is not to be sought for, therefore, *in* the consecrated bread and wine, but *in* the worthy receiver of them. . . . I see not which way (saith that exact divine Master Hooker) it should be gathered by the words of Christ, when and where the Bread is the Body, or the Cup the Blood, but only in the very heart and soul of him which receiveth them." (Bishop Field's Parasceve Paschæ, pp. 187, 134—137, London, 1624; see also pp. 112, 113.)

"Corpus et Sanguis Christi uniuntur pani et vino sacramentaliter, ita ut credentibus vere Christus exhibeatur, nullo tamen vel sensu vel ratione hujus sæculi, sed fide verbis Evangelii nitente, intuendus. Dicitur autem Christi Caro et Sanguis pani et vino uniri, quia in Eucharistiæ celebratione simul et semel cum pane Caro, et cum vino Sanguis, exhibentur et percipiuntur." " Hæc duo, ex divinâ ordinatione, ita unum fiunt, ut, quamvis unio ista non sit naturalis, aut substantialis, aut hypostatica, aut localis (per unius in altero existentiam) tamen, adeo concinna est, et vera, ut in comestione sacrati panis verum Christi corpus nobis communicetur, ac signi signatique nomina passim ultro citroque permutentur, et pani tribuatur quod est corporis, et contra corpori quod est panis; sintque simul tempore, quæ disjuncta sunt loco." (Cosin, Works, vol. iv. pp. 46, 48, Oxford, 1851.)

"The relation is the mystical union and conjunction of these two

And can the Christian's soul partake of this mystery—
receiving the *res sacramenti* from the very present living
Saviour—without adoring ? *

which is neither natural nor local, nor yet corporal, but merely sacramental." "The union of the things with the signs is altogether mystical and spiritual, and depends merely upon Christ the ordainer's will and counsel." "Faith, the instrument by which we receive the seal of the covenant, is a gift of the Spirit, which by apprehending and applying, unites the signs and the things signified, which, in their own nature, are far dissonant." (Nicholson's Exposition of Catechism, pp. 187, 188, 190, Oxford, 1866.)

"Hi qui vocem sacramenti pro signis usurpant, constituant quandam mysterii cum signo in sacramentis conjunctionem." (A Lasco, De Sacramentis, fo. 14, London, 1552.)

"The signs are joined with Jesus Christ by sacramental union, as the water in baptism is joined with the Blood of Jesus Christ." (Du Moulin, Buckler of the Faith, p. 466, London, 1623.)

Those who may desire further evidence may be referred to Bullinger, Decades V. pp. 278, 279, Parker Society.

Harmonia Confessionum, Hall's Eng. ed., London, 1842, p. 327, from the Confession of Bohemia; Ibid. p. 337, from the Belgian Confession.

Beza, Tractiones Theologicæ, tom. i. p. 244, Geneva, 1582; Ibid. tom. iii. p. 102.

Ursinus, Opera Theologica, tom. ii. c. 1446, Heidelberg, 1612 Ibid. c. 1366.

Index Errorum Gregorii de Valentia, Sadeel's Works, p. 382, 1593.

G. I. Vossius, Theses Theologicæ et Historicæ, Oxford, 1628, p. 324.

Turretin, Institutio Theol. Elencticæ, pars iii. loc. xix. pp. 379, 389, Geneva, 1686.

Alstedius, in Chamieri Panstratiâ Catholicâ, Supp. p. 15, 1629

Consensus Orthodoxus of Herdesian, p. 404, Zurich, 1605.

Hospinian, Works, vol. iii. p. 10; vol. iv. p. 282, 1681; Ibid. p. 265, " Declaratio Helveticarum Ecclesiarum."

* " As for our Church, which only adores Christ in the *Sacrament* (as that signifies the *action,* in which certainly Christ is), and not the elements themselves, nor Christ's Body locally present under the shape of those elements (as certainly it cannot be, without either being

Nay, there is nothing in the true view of the mystery that stands in opposition to the Eucharistic adoration of Ridley and Jewel and Hooker, of Andrewes and Hammond and Jeremy Taylor, of Cosin and Brevint, of Ken and Kettlewell and Spinkes.* What they contended for let

no longer in heaven, or being in more places than one at once) . . . . which . . . . allows the elements no more than a reverent usage proportionable to such instruments of God's worship . . . . there can be no show of charge against it for so doing, nor, consequently, for kneeling at the time of receiving the Sacrament, which is only a kneeling to God in prayer, ... unless it be a fault to worship Christ, or to choose that time or place to do it in the lowliest manner, when and where He is eminently represented by the priest, and offered by God to us." (Hammond's Works, vol. i. p. 264, London, 1684.)

"Our Church . . . commands all persons to receive the Sacrament kneeling, in a posture of adoration, as the Primitive Church used to to do, with the greatest expression of reverence and humility, τρόπῳ προσκυνήσεως καὶ σεβάσματος, as St. Cyril of Jerusalem speaks [Catech. Mystag. 5], and, as I shall show, is the meaning of the greatest authorities they produce out of the ancients for adoration not *to*, but *at* the Sacrament." (Prebendary Payne in Gibson's Preservative, vol. x. p. 117, 118, London, 1848.)

"No doubt they [Christ and His Body] may be adored in this Sacrament, in the Sacrament of Baptism, too, and in all the Offices of the Christian religion, wherein we pray to Christ, and kneel before Him : . . . . this adoration we give to Christ, who is God blessed for ever, and who sits at the right hand of God the Father." (Ibid., pp. 119, 120.) See Vogan's True Doctrine, pp. 278, 279.

* "And I also worship Christ in the Sacrament, but not because He is included in the Sacrament, like as I worship Christ also in the Scriptures, not because He is really included in them. Notwithstanding, I say that the Body of Christ is present in the Sacrament, but yet sacramentally and spiritually (according to His grace), giving life, and in that respect really, that is, according to His benediction, giving life. Furthermore, I acknowledge gladly the true Body of Christ to

us contend for. And never let us give just occasion for any to allege that they find no standing ground between

be in the Lord's Supper, in such sort as the Church of Christ (which is the spouse of Christ, and is taught of the Holy Ghost, and guided by God's word) doth acknowledge the same. But the true Church of Christ doth acknowledge a presence of Christ's Body in the Lord's Supper to be communicated to the godly by grace and spiritually, as I have often showed, and by a sacramental signification, but not by the corporal presence of the Body of His Flesh." (Ridley's Works, P.S. edit., pp. 235, 236.) For Jewel, see Papers on Eucharistic Presence, pp. 130, 132, 134, 135.)

"Our kneeling at communions is the gesture of piety. If we did there present ourselves but to make some show or dumb resemblance of a spiritual feast, it may be that sitting were the fitter ceremony; but coming as receivers of inestimable grace at the hands of God, what doth better beseem our bodies at that hour than to be sensible of minds unfeignedly humbled? Our Lord Himself did that which custom and long usage had made fit; we that which fitness and great decency hath made usual." (Hooker, Eccles. Pol., book v. ch. lxviii. § 3, edit. Keble, vol. ii. pp. 365, 366.)

When Bishop Andrewes wrote "Præsentiam (inquam) credimus, nec minus quam vos, veram. De modo præsentiæ nil temere definimus" (Ad Bell. Resp., A.C.L., p. 13), he was but making the same declaration which had been made by Grindal: "Christi præsentiam in suâ sacrâ cœnâ, eamque veram et salvificam omnes fatemur; de modo tantum est disceptatio" (Remains, P. S. edition, p. 248); and almost repeating the words of Perkins: "Thus far do we consent with the Romish Church touching Real Presence. We differ not touching the Presence itself, but only in the manner of the Presence." (Reformed Catholic, 10th Point, Works, vol. i. p. 590, London, 1616.)

This was teaching common to the English and foreign Reformed Churches. See Maresius, Confess. Eccles. Belgic. Exeg., pp. 531, 532, Gronin, 1652.

It is scarcely necessary to add that with these writers (as with Hooker, Jeremy Taylor, and the Reformed generally) to be present spiritually (*i.e.* not after the manner of spirits, but to our spirits only. See "Real Objective Presence," Mackintosh, p. 15; "Real Presence

a doctrine akin to Romish doctrine, and a teaching of
such a real absence as makes this holy ordinance of our

of the Laudian Theology," Macintosh, pp. 58, 60, 62) is all that pertains to the essence of the Real Presence. To affirm that there must be first a Real Presence in the elements, is, in their view, an unwarrantable definition of the mode. See " Essays on the Reformation" (Vivish, Maidstone), p. 19.

What Bishop Andrewes wrote on the adoration of Christ in the Sacrament is almost the echo of the language of Beza. See " Real Presence of the Laudian Theology," Macintosh, p. 57.

If Andrewes had held that adoration was due to the Real Objective Presence of Christ in the consecrated elements, he could never have stigmatised one holding the Romish doctrine as "pretium Redemptionis suæ ita temere inter Calicis labra positurum." (Ad Bell. Respon., p. 9, Oxford, 1851.) To one holding the Real Objective doctrine the *Presence* in the cup would have been *all the same*, the Romish peculiarity being only an unwarranted definition of the *mode*.

Neither could he have written: " Possumus ergo, ut in aliis Sacramentis, ita et in hoc *Figurate ;* et *nihil coactivum apparet*, ut aliter intelligamus" (p. 13). No teacher of the Real Objective Presence has ever contended for the figurative sense of the words, " Hoc est Corpus meum," as Andrewes does not only here, but more fully, and in the true fashion of Reformed theologians, in pp. 213, 214. Read in contrast, Note E (pp. 61—67) in Dr. Pusey's Doctrine of the Real Presence from the Fathers.

Neither could he have written, " Distinguat itidem, inter *res fidei*, in quibus ne ii quidem hic, quos *Puritanos* appellat (nisi plus etiam quam *Puritani sint*) a nobis, nec nos ab illis dissentimus; et *disciplinæ res ;* quam aliam ab Ecclesiæ prisca forma commenti sunt." (Ibid., pp. 290, 291.) Those who now teach Eucharistic Adoration would hardly speak thus of agreement with Puritans in matters of faith.

It would be easy to bring other evidence from the writings of Bishop Andrewes, but I must be content to refer to my " Real Presence of the Laudian Theology," pp. 56, 60, 61; to Archbishop Wake, in Gibson's Preservative, vol. x. pp. 68—70, 87, 88 ; Goode on Eucharist, ii. pp. 814—822, 960; Papers on Eucharistic Presence, pp. 417, 581;

Lord nothing more than a significant memorial with bare and empty signs, devoid of all sacred relationship to

and Dean Aldrich's Reply to Two Discourses, pp. 25, 34. For Hammond, see above, pp. 184, 185.

"We may not render divine worship to Him (as present in the blessed Sacrament, according to His human nature) without danger of idolatry; because He is not there according to His human nature and therefore you give divine worship to a *non ens*, which must needs be idolatry. For 'Idolum nihil est in mundo,' saith St. Paul; and Christ, as present by His human nature in the Sacrament, is a *non ens*, for it is not true; there is no such thing. He is present there by His divine power, and His divine blessing, and the fruits of His body, the real effective consequents of His passion; but for any other presence it is *idolum*—it is nothing in the world. Adore Christ in heaven; for the heavens must contain Him till the time of restitution of all things." (Jeremy Taylor, Works, edit. Eden, vol. vi. p. 669.) For Cosin, see above, pp. 38, 39. And as to the earlier series of notes in the Prayer-book, in Cosin's handwriting, see Papers on the Eucharistic Presence, p. 297. For Brevint see above, pp. 154, 155, and Dr. Stephens' Argument in Bennett Case, p. 256. For Ken, see Papers on Eucharistic Presence, pp. 155, 156; and Real Objective Presence, p. 16. For Kettlewell, see Papers on Eucharistic Presence, p. 573. The following is from Spinkes :—

"The question is whether the Romanists are not idolaters in worshipping the bread and wine? That we charge them with being so he [the author of Proposal for Catholic Communion, &c.] takes for granted, and I will not dispute it with him, but desire him rather to try what answer he can give to the doctrine of a late great prelate of our Church, whose words are these [Pearson on Creed, Art. ii.]: '*For a man to worship that for God which is not God, knowing that it is not God, is affected and gross idolatry; to worship that for God which is not God, thinking that it is God, is not the same degree, but the same sin.*' The consequence whereof is, that notwithstanding *Christ be solemnly professed by them to be the object of their worship in the Eucharist, and not the elements of bread and wine,* our charge against them still holds good, whilst they pay a religious adoration to what is before them on the altar, which they indeed deny, but we certainly know, to be bread and wine.

those most blessed gifts whose name they bear, and bear by His appointment who gave His blood of the New

"Nor will his former citation out of Bishop Andrewes make any alteration herein. For he only professes *the King* to own that *Christ is truly present and to be adored in the Eucharist.* And indeed what properer time of paying Him our devoutest and most humble adoration than when He condescends to meet us in this holy ordinance?" (Spinkes's Reply to Essay for Catholic Communion, &c., London, 1705, p. 118.)

"That those of the Roman Communion do actually pay divine worship to the host, and require it of all their converts, is not disputed; but only that they deny they intend this worship to the bread and wine, and therefore we ought to believe them in the right and comply with them accordingly. This, I confess, is a very expeditious way of despatching any difference. But in the mean time, how shall an honest man do, who believes nothing of Transubstantiation? Will he not be required to go to Mass? And must not all that come thither worship at the Elevation? Is not a bell rung to give them notice of the time? And not content with adoring the host at church only, do they not carry it in procession? And is not whosoever meets it to fall upon his knees and worship? And how shall they be excused that do it not? If a man will not worship he is to be looked upon as a heretic. And if he do, he contradicts his own principles, is guilty of a heinous offence against God, and pays such adoration as this author assures us themselves would disown and detest." (Ibid., pp. 120, 121.)

Dr. Vogan has truly said "that the great divines and authorities of the Church of England practised and taught adoration to our Lord in the Holy Communion, is of course indisputable. It is a necessary result of their belief that He is the Son of God. But that they practised and taught adoration after a doctrine which they did not believe, a doctrine of the nineteenth century, clearly does not follow. They believed our Lord Jesus Christ to be really present in the celebration of the Eucharist, with a presence which He promised, not with a presence which He did not promise. They believed Him to be present to give His flesh and His blood to His faithful people, to dwell in them, and to take them to dwell in Him; but they were too acute in their logic, too sound in their philosophy, too Scriptural and Catholic in their doctrine to believe in the presence of that which does not exist, or of

Testament to be shed for many for the remission of sins.

We may not, in our desire to shun superstition, make ourselves wiser than He, who knows what is in man, and has, in compassion to our weakness, ordained visible Sacraments to be received by all who would receive from Him the precious things of His Gospel, the purchase of His Blood.

We deprive ourselves of a merciful provision divinely ordered, if we would take a knife to cut the connexion between the free grace of the Gospel and the Sacraments of His grace.

The connexion is of God, the severance is of man. God's Spirit hath (in His way) joined them together; man's thoughts would sometimes put them asunder. Let man's thoughts give way to God's thoughts, and man's ways be content to follow God's ways.

But then, we may be sure God's thoughts and God's ways are not honoured nor submitted to, when human inventions, dissatisfied with God's way of joining together, would seek another way of their own; would make a quasi-physical or material conjunction, a sacramental union or identity on the visible altar, of things actually

that which is not promised; to pay adoration to that which is not, or to that in whose presence they could have no faith—the Body of our Lord which was given, and His blood which was shed; or the glorified Body of our Lord, the Blood being not shed; in the bread and wine, or with them, or under their form." (Vogan's True Doctrine, pp. 288, 289.)

distant in time and in place; a union the tendency of which is to destroy the faith of the Gospel, and the truth as it is in Jesus, and to bring the religion of Christ into conformity with those thoughts of man which have overspread the world with the vanities of the heathen, with ceremonies of idle superstition, and the festivals of pagan idolatry.

But I might—nay, I believe I ought to go further than this, and ask whether this is not a low and debasing view of the Presence of Christ which we are called to oppose, and whether it is not in maintenance of the true Real Presence of our Saviour that we are bound to contend against it.

There is something unspeakably grand—yes, grand and glorious and very blessed—in the conception of the man Christ Jesus—the man who bore our griefs and carried our sorrows, now exalted to God's right hand with all power in heaven and in earth, angels and authorities and powers subject to Him, and exalted for our sake, after purging our sins; and yet with all the compassion of His humanity and all the power of His Godhead still present in His Church with the real presence of His Divinity—that Divinity still (in some very true and real and blessed sense) the Divinity of the man Christ Jesus, and inseparable from His perfect humanity, and inseparable even from His human Body in heaven; still watching over His people—still Himself sustaining, strengthening, feeding them—as the

Good Shepherd leading them beside the waters of comfort, pouring the oil and wine of His grace into their wounded hearts, and still Himself saying to each contrite soul, "Thy sins be forgiven thee, go in peace," that they may return to follow Him—Himself the present Shepherd and Bishop of their souls, as truly the Saviour, the Friend, the Brother of each, as if He were not also the Saviour, the Friend, the Brother of all.

How can we put in front of this, to hide this real and living Presence, a presence of man's device; a localised presence (for it is idle to deny that it is in some sense localised); a presence on the altar of continued humiliation; a presence in the form of bread; a presence in the weakness of a wafer,* with a lighted taper going before it, or with rows of candles burning beside it?

---

* Some Romish divines teach very clearly that the very visible symbols are with Christ to be adored. See evidence of this as given in Aldrich's Reply to Two Discourses, p. 44, in Gibson's Preservative, vol. x. pp. 122—124, London, 1848. Indeed Gregory de Valentia regards the opposite opinion as heretical (p. 123), though others have spoken very differently (p. 120). See Dr. Stephens' Arg. in Bennett Case, 243; Forbes, Considerationes Mod., vol. ii. pp. 548, 551, A.C.L.; Papers on Eucharistic Presence, p. 470. The Council of Trent makes the Sacrament itself adorable, and Christ's Body without the species would not be a Sacrament (p. 122). The words are:

Nullus dubitandi locus relinquitur quin omnes Christi fideles pro more in Catholica Ecclesia semper recepto, latriæ cultum, qui vero Deo debetur, huic sanctissimo Sacramento in veneratione adhibeant; neque enim minus est adorandum, quod fuerit a Christo Domino, ut sumatur, institutum; nam illum eundem Deum præsentem in eo adesse credimus, quem," &c. (Sess. xiii. cap v.)

How can the hearts of Christian men bring themselves to offer their adoration and prayers to this so-

Gregory de Valentia writes: "Ex Concilii Tridentini doctrina illud ego collegi, adorationem Eucharistiæ, ut continet Christum, non esse ab adoratione Christi, ut est in Eucharistia, distrahendum, id est, ita separandam ut concessa una, negetur altera; non quia, Christus et Eucharistia idem sint, sed quia re ipsa idem adorationis motus ad utrumque spectat; tametsi non una prorsus et eadem ratione is ipse motus, adoratio Christi, et adoratio Eucharistiæ dicatur: Nam Christo divinitatis existimationem per se conciliat, ipsi vero Eucharistiæ, ut accidentibus panis et vini constat, minime, sed ad eam dicitur secundario spectare, ut continet Christum." (De Idolo., lib. iii. cap. vi. De Rebus Fidei, 1610, par. ii. p. 64.)

The rubric of the Roman Mass directs the priest "to lift the host on high, and with eyes fixed *upon it* (which he is to do also in the elevation of the cup) reverently to *show it* to the people to be worshipped." (See Notitia Euch., p. 550.)

Mark the words "eam [hostiam] reverenter populo, ut adoret, ostendit." (See Le Brun, Explicatio Lit. Miss., tom. i. p. 229.)

Mark also the words "Calicem . . . . extollit, ut a populo conspiciatur, et adoretur." (Ibid. p. 239.)

In the Missal "it is expressly said several times they shall worship the Sacrament." (See Gibson's Preservative, vol. x. p. 142, London, 1848.)

"But what, according to them, is this Sacrament? It is the remaining species of bread and wine, and the natural Body and Blood of Christ invisibly, yet carnally present under them; and these together make up one entire object of their adoration, which they call *sacramentum;* for Christ's Body without those species, and accidents at least of bread and wine, would not, according to them, be a sacrament; they being the outward and visible part, are, according to their schoolmen, properly and strictly called the *sacramentum*, and the other the *res sacramenti;* and to this external part of the sacrament, as well as to the internal, they give λατρεία and adoration; to these remaining species, which be they what they will are but creatures, religious worship is given together with Christ's Body, and they with that are the whole formal object of their adoration. *Non solum Christum sed totum visibile sacramentum unico cultu adorari* says

o

called Sacramental Presence in preference to that which is made known to us in the Scriptures?

Access into the holiest by the Blood of Jesus, does not mean admission near the steps or the rails of a chancel, nor to the view of any glittering tabernacle in which may be seen a consecrated host.

Heaven and earth are now brought together in a one-

Suarez, *quia est unum constans ex Christo et speciebus;* 'not only Christ but the whole visible sacrament (which must be something besides Christ's invisible Body) is to be adored with one and the same worship, because it is one thing (or one object), consisting of Christ and the species.'

" So another of their learned men: *Speciebus Eucharistiæ datur latria propter Christum quem continent;* 'the highest worship is given to the species of the Eucharist, because of Christ, whom they contain.' Now Christ, whom they contain, must be something else than the species that contain Him. Let Him be present never so truly and substantially in the Sacrament, or under the species, He cannot be said to be the same thing with that in which He is said to be present; and as subtle as they are, and as thin and subtle as these species are, they can never get off from idolatry upon their own principles in their worshipping of them; and they can never be left out, but must be part of the whole which is to be adored; *totum illud quod simul adoratur*, as Bellarmine calls it, must include these as well as Christ's Body. *Adorationem,* says Bellarmine, *ad symbola etiam panis et vini pertinere, ut quod unum cum ipso Christo quem continent,* ' Adoration belongs even to the symbols of bread and wine, as they are apprehended to be one with Christ, whom they contain,' and so make up one entire object of worship with Him, and may be worshipped together with Christ, as T. G. owns in his answer to his most learned adversary; and are the very term of adoration, as Gregory de Valentia says; who further adds, that they who think this worship does not at all belong to the species, in that heretically oppose the perpetual custom and sense of the Church." (Prebendary Payne in Gibson's Preservative, vol. x. pp. 122, 123, London, 1848.)

ness most blessedly to be realised indeed in the holy mystery of the Eucharist. There is now a Real Presence of the believing soul in heaven, and a very Real Presence of the living and exalted Saviour upon earth.

Full well did ancient liturgies bear witness to this truth. Well did they bid the communicants to hearken to the words " Sursum corda," and to cry aloud in response " Habemus ad Dominum."*

* " Quod ergo in sacramentis fidelium dicitur, ut sursum corda habeamus ad Dominum, munus est Domini, ... ut ascendat et quæ sursum sunt sapiat, ubi Christus est in dextra Dei sedens, non quæ super terram," &c. (Augustine, De Dono Persev., c. xiii. Opera, ed. Bened. 1690, tom. x. p. i. c. 839.)

See below, Appendix, Notes A. and B.

See also Harrison's " Dr. Pusey's Challenge Answered," pp. 541— 544, and Gibson's Preservative, vol. ix. p. 184, London, 1848.

"Ista formula [Sursum corda] omnibus toto orbe Ecclesiis communis est, et semper fuit, ut testimonia sanctorum Patrum palam faciunt." (Renaudot, Lit. Or. Col., tom. ii. p. 78.)

Mr. Milton truly remarks the great influence upon the whole Eucharistic doctrine of the ἀναφορά or "carrying up" of the whole transaction in spirit into heaven expressed by the Latin "Sursum corda;" and he very well observes: "The principle of Roman doctrine, and of the Corporal Objective Presence is, in fact, 'deorsum corda,' because the doctrine held is 'deorsum Corpus Christi.' " (Eucharist Illustrated, p. 83.)

In ridicule of the heathens who worshipped their gods as present in visible things on earth, the ancient Christians did not hesitate to mark the character of true Divine worship as that which looks upwards, and addresses itself to no object below the heavens.

Cyprian says: "Quid ante inepta simulachra, et figmenta terrena captivum corpus inclinas? Rectum te Deus fecit; et cum cætera animalia prona, et ad terram situ vergente depressa sint, tibi sublimis status, et ad cælum atque Deum *sursum* vultus erectus est. Illuc

Not well did men afterwards give order for the elevation of the host; as if Christian hearts might be content to rise no higher than the Presence of that* which was lifted up in the hands of the priest.

intuere; *illuc oculos tuos dirige,* in supernis Deum quære." (Ad Demetr., Op., edit. Baluzius, Venice, 1728, c. 438.)

Lactantius says: "Ne hunc cælestem vultum projiciamus ad terram, sed oculos eo dirigamus, quo illos naturæ suæ conditio direxit; nihilque aliud adoremus, nihil colamus, nisi solum artificis parentisque nostri unicum numen." (Inst., lib. vi. See also lib. ii. § 18, lib. iv. § 1, lib. vii. § 5, 9.)

Arnobius has similar language (Contra Gentes, lib. i.). And Clemens Alexandrinus is scarcely less distinct in condemnation of the worship directed towards that which is on earth. (Protrep. pp. 37, 38.)

Who can believe that the worship of the host, or of Christ as present in the Eucharistic elements, was a part of the religion of those who could write thus?

See this argument enforced in Dallæus, De Rel. Cultus Objecto, lib. i. cap. xx.

* The following is from the Syriac Liturgy which is called by the name of Pope Xystus (*i.e.* Sixtus):—

"*Sacerdos elevans corpus, dicit.* Sanctus, Sanctus, Sanctus, es Domine Deus potens Sabaoth, pleni sunt cæli et terra gloriæ tuæ. Elevare super cælos, Deus, et super omnem terram gloria tua. Ad te levavi oculos meos, *qui habitas in cœlis.*" (Renaudot, Lit. Orient. Col., tom. ii. p. 139.)

If these words are really *now* regarded as addressed to the elevated host, what strange perplexities, and (to an ordinary mind) contradictory notions they seem to suggest! The elevation to which the words would take the eyes of the heart—how high and lofty! The elevation of that to which the bodily eyes are directed, as containing the very presence of Christ, how mean and low!

There can be little doubt, however, that the prayer originally had no reference to the elevation of the elements. It is probably older than the doctrine of the Real Objective Presence, even if not older than the elevation.

Indeed in the Syriac Liturgy of St. James the Lord's brother is

Surely this is something of a going back from the liberty wherewith Christ hath made us free, to the weak and beggarly elements of a dispensation of ritual and bondage—a dispensation which was to be as a school for Christianity, that when the fulness of the time was come Christian men might put away these childish things.

Then, again, let me say, it is no low view of the Eucharist which we have to contend for. God forbid!

But it is a low view of Christianity itself which we have to protest against.

For, if the argument of this paper be not altogether mistaken, it is a low and debasing view of Christianity which grows, and must grow, however it may be lopped on this side and that, out of that view of the Eucharistic Presence which is inconsistent with the view of the truth of our Lord's human nature, and which has its natural development in that festival of the Romish Church in which the Sacramental Body of Christ is brought forth in solemn and gorgeous procession, to be set forth as the object of adoration to a multitude who

---

found nearly *verbatim* the same prayer, but *before* the priest takes the Eucharist into his hands. (See Renaudot, tom. ii. p. 40.)

In the same Liturgy is found "Te gesto, Deus, in manibus meis" (p. 141). And similar language occurs in the "Ordo Communis Liturg. Syr." (p. 23), on which Archdeacon Freeman observes: "It would be contrary to the analogy of all other Liturgies to doubt that this passage is of comparatively late introduction, as great part of the Syriac order confessedly is." (Principles of Divine Service, vol. ii. part i. p. 182.)

gaze, fall down and worship, but think not of obeying the Lord's direction, "Take, eat: this is My Body."

"It is," says Prebendary Payne, "out of the honour and respect that we bear to the Sacrament, that we are against the carrying it up and down as a show, and the exposing and prostituting it to so shameful an abuse, and so gross an idolatry."*

Was Christ's Sacrament ordained that His religion might thus be assimilated in outward show to the pageants of Gentile superstition?

Yet, if the so-called Catholic view of the Presence be true, there is nothing in all this which is not, to say the least, its suitable accompaniment.

But if this doctrine be not true,† then in all this there

---

* In Gibson's Preservative, vol. x. p. 118, London, 1848.

† "If the whole theory of the Roman Mass be a long dream of groundless impossibilities, there neither is, nor ever was, Pagan idolatry like the Roman, as even Jesuits sometimes confess; and those heathen, who worshipped senseless stocks and stones, can say a great deal more for themselves than they who worship a consecrated wafer. For they who worshipped wood and stone, as once most part of the world did; or rams and hawks and snakes, as the inhabitants of Egypt did; they were hereto persuaded in consideration of somewhat else, greater than anything that could be contained in them. Among the idolaters of all ages, except only the Manichees, whom St. Augustine makes worse than Pagans, because these worshipped always something that was, though 'twas not God; and those adored mere fictions (namely, Christ's hanging on tops of trees), which neither were gods, nor anything else: Except these Manichees, I say, the whole Vatican in all its ancient manuscripts cannot find one Pagan example, that ever adored, as the true direct object of devotion, such a small, senseless, ungodlike substance as is contained in a wafer." (Dean

is not only an outward approach to the likeness of heathen idolatrous rites,* but there is here unquestionably material idolatry ;† and not here only, but in every cognate form of Eucharistic adoration.

Brevint, " Depth and Mystery of the Roman Mass," pp. 108, 109, Oxford, 1673.)

* " The whole administration of it is so clogged, so metaphorized and defaced by the addition of a multitude of ceremonies, and those some of them more becoming the stage than the table of our Lord, that if the blessed Apostles were alive, and present at the celebration of the mass in the Roman Church, they would be amazed, and wonder what the meaning of it was; sure I am, they would never own it to be that same ordinance which they left to the Churches. *But the worst ceremony of all is the elevation of the Host, to be adored by the people,* as very Christ Himself under the appearance of bread, whole Christ, Θεάνθρωπος, God and man, while they neglect the old *sursum corda,* the lifting up of their hearts to heaven, where whole Christ indeed is. A practice this is, which nothing can excuse from the grossest idolatry but their gross stupidity, or rather infatuation, in thinking that a piece of bread can, by any means whatsoever, or howsoever consecrated and blessed, become their God and Saviour." (Bp. Bull, Corruptions of the Church of Rome, sect. iv. *sub fin.*, Works, vol. ii. pp. 309, 310, edit. Oxford, 1846.)

† " To make it such a continuing Shechinah as the Papists do, that Christ is present in it, not only in the action and solemn celebration, but *extra usum,* as they speak, and *permanenter,* even after the whole solemnity and use is over; that He should continue there, as a *præsens numen,* as Boileau expressly calls it, and be showed and carried about and honoured as such, and dwell in the species as long as they continue as truly as He dwelt in the flesh before that was crucified; this is strange and monstrous even to those who think Christ is present in the sacrament, but not so as the Papists believe, nor so as to be worshipped; I mean the Lutherans. But to bring the matter to a closer issue, the Papists themselves are forced to confess, that if the bread remain after consecration, and be still bread and be not transubstantiated into the Body of Christ, that they are then idolaters. So Fisher against Œcolampadius, l. i. c. 2, in express

Nor can we think this a matter to be lightly regarded because the idolatry may be excused as a devotion misdirected only because of a mistaken persuasion. Man's consciousness of the sinful is assuredly not the true measure of sin. Sins unknown and secret to us, are set by God in the light of His countenance.

When the Apostle says, "Flee from idolatry," he certainly does not mean, though he declares that an idol is nothing in the world, that there is no such real sin as idolatry apart from the sinful intention of the idolater.

A weak brother indeed might sin, through a needless scrupulosity, if, in doing what was sinless, he did so with a doubt as to its sinlessness. But it by no means follows that another brother might bow down in worship before an idol without sin, if he did so with a doubt as to its sinfulness, or with a mistaken persuasion that perchance (His own command notwithstanding) God might be worshipped under its form.

words. So Coster in his Enchiridion de Euch., c. 8: 'If the Body of Christ be not present in the Sacrament, then they are left in such an error and idolatry as was never seen or heard; for that of the heathens would be more tolerable, who worship a golden or silver statue for God, or any other image, or even a red cloth, as the Laplanders are said to do; or living animals, as the Egyptians, than of those who worship a piece of bread.' And again: 'Those infidel idolaters would be more excusable who worshipped their statues.' To whom I shall add Bellarmine, who says: 'It does not seem strange that they call the adoration of the Sacrament idolatry, who do not believe that Christ is there truly present, but that the bread is still true bread.'" (Prebendary Payne, in Gibson's Preservative, vol. x. p. 127, London, 1848.)

We are bound then to oppose the mistaken persuasion as itself the parent of idolatry*—of idolatry in itself hateful in the sight of a merciful but jealous God,† who knows the tendencies of human nature, and who will not be worshipped under the form of an image or the species of a creature.‡

We may not shrink from stating this view of the

---

* "All idolatry does proceed from a mistaken belief and a false support of the mind, which being gross and unreasonable, will not at all excuse those who are guilty of it; there never were idolaters but might plead the excuse of a mistake." (Prebendary Payne in Gibson's Preservative, vol. x. pp. 128, 129, London, 1848.) See Brevint, "Depth and Mystery," p. 109.

† "Against this the last refuge of Roman Catholics is to defend themselves by pleading good intention, and say they directly worship what is contained in this wafer, because they take it for their Saviour. So might they plead who worshipped the sun and moon (common idols of ancient times), for they would not have looked up twice towards them, as upon objects of supreme worship, if they had not thought them to be true gods. And in this case the Pagan hath this advantage for his excuse, that he can see in the splendour, motion, and influences of these great and noble bodies more probabilities to betoken a god, and so both to deceive, and defend himself, than the Roman can ever perceive in a wafer." (Dean Brevint, "Depth and Mystery of the Roman Mass," p. 109, Oxford, 1673.)

On the plea of ignorance as excusing the idolatry, see Turretin, De Necess. Secess., Disp. iii. § xviii. p. 70 *sqq.*, Geneva, 1588; Aldrich, Reply to Two Discourses, pp. 48, 49, 63—66; Hammond's Discourses, London, 1684, pp. 263, 264; Gibson's Preservative, Lond. 1848, pp. 98, 99; Valckenier's "Roma Paganizans," 1656, p. 349.

‡ "The Manichees in their idolatry .... of adoring the sun and moon, the object which they had in their minds, and thoughts, and purposes to worship, was Christ, as much as the Papists have Him in the Eucharist." (Prebendary Payne in Gibson's Preservative, vol. x. pp. 129, 130, London, 1848.)

matter.* It belongs to Christian controversy to set forth the truth, and the whole truth, but to set it forth in love. Thus conducted, controversy itself, though often a painful duty, is really a very sacred thing. And while earnestly contending for the faith once delivered to the saints, we may surely ask for God's blessing on consecrated controversy. And asking, we surely expect that in His own good way God will graciously employ feeble efforts made in a sacred cause.

God's truth will triumph over human error. God's light will shine out of darkness. The faith of Christ will scatter the idol-delusions of superstition.

"They are vanity, the work of errors: in the time of their visitation they shall perish."†

The Babel tower built up of man's thoughts, with their ever-changing aspects, and continual additions of growing corruption, if never before, in the day of His appearing must fall before the true knowledge of the Saviour, Jesus Christ, the same yesterday, and to-day, and for ever.

* See Archbishop Wake in Gibson's Preservative, vol. x. pp. 107—110, London, 1848; Prebendary Payne in Ibid., pp. 116, 117.
† Jer. li. 18.

APPENDIX.

NOTE A. (p. 10).
On the Testimony of the Fathers on the Subject of Eucharistic Worship.

THE quotations commonly adduced as evidence of the adoration of the host (or of Christ present under the form of the elements) from early Christian writers, seem to me, for the most part, to fall so obviously short of the point they should touch, that I can hardly regard them as less than damaging to a cause which can lean upon such support.*

The arguments built upon them have been more than sufficiently answered or exposed in the writings of divines of the Reformation. St. Ambrose, interpreting the 118th Psalm, says: " Videamus tamen ne terram illam dicat adorandam Propheta, quam Dominus Jesus in carnis adsumptione suscepit. Itaque per scabellum terra intelligitur: per terram autem caro Christi, quam hodieque in mysteriis adoramus, et quam Apostoli in Domino Jesu, ut supra diximus, adorarunt; neque enim divisus est Christus, sed unus: neque cum adoratur tamquam Dei filius, natus ex Virgine denegatur." (De Spiritu Sancto, lib. iii. cap. xi. § 79, Opera, tom. ii. c. 681, edit. Bened. Paris, 1690.)

To the argument built on these words of St. Ambrose, we have the obvious and sufficient answer in Jewel's controversy with Harding: " They will reply, St. Ambrose saith : ' We do adore Christ's flesh in the mysteries.' Hereof groweth their whole error. For St. Ambrose saith not, We do adore the mysteries, or the flesh of Christ really present, or materially contained in the mysteries; as it is supposed by M. Harding. Only he saith: ' We adore Christ's flesh in the mysteries,

---

* It has been well said by a very learned Lutheran divine: "Urgemus perpetuum silentium Patrum priorum seculorum, quorum monimenta hodienum supersunt certa et incorrupta. Eorum, nullus uspiam meminit Eucharistiæ abs se, aut ab auditoribus suis, vel aliis, adoratæ. ... Nec Bellarminus, Perronius, et Boilavius, qui hoc argumentum magna industria tractarunt, quidquam expectatione dignum, et quod examen sustineat, afferre potuerunt." (Deylingius, Observ. Sacr., par. iv. pp. 398, 390, Lips. 7.)

that is to say, in the ministration of the mysteries. And doubtless it is our duty to adore the Body of Christ in the word of God, in the sacrament of Baptism, in the mysteries of Christ's Body and Blood, and wheresoever we see any step or token of it, but specially in the holy mysteries; for that there is lively laid forth before us the whole story of Christ's conversation in the flesh. But this adoration, as it is said before, neither is directed to the sacraments, nor requireth any corporal or real presence. So St. Hierome * saith: 'Paula adored Christ in the stall,' and that he himself adored Christ in the grave. And St. Chrysostom † teacheth us to adore Christ's Body in the sacrament of Baptism. Yet neither was Christ's Body then really present in the stall, or grave; nor is it now present in the water of Baptism. Thus St. Ambrose saith: 'We adore the flesh of Christ in the mysteries.'" (Jewel's Works, edit. P. S. "Sermon and Harding," pp. 542, 543.)

St. Augustine, following the interpretation of St. Ambrose, says:

* "Cum eisdem Majis Deum puerum in præsepio adorasti." (Ad Paulam et Eustochium De Assumptione, &c.) The Epistle from which this is taken will be found in the edition of Jerome's works by Vallarsius, tom. xi. par. ii. c. 127 *sqq*. The passage cited is in col. 128. The Epistle must be of a much more recent date than the time of Jerome. See "Admonitio" in c. 127.

† " St. Chrysostom says : 'They fell down before Christ their King as captives in Baptism, and that they cast themselves down upon their knees before Him.' And yet no one would conclude, therefore, that they worshipped Him as corporeally present in Baptism, although Baptism made them partakers of His Body and Blood also. He says further: 'That the king himself bowed his body, because of God speaking in the holy Gospels.' But it would be ridiculous hence to infer, either that they worshipped the Gospels, or Christ as corporeally present in them. . . . Durantus undertakes to prove that the Body of Christ was not only worshipped as corporeally present in the Eucharist in the use and time of celebration, but at other times by non-communicants also. For this he alleges Chrysostom, who says : 'That the Energumens, at that time, were brought by the deacon, and made to bow their heads;' which Durantus interprets of bowing to the Eucharist. But Chrysostom, unluckily, spoils his argument; for at that time, he says, the Eucharist was not consecrated, but only about to be consecrated. . . . So that if they worshipped the host, it must be an unconsecrated host; which, according to Durantus himself, would be plain idolatry." (Bingham, Ant. of Chr. Ch., book xv. ch. v. § 5, vol. v. pp. 254, 255, 1844.) Of the quotations here made by Bingham, the first is found in the "Oratio Catechetica in diotum Evang., Simile est regnum Cœlorum homini patrifamilias," which appears to be the work of a later writer than Chrysostom (Op. Chrys., edit. Montfaucon, tom. viii. App. pp. 104, 105. See also p. 97); the second is found in the "Sermo in illum locum, Attendite ne Eleem. vestram faciatis c. h.," which is also now considered to be probably not Chrysostom's (Op., tom. viii. App. p. 93). It must be observed that the value of their testimony does not depend upon the authorship of these writings.

The place cited by Durantus is in Hom. iii. "De Incomprensibili Dei natura." (Op., edit. Montfaucon, tom. i. p. 470.) The passage alleged, by Bingham in proof of its referring to prayer before consecration, is in the following Homily. (P. 477.)

" Fluctuans converto me ad Christum, quia ipsum quæro hic ; et invenio quomodo sine impietate adoretur terra, sine impietate adoretur scabellum pedum ejus. Suscepit enim de terra terram: quia caro de terra est, et de carne Mariæ carnem accepit. Et quia in ipsâ carne hic ambulavit, et ipsam carnem nobis manducandam ad salutem dedit; nemo autem *illam carnem manducat nisi* prius adoraverit :* inventum est quemadmodum adoretur tale scabellum pedum Domini, et non solum non peccemus adorando, sed peccemus non adorando." (Enarr. in Ps. xcviii. § 9, Opera, tom. iv. pars ii. c. 1065, edit. Benedict., Paris, 1679—1700.)

Jewel † writes: "St. Ambrose and St. Augustine, as they agree together for the exposition of the psalm, so, touching the matter itself, neither do they any wise disagree from us, nor any wise agree with M. Harding. They teach us humbly to adore Christ's flesh; but they teach us not to adore the sacrament of Christ's flesh. . . . But M. Harding will say: We must adore the flesh of Christ. We grant, we believe it; it is our faith; we teach the people, as the old learned Fathers did, that no man eateth that flesh but first he adoreth it; and that he deadly offendeth God, and is wicked, and guilty of the Lord's Body, that adoreth it not." (Ibid., pp. 541, 542.) " Doth M. Harding think that the religion of Christ is so gross and so sensible that we cannot eat or adore His Body, unless it lie corporally present before our eyes? Verily St. Augustine saith : *Si resurrexistis cum Christo, dicit fidelibus, dicit corpus et sanguinem Domini accipientibus, Si resurrexistis cum Christo, quæ sursum sunt sapite, ubi Christus est in dextrâ Dei sedens: quæ sursum sunt quærite, non quæ super terram.*‡ . . . The godly being on earth, may likewise adore and honour Christ being in heaven." (Ibid., p. 542.)

Of these two passages from St. Ambrose and St. Augustine, Mr. Keble says: "If they are genuine—which no one disputes—they prove the fact; at least, as concerns the Churches of Italy and Africa, *i.e.* the whole West." (Eucharistic Adoration, p. 116, Oxford, 1867.) And no doubt they do prove the fact—the fact that early Christians adored, as all Christians desire to adore—but certainly not the fact that they directed Divine adoration to the consecrated

---

* "St. Augustine's 'nemo manducat nisi prius adoraverit illam carnem' has reference to the acknowledgment of our Lord's Divinity, not to any particular act of devotion. The Romish interpolation of *id* is exposed in Dr. Pusey's Letter to the Bishop of London, p. 76." (Canon Trevor, "Sacrifice and Participation," p. 47.)

† See also Cranmer's Reply to Gardener, P. S. edit., pp. 235, 236.

‡ See Aug., Enarr. in Ps. xxxix. § 28, Opera, tom. iv. pars i. c. 343, edit. Bened. Paris, 1679–1700.

ost,* or that they ever thought of worshipping Christ as present under the forms of bread and wine.

We are told that the Jews of old adored the flesh of Christ when they built an altar of earth to the Lord. "Ad Israel dicitur, *Altare de terra facietis mihi*. Altare enim de terrâ Deo facere est, incarnationem Mediatoris adorare." (Hincmari Opera, tom. ii. p. 86, edit. Sirmondi, 1645.) Yet the Jews did not fall down before the earthen altar, nor worship Christ's Body as present under its form.

Shall not Christians be much more truly said to worship the Incarnate Saviour in receiving the holy mysteries of His passion, though they know no real presence of His Body in the bread, and never think of adoring His flesh under the form of a wafer?

Mr. Keble further argues (p. 118), on behalf of what seems to some to look too much like a new adoration in the English Church, from the language of St. Augustine's Letter to Honoratus : " Neque enim frustra ita distincti sunt, ut de pauperibus supra diceretur, Edent pauperes, et saturabuntur; hic vero, Manducaverunt et adoraverunt omnes divites terræ. Et ipsi quippe adducti sunt ad mensam Christi, et accipiunt de corpore et sanguine ejus : sed adorant tantum, non etiam saturantur." (Ep. cxl. § 66, Op., ed. Ben. 1679, tom. ii. c. 447.)

So from the same words, on behalf of Romish adoration, had Harding argued before. And thus had he been answered by Jewel: " St. Augustine speaketh not one word of adoration, either of the sacrament, or of Christ's Body, as being really present in the sacrament. . . . It is said and proved before, we see Christ, and worship Christ, sitting in heaven. Certainly St. Augustine, who best knew his own mind, said thus : *Habes aurum, sed nondum tenes præsentem Christum*.† . . . St. Augustine saith: 'Christ is not here present.' M. Harding's commentary saith : 'Christ is here present.' Now let the reader consider whether of these two he will believe." ‡ (Jewel's Works, P. S. edit., " Sermon and Harding," p. 544.)

---

* Even if the adoration which St. Augustine speaks of should refer to the time of the celebration of the Eucharist, yet "will he not admit of any other *veneration* therein than what may be held as well in the Sacrament of Baptism ; he requiring that in both these the *veneration be not applied to the Sacrament itself, but to the things signified thereby*." (Morton on Eucharist, p. 509.)

"Qui veneratur utile signum divinitus institutum, cujus vim significationemque intelligit, non hoc veneratur quod videtur el transit, sed illud potius, quô talia cuncta referenda sunt." (Aug. de Doct. Chr., lib. iii. c. 9.)

† De Verbis Evangel. Matth., Sermo lxxxv. § 4, In Op., edit. Benedict., 1683, tom. v. par. 1. c. 454.

‡ If any shou desire a fuller answer, they may be referred to Albertinus, De Euch., pp. 730, 731.

More plausible, at first sight, appears the argument derived from the words of Theodoret: νοεῖται δὲ (τὰ μυστικὰ σύμβολα) ἅπερ ἐγένετο, καὶ πιστεύεται, καὶ προσκυνεῖται, ὡς ἐκεῖνα ὄντα ἅπερ πιστεύεται (Dial. ii. Inconfusus. tom. iv. p. 126, edit. Schulze), for almost immediately afterwards the very same word, προσκυνεῖται, is used of the Body of Christ to be adored by all creation at the right hand of God.

But is it possible for us to understand Theodoret as meaning that adoration such as this was addressed to the sacramental *symbols?*

Not, certainly, when we have marked how clearly Theodoret uses the expression τὰ σύμβολα as signifying something quite distinct from that adorable Body; as, for example, where he says, Μετὰ γὰρ δὴ τῆν αὐτοῦ παρουσίαν, οὐκέτι χρεία τῶν 'συμβόλων τοῦ σώματος, αὐτοῦ φαινομένου τοῦ σώματος· διὰ τοῦτο εἶπεν ἄχρις οὗ ἂν ἔλθῃ (In 1 Cor. xi., edit. Schulze, 1772, tom. iii. p. 238), words which are further valuable as bearing evidence as to the view of Theodoret with reference to the question of the Real Presence or Real Absence of Christ's Body in respect of their consecrated symbols.

Indeed, Theodoret, while constantly meaning by σύμβολα the elements of bread and wine received and eaten in the Eucharist, speaks of it as the extremest folly to adore (προσκυνεῖν) that which is eaten: 'Αβελτηρίας γὰρ ἐσχάτης, τὸ ἐσθιόμενον προσκυνεῖν. (Quæstiones in Genes., cap. ix. Inter. lv., Op., edit. Schulze, tom. i. p. 68.) In this he was but following the teaching of the heathen.

"As to that celebrated act of Popish idolatry, the adoration of the host, I must confess that I cannot find the least resemblance of it in any part of the Pagan worship; and as oft as I have been standing by at Mass, and saw the whole congregation prostrate on the ground, in the humblest posture of adoring, at the elevation of this consecrated piece of bread, I could not help reflecting on a passage of Tully, where speaking of the absurdity of the Heathens in the choice of their gods: 'But was any man,' says he, 'ever so mad as to take that which he feeds upon for a god?' ["Sed ecquam tam amentem esse putas, qui illud, quo vescatur, Deum esse credat?" Cic. De Nat. Deor. 3.] This was an extravagance reserved for Popery alone." (Middleton's "Letter from Rome, showing Conformity between Popery and Paganism," London, 1741, p. 179.) See above, p. 156.

When, therefore, he speaks of these σύμβολα as προσκύνητα,* and

* None, I suppose, would teach that *latria* is due to the *symbols* in themselves. Even Bellarmine denies "ipsa symbola externa proprie et per se adoranda esse cultu

says of them that προσκυνεῖται, we need not doubt that he is using latriœ, sed solum *veneranda* cultu quidem minore, qui omnibus sacramentis convenit." (De Euch., lib. iv. cap. 29.) Shall we believe, then, that Theodoret is teaching what Bellarmine will not allow? Of the *veneration* which Bellarmine claims for the symbols, Turretin writes : " Si per *cultum minorem* intelligit Bellarm. æstimationem et usum reverentem et sacrum symbolorum, hactenus nos habet assentientes ; nec enim diffitemur, sacra hæc sancte et maxima cum devotione tractanda esse." (De Necess. Seces., Disp. iii. § 10, p. 64, Genova, 1688.) In Theodoret's language there is nothing to suggest the idea of the presence of another Body to be adored in or under the form of the venerable symbols.

The symbols are venerable, no doubt, because they are symbols, and because of that which they symbolise. (See Papers on the Eucharistic Presence, p. 56.) But that the thing symbolised is substantially present in the symbols (except representatively by Christ's institution and efficaciously by His grace—as principals may be said to be present in their proxies) is a notion which not only the language of Theodoret does not suggest, but which, as it seems to me, it [can hardly, without force, admit of. See the context following.

According to his teaching the reverence is due to the symbols, not for what they *contain*, but what they *are called*, and for what (in some real sense, though *improprie* (see below, Note E) they *are*. And the symbols (still bread and wine) are what they are called (the Body and Blood of Christ), not by any change of nature, nor by the indwelling of that which they represent, but by the addition of grace.

If Theodoret had regarded the symbols as being the Body and Blood of Christ κυρίως he would hardly have used the expression *" are called."* But neither would he have used this expression "are called" if he had meant it to be understood that the symbols contained them.

If again Theodoret had regarded the symbols as *untruly* called by the name of the Body and Blood of Christ, he would hardly have used the words "they are " or "are understood to be." These words cannot well mean less than that the symbols themselves really are so in effectual representation, by the grace added to them. But then neither could he naturally have said of the symbols that they *are* what they are called, if his idea had been 'that the symbols bear the names of the Body and Blood—not (as in some sense) *being*, but as concealing under their forms that which they symbolise.

In answer to the argument (as urged by Perronius) that the words "intelliguntur *esse* quod facta sunt" must needs mean "*realiter esse*," Albertinus says : "Ambiguitate ludit. Nam, vel adverbium *realiter* simpliciter sumit pro *vere*, licet non propriè et substantialiter, vel pro *vere*, hoc est propriè et substantialiter. Si igitur intelligat, mentem Theodoreti esse, *symbola mystica* credi debere, propriè ac substantialiter esse corpus et sanguinem Domini, figmentum id esse dicimus, non Theodoreti sensum. Nam qualis, oro, est hæc consequentia. *Symbola mystica intelliguntur et creduntur esse quod facta sunt*, scilicet, corpus et sanguis Domini ; Ergo corpus et sanguis Ejus sunt proprie et substantialiter ? Præclare. Ergo, quando Gregorius Nyssenus de Christo ait, *Dextera Dei intelligitur et est*, pariter dixerim illum Dei dexteram proprie esse." (Albertinus, De Eucharistia, pp. 805, 806.)

The words quoted above p. 207 seem to make Theodoret's meaning still more clear, for they not only mark the distinction between the Body of Christ itself and its sacramental symbols, but they further evidently imply their *real absence* from one another. According to this teaching, when Christ Himself shall be *really present* His Body will be *visible*, and the symbols will have no more place. How can this be made to consist with the notion of Christ being with His Body *really present* in an *invisible* manner in the symbols *now* ? See also above, pp. 71, 74, 103.

For further evidence as to Theodoret's views see below, Note E.

the word in that more general sense in which it was used to express the reverence* due to all sacred things, as temples and vessels for ministration.† So Chrysostom uses it of the reverence paid by Christians to the cross,‡ and Nazianzen of that to the stall,§ and Isidore of Pelusium|| of that to the sepulchre.¶

Indeed, elsewhere, Theodoret uses language which seems very clearly to imply the distinction between the reverence due to the symbols and that which belongs to the Body of Christ: " Si corpus Christi exiguum tibi ac vile videtur, quomodo typum ejus venerabilem et salutarem existimas? quomodo enim archetypum, cujus typus

---

* Damascenus says : Προσκυνοῦμεν δὲ καὶ τὸν τύπον τοῦ τιμίου καὶ ζωοποιοῦ σταυροῦ. And again: Προσκυνητέον τοίνυν τὸ σημεῖον τοῦ Χριστοῦ [Crucis signum] ἔνθα γὰρ ἂν ᾖ τὸ σημεῖον, ἐκεῖ καὶ αὐτὸς ἔσται. (De Fide Orthodoxa, lib. iv. cap. xi., Opera, tom i. p. 265, edit. Lequien, 1712.) And in the same chapter (p. 264) he speaks of the worship due (προσκυνητέον) to the wood of the cross, the nail, the spear, the stall, the cave, the sepulchre, &c.

† See Prebendary Payne in Gibson's Preservative, vol. x. p. 150, London, 1848; and L'Aroque's History of the Eucharist, Walker's translation, pp. 560—563; Albertinus, De Euch., pp. 432, 822, 823; Bingham, Antiq. Chr. Ch., vol. v. pp. 252, 253, book xv. c. 5, § 5.

‡ Τὸ δὲ παρὰ τοῖς τὸν σταυρὸν προσκυνοῦσι . . . τοῦτ' ἔστι τὸ πολλῶν θρήνων ἄξιον. (In 1 Cor. Hom. xii. § 7, Op., ed. Montfaucon, tom. x. p. 107. So also Concil. Nic. II.; Mansi, tom. xiii. c. 268: cf. c. 273.)

§ Καὶ τὴν φάτνην προσκύνησον. (Oratio xxxviii. § xvii., Op., ed. Bened. tom. i. c. 674.) A little before (§ xiii. p. 671) Gregory had been condemning idolatry: τῇ μεταθέσει τῆς προσκυνήσεως ἀπὸ τοῦ πεποιηκότος ἐπὶ τὰ κτίσματα.

|| Liber iv. Epist. xxvii. Ad Olympiodorum, in Bibliotheca Max. Patr., Lugd. 1677, tom. vii. p. 695. "Venerandum [προσκυνούμενον] Christi sepulchrum cachinnis petulantibus excipiunt."

¶ "Since none of the witty and subtle adversaries of Christianity ever did or could make this defence by way of recrimination, it is certain there was no occasion given; and therefore those trifling pretences made out of some sayings of the Fathers pretending the practice of worshipping the Sacrament must needs be sophistry and illusion, and can need no particular consideration. But if any man can think them at all considerable, I refer him to be satisfied by Mich. le Faucheur in his voluminous confutation of Card. Perron. I for my part am weary of the infinite variety of argument in this question; and therefore shall only observe this, that antiquity does frequently use the words προσκύνητος, σεβασμιώτατος, θεῖος, προσκυνούμενος, 'venerable,' 'adorable,' 'worshipful,' to everything that ought to be received with great reverence, and used with regard; to princes, to laws, to baptism, to bishops, to priests, to the ears of priests, the cross, the chalice, the temples, the words of Scripture, the feast of Easter: and upon the same account by which it is pretended that some of the Fathers taught the adoration of the Eucharist, we may also infer the adoration of all the other instances. But that which proves too much, proves nothing at all." (Jeremy Taylor, Real Presence, xiii 4, Works, edit. Eden, vol. vi. p. 168.) The 2nd Nicene Council declares ὁ ἐνορῶν εἰκόνα τοῦ βασιλέως, ὁρᾷ ἐν αὐτῇ τὸν βασιλέα. ὁ γοῦν προσκυνῶν τὴν εἰκόνα, ἐν αὐτῇ προσκυνεῖ τὸν βασιλέα. (Mansi, tom. xiii. c. 273.)

adorandus (προσκύι ητος) et honorandus est, contemptibile et abjectum esse potest?"*

On this passage it is forcibly urged by Albertinus : "Manifeste argumentatur a minori ad majus, et ostendens cultum qui typo tribuetur, hoc est, symbolo Eucharistico, inferius esse cultui qui redditur Archetypo, id est proprio Christi Corpori, consequenter declarat symbolum mysticum licet corporis Dominici appellatione ab ipsomet Domino honoratum, inferius esse proprio Christi Corpore, ac proinde non proprie et substantialiter illud corpus. Gravissimum sane argumentum." (Albertinus, De Eucharistia, p. 822.)

Even if we were to allow a higher sense to Theodoret's use of the word προσκύνητα, it would be quite possible to understand his language of adoration paid not to the proxies, but to the things signified, whose names they bear. And, indeed, the evidence of his own writings would compel us so to understand it.† See J. Forbes of Corse,

---

* Dialog. iii. Impatibilis, Opera, edit. Schulze, tom. iv. p. 190.

† The following is from Bishop Jewel : "St. Augustine teacheth us, 'in sacraments we must consider, not what they be indeed, but what they signify.' And in this sense they are understanded and believed and adored, as by signification being or representing the things that are believed. St. Augustine saith: *Sacramenta* [*sunt*] . . . *verba visibilia*, 'Sacraments be visible words.' But words are oftentimes put for the things that are signified by the words. So saith St. Hilary : *Verba Dei sunt illa quæ enuntiant:* 'The words of God be the very things that they utter or signify.' So Christ saith : 'My words be spirit and life,' because they be instruments of spirit and life. And so Origen saith : *Hoc quod modo loquimur, sunt carnes Christi:* 'The very words that I now speak are the flesh of Christ.' Even in this sort the Sacraments are the flesh of Christ, and are so understanded and believed and adored But the whole honour resteth not in them, but is passed over from them to the things that be signified.

"M. Harding will say by this construction *adorantur* is as much to say as *non adorantur;* 'they are honoured,' that is, they are not honoured, but only lead us to those things that must be honoured. Herein is none inconvenience. For so it appeareth Theodoretus expoundeth his own meaning. His words immediately following are these : *Confer ergo imaginem cum exemplari, et videbis similitudinem. Oportet enim figuram esse veritati similem:* 'Compare therefore the image (that is, the sacrament) with the pattern (that is, with Christ's Body). For the figure must be like unto the truth.' Theodoretus calleth the sacrament an image, a resemblance, and a figure. I think M. Harding will not say that images, resemblances, and figures, be worthy of godly honour. And hereunto very aptly agreeth St. Augustine's lesson touching the same : *Qui . . . adorat utile signum divinitus institutum, cujus vim significationemque intelligit, non hoc veneratur quod videtur et transit, sed illud potius, quo talia cuncta referenda sunt:* 'He that worshippeth a profitable sign appointed by God, and understandeth the power and signification of the same, doth not worship anything that is seen with the eye and passeth away; but rather he worshippeth that thing unto which all such things have relation.' Here St. Augustine thinketh it no inconvenience to say, we worship the sign, and yet worship it not. And this he speaketh, not only of the sacrament of Christ's Body, but also of the sacrament of Baptism. For so he saith further in the same place : *Sicuti est baptismi sacramentum,* &c. : 'As is the sacrament of Baptism and the celebration of the Body and Blood of

Irenicon, lib. ii. cap. xvi. § 32, Opera, tom. i. pp. 469—471, Amsterdam, 1703; Chamier, Panstratia Catholica, lib. vii. cap. ii. § liv., tom. iv. p. 169; and 2nd Nicene Council as quoted above, p. 209.

The account of Gorgonia, as given by her brother Gregory of Nazianzum, has sometimes been alleged as evidence of Eucharistic adoration. Cardinal Allen says: " Maxime memorabilis est locus Gregorii Nazianzeni in epitaphio Gorgoniæ sororis. *Quæ* (inquit ille) *cum gravi morbo periclitaretur, ad medicum omnium mortalium confugit; cumque levius aliquantulum morbus urgeret, ad altare cum fide; eumque qui super illud colitur maximo clamore obtestans, omnibusque nominibus appellans, atque omnium rerum quas unquam mirifice gesserat commonefaciens, &c.* Legatur locus, notetur miraculo restituta sanitas, observetur omnibus Dei nominibus Christus in Eucharistia compellatus, agnitusque pro eo, qui omnia orbis miracula gesserat." (Libri Tres, p. 379, Antwerp, 1576; De Euch. Sacr., lib. i. cap. xxx.)

But the account goes on to say: Εἴ πού τι τῶν ἀντιτύπων τοῦ τιμίου σώματος, ἢ τοῦ αἵματος ἡ χεὶρ ἐθησαύριζεν, τοῦτο καταμιγνῦσα τοῖς δάκρυσιν. (Orat. viii. § xviii., Op., tom. i. p. 229, edit. Benedict., Paris, 1778.)

And surely this narrative, regarded as a whole, including the use*.

the Lord : which sacraments every man, when he receiveth them, being instructed, knoweth whereto they belong, that he may worship them, not with carnal bondage, but with the freedom of the spirit.' I might add hereto the words of that most fond and lewd Second Council of Nice : *Venerandas imagines perfecte adoramus ; et eos, qui secus confitentur, anathematizamus:* 'We do perfectly adore the reverend Images, and do accurse them that profess otherwise.' And yet afterward they say : *Honor imagini exhibitus refertur ad prototypum :* 'The honour given to the image [is not given to the image, but] redoundeth unto the pattern.'" (Jewel's Works, P. S. edit., Sermon and Harding, pp. 547, 548. See Mansi, tom. xiii. c. 273.)

* "Watering that with tears (not adoring it with Divine worship), she departed presently cured of her disease. That which you affirm to be the real and natural Flesh and Blood of Christ, she had about her, as many men and women used in the primitive Church to carry the same about them, and yet she did not adore that which she had in her hand, but Him that is served and honoured on the altar or table of the Lord." (Bp. Bilson's True Difference, 1585, p. 713.)

It is scarcely possible not to contrast the present Romish mode of treating the sacrament:—

" *C.* I observe that after the consecration, the priest holds the thumb and forefinger of each hand joined together. Why is this?

" *P.* Partly out of reverence to the adorable sacrament, in order that, after having handled the sacred Body of our Lord, he may touch no other object except itself till the fingers have undergone ablution: and partly in order to prevent minute portions of the Blessed Sacrament which may possibly have adhered to the fingers sustaining any irreverence by the fingers coming into contact with other substances." (Oakley's Ceremonial of the Mass, p. 63, 2nd edit.)

The above is from a manual, the chief part of which has "obtained, in the form of an accurate Italian translation, the official 'Imprimatur' of the Holy See." (See page v.)

which she made of the Sacramental Body (a use to which she could hardly without irreverence* have put anything higher than the sacred *symbols*—or, as St. Gregory himself here calls them, the *antitypes* †— of Christ's Body), not only refutes any argument which may be based on the earlier part, but furnishes an example showing how little value is to be attributed to the evidence brought in support of the Real Objective Presence, or its adoration, from practices springing out of a mistaken or excessive regard for holy things or places.‡

It is not easy to believe that such different views of what is fitting in conduct towards the sacrament do not proceed from fundamentally different views of what the sacrament really is.

Some have understood Gregory's words as implying that Gorgonia made a salve of the elements, which she applied to her body. (See Taylor's "True Doctrine of Euch." p. 221.) And this inference, as drawn by Basnage, is allowed by J. A. Assemani ("illud lacrymis miscuit, ut sibi medicamenta compareret." Codex Liturgicus, tom. iv. p. 108.) Even if this were so, it would but be a parallel case to that mentioned by St. Augustine, of the boy whose eyelids were opened (imposito ex Eucharistia cataplasmati) by a plaster made of the sacrament (Opus. Imperf. contra Julian, lib. iii. c. clxli., Op., edit. Benedict. 1690, tom. x. par. ii. c. 1114.)

* The old Hereford Missal, as given by Mr. Maskell, contains the following direction: "Nec aliquo modo corpus Christi osculetur; nec ab aliqua parte corpus Christi tangi debet : nisi tantum digitis ad hoc specialiter consecratis." (Ancient Liturgy of the Church of England, p. 41.)

† Gregory could hardly here have used the words *antitypes*, if he had intended to represent his sister as touching the *very, true* Body of Christ. Vasques maintains that by antitypes Gregory does not mean the Eucharist, adding: "Nonnihil esset irreverentiæ corpori et sanguini Christi ita faciem admovere." But the Benedictine editors determine nevertheless that the Eucharist is meant (see note *in loc.*), which is no doubt true, if understood not of the Body of Christ, but (according to the natural meaning of Gregory's words) of its sacramental signs.

Albertinus asks: "Quis negaverit Christum honorari in altari, hoc est in *sacra* mensa, ut ipsemet Gregorius alibi loquitur, cum in ea sacramentum corporis et sanguinis Ejus per ipsius invocationem conficitur et consecratur, ac rursum in Ejus gloriam fidelibus distribuitur? Verum damus Bellarmino Gregorium intelligere, Christum coli in altari per venerationem Eucharistiæ redditam : quo sensu dicitur ab Augustino (De Doctr. Christ., lib. iii. cap. 9) *qui operatur aut veneratur utile signum divinitus institutum cujus vim significationemque intelligit, non hoc veneratur quod videtur et transit, sed illud potius quo talia cuncta referenda sunt;* quid promovebit? (De Euch., p. 473. See also p. 468 *sqq.*)

‡ The argument derived from the words formerly attributed to Origen can scarcely need to be answered. It is said in the *Homiliæ in diversos* which have borne his name: "Quando ... manducas et bibis corpus et sanguinem Domini, tunc Dominus sub tectum tuum ingreditur. Et tu ergo humilians temetipsum imitare hunc centurionem, et dicito: Domine, non sum dignus ut intres sub tectum meum. Ubi enim indigno ingreditur ibi ad judicium ingreditur accipienti." (Hom. V.)

These homilies are now regarded as spurious.

As to Origen's views on the Eucharist, see above, pp. 66, 73, 97, 101.

Jewel truly says: "Origen in that whole place speaketh not one word, neither of worshipping the sacrament, nor of Christ's real or corporal being therein, nor of material entering into our bodies. . . . Whensoever Christ entereth thus into our house, whether it be by some holy man, or by the sacrament of His Body, or by the sign of the cross, or, as St. Augustine saith, by faith, or the sacrament of Baptism,

Indeed, if I mistake not, there were at this date many superstitious

Origen teacheth us to humble our hearts, and to say at every such coming or presence, 'O Lord, I am not worthy that Thou shouldest thus enter into my house.' If M. Harding will gather hereof that Origen teacheth us to adore the sacrament, then must he also say that Origen likewise teacheth us to adore bishops, or any other godly man, and that even as God, and with godly honour." (Jewel's Works, P. S. edit., Sermon and Harding, pp. 536, 537.)

Moehler is quoted as alleging in support of the adoration of the host, that "in the second century, St. Irenæus makes mention of the ἐπίκλησις." (Symbol., vol. 1. Appen., p. 4.)

"There is but one passage," says Mr. Faber, "in which Irenæus, when treating of the Eucharist, employs that word." (Difficulties of Romanism, book i. ch. iv. p. 90, 3rd edit.)

It is a passage which is thus translated by Dr. Pusey, who regards it as attesting he doctrine of the Real Presence: "He pretending to consecrate, as an Eucharist, a drink mingled with wine, and prolonging at great length the words of invocation [τὸν λόγον τῆς ἐπικλήσεως], makes it appear purple and red, so that it might be thought that the Grace from those above the universe through his Invocation [διὰ τῆς ἐπικλήσεως αὐτοῦ] distils Its own blood into that Chalice." (Real Presence from the Fathers, p. 325, from Irenæus, Contra Hær., lib. i. c. xiii. § 2, edit. Migne, c. 579.)

This is the account of Marcus the magician, whose ἐπίκλησις is clearly nothing more than an invocation, as if in parody of a prayer of consecration, by which he appeared to be a worker of miracles [θαυματοποιὸς ἀνεφάνη, c. 581]. Irenæus adds: καὶ ἄλλα τινὰ τούτοις παραπλήσια ποιῶν ἐξηπάτησε πολλούς. (c. 581.)

Possibly, however, Moehler may have been thinking of the following passage: "Quemadmodum enim qui est a terra panis, percipiens *invocationem* Dei, jam non communis panis est, sed Eucharistia, ex duabus rebus constans, terrena et cœlesti: sic et corpora nostra percipientia eucharistiam, jam non sunt corruptabilia, spem resurrectionis habentia." (Contra Hæreses, lib. iv. cap. xviii., § 5, edit. Migne, c. 1028.)

But here the Greek for "*invocationem*" is ἔκκλησιν; and it will hardly be maintained that it means or implies any invocation or adoration of the host.

The passage is parallel with other teachings, in which we are told "aquam baptismi et oleum quo baptizati ungebantur post *invocationem Dei* non esse amplius commune lavacrum et commune unquentum." (See Greg. Nys. and Cyril. Hier., as quoted in Albertinus, De Eucharistia, p. 303, and other quotations in p. 306. See also Waterland, Works, vol. iv. pp. 595, 596, Oxford, 1843; Morton on Eucharist, pp. 519, 520.)

I think it right to add, that in the 3rd edition of Robertson's Translation of Moehler's Symbolism, I have been unable to find the passage quoted. Probably, therefore, the argument has now been abandoned by the author.

Mr. Keble quotes from the Catechetical Lectures of St. Cyril of Jerusalem, who directs the communicant to receive the cup: κύπτων, καὶ τρόπῳ προσκυνήσεως καὶ σέβασματος λέγων τὸ Ἀμὴν. (Cate. xxiii. Myst. v. *sub fin.*, edit. Toutte'e, Paris, 1720, p. 332. Mr. Keble refers also (as evidence of the Real Presence) to such sayings as this—ἀπὸ τῆς πίστεως πληροφοροῦ ἀνενδοιάστως, σώματος καὶ αἵματος Χριστοῦ καταξιωθείς. (Cate. xxii. Myst. iv. § 6, p. 321, edit. Toutte'e.)

The deduction he draws from Cyril's language is thus expressed: "The tradition, then, of the mother Church of Christendom in the middle of the fourth century, was to receive with adoration, just because it is the Body and Blood of Christ. There are no subtilties, no explanations; the simple word of the Lord is support, exposition,

customs coming in, which were doubtless doing something towards

reason, and guidance sufficient. And it does not come at all as a portion of S. Cyril's own teaching, but as a rehearsal of the established custom of the Church of Jerusalem." (On Eucharistic Adoration, p. 107, Oxford, 1867.) And all this may very readily be allowed; only it might be well to guard the language against being understood of a Real Presence in the elements, or of adoration addressed to such a Presence.

Elsewhere Cyril expresses himself οὐκ ἄρτου καὶ οἴνου κελεύονται γεύσασθαι, ἀλλὰ ἀντιτύπου (or ἀντιτυπῶν, see note in Benedictine Edit.) σώματος καὶ αἵματος τοῦ Χρίστου. (Cate. xxiii. Myst., v. p. 331, edit. Paris. See also Albertinus, De Eucharistiâ, pp. 427 sqq.)

This furnishes the true interpretation of his words ἐν τυπῷ γὰρ ἄρτου, δίδοταί σοι τὸ σῶμα· καὶ ἐν τύπῳ οἴνου, δίδοταί σοι τὸ αἷμα (Myst. iv. § iii., Op., ed. Toute'e, p. 320), where the preposition ἐν does not necessarily imply anything as to place. It might very well be translated (as by Dr. Vogan) by. Nor is ἐν τυπῷ ἄρτου at all equivalent to ἐν ἀρτῷ. Compare, e.g. the words of St. Ambrose: "Hic est qui nunc in hædi typo, nunc in ovis, nunc in vituli offerebatur." (St. Ambrose, de Spir. S., lib. i. Prol. § 4, Op., edit. Bened., tom. ii. pp. 600, 601.) So Theodoret (In Cant. Cant., cap. i., edit. Schulze, tom. ii. p. 30) speaks of receiving the grace of the Spirit: ὡς ἐν τύπῳ τῷ μύρῳ (Lat. "sub eâ visibili unguenti specie"); and again says (In Zach., cap. v. tom. ii. p. 1618) that Zacharias sees τὴν ἁμαρτίαν ἐν τύπῳ γυναικὸς φαινομένην (Latin "sub specie mulieris"). And the Homily formerly attributed to Eusebius of Emessa says of Christ "latuit præfiguratus in manna." (Op. Hieron., edit. Vallarsius, tom xi. par. ii. c. 351.) Cyril here speaks of the Body and Blood as distinct —of the Blood as separate from the Body in death—not therefore of the living glorified Body, and therefore certainly not of any "Real Presence' of Christ's Body under the form of bread. (See Vogan's "True Doctrine," pp. 152, 153. See also Crakanthorp's " Defensio Ecclesiæ Angli.," p. 510, A.C.L.; and Dr. Harrison's "Dr. Pusey's Challenge Answered," pp. 364 - 369: also especially Albertinus, De Eucharistia, p. 658.)

L'Aroque says: "St. Cyril requires nothing of his communicants but what St. Chrysostom doth require of his also, and yet in stronger terms of his Catechumeny, when the time of their catechising was expired, that they presented themselves to be baptised. *When you shall* (saith he) *come into the Closet of the Holy Spirit, when you shall run into the Marriage-Chamber of Grace, when you shall be near unto that terrible and also desirable Pool, prostrate yourselves as captives before your King, cast yourselves all together on your knees ; and lifting up your eyes unto that Eye which never slumbers, use these words unto that Lover of Mankind, &c*. Is not this approaching unto Baptism in a way of worship and adoration, as St. Cyril desired one should approach unto the Holy Communion? And yet Christians never inferred from the words of St. Chrysostom that the water of this sacrament of our regeneration was to be adored. But what I say of the water of Baptism, the same Chrysostom requires we should also do of the hearing of the Word of God : *The King himself* (saith he) *will not have his diadem upon his head, but lays it aside, in reverence unto God, speaking in the holy Gospel. What* (saith he), *I know His dignity, which hath given me mine: I adore His kingdom, which hath been pleased to make me reign."* (History of Eucharist, Walker's translation, p. 568.)

These extracts from writings which have passed under the name of Chrysostom, but are not now reckoned among his genuine works, will be found in Montfaucon's edition, tom. i. pp. 93, 104, 105.

preparing or leading the way to the belief of the Real Presence,

The question of their authorship is immaterial to the argument derived from them. See above, p. 204.
Some have spoken as if the language of Pseudo-Dionys. Areop. proved conclusively the practice of adoring the host in the days of this writer. See Harding in Jewel's Works, P. S. edit., "Sermon and Harding," p. 534, and marginal note in Dion. Areop., edit. Corderius, Antwerp, 1634, tom. i. p. 286; and Alanus, "Libri Tres," p. 379, Antwerp, 1576, De Euch. Sacr. cap. xxx.
The words are Ἀλλὰ ὦ θειοτάτη καὶ ἱερὰ τελετή, τὰ περικείμενα σοι συμβολικῶς ἐμφιέσματα τῶν αἰνιγμάτων ἀποκαλυψαμένη, τηλαυγῶς ἡμῖν ἀναδείχθητι, καὶ τὰς νοερὰς ἡμῶν ὄψεις ἑνιαίου καὶ ἀπερικαλύπτου φωτὸς ἀποπλήρωσον. (De Eccles. Hierar. cap. iii. sec. iii. § 2, Op., tom. i. p. 286.)
It would, perhaps, be going a little too far to answer that Jerem. xxii. 29 proves quite as conclusively that the earth was adored by faithful Jews in the days of Zedekiah.
But at any rate, it may be fairly said, such salutations as : " O crux, ave . . . . auge piis justitiam, reisque dona veniam," serve as clearly to prove the Divine adoration of the cross by those who used them.
If further answer be thought necessary, it may be found in Jewel (P. S. edit., "Serm. and Hard." pp. 534, 535), and L'Aroque's History of Eucharist, Walker's Translation, pp. 566, 567.
See also Chamier, Panstratia Cath., tom. iv. p. 169, and Morton on Eucharist, p. 518.
Somewhat similar is the following impersonated address of St. Ambrose to water: " O aqua, quæ sacramentum Christi esse meruisti, quæ lavas omnia, nec lavaris! Tu incipis prima, tu comples perfecta mysteria. . . Tu nomen prophetis et apostolis, tu nomen Salvatori dedisti . . . te, cum de latere Salvatoris erumperes, percussores viderunt, et crediderunt: et ideo regenerationis nostræ de tribus una es testibus." (Expos. Evan. Luc., lib. x. § 48, Op., tom. i. c. 1514, edit. Benedict., Paris, 1686.)
Similar, also, is the language of Optatus : " O aqua quæ dulcis a Deo creata es, super quam ante ipsius natalem mundi Sanctus Spiritus ferebatur! O aqua, quæ ut purum faceres orbem, lavasti terram!" (Optati Afri Milevil. Episcop., De Schis. Don. lib. v., In Bibl. Max. Patr., Lugd. 1677, tom. iv. p. 365.)
Compare the following from Fulgentius : " O grande mysterium subvenientis olei sacramentum. . . . O olei sacramentum. Inde sapientes probatæ sunt virgines. Inde securæ redduntur et matres." (Hom. xviii. in Bibl. Max., tom ix. pp 126, 127.)
Bp. Morton has gone very fully into the subject of the language of Dionysius, arguing from the interpretation of the paraphrast. He concludes thus : " By all which you may clearly discern the true meaning of the first objected author *Dionysius* from his expositor *Pachymeres.* (2) The judgment of *Pachymeres*, by his reference to the sentence of *Gregory Nazianzen*. (3) The exact understanding of *Gregory Nazianzen*, by the commentary of Bishop *Nicetas*. And (4) the truth of that commentary by the tenor of Nazianzen's Oration itself." (On Eucharist, p. 523).
As to the quotation from St. Basil which is urged by Cardinal Allen ("Libri Tres," p. 380, Antwerp, 1576), and by Cardinal Bona (Rerum Liturg., lib. ii. cap. xiii., Opera, p. 349, 1723), as if in support of elevation and adoration, it will suffice to quote the following concession of Renaudot : " Locum Basilii libro de Spiritu sancto . . . qui meminit ἀναδείξεως panis et calicis, ad utriusque *ostensionem non* pertinere certissimum est, quamvis Bellarmino multisque aliis visum aliter fuerit. Nam eo loco ἀνάδειξις Basilio, est *consecratio* elementorum in corpus et sanguinem Christi." (Lit. Or. Coll., tom. i. p. 249.)
On this sense of ἀνάδειξις the reader may be referred to Dr. Covel's "Account

while they are actually themselves very strong testimonies against

of the Greek Church," pp. 60—62 ; Bingham, Antiq. of Chr. Ch., vol. v. pp. 248, 249, 1844, book xv. chap. v. § 4; Albertinus, De Euch., p. 446; Morton on the Eucharist, pp. 519, 520.

I hardly suppose that any will now need an answer to the argument sometimes urged from the words of St. Augustine in reply to the charge against the Christians of worshipping Ceres. (Contra Faust., lib. xx. c. 13.) At any rate the following extract from Albertinus will sufficiently dispose of this matter : " Augustinus in responsione sua, postquam ludibrio, excepisset eos, qui *nos*, inquit, *propter panem et Calicem Cererem ac Liberum colere existimant*, subjungit, *A Cerere et Libero Paganorum Diis longe absumus, quamvis panis et Calicis sacramentum quod ita laudatis, ut in eo nobis pares esse volueritis, nostro ritu amplectamur.* Quis dixerit, panis et calicis sacramentum Christiano ritu amplecti, illi esse panis et Calicis sacramentum adoratione summa colere ? Inepte sane.

" Hac enim ratione Catholici dici quoque possent baptismi sacramento adoratione summa esse prosecuti. Nam de schismaticorum baptismati loquens, *Sacramentum Dei*, inquit, *agnoscimus in eis, et veneramur, et amplectimur:* perspicue, ni fallor, indicans se utrobique, non adorationem, sed venerationem intelligere." (Albertinus, De Eucharistia, p. 629). See also Chamier, Panstratia Catholica, De Euch., lib. vii., cap. iii. § xvii. tom. iv. p. 170.

Muratori quotes the words of Chrysostom: "Hoc corpus etiam jacens in præsepio reveriti sunt sunt magi, et cum multo metu ac tremore adorarunt. Tu non in præsepi vides, sed in altari. Nos ergo longe majorem quam illi barbari ostendamus reverentiam." (De Rebus Liturg , cap. xix., In Migne, c. 1012.)

But (1) in the original the last sentence follows after a considerable interval ; (2) the word rendered by Muratori "reverentiam" is in the original τὴν εὐλάβειαν, which certainly implies no adoration of any present object; and the change from προσεκύνησαν is observable, though even that word would by no means necessarily have meant Divine adoration. Moreover the εὐλάβεια seems to be explained by the words immediately following, ἵνα μὴ ἁπλῶς, μηδὲ ὡς ἔτυχε προσελθόντες : of which it is too little to say that they do not suggest any adoration of the Eucharist; (3) the Homily is full of highly rhetorical language concerning the Sacrament, which can only be sacramentally understood, *e.g.* it represents Christ's Body not only as present and eaten, but as seen and touched (p. 219); (4) in the same Homily it is said, "Quid enim, inquit, dico communicationem ? Illud ipsum Corpus sumus. Quid est enim panis ? Corpus Christi. Quid autem fiunt communicantes (οἱ μεταλαμβάνοντες)? Corpus Christi, non corpora multa, sed unum Corpus . . . ex eodem, et idipsum efficimur omnes" (pp. 213, 214). (See Chrys. in Ep. i. ad Cor. Hom. xxiv., edit. Benedict., tom. x. pp. 211—219, Paris, 1732.) Yet Chrysostom certainly did not mean that Divine adoration was to be given to the communicants, or to Christ's Body, or Christ Himself as really present in them.

It has been well said by Prebendary Payne : "Some of the Fathers' words imply that when we come to the sacrament it should be with the greatest lowliness, both of body and mind ; and as the Primitive Church used to do, and as the Church of England does, in a posture of worship and adoration, in the form and manner of worship, as St. Cyril of Jerusalem speaks ; or as St. Chrysóstom, in the form and manner of supplicants and worshippers of Christ, as the Magi were when they came to bring their presents to Him : 'Do thou then present Him with humility and a lowly and submissive heart ; and be not like Herod, who pretended he would come to worship Him, but it was to murder Him ; but rather imitate the Magi, and come with greater fear and reverence to thy Saviour than they did.' This is the whole design and substance of what is produced out of St. Chrysostom ; and this is the

the existence of that belief at the time they began to be practised.*

It would seem to be altogether out of place to enter into anything like a minute examination here of the history of the Councils of Constantinople (754) and Nicæa (787), and of arguments which have been built on it, seeing these Councils belong to so late a date.

If even it could be proved that adoration of the host was practised in the latter part of the eighth century, it would go a very little way towards showing us anything concerning the Eucharistic faith or practice of the first century.

But believing that this history is good for very little except to prove how low the Eastern Church had already fallen,† I cannot but think that if there is *one thing* which it does seem to show pretty clearly, it is this : that, at this date, the Eastern Church knew nothing of any Divine adoration due to the Eucharistic symbols, or to any Real Presence of Christ in them. (See Papers on the Eucharistic Presence, pp. 135, 136 ; Romish Mass and English Church, pp. 62, 63.)

It is quite possible that the difference between the contending parties (for and against image worship) may have been very trifling on the subject of the Eucharist (though the Nicene Council rejected the expression $\theta\acute{\epsilon}\sigma\epsilon\iota$ used on the other side: see Labbæus, tom. vii.

plain meaning of Origen, that when we come to receive Christ in the sacrament, we should do it with all humility; 'for consider,' says he, 'that then the Lord enters under thy roof. Do thou therefore humble thyself, and imitate the centurion, and say, Lord, I am not worthy that Thou shouldest enter under my roof.' When the Fathers would give us the picture of a devout communicant, they draw him in the greatest posture of humility and reverence, looking upon and adoring the Saviour who died for him upon the cross, prostrating his soul and his body before Him, and exercising the highest acts of devotion to Him : and with tears in his eyes and sorrow in his heart, standing like a penitent before Him, trembling and afraid, as sensible of his own guilt ; with his eyes cast down and with dejected looks considering that he is but dust and ashes who is vouchsafed this honour, and inwardly groaning and sighing and panting in his soul, saying, 'Lord, I am not worthy that Thou shouldest enter under my roof ;' and the like. And thus they may find all devout communicants in our Church behaving themselves during the whole solemnity and celebration of that blessed sacrament, in which mystery they always adore Christ, and that flesh of Christ which was crucified. For then, as St. Ambrose and St. Austin speak, when their minds are all the while inflamed with the most devout affections, and they are performing all the inward and outward acts of the highest devotion to God and their Saviour, then they are upon their knees, offering up most ardent prayers and thanksgiving." (Prebendary Payne, in Gibson's Preservative,vol. x. pp. 151, 152, Lond.1848.)

* See, *e.g.*, Covel's Account of the Greek Church, p. 85.
† See Aldrich, Reply to Two Discourses, p. 54, and Neander's Church History, vol. v. pp. 297—299, 277, edit. Clark ; also Tillotson, Rule of Faith, part iv. sect. 1, Works, p. 747, 6th edit. London, 1710 ; and Weismann, Hist. Eccl. N. T., sect. viii. tom i. p. 746, Halle, 1745, and Du Pin, Eccles. Hist., vol. vi. pp. 133—142, English trans., London, 1699.

c. 452) : that both held something like the augmentation doctrine (see " Romish Mass and English Church," p. 62), or a cognate theory of adoption (θέσει: Labbæus, tom. vii. c. 448), or incorporation (Romish Mass, p. 62), or assumption (Ussher's Works, vol. ii. p. 212 , or, at any rate, regarded the elements after consecration as made to be, in some sense, the Body of Christ by the grace of a certain sanctification (ὡς διὰ τίνος ἁγιασμοῦ χάριτι θεουμένη: Labbæus, tom. vii. c. 448).

The difference may possibly have been mainly as to the question whether the true doctrine might be more suitably expressed by admitting or rejecting such terms as εἰκὼν and ἀντίτυπα.*

On both sides, no doubt, they regarded the elements with the greatest reverence. The one side regarded them as ἀψευδῆ εἰκόνα τῆς φυσικῆς σάρκος (Labbæus, tom. vii. c. 448); and the other side certainly had no lower conception of them. As to the use of the term *Deification*, see Albertinus, De Eucharistia, p. 914; Robertson's History of Christian Church, vol. iii. p. 236, 1874.

But it is one of the arguments used by the Council of Constantinople, A.D. 754, that in the Sacrament of the Lord's Supper (which was given εἰς τύπον καὶ ἀνάμνησιν ἐνεργεστάτην : Labbæus, tom. vii. c. 445). Christ ἄρτου οὐσίαν προσέταξε προσφέρεσθαι, μὴ σχηματίζουσαν ἀνθρώπου μορφήν, ἵνα μὴ εἰδωλολατρεία παρεισαχθῇ. (Labbæus, tom. vii. c. 448.) And it is difficult to see what force there can be in this argument if they regarded the Divine adoration as due to the host, or to Christ present under its form. How can the statement be understood that bread should have been chosen to be the Lord's Body θέσει, on account of its unlikeness to the human form, and this for the purpose of avoiding any furtive incoming of idolatry, if it were not idolatry to address Divine adoration to that which is thus Christ's Body in the Eucharist? (See Ussher's Works, edit. Elrington, vol. iii. pp. 79, 80; Mansi, tom. xiii. c. 204.)

There is, surely, in their statement no place for the idea of any *other* body (a proper object of adoration) having a real Presence under the form of that which they recognise as Christ's Body θέσει.

With the iconoclast party that θεῖος ἄρτος (Labbæus, tom. vii. c. 448) which is adopted to be the Lord's Body (θεῖον σῶμα, c. 448) is ὁ θεοπαράδοτος εἰκὼν τῆς σαρκὸς αὐτοῦ. (See Hardouin, Paris, 1714, tom. iv. c. 368, 369; Labbæus, tom. vii. c. 448; Mansi, tom. xiii. c. 264.)

* See Claude, Reply to Arnauld, part i. pp. 340, 341, 344, London, 1864 ; and Mansi, tom. xiii. c. 264, 265.

It is replied by their opponents, Εἰ εἰκὼν τοῦ σώματος ἐστιν, οὐκ ἐνδέχεται εἶναι αὐτὸ τὸ θεῖον σῶμα. (C. 372; Labbæus, tom. vii. c. 449.) And many similar sayings marking the distinction between *images, figures, likenesses, symbols*, &c., and the *truth* which they represent, may be quoted from the earlier Fathers. (See Albertinus, De Eucharistia, p. 274.) Notably, Theodoret says, ἡ εἰκὼν σχήματα ἀλλ' οὐ πράγματα ἔχει. (In Dan., lib. ii. cap. 2. See below, Note E.) On the whole subject see Goode on Eucharist, i. pp. 279, 28; Robertson's Hist. of Chr. Ch., vol. iii. p. 230, 1874; Albertinus. De Eucharistia, pp. 913—915; Hospinian's Works, tom. iii. p. 251; Neander's Church History, vol. v. pp. 277 *sqq.*, edit. Clark.

It is clear no valid argument can be made to rest on the use of the word σεβόμενοι (Labbæus, tom. vii. c. 445). "Do they believe that *Polemon*, the Heathen's picture, deserved any religious worship? It is true, St. Gregory Nazienzen says that picture was venerable (σεβασμία); but he means no more than this, that it was well done and did inspire some respect of the painting; which shows, though this kind of epithets (holy, venerable) were said somewhere else of the pictures of saints, that would not come up to an invincible proof that they ought to be honoured." (Du Pin, Eccles. Hist., vol. vi. pp. 139, 140, English transl., London, 1699.)

Against all that can be alleged from earlier writers as seeming possibly to indicate some special worship addressed to the Eucharistic Presence (even if it were of much greater weight than it seems to me to be) it would more than suffice to set one or two quotations from Agobard as evidence that in the early part of the ninth century no such practice was in use as the adoration of the host, or of Christ present under its form.

"Adoretur, colatur, veneretur a fidelibus Deus; illi soli sacrificetur, vel mysterio corporis et sanguinis, quo sumus redempti; vel in sacrificio cordis contriti et humiliati. Angeli vel homines sancti amentur, honorarentur, caritate non servitute. Non eis Corpus Christi offeratur, cum sint hoc et ipsi." (Liber De Imaginibus, ch. xxx., Op., edit. Baluze, tom. i. p. 264).

If in his time the Sacramental Body of Christ had been an object of Divine worship, is it conceivable that Agobard, arguing against the worship of saints or angels, after saying "Non eis Corpus Christi offeratur," should (following St. Augustine) have added the words "cum sint hoc et ipsi"? Would he not rather have written "cum hoc ipsi adorent"?

In the language used the Sacramental Body of Christ is surely not to be regarded as more adorable than the Spiritual Body, *i.e.* the saints, to whom Agobard will allow no adoration to be paid.

But further, I venture to think that Agobard could never have written the previous words if in "the mystery of Christ's Body and Blood" he had recognised not a *mean* only, but an *object* of Divine worship: if in his time it had been understood that not only was adoration to be offered to God in and by the Sacrament of Christ's Body and Blood, but that also in that Sacrament the Body and Blood of Christ, and Christ Himself, were to be adored under the form of bread and wine; that the consecrated elements contained not only the mystery of that which is offered in worship as sacrifice to God, but the very presence of Him to whom all worship and adoration is due.

And that Agobardus had no such view is made, I think, still more clear by the following extracts from his "Liber adversus Fredegisum: "

"*Omnes eundem potum spiritalem biberunt.* Quem potum? Illum quem in superiori sententiâ præmisit, uno Spiritu potati sumus, et quam escam spiritalem, nisi participationem Corporis Christi?" (Lib. Adv. Fredeg., ch. xx., Op., tom. i. p. 188.) "Nihil omnino differt aliud inter illos et nos, nisi quia sacramenta salutis quæ per mediatorem operata sunt propter nos et propter illos, nos salvant præterita, illos futura; quia quæ nos credimus et tenemus præterita, illi crediderunt et tenuerunt futura; et illi in sola conscientia et figuris futurorum, nos etiam in publica professione, votis et annunciatione præteritarum rerum cum significatione tractabilium sacramentorum ; sicut et illi duo qui unum botrum in falango portabant, unum opus faciebant indifferenter, nisi quia eundem botrum, unus post dorsum, alter ante faciem habebant." (Ibid., ch. xxi. p. 190.)

With this let the reader compare the teaching of Thomas Aquinas concerning the sacraments of the Old and New Law (see Summa, Par. iii., Quæst. lxi. Art. 4, Quæst. lxii., Quæst. lxxv. Art. 1), and he can hardly fail to observe that in the view of Agobard (as of St. Augustine) the Sacraments of the Gospel are lacking the *differentia*, which is now regarded as an essential part of Catholic truth, and which alone admits that doctrine of the Eucharist in particular which can justify the sacramental adoration of more modern times.

Romish theology teaches that the sacraments of the old law did not, that those of the new do, contain grace, and that the Eucharist contains Christ Himself really present. (See Vogan's True Doctrine, pp. 529, 361.)

In the theology of Agobard the only difference between the sacraments of the Old and New Testament is the difference which belongs to looking forwards to what has to be done in the future, and backwards on what is accomplished in the past.* And the participation or communion of the Body of Christ is, in his teaching, so far from requiring Christ Himself to be really contained in the elements, that the same " participation of the Body of Christ" is ascribed to the old Fathers, who before the incarnation of Christ did all eat the same spiritual meat. (Cf. Hincmar, Opera, tom. i, pp. 392, 393, pp. 396, 397, edit. Sirmondi, 1645.)

The fact of Agobard's tendency as a Reformer to make a stand against the growing superstition of his times, deducts nothing from the value of his testimony, so far as that testimony bears on the doctrine and practice of the Church in his day.†

There was an increasing disposition, as time went on, to contrast the sacraments of the Old Testament and the New, which makes the language of Agobard in the ninth century all the more striking.

It must not, however, be too hastily assumed that those Fathers who spoke of the Jews' sacraments as shadows of ours, and of ours as having the truth which theirs wanted, necessarily render any real support to the teaching of the Romish Church, or to the doctrine of the Real Objective Presence.

Sacraments are signs and types and figures alike in the Old and in the New Testament.‡ But there is a difference, which some of

* So Fulgentius : " In illis sacrificiis quid nobis esset donandum, figurate significabatur ; in hoc autem sacrificio quid jam nobis donatum sit, evidenter ostenditur." (De Fide, c. 19. See below, p. 222.)

On which Bertram's comment is : " Patenter innuit quod sicut illa figuram habuere futurorum, sic et hoc sacrificium figura sit prœteritorum." (De Corpore et Sanguine Dom., § xci., In Migne, c. 166.)

So also Berengarius : "Ut diceret [Petrus diaconus : *Si adhuc in figura sumus, quando rem tenebimus*, non attendente, quod dicit beatus Augustinus: hunc panem significavit manna, hunc panem significat altare Dei, *in signis diversa sunt, in re quæ significatur, paria*, et illud in psalmo iii. : *Corporis et sanguinis sui figuram discipulis commendavit*, non attendente, non interesse nihil *inter figuram vel signum rei, quæ nunquam fuit, rei nondum exhibitæ* prœnunciatoriam, et figuram vel signum *rei existentis*, rei jam exhibitæ commonefactoriam." (Berengarius, " De Sacra Cœna, adversus Lanfrancum," p. 43, Berlin, 1834.)

† It is said by Baluzius, in the dedicatory epistle of his edition of Agobardus, that in the Gallican Church "clarissimum lumen œvo suo fuit Agobardus."

"The reader," says Allix, "need not take much pains to apprehend why Rome thought fit to condemn these books of Agobardus ; though he may be at a loss how it comes to pass that, notwithstanding all this, he is at this day held for a saint, and publicly adored at Lyons under the name of St. Agobo. This is a riddle which has strangely perplexed that learned Jesuit, Theophilus Raynaldus, as well as Le Cointe, in his 'Annals of the Church of France ' But he is not the only person that has opposed the belief and worship of the Church of Rome, and is publicly adored by her." (Remarks on the Ancient Churches of the Albigenses, Oxford, 1821, p. 97.)

‡ " Eadem quippe sunt in veteri et novo [testamento] ibi obumbrata, hic revelata :

the later Fathers have expressed, perhaps sometimes in ambiguous or superlative terms,* in that ours are effectual signs of things which have been seen and handled in the past, and to the faith of the Church are really present still. The sacraments of the Jews were types or shadows of things promised indeed, but yet in the dark, unrevealed. Ours are exhibitive signs of things clearly revealed and brought into the light of day.†

Hence theirs are said to be types of ours—although ours are recognised as types also. So Gregory Nazianzen calls the Passover a more obscure type of a type. See below, Note F.

Moreover, the sacraments of the Jews had immediate relation to

ibi præfigurata, hic manifestata. Non solum sacramenta diversa sunt, verum etiam promissa." (Ven. Beda in 1 Cor. xi., Opera, tom. vi. c. 379, edit. Cologne, 1688.)

So also, following St. Augustine, Bede writes:—

"Hunc panem significavit manna, hunc panem significavit altare Dei. Sacramenta illa fuerunt, in signis diversa sunt, in re quæ significatur paria sunt." (Ven. Beda in 1 Cor. x., Opera, tom. vi. c. 356.)

"Ibi petra Christus. Nobis Christus, quod in altare Dei ponitur. Et illi pro magno sacramento ejusdem Christi biberunt aquam profluentem de Petra. Nos quid bibamus, norunt fideles. Si speciem visibilem intendas, aliud est. Si intelligibilem significationem, eundem potum spiritualem biberunt." (Ibid., c. 356.)

* So *e.g.* Isidorus Hispalensis writes: "Tantum interest inter propositionis panes et corpus Christi, quantum inter umbram et corpus, inter imaginem et veritatem, inter exemplaria futurorum et ea ipsa quæ per exemplaria præfigurabantur." (De Eccles. Officiis, lib. i. c. xviii., § 10, Op., edit. Migne, tom. vi. c. 756.)

Yet Isidore cannot be held to teach the Real Presence of Rome. (See Albertinus, De Eucharistia, pp. 899 *sqq.*)

See also above, pp. 75, 78, 120, 151.

† "Quanto magis nunc pro baptismo Christi, pro Eucharistia Christi, pro signo Christi ad omnia præferenda paratior debet esse Christianus, cum illa fuerint promissiones rerum complendarum, hæc sint indicia completarum?" (Augustine, Contra Faustum, lib. xix. c. xiv., Opera, edit. Benedict, 1688, tom. viii. c. 320.)

"Si enim soni verborum quibus loquimur, pro tempore commutantur, eademque res aliter enunciatur facienda, aliter facta, nec paribus morarum intervallis, nec iisdem vel totidem litteris syllabisve sonuerunt: quid mirum si aliis mysteriorum signaculis passio et resurrectio Christi futura promissa est, aliis jam facta annunciatur, quando quidem ipsa verba, futurum et factum, passurus et passus, resurrecturus et resurrexit, nec tendi æqualiter, nec similiter sonare potuerunt? Quid enim sunt aliud quæque corporalia sacramenta, nisi quædam quasi verba visibilia, sacro-sancta quidem, verumtamen mutabilia et temporalia?" (Ibid., cap. xvi. c. 321.)

See also Fulgentius: "In illis enim carnalibus victimis figuratio fuit carnis Christi quam pro peccatis nostris ipse sine peccato fuerat oblaturus, et sanguinis quem erat effusurus in remissionem peccatorum nostrorum, in isto autem sacrificio gratiarum actio atque commemoratio est carnis Christi, quam pro nobis obtulit, et sanguinis quem pro nobis idem Deus effudit. . . . In illis ergo sacrificiis quid nobis esset donandum, figurate significabatur. In hoc autem sacrificio quid nobis jam donatum sit, evidenter ostenditur." (Fulgentius, De Fide ad Petrum Diac. cap. xix. in "Heptas Presul. Christ.," edit. Raynaudus, Paris, 1661, pp. 494, 495.)

See also especially Fulgentius Ferrando, De Quinque Quæstionibus, § xxxviii.–xli., In Bibl. Max. Patr., Lugd. 1677, tom. ix. pp. 194, 195.

deliverances or redemptions, which were shadows of * our redemption and salvation. Ours stand in immediate relation to that which is as the substance of those † previous shadows. (See Isido. Hispal., Sent, lib. i. cap. xx. § 3.)

Hence, also, theirs are compared to the sketched outline in a picture, ours to the filling in of the colours which bring out the figures as in living reality, and yet but in a picture still. (See below, Note E.)

Those who desire further satisfaction on this point may be referred to Dr. Harrison's "Dr. Pusey's Challenge Answered," pp. 400—403, 624—626.

It may, however, very well be admitted that this growing tendency to contrast the sacraments of the Law and the Gospel was in time connected with some sort of superstitious approaches towards the Paschasian doctrine; and that the decided language of Agobard indicates a strong resolve to maintain the earlier and purer doctrine in its simplicity. The point to be insisted upon is that it would have been altogether impossible for him to maintain his position in this respect, in the face of anything like a general custom of adoring the Eucharist.

His teaching would have required of him a most uncompromising denunciation of such a custom if it had existed.

It may be observed how St. Augustine had exclaimed against the madness of those who could think of worshipping the sun, because in the Scriptures it signifies Christ. St. Augustine argues against such

* "Panem illum sacramentalem, quamvis Corpus Christi non proprie, sed figurate sit, *verum* appellat [Hieronymus] duplici de causa. Una est : quia Veteres testantur non modo in genere Sacramenta Vetera nostrorum figuras fuisse, sed et in specie manna figuram fuisse panis Eucharistici, quemadmodum mare per quod Israelitæ transierunt, baptismi typum. . . . Si baptismus noster, quamvis aqua substantialiter sit, respectu veterum baptismatum, *verum baptisma* et *veritas* appellatur, Cur non et panis Eucharistiæ, quamvis panis juxta substantiam proprie dictus sit, mannæ comparatus a quâ præfigurabatur, *verus panis* et *veritas* pariter indigetabitur ? Altera causa est, quia panis Eucharisticus ad animæ nutritionem propriè est ordinatus. . . . Manna autem per se et primario ad Corporis alimentum." (Albertinus, De Eucharistia, p. 582. See also p. 503.)

† So our translation in the heading of 1 Cor. x., " The Sacraments of the Jews are types of ours," which has been unduly objected to.

" Veteres docent, sacramenta vetera fuisse novorum typos, sed non eo sensu, quasi nostra sacramenta sint res significata. Id enim prorsus est alienum a rei natura, et mente Patrum. Nam in Sacramentis V. and N. T. est una et eadem res significata. . . . Quia vero differunt gradu claritatis, recte sacramenta vetera dicuntur typi, hoc est sciagraphia et imagines adumbratæ ; nova, antitypa, hoc est, imagines expressæ et illustratæ." (Supplementum Panstratiæ Catholicæ, cap. vi. § xvii., In Chamier, tom. ii. Append. p. 23.)

The Fathers not only spoke of manna as a type of the Eucharist, but of the Red Sea also as a type of Baptism. See Albertinus, De Euch., p. 589. See also especially Morton on Eucharist, p. 213, ed. 1635.

folly by a *reductio ad absurdum:* "Adorara ergo et petram, quia Christum significat." (In Ps. ciii. Enar., Serm. iii. § 20, Op., ed. Ben. 1081, tom. iv. par. ii. c. 1163.)

Yet St. Augustine had taught (not less plainly than Agobard) that the rock is called Christ because of a relationship to Christ similar to that borne by the Eucharistic elements. And it is incredible he could have argued thus if he had known anything of a Real Presence to which adoration is due in or under the consecrated symbols. See Dr. Harrison's " Dr. Pusey's Challenge Answered," p. 351. See also above, pp. 77, 78.

And certainly, if a custom of adoring the host had prevailed in Agobard's time, he would have been called to inveigh against it with as much vigour as that with which St. Augustine opposed the worship of the sun.

It should be observed that our Venerable Bede had also, in the previous century, insisted on the same view of the Sacraments of the New Testament. See note above, pp. 78, 221, 222. See also Harrison's " Dr. Pusey's Challenge Answered," pp. 224—227.

Very many similar passages might be quoted from Bertram also, which could hardly have been written, if anything like the adoration of Christ really present in the host had been known in his day: or which, at least, would have demanded that, in consistency, he should have denounced any approach to such a custom. (See *e.g.* Quotations in Harrison's " Dr. Pusey's Challenge Answered," vol. i. pp. 186, 187, 190—194, 201—204.)

And yet the opponents of Bertram are not found urging against his teaching or his arguments the prevalence, or even the existence anywhere, of such a custom. Nor does Bertram himself ever allude to any such practice.

Rabanus Maurus also taught the same view of the Christian Sacraments in relation to those of the law; adopting the language of St. Augustine. (Enar. in 1 Cor. x., Op., ed. Migne, tom. vi. c. 88, 89.)

I must add, that the same argument may be pressed with great force from the teaching of Elfric. Surely what Elfric wrote about the Eucharist must have been written before the worship of the host was known in England. When Elfric's doctrine had been superseded by the doctrine of Lanfranc, adoration, and elevation for purposes of adoration, may doubtless have crept into the English Church. But as long as the doctrine taught by Elfric prevailed, it is incredible that such practices could have stood side by side with it, or have been introduced without vehement opposition. (See above, pp. 122, 123, 131, 132.)

NOTE B (p. 11).

On the Testimony of the Liturgies on the Subject of Eucharistic Worship.

THE entire absence * of all support of Eucharistic adoration (as addressed to any presence in or under the elements) from anything that can be alleged out of the ancient Liturgies † is a fact of much significance.

* It is said, indeed, in Dr. Rock's Hierurgia, p. 98 (2nd edit.): "The elevation and adoration of the Body and Blood of Jesus Christ in the holy sacrifice of the Mass, are to be found in all the Oriental liturgies, whether Greek, Syriac, Egyptian, or Ethiopic, and are distinctly pointed out in the liturgies of St. James, St. Chrysostom, and St. Basil."

But, assuming that it is meant that the Divine adoration is addressed to the real objective Presence of Christ's Person under the form of the elements, one's wonder at the assertion is only surpassed by the astonishment felt at Dr. Rock's supposing that such an assertion is substantiated by the extracts which he gives.

They tell, indeed, of adoration—which needs, I hope, no proof and no recommendation; but where is the evidence to show that the object of a Divine adoration is present (body, soul, and divinity) in the consecrated elements?

Other writers have candidly admitted the absence from the ancient liturgies of all support of *such* Eucharistic adoration.

Mr. Keble writes: "The only plausible objection that I know of, to the foregoing statement, arises from the omission of the subject in the primitive liturgies, which are almost or altogether silent as to any worship of Christ's Body and Blood after consecration. We find in them neither any form of prayer addressed in special to His holy humanity so present, nor any rubric enjoining adoration inward or outward." (Eucharistic Adoration, p. 126, Oxford, 1867.)

Another writer says: "The liturgies, we are told, do not speak of the presence of His adorable Person. Was it necessary that they should do so? His ordinary language, as to the Eucharistic gift, spoke of His Body, or flesh, and His Blood. The liturgies reverently adopted this language; and they (as a rule) left the inferences regarding His Person to the unfailing logic of Catholic faith and love." (The Church and the World, p. 326, 3rd edition.)

But surely in the one fact that the Liturgies tell of no such presence of Christ's Person in the gifts, and the other fact that modern (so-called) Catholic worship makes so much of the adoration of this Presence, we have strong evidence of this further fact, that since the liturgies were written a great change has been made in the *rationale* of Eucharistic worship, and such a change as points clearly to a change of Eucharistic belief. And then—How is the significance of this change affected by attributing it to Catholic instinct or to the "logic of Catholic faith and love," unless we are prepared to maintain that Christianity is a revelation in which new doctrines were to be added to the faith, as they might be developed by the operations of the human soul; and thus to deny that the Christian faith in its simplicity and integrity was once for all delivered to the Saints?

† Dr. Neale, indeed, says of a prayer which follows the consecration in the Liturgy of St. Mark: "This is called the Prayer of Intense Adoration, and answers to the worship paid by the Western Church at the elevation of the host." (Neale's Liturgies, Gr., p. 35.)

If there were any real weight in the argument based upon the

It may seem presumptuous to question the statement of one so deeply versed in liturgical subjects as Dr. Neale. Yet it is impossible not to desire some explanation of this assertion—something to point out wherein is the correspondence between the prayer he refers to and the adoration of the host.

The prayer commences thus: Δέσποτα Κύριε ὁ Θεὸς, ὁ παντοκράτωρ, ὁ καθήμενος ἐπὶ τῶν χερουβὶμ, καὶ δοξαζόμενος ὑπὸ τῶν σεραφίμ . . . σοὶ ἐκλίναμεν τὸν αὐχένα τῶν ψυχῶν καὶ τῶν σωμάτων ἡμῶν, τὸ τῆς δουλείας πρόσχημα σημαίνοντες. Its principal petition is ὅπως . . . ἀξιώς μετάσχοιμεν τῶν προκειμένων ἡμῖν ἀγαθῶν, τοῦ ἀχράντου σώματος, καὶ τοῦ τιμίου αἵματος τοῦ μονογενοῦς σοῦ Υἱοῦ.

Now this prayer is not addressed to Christ as present in the consecrated elements. It is not even addressed as to Christ at all. It is a prayer to the First Person of the Holy Trinity; and the parallel prayer in the Coptic of St. Basil (as given by Dr. Neale) is introduced by this rubric: "The Priest saith the prayer of bowing down to the Father." (See Neale's Introduction, Hist. E. Ch., vol. ii. p. 632; and Renaudot, Lit. Orient. Col., tom. i. p. 21.)

In Mr. Malan's version the prayer is simply introduced by the words τὰς κεφάλας. See Divine Euchologion, p. 34. See also the Syriac Liturgy of St. James the Lord's Brother, in Renaudot, tom. ii. p. 39.

Even Renaudot, who strongly argues for Eucharistic adoration, confesses: "Inclinatio capitis quæ hic præscribitur . . . non refertur ad . . . Eucharistiœ adorationem, sed ad suscipiendam benedictionem Sacerdotis, qua populus præparetur ad confessionem sinceram fidei." (Lit. Or. Col., tom. ii. p. 113. See the passage commented on in p. 39, Lit. S. Jacobi Frat. Dom.)

Archdeacon Freeman says: "There was one very solemn part of the rite, common to all liturgies, the 'bowing down' in the prospect of reception of the mysterious gifts. This, in the West, had long ago lost its proper meaning by the desuetude of the people's communion. But to interpret it as an act of worship of the elements would not answer the purpose, since it came at some considerable interval after the consecration. A new act of this kind, for priest and people, following immediately upon consecration, was necessary to be introduced, and was introduced accordingly." (Principles of Divine Service, vol. ii. par. i. pp. 57, 58.)

It seems then to me that to describe this prayer as answering to the worship of the Western Church, is equivalent to saying that in the Eastern Liturgies that which comes *nearest* to the adoration of the sacramental Body of Christ is a prayer of humble adoration to God the Father, as throned in the glory of heaven. And surely this is only another way of saying that there is nothing whatever in the liturgies of the East which, regarding its true *differentia*, answers at all to that which in the middle ages was brought in to form so strange and prominent a part in the worship of the Church of Rome. (See the argument of Mr. Sadler in "The Church and the Age," p. 300.)

The truth which is thus brought out is one which, indeed, is otherwise sufficiently clear; but it is one of such great weight in the controversy, that every additional evidence is of value.

The whole Eastern Church is thus seen bearing witness against that worship of the Western which is certainly not primitive, and which could hardly not have been primitive if the doctrine out of which it springs had been primitive.

Nor will anything alleged from Eastern practices, or confessions of faith of more recent date than the Latin influence and Jesuit intrigues, avail anything as evidence on the other side. See Smith's Account of the Greek Church (1680), "To the Reader," also pp. 141—151, 248—284; Ricaut's Present State of the Greek and Armenian Churches (1679), pp. 183—185, 434; Renandot, Liturg. Orien:. Coll., tom. ii.

doubtful, or more than doubtful, expressions * used by some of the

pp. 567—602; Covel's Account of the Greek Church (1722), Pref. pp. xi.—xviii., also pp. 129—147.

The former faith of the Greeks concerning the Eucharist may have been mixed with grievous error and much superstition, which, doubtless, paved the way for Roman doctrine; but their present belief as to the Eucharistic Presence has not been derived from the same source as their liturgies, which give evidence against it. (See Kimmel's Monumenta Fidei Eccles. Orient., p. 458, and Freeman's Principles of Divine Service, vol. ii. part i. pp. 71—74.)

Surely it is a matter of no small moment that we look in vain in all ancient liturgies for any support of that Eucharistic *cultus* which, by the confession of Romish doctors, is now a chief part of the religion of Rome. (See Cardinal Allen as quoted above, pp. 12, 13.)

* Of these expressions Archdeacon Freeman writes: "It has been said indeed, with some plausibility, that they carry weight as seeming to describe, not a passing feeling towards the consecrated elements, but a *habit* of actual and proper worship of them. But this, for reasons already set forth, is exactly what they cannot possibly be held to convey. We know with the utmost precision what was prescribed in the matter of worship by the Eucharistic offices of the Churches to which these writers belonged, and that no such acts of worship of the elements are in any way recognised by them. We are under the absolute necessity, therefore, of giving up this view of the passages ; and it remains, that no feeling or practice beyond that of the deepest reverence can be grounded upon them. To build upon them anything further, is to represent these holy men of old time as teaching what the Church had never taught them, and to set the testimony of these few and equivocal passages against the tradition of the whole Church from the beginning." (Freeman's Principles of Divine Service, vol. ii. part i. pp. 184, 185.)

" When Scripture and all other reasons fail them, as they generally do, then they fly to the Fathers; as those who are sensible their forces are too weak to keep the open field, fly to the woods or the mountains, where they know but very few can follow them. I take it to be sufficient, that in any necessary article of faith, or essential part of Christian worship (which this of the sacrament must be, if it be any part at all), it is sufficient that we have the Scripture for us, or that the Scripture is silent, and speaks of no more than what we own and admit. In other external and indifferent matters relating merely to the circumstances of worship, the Church may, for outward order and decency, appoint what the Scripture does not. But as to what we are to believe, and what we are to worship, the most positive argument from any human authority is of no weight where there is but a negative from Scripture. But we have such a due regard to antiquity, and are so well assured of our cause, were it to be tried only by that, and not by Scripture—which the Church of Rome generally demurs to—that we shall not fear to allow them to bring all the Fathers they can for their witnesses in this matter, and we shall not in the least decline their testimony. Boileau musters up a great many, some of which are wholly impertinent and insignificant to the matter in hand, and none of them speaks home to the business he brings them for. He was to prove that they taught that the sacrament was to be adored, as it is in the Church of Rome; but they only teach as we do, ' that it is to be had in great reverence and respect,' as all other things relating to the Divine worship ; ' that it is to be received with great devotion, both of body and soul,' and in such a posture as is to express this, 'a posture of adoration'; that Christ is then to be worshipped by us in this office especially, as well as He is in all other offices of our religion ; that His Body and His Flesh, which is united to His Divinity, and which He offered up to His Father as a sacrifice for all mankind, and by which we are redeemed, and which we do spiritually partake of in the Sacrament,

ancient Fathers, it would be much more than counterbalanced by the argument which rests upon this Liturgical silence.*

that this is to be adored by us; but not as being corporeally present there, or that the sacrament is to be worshipped with that or for the sake of that; or that which the priest holds up in his hands or lies upon the altar, is to be the object of our adoration,—but only Christ and His blessed Body, which is in heaven." (Prebendary Payne, in Gibson's Preservative, vol. x. pp. 144, 145, London, 1848.)

* "It is difficult, if not impossible, to find in any really ancient liturgy, or portion of a liturgy, a single expression which *goes beyond* the recognition of the elements as the Body and Blood of Christ; any which identifies them with Christ Himself, much less with the triune God. It would not have been surprising had the glowing language, which has been now quoted, here and there overflowed in the liturgies the just bounds of the mystery, as unquestionably is sometimes the case with ancient writers on the Eucharist. But it should seem that the Church's conception of the true nature of that mystery was too fixed and clear to admit any such departure from correct Eucharistic language. Certain it is, that those who have searched most diligently for such expressions, and were every way concerned to produce them if possible, have failed in the attempt. Thus Muratori, than whom few had a more exact acquaintance with the subject, has only been able to produce three or four such expressions; and these are found either in confessedly late liturgies, bearing the marks of obscure and individual teachers, or in later additions to the ancient ones.

"It is in a prayer of comparatively late origin in St. Chrysostom's Liturgy—the present Greek rite—that he finds even the words: 'Thou art He that offered and art offered, and receivest and art distributed,—Christ our God'; expressions all defensible enough as the warm language of devotion, but a manifest departure from the general manner of the liturgies, and not capable of being insisted on in their literal signification. It is among the *cantica*, or hymns, of the Syriac Liturgy of St. James, known to be of more recent origin than the general structure of the rite, that such expressions occur as: 'Whom Moses saw in the bush, and Ezekiel upon the cherubim, He Himself is placed upon the holy altar, and the people receive Him and live.' And again, a 'Prayer of St. James the Doctor' has: 'Father of truth, behold Thy Son, a Victim well pleasing to Thee; receive Him who died for me.' So in an obscure liturgy, attributed to St. James: 'The living Lamb of God is offered on the altar'; in that of James Baradæus: 'We offer Himself (Thy Son) for us'; and similar passages are found in that of John Bassora (650). Lastly, it is in a very late Syrian Liturgy attributed to one Gregory (1220), that the words 'Adore the Word the Lamb,' follow shortly after the consecration.

"There is, indeed, in the regular Syriac Liturgy, though not noticed by Muratori, one passage of awful tenor. It is, however, among the private prayers of the priest before reception, and is probably as recent as it is exceptional. The first three of these prayers, as some in the Roman rite, are addressed to our Lord,—a circumstance in itself very unusual, such prayers being generally addressed to the Father: 'Grant me, O Lord, to eat Thee holily;' 'Grant, O Lord our God, that our bodies may be sanctified by Thy holy Body, and our souls illuminated with Thy propitious Blood.' But the last to which I allude actually addresses the element of bread as God in these words: 'I hold Thee, who containest the ends of the world; I have Thee in my hands, who rulest the deep; Thee, God, I place in my mouth.' It would be contrary to the analogy of all other liturgies to doubt that this passage is of comparatively late introduction as great part of the Syriac Order confessedly is. And the like account is doubtless to be given of certain private prayers of the priest found in the ancient English uses, similar to the first three here spoken of. The awful profanity of the last is happily unknown to them, and I believe to the rest of the Western Church." (Freeman's Principles of Divine Service, vol. ii. part i. pp. 180—182.)

For small as may be the value of many of the deductions drawn from the positive teaching of these Liturgies, on account of the difficulty of determining what is really ancient in the midst of so many interpolations, the argument derived from what they certainly do not teach is in no wise diminished in force by anything that may be said as to additions made to their doctrine in more recent times.*

---

* Bearing this in mind, the general structure of the ancient Liturgies (to which we may with confidence attribute an antiquity greater than we could venture to ascribe to most of the prayers) should be carefully observed.

It will be found that the *change* asked for the gifts (a *change* which the Fathers rank beside other changes, as Cyril of Jerusalem says of it: Πάντως γὰρ οὗ ἐὰν ἐφάψαιτο τὸ ἅγιον Πνεῦμα, τοῦτο ἡγίασται καὶ μεταβέβληται, Myst. v. § vii., edit. Toutte'e, p. 327) is not asked till after the oblation (most properly so called), and is asked for the purposes of communion.

Professor Heurtley says: "The liturgies of the Apostolical Constitutions of St. James, St. Basil, and St. Chrysostom are all cast in the same mould as that of Alexandria. The prayer for the descent of the Holy Spirit upon the elements, to make the bread the Body of Christ and the cup the Blood of Christ, is not offered till the oblation has been made. And in substance it is the same prayer in all, viz. that God would send His Holy Spirit, not upon the elements singly, but upon the communicants also—'upon us and upon these oblations,' and not simply that 'He would make the bread the Body of Christ, and the cup the Blood of Christ,' but that He would make them such in order that they might be to all who should partake of them, 'unto remission of sins, unto sanctification, unto eternal life'—language which is at least as consistent with what has been called the 'virtual' theory as with that of the so-called 'real objective Presence.'

"To understand, however, what the Fathers meant, when they prayed for the descent of the Holy Spirit upon the elements, it should be remembered that language of the same description was used in reference to the water in Baptism. Thus, for instance, Tertullian: 'Omnes aquæ de pristina originis prærogativa sacramentum sanctificationis consequuntur, invocato Deo. Supervenit enim statim Spiritus Sanctus de cœlis, et aquis superest, sanctificans eas de Semetipso : et ita sanctificatæ vim sanctificandi combibunt.' De Baptismo, c. iv. p. 225.

"See various other instances in Waterland on the Eucharist, ch. x. vol. iv. pp. 675, &c. Cyril of Jerusalem uses similar language of the chrism with which the newly baptised person was anointed: Ὅρα μὴ ὑπονοήσῃς ἐκεῖνο τὸ μῦρον ψιλὸν εἶναι· ὥσπερ γὰρ ὁ ἄρτος τῆς εὐχαριστίας, μετὰ τὴν ἐπίκλησιν τοῦ ἁγίου Πνεύματος, οὐκ ἔτι ἄρτος λιτός, ἀλλὰ σῶμα Χριστοῦ, οὕτω καὶ τὸ ἅγιον τοῦτο μύρον οὐκ ἔτι ψιλὸν, οὐδ᾽, ὡς ἂν εἴποι τίς, κοινόν, μετ᾽ ἐπίκλησιν, ἀλλὰ Χριστοῦ χάρισμα, καὶ Πνεύματος ἁγίου, παρουσίᾳ τῆς αὐτοῦ Θεότητος ἐνεργητικὸν γινόμενον. Catech. Myst iii. 3. See also ii. 3, where similar language is used of the oil of exorcism, wherewith the person about to be baptized was anointed before he entered the font: Τὸ ἐπιορκιστὸν τοῦτο ἔλαιον, ἐπικλήσει Θεοῦ καὶ εὐχῇ, δύναμιν τηλικαύτην λαμβάνει, ὥστε οὐ μόνον καῖον τὰ ἴχνη τῶν ἁμαρτημάτων ἀποκαθαίρειν, ἀλλὰ καὶ πάσας ἀοράτους τοῦ πονηροῦ ἐκδιώκειν τὰς ὑυνάμεις. Cyril speaks in like terms of Baptism, Catech. iii. 3.

"In the Salisbury Manual we have the following prayer at the consecration of the water to be used at Baptism : 'Descendat in hanc plenitudinem fontis virtus Spiritus Sancti, totamque hujus aquæ substantiam regenerandi fœcundet effectu.'" (Heurtley's Sermons on Recent Controversy, p. 58, 59)

The tendency of innovation was never to deduct from their doctrine.* Their silence, we may be sure, was never interpolated. And when it is pleaded, as in depreciation of this argument, that this silence may be accounted for by the prominence in these Liturgies of the sacrificial character † of the Eucharist, it deserves to

* "Now it has been before pointed out that for the determination of Eucharistic questions, the ancient liturgies are more weighty and trustworthy than ecclesiastical writers. What, then, is their testimony on this point? Nothing can be more unequivocal, nothing more unanimous. And be it observed, that their testimony on a point of this kind is beyond suspicion, since there was confessedly a tendency, as time went on, in the Churches to which these liturgies belong, to add to, rather than to diminish in the slightest degree, the reverence and awe with which the entire rite, and especially the consecrated elements, were viewed. Whatever aspect they exhibit, therefore, in that form which they had acquired by about the sixth or seventh century, and still retain, is likely to be an intensification rather than a relaxation of the earlier mind in point of reverent expression towards the elements. . . . Now it is clear, that if upon consecration a proper object of Divine worship is forthwith present, and demands and exacts such worship without fail; if it be so, that the majestical Throne of God is for the time transferred to the altar of the Church, or that the altar becomes His majestical Throne; then of necessity must real worship be *from that moment* obligatory. Nor could any feature be more indispensable or more universal than a provision for such immediate worship. But not only is such a provision not universal, but there is not, it is confessed on all hands, a single liturgy in the world that, within the period specified, contains such a direction for the faintest gesture of worship to be offered to the elements immediately on their consecration." (Freeman's Principles of Divine Service, vol. ii. part i. pp.170, 171.)

† Those who urge this argument (see Keble, Euch. Ador., p. 126), pleading the African rule, as set forth in the twenty-third Canon of the third Council of Carthage, A.D. 397, "Cum altari assistitur, semper ad Patrem dirigatur oratio," and alleging that "the *rationale* of the Holy Eucharist is to be a sacrifice offered by the Son to the Father," may be asked to observe in how many Eastern liturgies, as we have them now, are found prayers addressed evidently to the Saviour. (See *e.g.* Renaudot, Lit. Orient. Col., tom. i. pp. 15, 90, 91, 93, 96, 97, 98, 104, 105, 106, 107, 108, 109, 110, 111, 112, tom. ii. pp. 32, 128, 156, 165, 169, 183, 211, 224, 587.)

In some we find several prayers continuously addressed to Christ by name, while in not a few even the great oblation is offered to our Lord. This is the case with two Abyssinian forms, and with those ascribed to St. Gregory of the Coptic and Alexandrian Liturgies. It is so, also, with the two Syrian forms, in which the oblation is retained. Mr. Scudamore says he has not observed it in the Old Gallican Missals, but there are many instances of it in the Mozarabic. (See Notitia Eucharistica, pp. 564—567.)

Yet, if we except a prayer of comparatively late insertion in the Liturgy of St. Chrysostom, not found in the ancient Berberini MS.: "Thou art He that offerest and art offered, and receivest and art distributed, Christ our God" (see Freeman's Principles of Divine Service, vol. ii. part i. pp. 180, 181), which is very doubtfully an exception, and the Syriac prayers mentioned above pp. 197, 228, probably as recent as exceptional (see Freeman, Principles of Divine Service, vol. ii. part i. pp. 181, 182), in none of these cases (I believe) is prayer addressed to Christ as present after the consecration under the form of the host. At whatever date these prayers were added to the normal forms, they certainly bear witness that at *that* time and in that region the *rationale* of the Eucharistic service was not so understood as to make unsuitable direct addresses to the Incarnate Saviour. Surely then if, at that time, it was un-

be well considered whether this fact, as rightly understood, does not derstood that by the extension of the Incarnation, Christ (Body, Soul, and Divinity) was in the Eucharist really present after consecration, under the form of elements, we should expect to find all the prayers, after consecration, said to Him, bearing evident signs of being spoken to Him as thus sacramentally present in those visible signs. On such a supposition how is it to be accounted for that He should have been, in these prayers, addressed as in heaven, and not on the altar?

There is one prayer to which Mr. Sadler has directed special attention. It is in the Liturgy of St. James, and is addressed to Christ as "the heavenly bread," confessing that "I am not worthy to partake of Thy spotless mysteries," and asking Him "to make me worthy to communicate in the holy Body and precious Blood." Mr. Sadler says : "This is a prayer addressed to Christ, not as personally present in, or included under, the bread, but rather as external to it; external to it, I say, in this sense, that He who feeds us with bread (or prepares us to receive bread aright), must be in some sense external to the bread with which He feeds us ; and this prayer is addressed to Him as thus external. Whilst calling Him the Bread from heaven, it is plainly not addressed to Him as veiled under the bread in any sense, and it is the only prayer so addressed to Him in the Liturgy." (The Church and the Age, p. 301.

Not less observable is the prayer of the Mozarabic Liturgy (as given in Dr. Neale's "Tetralogia Liturgica," p. 130), which just precedes the consecration, and is probably of a comparatively recent date, see p. 252 : "Adesto, adesto, Jesu bone Pontifex, in medio nostri, sicut fuisti in medio discipulorum tuorum, et sanctifica hanc oblationem, ut sanctificata sumamus per manum sancti angeli tui, Sancte Domine et Redemptor æterne."

Here is, indeed, a prayer addressed to Christ, and asking His Presence, but it is certainly not addressed to Him as in the elements (for they are yet unconsecrated), nor does it ask Him to be present in the elements after consecration; but it asks Christ to be present as the *cause*, not the *consequence* of the consecration, the *consequence* of the consecration being simply "ut sanctificata sumamus."

And shortly after the consecration, before reception, the Priest says three times, in the chief festivals (see Neale, p. 255): "Vicit Leo de tribu Juda, radix David, alleluia ;" to which there is a response addressed to Christ, not as on the altar, but as in heaven : "Qui sedes super Cherubim, radix David, alleluia" (p. 168).

The following prayer (after consecration) from the Coptic Liturgy of St. Gregory the Theologian also deserves attention : "Cleanse us also, O our Master, *as* Thou hast *hallowed* THESE *gifts lying here*, and hast made them to become invisible out of that which is visible in them; and a mystery in that they *make one* THINK *of Thee*, O our Lord, and our God, and our Saviour Jesus Christ." Is it possible to read this prayer without observing how alien it is from that idea of Eucharistic worship which regards the Object of adoration as, in any way, personally united with the hallowed gifts? It is followed shortly by the "Prayer of bowing the head," the first division of which concludes thus : "Thou art King of us all, O Christ our God. And He to whom we *send up* glory, and honour, and worship, with Thy Good Father and the Holy Ghost." (Malan's Documents of the Coptic Church, pp. 79—81.)

Surely this praise is *sent* up, not to any presence in the host, but to a Presence on high, whose glory cannot be shared with any sacrament below.

Moreover, in the second division the prayer continues : "Thou art He who sits upon the Cherubim and Seraphim, and who looks upon the humble ones; Thou art He also, our Master, to whom we lift up the eyes of our hearts, O Lord our God.' (Ibid., pp. 81, 82.)

Thus with the consecrated sacrament before him, the Priest, addressing Christ, recognises no presence but that which from the height of heaven looks down upon the lowly, and to which His worshippers on earth are *to lift up* the eyes of their hearts.

in truth add force to the argument rather than detract anything from its cogency.

For it is, indeed, a very part of this sacrificial character of the Eucharist, as prominently seen not only in ancient Liturgies, but in the writings of the Fathers * since the time of Cyprian, that this sacrament bears so distinctly the mark of a mystical showing forth of the Lord's death till He come.

Hence Christ is here represented as the broken, the crucified, the sacrificed Saviour. This is, in mystical representation,† the slaying of the Lamb of God. The *res sacramenti* is here the sacrifice of Christ, or Christ evidently set forth crucified for sinners—His Body given as separate from His Blood outpoured.

And this being so, it must be obvious that this true *res sacramenti* is not only, as (in some sense) a lifeless thing, no true object of Divine adoration,‡ but also, however really present to the believing spirit, and however efficaciously present in its ordained proxies, in real substance distant, not in place only,§ but in time.

In this sacrifice all is what it is, not in real being, nor by any real objective presence, but in the way of vicarious representation, and ordained commemoration.

In those days (in the idolatry of the whole Pagan world, as well as in the ceremonial ordinances of the Jews), the very idea of worship was so bound up with the notion of sacrifice that the two terms might almost be said to be convertible; so that Divine worship was scarcely to be conceived without anything that should bear the name of sacrifice, and the character of an offering. To come in adoration before God with nothing, was abhorrent to the religious instincts of all people.

Christians had in the highest sense (and they readily acknowledged it, and endured ridicule for it) no real sacrifice to offer, because their one all-sufficient Sacrifice of propitiation had already, and once for all, been offered and accepted. They had learned to come before God as, in themselves, beggars, with nothing to give and all to receive. But

---

* See "Romish Mass and English Church," pp. 91—93.

† Ὁ γὰρ βασιλεὺς τῶν βασιλευόντων, καὶ Κύριος τῶν κυριευόντων Χριστὸς ὁ Θεὸς ἡμῶν προσέρχεται σφαγιασθῆναι καὶ δοθῆναι εἰς βρῶσιν τοῖς πιστοῖς. (Neale's Tetralogia Liturgica, p. 57. See below, Note F.)

The words of St. James's Liturgy: Ἴδε ὁ ἀμνὸς τοῦ Θεοῦ, ὁ Υἱὸς τοῦ Πατρὸς, ὁ αἴρων τὴν ἁμαρτίαν τοῦ κόσμου, σφαγιασθεὶς ὑπὲρ τῆς τοῦ κόσμου ζωῆς καὶ σωτηρίας (Neale's Liturgies, Gr., p. 73) should be read in connection with the report of Gelasius Cyz., quoted below, Note F.

‡ See above, p. 16.

§ See Papers on Eucharistic Presence, p. 401.

they had, in the language of Eusebius, "a * memorial instead of sacrifice," a pledge of Christ's love for the continual remembrance of His all-sufficient atonement and perfect redemption.

And this memorial was to be the memorial of Christ's *death*, and to be made by the *symbols* of His Body and Blood—of His Body as dead, and of His blood as poured out in sacrificial propitiation, as the Blood of the New Testament shed for the remission of sins.

Hence this true patristic view of the sacrificial character of this ordinance is really destructive † of that theory of the presence of Christ's Body and Blood which alone could justify the adoration of the host, or of Christ as really present therein. " Christ being raised from the dead dieth no more." His Body is not dead now, that it should be really present as dead anywhere.

It may, indeed, very well be that this sacrificial view of the Eucharist accounts for the fact that the worship of the Liturgies is chiefly addressed to the Father. It is, however, beyond dispute that some of the Liturgies contain prayers addressed also to Christ.

Now whatever may be the date at which these exceptional prayers were inserted (and they are doubtless no parts of the original Liturgies), they are certainly not addressed to Christ as on the altar, nor to Christ as present in the elements.‡

* See below, Note E. See also " Romish Mass and English Church," pp. 88, also pp. 85, 90 *sqq.*, 38, 39.

† " The Fathers look upon the bread and wine in the Eucharist as the representative Body of Christ, and thus Christ's Body is indeed present by that which is its proxy or pledge ; but this presence in a proper sense is absence, and does suppose it.

"I shall therefore here only insist upon one consideration of Christ's Body there, which can only agree to His representative Body, but not to the natural and glorified Body of Christ, viz. :—

"The presence of Christ's Body in the Eucharist, which the Fathers speak of, is of His Body as crucified, and slain, and dead. Now this cannot agree to His natural Body, which by our adversaries' confession is impassible and invulnerable, now it is glorified, and cannot admit any separation of parts, which crucifixion does suppose, nor die any more. It is plain by the words of institution, that the Body of Christ there spoken of is His broken Body, such as crucifixion caused, and His Blood is considered as shed and poured out of His veins, and separated from His Body, which our adversaries that speak of His Presence in the Sacrament do not believe." (Patrick in Gibson's Preservative, vol. ix. p. 179, London, 1848.)

‡ " But the truth is, as appears on the slightest examination, that devout prostration and adoration, which thus took place, was not addressed to the elements, or to any presence of God or of Christ on earth. It was, so far as it found utterance in words at all, expressly directed to God, or to Christ, in heaven, while its peculiarly profound character, and its outward gesture, were manifestly dictated by a sense of awe in the prospect of immediate *reception* of the awful gifts, and through them of Christ Himself.

" In the first place, this prayer of bowing the head, and this profound prostration, *take place before the elevation* (the real intention of which will be considered presently.) This alone entirely differentiates the action from the novel Western elevation

And this is in marked contrast to the adoration which has resulted from the Romish transubstantiation, and which naturally should result from kindred views of the Presence, such as are now being taught by some in the English Church.*

and worship immediately after the consecration, with which it has been usual to assume its identity or close resemblance. It is clear even from hence that it is not directed towards the elements at all. But next, the exhortation to the action is: 'Let us bow our heads to the Lord,' or 'to Jesus.' And *whither* the prayer was directed, the Liturgy of St. Chrysostom, the present Greek rite, plainly declares: 'Hear us, O Lord Jesus Christ, our God, out of Thy holy dwelling-place, and from the throne of the glory of Thy Kingdom, and *come* and sanctify us ; *Thou that sittest above with the Father,* and here unseen art present with us ; and *come* and *give us to partake* of Thy spotless Body and precious Blood.' Nothing could more distinctly exhibit the mind of the Eastern Church in reference to the nature and degree of our Blessed Lord's intervention and presence in the Eucharistic rite, than this prayer. He is addressed as in heaven, on the throne of His glory. ' He is prayed to *come and give* the worshippers of His own Body and Blood, then lying mysteriously on the altar. *They* are not deemed to be Christ Himself; they are clearly distinguished from Him. Yet all the time He is believed to be invisibly present: doubtless in that manner and sense in which He is present by His Divinity in all the ordinances of His Church; not in a peculiar manner, as the effect of the consecration of the elements. Both He Himself, as thus present, and His Body and Blood as sacramentally so, are recognised and reverenced ; but as in heaven, and as there only, is He worshipped." (Freeman's Principles of Divine Service, vol. ii. part i. pp. 173—175.)

* "In them" [the oldest liturgies and Eucharistic forms] "it appears that there was no such adoration to the sacrament till of late, for in none of them is there any such mention, either by the priest or the people, as in the Roman missal and ritual, nor any such forms of prayer to it as in their breviary. Cassander has collected together most of the old liturgies, and endeavours, as far as he can, to show their agreement with that of the Roman Church ; but neither in the old Greek, nor in the old Latin ones, is there any instance to be produced of the priests or the people's adoring the sacrament as soon as he had consecrated it; but this was perfectly added, and brought in anew into the Roman liturgy after the doctrine of transubstantiation was established in that Church, which has altered not only their liturgy, but even their religion in good part, and made a new sort of worship, unknown, not only in the first and best times of the Church, but for above a thousand years after Christ. Boileau finding this, though a negative argument, press very hard upon them (and sure it cannot but satisfy any reasonable man), that there is no direction in the ancient liturgies for adoring the sacrament; and it is very hard to require us to produce a rubric against it, when nobody thought of that which after-superstition brought in ; he would fain, therefore, find something in an old liturgy that should look like that of their own. And no doubt but he might have easily met with abundant places for their worshipping and adoring God and Christ at that solemn office of the Christian worship, the blessed sacrament; and therefore out of the liturgy called St. Chrysostom's—which he owns to be two hundred years later than St. Chrysostom—he produces a place, wherein it is said, that 'the priest and the deacons worship in the place they are in, and likewise the people,' But do they worship the sacrament? Is that, or only God and Christ, the object of their worship there? Is there any such thing to determine this, as they have taken there should be in their missal? Where it is expressly said several times, they shall worship the sacrament; but here in St. Chrysostom's Liturgy it is God who is to be worshipped : 'God be merciful to me a

The argument, however, from the ancient Liturgies should by no means be weighed alone.

The ninth century, which saw the birth of the Paschasian doctrine, and the commencement of the Eucharistic controversy, saw also, not indeed strictly the commencement,* but the development of a literature " de rebus Liturgicis."

This new science (if it may be so called) may doubtless be regarded as indicative of something like a new phase of development on which Christianity was entering.

Yet the earlier Liturgical writers yield no support whatever to the new theories of Eucharistic adoration. And if they yield it no support, they certainly thereby add vast weight to the argument built on the absence from the Liturgies of anything which can be urged in their favour.

It is acknowledged that there is not a word to be found as to the elevation of the host immediately after consecration, for purposes of

sinner ;' but in the Roman it is the 'Sacrament is prayed to,' and they would reckon and account it as true religion not to worship and pray to that as not to worship God and Christ. So in the liturgy that goes under the name of St. James, the worship is only before the holy table, as it is in the Church of England; and I hope Boileau will not pretend that this is to the holy table itself. If whatever we worship before is the very object of our worship, then the priest is so, as well as the table ; but it is neither he, nor the table, nor the sacrament, but only Christ Himself, to whom this worship is or ought to be given at the celebration of the Eucharist; and therefore this adoration was as well before as after the consecration of the sacramental elements, and so could not be supposed to be given to them." (Prebendary Payne, Discourse on the Adoration of the Host, in Gibson's Preservative, vol. x. pp. 141, 142, London, 1848.)

* Before this (not to mention the works of P. eudo-Dionysius and others', two books "De Ecclesiasticis Officiis" had been written by Isidore Hispalensis in the early part of the seventh century.

Maximus, the Scholiast on Pseudo-Dionysius Areop., is also supposed to have written in the seventh century.

Alcuin died very early in the ninth century. But the " De Divinis Officiis Liber," which passed under his name, was not his.

The "Ordo Romanus " (in its present form) appears to belong to the eleventh century. (See Claude, Cath. Doct. of Euch., part ii. p. 71.) But it originally appeared in the eighth century. Cave says: " Usserium sicuti circa annum 730 collocamus." (Hist. Lit., p. 342.) He adds: " Non pauca observari possunt, quœ tempora ævum Carolinum sequentia manifesto sapiunt." See also Albertinus, De Eucharistia, p. 917.

Morinus says : " Posterior " [Henrico primo Francorum Rege] "est Ordo Romanus in Bibliotheca Patrum editus, cujus scriptio . . . vix ad ætatem illam pertingit. Id ex fine non inevidenter constat." (De Sacris Ordinationibus, pars iii. exercit. ix., De Diaconatu, cap. i. p. 133, Antwerp, 1685.)

The " Theoria rerum Ecclesiasticarum " of Germanns is of uncertain date, seeing it is a question whether it was written by the Patriarch of Constantinople in the eighth century, or by one of the same name in the thirteenth. Cave attributes it to the latter. (See Hist. Lit., p. 493.)

adoration, in the writings attributed to Alcuinus, nor in those of Amalarius,* or Florus Magister. Rabanus Maurus,† in his work

* Amalarius has a chapter "De adoratione Sanctæ Crucis" (Hittorpius, De Cath. Eccles. Divinis Officiis, pp. 108 sqq , Rome, 1591), but nothing on the adoration of the host.
Muratori, indeed, quotes from Amalarius (De Divin. Offic., lib. iii. c. 23): "Perseverant retro stantes inclinati, usque dum dicatur, Sed libera nos a malo" (see Hittorpius, p. 165, Rome, 1591), and then he adds: "Hoc est, adorationem per totum canonem continuabant." (De Rebus Liturg., cap. xix., In Migne, c. 1008, In Lit. R. Vet., c. 234.) But it might with equal force be argued that the adoration of the host is practised in the English Church throughout the Communion service. (See Papers on the Eucharistic Presence, p. 575.)
Indeed Amalarius himself gives his reasons for this *inclination*, and they have nothing whatever to do with adoration of the Eucharist. He says: "Quod enim sequitur, usque, Per omnia sæcula sæculorum, expositio est novissimæ petitionis Dominicæ orationis. . . . Ipsi stant inclinati, donec liberarentur a malo. Hi enim sunt Apostoli, qui magna tribulatione erant oppressi: Antequam audirent Domini resurrectionem non se audebant erigere. . . . Sua inclinatione subdiaconi mæstitiam . . . signant." (Hittorpius, p. 165.)
These notions of Amalarius are ridiculed by Florus Magister (Advers. Amalarium, cap. ii. § 5, Op., edit. Migne, c. 81), but without a word to suggest the idea that a truer account of these ceremonies could be found in the doctrine of the Real Presence of Christ to be adored on the altar.
When therefore Mabillon (In Ord. Rom. Com. § vii., Mus. Itali, tom. ii. p. xlix.), followed by Lambertinus (De Sacr. Mis., sect. i. ch. cclxviii. p. 102, Patav. 1745), says "Hac corporis inclinatione *adorabant* sacram *actionem*, et sacra mysteria," we must understand (as in many early writings) the word "*adoro*" in that wider sense in which alone, I suppose, it can be applied to the "*sacra actio*." (See Dean Aldrich, Reply to Two Discourses, p. 39.) And even so, his assertion can scarcely be said to be fully supported by the words of Amalarius.
As to what Amalarius says in the preceding chapter (xxii.) of the veneration of the Divine Majesty and the Incarnation (which is relied upon by Le Brun, Expli. Miss., tom. i. p. 232), it obviously has reference likewise to mystical interpretation. Mark the words: "Angelorum concentus, dicendo Sanctus, &c. Majestatem Divinam introducit : Turbarum vero, Domini Incarnationem, dicendo : Benedictus qui venit in nomine Domini." And observe that all this is before entering on the Canon.
Muratori further quotes from the "Eclogæ" which bear the name of Amalarius (c. 1009). But the authenticity of these "Eclogæ" is questioned. (See Du Pin, Eccles. Hist., English trans., 1699, vol. vii. p. 159) Moreover in them the *adoring* of the "*Sancta*" should much rather, I think, be understood of the highest reverence towards sacred *things*, as effectual proxies representing the crucified Body and outpoured Blood of Christ, than of Divine adoration addressed to the Person of the Son, as really present under their forms.
† There is found indeed at the end of the first Book of Rabanus, "De Institutione Clericorum," a certain short chapter added, in which the elevation is spoken of and mystically interpreted. The words are: "Elevatio sacerdotis et diaconi corporis et sanguinis Christi, elevationem ejus ad crucem insinuat pro totius mundi salute." (Hittorpius, p. 279; Rabanani Mauri Opera, edit. Migne, tom. i. c. 324.)
But the genuineness of this fragment is very doubtful. Hittorpius says of it : "Additio quæ sequitur, in duobus quibus nos usi sumus exemplaribus, non erat." (See also L'Aroque's History of the Eucharist, Walker's translation, p. 103 ; Dallæus, De Rel. Cult. Obj., p. 237.)
Even if it were genuine, it would but support the statements of Germanus of

"De Institutione Clericorum," and in that "De Sacris Ordinibus," is equally silent. And so is Walafrid Strabo in his book "De Rebus Ecclesiasticis."

Yet in the works of these writers will be found, treated at some length, various parts of the Liturgy in use in their days, not omitting such ceremonial particulars as in after times were embodied in rubrical directions.[*]

Nor are we dependent entirely on these later writers "de ecclesiasticis officiis" for our acquaintance with the usages of the Christian Church in the celebration of the Lord's Supper.

Constantinople, that the elevation of the host was for a commemoration of the lifting up of the Body of Christ on the cross.

Germanus says: "Elatio autem in altum venerandi corporis repræsentat Crucis elationem, et mortem in ea, et ipsam resurrectionem." (Germanus Constant., Theoria Rer. Eccles., In Bibl. Max. Patr., Lugd. 1077, tom. xiii. p. 61.)

So Hugo de Santo Victore: "Post signa Crucis utraque manu elevat sacramentum corporis et sanguinis Christi, et paulo post deponit: quod significat elevationem corporis Jesu Christi in cruce, et ejusdem in sepulchrum depositionem, unde et calicem corporali palla tegit, quod significat sindonis involutionem." (De Offic. Eccles., lib. ii. cap. xxxviii., Opera, tom. iii. fol. 172, Venice, 1588.)

In this view of the elevation there is nothing to support the teaching of the adoration of the host, or of any similar doctrine. See below, p. 245.

[*] In the "Ordo de Feria VI. Passione Domini" of the "Sacramentarium Gelasianum" in the following rubric: "Istis orationibus suprascriptis expletis, ingrediuntur Diaconi in Sacrarium. Procedunt cum Corpore et Sanguine Domini, quod ante die remansit; et ponunt super altare. Et venit sacerdos ante altare, adorans crucem Domini et osculans. Et dicit: *Oremus*, et sequitur: *Præceptis saltaribus moniti*. Et oratio Dominica. Inde, '*Libera nos, Domine, quæsumus*. His omnibus expletis adorant omnes sanctam crucem, et communicant." (Muratori, Lit. Rom., tom. i. c. 562.)

This mention of the adoration of the cross makes very observable the omission of all adoration of the host. And this adoration of the cross follows immediately upon the placing of the consecrated elements on the altar, the priest then coming in front of the altar to adore not the host but the cross. And this adoration of the cross is repeated immediately before communicating.

This would little accord with the *rationale* of the Mass service as now expounded: "Whereas up to the consecration the priest inclined towards the crucifix, he makes his reverence after it to our Lord in the Blessed Sacrament." (Oakley's Ceremonial of the Mass, p. 63, second edition.)

Alluding to the prayer which anciently had place in the Sacramentary of Gregory (see below, Note E), in which the Eucharist is regarded as a "pledge and an image," Soames says: "Hence we can understand sufficiently why this pontiff's liturgical productions, like those of earlier periods, offer no directions for adoring the holy Sacrament. Fond as Gregory was of ritual pomp, who would expect him to enjoin the worship of a pledge and an image?" (Bampton Lectures, p. 371.) And he adds, in a note, "Of this fact anyone may satisfy himself who will consult Menard's *Sacramentary of Gregory the Great*. No rubric directing the adoration of the Eucharist will be found in that work. Nowhere is this omission more strikingly exemplified than in the rubric relating to the observance of Good Friday (p. 69). Among the ceremonies provided for that solemnity, are the adoration of the cross, and the

Beginning with Justin Martyr* (who gives us a somewhat detailed account of the custom in the second century), we have various notices of such observances as were practised by Christians in the Eucharistic service, and frequent interspersed allusions, in the writings of the Fathers; but among all these we find nothing to lead us to suppose that anything like the adoration of the host,† or its elevation for purposes of adoration, was known at all for many centuries in the Christian Church.

receiving of the Eucharist consecrated on the day before, and reserved for the express purpose of administration on that day. There is certainly, therefore, a sufficient opening here for any of those Romish usages which Protestants charge with superstition. . . . Who would have expected, at least who believes in the complete antiquity of Romanism, that these directions for carrying about the consecrated elements should have exhibited no trace of any direction for adoring them?" (Soames, Bampton Lectures, pp. 396, 397.)

* "Those most ancient writers, Justin Martyr, the author of the Apostolic Constitutions, and St. Cyril of Jerusalem, who acquaint us with the manner how they celebrated the Eucharist, which was generally then one constant part of their public worship; they give no account of any adoration given to the sacrament, or to the consecrated elements, though they are very particular and exact in mentioning other less considerable things that were then in use, the kiss of charity, in token of their mutual love and reconciliation; this Justin Martyr mentions as the first thing just before the sacrament. In St. Cyril's time, the first thing was the bringing of water by the deacon, and the priests washing their hands in it, to denote that purity with which they were to compass God's altar; and then the deacon spoke to the people, to give the holy kiss; then bread was brought to the bishop or priest, to which the people joined their Amen, the deacons gave everyone present of the blessed bread, and wine, and water; and to those that were not present, they carried it home. 'This,' says Justin Martyr, 'we account not common bread, or common drink, but the Body and Blood of Christ, the blessed food, by which our flesh and blood is nourished, that being turned into it,'—which could not be said of Christ's natural Body; nor is there the least mention of any worship given to that, as there present, or to any of the blessed elements. The others are longer and much later, and speak of the particular prayers and thanksgivings that were then used by the Church: of the Sursum Corda, Lift up your heart, which St. Cyril says followed after the kiss of charity; of the *Sancta Sanctis*, Things holy belong to those that are holy; then they describe how they came to communicate, how they held their hand when they received the elements, how careful they were that none of them should fall upon the ground; but among all these most minute and particular descriptions of their way and manner of receiving the sacrament, no account is there of their adoring it, which surely there would have been had there been any such in the Primitive Church, as now in the Roman." (Prebendary Payne, Discourse on the Adoration of the Host in Gibson's Preservative, vol. x. pp. 139—141, London, 1848.)

† " Ex Indiis et Japonibus in Europam per Jesuitas invecta illa Eucharistiæ glorificanda formula ita apud multos, præsertim Hispanos, invaluit, ut nihil nunc sit in omni eorum sermone crebrius. Jam si idem fuisset primi Christianismi sensus atque usus, extarent itidem in veris primæ antiquitatis monumentis aliquæ piorum illius memoriæ preces et gratiarum actiones ad sacramentum Eucharisticum directæ. At nullas extare videmus. Multas confessorum et martyrum veterum preces et gratiarum actiones in superiori disputationis parte attulimus, plures piorum ejusdem ævi infra opportunius ubi de Sanctorum cultu dicemus allaturi sumus. Omnes ad Deum

NOTE C (p. 14).

On Elevation, and its Relation to Eucharistic Worship.

IT must by no means be supposed that the elevation of the host, whenever it began to be practised, implied of necessity anything like an intention of demanding from the people the adoration of a Presence of Christ under its form.

Neither may it be thought that the practice of prostration, or other excessive signs of reverence, are any sufficient evidence of an intent to give Divine worship to any present object.*

If no other proof of this were forthcoming, it would suffice to point to the fact of the Eastern elevation† of the Gospel, and the signs of

directæ sunt; nulla plane ad sacramentum. Illam vero nunc apud Latinos frequentissimam, δοξολογίαν, Laus sanctissimo sacramento, non modo in vetustissimis Christianorum libris non extare; sed ne sequentium quidem ad nostram pœne memoriam sæculorum monumentis uspiam inveniri, ipsi in fallor, Jesuitæ confitebuntur, suamque hanc propriam esse laudem agnoscent, quod omnium mortalium primi tradiderint, quæ vera ac legitima sit glorificandi sacramenti ratio, ac formula. Etiam qui ante eos Eucharistiam adoraverant, hoc tametsi claro ac necessario adorationis (ut sic dicam) consectario abstinuerant tamen, pudore credo, deterriti, ne Deum de eo loco pellere viderentur, qui ejus apud omnes pios, et Judæos primum ; et deinceps etiam Christianos semper proprius in omni retro ecclesia fuerat. Cæteros mitto. Primis quidem tribus Christianismi sæculis, de quorum traditione nunc disputamus, nullam hujus glorificationis formulam, nullas ad sacramentum directas preces, aut gratiarum actiones occurrere, certum clarumque est ; unde illud porro quod concludebamus, sequitur, illum Eucharistiæ divinum cultum, ex quo omnis hæc tum glorificandi, tum precandi sacramenti consuetudo apud Latinos profluxit, nondum fuisse toto illo tempore apud Christianos cognitum aut factitatum." (Dallæus, De Cultus Religiosi Objecto, pp. 288, 289.)

* The words which are quoted as from Gregory I. go to show, that according to the theory by which image-worship was supported, prostration before a visible object may mean only adoration of an object called to mind thereby : " Et nos quidem non quasi ante Divinitatem, ante illam prosternimur, sed illum adoramus, quem per imaginem, aut natum, aut passum, sed et in throno sedentem recordamur." This language, however, is probably not Gregory's. (See James's "Corruption of S. Councils and Fathers," p. 144, London, 1843.)

This is still the theory on which image-worship seems to rest. (See Concil. Trid. Sess. xxv.) If then the elements solemnly carried in to be consecrated may so far only be regarded as signs of Christ, that they may avail to call Him to mind, I scarcely see why Romish divines, on their own theory, may not consistently allow the prostration of the Easterns at the Greater Entrance to be altogether freed from the charge of idolatry.

Of course, the soundness of the theory is quite another question. So is its relation to the Second Commandment.

† Of the Eastern elevation Cardinal Bona writes: " Habet exemplum in veteri Testamento hæc hostiæ elevatio : nam passim legimus partem victimæ a sacerdotibus

excessive veneration, amounting sometimes to prostration,* which are exhibited at its entrance.

But, in fact, we have abundant evidence that other causes were formerly assigned for the elevation of the sacramental Body of Christ; and that excessive† reverence, with every outward sign, at least, of elevatam coram Domino." (Rerum Liturgicarum, lib. ii. cap. xlii., Opera, p. 349, Antw. 1723.)

" Elevata est Eucharistia. Ergo adorata. Perpetuæ nugæ. Nonne enim elevatio in lege usitatissima inter sacrificandum?" (Chamier, Panstratia Cath., De Euch., lib. vii. cap. ii. § xvi. tom. iv. p. 166.)

"Elevationem legis; etiam Evangelii in Chrysostomi [liturgiâ]: et quidem ita, ut τὸ ὑψοῦν, quomodo sit accipiendum facile doceat, εἰσέρχεται ὁ διάκονος εἰς τὸ μέσον, καὶ στὰς ἔμπροσθεν τοῦ ἱερέως ἀνυψοῖ μικρὸν τὰς χεῖρας, καὶ δεικνύων τὸ ἅγιον εὐαγγέλιον, λέγει ἐκφώνως, Σοφία ὀρθή. (Ibid., § xliii. p. 168.)

"The deacon having received the book of the Gospel from the hands of the priest, *holding it on high*, that the people may the better see it, goes out at the north door of the chancel." (Smith's Account of the Greek Church, 1680, p. 130.)

Ὁ Διάκονος εἰπὼν τὸ, Ἀμὴν, καὶ προσκυνήσας μετ᾽ εὐλαβείας τὸ ἅγιον Εὐαγγέλιον, αἴρει αὐτό. (Rubric of St. Chrysostom's Liturgy. See Neale's Liturgies, Gr., p. 123 : see also p. 120. See also Fortescue's Armenian Church, p. 154.)

So also in the Roman Church, according to the "Ordo Romanus," the Book of the Gospel was "lift up by the hands of the deacon, and carried on his right shoulder." (See Morton on the Eucharist, p. 513.)

In the Clementinarum Liber V. tit. iv. cap. iii. is a condemnation of the Biguardi and Beguinæ for asserting "quod in elevatione corporis Jesu Christi non debent assurgere, nec eidem reverentiam exhibere." And the gloss on this alleges " Nam etiam cum evangelium legitur, curvari debemus." (Clementinæ, Antwerp, 1572, c. 297.)

"The copies [of St. Chrysostom's Liturgy] are very different ; for in that amongst the works of St. Chrysostom there is no mention made of adoring but once, when the Gospel is carried, and when 'tis lifted up ; because then the *choir* saith, *Come, let us worship and kneel down before Jesus Christ;* excepting that the priest and deacon bow the head, in several places of the Liturgy, before and after the consecration, and that the people are once warned to bow the head to give thanks unto God. Cassander represents another unto us in his Liturgies, of the version of Leo Tuscus, wherein there is no mention of adoration ; but is not so of two others which we have, one in the Library of the Holy Fathers, and the other in the Ritual of the Greeks by *James Goar*, of the order of Preaching Friars, for in both these there is frequent mention made of adoring. It is true these sorts of adorations are there practised before the consecration and after, which plainly showeth they were addressed unto God, and unto Jesus Christ, because the Bread and Wine by the doctrine itself of the Church of *Rome*, are not to be adored until after consecration. The thing will appear yet plainer, if we consider the prayers which be there made when they dispose themselves unto the Communion. *Lord Jesus* (saith the priest), *behold us from thy holy habitation, and from the Throne of thy Glory, and come sanctifie us, thou who art in the Heavens sitting with thy Father, and art here present with us in an invisible manner, be pleased to give us by thy powerful hand, thy pure and unspotted Body, and thy precious Blood ; and by us unto all the people.*" (L'Aroque's History of Eucharist, Walker's translation, pp. 558, 559.)

* See Romanoff's Liturgy of St Chrysostom, pp. 46, 49, 50 ; Neale's Tetralogia Lit. p. 227.

† Arcudius writes : "Populus . . . in Russiâ prosternit se, terram fronte percutit ac veluti præsentem in ea oblatione cœlorum Regem alloquitur, et adorat. Sic enim communiter populus credit. Quem divinum cultum, huic rei minime debitum, Græci

adoration, was exhibited at the entrance of the elements in the

... adeo tenaciter imbiberunt, ut si quis velit eos verum docere, atque ab hac corrupta consuetudine dimovere, omnino ipsis execrandus iste sit, et detestabilis, ac veluti hæreticus habeatur." (De Concordia Eccles. Occ. et Ori., Paris, 1672, p. 220, lib. iii. cap. xix.) "Populus Græcorum in eo vehementer errat, quod suis verbis dona, non Deum invocat et alloquitur. Non enim secus atque si esset præsens sacramentaliter Christus Dominus sub illis speciebus, eos populus respiciens et adorans ait, *Memor sis mei Domine in regno tuo.*" (Ibid., p. 221.)

Smith says: "The people during this procession show all imaginable reverence, bowing their heads, bending their knees, and sometimes prostrating themselves upon the pavement,... repeating these words, *Remember me, O Lord, in Thy kingdom.*.. This seems to be, and really is, ... the most solemn part of the Grecian worship.... After the consecration, when the symbols are exposed and shown to the people, the reverence is not half so great; only a little bowing of the body, which is soon over." (Smith's Account of the Greek Church, 1680, pp. 133, 135.) "When they receive the Sacrament they do not kneel, but only incline their body." (Ibid., p. 159. See also Ricaut's Present State of the Greek and Armenian Churches, 1679, p. 196.)

Dr. Neale writes: "The adoration of the unconsecrated elements by the people has given great scandal to many Latin, and some Greek, writers. It, however, is not a peculiarity of Constantinople, for we find it to exist in Ethiopia, where, as Alvarez informs us, the people fall down in reverence, and the bells are rung; in the Coptic Church, and, it appears, in the Syro-Jacobite." (Introduction, History of the Eastern Church, vol. i. p. 375. See also Tetralogia Liturgica, p. 242.)

Goar has laboured to excuse the Greeks from the inculpation of idolatry. One of his arguments is observable: "Nec si regis thronum, absente rege, venerentur Britanni concessi inanimæ rei regii honoris, confestim sunt accusandi." (Euchologion, p. 114.)

However, he has failed to give satisfaction on this point to doctors of his own Church.

But the important matter in this controversy is entirely untouched by the question of the Greeks' idolatry.

The only point which concerns us is clear. After such outward excessive tokens of veneration at the bringing in of the unconsecrated elements, no valid argument can possibly be built on any similar tokens afterwards in support of the adoration of the Host, or of Christ present under the form of the elements.

As a matter of fact the προσκύνησις of the Greeks after consecration appears to be far less conspicuous, and to have less of the character of true and proper adoration, than that before consecration. See Scudamore, Notitia Eucharistica, pp. 342, 596.

Dr. Covel, who had opportunities of observation, writes: "In the common daily Liturgies the elements are worshipped as they pass by *unconsecrated*, but are never worshipped by them after they are consecrated." (Account of the Greek Church, p. 102.)

And he tells us: "The laymen always stand upright at the Communion, without any sign of adoration at all." (Ibid.)

Again he declares: "The Greeks show such reverences for many, many other things which they count either sacred or highly good. Thus the priest and deacon in the Liturgy often bow *to the prothesis;* to the holy table, or high altar; to the holy things upon it; to one another; to the Gospel, and all the people do the like as it pass by in the procession, and the bishop or priest kiss it. And I have often seen Greeks, of good sense and quality, take up common bread that is fallen down and kiss it, and put it to their forehead. They will do the like to the Bible when they take it up; all bow to a cross; to pictures. ... Gabriel Philadelph saith the elements once offered to God are no more simple bread and wine, but have received more

R

Eastern Church, even before consecration.*

worth and honour as being a Divine gift, and therefore all orthodox Greeks adore them. . . . Gabriel Philadelph argues warmly, that they might as well worship the elements as the picture of Christ; and I must say the same of the saints' portions; they might as well (and surely they did as easily) worship them as they worshipped their picture." (Pp. 103, 104. See also pp. 34 and 102.)

So of the *ark*, whatever it be, which Dr. Neale (against the opinion of Renaudot) considers to be the *tabout*, "used for the reservation of the blessed Sacrament" in Ethiopia, we are told that "young and old, rich and poor prostrate themselves on the ground," as it is "carried in procession through the streets under the great umbrellas." (See Neale's Introduction, History of the Eastern Church, p. 186, note.)

Yet in the seventeenth century they seem to have had no elevation or adoration of the host after the manner of Romish mass.

Dr. Geddes says: "They do not elevate, nor worship the consecrated elements, neither are they kept after the Communion." (Church History of Ethiopia, London, 1696, p. 33.)

* This argument is obviously not at all weakened by the plea that such prostration, whether at the Lesser or the Greater Entrance, may have reference to a mystical signification in the entrance as representing the Advent of Christ, or His Ascension (Fortescue's Armenian Church, p. 153), or His triumphant entry into Jerusalem (see Goar, Euch., p. 114), or of His going to judgment and to death (Romanoff, Lit. of Chrys., p. 63), or of His Body being taken from Calvary to the sepulchre (Arcudius, p. 224). The point to be insisted on is this, that that which calls it forth is unquestionably not the *Real Presence* of the Body and Blood of Christ.

One account (as given by Symeon of Thessalonica) of the outward signs of adoration at the Greater Entrance is this—that it is a fitting prostration of the faithful to the priests, to beg their prayers in the sacred service. (See Neale's Tetralogia Liturgica, p. 242.)

Neither will the argument be deprived of its force by alleging an ignorant supposition of such a Real Presence.

Now, indeed, the uneducated may fall down as before the unconsecrated gifts, or address themselves as to a Real Presence in them. This is only what, from the natural growth of superstition, we should expect. But it is surely quite incredible that this was the original theory of the ceremonial. None will maintain that the Greek Church ever meant to teach a Real Presence in the symbols before consecration. Whereas to connect this prostration with some event mystically symbolised by the Greater Entrance would be entirely in accord with the genius of the Oriental Liturgies.

Raulin (as quoted in Scudamore's Notitia Euch., p. 380, 2nd edit.) maintains that such worship is merely $προσκύνησις$, and that any act of Latria would only be directed to that which is represented—a plea by which this prostration might be as fairly defended as that before images. See above, p. 239.

In the "Dux Viæ" of Anastasius Sinaita we find it said under Quæstio cliv.: Quando sacra synaxis seu Missa perficitur, primus introitus sacerdotis repræsentat primam Christi præsentiam." (In Bibl. Max. Patr., Lugd., 1677, tom. ix, p. 1040.)

In the *Chronicon Alexandrinum* it is said: "Cum Abraham Melchisedecem sibi occurrentem cum pane Eucharistiæ et calice benedictionis videret, pronus in terram Abraham in faciem procubuit, atque adoravit, gavisus quod videret diem Domini." (De Melchisedece.)

Here we have an example of prostration and adoration described with approval before that which was only a sign or figure, containing no Real Presence of the object of adoration. It seems analogous to the adoration and prostration of the Easter Christians at the Greater Entrance.

243

A certain lifting up and showing of the elements at the τὰ ἅγια τοῖς ἁγίοις* appears, indeed, to have been an ancient practice. †

  The marginal note on the passage in the *Bibliotheca Maxima Patrum* (Lugd. 1677, tom. xii. p. 383) is remarkable: "Figura Eucharistiœ adoratur ab Abrahamo, quanto magis ipsa Eucharistia est adoranda." The argument may be allowed if by adoration is meant only reverence due to sacred signs. But it is impossible not to observe how little may be meant by "adoration," and how futile is the argument from excessive tokens of veneration to a faith in the Real Objective Presence.

  * "*Sancta Sanctis*. Vix ulla cæremoniarum Liturgicarum pars est, quæ cum ista possit de antiquitate contendere, præsertim in Ecclesiis Orientalibus. Nam de illa formula, qua, ut ait Chrysostomus, sancti ad Eucharistiœ communionem soli vocantur, et illius et omnium aliorum Patrum Græcorum infinita extant testimonia. Illam disciplinam imitatœ sunt et huc usque retinuerunt omnes Orieutales Ecclesiœ." (Renaudot, Lit. Orient. Coll., tom. ii. p. 114.)

  Archdeacon Freeman's interpretation of these words, as if signifying or praying that these holy gifts might be accepted in the Most Holy Place (Principles of Divine Service, vol. ii. part i. pp. 175, 176) seems to be contradicted by the teaching of the Greek Fathers. "Chrysostomus fusa disertaque oratione hæc verba explicans, Homil. 17 in Epist. ad Hebræos tandem concludit εἴ τις οὐκ ἔστιν ἅγιος μὴ προσίτω. οὐχ ἁπλῶς φησιν ἁμαρτημάτων καθαρός. ἀλλ' ἅγιος. τῶν γὰρ ἁγίων οὐχ ἡ ἁμαρτημάτων ἀπαλλαγὴ ποιεῖ μόνον, ἀλλὰ καὶ ἡ τοῦ πνεύματος παρουσια, καὶ ὁ τῶν ἔργων πλοῦτος . . . Et S. Germanus paucis τοῖς καθαροῖς τῇ καρδίᾳ ἀξιοῖ ὁ Θεὸς δοῦναι τὰ ἅγια. . . . Cyrillus Hieros., Catech. 5, Myst. ἅγια τὰ προκείμενα, ἐπιφοίτησιν δεξάμενα ἁγίου πνεύματος, ἅγιοι καὶ ὑμεῖς πνεύματος ἁγίου καταξιωθέντες· τὰ ἅγια οὖν τοῖς ἁγίοις κατάλληλα." (Goar, Euchologion, In S. Joan. Chrysost. Missam, Not. 159, p. 126, Venice, 1730. See also Renaudot, tom. ii. pp. 114, 116, 607.)

  In the West the words seem to have been misunderstood sometimes of the "conjunction" of the elements, and in some of the provincial French missals *Sancta Sanctis* was altered to *Sancta cum Sanctis* to suit this misinterpretation. (See Scudamore's Notitia Eucharistica, p. 594; and Arevalus, as quoted in Neale's Tetralogia Liturgica, pp. 256, 257.)

  In the Armenian Liturgy, as translated by Mr. Malan, the formula is represented by the words "Unto the Holiness of the Holy" (literally "Holies"). See p. 47.

  † "In primitiva Ecclesia . . . Symbola Eucharistica, panis niinirum et vinum, paululum elevata et populo ostensa non autem supra caput ad adorationem elata fuerunt. Dionys. enim lib. iii. de Ecclesiast. Hierarchia sic scribit : 'Pontifex divina munera seu dona laude prosecutus, sacrosancta et augustissima mysteria conficit, et collaudata εἰς ὄψιν ἄγει in conspectum agitas, producit, per symbola reverenter proposita: et dona sacrificiorum commonstrans et sacram illorum communionem et ipse accedit et hortatur alios.' Sacerdos igitur non supra caput extulit aut elevavit symbola illa, sed in conspectum solum produxit, hoc est, commonstravit populo. . . . Neque enim ostendit, ut adorarentur, sed ut consecratum panem, adeoque paratam communionem indicaret, et ut populus ad communionem se pararet, atque ad mensam accederet : Hoc ex verbis Dionysii clare perspicitur, inquit enim *Dona sacrificiorum commonstrans ad sacram illorum communionem et ipse accedit et hortatur alios*." (Hospinian, Hist. Sacra, lib. ii. cap. i., Op., tom. iii. p. 27.)

  The following is from the paraphrase by Pachymeres of the Ecclesiastical Hierarchy of the Pseudo-Dionysius: "Hierarcha stans in medio selectos illos Diaconos sibi habet assistentes, hymnoque dicto divinissima consecrat sacramenta, et sub aspectum ducit ea quæ celebrata sunt, declarans ea Christi esse symbola [ὡς Χριστοῦ εἰσι τὰ τοιαῦτα σύμβολα], quoniam post cœnam *accepto pane* et quæ sequuntur item, *Hoc*

But it was certainly not anciently connected with any intention of exhibiting them for purposes of worship.*
In the Latin Church various † writers have given various reasons

facite in meam commemorationem. Ostendit autem, id est, tunc detecta sancta dona post preces attollit seu elevat, de cetero tecta manent usque ad tempus sumptionis." (Eccles. II., cap. iii. § ii. Par. Pac., tom. i. p. 316, edit. Corderius, Antwerp, 1634.)

Smith says: "The priest comes to the middle door of the chancel, and elevates the bread, which he afterwards breaks and divides into four parts." (Account of Greek Church, 1680, p. 140.) And Ricaut: "So covering again the chalice, which contains both species, he elevates it, and the people worship." (Present State of the Greek and Armenian Church, 1679, p. 198.) It has been inferred that, in earlier times, at this point the veil was drawn aside and the chancel gates opened, and the symbols shown to the people. Le Brun says: "S. Joannes Chrysostomus reclusum sanctuarium ait proinde spectandum fuisse, ac si cœli recluderentur ut Christus et Angelorum Chori Fidei oculis cernerentur; 'Vobis' inquit 'ipsi Regis mensam proponite; deserviunt ibidem Angeli, Rex adest; si mundis vestibus induti estis, adorate, et ad Communionem accedite.' Neque vero cæremonia hæc intermissa fuit; cum S. Germanus Constantinopolitanus viii. sæculo asseret adorandi Corporis elevatione Crucis elevationem, et Resurrectionem exhiberi." (Explicatio Literalis Miss., tom. i. p. 231.) See Chrysost., Hom. iii. in Ep. ad. Ephes., § 5, Op., ed. Montfaucon, tom. xi. p. 23.

Dr. Harrison, however, has given his reasons for thinking that Chrysostom's lang iage points rather to what took place before the elements were consecrated. (Eastward Position, p. 130.)

* "It seemeth likely that as well this usage, as also sundry others of apparel, of oil, &c., grew first from the imitation of the ceremonies of the Jews, among whom the priest, in the time of their sacrifices, held up the oblation before his breast. So in the primitive Church, whatsoever was offered by any man to the relief of the poor, it was taken by the priest, and holden up and presented to the Church, as a pleasant sacrifice before God. So Chrysostom saith, the priest in the time of the holy ministration lifted up the Gospel. His words be these: *Sacerdos in altum tollit evangelium.* And Nicolas Cabasilas likewise saith: *His ... peractis, sacerdos stans super altare, in altum tollit evangelium, et ostendit:* 'These things being done, the priest, standing over the altar, lifteth the Gospel on high, and showeth it.'

"But, that the holding up of the Sacrament should import adoration to the same, as Mr. Harding surmiseth, neither is it thought true by all others of that side, nor hath it any good savour or show of truth. Indeed great pardons and charters have been liberally given of late years for the better maintenance thereof. And Durandus saith, therefore elevation is made, *ut populus intelligat, Christum venisse super altare,* 'that the people may understand that Christ is come down upon the altar. But the old learned Fathers, both Greeks and Latins, when they held up a little, or showed the Sacrament, evermore they called the people to draw near, to receive, to be partakers of the holy mysteries, and to lift up their hearts; but in the time of the same ceremony they never spake one word of adoration. Pachymeres saith: *Sacerdos ostendit, hæc esse Christi symbola:* 'The priest showeth that these be tokens or signs of Christ.' He saith not, the Sacraments be Christ Himself, but tokens and signs of Christ. Maximus saith, ὅτι σύμβολα ταῦτα καὶ οὐκ ἀλήθεια: Symbola ista sunt, non autem veritas: 'These be tokens (of the truth), but not the truth itself.' And perhaps upon this occasion Beguinæ and Reguardi held, that no man ought to rise up or to give reverence at the elevation of the Sacrament." (Jewel, Works, P. S. edit., "Serm. and Hard.," pp. 512, 513.)

† "As for the Latins, the first that I remember, who bethought himself of finding

for elevation ;* but no writer seems to have distinctly connected the elevation with any purpose of adoration before Durandus,† in the thirteenth century; and he connects with it various other reasons. Nor has the vast amount of ability and learning devoted to the subject availed to bring any real support from antiquity for the elevation and adoration which are maintained in the Church of Rome.‡

out a mystery in the same elevation, was *Ives* of Chartres, at the end of the eleventh century; . . . when the Bread and the Cup (saith he) are lifted by the ministry of the deacon, there is commemoration made of the lifting up of the Body of Christ upon the cross." (L'Aroque, History of Eucharist, Walker's translation, p. 102.) See above, p. 237.

* "Yet are not they all of that side hitherto fully resolved touching their own elevation, neither when, nor where, nor wherefore it first came in use, nor what it meaneth. Some of them say the lifting up of the Sacramental Bread signifieth Christ's incarnation; some of them say it signifieth Christ hanging upon the cross: some of them, that it signifieth the taking down of His Body from the cross ; some His resurrection; some His ascension into heaven; some that it signifieth a sacrifice special, above all sacrifices : some others say that the priest lifteth up the chalice to signify that Christ, crying out with a loud voice, gave up the spirit. M. Harding saith : 'It is lifted up doubtless to the intent the people may adore.' Thus many and more mysteries they have imagined in one thing, and yet the same, as it is confessed, no key of their religion. Disagreement evermore argueth ignorance. St. Augustine saith : *Si vix aut omnino nunquam inveniri possint causæ, quas in istis rebus instituendis homines sequuti sunt, ubi facultas tribuitur, sine ulla dubitatione resecanda existimo:* 'If the causes which men followed in devising such things can hardly or never be found, I think it best, when opportunity and occasion is given, they be abolished and put away without scruple or staggering.'
"They have assayed earnestly to prove this ceremony by the warrant of God's word, as if God Himself had commanded it. Gerardus Lorichius saith : *Hunc ritum David videtur prævidisse in spiritu:* 'David seemeth to have foreseen this order in the spirit.' And to this purpose he allegeth the authority of Rabbi Johai, whom I marvel M. Harding had forgotten. Durandus, for the same, allegeth the words of Christ: *Ego si exaltatus fuero a terra, omnia trahem ad meipsum:* 'If I be once lifted up from the earth, I shall draw all things to Myself.' And to speed the matter the better forward, Linwood saith : 'The Pope hath given liberal dole of pardons.'" (Jewel, Works, P. S. edit., "Serm. and Hard.," pp. 508, 509.)

† "Sane, dictis verbis illis : *Hoc est corpus meum*, sacerdos elevat Corpus Christi. Primo, ut cuncti adstantes illud videant, et petant quod proficit ad salutem, juxta illud : *Ego si exaltatus fuero a terra, &c.* Secundo, ad notandum quod non est aliud dignum sacrificium, imo est super omnes hostias. Tertio, exaltatatio Eucharistiæ in manu sacerdotis signat Christum verum panem, per prophetas in Scripturis exaltatum, quando scilicet ejus incarnationem prophetizabant, unde Isaias : *Ecce virgo concipiet;* et hunc cibum fore cæteris excellentiorem. Similiter et de potu. Quarto, significat, resurrectionem. Quinto, hostia elevatur ut populus non præveniens consecrationem, sed ex hoc cognoscens illam factam esse, et Christum super altare venisse, reverenter ad terram prosternantur, juxta illud ad Philippenses : *In nomine Jesu omne genu flectatur, &c.*; et illum corde et ore adorent, juxta illud Apostoli ad Romanos : *Corde creditur ad justitiam, ore autem confessio fit ad salutem.*" (Durandus, Rationale D. Off., lib. iv. cap. xli. § 51, p. 265, Naples, 1859.)

‡ The uncertainty of the date at which the Latin elevation after consecration came into use is acknowledged by Romish divines. There is certainly no satisfactory evidence of anything like it for many centuries after the time of the Apostles.

246

That the practice of adoration addressed as to the host should have arisen after the prevalence and dominance of anti-Berengarian views

Goar says: "Longe post orationem Dominicam, brevi tamen ante communionem spatio, juxta Jacobi, Basilii, et Chrysostomi liturgias Dominicum corpus, non ita tamen ut a populo conspiciatur, elevat Græcus sacerdos. Ita ab antiquo fieri solitum indicat Dionysius 3 cap de Eccles. Hierar: τὰς δωρεὰς τῶν θεουργιῶν ὑποδείξας, εἰς κοινωνίαν αὐτῶν ἱερὰν αὐτός τε ἔρχεται. ... Sacer itaque panis (major Hostia) est qui elevatur: particulæ autem benedictionis nomine hic intellectæ, populo sacræ communionis cupido, voce τὰ ἅγια τοῖς ἁγίοις, promittuntur sumendæ. Cæterum de majoris Hostiæ a populo completa consecratione per elevationem conspiciendæ nihil apud antiquos rituum expositores Alcuinum, Valafridum Strabonem, et Micrologum legimus: licet hic de Hostia cum calice levanda, in fine Canonis proxime ad Orationem Dominicam non taceat, cap. 15 et 23, eo quod verba ista: Per ipsum, et cum ipso, et in ipso: est tibi Deo Patri omnipotenti, in unitate Spiritus Sancti: omnis honor et gloria, Corporis Christi ostensionem, et ex animo adorationem secum inferre videntur. Ibidem Ordo Romanus annotat Pontificem oblatam levare, et Archidiaconum attollere calicem. Quando vero consecrationi apud Latinos juncta fuerit Hostiæ elevatio, non plane constat. Stephanus Durantus ab ea numquam fuisse divisam contendit, sed infirmo juxta suam sententiam Dionysii et Maximi fundamento, qui scriptis suis, nonnisi Græcis ritibus suffragantur." (Euchologion, In S. Joan. Chrysost. Missam, Not. 157, p. 125, Venice, 1730.)

There seems a slight inaccuracy in the words "Pontificem oblatam levare" (as observed by Dallæus, De Rel. Cul. Obj., p. 237); the words of the Ordo Rom. are: "Archidiaconum levare calicem per ansas." (See Mabillon, Mus. Ital., tom. ii. p. xlix. See also L'Aroque's Hist. of Eucharist, Walker's translation, p. 103.)

Cardinal Bona declares: "Nec etiam liquet, quæ prima origo fuerit in Ecclesia Latina elevandi sacra mysteria statim ac consecrata sunt: in antiquis enim sacramentorum libris et in Codicibus Ordinis Romani tam excusis, quam MSS. nec in priscis rituum expositoribus, Alcuino, Amalario, Walfrido, Micrologo, et aliis aliquod ejus vestigium reperitur." (Rerum Liturg., lib. ii. cap. xiii., Opera, p. 349, Antwerp, 1723.)

And to the same effect Hugo Menardus says of the Roman elevation immediately after consecration: "Quem ritum non puto adeo esse antiquum, cum in nostris Sacramentariis MSS., et excusis et apud Pamelium nihil simile reperire sit, quemadmodum nec in veteribus Ordinibus Romanis, nec apud Alcuinum, Amalarium, Walfridum, et Rabanum, qui ordinem Missæ enucleate persecuti sunt: neque apud Micrologum, qui in eadem materia egregiam operam navavit." (In Gregorii Libr. Sacramentor., Paris, 1642, p. 373.)

The same testimony is given by Catalanus (Sacræ Cæremoniæ, tom. ii. p. 76, Rome, 1750).

Mabillon claims for the practice no higher antiquity than the middle of the eleventh century. He says: "Non statim post consecrationem in altum a sacerdote hostia, itemque calix primis illis temporibus efferebatur, sed sub finem canonis, cum diceret sacerdos: *Per quem hæc omnia, &c.*, erigebat se Archidiaconus solus: et cum diceretur: *Per ipsum et cum ipso*, levabat cum offertorio calicem per ansas, et tenebat exaltans illum juxta Pontificem. Micrologus, corpus cum calice tunc levatum fuisse, dicit in cap. 15, ubi nullam alterius post consecrationem levationis mentionem fecit. Orientales id præstant paulo ante communionem. Porro elevationem post consecrationem in Gallia, post *medium sæculum undecimum* videtur fieri cœpta, haud scio an paulo serius *in Ecclesia* Romana, tametsi utrobique ad consecrationem sacra mysteria adorarentur." (Mabillon, Mus. Ital., tom. ii. p. xlix. In Ordin. Rom., Com. vii.)

That there is mention made in Micrologus (eleventh or twelfth century: see Cave, Hist. Lit., p. 434; Soames's Mosheim, ii. p. 346), and in the "Ordo Romanus,"

is but natural,* and it may well be supposed to have preceded the decree of Honorius III. in 1219, enjoining that it should be encouraged by the instructions of the Priests. Yet there is some reason

of quite another elevation (if it may be so called), makes the evidence derived from the omission of all mention of *this* far more forcible.

Le Brun says: "Facile intellectu est, veram Christi præsentiam in Eucharistia a Berengario impugnatam esse xi. ecclesiæ sæculo; ac post ejus pœnitentiam, et mortem quæ in anno 1088 incidit, bene multos sanctitate præstantes viros non una ratione uti cæpisse, ut in erroris execrationem quem Berengarius disseminaverat, ac publicam veræ Christi in Eucharistia præsentiæ professionem Fideles adducerent ; et hanc quidem elevandæ Hostiæ originem, non aliam fuisse." (Explicatio Lit. Miss., tom. i. Præf., p. xxiv. See also tom. i. p. 232, and tom. iii. p. 277 ; and Alanus as quoted above, pp. 12, 13.)

The opinion of Le Brun is followed by Lambertinus (Pope Benedict XIV.), De Missa, sect. i. ch. cclxix. pp. 103, 104, 1745.

* The custom of elevation immediately after consecration appears to have originated with the Carthusians, about the middle of the twelfth century.

The first episcopal or synodical decree on the subject appears to be found in the Constitutions of Odo of Paris, 1197. Guido, a Papal Legate, being at Cologne in 1208, ordered "that at the elevation of the host all the people in the church should, at the sound of the bell, pray for forgiveness, and so lie prostrate until the benediction of the chalice." This was followed in 1219, by instructions of Honorius III. to the bishops of Ireland, that the priests should often teach the people that "when the salutary host is lifted up in the celebration of masses, everyone should bow reverently." And this rule was admitted into the Decretals by his successor Gregory IX. The Council of Mayence in 1261 ordered the people to be instructed that at the elevation everyone should devoutly bend his knees, or at least bow reverently. At first the purpose of this elevation appears to have been rather to quicken devotion than to present an object for adoration. But the transition was easy to an actual worship of the consecrated symbols. In 1287 we find a decree of the Synod of Exeter : " Let not the priest elevate the host until he has fully brought out those words [This is My Body], lest the creature be worshipped by the people for the Creator." Similar prohibitions in other Councils had preceded this. (See Scudamore's Notitia Eucharistica, pp. 547—549, where will be found much interesting information on this subject. See also Freeman's Principles of Divine Service, vol. ii. part i. pp. 87, 88.) Mr. Scudamore says (p. 546) : " This elevation and worship of the consecrated elements were unknown for more than a thousand years after Christ. They naturally followed on the reception of the mediæval dogma of transubstantiation, though they seem to have had very little authoritative sanction before that doctrine was formally adopted by the Church of Rome in 1215."

Before this, no doubt, the custom had arisen of suiting the action to the word " took bread " (as ordered in our Rubric), and then (more or less observably) raising the paten. But though this has sometimes been called the elevation, it must by no means be confounded with the subsequent Roman custom of elevating the host on high after the words *This is My Body*. (See Scudamore's Notitia Eucharistica, 2nd edit., pp. 602, 617.)

"Eodem propemodum tempore in scenam simul prodierunt fœdissimæ superstitiones ac corruptelæ, de Transubstantiatione, ac hostiæ adoratione, seculo perobscuro, barbaro, et Christianæ Reipublicæ multis de causis exitiali, ortæ. Par igitur erat, ut his inventis novellum εὕρημα adderetur, solemnis nempe hostiæ ostentatio, ut a populo, tanquam summum Numen, publice adoraretur." (Deylingius, Observ. Sacr., Par. iv. p. 395, Lips. 1757.

to think that such adoration did not very readily obtain footing in England;* at least not to the extent of setting its mark so distinctly as in continental churches, on the ceremonial of the Mass.

All elevation was distinctly prohibited in the first Prayer-book of Edward VI. And there is evidence of its being since regarded as a thing only not distinctly forbidden because of its being too obviously contrary to the doctrines and principles of the Church of England. (See Papers on the Eucharistic Presence, pp. 501—504.)

Renaudot has a long note on the Coptic Liturgy of St. Basil (Liturgiarum Orient. Collectio, tom. i. 244—250), which contains perhaps one of the ablest defences of the Roman elevation and adoration.

The attentive reader, however, cannot fail to remark that this note contains *two assumptions*, which, if they were granted, would doubtless remove all just cause of objection to the Romish practice, but against which we most strongly protest, and put in our appeal to the testimony of antiquity.

(1) It is assumed that the Real Presence in the elements was undoubtedly and universally held by faithful Christians from the beginning (p. 249)—an assumption of which it would be easy to say that it has certainly never yet been proved, and has, we believe, been many times effectually disproved. The reader may be asked to mark how Romish theologians have shown their perception of the evidence which lies against it, as indicated above, pp. 77, 83, 93, 95, 98, 102, 104, 106, 110, 124.

(2) It is assumed that the fact of adoration addressed to the Sacramental Presence in the elements by Christians of old time is clear from the testimonies of the Fathers (p. 249); whereas all attempts to prove this have resulted, as we are persuaded, in failure. (See above, pp. 203—224.)

* "The direction which was embodied in the rubrics of all other Churches and monastic bodies of the West, for the celebrant to kneel and worship the element, never found footing in those of the English Church. . . . And this peculiarity continued down to the very time of the revision of the offices in the sixteenth century." (Freeman, Principles of Divine Service, vol. ii. part i. pp. 84, 85.)

Elsewhere also some of the new customs were not always readily admitted. Martene says: "Canonici Lugdunenses ex antiqua ecclesiæ suæ consuetudine, hactenus stando Christum adorant, nec ullis unquam adduci potuere precibus ut priscum ritum immutarent: quibus superiori sæculo faverunt Cardinales Lotharingus et Turnonius, cum in regio Henrici II. consilio impetiti a decano urgerentur, ut propter invalescentes hæreses prostratione seu genuflexione eucharistiam venerarentur." (Martene, De Antiquis Ecclesiæ Ritibus, lib. i. cap. iv. Art. viii. § xxii., Antwerp, 1730, tom. i. c. 414.)

But if, putting aside these assumptions, and what is made to rest upon them, we examine the note carefully, with a view to ascertain what beyond this it is which Renaudot desires to prove historically, we are led to ask: What does the whole amount to, even supposing we accept all his conclusions? And the answer will be this : that

(1) As regards the Easterns there was a custom of raising the host (or rather the *spodicon* or *media hostiæ pars*) at the words τὰ ἅγια τοῖς ἁγίοις (which was a sort of invitation to the communicants to come up and receive τὰ ἅγια, see pp. 246, 247, and p. 114, and which was shortly followed by the Communion); and that for this custom may be pleaded considerable antiquity—which none, I imagine, will care to question; and further, that this ceremony was accompanied by some sort of outward signs of veneration or adoration on the part of the people, which is certainly not improbable, seeing it is nothing more (and seems to be decidedly much less) than is exhibited at the carrying of the Book of the Gospels, and at the bringing in of the unconsecrated elements.

(2) As regards the Latins there was a custom of some antiquity of raising moderately the host and chalice before the Lord's Prayer (*hostia cum calice elevatur modice, paulo ante orationem Dominicam*, p. 248), which few, I imagine, would care to dispute.

But there are also some important concessions made in this same note—if indeed, as I suppose, the following statements may fairly be regarded as concessions.

(1) That the Roman elevation, immediately after the consecration, is an innovation, as late probably as the eleventh century. (P. 248.)

(2) That the elevation of the Greeks at the τὰ ἅγια τοῖς ἅγιος was not for the purpose that the elevated Sacrament might be seen by the people; and that, in fact, they were quite unable to see it (see Statement from Goar, p. 245, which I understand Renaudot to accept), though it is not to be concluded that this was *always* so. (See Le Brun, Explicatio Lit. Miss., tom. i. p. 231.)

Three observations on the note may suitably be added.

(1) The fact of the Greeks not being able to see this elevation (such as it is) is a very strong presumption against the notion of this elevation being originally for purposes of adoration, and against the supposition of the προσκύνησις (such as it was) being intended as divine worship addressed to Christ as present under the form of the elements. Mark the contrast with the Romish custom. There is good reason, indeed, to think that the custom which Goar describes is an innovation on an earlier practice which knew no such conceal-

ment. But it may be confidently argued that such an innovation never could have found place if this raising of the elements had ever been intended as an elevation for purposes of adoration.

(2) The oldest authority quoted by Renaudot for the elevation, "Severus, Episcopus Aschmonin," does suggest a reason for it, and that reason has no relation to adoration, but is that of representing Christ on the cross (*sicut olim elevatus est in ligno crucis*, p. 246), which seems also to have been among the older ideas in the Latin elevation. (See above, pp. 236, 237, 245.)

(3) This reason is quite sufficient to account for, and is probably the true explanation of, the fact that this elevation was accompanied by the prayer of the penitent thief on the cross (p. 246), which would naturally be suggested by it, or by the prayer "God be merciful to me a sinner," p. 245, or Kyrie Eleison (p. 246), and by the ὁμολογία (pp. 246, 251)*; neither the prayer nor the ὁμολογία giving any evidence of being addressed as to the host, or to Christ really present under its form.† (See quotation from the Patriarch Gabriel in p. 245, and from the Liturgy of St. Chrysostom, p. 246. See also Scudamore, Notitia Eucharistica, p. 596.)

Indeed it is worthy of special observation that in the Liturgy of St. Chrysostom this short ejaculation is immediately preceded by a longer prayer, addressed indeed to the Second Person of the Trinity, but not at all as present on the altar, though it seems by Le Brun (Expl. Lit. Missæ, tom. iii. p. 279) to be so understood. It evidently has respect to Him (while recognising His spiritual presence in the midst) as looking down "from His holy dwelling, and from the throne of His glory." Πρόσχες, Κύριε Ἰησοῦ Χριστὲ ὁ Θεὸς ἡμῶν, ἐξ ἁγίου κατοικητηρίου σου, καὶ ἀπὸ θρόνου δόξης τῆς βασιλείας σου, καὶ ἐλθὲ εἰς τὸ ἁγιάσαι ἡμᾶς, ὁ ἄνω, τῷ Πατρὶ συγκαθήμενος, καὶ ὧδε ἡμῖν ἀοράτως συνών· καὶ καταξίωσον τῇ

* So Angelus describing the manner of reception says : Ὁ δὲ μέλλων μεταλαβεῖν, ἐν τῇ στυγμῇ, ἐν ᾗ μέλλει μεταλαβεῖν, λέγει πρὸς τὸν Χριστὸν· οὐ φίλημα σοὶ δώσω καθάπερ ὁ Ἰούδας, ἀλλ' ὡς ὁ λῃστὴς ὁμολογῶ σοὶ, Μνήσθητί μοι, Κύριε, ὅταν ἔλθῃς ἐν τῇ βασιλείᾳ σοῦ (Enchiridion, Lips. 1600, § cccxxiii. p. 348), where there is nothing to imply that the words addressed to Christ are addressed to Him as really present in the bread.

† It may be observed that in St. Chrysostom's Liturgy we have this rubric, following upon the completion of the consecration : Καὶ τὴν κεφλὴν ὑποκλίνας ὁ διάκονος τῷ ἱερεῖ, καὶ εἰπὼν τὸ Μνήσθητί μου, ἅγιε Δέσποτα, τοῦ ἁμαρτωλοῦ, ἵσταται ἐν ᾧ πρότερον τόπῳ. (Neale's Tetralogia Lit., p. 142.) And the same direction is given in the Liturgy of St. Basil (Neale's Liturgies, p. 164).

It must be allowed, I think, to be a most extraordinary direction on the hypothesis of Christ Himself being just made present—Body, Soul, and Divinity—under the form of the elements.

κραταιᾷ σου χειρὶ, μεταδοῦναι ἡμῖν τοῦ ἀχράντου σώματός σου καὶ τοῦ τιμίου αἵματος, καὶ δἰ ἡμῶν παντὶ τῷ λαῷ. (See Neale's Tetralogia Liturgica, p. 172). And it is to be observed that this very same prayer, with slight alteration, is said by the Priest, prostrating himself, in the Armenian Liturgy, as given by Dr. Neale (Introduction, Hist. of Eastern Church, p. 642. See also Malan's Divine Liturgy of the Armenian Church, p. 47.) It has place also in the Liturgy of St. Basil.

Moreover the same prayer of the penitent thief is made at the Greater Entrance, when the unconsecrated elements are brought in in procession. Goar tells us: " Quidam inclinant, alii procumbunt in genua, in quibusdam etiam locis nonnulli, maxime ægritudine afflicti, pedibus se transeuntium substernunt: cuncti vero vel precantur, vel se celebrantium orationibus commendant, vel quod frequentius est, Christum quasi præsentem, *latronis in cruce penitentis* voce alloquuntur ... a qua voce repetenda nullatenus desistunt, usque dum stantibus ad sacras fores Lectoribus, ipsi per medios eorum ordines pertranseuntes, ad sanctum Tribunal pervenerint. Ibi a Pontifice, ordine, mutuisque precibus excipiuntur." (Euchologion, p. 113.)

As to the practice of the Greeks in the latter half of the seventeenth century in the matter of elevation, the following is the testimony of Dr. Covel: "There is no such elevation of the bread made by the Greek priest over his head, as is made in the Latin Church, but only he takes it up in his hand before him, as being ready to divide it, as followeth. And it is remarkable that in the Liturgy of the *Presanctified*, by an express rubric, *when the Priest is to elevate the Holy Bread, it is to be covered with the Aer*, and he only puts it in his hand and touches it warily; so that this is far enough from *showing it to the people*. I myself have been often an eye-witness of this, being permitted to stand by in the ἅγιον βῆμα, *Chancel*, and at their altars at Holy Fountains, during the whole service. Next there is no elevation of the cup at all amongst the Greeks, either anywhere mentioned or ever practised, as it is amongst the Latins. Again the Greek priest takes up only the biggest piece, or Christ's portion, to break it. . . . Goar himself confesseth that this elevation or taking up is not made so high as that the people may see it. And *Arcudius* says, indeed, an elevation is made at those words *Holy things to the Holy*, but the Eucharist is *not shown to the people*. Therefore if the word ὕψωσις, elevation or lifting up, and this ceremony or rubric, were at first here, I fancy it meant no more than to take the bread up to divide it."

(Account of the Greek Church, p. 76.) On this subject see also L'Aroque's History of the Eucharist, Walker's translation, pp. 104, 105. Also see above, p. 243 *sqq.*

In the Armenian Liturgy (as printed by Mr. Malan) the priest (just before the drawing of the curtain) raises the Holy Bread "*in the eyes of the congregation;*" but this is followed by an address to the people, which seems to be suggestive not of adoration but of the original object of the ostension—" Let us taste in holiness of the Holy, holy, and honourable Body and Blood of our Lord and Saviour Jesus Christ, who came down from heaven, and is now parted among us." (Malan's Divine Liturgy of the Armenian Church, p. 47.)

There is also in the Armenian Church a showing of the elements (or the vessels containing them) just *before* consecration. (Ibid., p. 10.)

Mr. Scudamore says: " The elevation of the bread, which takes place here in the Greek and Oriental rites, is not with a view to adoration. It is *only seen by those within the Bema*, the doors of which are still closed. The pure Armenian Liturgy merely directs the priest to ' lift up the sacrifice before his eyes' (see Dr. Neale's Introduction, Hist. of Eastern Church, p. 595); but there are copies, accommodated to Roman notions, which order him to ' show it to the people.' Pseudo-Dionysius only, about 450, speaks of the elevation (if in his time it could be so called) as a ' showing of the gifts.' At a much later period it is thus referred to by Symeon of Thessalonica : ' Having robed and lifted up the Bread, and proclaimed Holy things &c., he *invites* all holy persons to that Divine lively food of the Sacred Table, (that is) when he says, Holy things for the holy !' Dionysius Bar Salib : ' The priest lifts up and carries about the Sacraments, crying out and saying, Holy things for the holy.' James of Edessa : ' The priest shall proclaim to the people that the holy things of the Body and Blood are for those who are pure and holy, not for those who are not cleansed ; and, uttering these words with a loud voice, he lifts the Sacraments on high *for a witness* of that which he has just announced.' " (Notitia Eucharistica, p. 595. See also Patrick in Gibson's Preservative, vol. ix. pp. 246, 247, London, 1848.)

" There is no rubric prescribing, or prayer embodying, the adoration of the elements in any Greek or Oriental Liturgy." (Ibid., p. 596.)

" In the seventeenth century, however, the Greek Church became formally responsible for the same high worship of the elements as is practised in the Roman." (Ibid., p. 597.)

NOTE D (p. 47).

On Interpretative Dicta of the Fathers.

These interpretative *dicta* are chiefly, though by no means exclusively, found in the writings of St. Augustine. But, as propounded by him, they bear on their face the character, not of questionable or controverted statements, but of incontrovertible truths. Nor were they, so far as we know, in his days ever called in question by anyone.

Such are the following :—

I.

"Sacramentum, id est, sacrum signum." (Augustine, De Civitate Dei, lib. x. cap. v. See below, p. 276.)

II.

"Corporis autem ejus sacramentum multi accipiunt: sed non omnes qui accipiunt sacramentum, habituri sunt apud eum etiam locum promissum membris ejus. Pene quidem *sacramentum omnes corpus ejus dicunt*, quia omnes in pascuis ejus simul pascunt." (Ibid., Sermo cccliv. ad Continentes, Op., tom. v. par. 2, c. 1375, edit. Benedict., Paris, 1683.)

III.

"*Hujus rei sacramentum*, id est, unitatis corporis et sanguinis Christi alicubi quotidie, alicubi certis intervallis dierum in Dominica mensa præparatur, et de mensa Dominica sumitur; quibusdam ad vitam, quibusdam ad exitium : *res* vero *ipsa cujus sacramentum* est, omni homini ad vitam, nulli ad exitium, quicumque ejus particeps fuerit." (Ibid., In. Johan. Evang., cap. 6, Tract. xxvi. § 15, Op., tom. iii. par. 2, c. 500.)

IV.

"Quoniam omnia significantia videntur quodam modo earum rerum, quas significant, sustinere personas: sicut dictum est ab Apostolo, *Petra erat Christus*; quoniam petra illa, de qua hoc dictum est, significabat utique Christum." (Ibid., De Civitate Dei, lib. xviii. cap. xlviii.)

V.

"Videte ergo, fide manente signa variata. Ibi petra Christus, nobis Christus quod in altari Dei ponitur." (Ibid., In Johan. Evang., cap. 10, Tract. xlv., § 9, Op., tom. iii. par. 2, c. 598.)

VI.

"Solet autem res quæ significat, ejus *rei nomine quam significat nuncupari.** . . . Hinc est quod dictum est, Petra erat Christus. Non enim dixit, Petra significat Christum, sed *tamquam hoc esset,* quod utique, *per substantiam* non hoc erat, sed *per significationem.*" (Augustine, Quæstiones in Levit., lib. iii., Quæst. lvii. § 3, Op., tom. iii. par. 1, c. 516.)

VII.

"Non est dictum, Petra significabat Christum, sed Petra erat Christus. Nec dictum est, Bonum semen significabat filios regni, aut zizania significabant filios maligni: sed dictum est, Bonum semen hi sunt filii regni, zizania autem filii maligni. Sicut ergo *solet loqui Scriptura*, res significantes tamquam illas quæ significantur appellans, ita locutus est Dominus dicens, *Nunc clarificatus est filius hominis.*" (Ibid., In Joan. Ev., cap. 13, Tract. lxiii. § 2, Op., tom. iii. par. 2, c. 671.)

VIII.

"Omnes eundem potum spiritalem biberunt. Aliud illi, aliud nos, sed specie visibili, quod tamen hoc idem significaret virtute spiritali. Quomodo enim eundem potum? Bibebant, inquit, de spiritali sequente petra: petra autem erat Christus. Inde panis, inde potus.

---

* So another writer: "In multis sacræ Scripturæ imaginatis rebus verarum rerum nomina sæpe adscribuntur: Quomodo et prædicta virga in similitudinem serpentis imaginata, et phantastica illa majorum serpentium in Ægypto, et ille æneus in deserto serpens nominatur. Duo quoque Cherubim pro similitudine obumbrare propitiatorium memorantur. Quinque mures, et quinque anuli de terra Philistium in capsella cum arca Domini referuntur. Duodecim boves sub mari æneo, et quatuordecim leones in throno Solomonis eburneo statuuntur. Cherubim quoque et palmæ, et mala granata, et retia in templi ædificio depicta describuntur, cum hæc omnia non ipsa rerum veritate, sed pro similitudine ista nomina recipiunt. Ipsæ tamen Scripturæ sine ullo incertitudinis respectu quasi res veras hæc nominatim ponunt." (De Mirabilibus Sacræ Script., lib. ii. cap. xi., In Works of St. Augustine, edit. Benedict., Paris, 1630, tom. iii. par. 1, Appendix, c. 19.)

Of the freedom with which such language was used, let the following be taken as an example:—

"Melchisedech . . . in typo Christi panem et vinum obtulit; et mysterium Christianum in Salvatoris sanguine et corpore dedicavit." (Paulæ et Eustoch. Epist. ad Marcellam, Op. Hieron., edit. Vallarsius, Ep. 46, tom. i. p. 200. See Goode on Euch., i. 238.)

See other quotations in Albertinus, De Euch., pp. 395, 531. See also "Romish Mass and English Church," pp. 3, 4.

How easily such language might be quoted as good evidence of the primitive belief in the Real Presence of Christ's Body and Blood in the bread and wine which Melchizedek brought forth!

Yet how naturally such expressions are used by those to whom such a notion would certainly have seemed a strange conception indeed!

Petra Christus in signo verus Christus in verbo et in carne." (Augustine, In Johan. Evang., cap. 6, Tract. xxvii., Op., tom. iii. § 12, par. ii. c. 499.)

IX.

"*Hic est panis qui de cœlo descendit.* Hunc panem significavit manna, hunc panem significavit [*or*, significat] altare Dei. Sacramenta illa fuerunt, in signis diversa sunt: in re quæ significatur, paria sunt * . . . omnes eamdem escam spiritalem manducaverunt. Spiritalem utique eamdem: nam corporalem alteram, quia illi manna, nos aliud : spiritalem vero, quam nos." (Ibid., c. 498.)

X.

"Sæpe ita loquimur, ut Pascha propinquante dicamus, crastinam vel perendinam Domini passionem . . . . ipso die dominico dicimus, Hodie Dominus resurrexit. . . . . Cur nemo tam ineptus est, ut nos ita loquentes arguet esse mentitos, nisi quia istos dies secundum illorum, quibus hæc gesta sunt, *similitudinem* nuncupamus, ut dicatur ipse dies qui non est ipse, sed revolutione temporis *similis* ejus? . . . . Nonne semel immolatus est Christus in seipso, et tamen . . . . omni die populis immolatur, nec utique mentitur, qui interrogatus eum responderit immolari. Si enim sacramenta † quandam *similitudinem*

---

* It is evident that these words were relied upon in after ages by those who opposed the Real Objective doctrine, and that their force was felt by the opponents of Berengarius as yielding decided support to his views. See Rupertus Tuitiensis, In Joan., lib. vi., Opera, edit. Migne, tom. lii. c. 463.

Rupert, for the malutenance of his own position, finds himself obliged to bend his arguments against the teaching of St. Augustine himself. See especially c. 464, 469.

† With this compare the words of Amalarius: "Quæ aguntur in celebratione Missæ, in Sacramento Dominicæ passionis aguntur, ut ipse precepit, dicens : Hæc quotiescunque feceritis in mei memoriam facietis. Idcirco presbyter immolans panem, et vinum et aquam in sacramento est Christi : Panis vinum et aqua in sacramento carnis Christi et ejus sanguinis. *Sacramenta debent habere similitudinem aliquam earum verum, quarum sacramenta sunt.* Quapropter similis sit sacerdos Christo, sicut panis et liquor similia sunt Corpori Christi. Sic est immolatio sacerdotis in altari quodammodo ut Christi immolatio in cruce." (De Eccl. Offic., Præf. altera, in Hittorpius, p. 87.)

Let it be well observed how Amalarius, adopting the language of Augustine concerning the nature of Sacraments, follows out the idea into these particulars, in which he makes a parity of relationship, (1) of the Priest to Christ, (2) of the element to the Body and Blood of Christ, (3) of the act of the Priest in the *immolation* of *bread* to the immolation of Christ on the cross.

If, then, there is no real death of Christ on the altar, and no real presence of Christ in the priest, neither can there be a Real Objective Presence of the Body and Blood of Christ in the consecrated elements.

Moreover, the idea which Amalarius thus gives of the relation of the elements after consecration to the Body and Blood of Christ, viz. that of vicarious representatives, he expresses more distinctly in lib. iv. cap. xxv. of the same treatise (In Hittorpius, p. 169), where he says, "Sacerdos inclinat se, et hoc, quod *vice Christi*, immolatum est, Deo patri commendat."

earum rerum, quarum sacramenta sunt, non haberent, omnino sacramenta non essent. Ex *hac* SIMILITUDINE *plerumque etiam* ipsarum rerum nomina accipiunt.* Sicut enim secundum quendam modum sacramentum Corporis Christi Corpus Christi est, ita et Sacramentum Fidei Fides est. Nihil est autem credere quam fidem habere. Ac per hoc cum respondetur parvulus credere, qui fidei nondum habet affectum, respondetur fidem habere propter fidei sacramentum, et convertere se ad Deum propter conversionis sacramentum, quia et ipsa responsio ad celebrationem pertinet sacramenti. Sicut de ipso baptismo Apostolus, *Consepulti,* inquit, *sumus Christo per baptismum in mortem.* Non ait, Sepulturam significamus : sed prorsus ait, *Consepulti sumus.* Sacramentum ergo tantæ rei nonnisi ejusdem rei vocabulo nuncupavit." (Augustine, Epist. ad Bonifacium, Ep. xcviii., § 9, Op., tom. ii. c. 267, 268.)

XI.

Τῷ δὲ τῆς σαρκὸς ὀνόματι πάλιν καὶ τὰ μυστήρια καλεῖν εἴωθεν ἡ γραφὴ, καὶ τὴν ἐκκλησίαν ἅπασαν, σῶμα λέγουσα εἶναι τοῦ Χρίστοῦ. (Chrysostom, in Cap. v. Epist. at Galat. Comment., Opera, tom. x. p. 720, edit. Montfaucon.)

Elsewhere also Amalarius uses language expressive of the figurative relation of the *sacramentum* to the *res sacramenti.*
See Romish Mass and English Church, p. 66, and Claude's Answer to Arnold, par. 2, pp. 243, 245 ; Albertinus, De Eucharistia, pp. 925, 923.
With the language of Amalarius may be compared that of an author regarded by some as Joannes Hierosolymitanus (successor of Cyril, 386), blaming some Christians "qui nec considerant, nec intelligunt sacerdotes Christi, vicarios esse Christi, et Christum." (Com. in Matth. cap. vii. v. 6, Op., edit. Wastelius, 1643, tom. 1. p. 183.)

* With this the following should be compared : "Solent imagines rerum earum nominibus, appellari quarum imagines sunt. Sicut omnia quæ pinguntur atque finguntur ex aliqua materie metalli aut ligni, vel cujusque rei aptæ ad opera hujusmodi, quæque etiam videntur in somnis, et omnes fere imagines, earum rerum quarum imagines sunt, appellari nominibus solent. Quis est enim, qui hominem pictum dubitet vocare hominem ? Quando quidem et singulorum quorumque picturam cum aspicimus, propria quoque nomina incunctanter adhibemus : velut cum intuentes tabulam aut parietem, dicimus, Ille Cicero est. . . . . Et Pharao spicas se dixit vidisse in somnis et boves, non spicarum aut bovum imagines. Si igitur liquido constat nominibus earum rerum, quarum imagines sunt, easdem imagines appellari, non mirum est quod Scriptura dicit Samuelem visum, etiamsi forte imago Samuelis apparuit." (Augustine, "De Diversis Quæst. ad Simplicianum," lib. ii. Quæst. iv. § 2, Opera, edit. Benedict., Paris, 1685, tom. vi. c. 116.) See also "De Octo Dulcitii Quæst.," Qn. vi. § 3, Op., tom. vi. c. 134, where the same words are repeated. See also Isidore Hisp., Quæst. in Vet. T., Reg. ii. cap. xx. Op., edit. Migne, tom. v. c. 407, 408, where the words are quoted. In view of the comparison of St. Augustine's words concerning pictures or images, and concerning sacraments, the words of Theodoret should be noted as quoted below, Note E, in which is seen the natural transition of thought from the sacramental symbol—in its relation to the *res sacramenti*—to the picture of the painter in its relation to the ἀρχέτυπον.

XII.

Μυστήριον κιλεῖται ὅτι οὐχ ἅπερ ὁρῶμεν πιστεύομεν, ἀλλ' ἕτερα ὁρῶμεν, καὶ ἕτερα πιστεύομεν. τοιαύτη γὰρ ἡ τῶν μυστηρίων ἡμῶν φυσὶς . . . οὐ γὰρ τῇ ὄψει κρίνω τὰ φαινόμενα, ἀλλὰ τοῖς ὀφθαλμοῖς τῆς διανοίας. ἀκούω σῶμα Χρίστοῦ· ἑτέρως ἐγὼ νοῶ τὸ εἰρημένον, ἑτέρως ὁ ἄπιστος. (Chrysost., in Ep. ad Cor., Hom. vii., Opera, tom. x. p. 51.)

XIII.

"Hæc sacramenta sunt, in quibus non quid sint, sed quid ostendant semper adtenditur, quoniam signa sunt rerum, aliud existentia, et aliud significantia." (Augustine, Contra Maximum, lib. ii. cap. xxii. § 3, Op., tom. viii. c. 725, edit. Benedict., Paris, 1688.)

XIV.

"De signis disserens hoc dico, ne quis in eis adtendat quod sunt, sed potius quod signa sunt, id est, quod significant. Signum est enim res præter speciem, quam ingerit sensibus, aliud aliquid ex se faciens in cogitationem venire. . . . . Signorum alia sunt naturalia, alia data. . . . . Data signa sunt, quæ sibi quæque viventia invicem dant ad demonstrandos, quantum possunt, motus animi sui, vel sensa, aut intellecta quælibet. . . . . Odore unguenti Dominus, quo perfusi sunt pedes ejus, signum aliquod dedit: et *sacramento corporis et sanguinis* sui prægustato, significavit quod voluit." (Ibid., De Doctrina Christ., lib. ii. § 1—4, Op., tom. iii. par. i., c. 19, 20.)

XV.

"Quid mirum si aliis *mysteriorum signaculis* passio et resurrectio Christi *futura* promissa est, aliis *jam facta* annunciatur, quando quidem ipsa verba, futurum et factum, passurus et passus, resurrecturus et resurrexit, nec tendi æqualiter, nec similiter sonare potuerunt? Quid enim sunt aliud quæque *corporalia sacramenta*, nisi quædam quasi *verba visibilia*, sacro-sancta quidem, verumtamen mutabilia et temporalia." (Ibid., Contra Faustum, lib. xix. cap. xvi., Op., tom. viii. c. 321.)

XVI.

"Nimis longum est, convenienter disputare de varietate signorum, quæ cum ad res divinas pertinent, Sacramenta appellantur." (Ibid., Ad Marcellinum, Epist. cxxxviii. § 7, Op., tom. ii. c. 412.)

S

XVII.

"Hoc vero tempore postea quam resurrectione Domini nostri manifestissimum indicium nostræ libertatis illuxit, nec eorum quidem signorum, quæ jam intelligimus, operatione gravi onerati sumus; sed quædam pauca pro multis, eademque factu facillima, et intellectu augustissima, et observatione castissima ipse Dominus et Apostolica tradidit disciplina: sicut est *baptismi Sacramentum*, et celebratio *Corporis et Sanguinis Domini*. Quæ unusquisque cum percipit, quo referantur imbutus agnoscit, ut ea non carnali servitute, sed spiritali potius libertate veneretur. Ut autem literam sequi, et *signa pro rebus quæ iis significantur accipere*, servilis infirmitatis est; ita inutiliter signa interpretari, male vagantis error est." (Augustine, De Doctrina Christianâ, lib. iii. cap. ix., Op., tom. iii. par. i. c. 49.)

XVIII.

"Est miserabilis animæ servitus signa pro rebus accipere."* (Ibid., De Doctrina Christianâ, lib. iii. c. v. § 9, tom. iii. par. i. c. 47.)

XIX.

"Si ergo signum utiliter institutum pro ipsa re sequi, cui significandæ institutum est, carnalis est servitus, quanto magis inutilium rerum signa instituta pro rebus accipere?" (Ibid., cap. vii. § ii. c. 48).

XX.

"Hoc quod videtis in altari Dei, etiam transacta nocte vidistis: sed quid esset, quod sibi vellet, quam magnæ rei sacramentum contineret, nondum audistis. Quod ergo videtis, panis est et calix, quod vobis etiam oculi vestri renunciant: quod autem fides vestra postulat instruenda, *panis est corpus Christi, calix sanguis Christi*. Breviter quidem hoc dictum est, quod fidei forte sufficiat: sed fides instructionem desiderat . . . . quomodo est·panis corpus ejus? et calix, vel quod habet calix, quomodo est sanguis ejus? Ista, Fratres, ideo dicuntur Sacramenta, quia in eis aliud intelligitur. Quod videtur, speciem habet corporalem, quod intelligitur, fructum habet spiritalem. . . . . Si ergo vos estis corpus Christi et membra, mysterium vestrum in mensa Dominica positum est: mysterium vestrum accipitis. Ad id quod estis, Amen respondetis, et respon-

---

* Compare the following: Διαγελᾷν οἶμαι πρέπειν τοὺς ἀνοήτως αἱρετικούς, τὸ ἐν τάξει σημείου τεθὲν, εἰς ἀλήθειαν πράγματος ἐκλαμβάνοντας. (Cyrillus Alex., In Joan. i. 32, 33, Com., lib. ii. cap. i., Opera, edit. Migne, tom. vi. c. 213.)

This is spoken with reference to the appearance of the Holy Spirit ἐν τῷ τῆς περιστερᾶς σχηματισμῷ.

dendo subscribitis. Audis enim, Corpus Christi, et respondes, Amen. Esto membrum corporis Christi, ut verum sit Amen." (Augustine, Sermo cclxxii. Ad Infantes, Op., tom. v. par. i. 1104.)

XXI.

"Aliquando ad hoc fit eadem species, vel aliquantulum mansura, sicut potuit serpens ille æneus exaltatus in eremo, sicut possunt et literæ; vel peracto ministerio transitura, sicut *panis* ad hoc factus in *accipiendo sacramento consumitur.*

"Sed quia hæc hominibus nota sunt, quia per homines fiunt, honorem tamquam religiosa possunt habere, stuporem tamquam mira non possunt." (Ibid., De Trin., lib. iii. § 19, 20, Op., tom. viii. c. 803).

XXII.

"Potest sacramentum adoptionis adoptio nuncupare: sicut sacramentum corporis et sanguinis ejus, quod est in pane et poculo consecrato, corpus ejus et sanguinem dicimus : non quod proprie corpus ejus sit panis, et poculum sanguis, sed quod in se mysterium corporis ejus sanguinisque contineant." (Facundus Hermianensis, Pro Defensione Trium Cap., lib. ix. c. 5.)

XXIII.

"Sacrificium dictum, quasi *sacrum factum*, quia prece mystica consecratur in memoriam pro nobis Dominicæ passionis; *unde hoc eo jubente Corpus Christi et* sanguinem dicimus, quod, dum sit ex fructibus terræ, sanctificatur, et fit sacramentum." (Isidore Hispalensis, Etymol., lib. vi. cap. xix., Opera, edit. Migne, tom. iii. c. 255.)

XXIV.

"Multum hæc locutio notanda est, ubi aliqua significantia earum rerum, quas significant, nomine appellantur. Inde est, quod ait Apostolus: *Petra autem erat Christus.* Non ait, Petra significabat Christum. Solet res, quæ significat ejus rei nomine, quam significat nuncupari, sicut scriptum est, *Septem spicæ septem anni sunt.* . . . . Omnia significantia videntur quodammodo earum rerum, quas significant sustinere personas." (Beda in 1 Cor. x., Op., tom. vii. c. 357, 358, edit. Cologne, 1688.)

XXV.

Ἐν τῇ εἰκόνι ἄλλο οὐδὲν ὁ ἀληθὴς λόγος γινώσκει ἢ κατὰ τὸ ὄνομα κοινωνεῖν, οὗ τινός ἐστιν εἰκὼν, καὶ οὐ κατὰ τὴν οὐσίαν.* (Second Nicene Council, in Labbæus, tom. vii. c. 441.)

* This, of course, was not written with reference to the Eucharist; but when viewed in connection with previous extracts (especially Nos. vi., ix., xvii.), and the

It is important to direct attention to the fact that these *are* interpretative *dicta*. We appeal with confidence to the verdict of common intelligence, to say whether they are not so. And if they are, we assert with equal confidence, that it is impossible fairly to deal with them in the way of any such numerical calculation as would result in its being said, " Yes, it is granted there are a certain number of doubtful expressions which would seem to favour the notion of a Real Absence ; but see how they are outnumbered by passages which declare so plainly for the Real Presence." They may be vastly outnumbered by passages which call the bread and wine the Body and Blood of Christ; but these' interpretative *dicta* are *not doubtful expressions*, and if true, they have power to bring the others into harmony by a simple explanation—nay, they necessitate such an understanding of them, whereas all the others together can never explain away the one natural and obvious meaning of these. One saying truly interpretative, demolishes the argument built on the misinterpretation of any number of sayings, however natural or literal such a mistaken interpretation may have been.

As in answer to the charge, "You may pervert all the Fathers' writings, and make what sense you list of their sayings," it was well said by Bishop Bilson : " We measure their words by their own warrant, and suffer not a phrase here and there, which may be well revoked by their rules, to undermine the chief grounds of their faith. .... We show you the general admonition of the Fathers themselves, that after consecration they call the visible figures no longer by their wonted names, but by the names of those things whose signs they are and whose virtues they have. This rule we say is then to take place, when the speech which we find in a Father, 'if it should be referred to the things themselves, would be both absurd and repugnant to the rest of his doctrine, and to himself in other places. This is not to turn the Fathers whither we will, but to take heed we fall not into the pit, which they warn us to avoid." (True Difference, 1585, p. 768.)

Dean Goode says of the Fathers : " They viewed the elements as *representatively* and *in operation and effect* the Body and Blood of Christ, and spoke of them as such, freely calling them by the names of those things which they signified.

" They evidently considered this to be the language which was due to their *character* and *use*, and sanctioned by the example of our earlier application of the term εἰκών to the Eucharist (see below, Note E.), it may fairly, I think, be regarded as interpretative of those sayings in which the symbol is called by the name of Christ's Body.

Blessed Lord, and would have considered themselves as failing in the respect due to them, if they had not spoken of them in this way. And such language might have continued to be freely used, if the awful corruption of doctrine that has since taken place had not rendered it dangerous to do so. To a certain extent it is, and may properly be, used now; but not as it was in earlier times." (Goode on Eucharist, i. 321, 322.)

It will hardly be out of place to add here a few examples of what may be termed *interpretative modes of expression*—of sayings concerning the elements in their relation to the Body and Blood of Christ, such as could hardly have been used on the hypothesis of the Real Objective Presence, but such as square well with the words of Institution as interpreted by the *dicta* given above, illustrating and illustrated by the sacramental language of the Fathers.

I.

Ὅπως ἀποφήνῃ τὸν ἄρτον τοῦτον σῶμα τοῦ Χριστοῦ σου, καὶ τὸ ποτήριον τοῦτο αἷμα τοῦ Χριστοῦ σου, ἵνα οἱ μεταλαβόντες αὐτοῦ βεβαιωθῶσι πρὸς εὐσέβειαν, κ.τ.λ. (Liturg. of Apost. Const.* in Cotelerius, Autw. 1670, tom. i. p. 403.)

II.

"Cum dicat Christus, *Ego sum vitis vera*, sanguis Christi non aqua est utique, sed vinum.

"Nec potest videri sanguis ejus quo redempti et vivificati sumus esse in calice, quando vinum desit calici, quo Christi sanguis *ostenditur*."† (Cyprian, Epist. ad Cæcilium, Op., edit. Baluzius, c. 225).

* Compare Pfaffian fragment of Irenæus, quoted below, p. 287.

† "Cyprian, in a letter addressed to Cæcilius, is contending against the practice of certain heretics or innovators, who, in celebrating the Sacrament of the Lord's Supper, made use of water only, instead of water and wine mixed (for it was the custom to mix those elements in the Eucharist at that time, as it was in our own Church, till the Prayer-book of 1549 was superseded by that of 1552, not in all respects perhaps for the better). Now, argues Cyprian, 'Since Christ said, I am the true *vine*, the Blood of Christ is not water, but *wine*. Nor can His blood, by which we are redeemed and quickened, *seem* to be in the cup, when there is no wine in the cup, by which Christ's Blood is represented, and of which there is a mystical mention made all Scripture through :'—' Nec potest videri sanguis ejus, quo redempti et vivificati sumus, esse in calice quando vinum desit calici, quo Christi sanguis ostenditur.' And again in the same Epistle : ' For as Christ bare us all, since He bare our sins, we perceive that the people is *understood* in the water ; the Blood of Christ is *represented* by the wine:'—' Nam quia nos omnes portabat Christus, qui et peccata

III.

"Quæ [aqua] sola Christi sanguinem non possit exprimere."
(Cyprian, *ut sup.*, c. 229.)

IV.

"Invenimus calicem mixtum fuisse quem Dominus obtulit, et vinum fuisse quod sanguinem suum *dixit*. Unde apparet sanguinem Christi non offerri, si desit vinum calici; nec sacrificium Dominicum legitima sanctificatione celebrari, nisi oblatio et sacrificium nostrum *responderit* Christi passioni." (Ibid., c. 228.)

V.

"Videmus in aqua populum intelligi, in vino ostendi sanguinem Christi." (Ibid., c. 229.)

VI.

"Non reprobavit panem, quo ipsum corpus suum repræsentavit." (Tertullian, Contra Marcionem, lib. i. cap. xiv., Opera, edit. Rigaltius, 1689, p. 372).

VII.

"Panem Dominicum, quo Salvatoris Corpus *ostenditur*, et quem frangimus in sanctificatiouem nostri." (Theophili Alex. Paschalis ii. § 13, In Op. Hieronymi, edit. Vallarsius, tom. i. c. 595.)

VIII.

"Quæ [signa] unusquisque cum percipit, quo *referantur* imbutus agnoscit, ut ea non carnali servitute, sed spiritali potius libertate veneretur." (August., De Doct. Christ., lib. iii. cap. ix. § 13, Op., ed. Bened. 1680, tom. iii. par. i. c. 49. See above, p. 258, No. xvii.)

IX.

"Recte vini specie* sanguis ejus *exprimitur*." (Gaudentius Brix., Serm. ii., Op., edit. Galeardus, p. 33.)

nostra portabat, videmus in aquâ populum *intelligi*, in vino vero *ostendi* sanguinem Christi,—the word *ostendi* in the latter clause clearly in apposition to the word *intelligi* in the former, *i.e.* the element in either case is used *figuratively*; and to make the matter still more clear, Cyprian, having quoted a well-known text in the Epistle to the Galatians, adds: 'Since, therefore, neither the Apostle himself, nor an angel from heaven could preach any other doctrine, than that which Christ and His Apostles preached once for all, I marvel more than a little, whence it could come to pass, that in some places, contrary to the Evangelical and Apostolical discipline, water should be offered in the Lord's cup, when water alone cannot possibly express the Blood of Christ'—'quæ sola Christi sanguinem non possit exprimere;'—evidently implying that wine did *express* that Blood; not that it was the Blood itself." (Blunt's Early Fathers, p. 34.)

* On the sense of *species* see below, p. 276.

X.

"Panis, quia corpus confirmat, ideo Corpus Christi *nuncupatur*, vinum autem, quia sanguinem operatur in carne, ideo ad sanguinem Christi *refertur*." (Isidorus Hisp., De Eccles. Officiis, lib. i. cap. xviii. § 3, Opera, edit. Migne, tom. v. c. 755.)

XI.

"Sexta exhinc succedit conformatio sacramenti, ut oblatio, quæ Deo offertur, sanctificata per Spiritum sanctum, Christi corpori ac sanguini *conformetur*."* (Ibid., lib. i. c. xv. § 3, Opera, edit. Migne, tom. v. c. 753.)

XII.

"Calix enim Dominicus vino et aqua permistus debet offerri; quia videmus in aqua populum *intelligi*, in vino vero *ostendi* sanguinem Christi. Ergo, quando in calice vino aqua miscetur, Christo populus adunatur." (Concilium Bracarense III. A.D. 675, Can. i., In Carranza, Sum. Con., edit. 1778, tom. ii. p. 102.)

XIII.

"Quia ergo panis carnem conformat, vinum vero sanguinem operatur in carne, hic ad Corpus Christi mystice, illud *refertur* ad sanguinem verum, quia et nos in Christo, et in nobis Christum manere oportet." (Ven. Beda, in Matt. xxvi. Opera, edit. Cologne, 1688, tom. v. c. 77.)

XIV.

"Ergo quia panis corporis confirmat, ideo ille Corpus Christi congruenter *nuncupatur*. Vinum autem quia sanguinem operatur in carne, ideo ad sanguinem Christi *refertur*." (Rabanus Maurus, De Clericorum Institu., lib. i. cap. xxxi., Opera, edit. Migne, tom. i. c. 319.)

XV.

"Advertimus in aquis *figuram* gentium *demonstrari*, in vino autem sanguinem Dominicæ passionis *ostendi*." (Hom. de Corp. et Sang. Dom., formerly attributed to Eusebius Emissenus, in Op. Hieron., edit. Vallarsius, tom. xi. par. ii. c. 352.)

XVI.

"Videmus in aqua populum *intelligi*, in vino vero ostendi sanguinem Christi. Ergo cum in calice vino aqua miscetur, Christo populus adunatur, et credentium plebs ei in quem credit, copulatur et jungitur." (Gratian, Decret., par. iii. De Consecr., Dist. ii. can. vi. al. vii. p. 1264, Venice, 1567, as from Julius Papa.)

* See Claude, Cath. Doctr. of Euchar., par. ii. p. 92, London, 1684.

XVII.

" Ante benedictionem . . . alia species *nominatur*, post consecrationem corpus *significatur*." (De Myster. cap. ix. § 54, in Op. Ambros., ed. B., tom. ii. c. 339.)

To the argument from these modes of expression might suitably be added another from the use of such terms as *intelligibilis*, νοητός, νοούμενος, &c., as applied to the sacrament of the Eucharist.*
So Gregory of Nyssa: Ὁ γὰρ οἶνος τε καὶ γάλα τῇ γεύσει κρίνεται· νοητῶν δὲ ὄντων ἐκείνων, νοητὴ πάντως καὶ ἡ ἀντιληπτικὴ τούτων τῆς ψυχῆς ἐστι δύναμις.† (In Can. Cant., Hom. i., Op., ed. Migne, tom. i. c. 780.)

So Cyril of Jerusalem: Ἡτοίμασας ἐνώπιον μοῦ τράπεζαν· τί ἄλλο σημαίνει ἢ τὴν μυστικὴν καὶ νοητὴν τράπεζαν. (Myst. iv. § vii., ed. Bened., p. 321.)

So Chrysostom: Νοητοῖς αὐτὸ βλέπωμεν ὀφθαλμοῖς, οὐδὲν γὰρ αἰσθητὸν παρέδωκεν ἡμῖν ὁ Χριστός, ἀλλ' αἰσθητοῖς μὲν πράγμασι, πάντα δὲ νοητά. (Chrysostom, In Matt., Hom. lxxxii. al. lxxxiii. § 4, Op., ed. Montfaucon, tom. iii. p. 787.)

So St. Augustine: " Ibi petra Christus, nobis Christus quod in altari Dei ponitur, et illi pro magno sacramento ejusdem Christi biberunt aquam profluentem de petra, nos quid bibimus norunt fideles : si speciem visibilem intendas aliud est, si intelligibilem significationem eumdem potum spiritalem biberunt."‡ (Augustine, In Joan., Tract. xlv. § 9, Opera, tom. iii. par. 2, c. 598.)

* " Veteres quidem nonnunquam dixerunt, *Corpus Christi in pane esse intelligendum*, quemadmodum aiunt *Christum in petra fuisse intellectum*, ad designandum concipi debere velut ab iis significatum. Ac rursum, per *rem intelligibilem* Eucharistiæ interdum designarunt rationem formalem sacramenti qua sacramentum est, hoc est ipsius significationem . . . interdum *virtutem* sacramenti . . . quia tum *significatio*, tum *virtus sacramenti* non sunt res sensu perceptibiles, sed intellectu tantummodo comprehenduntur." (Albertinus, De Euch., pp. 5, 6.)

See Claude's Cath. Doctr. of Euch., London, 1684, part i. p. 157, who says: "Cabasilas speaks of the gifts, and says that the faithful adore, bless, and praise Jesus Christ, who is understood in them τὸν ἐν αὐτοῖς νοούμενον Ἰησοῦν. Now a man must be very little conversant amongst Greek authors not to know, that when a question is concerning the symbols, νοούμενον, or the τὸ νοητὸν, signifies the spiritual and mystical object represented by the outward sign."

† This is given as an illustration of the assertion διπλῆ τίς ἐστιν ἐν ἡμῖν αἴσθησις, ἡ μὲν σωματική, ἡ δὲ θειοτέρα.

‡ Hugo Lingonensis, writing to Berengarius, charges him with giving to the sacrament a *corpus intellectuale*. See Neander, Church History, vol. vi. p. 314, edit. Clark. His words are : "Corpus quod dixeras crucifixum intellectuale constituis. In quo evidentissime patet, quod incorporeum confiteris. Qua in re universalem Ecclesiam scandalizas" (De Corp. et Sang. Christi, In Bibli. Max. Patr., Lugd. 1677, tom. xviii. p. 417)—words which could hardly have been written when the faith of the Church was in agreement with the language of St. Augustine.

So *e.g.* Hesychius of Jerusalem : " Ipse Dominus primus in Cœna mystica intelligibilem* accepit sanguinem, atque deinde calicem Apostolis dedit." (In Levit., lib. ii., In Bibl. Max. Patr., tom. xii. p. 84*b*.

Again: "Tunc intelligibilem sanguinem super altare, videlicet suum corpus, effudit, corpus autem Christi Ecclesia est." (P. 85.)

And again : "Intelligibilem agnum,† Domini traditionem immolantes mystice." (Lib. vi. p. 153*b*.)

And again : " Neque enim aliter, sed per Ejus mediationem, et virtutem a sensibilibus ad intelligibilia transferuntur ea quæ in illo sacrificio peraguntur." (Lib. vi. pp. 153*b*.)

For illustration and evidence of the sense in which these terms are used by the Fathers, the reader may be referred to the work of Hesychius of Jerusalem, on Leviticus.

In this treatise, which is much occupied in interpreting legal types, he will find the thing or person signified constantly called by the name of the sign, with the addition of the adjective "intelligibilis."

Thus Christ is said to be the "intelligibilis Melchizedek" (In Levit., lib. vi. In Biblio. Max. Patr., Lugd. 1677, p. 153*b*); the "intelligibilis Aaron" (pp. 88*b*, 89*b*, 122*a*, 125*a*, 159*a*); the "intelligibilis Moses" (p. 91*b*); the "intelligibilis Agnus" (p. 153*b*); the "intelligibilis Aries (p. 120*b*); the "intelligibilis Sacerdos" (pp. 148*a*, *b*, 158*a*); the "intelligibilis Solomon" (p. 179*a*).

There we read also of the "intelligibilis hostis," *i.e.* the devil (p. 184*a*); the "intelligibiles inimici," *i.e.* "dæmones" (p. 184*a*); the "intelligibilis requies" (pp. 157*a*, 159*b*); the "intelligibile Sabbatum" p. 91*b*); the "intelligibilis Pharaoh" (p. 158*a*); the "intelligibile tabernaculum" (p. 124*a*); the "intelligibilis Ægyptus" (pp. 151*b*, 158*a*); the "intelligibile Pascha," *i.e.* the Lord's Supper (p. 151*a*); the "intelligibilis Ager," *i.e.* the Scripture (p. 182*a*); the "intelligibiles civitates," *i.e.* Prophetæ (p. 175*b*); the "intelligibile altare," *i.e.* Corpus Domini ‡ (pp. 64*b*, 89*a*, 122*b*) ; the "intelligibilis

---

* This, doubtless, furnishes the explanation of Chrysostom's διὰ τοῦτο τὸ ἑαυτοῦ αἷμα αὐτὸς ἔπιε (Hom. in Matt. lxxxii. al. lxxxiii. § 1, Op., ed. Montfaucon, tom. vii. p. 783), words which cannot be understood in the Romish and literal sense without doing violence to the teaching of the Fathers (see Albertinus, De Euch., pp. 538, 849), but which he himself interprets when he asks almost immediately afterwards τίνος σύμβολα τὰ τελούμενα;

† Compare Cyril. Alex. of the Ethiopian Eunuch: μέτοχος ἤδη τοῦ νοητοῦ προβάτου. (Glaphyr. in Exod., lib. ii. § 2, p. 270, Op., ed. Migne, tom. ii. c. 425.)

‡ It may be worth noting that in this sense Hesychius understands Heb. xiii. 10. He says: "Quia autem intelligibile altare Corpus Domini, et B. Paulus intelligit, ipso dicente cognosce, ait enim : *Habemus altare, de quo edere non habent potestatem, qui*

ignis," *i.e.* Spiritus (p. 89*a*); the "intelligibilis Cydaris," *i.e.* Christ's Divinity and Humanity (p. 90*a*); the "intelligibilis paupertas" (p. 183*a*); the "intelligibilis terra" (p. 183*a*).

So Origen writes: " Hoc est ergo signum ubi Jonas videbatur, et Christus intelligebatur." (Com. in Ep. ad Rom., lib. iv. § 3, p. 525, Op., ed. Migne, tom. iv. c. 968. See also below, p. 269.)

NOTE E. (p. 71).

On the Patristic Use of the terms FIGURE, TYPE, *and the like, as applied to the Eucharist.*

WITH a view to contribute something towards a just appreciation (in its bearing on the controversy concerning Transubstantiation*

tabernaculo deserviunt, corpus videlicet Christi dicens, de illo enim comedere Judæis fas non est." (P. 64.)

So Hugo Lingonensis writes: "In Christo hæc omnia. Ipse enim est sublime altare Patris, sicut Scriptum est. Putasne aliud esse altare ubi Christus pontifex adstitit, quam Corpus suum per quod, et in quod Deo Patri vota fidelium, et fides offeruntur?" (De Corp. et Sang. Christi, In Bibli. Max. Patr., tom. xviii. p. 419.)

* Bishop Cosin says: "Quum iidem ipsi sancti patres, qui de pane et vino S. Eucharistiæ, quasi de ipso corpore ipsoque sanguine Domini, quandoque loquuntur (usitatâ scilicet, ubi de sacramentis sermo fit, phraseologiâ,) eundem panem et vinum Eucharisticum, typos, symbola, signa, figuram corporis et sanguinis Christi, sæpissime vocent,—vel hinc manifesto liquet, eos cum protestantibus, non cum transubstantiatoribus, sentire. Possumus enim, incolumi nostrâ de sacramento Eucharistiæ sententiâ, prioribus illis uti locutionibus, quas sibi favere pontificii arbitrantur, modo eas (uti par est) sacramentaliter intelligamus. Posterioribus vero uti nemo potest, quin eo ipso, quod iis utatur, figmentum transubstantiationis evertet; quum ista duo, panem in corpus transubstantiari, et esse simul typum, symbolum, signum, figuram corporis Christi,—sint prorsus ἀσύστατα. Nam res, quæ desiit esse, alterius rei symbolum ac figura esse nequit; nec res ulla sui ipsius typus aut signum esse potest." (Works, A. C. L., vol. iv. pp. 105, 106.)

Dr. Pusey says: "This class of title, figure, type, image, symbol, were used by minds of every character in the ancient Church freely, naturally. The writers use them, moreover, not as if they were saying anything of their own, but as employing a current language. It is, so to speak, almost a technical, certainly a received language. ... There is no reason to question the genuineness of the fragment of Irenæus in which the expression [antitypes] occurs. Corresponding language is used by Tertullian; and the use of the term both in S. Basil's Liturgy and Apostolic Constitutions makes it probable that it was a received expression." (Real Presence from the Fathers, pp. 95, 96).

Dr. Pusey understands these terms as asserting "the actual presence both of the inward and outward part" (p. 96). It is no doubt true that they are quite consistent with the Real Presence to faith, and the Real giving to and receiving by faith of the "res sacramenti," with its "sacramentum" or "symbolum." But it can scarcely be maintained that they at all naturally imply, nor even that in their natural sense they are consistent with the Real Objective Presence of the "res sacramenti" in the "sacramentum."

and the Real Objective Presence) of the use made by the Fathers of the terms *type, symbol,* and the like, as applied to the Eucharistic

Turrian contended that the term ἀντίτυπον had such a force. He maintained "antitypum proprie significare figuram quæ rem in se habet ad differentiam typi qui rem in se non continct." And he appealed to the use of the term by Cyril of Jerusalem. (See also Toutte'e, in Op. Cyril., Disser. iii. cap. xi.) But he was answered by Vasquez, who says: "Hæc opinio de significatione vocis *antitypum* ex nullo probato auctore confirmari potest. Quod vero adducit ex Cyrillo potius contra ipsum est, quoniam baptismus qui a Cyrillo dicitur *antitypum passionis et sepulturæ Christi,* non continet reipsa mortem et sepulturam illius, sed effectum, nempe remissionem peccatorum, &c. Similiter non dicitur a Cyrillo sacramentum confirmationis antitypum ejus nimirum olei quo Christus unctus est, quod illud oleum reipsa, et non secundum significationem contineat, sed quod effectum aliquem illius, eique similem unctionem habeat." (See Albertinus, De Eucharistia, p. 279. See also Goar, Euchologium, p. 158.)

And though, doubtless, examples may be quoted of the use of the term *antitype* in connection with an idea of some sort of spiritual incorporation (see *e g.* Pusey's "Real Presence from the Fathers," pp. 113, 114), it will be found that in such cases the notion is rather an addition to the meaning of the term than at all involved in it.

The term is used of the bread and wine of Melchizedek.

And, indeed, the examples cited below will, it is believed, sufficiently show that no such *inclusive* idea is contained in its usual sense.

J. A. Assemani, after giving various other modes by which Romish divines have laboured to bring the use of this term into harmony with the Romish doctrine, adds: "Vel demum per Antitypum Isotitypum intelligunt, siquidem de magnis illis mysteriis, hoc est de sanctissimo Christi corpore, et pretioso sanguine istud accipias, proposito enim hæc *anti* nonnunquam æqualitatem etiam significat, ita Elias Creten. in Orat. i. Apologet. Nazianz. pag. edit. Morell. 201. Ex dictis conciliantur Patres Græci, quorum aliqui post consecrationem divina appellant *antitypa,* permulti vero negant ita esse appellanda." (Codex Liturgicus, tom. iv. p. 73, Diss. De Liturg. Origine, Art. iv. § vii.)

But the very many who in later times refused this title to the mysteries are good witnesses to the fact that this was not the natural or usual sense of the word.

They never seem to have thought of thus reconciling their language with the language of earlier times and purer faith.

Even Theophylact, whose view, if I understand it aright, fell entirely short of the doctrine of Paschasius, from the standpoint of *his* doctrine, denied that the elements were antitypes. His words are: Πρόσχες δὲ, ὅτι ὁ ἄρτος ὁ ἐν τοῖς μυστηρίοις ὑφ' ἡμῶν ἐσθιόμενος, οὐκ ἀντιτυπόν ἐστι τῆς τοῦ Κυρίου σαρκός, ἀλλ' αὐτὴ ἡ τοῦ Κυρίου σάρξ. (In Joan. cap. vi. In Evang., Paris, 1631, pp. 651, 652.)

For the opinion of the second Nicene Council see above, p. 218, and "Romish Mass and English Church," p. 63.)

Suicer says: "Eodem prorsus sensu dicuntur ἀντίτυπα panis et vinum corporis et sanguinis Christi, quo σύμβολα, τύποι, figura, σημεῖον, signum, εἰκών, imago, similitudo, &c. An vero his vocibus ideo usos dicemus veteres, et indicarent, *symbolum, typum, figuram, signum, imaginem, similitudinem, &c. corporis Christi, esse ipsum corpus*? Non existimarim ego. Juxta Allatium ad Hebr. ix. 24: χειροποίητα ἅγια, quæ Apostolo dicuntur ἀντίτυπα τῶν ἀληθινῶν, erunt ipsa ἀληθινὰ ἅγια, ac proinde cœlum; quo quid absurdius fingi queat? . . . Juxta Allatium, 1 Petri iii. 21. Baptismus et arca Noachi erunt ἰσότυπα, Baptismus erit ipsa Arca. Aliter longe Apostolus. . . . Profecto, si ἀντίτυπα, essent ἰσότυπα, stulte omnino

elements, I give here the principal passages in which such use is made, arranged under the heads of the various terms.

ΕΙΚΩΝ.

I.

Εἰ δ', ὡς οὗτοί φασὶν ἄσαρκος καὶ ἄναιμος ἦν· ποίας σαρκὸς, ἢ τίνος σώματος, ἢ ποίου αἵματος ΕΙΚΟΝΑΣ διδοὺς, ἄρτον τε καὶ ποτήριον, ἐνετέλλετο τοῖς μαθηταῖς διὰ τούτων τὴν ἀνάμνησιν αὐτοῦ ποιεῖσθαι; ὧν καὶ ὁ Ἀπο*τ*τολός ἐστι· μαρτυρῶν γὰρ τούτοις φησὶ τόν τε ἄρτον καὶ τὸ ποτήριον τῆς εὐλογίας κοινωνίαν αἵματος τε εἶναι καὶ σάρκος. (Adamantius, Dialogus De Recta in Deum Fide, Sect. iv. in Op. Originis, tom. i. c. 1840, edit. Migne.)

II.

Αὐτὸς τὰ σύμβολα τῆς ἐνθέου οἰκονομίας τοῖς αὐτοῦ παρεδίδου μαθηταῖς, τὴν ΕΙΚΟΝΑ τοῦ ἰδίου σώματος ποιεῖσθαι παρακελευόμενος ... ἄρτῳ χρῆσθαι συβόλῳ τοῦ ἰδίου σώματος παρεδίδου.* (Eusebius, Demonstratio Evang., lib. viii. a Genesi, p. 380, edit. Paris, 1628.)

III.

Οὐδὲ γὰρ μετὰ τὸν ἁγιασμὸν τὰ μυστικὰ σύμβολα τῆς οἰκείας ἐξίσταται φύσεως ... παράθες τοίνυν τῷ ἀρχετύπῳ τὴν ΕΙΚΟΝΑ, καὶ ὄψει τὴν ὁμοιότητα. χρὴ γὰρ ἐοικέναι τῇ ἀληθείᾳ τὸν τύπον.† (Theodoret., Dial. ii. Inconfusus, Opera, edit. Schulze, tom. iv. p. 126.)

Theophylactus, strenus ille μετουσίας πρόμαχος, negaret, panem et vinum esse ἀντίτυπα corporis et sanguinis Christi. At negat ... cum Theophylacto etiam delirat Samona, Archiepiscopus Gazæ, qui in Liturgiis, p. 136, negat, κοινωνίαν esse ἀντίτυπον τοῦ σώματος τοῦ Χριστοῦ, ἢ τύπον, ἢ εἰκόνα. Annon vero hoc est reliquis in faciem contradicere Patribus?" (Thesaurus, tom. i. c. 385. See also quotations in Dr. Harrison's "Dr. Pusey's Challenge Answered," pp. 64, 65; and Albertinus, De Eucharistia, pp. 275—278.)

The following extract from St. Chrysostom is decisive as to his use of Ἀντίτυπον:
—καλῶς εἶπεν ἐκεῖνα ἀντίτυπα, ἆρα τύπον ἔχει μόνον, οὐχὶ δὲ καὶ τὴν ἰσχύν· ὥσπερ ἐπὶ τῶν εἰκόνων, τύπον ἔχει τοῦ ἀνθρώπου ἡ εἰκών, οὐχὶ τὴν ἰσχύν. ὥστε τὸ ἀληθὲς καὶ ὁ τύπος κοινωνοῦσιν ἀλλήλοις. ὁ γὰρ τύπος ἴσος. ἡ δὲ ἰσχὺς οὐκέτι. (In Epist. ad Hebræos, cap. x., Hom. xvii. § 3, Opera, edit. Montfaucon, tom. xii. p. 163.)

See also examples below, under ἀντίτυπον.

It is, however, not to be forgotten that the sacramental *antitypes* are representative signs for an effectual purpose. See above, p. 180.

Albertinus says: "Antitypa corporis et sanguinis Christi dicuntur, tum ratione *similitudinis* ... tum ratione *conversionis*, non in substantiam corporis et sanguinis ejus, sed in virtutem seu efficaciam eorum ut Cyrillus Alexandrinus loquitur. (De Eucharistia, p. 427.)

* See above pp. 69, 70; and mark here the equivalent use of εἰκών and σύμβολον.

† The terms εἰκων and τύπος here are both used as corresponding with τὰ

IV.

Παρέδωκε γὰρ ΕΙΚΟΝΑ τοῦ ἰδίου σώματος μαθηταῖς.* (Procopius of Gaza, Comment. in Gen., cap. xlix. v. 12, Opera, edit. Migne, tom. i. p. 502.)

V.

Διαγράφει γὰρ ἐν τούτοις αἰσθητῶς, ὑπ' ὄψιν ἄγων Ἰησοῦν τὸν Χριστόν, τὴν νοητὴν ὑμῶν ὡς ἐν ΕΙΚΟΣΙ ζωήν.† (Pseudo-Dionysius,

μυστικὰ σύμβολα. The ἀρχέτυπον and the ἀλήθεια, which are to be compared with them (but clearly not identified with them), are the Body of Christ (not on the altar, but) now at God's right hand (τῆς ἐκ δεξιῶν ἠξιώθη καθέδρας), retaining still its former form and circumscription (or local limitations), and these as a part of its very substance or nature as a Body (τὸ μὲν πρότερον εἶδος ἔχει, καὶ σχῆμα, καὶ περιγραφήν, καὶ ἀπαξαπλῶς εἰπεῖν, τὴν τοῦ σώματος οὐσίαν.)

* This is the Greek as given by Coffetel from a manuscript. See above, p. 60.

† This is the author's account of the distribution. The paraphrase of Pachymeres runs thus: Ἀναζωγραφεῖ γὰρ ἐν τοῖς συμβόλοις αἰσθητῶς τὴν νοητὴν ἡμῶν ζωήν, τὸν Κύριον ἡμῶν Ἰησοῦν Χριστόν. (P. 327.)

In Chapter iii., after the description of the Eucharistic service, the Θεωρία commences "Agedum ergo . . . post figuras ordine sancteque digestas (μετὰ τὰς ΕΙΚΟΝΑΣ ἐν τάξει) . . . veritatem . . . declarabo" (§ 1, p. 285), on which the Scholiast Maximus remarks: ΕΙΚΟΝΑΣ ἐκάλεσε τῶν ἀληθῶν, τὰ νῦν τελούμενα ἐν τῇ Συνάξει. (P. 306). The sixth section commences: "Qui quidem horum sacramentorum penitus ignari sunt, illi ne imagines quidem cernunt" (οὐδὲ τὰς ΕΙΚΟΝΑΣ ὁρῶσιν, p. 289). The third section commences: "Sancta itaque nobis penetranda censeo, ut, intelligentiâ primi simulacri detectâ (τὸ νοητὸν τοῦ πρώτου τῶν ἀγαλμάτων ἀπογυμνώσαντας) deiformem ejus pulchritudinem intueamur" (p. 286); on which the Scholium of Maximus is Ἀγάλματα μὲν φησὶ τὰς ΕΙΚΟΝΑΣ τῶν ἀοράτων καὶ μυστικῶν. ἤγουν τὰ συμβολικῶς τελούμενα (p. 307). And so the paraphrase of Pachymeres: Ἀγάλματα δὲ φησὶ τὰς εἰκόνας τῶν μυστικῶν. (P. 318.)

It is not intended that these expressions have any exclusive reference to the Eucharistic elements. I believe, however, that it will scarcely be found possible, in a fair interpretation of the words of Pseudo-Dionysius and his interpreters, to exclude the elements from the general application. (See above, p. 133.)

And this being so the following illustrative language should be taken into the same view: "Sicut in imaginibus (καθάπερ ἐπὶ τῶν αἰσθητῶν εἰκόνων), si pictor ad primævam speciem (ἀρχέτυπον εἶδος) constanter intendat, nullâ re aliâ visibili distractus, neque secundum quidpiam divisus, illum ipsum qui depingendus est (si ita placet liceat) quodammodo replicabit, atque ipsam veritatem in similitudine, et archetypum in imagine (τὸ ἀρχέτυπον ἐν τῇ εἰκόνι) exprimet, alterumque in altero citra substantiæ differentiam referet: sic honesti amantibus in mente pictoribus, suaveolentis et arcanæ pulchritudinis intenta constansque contemplatio infallibilem indet maximeque deiformem imaginationem" (cap. iv. § 1, p. 331). It should be observed that this occurs in the chapter which is specially concerned with the sacred ointment, which is called an εἰκών (p. 331). But then it is also to be very specially observed that the following words in section 3 (p. 333) bring this ointment into the same generic rank with the Eucharist: "Divini præceptores nostri, tamquam ejusdem ordinis et operationis cum sacrosancto Synaxeos sacramento, iisdem imaginibus ut plurimum (ταῖς αὐταῖς ΕΙΚΟΣΙΝ ὡς τὰ πολλὰ) mysticisque distinctionibus ac sacris verbis descripserunt."

Areop., De Eccles. Hierar., cap. iii. § 13, Opera, edit. Corderius, Antw. 1634, tom. i. p. 300.)

VI.

Οἱ τὴν ἀληθῆ τοῦ Χριστοῦ ΕΙΚΟΝΑ εἰλικρινεστάτῃ ψυχῇ ποιοῦντες καὶ ποθοῦντες καὶ σεβόμενοι. (Concil. Constant., 754,* in Labbæus, tom. vii. c. 445, Mansi, tom. xiii. c. 261.)

VII.

'Ιδοὺ οὖν ἡ ΕΙΚΩΝ τοῦ ζωοποιοῦ σώματος. (Ibid., c. 445, 262.)

VIII.

Ὡς ἀψευδῆ ΕΙΚΟΝΑ τῆς φυσικῆς σάρκος. (Concil. Constant. 754, in Labbæus, tom. vii. c. 448, Mansi, tom. xiii. c. 264.)

IMAGO AND SIMILITUDO.

I.

"Tuam, oro, *imaginem* repræsentet panis ac mens; morare in pane, et in comedentibus illum, in utroque objecto, manifesto atque occulto videat te, ut Mater, sic Ecclesia tua." (Ephrem Syrus, In Natalem Domini, Serm. xi. Version of Petrus Benedictus, Opera, tom. ii. p. 416, edit. Venice, 1756.)

II.

" Videmus per *imaginem* bona: et tenemus *imaginis* bona. . . . Ipse quidem nobis apud Patrem advocatus adsistit: sed nunc eum non videmus. Tunc videbimus, cum *Imago* transierit, *veritas*, venerit. Ascende ergo, homo, in cœlum : et videbis illa, quorum *umbra* hic erat vel *imago*, videbis perfectum hominem, jam non in *imagine*,† sed in veritate." (Ambrose, Enarr. in Psalm. xxxviii. § 25, 26, Opera, edit. Benedict. 1686, tom. i. c. 853.

III.

" Umbra in lege, *imago*‡ in Evangelio, veritas in cœlestibus. Ante agnus offerebatur, offerebatur et vitulus, nunc Christus offertur : sed

* See above, pp. 217—219.

† Bertram says: "In orationibus quæ post mysterium corporis sanguinisque Christi dicuntur, et a populo respondetur, *Amen*|: sic sacerdotis voce dicetur: *Pignus æternæ vitæ capientes, humiliter imploramus ut quod in* IMAGINE *contingimus sacramento manifesta participatione sumamus.*" (De Corpore et Sanguine Dom., c. lxxxv. See note in Migne, c. 162, 163, and especially Soames's Bampton Lectures, p. 395.)

‡ The Benedictine editors would claim for *Imago* here a sense inclusive of "Real Presence." (Note *c*, 63.) But the whole passage, and the preceding extract, refute the claim. See Harrison's "Fathers *versus* Dr. Pusey," pp. 133, 134, and "Challenge Answered," pp. 399, 400.

The reference is to Heb. x. 1, where the distinction between the shadow (σκιά) and the image (εἰκών) is by Chrysostom, and other ancient expositors, explained as that between a sketched outline and a coloured picture. See Wordsworth *in loc.*

offertur quasi homo, quasi recipiens passionem ; et offert se ipse quasi sacerdos, ut peccata nostra dimittat : hic in *imagine*, ibi in veritate, ubi apud Patrem pro nobis quasi Advocatus intervenit. (Ambrose, De Offic. Minist., lib. i. cap. xlviii. § 248, Opera, tom. ii. c. 63.)

IV.

"Certe sacramenta, quæ sumimus, corporis et sanguinis Christi, divina res est, propter quod et per eadem Divinæ efficimur consortes naturæ, et tamen esse non desinit substantia vel natura panis et vini. Et certe *imago et similitudo* corporis et sanguinis Christi in actione mysteriorum celebrantur."* (Gelasius I., De Duabus Naturis, In Bibliotheca Maxima, Lugd. 1677, tom. viii. p. 703.)

V.

"Quia istam mensam præparavit servis et ancillis in conspectu eorum, ut quotidie in *similitudinem* corporis et sanguinis Christi, panem et vinum secundum ordinem Melchizedek nobis ostenderet in sacramento, ideo dicit : Parasti in conspectu mensam," &c.† (Hom. in Ps. xxii., published among the works of Chrysostom in the Paris edition of 1588, tom. i. col. 703.)

VI.

"Dedit sui corporis *imaginem* vel effigiem vel typum discipulis, haud amplius admittens et acceptans legis cruenta sacrificia."‡

The εἰκών is a *vivid resemblance* in contrast with the *faint and imperfect figuring* of the σκιά.

See especially Chrysostom, In Heb., Hom. xvii., Opera, edit. Montfaucon, tom. xii. p. 167.

See also Albertinus, De Eucharistia, pp. 857, 858.

This εἰκών may also doubtless be called ἀλήθεια ; but then the ἀλήθεια is the lifelike reality of the coloured picture, which implies no Real Objective Presence of the ἀρχέτυπον. So Chrysostom : Ἡλίου γὰρ ἀνίσχοντος, κρύπτεται ἡ σκιά. διὰ τοῦτο γὰρ ἐν αὐτῇ τῇ τραπέζῃ ἑκάτερον γίνεται πάσχα, καὶ τὸ τοῦ τύπου, καὶ τὸ τῆς ἀληθείας. καθάπερ γὰρ οἱ ζωγράφοι ἐν αὐτῷ τῷ πίνακι καὶ τὰς γραμμὰς περιάγουσι καὶ τὴν σκιὰν γράφουσι, καὶ τότε τὴν ἀλήθειαν τῶν χρωμάτων αὐτῷ ἐπιτιθέασιν· οὕτω καὶ ὁ Χριστὸς ἐποίησεν. ἐπ' αὐτῆς τῆς τραπέζης καὶ τὸ τυπικὸν πάσχα ὑπέγραψε καὶ τὸ ἀληθινὸν προσέθηκε. (De Prodit. Judæ, Homil. i. § 4, Opera, edit. Montfaucon, Paris, 1718, tom. ii. p. 383.)

See Gregor. Nazianz., as quoted below, p. 273.

See also Euthymius Zigabenus, Comment. in quatuor Evangelia, cap. lxiv. (In Bibl. Max. Patr., Lugd. 1677, tom. xix. p. 578.)

* See Routh's Opuscula, tom. ii. pp. 139 *sqq.*, and Albertinus, De Eucharistia, pp. 858—876. For evidence of the sense of *similitudo* in its bearing on the controversy, see Albertinus, pp. 858 *sqq.*

† See Goode on Eucharist, i. p. 272.

‡ This is the Latin version of C. Thrasybulus. See above, p. 268. The Greek *in the editions* is here deficient.

(Procopius of Gaza, Comment. in Genesin, cap. xlix. v. 12, Opera, edit. Migne, tom. i. p. 502.)

VII.

"Lætentur et exultent et præsumant qui veram Christi *imaginem* benigno animo facientes et diligentes et venerantes ad salutem animæ et corporis offerentes, quam ipse sacrificii perfector et Deus nostram ex nobis ex toto suscipiens massam secundum tempus voluntariæ passionis in signum et in memoriam manifestam suis tradidit discipulis." (Latin version of Conc. Const. 754, as read in 2nd Nicene Council by Gregory, Bp. of Neocæsarea.)*

VIII.

"Corporis et sanguinis Christi antitypa . . . quæ *imaginem* ac veram illorum figuram teneant." (Stephanus Junior, in Surius, Nov. 28, cap. xxxvi., De Sanct. Vitis, Col. 1618, tom. iv. p. 633.)

IX.

"Sicut enim mortis *similitudinem* sumpsisti, ita etiam *similitudinem* pretiosi sanguinis bibis." (De Sacramentis, In Op. Ambrosii, lib. iv. cap. 4, § 20, edit. Benedict., Paris, 1690, tom. ii. c. 370, 371.)

X.

"In *similitudinem* accipis sacramentum." (Ibid., lib. vi. cap. 1, § 3, tom. ii. c. 380.)

---

* Quoted as from him, and with decided disapproval, by Charlemagne, De Imag., lib. iv. cap. xiv., Op., ed. Migne, tom. ii. c. 1213. See Mansi, tom. xiii c. 262, 677.

As applied by early writers to the Eucharist, the word *Imago* of course conveys the idea of *representation* rather than actual or physical *likeness*. Du Cange interprets "Imaginarius" by "Vicarius, Locum-tenens, qui vices alterius in rebus gerendis implet, et *imaginem* quodammodo refert." He quotes from Petrus de Vincis, lib. ii. Ep. 9 : "Filium nostram ad vos tanquam Imaginarium nostræ præsentiæ destinamus." (Glossarium in voc. *Imaginarius*.) And this sense is doubtless derived from an older meaning of *Imago*.

With Charlemagne, on the contrary, the prominent question of Image-worship would seem to have given to *Imago* the sense of physical and *artificial likeness*, to the exclusion of the idea of divinely appointed representation. See below, under *Figura*, pp. 279, 280.

Doubtless, also, the sacramental union (see above, p. 182 *sqq.*), in its relation to the Incarnation, and the fraction of the bread in its ordained relation to the passion of Christ, appear sometimes to come into the idea of the representation understood by the terms εἰκών, *Imago*, and the like.

But the central point of real similitude is the correspondence between natural bread and wine in their relation to the hunger and invigoration of the body, and the true bread and wine of Christ's Flesh and Blood, given and shed for the life of the world in their relation to the hunger of man's soul, and the support of his spiritual life. This analogy makes the sign as delivered to the body so suitable to represent as a true image and convey to faith the thing signified, that which is to man meat indeed and drink indeed.

ΤΥΠΟΣ.

I.

Πρόσεχε, πῶς τὸν ἄρτον εὐλογῶν κλάει αὐτὸν ἐν ΤΥΠΩ τοῦ σώματος τοῦ ἰδίου ἀχράντου· καὶ τὸ ποτήριον πάλιν, πῶς ἐν τύπῳ αἵματος εὐλογεῖ, καὶ δίδωσιν τοῖς ἑαυτοῦ μαθηταῖς. (Homily among the Works of Ephrem Syrus, "De lis qui Naturam Dei scrutantur," Opera, tom. i. p. 497, edit. Venice, 1755. In the Roman edition of Asseman, 1732, the Homily will be found in tom. iii. pp. 418 sqq. The extract is from writings not found in the Syriac, and whose authenticity is not unquestioned. If not the writing of Ephrem, though it will lose the weight of his high authority, it will still bear witness to the faith of the Church at a later period.)

II.

Ἐὰν σε ὁ Κύριος καταξιώσῃ, εἰς τὸ ἔμπροσθεν γνώσῃ, ὅτι τὸ σῶμα αὐτοῦ κατὰ τὸ εὐαγγέλιον ΤΥΠΟΝ ἔφερεν ἄρτου.* (Cyril. Hieros., Catech. xiii. § xix., Opera, edit. Ben., p. 192.)

III.

Μεταληψόμεθα δὲ τοῦ Πάσχα, νῦν μὲν ΤΥΠΙΚΩΣ ἔτι, καὶ εἰ τοῦ παλαιοῦ γυμνότερον· τὸ γὰρ νομικὸν Πάσχα, τολμῶ καὶ λέγω ΤΥΠΟΥ τύπος ἦν ἀμυδρότερος.† (Gregor. Nazianz., Orat. xlv. § xxiii., Opera, edit. Benedict., Paris, 1778, tom. i. p. 863.)

IV.

"*Super frumento*, inquit, *et vino, et oleo*, de quo conficitur panis Domini, et sanguinis ejus impletur *typus*, et benedictio sanctificationis ostenditur." (Hieronymus, Comment. in Jeremiam, lib. vi. cap. xxxi. vs. 10, 11 *sqq*., Opera, edit. Vallarsius, tom. iv. c. 1063.)

V.

"*In typo* sanguinis sui non obtulit aquam sed vinum." ‡ (Ibid.,

---

* Commenting on Jerem. xi. 19, according to the version "lignum injiciamus in panem ejus;" on which passage Tertullian has the similar note, "Sic enim Deus in evangelio quoque vestro revelavit panem corpus suum appellans, ut et hinc jam eum intelligas corporis sui figuram pani dedisse." (Adv. Marcio., § xix., Opera, edit. Rigaltius, 1689, p. 408. See above, pp. 66, 92, 94, and below, p. 277.)
So on the same passage Theodoret writes: Τῷ δὲ Δεσπότῃ Χριστῷ καὶ μάλα τῆς προφητείας ὁ λόγος προσήκει· ἄρτον γὰρ τὸ ἑαυτοῦ προσηγόρευσε σῶμα. ὁ ἄρτος γὰρ φησὶν, ὃν ἐγὼ δώσω, ἡ σάρξ μοῦ ἐστιν. (In Hierem., cap. xi., Opera, edit. Schulze, tom. ii. pp. 472, 473.)

† It may be observed that elsewhere Gregory uses language which implies that all that is offered on the tables of Christian Churches may be regarded as a σκιά. He says that if driven from the altars he knows another—the work of the mind: Τούτῳ θύσω δεκτά, θυσίαν, καὶ προσφοράν, καὶ ὁλοκαυτώματα, κρείττονα τῶν νῦν προσαγομένων, ὅσῳ κρεῖττον σκιᾶς ἀλήθεια. (Orat. xxvi. § 16, Opera, edit. Benedict., tom. i. p. 483.)

‡ On this extract see above, p. 116.

Adv. Jovin., lib. ii. § 5, quoting from Jovinianus, Opera, edit. Vallarsius, tom. ii. c. 330.)

VI.

"Ότι γὰρ ἡ κοινωνία τῆς μυστικῆς εὐλογίας ὁμολογία τίς ἐστι τῆς ἀναστάσεως τοῦ Χριστοῦ, σαφὲς ἂν γένοιτο, καὶ μάλα ῥᾳδίως, δι' ὧν αὐτὸς ἔφη τὸν τοῦ μυστηρίου TYΠON ἐπιτελέσας δι' ἑαυτοῦ. Διακλάσας γὰρ τὸν ἄρτον, καθὰ γέγραπται, διεδίδου, λέγων· τοῦτο μου ἐστὶ τὸ σῶμα, κ.τ.λ. (Cyril. Alex., In Joan. Evang., lib. xii. 1104, 1105, Opera, edit. Migne, tom. vii. c. 725.)

VII.

Εἰ δὲ ἡ σὰρξ εἰς θεότητος μετεβλήθη φύσιν, οὗ δὴ χάριν μεταλαμβάνουσιν τῶν ἀντιτύπων τοῦ σώματος; περιττὸς γὰρ ὁ TYΠOΣ* ἀνῃρημένης τῆς ἀληθείας. (Theodoret., Demonstratio, Quod Unio sit Inconfusa, Opera, tom. iv. p. 269, edit. Schulze.)

VIII.

Τίνος ἡγῇ σύμβολόν τε καὶ TYΠON τὴν παναγίαν τρόφην;† (Ibid. Dial. i. *Immutabilis*, Op., tom. iv. p. 27.)

IX.

" Dedit sui corporis imaginem vel effigiem vel *typum* discipulis." ‡ (Procopius of Gaza, Comment. in Genesin, cap. xlix. v. 12, Opera, edit. Migne, tom. l. p. 502.)

X.

" Non oportet, inquiunt [Nestoriani] te moleste ferre hanc œconomiam. Panis enim in *typum* Corporis Christi propositus plus benedictionis participavit quam panis, qui in foro venditur, et quam panes, quos Philomarianitæ offerunt in nomine Mariæ." § (Leontius Byzant., Contra Nestor. et Eutych., lib. iii. " De Nestorianorum Impietate," In Biblioth. Max. Patr., Lugd. 1677, tom. ix. p. 696.)

XI.

Ὡς οὐκ ἄλλου εἴδους ἐπιλέχθεντος παρ' αὐτοῦ ἐν τῇ ὑπ' οὐρανον, ἢ TYΠOY, εἰκονίσαι τὴν αὐτοῦ σάρκωσιν δυναμένου. (Concil. Constant. 754, in Labbæus, tom. vii. c. 445 ; Mansi, tom. xiii. c. 264.)

* It is to be specially noted here how Theodoret uses the terms τύπος and ἀντίτυπον as equivalent alternatives.

The reader may also be asked carefully to weigh the language here used, in view of the questions—(1) Does Theodoret regard these terms as inclusive of that which they symbolise? (2) Does his view recognise the real presence of the thing typified in or under the form of the type?

† Here again it may be observed how the terms σύμβολον and τύπος are classed together apparently as equivalents.

‡ See above, p. 272.

§ See Claude, "Catholic Doctrine of Euch.," London, 1684, book v. ch. vi. part ii. p 52. See also above, p. 64.

XII.

Εἰς ΤΥΠΟΝ καὶ ἀνάμνησιν ἐναργεστάτην . . . παραδέδωκεν. (Concil. Constant. 754, in Labbæus, tom. vii. c. 445; Mansi, tom. xiii. c. 261.)

XIII.

"Testamentum ergo sanguine constitutum est, quia beneficii divini sanguinis testis est. In cujus *typum*, nos calicem mysticum ad tuitionem corporis et sanguinis, et animæ nostræ percipimus; quia sanguis Domini sanguinem nostrum redemit." (Rabanus Maurus, Comment. in Epist. Paul., lib. xi., In 1 Cor. xi., Opera, edit. Migne, tom. vi. c. 103.)

XIV.

"Et qui proposuimus *typum* Corporis et Sanguinis Christi Tui, adoramus; ac supplices rogamus Te per bonitatis Tuæ benignitatem, veniat Sanctus Tuus Spiritus super nos, et super hæc quæ proposuimus dona, et sanctificet ipsa." (Anaphora D. Basilii, ex Codice Syriac., transl. per Andr. Masium, Ant. 1569, p. 243. See Cosin's Works, A.C.L., vol. iv. p. 66.)

XV.

"Non oportet aliquid aliud in sacramento offerri præter panem vinum et aquam, quæ in *typo* Christi benedicuntur." (Gratian, Decret., Pars iii. De Consecr. Dist. ii. can. iii. * Venice, 1567, col. 1262.)

SIGNUM.

I.

"Quapropter a sacris vinculis soluti, ad *signa* Dominica confirmatis animis accedite." (Innocentius I. Papa in Epist. ad Arcadium Imperatorem.†)

II.

"Ex eo quod scriptum est, sanguinem pecoris animam ejus esse, præter id quod supra dixi, non ad me pertinere quid agatur de pecoris anima, possum interpretari illud in signo esse positum. Non enim Dominus dubitavit dicere, Hoc est corpus meum: cum *signum* daret corporis sui." (Augustin., Contra Adimantum, cap. xii. § 3, tom. viii. col. 124, edit. Benedict., Paris, 1688.)

III.

"De *signis* disserens hoc dico, ne quis in eis adtendat quod sunt, sed potius quod *signa* sunt, id est, quod *significant*. . . . Nam et odore unguenti Dominus, quo perfusi sunt pedes ejus, *signum* aliquod

* Can. lv. in edit. Migne, col. 1732.
† See Hospinian, Opera, tom. iii. p. 123, edit. 1681.

dedit; et *sacramento* corporis et sanguinis sui prægustato, *significavit quod voluit.*"* (Augustine, De Doctr. Christ., lib. ii. cap. iii. tom. iii. p. 1, c. 19, 20, edit. Benedict. 1680.)

IV.

" Ante benedictionem verborum celestium alia species † nominatur, post consecrationem corpus *significatur*. Ipse dicit sanguinem suum. Ante consecrationem aliud dicitur, post consecrationem sanguis nuncupatur. Et tu dicis, Amen : hoc est, verum est." (De Mysteriis Liber, cap. ix. § 54, Opera Ambrosii, edit. Benedict., Paris, 1690, tom. ii. c. 339, 340.)

V.

" Quam [imaginem] . . . . in *signum* et in memoriam manifestam suis tradidit discipulis." (Greg. Bp. of Neocæsarea ‡ as quoted by Charlemagne.)

VI.

" Dicitur Corpus Christi, sed improprie. Unde dicitur suo modo, sed non rei veritate, sed significati mysterio; ut sit sensus, Vocatur Christi corpus, id est, *significat*." (Gloss. § in Gratian, Decret., Pars iii. De Consec., Dist. ii. c. xlviii.)

FIGURA.

I.

" Professus itaque se concupiscentia concupisse edere Pascha ut suum (indignum enim ut quid alienum concupisceret Deus) acceptum panem, et distributum discipulis, corpus illum suum fecit, hoc est corpus meum dicendo, id est. *figura* ‖ corporis mei. *Figura* autem non fuisset, nisi veritatis esset corpus. Ceterum vacua res, quod est phantasma, figuram capere non posset." (Tertullian, Adv. Marc., lib. iv. xl. edit. Paris, 1689, pp. 457, 458.)

* With this passage should be compared the following : " Tantæ rei *sacramenta*, id est, *sacra signa*." (Ibid., Contr. Adv. Legis, lib. ii. c. 9, § 33, Opera, tom. viii. c. 599, edit. Benedict. 1688.)
"Nimis longum est, convenienter disputare de varietate signorum, quæ cum ad res divinas pertinent, Sacramenta appellantur." (Ibid , Ad Marcellinum, Ep. cxxxviii., Opera, tom. ii. c. 412, edit. Benedict. 1679.)

† The reader may be cautioned against attributing to *species* a modern sense. The Fathers sometimes use it as equivalent to *substantia*. Ambrose speaks elsewhere of our Lord as changing "aquæ substantiam in vini speciem " ; and again he says : " Gravior est ferri species quam aquarum liquor." See Albertinus, De Eucharistia, pp. 512, 515, 518.

‡ See above, p. 272. § See above, p. 129.

‖ In the report to Pope Benedict XII. of the faith of the Armenians, it is alleged as among their *errors*, that they hold that the Sacrament is " a representation, a resemblance, or a *figure* of the true Body and Blood of our Lord." " They say likewise that when our Saviour instituted this Sacrament, He did not transubstantiate the

II.

" Sic enim Deus in Evangelio quoque vestro revelavit panem corpus suum appellans, ut et hinc jam eum intelligas corporis sui *figuram* pani dedisse, cujus retro corpus in panem Prophetes figuravit, ipso Domino hoc sacramentum postea interpretaturo." * (Tertullian, Adv. Marci. lib. iii. xix. edit. Paris, 1689, p. 408. See also Adv. Judæos, x. p. 196.)

III.

" Who gave to . . . . His Church mystical corn and wine and oil; corn which [mystically] *figures* His holy Body, and wine, His atoning Blood; and again, oil for the fragrant ointment, wherewith the baptized are sealed, and put on the armour of the Holy Spirit." † (Ephrem Syrus, in Joel ii. 24, Op., edit. Venice, tom. ii. p. 340, edit. Rome, 1732, tom. v. p. 252.)

IV.

" In historia Novi Testamenti ipsa Domini nostri tanta et tam miranda patientia, quod eum tamdiu pertulit tanquam bonum, cum ejus cogitationes non ignoraret, cum adhibuit ad convivum, in quo corporis et sanguinis sui *figuram* discipulis commendavit et tradidit; quod denique in ipsa traditione osculum accepit, bene intelligitur pacem Christum exhibuisse traditori suo." (Augustin., Enarr. in Psalm. iii. § 1, tom. iv. par. i. col. 7, edit. Benedict., Paris, 1688.)

V.

" Labores passionis Christi . . . . in *figurá* corporis ejus ac sanguinis pro salubritate vitæ communis afferimus, ad agnitam dulcedinem mysteriorum conscio ore testamur." (Gaudentius Brix., Serm. xix. p. 198, edit. Galeardus, 1757.)

bread and wine into His Body, but only instituted a representation or a resemblance of His Body and Blood." "The Armenians likewise say we must expound that which is said in the Canon of their Mass: *by which Holy Spirit the bread is made the real Body of Jesus Christ* in this sense, that by the *real Body of Jesus Christ*, we must understand the real resemblance or representation of the Body and Blood of Jesus Christ." (See Claude's "Catholic Doctrine of Euch.," London, 1684, part ii. p. 29.)

* On this passage see Morton on Eucharist, p. 492, edit. 1635, and Albertinus, De Eucharistia, p. 324 *sqq.*

† Quoted from Dr. Pusey's translation in "Real Presence from Fathers," pp. 414, 415.

I have inserted the word "mystically" at the suggestion of the Dean of Canterbury. The Syriac verb is from the same root as the adjective *mystical*. The corresponding noun seems to have much the same variety of sense as the Greek μυστήριον.

The Latin version of Petrus Benedictus renders " quod est mysterium corporis ipsius sanctissimi."

VI.

"Recte etiam vini specie tunc sanguis ejus exprimitur, quia cum ipse in Evangelio dicit : 'Ego sum vitis vera ;' satis declarat sanguinem suum esse omne vinum quod *in figurá* passionis ejus offertur." (Gaudentius Brix., Serm. ii. p. 33.)

VII.

" Quomodo panem de multis tritici granis in pollinem redactis per aquam confici, et per ignem necesse est consummari, rationabiliter in eo *figura** accipitur corporis Christi, quem novimus ex multitudine totius humani generis unum esse corpus effectum, per ignem sancti Spiritus consummatum. . . . . Similiter et sanguinis ejus vinum ex pluribus acinis, id est uvis vineæ ab ipso plantatæ, collectum, in torculari Crucis exprimitur, et per capacia vasa fideli corde sumentium propria virtute fervescit." (Ibid., Serm. ii. pp. 39, 40.)

VIII.

" Corporis et sanguinis sui *figuram* discipulis commendavit et tradidit." (Isidorus Hispalensis, Quæstiones in Vet. Test., Reg. ii. cap. iii., Opera, edit. Migne, tom. v. c. 413.)

IX.

" Ejus [Judæ] nefanda consilia cognoscens ejus præsentiam pertulit, nec a sacratissima coenâ in quâ *figuram* sacrosancti corporis sanguinisque suis Discipulis tradidit,† ipsumque exclusit." (Ven. Beda, in Psalm. iii., Opera, edit. Colon., 1612, tom. viii. c. 324.)

X.

" Transiit [Dominus] ad novum [Pascha] quod in suæ redemptionis memoriam Ecclesia frequentare desiderat, ut videlicet pro agni carne vel sanguine suæ carnis sanguinisque sacramentum in panis ac vini *figura* substituens, ipsum se esse monstraret cui juravit Dominus, et

---

* The words following might seem to represent the *thing figured* here as Christ's Spiritual Body, the Church. But the preceding and subsequent context seem to show that this is so only because the sacrament of the Lord's Supper is as a bond of union of the two senses of Christ's Body, making the recipients to be "One bread and One Body," because "partakers of that One bread." St. Augustine says : " Dominus noster Jesus Christus, Corpus et Sanguinem suum in eis rebus commendavit quæ ad unum aliquid rediguntur ex multis. Namque aliud in unum ex multis granis confit aliud in unum ex multis acinis confluit." (August. in Joan., Tract. xxvi., Opera, tom. iii. par. ii. c. 500.) See Cyprian, Ep. ad Cæcilium (p. 230, edit. Venice, 1728.) "Ipso sacramento populus noster ostenditur adunatus, ut quemadmodum grana multa in unum collecta, et commolita et commixta panem unum faciunt, sic in Christo, qui est panis coelestis, unum sciamus esse corpus, cui conjunctus sit noster numerus et adunatus." See below, Note G.

† Cf. Augustine, as quoted above, p. 277, and see Soames's Bampton Lectures, p. 405.

non pœnitebit eum, tu es sacerdos in æternum secundum ordinem Melchisedek." (Ven. Beda, In Luc. xxii., Opera, tom. v. c. 424)

XI.

" An tu quoque corporis et sanguinis Christi antitypa ab Ecclesia proscribes, ut quæ imaginem ac veram illorum *figuram* teneant?"* (Stephanus Junior, in Surius, Nov. 28, cap. xxxv. De Sanct. Vitis, Colon., 1618, tom. iv. p. 633.)

XII.

"[Dominus], cœnando cum Discipulis, panem fregit, et calicem pariter dedit eis in *figuram* † corporis et sanguinis sui, nobisque profuturum magnum exhibuit sacramentum." (Carolus Magnus, De ratione Septuages. ad Alcuinum, In Alcuini Opera, c. 1150, edit. Paris, 1617.)

* See below, under ἀντίτυπον, p. 291.
† It should be noted, however, that elsewhere, in the book "De Imaginibus," Charlemagne (or the author of the "Libri Carolini"), in this particular following the lead of the second Nicene Council, objects to the term *imago* as applied to the Eucharist. It would appear from his language (see lib. iv. cap. xiv., Opera, ed. Migne, tom. ii. c. 1214), that he distinguished between *figura* and *imago*; regarding the latter term either as implying or referring to an object having as yet no real existence, or as signifying a mere *likeness* of man's device and art. Accordingly, Albertinus says : " Innovatio igitur est in loquendi forma potius quam in re : sed periculosa tamen, et quæ sequentibus sæculis errandi non levem ansam incautis subministravit. Præstitisset semper loqui cum veteribus qui Eucharistiam corporis et sanguinis Dominici imaginem liberrime nominarunt." (De Eucharistia, p. 917.)
As to the views maintained in the "Caroline Books," see Canon Robertson's "Hist. of Ch. Ch.," vol. iii. pp. 143—146, 1874.
" In the 27th chapter of the 2nd book of the Caroline Books, the term *sacramentum* is used repeatedly and plainly to designate a *figure*, or *sacred sign*. ' Corporis et sanguinis Dominici sacramentum ad commemorationem suæ passionis, et nostræ salutis nobis concessum.' ' Corporis et sanguinis Dominici *sacramentum non omni sacramento æquiperandum, sed* pene omnibus præferendum.' Imperialia Decreta de Cult. Imag., ex. edit. Melch. Haim. Goldast, Francof., 1608, pp. 274—277." (Soames's Bampton Lectures, p. 411.)
The true key to the understanding of Charlemagne's objection to the word *imago* will be found, I believe, in the following words : "Multum igitur, et ultra quam mentis oculo perstringi queat, distat sacramentum Dominici corporis et sanguinis ab imaginibus pictorum arte depictis : cum videlicet illud efficiatur operante invisibiliter spiritu Dei, hæ visibiliter manu artificis ; illud consecratur a sacerdote Divini nominis invocatione, hæ pingantur a pictore humanæ artis eruditione." (Caroli Magni Opera, edit. Migne, tom. ii. c. 1095.)
It was, in fact, the rise of Image-worship which necessitated the drawing a clear line of demarcation to separate sacramental figures from images set up in churches, painted or graven by art and man's device. (See above, p. 272.)
The distinction is, in truth, very real and important between a representation made by an image or likeness the result of mere human skill, and that which results from an appointed sign (with no *likeness* of such sort) fitly ordained to signify by Divine institution and represent (not φύσει, but θέσει) to the faith of Christian men

XIII.

"Dicit Sacerdos: Fac nobis, inquit, hanc oblationem adscriptam, ratam, rationabilem, acceptabilem; quod *figura* * est corporis et sanguinis Domini nostri Jesu Christi." (De Sacramentis, in Op. Ambrosii, lib. iv. cap. v. § 21, edit. Benedict., 1690, tom. ii. col. 371.)

that which by faith is verily and indeed taken and received in the Eucharist. (See Papers on Eucharistic Presence, pp. 135, 136.)

And it was just this distinction which was called for by the claim, which Charlemagne is refuting, that *Images* might be put on a par with the Sacramental Body of Christ—a claim expressed in these words: "Sicut Corpus Dominicum et sanguis a fructibus terræ ad insigne mysterium transit, ita et imagines artificum industria compaginatæ ad earum personarum in quarum similitudinem compaginantur, transeant venerationem." (Car. Magni, Opera, edit. Migne, tom. ii. c. 1092.)

Let it be noted how not only Charlemagne's answer (see c. 1095), but this very claim itself, refutes the idea of Divine adoration due to a Real Objective Presence of Christ in the Elements. (See also Claude's Catholic Doctrine of Euch., part ii. p. 97, London, 1684.)

It may be observed that by others the term *image* was rejected as applied to the Eucharist, while *symbol* was accepted; and by others both *image and figure* were refused, yet *representation* was admitted. (See Claude's Cath. Doct. of Euch., part i. pp. 341, 344, London, 1684.) All these distinctions seem to indicate steps in departure from the earlier faith which admitted all these terms indiscriminately.

Yet again, in a new sense, the term *figure* was used by Paschasius and his followers. (See Claude, x. part ii. pp. 255, 256, and Anselm, Epist. cvi., Opera, pp. 452, 453. Paris, 1721.) But this sense was altogether unknown to the earlier Fathers. (See Albertinus, De Euch., pp. 5, 389, 621.)

And yet again, a new sense has been given even to *imago* with a view to make it admissible in Romish theology. (See Albertinus, p. 857.)

* This is doubtless a prayer before consecration. But it can hardly be doubted that it has respect to the effect of consecration. Compare the following from Florus Magister: "Oratur omnipotens, ut oblationem suis altaribus impositam, et tantis precibus commendatam, ipse per virtutem Spiritus descendentis ita legitimam et perfectam Eucharistiam efficiat, ut in omnibus sit adscripta, id est in numerum placitorum sibi numeretur recepta, sit etiam rata, id est, immobili firmitate perpetua . . . . . ut efficiatur corpus et sanguis unigeniti filii Dei. . . . . Hæc est rationabilis hostia, plena videlicet rationis, plena mysterii." (De Expositione Missæ, § 59, Opera, edit. Migne, c. 51.) See also the Liber "De Divinis Officiis" in the Works of Alcuin, c. 1111, edit. Paris, 1617.

Dr. Pusey has observed that the words "quod figura est corporis et sanguinis Domini Nostri Jesu Christi" occupy the same place as the words "ut nobis corpus et sanguis fiat dilectissimi Filii tui Domini Dei nostri Jesu Christi," in the old Roman Missal. (Real Presence from the Fathers, p. 105.)

Mr. Scudamore writes: "For the proof that this work [De Sacramentis] belonged to the Gallican Church, see Oudin, tom. i., Col. 1861. Ambrose of Cahors, its supposed author, wrote at the end of the eighth century, after the introduction of the Roman Liturgy by Charlemagne. Observe the qualification of the Roman original: 'Quod figura est corporis,' &c." (Notitia Eucharistica, p. 522.)

See also note in Benedictine edition of St. Ambrose, tom. ii. c. 371 ; Albertinus, De Eucharistia, pp. 275, 513, 730 ; Hospinian, Works, tom. iii. pp. 231, 232 ; Allix's Churches of Piedmont, p. 45 ; Goode on Eucharist, i. pp. 267—268 ; Dr. Harrison's Reply to Dr. Pusey's Challenge, vol. i. p. 549, vol. ii. p. 78.

XIV.

"Corpus Christi * quod sumitur de altari *figura* est dum panis et vinum videtur extra: veritas autem dum corpus et sanguis Christi, in veritate interius creditur." (Hilarius Papa? in Gratian, Decret., pars iii., De Consecratione, Dist. ii. cau. lxxviii. p. 1290, Venice, 1567.)

XV.

"Dedit discipulis suis sacramentum corporis sui .... ut memores illius facti, semper hoc in *figurâ* facerent, quod pro eis acturus erat non obliviscerentur. Hoc est corpus meum, id est, in sacramento. ... Vinum ... lætificat, et sanguinem auget. Et idcirco non inconvenienter sanguis Christi per hoc *figuratur*. ... Sicut denique si aliquis peregre proficiscens † dilectoribus suis quoddam vinculum dilectionis relinquit .... ita Deus præcepit agi a nobis, transferens spiritaliter corpus in panem, vinum in sanguinem, ut per hæc duo memoremus quæ fecit pro nobis de corpore et sanguine suo, et non simus ingrati tam amantissimæ charitati."‡ (Christian Druthmar, in Matth. Evang., fo. lxxxiv., edit. 1514.)

* On these words the gloss says: "Corpus Christi, &c.: Id est, sacrificium corporis Christi: alias falsum est quod dicit." On the writings of Hilary, see Cave's Historia Literaria, Ann. 461, p. 256, Geneva, 1694. On this quotation, which is probably not from Hilary, see Albertinus, De Eucharistia, p. 472. Compare Paschasius as quoted in "Romish Mass and English Church," p. 73.

† See below, under *Memoria*.
Compare also the following from Florus Magister: "Propterea et iturus ad passionem, et per resurrectionis et ascensionis gloriam discessurus e mundo, hoc sacramentum ultimum discipulis tradidit, ut memoriam tantæ charitatis, per quam solam salvamur, arctius eorum mentibus infigeret; quatenus semper memores simus, et quales et quantum ab eo dilecti simus." (Florus, De Expositione Missæ, § 63, in Migne's Patrologia, tom. cxix. c. 55.)
"Quantum est istud et ineffabile salutis mysterium et pietatis sacramentum, tanta contestatione prædictum, tanta veritate commendatum, ut prius hoc Dominus corpus et sanguinem suum assereret, quam pro nobis suum corpus et sanguinem traderetur." (Ibid., § 6, c. 23.)

‡ There is a history connected with this extract from Druthmar which is worth noting.
Sixtus Senensis (followed by Cardinal Du Perron) charged the Protestants with having corrupted the text to make it read as quoted above, alleging that "pro eo, quod codices in Germania excusi habent, Hoc est corpus meum, hoc est, in sacramento: Lugdunense exemplar plus habet, Hoc est corpus meum, hoc est, vere in sacramento subsistens; rursum ubi in impressis voluminibus legimus, Transferens spiritualiter corpus in panem, in vinum sanguinem: in Lugdunensi legitur, transferens panem in corpus, et vinum in sanguinem." (Biblioth. Sancta, lib. vi., Annot. cxii., Colon. 1586, pp. 475, 476.)
Hence arose the question—by no means an unimportant one in its bearing on the doctrine of Paschasius and of the ninth century—Was the genuine writing of Druthmar faithfully represented in the books printed by Protestants (in which case the Lyons MS., if truly reported by Sixtus Senensis, must have been interpolated to support

ΣΥΜΒΟΛΟΝ.

I.

Μυστικὸν ἄρα ΣΥΜΒΟΛΟΝ ἡ γραφὴ αἵματος ἁγίου, οἶνον ὠνόμασεν.* (Clemens Alexandrinus, Pædagogus, lib. ii. cap. ii., Opera, edit. Potter, Venice, 1757, tom. i. p. 184.)

II.

Ἀντὶ θυσίας τῆς δι' αἱμάτων, λογικὴν καὶ ἀναίμακτον, καὶ τὴν μυστικὴν, ἥτις εἰς τὸν θάνατον τοῦ Κυρίου ΣΥΜΒΟΛΩΝ χάριν

Romish doctrine)—or was it rightly given in the words as quoted by Sixtus Senensis as from the Examplar of Lyons (in which case the crime of tampering with his language would have to be laid to the charge of the Protestants)?

To this question an answer was given by Aubertin in his work on the Eucharist, who declared that the passage, in what Du Perron regarded its heretical form, was to be found in an early edition, printed, with every mark of orthodoxy and authority, in 1514, before Luther even had been heard of. (See Albertinus, De Eucharistia, pp. 863, 933, 934.)

This, however, by no means settled the question. It became now a question of Aubertin's veracity. Father Labbe reported, as the result of diligent inquiries, that no trace of the edition had been found, adding the words "Mihi Albertini hominis hæretici et a fide ac religione majorum suorum παραβάτου valde suspecta sit fides."

I am myself in possession of one of the copies of this curious edition, from which the quotation in the text is taken verbatim, and which fully supports the reading of the Protestants and the accuracy of Aubertin.

A note on the subject, well worth reading, will be found in Maitland's "Early Printed Books in Lambeth Library," p. 368 *sqq*. Mr. Maitland says: "It is strange indeed that a book of such size, which bore on its title-page an extract from the Pope's bull, and on the reverse of that title the license of the imperial censor, and which continued to be so known as that it was reprinted in sixteen years, should have been wholly unknown to such men as Father Labbe, and those whom he names. It is one of many almost incredible facts which show the value of catalogues. It is, at the same time, very remarkable, that all the controversy about it has not, so far as I can see, led to the discovery of half a dozen copies; perhaps not of more than three or four." (Pp. 370, 371.)

Cave notes (Historia Literaria, p. 371, edit. 1694), after quoting the words of Labbe: "Quo vero in posterum omnis hac de re dubitandi, vel calumniandi ansa tollatur, monemus æquum lectorem hanc ipsam Winphelingii editionem extare penes eximium virum Thomam Tenison, Ecclesiæ Anglicanæ Theologum celeberrimum, in cujus proinde instructissima Bibliotheca videri potest."

This copy of Archbishop Tenison, noted in his handwriting, is now in the Lambeth Palace Library. (See Maitland's Early Printed Books, No. 283, p. 126.)

Allix says that the Lyons copy mentioned by Sixtus Senensis "was never yet produced, though they who reprinted the work of Druthmarus, in the Bibliotheca Patrum, of the Cologne edition, have been pleased to put this falsification of Sixtus Senensis in the margent." (Remarks on the Ancient Churches of the Albigenses, Oxford, 1821, p. 100.) He says also that "Cardinal Perron, who was as able as any man of France to justify the fair dealing of Sixtus Senensis in the business of this manuscript of Lyons, did not care to concern himself about it." (Ibid.)

* See above, p. 72.

ἐπιτελεῖται, τοῦ σώματος αὐτοῦ καὶ τοῦ αἵματος.* (Constit. Apost., lib. vi. cap. xxiii., Cotelerius, tom. i. p. 353, Antwerp, 1700.)

III.

Τούτου δῆτα τοῦ θύματος τὴν μνήμην ἐπὶ τραπέζης ἐκτελεῖν διὰ ΣΥΜΒΟΛΩΝ, τοῦ τε σώματος αὐτοῦ, καὶ τοῦ σωτηρίου αἵματος, κατὰ θέσμους τῆς Καινῆς Διαθήκης παρειλήφοτες.† (Eusebius Cæs., Dem. Evang., lib. i. cap. 10, p. 39, edit. Paris, 1628.)

IV.

Αὐτὸς τὰ ΣΥΜΒΟΛΑ τῆς ἐνθέου οἰκονομίας τοῖς αὐτοῦ παρεδίδου μαθηταῖς, τὴν εἰκόνα τοῦ ἰδίου σώματος ποιεῖσθαι παρακελευόμενος. Ἐπειδὴ γὰρ οὐκέτι τὰς δί αἱμάτων θυσίας, οὐδὲ τὰς παρὰ Μωσεῖ ἐν διαφόρων ζώων σφαγαῖς νενομοθετημένας προσίετο, ἄρτῳ δὲ χρῆσθαι ΣΥΜΒΟΛΩ τοῦ ἰδίου σώματος παρεδίδου, εἰκότως τὸ λαμπρὸν καὶ καθαρὸν ἠνίξατο τῆς τροφῆς, εἰπὼν, καὶ λευκοὶ, κ.τ.λ. (Ibid., lib. viii. a Genesi, p. 380.)

V.

Εἰ γὰρ μὴ ἀπέθανεν ὁ Ἰησοῦς, τίνος ΣΥΜΒΟΛΑ τὰ τελούμενα ; (Chrysostom, In Matth., Hom. lxxxii. al. lxxxiii. § 1, Opera, edit. Montfaucon, tom. vii. p. 783.)

VI.

Πόσης ἐννόησον ἁγιωσύνης σοὶ δεῖ τῷ πολλῷ μείζονα ΣΥΜΒΟΛΑ ‡ δεξαμένῳ, ὧν ἐδέξατο τὰ ἅγια τῶν ἁγίων τότε . . . ὅσῳ γὰρ μειζόνων ἠξιώθης ΣΥΜΒΟΛΩΝ, καὶ φρικτῶν μυστηρίων, τοσούτῳ μείζονος εἶ

---

* Passages which speak of the *offering* of the symbols or antitypes, are insufficient by themselves to prove that the *consecrated* elements were thus regarded. Dean Goode says: "In all the Greek and Oriental Liturgies, as far as I can find, the offering of the elements takes place *before* their complete consecration, and supposed change by the descent of the Holy Spirit upon them, as there invoked." (On Eucharist, i. p. 279. See also Heurtley's Sermons on Recent Controversy, p. 54, and Albertinus, De Eucharistia, p. 443 *sqq.*)

Nevertheless, in connexion with other extracts, such passages are not without their value. See above, p. 280.

† Etsi demus symbola aliqua esse inclusiva rerum earum quas designant, illa tamen de quibus agimus, Eucharistica videlicet, alterius generis esse, probatu facillimum est. Eusebius enim per symbola corporis et sanguinis Domini intelligit illud ipsum quod memoriam seu memoriale quoque nominat: adeo ut si memoria excludat rei præsentiam cujus memoria habetur, itidem et signum seu symbolum memoriale quod illius memoriam per aliquid visibile renovat et excitat. Memoriam autem præsentiam rei excludere, verbis fere totidem docent Nyssenus et Augustinus." (Albertinus, De Eucharistia, p. 394.)

‡ These σύμβολα are immediately afterwards spoken of as σῶμα καὶ αἷμα δεσποτικόν.

ὑπεύθυνος τῆς ἁγιωσύνης. (Chrysostom in Psalm. cxxxiii., edit. Montfaucon, tom. v. p. 382.)

VII.

Συγκαύσας τὰς βίβλους πάσας ἐνδιαθέτους καὶ σπουδαίας, καὶ παιδίον ἕν, ὡς ἔφασαν οἱ ἑωρακότες, καὶ τὰ ΣΥΜΒΟΛΑ τῶν μυστηρίων. (Palladius. Dial. de Vit. J. Chrysostomi, In Op. Chrys., edit. Montfaucon, tom. xiii. p. 23.)

VIII.

Παρῄνει πᾶσι μετὰ τὴν κοινωνίαν ἀπογεύεσθαι ὕδατος ἢ παστίλου, ἵνα μὴ ἀκουσίως τῷ σιέλῳ ἢ τῷ φλέγματι συνεκπτύσωσι τι τοῦ ΣΥΜΒΟΛΟΥ. (Ibid., p. 26.)

IX.

Καὶ τῷ μὲν διακόνῳ θρασέως ἐντιναχθεὶς, τὰ ΣΥΜΒΟΛΑ* ἐκχέει. (Ibid., p. 34.)

X.

" Cum autem ad Apostolos dicit: Hoc est corpus meum. Item: Hic est sanguis meus; certo apud se statuant vult, posteaquam benedictio, et gratiarum actio, ad panem vel calicem propositum accesserit, per panis quidem *symbolum* corporis Christi; per calicem vero ejusdem sanguinis participes se fieri." (Victor Antiochenus, In Evang. Marci, cap. xiv., In Bibliotheca Max. Patr., Lugd. 1677, tom. iv. p. 407.)

XI.

Σκιά, φησὶ, τὰ παρόντα τῶν μελλόντων. ἐν γὰρ τῷ παναγίῳ βαπτίσματι τὸν τύπον ὁρῶμεν τῆς ἀναστάσεως, τότε δὲ αὐτὸν ὀψόμεθα τὴν ἀνάστασιν. ἐνταῦθα τὰ ΣΥΜΒΟΛΑ τοῦ δεσποτικοῦ θεώμεθα σώματος, ἐκεῖ δὲ αὐτὸν ὀψόμεθα τὸν Δεσπότην.† (Theodoret., In Epist. i. ad Cor. cap. xiii., Opera, edit. Schulze, tom. iii. p. 255.)

XII.

Κἀν τῇ τῶν θείων μυστηρίων παραδόσει, λαβὼν τὸ ΣΥΜΒΟΛΟΝ ἔφη, τοῦτο ἐστὶ τὸ σῶμά μοῦ, τὸ ὑπὲρ ὑμῶν διδόμενον, ἢ κλώμενον,

* Dr. Pusey has observed, that while Palladius here uses the word σύμβολα, St. Chrysostom speaks plainly of the "Blood of Christ." (See Real Presence from the Fathers, p. 109.) His words are: Καὶ τὸ ἁγιώτατον αἷμα τοῦ Χριστοῦ ... εἰς τὰ ἱμάτια ἐξεχεῖτο. (Epistola ad Innocentium Papam, § 3, In Op. Chrys., edit. Benedict., tom. iii. p. 519.)

† In this passage four points seem especially worthy of observation—(1) The apparent distinction of the Body symbolised from the Person of Christ; (2) The distinction of the symbols from that Body; (3) The parallelism of the type of the resurrection in Baptism, and these symbols in the Eucharist; (4) The bringing of both together to illustrate the statement Σκιά, φησὶ, τὰ παρόντα τῶν μελλόντων.

κατὰ τὸν ἀπόστολον.* (Theodoret., Epist. cxxx. Timotheo Episcop., tom. iv. p. 1218.)

XIII.

Καὶ τὰ θεῖα δὲ παραδοὺς μυστήρια, καὶ τὸ ΣΥΜΒΟΛΟΝ κλάσας καὶ διανείμας, ἐπήγαγε· τοῦτο μοῦ ἐστὶ τὸ σῶμα, τὸ ὑπὲρ ὑμῶν θρυπτόμενον εἰς ἄφεσιν ἁμαρτιῶν. (Ibid., Epist. cxlv. Monachis Constantinopolitanis, tom. iv. p. 1251.)

XIV.

Προσφέρει δὲ ἡ ἐκκλησία τὰ τοῦ σώματος αὐτοῦ καί τοῦ αἵματος ΣΥΜΒΟΛΑ, πᾶν τὸ φύραμα διὰ τῆς ἀπαρχῆς ἁγιάζουσα. (Ibid., In Psalm. cix., tom. i. p. 1397.)

XV.

Τίνος ἡγῇ ΣΥΜΒΟΛΟΝ καὶ τύπον τὴν παναγίαν τρόφην; τῆς θεότητος τοῦ Δεσπότου Χριστοῦ, ἢ τοῦ σώματος καὶ τοῦ αἵματος; (Ibid., Dial. i. Immutabilis, tom. iv. pp. 26, 27.)

XVI.

Ὁ Κύριος τὸ ΣΥΜΒΟΛΟΝ λαβὼν, οὐκ εἶπε, Τοῦτο ἔστιν ἡ θεότης μοῦ· ἀλλὰ τοῦτό ἐστι τὸ σῶμά μοῦ. (Ibid., p. 27.)

XVII.

Μετὰ γὰρ δὴ τὴν αὐτοῦ παρουσίαν, οὐκέτι χρεία τῶν ΣΥΜΒΟΛΩΝ τοῦ σώματος, αὐτοῦ φαινομένου τοῦ σώματος· διὰ τοῦτο εἶπεν ἄχρις οὗ ἂν ἔλθῃ. (Ibid., in 1 Cor. xi., tom. iii. p. 238.)

XVIII.

ΟΡΘ. Οἶσθα ὅτι ἄρτον ὁ Θεὸς τὸ οἰκεῖον προσηγόρευσε σῶμα;
ΕΡΑΝ. Οἶδα.
ΟΡΘ. Καὶ ἑτέρωθι δὲ τὴν σάρκα σῖτον ὠνόμασεν;
ΕΡΑΝ. Οἶδα καὶ τοῦτο...
ΟΡΘ. Ἐν δὲ γε τῇ τῶν μυστηρίων παραδόσει, σῶμα τὸν ἄρτον ἐκάλεσε καὶ αἷμα τὸ κρᾶμα.
ΕΡΑΝ. Οὕτως ὠνόμασεν.
ΟΡΘ. Ἀλλὰ καὶ κατὰ φύσιν τὸ σῶμα σῶμα ἂν εἰκότως κληθείη καὶ τὸ αἷμα αἷμα.
ΕΡΑΝ. Ὁμολόγηται.
ΟΡΘ. Ὁ δὲ γε Σωτὴρ ὁ ἡμέτερος ἐνήλλαξε τὰ ὀνόματα· καί τῷ μὲν σώματι τὸ τοῦ ΣΥΜΒΟΛΟΥ τέθεικεν ὄνομα· τῷ δὲ ΣΥΜΒΟΛΩ τὸ τοῦ σώματος. οὕτως ἄμπελον ἑαυτὸν ὀνομάσας, αἷμα τὸ ΣΥΜΒΟΛΟΝ προσηγόρευσεν.

* See Scrivener's Lectures on the Text of the New Testament, pp. 181, 182.

ΕΡΑΝ. Τοῦτο μὲν ἀληθῶς εἴρηκας· ἐβουλόμην δὲ τὴν αἰτίαν μαθεῖν τῆς ὀνομάτων ἐναλλαγῆς.

ΟΡΘ. Δῆλος ὁ σκοπὸς τοῖς τὰ θεῖα μεμυημένοις. ἠβουλήθη γὰρ τοὺς τῶν θείων μυστηρίων μεταλαγχανοντας, μὴ τῇ φύσει τῶν βλεπομένων προσέχειν, ἀλλὰ διὰ τῆς τῶν ὀνομάτων ἐναλλαγῆς, πιστεύειν τῇ ἐκ τῆς χάριτος γεγενημένῃ μεταβολῇ· ὁ γὰρ δὴ τὸ φύσει σῶμα σῖτον καὶ ἄρτον προσαγορεύσας, καὶ αὖ πάλιν ἑαυτὸν ἄμπελον ὀνομάσας, οὗτος τὰ ὁρώμενα ΣΥΜΒΟΛΑ τῇ τοῦ σώματος καὶ αἵματος, προσηγορίᾳ τετίμηκεν οὐ τὴν φυσὶν μεταβαλὼν, ἀλλὰ τὴν χάριν τῇ φύσει προστεθεικώς. (Ibid., Dial. i. Immutabilis, tom. iv. pp. 25, 26.)

XIX.

ΟΡΘ. Εἰπὲ τοίνυν, τὰ μυστικὰ ΣΥΜΒΟΛΑ παρὰ τῶν ἱερωμένων τῷ Θεῷ προσφερόμενα τίνων ἐστὶ ΣΥΜΒΟΛΑ;*

ΕΡΑΝ. Τοῦ δεσποτικοῦ σώματός τε καὶ αἵματος.

ΟΡΘ. Τοῦ ὄντως σωμάτος ἢ οὐκ ὄντως;

ΕΡΑΝ. Τοῦ ὄντως.

ΟΡΘ. Ἄριστα. χρὴ γὰρ εἶναι τὸ τῆς εἰκόνος ἀρχέτυπον. καὶ γὰρ οἱ ζωγράφοι τὴν φυσίν μιμοῦνται, καὶ τῶν ὁρωμένων γράφουσι τὰς εἰκόνας.

ΕΡΑΝ. Ἀληθές.

ΟΡΘ. Εἰ τοινύν τοῦ ὄντως σώματος ἀντιτυπά* ἐστὶ τὰ θεῖα μυστήρια, σῶμα ἄρα ἐστὶ καὶ νῦν τοῦ Δεσπότου τὸ σῶμα, οὐκ εἰς θεότητος φυσίν μεταβληθὲν, ἀλλὰ θείας δόξης ἀναπληθέν. (Ibid., Dial. ii. Inconfusus, tom. iv. p. 125.)

XX.

Ἐπιθέντων τῷ θείῳ θυσιαστηρίῳ τῶν σεβασμίων ΣΥΜΒΟΛΩΝ, δι' ὧν ὁ Χριστὸς σημαίνεται καὶ μετέχεται. (Pseudo-Dionysius, Eccles. Hierar., cap. iii. § 9, tom. i. p. 295, Opera, edit. Corderius, Antw., 1634.)

XXI.

Ἑστὼς ἐπίπροσθεν τῶν ἁγιωτάτων ΣΥΜΒΟΛΩΝ, ὕδατι τὰς χεῖρας ὁ Ἱεράρχης νίπτεται.† (Ibid., § 10, p. 295.)

* In this passage should be noticed — (1) The equivalent use of the terms σύμβολα and ἀντίτυπα; and (2) The illustration of their meaning in the εἴκων and ἀρχέτυπον of the painter. And again, the reader should be asked to view the language of Theodoret with reference to the questions — (1) Does Theodoret use these terms as including in their sense the thing symbolised? (2) Does his language lead us to suppose that in his view he recognised the Real Objective Presence of the ἀρχέτυπον in or under the form of the σύμβολον or εἴκων?

† Here Maximus the Scholiast explains συμβόλων — τοῦ σώματος καὶ αἵματος (p. 311). See above, pp. 133, 269.

XXII.

Ἡ ... ἀπόνιψις ἐπιπροσθεν γίγνεται τῶν ἁγιωτάτων ΣΥΜΒΟΛΩΝ, ὡς ἐπὶ Χριστοῦ τοῦ πάσας ἐφορῶντος ἡμῶν τὰς κρυφιωτάτας ἐννοίας. (Ibid., § 10, p. 296.)

XXIII.

Σημείωσαι δὲ, ὅτι πανταχοῦ συμβολικὴν λέγει τὴν θείαν ἱερουργίαν, καὶ τὰ ἅγια δῶρα ΣΥΜΒΟΛΑ τῶν ἄνω καὶ ἀληθινωτέρων. (Maximi Schol. in Pseudo-Dionys., De Eccles. Hier., cap. iii. § 12, p. 313.)

XXIV.

Ὁ Ἱεράρχης ... ὑπ' ὄψιν ἄγει τὰ ὑμνήμενα, σαφηνίζων, ὡς Χριστοῦ εἰσὶ τὰ τοιαῦτα ΣΥΜΒΟΛΑ· ὅτι μετὰ τὸ δεῖπνον λαβὼν ἄρτον, καὶ τὰ ἑξῆς. (Pachymeres, Paraph. in Pseudo-Dionysius, De Eccles. Hierar., cap. iii. § ii., Opera, edit. Corderius, Antwerp, 1634, tom. i. p. 316.)

ΑΝΤΙΤΥΠΑ.

I.

Ἡ προσφορὰ τῆς εὐχαριστίας οὐκ ἔστι σαρκικὴ, ἀλλὰ πνευματικὴ καὶ ἐν τούτῳ καθαρά. Προσφέρομεν γὰρ τῷ Θεῷ τὸν ἄρτον καὶ τὸ ποτήριον τῆς εὐλογίας εὐχαριστοῦντες αὐτῷ, ὅτι τῇ γῇ ἐκέλευσεν ἐκφῦσαι τοὺς καρποὺς τούτους εἰς τροφὴν ἡμετέραν, καὶ ἐνταῦθα τὴν προσφορὰν τελέσαντες ἐκκαλοῦμεν τὸ Πνεῦμα τὸ ἅγιον, ὅπως ἀποφήνῃ τὴν θυσίαν ταύτην καὶ τὸν ἄρτον σῶμα τοῦ Χριστοῦ καὶ τὸ ποτήριον τὸ αἷμα τοῦ Χριστοῦ, ἵνα οἱ μεταλαβόντες τούτων τῶν ΑΝΤΙΤΥΠΩΝ, τῆς ἀφέσεως τῶν ἁμαρτιῶν καὶ τῆς ζωῆς αἰωνίου τύχωσιν.* (Irenæus, Fragm., edit. Migne, No. xxxvii., Opera, c. 1253.)

II.

Τὰ ἐπὶ τοῦ λογικοῦ ἡμῶν θυσιαστηρίου ἐπιτελούμενα ἁγιάζει τὴν τράπεζαν, καὶ τὰ ἐν αυτῇ σκεύη, ΑΝΤΙΤΥΠΑ γὰρ εἰσὶ τοῦ δεσποτικοῦ σώματος. (Origen, as quoted by Julius Cæsar Bulenger† in his "Diatribe contra Casaubonum, iii. p. 166.)

---

* This is one of the Pfaffian fragments, the genuineness of which, on account of the loss of the Turin MS., Professor Lightfoot says "must always remain doubtful." (On Phillip., p. 202). Its remarkable verbal agreement with this Liturgy of the Apostolical Constitutions has been pointed out by Professor Heurtley (Sermons on Recent Controversy, pp. 53, 54).

† See also Huetius, Origeniana, lib. ii. Quest. xiv. § 2, in Origen. Comment., tom. i. p. 182.

III.

Παραδούς δὲ ἡμῖν τὰ ΑΝΤΙΤΥΠΑ μυστήρια τοῦ τιμίου σώματος αὐτοῦ καὶ αἵματος. (Pseudo-Clem. Rom., Const. Apost. v. c. 14, Cotel., Antwerp, 1700, tom. i. p. 317.)

IV.

Ἔτι εὐχαριστοῦμεν, πάτερ ἡμῶν, ὑπὲρ τοῦ τιμίου αἵματος Ἰησοῦ Χριστοῦ τοῦ ἐκχυθέντος ὑπὲρ ἡμῶν καὶ τοῦ τιμίου σώματος· οὗ καὶ ΑΝΤΙΤΥΠΑ ταῦτα ἐπιτελοῦμεν, αὐτοῦ διαταξαμένου ἡμῖν καταγγέλλειν τὸν αὐτοῦ θάνατον. (Ibid., lib. vii. c. 25, Cotel., tom. i. p. 370.)

V.

Τὴν ΑΝΤΙΤΥΠΟΝ τοῦ βασιλείου σώματος Χριστοῦ δεκτὴν εὐχαριστίαν προσφέρετε ἔν τε ταῖς ἐκκλησίαις ὑμῶν, καὶ ἐν τοῖς κοιμητηρίοις. (Ibid., lib. vi. cap. xxx. Cotel., tom. i. p. 358.)

VI.

Διὰ τοῦ οἴνου καὶ τοῦ ἄρτου τὰ ΑΝΤΙΤΥΠΑ τῶν σωματικῶν τοῦ Χριστοῦ κηρύττει μελῶν. (Eustathius Antiochenus.)*

VII.

Μὴ τῷ λάρυγγι τῷ σωματικῷ ἐπιτρέπητε τὸ κριτικόν· οὐχὶ, ἀλλὰ τῇ ἀνενδοιάστῳ πίστει. γενόμενοι γὰρ, οὐκ ἄρτου καὶ οἴνου κελεύονται γεύσασθαι, ἀλλὰ ΑΝΤΙΤΥΠΟΥ† σώματος καὶ αἵματος τοῦ Χριστοῦ.‡ (Cyril. Hierosol., Cateches. xxiii. Mystag. v. § xxi., Opera, p. 331, edit. Benedict.)

* Interpreting Prov. ix. 5, as alleged by Epiphanius the Deacon, in the second Nicene Council, Act. vi. On this passage see Albertinus, De Eucharistia, pp. 388, 389.

† Or perhaps ἀντιτύπων, as quoted by Dositheus Hieros. See note in Benedictine edition.

‡ For a defence of the Romish sense of these words see Toutte'e in Oper. Cyrill., Diss. iii. cap. xi. p. ccxxiv. sqq.; and for an answer to his arguments here, and elsewhere in this Dissertation "De doctrina Cyrilli," see Deylingius, Observ. Sacr. et Misc. pars iv. Cyrill, Vindic. xxx.—xxxviii. pp. 160—178. See also Albertinus, De Eucharistia, p. 427.

Waterland says: "Here our author plainly owns the elements to be *types*, or *symbols* (as he had done before), and therefore not the very things whereof they are symbols not literally and strictly, but interpretatively, mystically, and to all saving purposes and intents; which suffices. It is no marvel if Mr. Toutte'e and other Romanists interpret Cyril to quite another purpose. . . . As to believing, he very well knew that every one would believe his senses, and take bread to be bread, and wine to be wine, as himself believed also; but he was afraid of their *attending* so entirely to the report of their *senses*, as to forget the reports of *sacred Writ*, which ought to be considered at the same time, and with closer attention than the other, as being of everlasting concernment. In short, he intended no lecture of *faith* against *eye-sight*; but he endeavoured, as much as possible, to draw off their attention from the object

VIII.

Θαρρούντες προσεγγίζομεν τῷ ἁγίῳ σου θυσιαστηρίῳ, καὶ προσθέντες τὰ ΑΝΤΙΤΥΠΑ (configuralia, vetus versio) τοῦ ἁγίου σώματος καὶ αἵματος τοῦ Χριστοῦ σου, σοῦ δεόμεθα καὶ παρακαλοῦμεν, ἅγιε ἁγίων, εὐδοκίᾳ τῆς σῆς ἀγαθότητος, ἐλθεῖν τὸ Πνεῦμα σου τὸ ἅγιον ἐφ' ἡμᾶς, καὶ ἐπὶ τὰ προκείμενα Δῶρα ταῦτα, καὶ εὐλογῆσαι αὐτὰ, καὶ ἁγιάσαι, καὶ ἀναδεῖξαι. (Liturgy of St. Basil,* Neale's Liturgies, p. 163; Goar's Euchologium p. 144.)

IX.

Ἐν τῇ Ἐκκλησίᾳ προσφέρεται ἄρτος καὶ οἶνος, ΑΝΤΙΤΥΠΟΝ τῆς σαρκὸς αὐτοῦ καὶ αἵματος· καὶ οἱ μεταλαμβάνοντες ἐκ τοῦ φαινομένου ἄρτου, πνευματικῶς τὴν σάρκα τοῦ Κυρίου ἐσθίουσι.† (Macarius Ægypt., Hom. xxvii. § 17, Opera, edit. Migne, c. 705.)

X.

Καὶ εἴ πού τι τῶν ΑΝΤΙΤΥΠΩΝ τοῦ τιμίου σώματος, ἢ τοῦ αἵματος ἡ χεὶρ ἐθησαύριζεν, τοῦτο καταμιγνῦσα τοῖς δάκρυσιν, ὦ τοῦ θαύματος· ἀπῆλθεν εὐθὺς αἰσθομένη τῆς σωτηρίας.‡ (Gregory Nazianz., Orat. viii. § xviii., Opera, tom. i. p. 229, edit. Bened.)

XI.

Ὁ Μελχισεδὲκ αὐτῷ ἀπήντα τότε, καὶ ἐξέβαλεν αὐτῷ ἄρτον καὶ οἶνον, προτυπῶν τῶν Μυστηρίων τὰ αἰνίγματα, ΑΝΤΙΤΥΠΑ τοῦ Κυρίου ἡμῶν, λέγοντος· ὅτι ἐγώ εἰμι ὁ ἄρτος ὁ ζῶν. καὶ ΑΝΤΙΤΥΠΑ τοῦ αἵματος τοῦ ἐκ τῆς πλευρᾶς αὐτοῦ νυχθέντος, καὶ ῥεύσαντος εἰς

of sense to the object of faith, and from the signs to the things signified." (Waterland, vol. iv. pp. 597, 598, 1343.)

See also Morton on Eucharist, pp. 496, 497, edit. 1635.

* Albertinus regards this Liturgy as "valde suspecta, eo quod Græca quam nunc habemus non conveniat, nec cum Latina veteri translatione, nec cum ea quam Syri habent ab Andrea Masio Latine reddita." (De Eucharistia, p. 442.)
On this prayer see Dr. Heurtley's observations quoted above, p. 229; and Dean Goode, as quoted p. 283.

† From this passage it is argued by J. C. Bulenger: "Qui manducarent eum qui appareret panis, spiritualiter comedere Christi carnem, quia scilicet spiritali quodam, et invisibili modo Christi caro sub specie panis subest." (Diatrib. ad Is. Casauboni, Exercit. adv. Card. Barronium, Lugduni, 1617, Dial. iii. ad cap. xxxiii. Exer. vi. p. 166. See also note in Migne.)
But this is to force Macarius to use the word ἀντίτυπον in the unnatural sense he desires to fasten on the term, by forcing on the context a meaning not only unnatural but alien from the whole tenor of Patristic teaching. See Goode on Eucharist, i. p. 334; and see above, pp. 65—67, 206—268.

‡ See above, p. 212. See also Albertinus, De Eucharistia, p. 468. The note of the Benedictine editors is: "Per ἀντιτύπα, recte Elias ipsam Eucharistiam intelligit, et ipsum vere corpus Christi exponit."

U

κάθαρσιν τῶν κεκοινωμένων, καὶ ῥαντισμὸν, καὶ σωτηρίαν τῶν ἡμετέρων ψυχῶν. (Epiphanius, Adv. Hæreses, lib. ii. tom. i. § 6, ch. xxxv. vel lv., Opera, tom. i. p. 472. edit. Patavius, Cologne, 1682.)

XII.

Ὅν τρόπον οὐ δυὸ βασιλεῖς, αὐτὸς βασιλεὺς καὶ ἡ τούτου εἰκὼν,* οὐδὲ δυὸ σώματα, αὐτὸ τὸ χριστοῦ σῶμα ὑπόστατον ἐν οὐρανοῖς ὂν, καὶ ὁ τούτου ΑΝΤΙΤΥΠΟΣ ἄρτος ἐν ἐκκλησίας παρὰ τῶν ἱερέων διαδιδόμενος τοῖς πιστοῖς.† (Theodotus Antiochenus, as quoted by Julius Cæsar Bulenger in his "Diatribæ ad Casauboni Exercitationes adv. Cardinalem Baronium," Lugduni, 1617, p. 166, Diatribe iii., ad cap. xxxiii. Exercit. vi.)

* Solemne est apud veteres asserere, imaginem et id cujus imago est, unum atque idem esse, non multa. Eusebius: *Nemo sanus dixerit Regem et Regis imaginem ubique circumlatam duos esse Reges. Unus enim est in imagine sua honoratus.* [Contra Marcell. de Eccl. Theod., lib. ii. c. 23.] Athanasius: *In imagine species et forma Regis est et in Rege imaginis species. . . . Quoniam autem non est dissimilitudo, ei, qui post visam imaginem vellet Regem videre, imago recte diceret, Ego et Rex unum sumus; ego enim in illo sum, et ille in me.* [Contra Arian. Orat. iv.] Et rursum: *Qui videt imaginem Regis Regem videt. . . . Nec ideo duos facit reges.* [Contra Sabell. Greg.] Basilius: *Imago Regis Rex quoque dicitur, nec ideo duo sunt reges.* [De Sp. S. c. 18.] Et rursum: *Qui in foro Regis imaginem intuetur, et Regem dicit eum qui in tabula est, non propterea duos agnoscit Reges. . . .* [Contra Sabell.] Cyrillus Alexandrinus: *Si quis imaginem optime depictam videat ac admiretur . . . ac nihilominus cupiditas illum incessat Regem ipsum videndi, conveniente ei tabula dixerit, vidisti me, vidisti Regem. Et rursum: Ego et Rex unum sumus, quantum ad perfectam similitudinem attinet.* [In Thesaur., Assert. xii.] Nicephorus denique Constantinopolitanus: *Similitudo communitatem nominis largetur . . . Rex quippe dicitur etiam imago Regis, quæ dicere posset, Ego et Rex unum sumus, præter substantiæ differentiam.*" (Albertinus, De Eucharistia, p. 562.)

† "Proxime addemus Theodotum Antiochenum mirum in modum a Theodoreto laudatum, cujus hæc verba Bulengerus contra Casaubonum scribens e manuscriptis proferre se profitetur: *Quemadmodum ipse Rex et ejus imago non sunt duo Reges, nec quoque duo corpora sunt ipsum Christi corpus personale in cœlis existens, et panis antitypus ipsius in ecclesiis per sacerdotes fidelibus traditus.* Illustrissimum sane locum, et cujus nobis suppeditati Bulengero gratias agimus. Theodotus enim non modo confert panem Eucharistiæ qui in ecclesiis distribuitur, cum proprio corpore, tanquam typum cum veritate cujus typus est: unde sequitur illum corpus id non esse, cum typus non sit veritas cujus typus est; sed et innuit, panem illum, et proprium Domini corpus, unum ac idem corpus esse, eo modo quo Imago Regis et Rex, unus et idem Rex sunt." (Albertinus, De Eucharistia, p. 744.)

This is a very noteworthy passage; and, considering the scant remains of Theodotus known to exist, it seems strange that Bulenger does not state from what MS. source he derived it. This, however, is according to his wont.

But the strangest thing by far is this—that it is alleged by Bulenger (with other quotations) in evidence, to support this position: "Patres signum ac sacramentum pro verissimo corpore Christi posuisse, quod sub signis latet." (P. 165.)

For this purpose he adds this gloss to his translation: "Antitypum panem vocat speciem panis sub quo revera est corpus Christi."

XIII.

Εἰ τοίνυν τοῦ ὄντως σώματος ΑΝΤΙΤΥΠΑ ἐστί τὰ θεῖα μύστηρια, σῶμα ἄρα ἐστὶ καὶ νῦν τοῦ Δεσπότου τὸ σῶμα, οὐκ εἰς θεότητος φύσιν μεταβληθέν. (Theodoret, Dial. ii. Inconfusus, edit. Schulze, 1772, tom. iv. p. 125.)

XIV.

Εἰ δὲ ἡ σὰρξ εἰς θεότητος μετεβλήθη φυσὶν, οὗ δὴ χάριν μεταλαμβάνουσι τῶν ΑΝΤΙΤΥΠΩΝ τοῦ σώματος; περιττὸς γὰρ ὁ τύπος ἀνῃρημένης τῆς ἀληθείας. (Ibid., Demonstratio, Quod unio sit Inconfusa, tom. iv. p. 269.)

XV.

"An tu quoque corporis et sanguinis Christi *antitypa* ab ecclesiâ proscribes, ut quæ imaginem ac veram illorum figuram teneant quæ et adoramus, et osculamur, et eorum participatione sanctitatem consequimur."* (Stephanus Junior, In Surius, ad 28 Nov., cap. 36, Sanctorum Vitæ, Col. 1618, tom. iv. p. 633.)

XVI.

"Pretiosum suum corpus et sanguinem nobis dedit inquiens:

But what is there in the language of Theodotus to give the slightest colour to such an unnatural interpretation?

In the statue of a king is there only the *species* of the marble which represents? And is the king really present under the form of the image or picture?

Goar endeavouring to maintain for ἀντίτυπον such a sense as Bulenger would give it, distinguishes between two kinds of *figure*, that he may altogether separate from ἀντίτυπον the very notion which Theodotus connects with it. His words are: "Cum duplex sit figura, una quæ umbram tantum et speciem referat, alia quæ veritatem ipsam ita adumbrat ut etiam contineat: illa, quæ extranea est, et diversæ penitus naturæ a re per eam repræsentata, sicut, *ab homine pictura:* hæc, quæ nullam in substantia diversitatem agnoscit," &c. (Euchologium, p. 158.)

The second Nicene Council declares: Ἀρίδηλον γὰρ πᾶσιν ὑπάρχει, ὅτι ἄλλο ἐστὶν εἰκὼν καὶ ἄλλο πρωτότυπον· τοῦτο μὲν ἔμψυχον, ἐκεῖνο δὲ ἄψυχον. ... Πέτρος γὰρ καὶ Παῦλος ἀναζωγραφόμενοι βλέπονται, αἱ δὲ ψυχαὶ αὐτῶν ἐν ταῖς εἰκόσιν οὐ πάρεισιν. (Lab., tom. vii. c. 445.) And again: Τὰ ἰδιώματα τοῦ πρωτοτύπου οὐδαμῶς τίς τῶν εὖ φρονούντων ἐν τῇ εἰκόνι ἐπιζητεῖ· ἐν γὰρ τῇ εἰκόνι ἄλλο οὐδὲν ὁ ἀληθὴς λόγος γινώσκει ἢ κατὰ τὸ ὄνομα κοινωνεῖν, οὗ τινός ἐστιν εἰκών, καὶ οὐ κατὰ τὴν οὐσίαν. (Ibid., c. 441.)

In like manner Chrysostom speaks of the εἰκὼν of a man, by which he also (like Theodotus) illustrates the sense of ἀντίτυπα. See quotation above, p. 268.

So also Theodoret speaks of the εἰκόνες of a king, illustrating the sense of τύπος. Dial. ii. Inconfusus, Opera, edit. Schulze, tom. iv. p. 86. See also above, pp. 269, 286.

On the character and writings of Theodotus Antiochenus, see Cave, Hist. Lit., 2d edit. *sub voce.*

* The words are addressed to the Emperor in support of image-worship. They are immediately preceded by the words "Sacrosancta vasa a nobis adorata nullam nobis reprehensionis notam inurunt. Siquidem ea per Christi invocationem in sancta mutari persuasum habemus." See above, pp. 116, 117.

Hoc facite in mei recordationem, nos autem memores ejus mandati, ANTITYPA (id est Configuralia) offerimus." (Germanus Constant., Theoria Rer. Eccles., In Bibliotheca Max. Patr., Lugd. 1677, tom. xiii. p. 59.)

PIGNUS, ΑΝΑΜΝΗΣΙΣ, ΜΝΗΜΟΣΥΝΟΝ, MEMORIA, ETC.*

I.

"Ότι μὲν οὖν καὶ ἐν ταύτῃ τῇ προφητείᾳ περὶ τοῦ ἄρτου ὃν παρέδωκεν ἡμῖν ὁ ἡμέτερος Χριστὸς ποιεῖν εἰς ΑΝΑΜΝΗΣΙΝ τοῦ τὲ σωματοποιήσασθαι αὐτὸν διὰ τοὺς πιστεύοντας εἰς αὐτὸν, δι' οὓς καὶ παθητὸς γέγονε· καὶ περὶ τοῦ ποτηρίου ὃ εἰς ΑΝΑΜΝΗΣΙΝ τοῦ αἵματος αὐτοῦ παρέδωκεν εὐχαριστοῦντας ποιεῖν, φαίνεται. (Justin Martyr, Dial. cum Tryph., § 70, Opera, edit. Benedict., Hagæ C., 1742, pp. 168, 169.)

II.

" Non licet nobis in dubium sensus istos devocare, ne et in Christo de fide eorum deliberetur ; ne forte dicatur, quod falso Satanam prospectarit de cœlo præcipitatum ; aut falso vocem Patris audierit de ipso testificatam : aut deceptus sit cum Petri socrum tetigit: aut alium postea unguenti senserit spiritum, quod in sepulturam suam acceptavit: alium postea vini saporem, quod in sanguinis sui *memoriam* consecravit."† (Tertullian, De Anima, cap. xvii., Opera, p. 276, edit. Rigaltius, 1689.)

III.

" Calicem in *commemorationem* Domini et passionis ejus offerimus." (Cyprian, Epist. ad Cæcilium, Epist. lxiii., Opera, edit. Baluzius, Venice, 1728.)

IV.

Ἐνέτελλετο τοῖς μαθηταῖς διὰ τούτων ΑΝΑΜΝΗΣΙΝ αὐτοῦ ποιεῖσθαι.‡ (Adamantius, in Op. Origenis, tom. i. c. 1840, edit. Migne.)

---

* It would be easy to multiply extracts in which the Eucharist is spoken of as a memorial of Christ's *passion*. Such quotations are not given, because the Real Presence of Christ's suffering and death is not in question in the present controversy.

The passages which are given (*taken together*) will be found to have a very important bearing on that which is in question—the Real Objective Presence under the form of bread and wine of Christ's Body and Blood, Soul and Divinity.

† On this passage see above, p. 24. See also Albertinus, De Euch., pp. 337 *sqq*.
‡ See above, pp. 61, 268.

V.

Ἵνα ἐσθίοντες τε καὶ πίνοντες, ἀεὶ ΜΝΗΜΟΝΕΥΩΜΕΝ τοῦ ὑπὲρ ἡμῶν ἀποθανόντος καὶ ἐγερθέντος . . . ὁ γὰρ ἐσθίων καὶ πίνων, δηλονότι εἰς ἀνεξάλειπτον ΜΝΗΜΗΝ τοῦ ὑπὲρ ἡμῶν ἀποθανόντος . . . τὸν δὲ λόγον τῆς ΜΝΗΜΗΣ . . . μὴ πληρῶν . . . οὐδὲν ἔχει ὄφελος.* (Basil. Cæsar.? De Baptismo, lib. i. cap. iii. § 2, Opera, edit. Garnier, Paris, 1722, tom. ii. Append., pp. 650, 651.)

VI.

Ὥσπερ οὖν ἐπὶ τῶν Ἰουδαίων, οὕτω καὶ ἐνταῦθα τῆς εὐεργεσίας ἐγκατέδησε† τὸ ΜΝΗΜΟΣΥΝΟΝ τῷ μυστηρίῳ. (Chrysostom, In Matth., Hom. lxxxii. al. lxxxiii. § 1, Opera, edit. Montfaucon, tom. vii. p. 783.)

VII.

" Hujus sacrificii caro et sanguis ante adventum Christi per victimas similitudinum promittebatur, in passione Christi per ipsam veritatem reddebatur; post adscensum Christi per Sacramentum *memoriæ* celebratur." (Augustin., Contra Faustum, lib. xx. cap. xxi., Opera, edit. Benedict., 1688, tom. viii. c. 348.)

VIII.

" *Accepit panem, et gratias agens fregit, et dixit: Accipite et manducate.* Hoc est, benedicens, etiam passurus, ultimam nobis commemorationem, sive memoriam dereliquit. Quemadmodum si quis peregre proficiscens aliquod *pignus* ei, quem diligit, derelinquat. .... Ideo hoc Salvator tradidit‡ sacramentum, ut per hoc semper commemoremus, quia pro nobis est mortuus. Nam et ideo cum accipimus, a sacerdotibus commonemur, quia corpus et sanguis est Christi: ut beneficiis ejus non existamus ingrati." (Commentary in 1 Cor. xi.—probably the work of Pelagius—among the works of St. Jerome, tom. xi. par. iii. c. 259, 260, edit. Vallarsius, Venice, 1771.)

IX.

" Vere istud est hæreditarium munus Testamenti ejus novi, quod

---

* See on this extract Albertinus, De Euch., p. 440. It will be found also in Homil. in Aliquot Sc. loc. De Spiritu Sancto, sub fin., Opera, tom. ii. p. 586.

† Shortly before Chrysostom had said . Καθάπερ Μωσῆς φησὶ, τοῦτο μνημόσυνον ὑμῖν αἰώνιον· οὕτω καὶ αὐτὸς, εἰς ἐμὴν ἀνάμνησιν, ἕως ἂν παραγένωμαι.

‡ Compare the following from Florus Magister: " Propterea et iturus ad passionem, et per resurrectionis et ascensionis gloriam discessurus e mundo, hoc sacramentum ultimum discipulis tradidit, ut memoriam tantæ charitatis, per quam solam salvamur, arctius eorum mentibus infigeret." (De Expositione Missæ, § 63, Opera, edit. Migne, c. 55), which words are found also in Hincmar (Opera, tom. ii. p. 92, edit. Paris, 1645).

Elsewhere Florus writes : " Panis ille sacrosanctæ oblationis corpus est Christi, non materie vel specie visibili, sed virtute et potentia spirituali." (Adversus Amalarium, ib. i. § 9, Opera, edit. Migne, c. 77.)

nobis ea nocte qua tradebatur crucifigendus, tanquam *pignus** suæ præsentiæ dereliquit." (Gaudentius Brix., Serm. ii., Opera, p. 38, edit. Galeardus, 1757.)

X.

" Suam *memoriam* nobis reliquit, quemadmodum si quis peregre proficiscens, aliquod *pignus* ei quem diligit derelinquat, ut quotiescunque illud viderit, possit ejus beneficia et amicitias recordari."†

* Dr. Pusey (Real Presence from the Fathers, p. 110), argues from this : "If Christ were not present, the Eucharist could be no 'pledge of His Presence,'" which is, doubtless, quite true, if understood of the Presence of His Deity, which the Fathers have so carefully distinguished from His corporal presence. (See above, p. 149 *sqq.*) But to understand it of a Real Objective Presence of Christ's Body would not only be at variance with the sense in which the word *pignus* is used by the Fathers (see, in addition to other passages under this head, Bertram, as quoted below, p. 302) ; but to the language of Gaudentius himself, who goes on (p. 38) to speak of the mysteries, "quæ necesse est a cunctis sacerdotibus per singulas totius orbis Ecclesias celebrari, usquequo iterum Christus de cœlis adveniat."

† Compare Christian Druthmar, quoted above, p. 281.

Compare also the following from the Commentary on St. Paul's Epistles, probably the work of Remigius of Auxerre : " Relinquens Dominus hoc sacramentum salutiferum omnibus fidelibus, ut illud infingeret cordibus et memoriæ eorum, egit more cujuscunque hominis inquiens, qui appropinquans morti aliquod munus pretiosum dimittit alicui amicorum suorum in memoriam suam, inquiens : accipe hoc munus, amice charissime, et tene illud cum omni diligentiâ penes te in memoriam mei, ut quotiescunque illud videris, recorderis mei. Qui amicus admittens illud munus amici sui charissimi, si eum toto animo dilexit, non potest non dolere et tristari de morte amici quotiescunque munus sibi conspicit dimissum." (In Bibliotheca Max. Patr., Lugd. 1677, tom. viii. p. 971. See Albertinus, De Eucharistia, p. 939.)

These are assuredly not the words of one holding the doctrine of the Real Presence of Christ Himself in the Elements ; although they may very well consist with the belief of an assumption of the Elements into spiritual union with Christ's Body, which appears to have been the view of Remigius, who was probably also the author of the book " De Divinis Officiis," among the works of Alcuin, in which this notion is very clearly expressed. (See Romish Mass and English Church, p. 62, and Albertinus, De Eucharistia, p. 958. Gratian has quoted from this work as from Gregory I. See Hospinian, tom. iii. p. 216.)

The same view was probably held by Fulbert of Chartres, who writes : " Ne sublati corporis præsenti fraudaremur munimine corporis nihilominus et sanguinis sui *pignus* salutare nobis reliquit, non inanis mysterii symbolum, sed compaginante Spiritu Sancto corpus Christi verum." (Epistola ad Adeodatum, in Migne's Patrologia, tom. cxli. c. 202. See Albertinus, De Eucharistia, pp. 944—946.)

Indeed, the passage of Remigius which most clearly expresses his view, and which presents so many points of resemblance to a passage in the treatise " De Divinis Officiis " (part of which is quoted in " Romish Mass and English Church," p. 63), is quoted by Fulbert as from "Haymo super Epist. ad Corinth." in his Sermo viii. (Opera Varia, edit. De Villiers, 1608, fo. 169 ; Patrologia, Migne, tom. cxli. c. 355.)

The passage is as follows : " Caro quam Verbum Dei Patris assumpsit in utero virginali in unitate suæ personæ, et panis qui consecratur in Ecclesiâ, unum corpus Christi sunt. Sicut enim illa caro corpus Christi est, ita iste panis transit in corpus Christi, nec sunt duo corpora sed unum corpus. Divinitatis enim plenitudo, quæ fuit in illo, replet istum panem ; et ipsa divinitas Verbi, quæ implet cœlum et terram et

(Sedulius Scotus, in 1 Cor. xi., Migne's Patrologia, tom. ciii. c. 151, In Bibliotheca Max. Patr., Lugd. 1677, tom. vi. p. 545.)

XI.

"Quia corpus assumptum ablaturus erat ex oculis nostris, et sideribus illaturus, necessarium erat ut nobis in hac die Sacramentum corporis et sanguinis sui consecraret : ut . . . . perennis illa victima viveret in *memoria*, et semper præsens esset in gratia." (* Homilia V. "De Pascha," in Bibl. Max. Patr., Lugd. 1677, tom. vi. p. 636.)

XII.

"In illis enim carnalibus victimis figuratio fuit carnis Christi quam pro peccatis nostris ipse sine peccato fuerat oblaturus, et sanguinis quem erat effusurus in remissionem peccatorum nostrorum; in isto autem sacrificio† gratiarum actio atque *commemoratio* est carnis Christi, quam pro nobis obtulit, et sanguinis quem pro nobis idem Deus effudit." (Fulgentius, De Fide ad Petr. Diac., cap. xix. In " Heptas Præsulum," Paris, 1661, p. 495.)

XIII.

"Salvator Deus exemplum dedit, ut quotiescunque hoc facimus, in mente habeamus quod Christus pro nobis omnibus mortuus est. Ideo nobis‡ dicitur, Corpus Christi, ut cum hoc recordati fuerimus, non simus ingrati gratiæ ejus; quemadmodum si quis moriens relinquat ei quem diligit aliquod *pignus*, quod ille, post mortem ejus,

omnia quæ in eis sunt, ipsa replet corpus Christi quod a multis sacerdotibus per universum orbem sanctificatur, et facit unum corpus Christi esse. Et sicut ille panis et sanguis in corpus Christi transeunt, ita omnis qui in Ecclesia digne comedit illud, unum corpus Christi est, sicut ipse dixit : *Qui manducat carnem meum et bibit meum sanguinem, in me manet, et ego in illo* (Joan. vi. 57). Tamen illa caro quam assumpsit, et iste panis, omnisque Ecclesia, non faciunt tria corpora Christi, sed unum corpus. Et sicut qui corpore et sanguine Christi communicant, unum corpus cum eo efficiunt, sic et qui communicant de idolothytis, unum cum diabolo corpus existunt." (Bibl. Max., tom. viii. pp. 967, 968.)

* This is the Homily formerly attributed to Eusebius Emissenus. It is, perhaps, the work of Faustus Rhegiensis.
† This had been called just before "Sacrificium panis et vini."
On this passage see Albertinus, De Eucharistia, p. 884.
‡ These words of Primasius, alleging a reason for the sacrament being called the Body of Christ, are worthy of special observation.
Bishop Morton (after showing that the expression "pledge of resurrection to immortality ¡ is applied to Baptism as well as the Eucharist) says : "All these holy Fathers (you see) interpret this sacrament to be unto us a *present pledge* of a *Friend absent*, whether he be a living traveller, or one departed this life. Primasius's observation of the [*Pledge*] is very remarkable, when he saith of this sacrament (thus called a *Pledge*) that it is *therefore called* the Body of Christ, giving the name of the *Thing* to the token thereof : than which similitude what can be more pregnant and pertinent for the confuting of your Tridentine faith, concerning the corporal Presence of Christ in the Eucharist?" (Morton on Eucharist, book v. c. ix. § 2, p. 369, London, 1655.)

quandocunque viderit, nunquid potest lacrimis continere, si eum perfecte dilexerit?" (Primasii Com. in 1 Cor. xi., In Bibliotheca Max. Patr., Lugd. 1677, tom. x. p. 189.)

XIV.

"Cujus et nunc sacramentis carnis et sanguinis *pignus* vitæ accipit [ecclesia] et in futuro præsenti beatificabitur aspectu." (Ven. Beda, In Prov., lib. i. c. iii., Opera, edit. Colon. 1688, tom. iv. c. 645.)

XV.

Εἰς τύπον καὶ ΑΝΑΜΝΙΙΣΙΝ ἐναργεστάτην ... παρέδωκεν. (Concil. Constant. 754, In Labb., tom. vii. c. 445; Mansi, tom. xiii. c. 261.)

XVI.

"Nec offerens victimas legales, sed instar illius panem et vinum. carnem videlicet et sanguinem suum,* unde dixit : Caro (inquiens) mea vere est Cibus, et sanguis meus vere est potus. Ista quoque duo munera panem videlicet et vinum commisit Ecclesiæ suæ *in memoria* sui offerenda."† (Primasius, ? Comment. in Epist. ad Hebræos, cap. v., In Biblioth. Max. Patr., Lugd. 1677, tom. x. p. 258.)

XVII.

"Hujus sacrificii caro et sanguis ante adventum Christi per victimas similitudine promittebatur, in passione Christi per ipsam veritatem reddebatur, post ascensum Christi per sacramentum *memoria* celebratur.‡ Proinde prima sacramenta, quæ observantur et celebrantur ex lege, prænuntiativa erant Christi venturi, quæ cum suo adventu Christus implevisset, oblata sunt ; et ideo oblata quia impleta, non enim venit solvere legem sed adimplere. Alia sunt instituta virtute majora, utilitate meliora, actu faciliora, numero pauciora, tanquam justitia fidei revelata, et in libertate vocatis filiis Dei jugo servitutis ablato, quod duro et carni dedito populo congruebat, qualia sunt in Ecclesia baptismus Christi, Eucharistia Christi, signaculum Christi. Hinc est quod cautissimo divisionis ordine Ecclesia Dei vivi, quæ est columna et firmamentum veritatis, tempora venturi Christi venientisque discernit, et omissis sacrificiis quibus Christus passurus promittebatur, hoc sacrificium offert, quo Christus *passus ostenditur,* qui propterea verus est sacerdos,

---

* See Romish Mass and English Church, pp. 3, 4.

† See Albertinus, De Euch., p. 305. This commentary on the Hebrews is by mistake attributed to Primasius. It is probably the work of Rhemigius of Auxerre. See Albertinus, p. 891.

‡ Compare above, p. 293, No. VII. The teaching of the whole of this extract is substantially St. Augustine's.

quia semetipsum veram pro nobis hostiam obtulit." (Florus Magister, De Expositione Missæ, § 4, Op., ed. Migne, c. 20.)

XVIII.

" Et hoc corpus *pignus* est et species: illud vero ipsa veritas. Hoc enim geritur, donec ad illud perveniatur. Ubi vero ad illum perventum fuerit, hoc removebitur." (Bertram, De Corpore et Sanguine Christi, § lxxxviii., Migne's Patrologia, tom. cxxi. c. 164, 165.)

XIX.

"Apparet itaque, quod multa inter se differentia separantur, quantum est inter *pignus* et eam rem pro qua pignus traditur: et quantum inter imaginem, et rem cujus est imago : et quantum inter speciem et veritatem." (Ibid., § lxxxix. c. 165.)

XX.

"Igitur cum ipse filius Dei dicat, Caro mea vere est cibus, et sanguis meus vere est potus : ita intelligendum est, eadem redemptionis nostræ mysteria, et vere esse corpus et sanguinem Domini, ut illius unitatis perfectæ, quam cum capite nostro, jam spe, postea re, tenebimus, *pignora* credere debemus. Inde et sacramenta, a sanctificatione vel secreta virtute, dicuntur." (Walafrid Strabo,[*] De Rebus Eccles., cap. 17, In Hittorpius, p. 342.)

XXI.

" This mystery is a *pledge* and a figure : Christ's Body is truth itself. This *pledge* we do keep mystically until that we be come to the truth itself ; and then is this pledge ended. (Elfric's Saxon Homily, in " A Testimony of Antiquity," Haviland, 1623, p. 7, L'Isle's Reprint.)

XXII.

" Sacrificii placabilis nobis providit expiamenta, ut, quia corpus suum, quod semel pro nobis offerebat in pretium, paulo post a nostris visibus sublaturus fuerat in cœlum, ne sublati corporis fraudaremur præsenti munimine, corporis nihilominus et sanguinis sui *pignus* salutare nobis reliquit, non inanis mysterii symbolum, sed compaginante Spiritu Sancto corpus Christi verum,[†] quod quotidiana venera-

---

[*] In the preceding chapter (p. 341) it is said : " Novi vero testamenti, nova mysteria ad instruendum novum hominem tradidit : Et morte sua vetera perficiens, resurrectione sua, nova firmavit. In cœna siquidem, quam ante traditionem suam ultimam cum discipulis habuit, post Paschæ veteris solemnia, corporis et sanguinis sui sacramenta in panis et vini substantia eisdem discipulis tradidit, et ea in commemorationem sanctissimæ suæ passionis celebrare perdocuit. Nihil ergo congruentius his speciebus, ad significandam capitis atque membrorum unitatem, potuit inveniri."

[†] See above, p. 294. Gieseler says that Fulbert " cannot have expressed himself decidedly against the transformation doctrines, since Adelmann, in his letters, refers Berenger to their common teacher." (Eccles. Hist., vol. II. p. 398, edit. Clark. See also Hospinian, Opera, tom. iii. p. 237, Geneva, 1681.)

tione, sub visibili creaturæ forma invisibiliter virtus secreta in sacris solemnibus operatur." (Fulberti Carnotensis Epistolæ, in Migne's Patrologia, tom. cxli. c. 202.)

XXIII.

" Sed quodammodo aliud esse dicitur, quod virginali utero sumpta carne crucis injuriam sustinuit, de sepulcro resurgens discipulis apparuit, cujus *memoriam* in pane presbyteris collato Episcopus agere videtur: aliud quod per mysterium agitur," &c. (Fulberti Carnotensis Epistolæ, in Migne's Patrologia, tom. cxli c. 194.)

This note would be incomplete without the addition of certain other extracts marking clearly the sense in which such terms were used by ancient Christians. Such are the following :—

ΕΙΚΩΝ.

I.

Αἱ εἰκόνες τούτων ὧν εἰσὶν εἰκόνες, καὶ ἀπόντων δεικτικαί εἰσίν· ὥστε καὶ τόν ἀπόντα δι' αὐτῶν φαίνεσθαι δοκεῖν. (Marcellus Ancyranus, as quoted by Eusebius Contra Marcel., lib. i. cap. iv. p. 24, as appended to Demonstr. Evaugel., Paris, 1628.)

II.

Ὥστε εἰ μὲν εἰκὼν οὐ Κύριος. (Ibid., p. 24.)

III.

Οὐ δὴ ποῦ δὲ ἡ εἰκὼν καὶ τὸ οὗ ἐστὶν ἡ εἰκών, ἓν καὶ ταὐτὸν ἐπινοεῖται. (In Ibid., p. 25.)

IV.

Πολὺ τὸ μέσον ἐστὶ, τοῦ τε κατὰ τὸ ἀρχέτυπον νοουμένου, καὶ τοῦ κατ' εἰκόνα γεγενημένου. Ἡ γὰρ εἰκών, εἰ μὲν ἔχει τὴν πρὸς τὸ πρωτότυπον ὁμοιότητα, κυρίως τοῦτο κατονομάζεται. (Gregorius Nyss., De Hominis Opificio, cap. xvi., Op., edit. Migne, tom. i. c. 180.)

V.

Ἔστι εἰκὼν δηλοῦσα τὸ ὁμοούσιον· αἱ μὲν γὰρ ἄψυχοι εἰκόνες οὐκ ἔχουσι τὴν οὐσίαν τούτων ὧνπερ εἰκόνες εἰσίν. (Theodoret., Epist. ad Coloss. cap. i., Opera, tom. iii. p. 477, edit. Schulze).

VI.

Ἡ εἰκὼν σχήματα, ἀλλ' οὐ πράγματα ἔχει. (Ibid., in Dan., lib. ii. c. 2, Opera, tom. ii. p. 1091.)

VII.

Πολλάκις ἔφην, ὡς οὐχ οἷόντε τὴν εἰκόνα πάντα ἔχειν ὅσα τὸ ἀρχέτυπον ἔχει. (Ibid., Dial. iii., Impatibilis, Op., tom. iv. p. 203.)

VIII.

Εἰ εἰκὼν τοῦ σώματος ἔστι, οὐκ ἐνδέχεται εἶναι αὐτὸ τὸ θεῖον σῶμα.
(2nd Nicene Council, in Labbæus, tom. vii. c. 449.)

IMAGO AND SIMILITUDO.

I.

" Typus enim et *imago* secundum materiam, et secundum substantiam aliquoties a veritate diversus est; secundum autem habitum et lineamentum, debet servare similitudinem, et similiter *ostendere per præsentia illa quæ* NON * *sunt* PRÆSENTIA." (Irenæus, Contra Hæreses, lib. ii. cap. xxiii., Opera, edit. Migne, c. 786.)

II.

"*Imago* veritati non usquequaque adæquabitur, aliud enim est secundum veritatem esse, aliud ipsam veritatem esse." (Tertullian, Cont. Marci., lib. ii. c. 9, edit. Rigaltius, 1689, p. 386.)

III.

"*Imago*, quum omnes lineas exprimat veritatis, vi tamen ipsa caret, non habens motum." (Ibid., p. 386.)

IV.

" Neque ipse sibi quisquam *imago* est; sed eum, cujus *imago* est, necesse est ut *imago* demonstret." (Hilary Pict., Liber de Synodis, § 13, Opera, edit. Benedict., Paris, 1693, c. 1159.)

V.

"Nemo potest ipsi sibi *imago* sua esse." (Ambrose, De Fid., lib. i. cap. vii., Opera, edit. Benedict., tom. ii. c. 453.)

VI.

" Quid absurdius quam *imaginem* ad se dici?" (Aug., De Trin., lib. vii. c. i. §2, Opera, edit. Benedict., 1688, tom. viii. c. 853.)

VII.

" Aliud est veritas, aliud *imago* veritatis." (Claud. Mamertus, De Statu Animæ, lib. i. c. v., In Bibl. Max., Lugd. 1677, tom. vi. p. 1048.)

* It is very truly stated by J. A. Assemani: "Disputatum aliquando fuit, an Eucharistia dici possit *Imago Corporis Christi*. Negaverunt id Nicephorus Patriarcha Constantinopolitanus Antirrhetico 2, contra Iconomachos, Epiphanius Diaconus in 7, Synodo Act. 6, et alii subsecuti hæresim Iconoclastarum: alii tamen vetustiores, id affirmaverunt." (Codex Liturgicus, tom. iv. p. 73, Diss. De Liturg. Origine, Art. iv. § viii.)

We can very well understand why in more recent times Christians may have objected to the term, even without supposing their views to have approached to the Real Objective Presence. (See above, p. 279.)

But it is impossible, fairly and reasonably, to account for the use of the term by Christians of earlier times, on the hypothesis of their believing the Eucharist to be, or to contain, the very present Body and Blood of Christ.

VIII.

"Constantinus Iconomachus, imaginem Christi vocat, quod nobis dedit Christus ad manducandum, quomodo igitur idem dicitur Corpus Christi et *imago* Christi? Quod enim est alicujus *imago*, corpus ejus esse non potest? Et rursus, quod est corpus, non potest esse ejus *imago*. Omnis esse *imago* alia est ab eo, cujus *imago* est."* (Nicephorus Constantinopolitanus, De Cherubim, cap. vi., De Adoratione, In Bibliotheca Max. Patr., Lugd. 1677, tom. xiv. p. 94.)

IX.

"*Imago* veritas non est, etiam cum de veritate est." (Hugo, as quoted by Thomas Waldensis, De Sac. Euch., cap. lxxxvi., Opera, tom. ii. fo. 145, Venice, 1571.)

X.

"*Similia*, quæcunque alia sunt, inter se etiam dissimilia ex aliqua, parte sunt." (St. Augustine, De Genesi ad lit. Lib. Imperf. §60, Op., edit. Bened. 1680, tom. iii. par. i. c. 114.)

XI.

"*Similitudo* † rei veri imitatio est." (Cassiodorus in Ps. xlviii. v. 4, Op., edit. Garetius, Rotom. 1679, tom. ii. p. 161.)

ΤΥΠΟΣ.

I.

"*Typus* . . . debet . . . . ostendere per præsentia illa quæ non sunt præsentia."‡ (Irenæus, Contra Hæreses, lib. ii. cap. xxiii., Opera, edit. Migne, c. 786.)

II.

"*Typus* autem umbra est veritatis." (St. Ambrose, De Fide, lib. iii. cap. xi., Op., edit. Benedict., tom. ii. c. 513.)

III.

Ὁ ΤΥΠΟΣ οὐκ ἀλήθεια, μόρφωσιν δὲ μᾶλλον τῆς ἀληθείας εἰσφέρει. (Cyril. Alex. in Amos, cap. vi. v. 3, § lviii., Op., edit. Migne, tom. iv. c. 520.)

---

* On this passage see Albertinus, De Eucharistia, p. 919.

† So of ὁμοίωσις, Clemens Alexandrinus says: Ἄλλο ὁμοίωσις, ἄλλο αὐτὸ τὸ ὄν. (Stromat., lib. i. § vii., Op., edit. Potter, tom. i. p. 338.)
And another writer: Τὸ ὅμοιον τινὶ οὐκ ἔστιν αὐτὸ ἐκεῖνο ᾧ ὁμοιοῦται. (Refutatio hypocrisis Meletii, In Op. Athanasii, Op., edit. Benedict., tom. ii. p. 24.)

‡ See above under *Imago*, No. I.
Of τύπος Dr. Vogan says: "I find no proof that it 'stands for a thing present.' Nor do I find in Dr. Pusey's Note I. any such proof, except upon the assumption of 'the Real Presence.'" (True Doctrine, p. 152. See also Dr. Harrison's "Dr. Pusey's Challenge Answered," p. 366.)

IV.

Περιττὸς ὁ τύπος, ἀνῃρημένης τῆς ἀληθείας. (Theodoret, Op., tom. iv. p. 209, edit. Schulze.)

V.

Ὁ δὲ τύπος οὐκ ἔχει πάντα ὅσαπερ ἡ ἀλήθεια. οὗ δὴ χάριν ἐκεῖνος [Μωϋσῆς] οὐκ ἦν μὲν φύσει Θεὸς, ὠνομάσθη δὲ ὅμως Θεὸς, ἵνα πληρώσῃ τὸν τύπον. (Ibid., p. 85.)

SIGNUM.

I.

"*Signum* dicitur, cum per hoc quod videtur, aliud aliquid indicatur." (Origen, in Ep. ad Rom., lib. iv. § 2, p. 525, Op., ed. Migne, tom. iv. c. 968).

II.

"*Signum* est res, præter speciem quam ingerit sensibus, aliud aliquid ex se faciens in cogitationem venire." (Augustine, De Doctrina Christ., lib. ii. cap. i., Opera, tom. iii. par. 1, c. 19, edit. Benedict., 1680).

III.

"Aliud est veritas, aliud *signum* veritatis, quia signum veritas non est, etiam cum veritatis signum est, et verum est." (Hugo, as quoted by Thomas Waldensis, De Sac. Euch., cap. lxxxvi., Opera, tom. ii. fo. 145, Venice, 1571.)

FIGURA.

I.

"*Figura* etenim non est veritas, sed imitatio veritatis."* (Gaudentius Brix., Ep., Sermo ii., Op., p. 33, edit. Galeardus, 1757.)

II.

"Quæcunque mystica, quæcunque alta, quæcunque divina sunt, hæc de Christo a Moysa in umbra, et *figura*, et imaginibus dicebantur." (Hesychius Hieros., In Levit., lib. v. cap. xvi., In Bibl. Max. Patr., tom. xii. p. 125a.)

III.

"*Figura* est, superficie sua nihil afferens ædificationis: si tamen intelligatur, multum conferens utilitatis." (Radulphus Flaviacensis, In Levit., lib. xiii. cap. ii., In Bibl. Max. Patr., Lugd. 1677, tom. xvii. p. 167).

* For an answer to the objection taken from the words "in figura inventus ut homo," and Tertullian's language in reply to Marcion on this point (Contra Marc., lib. v. c. 20), see Albertinus, De Eucharistia, p. 329.

The passage from Gaudentius quoted in the text is immediately followed by the words "Nam et homo ad imaginem Dei factus est, nec tamen idcirco Deus est: tametsi ea ratione qua imago Dei dicitur, dicatur et Deus, quomodo natura unus Deus est, positione plures."

PIGNUS, MEMORIA, ETC.*

I.

" Hoc corpus [quod in ecclesia geritur] *pignus* est et species, illud vero [quod jam glorificatum cognoscitur] ipsa veritas." (Bertram, De Corp. et Sang. Dom., § lxxxviii., ed. Migne, c. 164.)

II.

" "*Pignus* et imago alterius rei sunt, id est, non ad se, sed ad aliud aspiciunt." (Ibid., lxxxvi. c. 163. See also Albertinus, De Eucharistia, p. 598.)

III.

"Nemo *recordatur* nisi quod in præsentia non est positum." (St. Augustine in Ps. xxxvii. § 2, Op., ed. Bened. 1681, tom. iv. par. i. c. 294.)

---

* For ἀντιτύπον see above, pp. 267, 268, also 286, 289.
With reference to the sense of σύμβολον Albertinus writes: "Veteres testantur, se illud pro signo et figurâ usurpasse, ut patet ex Bellarmino observante, *Patres Græci sacramenta vocant σύμβολα, id est, signa* [De Sacr. in Gen., lib. i. c. 9] et aliis Adversariorum in Græcorum Patrum versionibus σύμβολον per signum communiter reddentibus; tum ex ipso loco Isidori Pelusiotæ a Chrysostomo mutuato, ubi illud pro signo esse sumendum apparet ex Chrysostomo, modo σύμβολον modo σημεῖον usurpante, et Billio *signa* vertente; tum denique ex ipsomet Theodoreto illud per *typum* exponente et dicente *cujus putas symbolum et typum esse sanctissimum cibum !*" (De Eucharistia, p. 793. See pp. 394, 794. See also Dr. Harrison's "Dr. Pusey's Challenge Answered," vol. ii. p. 201.)
Maximus, the Scholiast on Pseudo-Dionys., says: Σύμβολα ταῦτα καὶ οὐκ ἀλήθεια. (In cap. iii. Ecc. Hier. See above, p. 133.)
And Chrysostom clearly marks the same sense when he says: Τὸ δὲ πᾶν ὁ θεὸς ἐργάζεται, σύμβολον οὗτος πληροῖ μόνον (In ii. Epist. ad Timoth., cap. i. Hom. ii., Opera, tom. xi. p. 671, edit. Montfaucon, 1734), which again is expressed thus: ὅτι σύμβολον ὁ ἱερεὺς πληροῖ (Ibid.), and which has its parallel in σχῆμα πληρῶν μόνον ἕστηκεν ὁ ἱερεύς. (De Prodit. Jud., Hom. ii., Op., tom. ii, p. 394; also in p. 384.

NOTE F (p. 137).

On the Res Sacramenti of the Eucharist, as in the condition of Death.

I QUOTE the following very forcible language from a work which contains much which is scarcely less forcible, and which seems to me to demand attention far beyond what it has hitherto received:—
"The letter does not speak of the Lord's body in any other condition than in that of 'being given for us;' or of His blood in any other condition than in that of being poured out for sin. The letter sets forth the Lord's body as a sacrifice for sin: it sets forth His blood as poured out from His body for sin. It sets forth His body and His blood separated from each other; and since blood is the life of the body, the body from which the blood is poured out has its life taken away, and is dead." (Prebendary Vogan's True Doctrine of the Eucharist, preface, p. ix.) "The bread is the body of Christ, and the wine is the blood of Christ, in a way beyond the nature of earthly things. The bread and the wine are the body and blood of Christ, so far as one thing can be another; the nature of each being unchanged. They are what He called, and by calling made, them, to all the intents and purposes for which He so made them. The wine is His blood poured out, the bread is His body given, the life being taken from it, and the body therefore dead; but both in spiritual effect, not in positive and absolute reality." (Ibid., p. x.) "His dead body is no more: His poured-out blood is no more. They are not anywhere, they cannot be present anywhere. They were not when He first gave them. His body was not broken; it was alive and unhurt, when He gave His dead body: His blood was not shed; it was all still flowing in His veins, when He gave His poured-out blood. Yet He gave, and it was in most real truth that He gave, His dead body and His outshed blood. And now He gives the same: His dead body, though His body is alive for evermore; His outshed blood, though it is impossible, and, since the day that it was

shed upon the Cross, has been impossible, for it ever to be shed again. Neither the blood remains poured out, nor the body dead. One is no more in the condition of being given, the other is no more in the condition of being shed. They are no more. His dead body is nowhere to be found, His poured-out blood is nowhere to be found. In most certain and absolute fact and reality, they are not. And as that which is not, cannot be present anywhere; the dead body of our Lord, and His blood shed, cannot be, and therefore are not, present either in the Eucharist, or in its elements." (True Doctrine, preface, p. xi.)

"From this it is necessarily to be concluded, that it was not by a real presence of His body and blood, but spiritually and effectually, that they were given. It was to the faith that His body—was—to be broken, that He gave it: it was to the faith that His blood—was—to be shed, that He gave it. And now that His body has been given and His blood has been shed; they are no longer in those conditions. They now are not. But to faith, and to the faith only, that His body has been given, and that His blood has been shed, He now imparts His body given and His blood shed, just as He imparted them to His Apostles, the night before He suffered. And this He did and now does, although the presence of His broken body and His outpoured blood was then, and now is, impossible." (Ibid., p. xii.)

"It follows that the bread was the body of our Lord, and the wine was His blood, by His will and all-powerful word, in a mystery, by effectual substitution and representation, in spiritual and lifegiving power; but not in literal fact." (Ibid., ch. x. p. 116.)

"Our Lord said nothing of His glorified body; nor will the literal interpretation [of the words of institution] admit the notion of His glorified body being in the Sacrament, in or under or with the outward forms. True, it is the body which is now glorified; but, as Bishop Andrewes well said, not in that state or condition. We cannot eat the glorified body—at least, it is contrary to the analogy and all notions of His glorified body; neither can we drink of the blood of His glorified body, for it cannot be poured out. We eat not a living body, but a dead body. It is therefore utterly beyond the question to speak of the capabilities and powers of the risen or glorified body of Christ; and all the subtle metaphysics which have been employed to prove that it can be in heaven unmoved, at the right hand of God, and yet can also be in thousands of places upon the earth, that it can remain, whole and perfect, in those places, and that it can be in or under innumerable millions of pieces of bread in those places,—all is to no purpose." (Ibid., pp. 104, 105.)

Dr. Vogan says: "The authorities cited by Dr. Pusey speak throughout of the body and blood of Christ, clearly in the meaning not of His body with the blood in it, circulating and enlivening it, and therefore not shed, but of His body given for us, as given; and His blood shed for us, as poured out from the body, and therefore leaving it dead. They had no notion of such a contradiction as a living, much more a glorified body, the blood being separated and poured out from it; nor of so doubly revolting a thing as eating a living body, or so impossible a thing as the blood being shed from our Lord's glorified body. . . . . . They would have seen the self-evident, but now for centuries the strangely overlooked fact, that a body is necessarily dead if the blood be poured out from it; that the sacrifices died from the shedding of their blood: that, therefore, our Lord Jesus Christ died, when His blood was poured out; and that when we receive His blood shed for us, His body which we receive is therefore dead." (True Doctrine, p. 107.)

It must by no means, however, be supposed that there is anything of novelty in the essential point of Dr. Vogan's contention. It is nothing more than has been continually urged by our Reformers, and by subsequent English divines.*

Moreover, the same teaching, subversive as it is of the Real Objective theory, is seen very clearly appearing here and there, as the recognised doctrine of the Christian Church in the writings of the Fathers.

As evidence of this the following quotations may suffice :—

I.

" Quomodo ad potandum vinum veniri non potest, nisi botrus calcetur ante, et prematur ; sic nec nos sanguinem Christi possemus bibere, nisi Christus calcatus prius fuisset et pressus." (Cyprianus, Ep. ad Cæcil., Ep. lxiii., Opera, c. 227, edit. Baluzius, Venice, 1728.)

II.

" From that place where He kept the Passover, and gave His Body that they should eat, and His Blood that they should drink, He went away and departed thither with His disciples where they took Him. When, then, His Body was eaten and His Blood drunk, He was 'counted among the dead' [*rather*, For whosoever hath eaten His Body and drunk His Blood, is counted among the dead]. For our

---

* See Papers on the Eucharistic Presence, pp. 43, 47, 401, 408, 415—420, and Real Presence of the Laudian Theology, pp. 52, 53, and Vogan's True Doctrine, pp. 103, 104, 109, 110, 132, 133. See also pp. 361—578.

Lord with His own hands gave His Body for food [*or*, to eat], and when He was not yet crucified, He gave His Blood for drink." * (Serm. xiv. De Pasch. § 4, formerly attributed to James of Nisibis,† Antonelli's edit. p. 341.)

III.

"They keep His watch, and bark against thieves, like dogs, and love our Lord, and lick His wounds when they receive His Body, and place it on their eyes, and lick it with their tongue as a dog licketh his master." (Ibid., Serm. vii. De Pœnit., § 8, p. 248, of Antonelli. See below, p. 315, No. xix.)

IV.

"Offertur quasi homo, quasi recipiens passionem." (Ambrose, De Offic. Minist., lib. i. c. xlviii.§ 248, Opera, edit. Benedict. 1686, tom. ii. c. 63.)

V.

Τῶν ἁγίων σαρκῶν αὐτοῦ ἐμπλησθῆναι ἔδωκεν ἡμῖν, ἑαυτὸν παρέθηκε τεθυμένον. (Chrysost., In Matt., Hom. l. § 3, Op., edit. Montfaucon, tom. vii. c. 517.)

VI.

Ὅταν γὰρ λέγωσι, πόθεν δῆλον ὅτι ἐτύθη ὁ Χριστός ; μετὰ τῶν ἄλλων καὶ ἀπὸ τῶν μυστηρίων αὐτοὺς ἐπιστομίζομεν· εἰ γὰρ μὴ ἀπέθανεν ὁ Ἰησοῦς τίνος σύμβολα τὰ τελούμενα ; (Ibid., In Matth., Hom. lxxxii. § 1, Op., tom. vii. 789.)

VII.

Τοῦ αἵματος ἐν τῷ κρατῆρι εἰς σὴν κάθαρσιν ἐκ τῆς ἀχράντου πλευρᾶς κενουμένου. (Ibid., De Pœnit., Hom. ix., Op., tom. ii. p. 349.)

VIII.

Οὐ γὰρ ἂν ἦν σῶμα τοῦ ἱερείου πρὸς ἐδωδὴν ἐπιτήδειον εἴπερ ἔμψυχον ἦν. Οὐκοῦν ὅτε παρέσχε τοῖς μαθηταῖς ἐμφαγεῖν τοῦ σώματος, καὶ τοῦ αἵματος ἐμπιεῖν, ἤδη κατὰ τὸ θελητὸν τῇ ἐξουσίᾳ τοῦ τὸ μυστήριον οἰκονομοῦντος ἀῤῥήτως τε καὶ ἀοράτως τὸ σῶμα ἐτέθυτο.‡ (Gregory Nyss., In Christi Resurrectionem, Orat. i., edit. Migne, tom. iii. p. 611, c. d.)

---

* The above is Dr. Pusey's translation of the Latin version made by Antonelli from the Armenian. (See "Real Presence from Fathers," p. 271.)
The words within brackets [ ] are emendations suggested by the Dean of Canterbury, who has kindly collated the passage with the Syriac of Aphraates.

† There is now no doubt that the name of the real author is Aphraates, concerning whom there is not much known. Some account of him and his writings will be found in the preface to volume 1. of Aphraates, edited by Mr. Wright (Williams and Norgate). See especially pp. 8, 9.

‡ On this passage see Albertiuus, De Eucharistiâ, p. 487.

IX.

"Labores enim *Passionis* Christi, quem velut apem, virginem permansurum Virgo edidit Mater, tam reges a regendo (summi videlicet sacerdotes) quam mediocres quique sequentium vel ordinis Levitici, vel fidelium plebis, in figura corporis ejus, ac sanguinis, pro salubritate vitæ communis afferimus, et agnitam dulcedinem mysteriorum conscio ore testamur: *Gustate, et videte, quoniam suavis est Dominus.* Sed væ hæreticis, qui id quod dulce est, amarum conantur asserere, ibi æqualitatem subtrahere de Filio gestientes, ubi totus in gloria Dei Patris manere cognoscitur, consummato mysterio Passionis." (Gaudentius Brix., Ep., Sermo xix., Op., p. 198, ed. Galeardus, 1757.)

X.

"Ergo in hac veritate qua sumus, *unus pro omnibus mortuus est;* et idem per singulas Ecclesiarum domos, in mysterio panis ac vini, *reficit immolatus,* vivificat creditus, consecrantes sanctificat consecratus. Hæc *agni caro,* hic *sanguis* est. Panis enim qui de cœlo descendit, ait: *Panis quem ego dabo, caro mea est pro sæculi vita.* Recte enim vini specie sanguis ejus exprimitur, quia cum ipse in Evangelio dicit: *Ego sum vitis vera,* satis declarat sanguinem suum esse omne vinum quod in figura *Passionis* Ejus offertur: unde beatissimus Patriarcha Jacob de Christo prophetaverat dicens: *Lavabit in vino stolam suam, et in sanguine uvæ amictum suum.* Stolam quippe nostri corporis indumentum suum, proprio erat sanguine abluturus." (Gaudentius Brix., Sermo ii. pp. 33, 34, edit. Galeardus, 1757.)

XI.

"Nam vere istud est hereditarium munus Testamenti Ejus novi, quod nobis ea nocte qua tradebatur crucifigendus, tamquam *pignus suæ præsentiæ* dereliquit. Hoc illud est viaticum nostri itineris, quo in hac via vitæ alimur ac nutrimur, donec ad ipsum pergamus de hoc sæculo recedentes, unde dicebat idem Dominus: *Nisi manducaveritis meam carnem, et biberitis meum sanguinem, non habebitis vitam in vobis ipsis.*

"Voluit enim *beneficia sua* permanere apud nos, voluit animas pretioso sanguine suo sanctificari per *imaginem propriæ Passionis,* et ideo discipulis fidelibus mandat, quos primos Ecclesiæ suæ constituit sacerdotes, ut indesinenter ista vitæ æternæ mysteria exercerent, quæ necesse est a cunctis sacerdotibus per singulas totius orbis Ecclesias celebrari, *usquequo iterum Christus de cælis adveniat* quo et ipsi sacerdotes, et omnes pariter fidelium populi, *exemplar Passionis* Christi ante oculos habentes quotidie, et gerentes in manibus, ore etiam sumentes, ac pectore redemptionis nostræ indelebilem memoriam teneamus." (Gaudentius Brix., Sermo ii., pp. 38, 39.)

XII.

"Mensa jucunditatis Passio Christi est, qui se pro nobis in *mensa Crucis* obtulit sacrificium Deo Patri, donans Ecclesiæ suæ Catholicæ vitale convivium, corpore suo nos videlicet satians, et inebrians sanguine. . . . Propter *hanc mensam*, corripiebat in idolis recumbentes Corinthios Apostolus dicens, *Non potestis* communicare mensæ Domini et mensæ dæmoniorum." (Serm. ccclxvi. de Ps. xxii. § 6, In Op. Aug., edit. Benedict. 1688, tom. v. par. ii. c. 1451.)

XIII.

"Cœnam suam dedit, passionem suam dedit." (Augustinus, In Psalm xxi. Enar. ii. § 27, Opera, tom. iv. par. i. c. 100.)

XIV.

"Gentes . . . passiones Domini in sacramentis corporis et sanguinis ejus per totum jam orbem suavitate lambunt devotissima." (Ibid., Quæsti. Evang., lib. ii. Quæst. xxxviii. § 5, Op., tom. iii. par. ii. c. 266.)

XV.

"Nos de cruce Domini pascimur, quia corpus ipsius manducamus." (Ibid., in Ps. c. § 9, Op., tom. iv. par. ii. c. 1088.)

XVI.

"Sicut ergo cœlestis panis, qui vére Christi caro est, suo modo vocatur Corpus Christi, quum revera sit sacramentum Corporis Christi, illius videlicet, quod visibile, palpabile, mortale in cruce est suspensum, vocaturque ipsa immolatio carnis quæ sacerdotis manibus fit, Christi passio, mors, crucifixio, non rei veritate, sed significante mysterio: sic sacramentum fidei, quod baptismus intelligitur, fides est."* (Gratian, Decret., Pars ii., De Consecr., Dist. ii. c. xlviii., as from August. in libro Sent. Prosperi, ed. Migne, c. 1754. 1755.)

* This passage, though probably corrupt (see above, p. 129), bears witness, even in its corrupted form, to two truths, each of which is destructive of the Real Objective Presence.

(1) The Eucharist is, and is called, the Body of Christ, in the same way as Baptism is, and is called, faith. Compare the language of St. Augustine's letter to Boniface: "Sicut ergo secundum quendam modum Sacramentum Corporis Christi, Corpus Christi est: Sacramentum Sanguinis Christi, Sanguis Christi est, ita Sacramentum fidei fides est." (Epist. xcviii. § 9, Op., ed. Bened. 1679, tom. ii. c. 267.)

(2) In the celebration of the Eucharist the act of the Priest is, and is called, the crucifying of Christ, in the same way as that which is in the hand of the Priest is, and is called, the Body of Christ. Compare, again, the Epistle to Boniface: "Nec utique mentitur, qui interrogatus eum responderit immolari. Si enim Sacramenta quamdam similitudinem earum rerum, quarum sacramenta sunt, non haberent, omnino sacramenta non essent. Ex hac autem similitudine plerumque etiam ipsarum rerum nomina accipiunt." (Ibid., c. 267.) See above, pp. 255, 256.

XVII.

ΟΡΘ. Οὐ τοίνυν θεότητος ἐμνημόνευσε, τοῦ πάθους τὸν τύπον ἐπιδεικνύς;
ΕΡΑΝ. Οὐ δῆτα.
ΟΡΘ. Ἀλλὰ σώματός γε, καὶ αἵματος;
ΕΡΑΝ. Ἀληθές.
ΟΡΘ. Σῶμα ἄρα τῷ σταυρῷ προσηλώθη;
ΕΡΑΝ. Ἔοικεν.*
(Theodoret, Dial. iii. Impatibilis, Opera, edit. Schulze, tom. iv. p. 220.)

XVIII.

" Ipse Dominus calicem, quem bibendum dedit, novum appellare dignatus est testamentum.... Etiam B. Paulus commemorans sacratissimum illius cœnæ mysterium, non aliud calicem quam novum a Domino nuncupatum insinuat testamentum.... Non aliud quam divinum permittitur accipere testamentum. Neque enim dubium est, aliis locis a Domino nomine calicis significatam gratiam passionis.... *Calicem quem dedit mihi Pater, non bibam illum?* In quo calice passionem esse intelligendam etiam illic ostendit.... *Pater si vis, transfer calicem istum a me.*... Manifestum est, hoc fuisse orare ut transiret ab eo hora, quod erat dicere ut calix transferretur ab eo. ... Ex hac regula qua iste calix testamentum dicitur novum, in illo calice quem prius dedit non absque ratione vetus intelligitur testamentum."† (Fulgentius Rusp., Ferrando, De Quinque Quæstionibus, § xxxv.—xxxviii., In Bibliotheca Max. Patr., Lugd. 1677, tom. ix. p. 193-4.)

XIX.

" Carnem ejus, quæ ad comedendum inepta erat ante passionem (quis enim comedere cupiebat carnem Dei?) aptam cibo post passionem fecit. Si enim non fuisset crucifixus, sacrificium corporis ejus minime comederemus." (Hesychius Hieros., In Levit. lib. i. cap. ii., In Bibliotheca Max. Patr., Lugd. 1677, tom. xii. p. 59.)

XX.

" Nisi [Caro Dominica] superimposita fuisset cruci, nos corpus Christi nequaquam mystice percepissemus." (Ibid., lib. ii. p. 74.)

* It should be observed that this argument is built on the words of institution in the context preceding.
Compare Chrysostom as quoted below, pp. 312, 313, No. xi., and above, p. 306, No. vi.
† The passage should be read entire in the original in order to appreciate its value, as an answer to the question, "Could this have been written by one who believed the Real Objective Presence of the Blood of Christ, and of Christ Himself in the cup of blessing"?

XXI.

"Pascha proprium præveniens, crucem suam Christus celebravit." (Hesychius Hieros., In Levit., lib. vi. p. 152.)

XXII.

"Intelligibilem agnum Domini traditionem immolantes mystice." (Ibid., lib. vi. p. 153.)

XXIII.

"Quotidie nobis agnus occiditur, et pascha quotidie celebratur, si fermentum malitiæ et nequitiæ non habemus." (Isidore Hispal., In Exod., cap. xvii., Opera, edit. Migne, tom. v. c. 295.)

XXIV.

"Quod semel fecit, nunc quotidie frequentat. Semel enim pro peccatis populi se obtulit, celebratur tamen hæc eadem oblatio singulis per fideles diebus, sed in mysterio, ut quod Dominus Jesus Christus semel se offerens adimplevit, hoc in ejus passionis memoriam quotidie geratur per mysteriorum celebrationem. Nec tamen falso dicitur quod in mysteriis illis Dominus vel immoletur vel patiatur; quoniam illius mortis atque passionis habens similitudinem, quarum existunt repræsentationes. Unde Dominicum corpus et sanguis Dominicus appellantur; quoniam ejus sumunt appellationem, cujus existunt Sacramentum." (Bertram, De Corp. et Sang. Dom., § xxxix. xl., edit. Migne, c. 144.)

XXV.

"In sacramento panis et vini, necnon etiam in memoria mea, passio Christi in promptu est." (Amalarius, De Eccles. Offic., lib. iii. cap. xxv., in Hittorpius, p. 168.)

XXVI.

"Sicut in superioribus Christi Corpus est vivum in sacramento panis et vini, atque in memoria mea, ita in præsenti ascendit in crucem." (Ibid., cap. xxv. p. 168.)

XXVII.

"De cujus sponsi carne Ecclesia prodiit, quando ex latere crucifixi, manante sanguine et aqua, sacramentum redemptionis et regenerationis accepit. Et quotidie lavacro rigatur ac poculo, baptismatis scilicet abluta mysterio, Corpus crucifixi in ara crucis torridum sumens, una cum ejus cruore roseo de latere crucifixi profuso."*

---

* In giving this citation as a witness to the faith in this particular, I must not be understood as claiming Hincmar as bearing anything like a distinct and consistent testimony against the Paschasian doctrine. Whatever may have been his Eucharistic views, many of his statements are of too ambiguous a character.

(Hincmar Rem., Ep. ii. Ad Carolum Calvum, § xii., Opera, edit. Sirmondi, Paris, 1645, tom. ii. p. 101.)

XXVIII.

"Totus adest, totus sancto incumbit altari, non ut iterum patiatur, sed ut fidei, cui præsentia sunt omnia præterita, ejus passio memoriter repræsentetur. Ita et Christus et iterum immolatur, et tamen impassibilis permanet et vivus." (*Rupertus Tuitiensis, De Trin., In Genes., lib. vi. cap. xxxii., Opera, edit. Migne, tom. i. c. 431.)

XXIX.

"Qui mactatus, carnem suam et sanguinem in cibum et potum vitæ æternæ proposuit fidelibus." (Germanus Constant., Theoria Rer. Eccl., In Bibliotheca Max. Patr., Lugd. 1677, tom. xiii. p. 51.)

XXX.

"Panis et poculum, proprie et vere, ad imitationem mysticæ illius cœnæ in qua Christus accepit panem et vinum, et dixit: *Accipite manducate, et bibite ex eo omnes, hoc enim est Corpus meum et sanguis:* ostendens se nos participes fecisse mortis, et resurrectionis, et gloriæ suæ." (Ibid., p. 53.)

XXXI.

"Bibite sanguinem ejus cum fide, et canite gloriam, hic est calix quem miscuit Dominus noster super lignum Crucis: accedite mortales, bibite ex eo, in remissionem delictorum." (Syriac Liturgy of St. James the Lord's brother, in Renaudot, Lit. Orient. Col., tom. ii. p. 41.)

Hence with the Fathers, as with the Liturgies, the celebration of the Eucharist brings near to the faithful as much the death of Christ as His Body and Blood; there is in it the Real Presence of His Passion and blood-shedding as well as of Himself. It is with them the slaying of the Lord and the shedding of His Blood. It is all this in mystical representation. Christ is crucified in sacramental commemoration.† It is the showing forth not of the Lord only, but of the Lord's death as the ransom of His people, that they may communicate sacramentally not only in the representing signs but in the represented death, not only in the commemoratory tokens

---

* On the Eucharistic doctrine of Rupert see "Romish Mass and English Church," p. 62.

Dr. Pusey ("Real Presence from the Fathers," pp. 5—9) fails to satisfy me that the view of Rupertus had not been more truly apprehended by Bellarmine (De Sacram. Euch., lib. iii. cap. xi. xv., Disp. 1701, c. 712, 713, 720), Cave (Hist. Litur., Geneva, 1694, p. 447), and others.

† See "Romish Mass and English Church," pp. 37, 38.

but in the Redemption commemorated, in the Body and Blood of the true Paschal Lamb which taketh away the sin of the world.

Let the following extracts bear witness to these assertions:—

I.

" Apparet sanguinem Christi non offerri, si desit vinum calici, nec sacrificium dominicum legitima sanctificatione celebrari, nisi oblatio et sacrificium nostrum responderit passioni." (Cyprian, Epist. ad Cæcilium, Ep. lxiii., Opera, c. 228, edit. Baluzius, Venice, 1728.)

II.

" Quia passionis ejus mentionem in sacrificiis omnibus facimus (passio est enim Domini sacrificium quod offerimus) nihil aliud quam quod ille fecit facere debemus." (Ibid., c. 231.)

III.

Διὰ τί δὲ προσέθηκεν, ὃν κλῶμεν; τοῦτο γὰρ ἐπὶ μὲν τῆς εὐχαριστίας ἐστὶν ἰδεῖν γινόμενον· ἐπὶ δὲ τοῦ σταυροῦ οὐκέτι, ἀλλὰ καὶ τοὐναντίον τούτῳ. ὀστοῦν γὰρ αὐτοῦ, φησὶν, οὐ συντριβήσεται. ἀλλ' ὅπερ οὐκ ἔπαθεν ἐπὶ τοῦ σταυροῦ, τοῦτο πάσχει ἐπὶ τῆς προσφορᾶς διὰ σε, καὶ ἀνέχεται διακλώμενος ἵνα πάντας ἐμπλήσῃ. (Chrysostom., In Epist. i. ad Cor., Hom. xxiv. § 2, Opera, edit. Montfaucon, tom. x. p. 213.)

IV.

Ἐπεὶ τὸν ἐν σταυρῷ προσηλωμένον μέλλομεν καὶ ἡμεῖς κατὰ τὴν ἑσπέραν ταύτην ἰδεῖν ὡς ἀμνὸν ἐσφαγμένον καὶ τεθυμένον. (Ibid., De Cæmeterio et Cruce, § 3, Opera, edit. Montfaucon, tom. ii. p. 401.)

V.

Ἐκφερομένης τῆς θυσίας, καὶ τοῦ χριστοῦ τεθυμένου τοῦ προβάτου τοῦ δεσποτικοῦ. (Ibid., In Epist. ad Ephes., Hom. iii. § 5, Op., tom. xi. p. 23.)

VI.

Ἔνθα ὁ χρίστος κεῖται τεθυμένος. (Ibid., Ad Popul. Antioch., Hom. xv. § 5, Op., tom. ii. p. 158.)

VII.

Ὅταν ἴδῃς τὸ προβάτον ἐσφαγιασμένον καὶ ἀπηρτισμένον. (Ibid., De Cæmet. et Cruce, § 3, Op., tom. ii. p. 401.)

VIII.

Ὁρᾷς αὐτὸν κείμενον. (Ibid., In Matth., Hom. l. al. li., § 2, Op., tom. vii. p. 517.)

IX.

Τοῦ ἀμνοῦ τοῦ Θεοῦ ὑπὲρ σοῦ σφαγιάζομενου . . . οὐ φοβῇ.
(Chrysostom., De Pœnit., Hom. ix., Op., tom. ii. p. 849.)

X.

Ὅταν ἴδῃς τὸν Κύριον τεθυμένον καὶ κείμενον, καὶ τὸν ἱερέα ἐφεστῶτα τῷ θύματι καὶ ἐπευχόμενον, καὶ πάντας ἐκείνῳ τῷ τιμίῳ φοινισσομένους αἵματι. (Ibid., De Sacerdotio, l. iii. § 4, Op., tom. i. p. 382.)

XI.

Μυστήριόν ἐστι τὸ πάθος καὶ ὁ σταυρός.* (Ibid., In Matth., Hom. lxxxiii., Op., tom. vii. p. 783.)

XII.

Χριστὸς ἡμᾶς σήμερον ἑστιᾶται, Χριστὸς ἡμῖν σήμερον διακονεῖ, Χριστὸς ἀναπαύει ὁ φιλάνθρωπος. Φοβερὸν τὸ λαλούμενον, φοβερὸν τὸ τελούμενον· ὁ μόσχος ὁ σιτευτὸς θυσιάζεται, ὁ ἀμνὸς τοῦ Θεοῦ ὁ αἴρων τὴν ἁμαρτίαν τοῦ κόσμου σφαγιάζεται. (Cyrillus Alex., Hom. x., In Mysticam Cœnam, Opera, edit. Migne, tom. x. c. 1017.)

XIII.

" Unus pro omnibus mortuus est; et idem per singulas ecclesiarum domos, in mysterio panis ac vini, reficit *immolatus*, vivificat creditus, consecrantes sanctificat consecratus." (Gaudentius Brix., Serm. ii., Opera, p. 33, edit. Galeardus, 1757. See above, p. 307.)

XIV.

Ἐπὶ τῆς θείας τραπέζης πάλιν κἀνταῦθα μὴ τῷ προκειμένῳ ἄρτῳ καὶ τῷ ποτηρίῳ ταπεινῶς προσέχωμεν. ἀλλ' ὑψώσαντες ἡμῶν τὴν διάνοιαν πίστει νοήσωμεν κεῖσθαι ἐπὶ τῆς ἱερᾶς ἐκείνης τραπέζης τὸν Ἀμνὸν τοῦ Θεοῦ τὸν αἴροντα τὴν ἁμαρτίαν τοῦ κόσμου, ἀθύτως ὑπὸ τῶν ἱερέων θυόμενον· καὶ τὸ τίμιον αὐτοῦ σῶμα καὶ αἷμα ἀληθῶς ·λαμβάνοντας ἡμᾶς πιστεύειν ταῦτα εἶναι τὰ τῆς ἡμετέρας ἀναστάσεως σύμβολα.† (Gelasii Hist. Conc. Nic. See Mansi, tom. ii. c. 887.)

* This is given as teaching contained in the words of institution.

† There has been much controversy on this passage, which was frequently appealed to by the Reformers and subsequent Reforming divines. Gelasius lived a century and a half after the first Council of Nice, and his *Diatyposis*, from which this is extracted, though attributed to the Fathers of that Council, is not mentioned by Eusebius, nor in any of the Canons of the Council. (See Albertinus, De Eucharistia, p. 384, and Cave, Hist. Lit., pp. 259, 260.)

Whatever may be its history, and whatever questions may be made as to the interpretation of some parts of it, it assuredly bears witness—(1) to the faith which regards the *res sacramenti* as in the state of death ; (2) to the fact that this *res sacramenti* is to be apprehended by faith and by a lifting up of the mind, while

XV.

"Unus calix est, in quo sumus, quia una passio est Christi, et una mors, qua omnes redempti sumus." (Etherius et Beatus, Contra Elipandum, lib. i., In Bibliotheca Max. Patr., Lugd. 1677, tom. xiii. p. 371.)

XVI.

Τίνας λέγει ληνοὺς ; τὰς ἐκκλήσιας, ἐν αἷς ἐκχεῖται ὁ οἶνος, ἤτοι τὸ ἅγιον αἷμα τοῦ Κυρίου Ἰησοῦ Χριστοῦ, καὶ θύεται καὶ τὸ ἅγιον σῶμα αὐτοῦ. (Interpretationes ex Vet. Test., In Op. Athanasii, "Ps. pro Torcularibus," Q. lxxvii., Opera, edit. Benedict., tom. ii. p. 269.)

XVII.

"Ideo autem hoc sacramentum de vino fit, quia Christus se vitem dixit, et Scriptura eum vinum jucunditatis asseruit. Uva autem in prælo duobus lignis expressa in vinum liquatur, et Christus duobus *lignis crucis pressus, sanguis ejus in potum fidelibus fundebatur.*" (Honorius Augustodunensis, Gemma Animæ, cap. xxxiii., In Bibliotheca Max. Patr., Lugd. 1677, tom. xx. p. 1051.)

XVIII.

"Ego omnipotenti Deo agnum immaculatum quotidie in altari Crucis sacrifico." (Pseudo-Apostolus Andreas,* in "Passio S. Andreæ.")

nothing but bread and wine are recognised in the object of sight below. Mr. Milton has an interesting note on it in "The Eucharist Cleared from Error," pp. 77—80; and an able argument on it will be found in Albertinus, pp. 384—388. See also Ridley's Works, P. S. edit., pp. 248, 249; and Papers on the Eucharistic Presence, pp. 53, 54.

The language may be illustrated, and the sense cleared, by the following from St. Chrysostom: Πνευματικῶς δεῖ τὰ περὶ ἐμοῦ ἀκούειν . . . τί δέ ἐστι τὸ σαρκικῶς νοῆσαι; τὸ ἁπλῶς εἰς τα προκείμενα ὁρᾶν, καὶ μὴ πλέον τι φαντάζεσθαι. τοῦτο γάρ ἐστι σαρκικῶς. χρὴ δὲ μὴ οὕτω κρίνειν τοῖς ὁρωμένοις, ἀλλὰ πάντα τὰ μυστήρια τοῖς ἔνδον ὀφθαλμοῖς κατοπτεύειν. τοῦτο γάρ ἐστι πνευματικῶς. (Hom. in Joan. xlvii. al. xlvi., Opera, tom. viii. pp. 277, 278, edit. Montfaucon, 1728.)

And this again may be fortified by comparing the words of St. Augustine: "In signis ne quis attendat quod sunt, sed potius quod signa sunt, id est, quod significant." (De Doct. Christ., lib. ii. c. i. See above, p. 257.)

The passage may (as Mr. Milton remarks, p. 79) be further illustrated from the Liturgies. See the quotations below, pp. 315, 316.)

On the whole subject see Bp. Morton on Eucharist, book iv. cap. xi. pp. 301—307, edit. 1635.

* See Albertinus, De Eucharistia, pp. 258, 259. This extract from a supposititious work is of value only as evidencing the belief of Christians some centuries after Apostolic times. It is quoted by Bellarmine with the omission of the words which so clearly mark the mystical sense, "in altari crucis." Arnauld followed the example.

XIX.

" Cruci hæremus, sanguinem sugimus, et intra ipsa Redemptoris nostri vulnera figimus linguam, quo interius et exterius rubricati " &c. (Sermo " De Cœnâ Domini," * formerly found among the writings of Cyprian: Opera Cypriani, c. xcix., edit. Baluzius, Venice, 1728.)

XX.

Ὁ γὰρ βασιλεὺς τῶν βασιλευόντων καὶ Κύριος τῶν κυριενόντων, Χριστὸς ὁ Θεὸς ἡμῶν, προέρχεται σφαγιασθῆναι καὶ δοθῆναι εἰς βρῶσιν τοῖς πιστοῖς.† (Liturgy of St. James, in Neale's Tetralogia Liturgica, p. 57.)

Claude replied : "The author of the relation of the martyrdom of St. Andrew makes this saint say, not what Mr. Arnauld imputes to him, *that he sacrificed every day to God the immaculate Lamb*, but *that he sacrificed every day to God* ON THE ALTAR OF THE CROSS the immaculate Lamb. Where I pray is Mr. Arnauld's fidelity thus to eclipse these words, *on the altar of the cross*, to make the world believe this Author means the sacrifice which is offered every day in the Eucharist?" (Reply to Arnauld, part ii. p. 86, London, 1684.) Albertinus argues "illud *sacrifico* intelligendum esse, non de sacrificio in ipsa rei veritate ; sed tum de sacrificio in mysterio, id est, in signo, quo sensu Isidorus Hispalensis ait, *quotidie nobis agnus occiditur, et pascha quotidie celebratur* [In Exod. cap. 17] ; tum de interna commemoratione veri ac realis sacrificii in cruce peracti per mentis apprehensionem et intuitum. Sic enim Hesychius : *Intelligibilem agnum Domini traditionem immolantes mystice*. [In Levit. l. 6.]" (P. 259.)

* Probably the work of Arnoldus Bonævallensis. See Albertinus, De Eucharistia, p. 304.

† Dr. Neale immediately after quoting this passage (Preface to Tetralogia Lit., pp. xvi. xvii.) uses strong language concerning those who understand some parts of the Liturgies "metaphorice dici."

It is to be regretted that Dr. Neale seems grievously to misunderstand the views of the Reformed. But he is quite right in supposing that they do not think that all parts of the Liturgies are to be interpreted as spoken κυρίως.

But how, in this passage, does Dr. Neale himself understand προέρχεται σφαγιασθῆναι ?

If it is to be understood κυρίως, then must it not follow, in the words of Bellarmine : "Ergo verum erit dicere, a sacerdotibus Christianis vere et realiter Christum occidi ; at hoc sacrilegium, non sacrificium esse videtur"? (De Missa, lib. l. cap. xxvii. c. 1041.)

Then also must it not follow that many of the sayings of the Fathers must be brought to nought? (See "Romish Mass and English Church," pp. 85, 90—94, 37—39, 41.)

Then *e.g.* what can be made of the declaration of Eusebius that Christ delivered us a memorial to offer *instead of* sacrifice? (μνήμην ἡμῖν παραδοὺς ἀντὶ θυσίας τῷ Θεῷ διενεκῶς προσφέρειν. Dem. Ev. c. x. p. 38, 1628.)

And what of his statement following (p. 39) that this memorial is to be made by the *symbols* of His Body and Blood? (διὰ συμβόλων τοῦ τε σώματος αὐτοῦ, καὶ τοῦ σωτηρίου αἵματος. See above, p. 283.)

Is there any greater violence to language in understanding the *symbols* to be in the stead of the Body and Blood than in understanding the *memorial* to be in the stead of the *sacrifice*?

XXI.

῎Ιδε ὁ ἀμνὸς τοῦ Θεοῦ, ὁ Υἱὸς τοῦ Πατρὸς, ὁ αἴρων τὴν ἁμαρτίαν τοῦ κόσμου, σφαγιασθεὶς ὑπὲρ τῆς τοῦ κόσμου ζωῆς καὶ σωτηρίας. (Liturgy of St. James, in Neale's Tetralogia Liturgica, p. 170.)

XXII.

Καὶ τιθεὶς αὐτὸν [τὸν ἅγιον ἄρτον] ὕπτιον ἐν τῷ ἁγίῳ δίσκῳ, εἰπόντος τοῦ διακόνου. Θῦσον δέσποτα. Ὁ ἱερεὺς θύει αὐτὸν σταυροειδῶς, λέγων, Θύεται ὁ ἀμνὸς τοῦ Θεοῦ.* (Chrysostomi Divina Missa, in Goar's Euchologion, p. 57.)

XXIII.

"Misce, quæsumus, Domine, in calice isto quod manavit ex latere tuo, ut fiat in remissionem peccatorum nostrorum." (Lit. Mozarabic, in Neale's Tetralogia Lit., p. 32.)

Yet doubtless by degrees this truth became less prominent, as the Eucharistic doctrine of earlier times passed into some form of, or approach to, the augmentation doctrine, which connected itself especially with the four first words of Institution, "Hoc est corpus meum," and practically dropped the remainder; suffering the idea of spiritual union with the glorified Body of Christ, by partaking of the deified Sacramental Body, or the Sacramental Bread spiritually adopted or assumed into union with Christ's Body, to obscure the scriptural view, in which the first and prominent idea is the Communion, or partaking in all its peace-giving, life-giving power of the atoning sacrifice of Christ's Body and Blood, which is the meat indeed, and the drink indeed, for that which is the sinful soul's hunger indeed and thirst indeed; upon which follows the spiritual union with the glorified Saviour in heaven.

* Goar's explanatory note is this: "Panis sive hostia, Christi velut agni immolandi vices nomenque sustinet, et ut mactetur, crusta inversa, mica sursum spectante, in disco velut agnus supinus ictum præstolans, extenditur" (p. 100).
See Dr. Covel's "Account of the Greek Church," p. 15. It is to be observed that all this takes place at the *prothesis*, before the unconsecrated elements are carried, at "the great entrance" to the holy table.

NOTE G. (p. 175).

On the Sayings of the Fathers concerning the Sacramental Body of Christ, and concerning His Church and His Poor.

ONE argument of very considerable weight, which has not been alluded to in the text, may be briefly touched upon here. It is this. The Fathers habitually speak of the Body of Christ which is the Sacrament of His Body, and the Body of Christ which is His Church, in such connexion one with another, and in such respect the one to the other, as to show clearly that they regarded the propositions "The consecrated bread is the Body of Christ," and "the Church of Christ is His Body," as being *ejusdem generis*, so far at least as not to admit any more literal sense for the first than for the second.

And this is surely equivalent to saying that the Fathers did not regard the Eucharist as being in any more proper sense Christ's Body than His faithful people are; and that they did not allow any Real Presence nor any adoration to the one, which does not also belong to the other.

Now this may indeed be perfectly consistent with the view of the consecrated elements, as possessing an inherent indwelling of the Spirit, or of some spiritual influence uniting them in some sort to Christ for the purposes of Sacramental Communion; and I think it may perhaps be admitted that some such view—the first step in the course of superstition—became in time more prevalent than has commonly, perhaps, been supposed; * but this teaching of the

---

* It should, however, be observed that we find in some of the Fathers teachings concerning the sacraments in general, and concerning the Eucharist in particular, which, if carried out to the results to which they most naturally point, would seem to be destructive of such a view.

Observe especially the words of Chrysostom : Πάρεστι καὶ νῦν ὁ Χριστὸς τὴν τράπεζαν κοσμῶν. οὐ γὰρ ἄνθρωπός ἐστιν ὁ ποιῶν τὰ προκείμενα γινέσθαι σῶμα καὶ αἷμα τοῦ Χριστοῦ. σχῆμα πληρῶν μόνον ἕστηκεν ὁ ἱερεύς, καὶ δέησιν προσφέρει· ἡ δὲ χάρις καὶ ἡ δύναμίς ἐστιν ἡ τοῦ Θεοῦ . . . καθάπερ ἐκείνη ἡ φωνὴ, ἡ λέγουσα, αὐξάνεσθε . . . οὕτω καὶ αὕτη ἡ φωνὴ, ἡ λέγουσα, διαπαντὸς αὔξει τῇ χάριτι τοὺς ἀξίως μετέχοντας. (De Prod. Jud., Hom. ii. § 6, Op., edit. Montfaucon, tom. ii. p. 394. Compare quotations above, p. 302.)

Perhaps still more distinct is the language of St. Augustine : "Semper Dei est illa gratia et Dei sacramentum, hominis autem solum ministerium ; qui si bonus est, adhæret Deo, et operatur cum Deo ; si autem malus est, operatur per illum Deus visibilem sacramenti formam: ipse autem donat invisibilem gratiam." (Ep. cv. § 12, Op., ed. Ben., 1679, tom. ii. c. 301.)

Fathers (though it has, doubtless, outlived the change of faith in the Western Church) is really inconsistent with the belief of the elements being by consecration either changed into the natural Body of Christ or possessed with the Real Objective Presence of that Body with His soul and divinity under their forms.

I add some quotations which may be useful in assisting the inquirer to appreciate the force of this argument.

I.

Ὁ δὲ ἄρτος ὃν ἐγὼ δώσω, φησὶν, ἡ σάρξ μοῦ ἐστίν, ἤτοι ᾧ τρέφεται ἡ σὰρξ διὰ τῆς εὐχαριστίας· ἢ, ὅπερ καὶ μᾶλλον, ἡ σὰρξ τὸ σῶμα αὐτοῦ ἐστὶν, ὅπερ ἐστὶν ἡ Ἐκκλησία, ἄρτος οὐράνιος, συναγωγὴ εὐλογημένη. (Theodoti * Excerpt. ad fin. Clem. Alex., Opera, edit. Potter, tom. ii. p. 971.)

II.

"Quando Dominus corpus suum panem vocat, de multorum granorum adunatione congestum, populum nostrum quem portabat, indicat adunatum." (Cyprian, Epist. lxxvi., Opera, edit. Venice, 1728, c. 318.)

III.

"Quemadmodum grana multa in unum collecta et commolita et commixta panem unum faciunt sic in Christo, qui est panis cœlestis, unum sciamus esse corpus, cui conjunctus sit noster numerus et adunatus." (Cyprian, Epist. lxiii. ad Cæcil., Op., c. 230.)

IV.

Καὶ αὕτη τοῦ μακαρίου Παύλου ἡ διδασκαλία, ἱκανὴ καθέστηκε πληροφορῆσαι ὑμᾶς περὶ τῶν θείων μυστηρίων, ὧν καταξιωθέντες, σύσσωμοι καὶ σύναιμοι τοῦ Χριστοῦ γεγόνατε. (Cyril. Hierosol., Mystag. iv. § 1, Opera, edit. Ben., p. 319.)

V.

Αὐτό ἐσμεν ἐκεῖνο τὸ σῶμα· τί γὰρ ἐστὶν ὁ ἄρτος; σῶμα Χριστοῦ. τί δὲ γίνονται οἱ μεταλαμβάνοντες; σῶμα Χριστοῦ· οὐχὶ σώματα

So Optatus had said: "Concedite Deo præstare quæ sua sunt. Non enim potest munus ab homine dari quod divinum est" (Opati Afri Milevit., Epis. De Schism. Dom., lib. v., In Bibliotheca Max. Patr., Lugd. 1677, tom. iv. p. 361); and again: "Ipse est ergo qui dat, ipsius est quod datur." (Ibid., p. 361.)

Such sayings, at least, seem rather to point to that view of sacramental efficacy which is expressed in the words of Hooker: "Which grace also they that receive by sacraments or with sacraments, receive it from Him and not from them" (Eccl. Pol., book v. ch. lvii. § 4, Keble's edit., vol. ii. p. 258), and which seems to be most consistent with the true Real Presence of Christ as the living Saviour, the Giver of the Feast, the Lord of the table. See above, pp. 32—35.

* This is Theodotus the heretic. (See Cave's Historia Literaria, 1694, p. 39, and Goode on Eucharist, i. p. 287.) But no mark of heresy is on this saying.

πολλὰ, ἀλλὰ σῶμα ἕν. (Chrysostom., In Ep. i. ad Cor. Hom. xxiv. § 2, Opera, edit. Montfaucon, tom. x. p. 213.)

VI.

Μηδεὶς λαμβανέτω Ἰούδας, ἵνα μὴ τὰ Ἰούδα πάθῃ· σῶμα ἐστὶ Χριστοῦ καὶ τουτὶ τὸ πλῆθος. (Ibid., In Matth., Hom. lxxxii. al. lxxxiii. § 6, Op., tom. vii. p. 790.)

VII.

Τῷ τῆς σαρκὸς ὀνόματι πάλιν καὶ τὰ μυστήρια καλεῖν εἴωθεν ἡ γραφή, καὶ τὴν ἐκκλησίαν ἅπασαν, σῶμα λέγουσα εἶναι τοῦ Χριστοῦ. (Ibid., In Gal., cap. v., Op., tom. x. p. 720.)

VIII.

"Corpus Christi si vis intelligere, Apostolum audi dicentem fidelibus, ' Vos autem estis Corpus Christi et membra.' Si ergo vos estis corpus Christi et membra, mysterium vestrum in mensa Dominica positum est: mysterium vestrum accipitis. Ad id quod estis, Amen respondetis, et respondendo subscribitis. Audis enim, Corpus Christi * et respondes, Amen. Esto membrum Corporis Christi, ut verum sit Amen." (Augustine, Serm. cclxxii., Opera, edit. Benedict. 1683, tom. v. par. i. c. 1104.)

IX.

"Estote quod videtis, et accipite quod estis." (Ibid., c. 1104.)

X.

"Dominus Christus nos significavit, nos ad se pertinere voluit, mysterium pacis et unitatis nostræ in sua mensa consecravit." (Ibid., c. 1104.)

XI.

"Quia passus est pro nobis, commendavit nobis in isto sacramento corpus et sanguinem suum ; quod etiam fecit et nos ipsos. Nam et nos corpus ipsius facti sumus, et per misericordiam ipsius quod accipimus, nos sumus." (Ibid., Serm. ccxxix., Op., tom. v. par. i. c. 976.)

XII.

"Ibi vos estis in mensa, et ibi vos estis in calice. Nobiscum vos estis." (Ibid., c. 976.)

---

* Compare the following: "Sumunt ergo fideles bene et veraciter corpus Christi, si corpus Christi non negligant esse. Fiant Corpus Christi si volunt vivere de Spiritu Christi." (Rabanus Maur., De Inst. Cler., lib. i. c. 31, Opera, edit. Migne, tom. i. c. 318.)

XIII.

"Hunc itaque cibum et potum societatem vult intelligi corporis et membrorum suorum, quod est sancta Ecclesia." (Augustine, In Johan., Tract. xxvi. § 15, Op., tom. iii. par. ii. c. 500.)

XIV.

"Hujus rei sacramentum, id est unitatis corporis et sanguinis Christi alicubi quotidie, alicubi certis intervallis dierum in Dominica mensa præparatur; et de mensa Dominica sumitur; quibusdam ad vitam, quibusdam ad exitium: res vero ipsa cujus sacramentum est, omni homini ad vitam, nulli ad exitium, quicunque ejus particeps fuerit." (Ibid., c. 500.)

XV.

"Eucharistia panis noster quotidianus est: sed sic accipiamus illum, ut non solum ventre, sed et mente reficiamur. Virtus enim ipsa quæ ibi intelligitur, unitas est, ut redacti in Corpus Ejus, effecti membra ejus, simus quod accipimus." (Ibid., Serm. lvii., Op., tom. v. par. i. c. 334.)

XVI.

"Hoc est sacrificium Christianorum. Multi unum corpus sumus in Christo, quod etiam sacramento altaris fidelibus noto frequentat Ecclesia, ubi ei demonstratur quod in ea oblatione quam offert ipsa offeratur." (Ibid., De Civit. Dei, lib. x. cap. vi.)

XVII.

"Benedicens fregit, transfigurans * corpus suum in panem, quod est ecclesia præsens." (Com. in Mar., cap. xiv., In Op. Hieronymi, edit. Vallarsius, tom. xi. par. ii. c. 118.)

XVIII.

"Quædam species mortis et quædam similitudo resurrectionis intervenit, ut susceptus a Christo, Christumque suscipiens non idem sit post lavacrum, qui ante baptismum fuit, sed corpus regenerati fiat caro crucifixi." (Leo Magn., De Pass. Dom., Serm. xiv. In Heptas Præsulum, p. 62.)

XIX.

"Cujus [Christi] caro de utero virginis sumpta nos sumus." (Ibid., De Nativ. Dom., Serm. x. p. 24.)

XX.

"Sicut factus est Dominus caro nostra nascendo, ita et nos facti

---

* Compare the language of St. Augustine: "The Head transfigured (*transfigurabat*) the members into Himself." See above, p. 70.

sumus ipsius renascendo." (Leo Magn., De Nativ. Dom., Serm. iii. p. 16.)

XXI.

"Non enim aliud agit participatio corporis et sanguinis Christi, quam ut in id quod sumimus transeamus." (Ibid., De Pass. Dom., Serm. xiv. p. 62.)

XXII.

" In illa mystica distributione spiritualis alimoniæ, hoc impertitur, hoc sumitur, ut accipientes virtutem Cœlestis cibi in carnem ipsius, quia caro nostra factus est, transeamus." (Ibid., Epist. xxiii., In Bibliotheca Max. Patr., Lugd. 1677, tom. vii. p. 1080.)

XXIII.

" Ut nos esse ipsum verum panem verumque corpus ostenderet, continuo subjunxit, *quoniam unus panis, unum corpus multi sumus omnes qui de uno pane participamus.* . . . Nam et carnem Domini nos esse confirmans, ait, *Nemo enim unquam carnem suam odio habuit,* &c. . . . Quocirca quoniam unus panis et unum corpus multi sumus, tunc incipit unusquisque particeps esse illius unius panis, quando cœperit membrum esse illius unius corporis, quod in singulis membris, quando in baptismo * capiti Christo subjungitur, tunc jam Deo viva hostia veraciter immolatur." (Fulgentius Rusp., De Baptismo Æthiopis, cap. xi., In Heptas Præsulum, p. 612. See above, pp. 82, 83.)

XXIV.

" Hoc ergo fit ille regeneratione sancti baptismatis, quod est de sacrificio sumpturus altaris. Quod etiam sanctos Patres indubitanter credidisse ac docuisse cognoscimus." (Ibid., p. 612.)

XXV.

"Ipsum Apostolum . . . audiamus cum de isto Sacramento loqueretur, unus panis, unum corpus multi sumus. Intelligite et gaudete, unitas, pietas, veritas, charitas, unus panis, unum corpus multi sumus. . . . Dominus Christus significans nos ad se pertinere. voluit mysterium pacis et unitatis nostræ in sua mensa consecrare." (Ibid., Hom. xxxiv., In Bibliotheca Max. Patr., Lugd. 1677, tom. ix. p. 134.)

* So the writer of the Homily "De Corpore et Sang. Christi," formerly attributed to Eusebius of Emessa, argues the need of Baptism from the words, "Except ye eat the flesh of the Son of Man, &c., ye have no life in you." He says: "Sub his enim Dei verbis, quibus Evangelista pronunciat: *Non habebitis vitam in vobis:* aperte intelligendum est, quod omnis anima munere baptismi vacua, non solum gratia careat, sed et vita." (In Op. Hieron., edit. Vallarsius, tom. xi. par. ii. c. 352. See above, p. 83.)

XXVI.

"Quando autem congruentius quam ad consecrandum sacrificium corporis Christi, sancta Ecclesia (quæ corpus est Christi) Spiritus Sancti deposcat adventum?" (Fulgentius Rusp., Ad Monimum, lib. ii. cap. x., In Bibliotheca Max. Patr., Lugd. 1677, tom. ix. p. 29.)

XXVII.

"Ipsa ergo *gratia spiritalis* per unitatem pacis et charitatem, corpus Christi per dies singulos ædificare non desinit. . . . Hæc itaque spiritalis ædificatio corporis Christi . . . nunquam opportunius petitur, quam cum ab *ipso Christi corpore* (quod est Ecclesia) in sacramentum panis et calicis *ipsum Christi corpus et sanguis* offertur. . . . Unde manifestum est . . . neque *spiritalis gratiæ* sanctificationem sacrificiis eorum tribui, qui offerunt ab Ecclesiastici corporis unitate disjuncti. . . . Solius itaque Catholicæ veritatis et communionis sacrificium Deus libenter accipit: quia dum charitatem suam per Spiritum Sanctum diffusam, in ea custodit, *ipsam Ecclesiam* sibi gratum sacrificium facit." (Ibid., cap. x. xi. xii. pp. 29, 30.)

XXVIII.

"Proprietas multis intelligitur modis. Nam et Ecclesia corpus ejus dicitur, ejusdemque Ecclesiæ facit Deus proprias passiones, pro qua etiam in cœlo positus clamat: Saule, Saule, quid me persequeris? Et unusquisque fidelium membrum ejus est, sicut idem docet Apostolus, dicens: Vos estis Corpus Christi, et membra de membro: sed et panis ille, quem universa Ecclesia in memoriam Dominicæ passionis participat, corpus ejus est."* (Joannes Maxentius, Dial. lib. ii., In Bibliotheca Max. Patr., Lugd. 1677, tom. ix. p. 555.)

XXIX.

"Hic panis, et vinum cum comeditur, et bibitur, fit corpus Christi, et sanguis Verbi. . . . Propter hoc, quia factus est homo pro nobis, commendavit nobis isto sacramento corpus et sanguinem suum, quod etiam fecit, et nos ipsos. Et nos corpus ipsius facti sumus per misericordiam ipsius quod accepimus, nostrumque corpus Christi accipimus et audi, quid dicit : *quia ipsum corpus nos sumus.* . . . Postea ad aquam venistis conspersi estis, et unus panis facti estis." (Etherius et Beatus, Contra Elipandum, lib. i., In Bibliotheca Max. Patr., Lugd. 1677, tom. xiii. pp. 370, 371.)

* This is a passage worthy of careful attention; especially in view of the interpretation of the words of institution, as understood by Maxentius to be an illustration of his *dictum:* "Proprietas multis intelligitur modis."

XXX.

Τοῦ Δεσπότου κατεπιστεύθης σῶμα, μᾶλλον δέ τι λέγω, γέγονας σῶμα δεσποτικόν. (Sermo in S. Pascha et in recens illuminatos, In Op. Athanasii, edit. Benedict., tom. ii. p. 398.)

XXXI.

"Angeli vel homines sancti amentur, honorarentur, caritate non servitute. Non eis Corpus Christi offeratur, cum sint hoc et ipsi." * (Agobardus, Liber De Imaginibus, ch. xxx., Opera, edit. Baluze, tom. i. p. 264.)

XXXII.

"Considerandum quoque quod in pane illo non solum corpus Christi, verum etiam in eum credentis populi figuretur: unde multis frumenti granis conficitur, quia corpus populi credentis multis per verbum Christi fidelibus augmentatur." (Bertram, De Corp. et Sang. Dom. lxxiii., Opera, edit. Migne, c. 139.)

XXXIII.

"Sicut non corporaliter sed spiritualiter panis ille credentium corpus dicitur, sic quoque Christi corpus non corporaliter sed spiritualiter necesse est intelligatur." (Ibid., lxxiv. c. 139.)

XXXIV.

"Accipitur spiritualiter quidquid in aqua de populi corpore significatur. Accipiatur ergo necesse est spiritualiter quidquid in vino de Christi sanguine intimatur." (Ibid., lxxv. c. 160.)

XXXV.

"In isto quod per mysterium geritur figura est non solum proprii corporis Christi, verum etiam credentis in Christum populi: utriusque namque corporis, id est, et Christi, quod passum est et resurrexit; et populi in Christo renati atque de mortuis vivificati, figuram gestat." (Ibid., xcviii. c. 169.)

XXXVI.

"Qui passus est pro nobis, commendavit nobis in isto sacramento corpus et sanguinem suum, quod etiam fecit et nos ipsos. Nam et nos corpus ipsius facti sumus, et per misericordiam ipsius quod accepimus nos sumus." (Rabanus Maurus, Enarr. in Ep. Pauli, lib. x., In Ep. 1 Cor. x., Opera, edit. Migne, tom. vi. c. 94. See above, p. 319.)

XXXVII.

"Corpus Christi est, quod assumpsit in utero virginali, Corpus Christi est tota Ecclesia fidelium, Corpus Christi est quod quotidie consecratur in Ecclesia. (Remigius Antiss., In cap. vii. Epist. ad Rom., In Bibliotheca Max. Patr., Lugd. 1677, tom. viii. p. 911.)

* See above, p. 219 sqq.

XXXVIII.

"Sicut ille panis et sanguis in Corpus Christi transeunt; ita omnes qui in Ecclesia digne comedunt illud, unum Corpus Christi sunt." (Remigius Antiss., In 1 Cor. x., In Bibliotheca Max. Patr., Lugd. 1677, tom. viii. p. 968.)

XXXIX.

Μετέχοντες γὰρ τοῦ σώματος τοῦ Χριστοῦ καὶ ἡμεῖς ἔκεινο γινόμεθα, ἐπειδὴ εἷς ἄρτος ὁ Χρίστος. (Œcumenius, In 1 Cor. x., Opera, Paris, 1631, tom. i. p. 515.)

XL.

"Ita enim tanquam suavis panis in Christi Corpus transibimus." Ivo Carnotensis, In Die Paschatis, In Hittorpius, p. 451.)

XLI.

"Ideo et Corpus Christi de pane fit, qui ex multis granis conficitur, quia Ecclesia Corpus Christi per illud reficitur, quæ ex multis electis colligitur." (Honorius Augustodunensis, Gemma Animæ, cap. xxxii., In Bibliotheca Max. Patr., Lugd. 1677, tom. xx. p. 1051.)

XLII.

"Ipse enim et panis, et caro et sanguis, idem cibus et substantia, et vita factus est Ecclesiæ suæ; quam corpus suum appellat, dans ei participationem Spiritus." (De Cœna Domini, In Op. Cypr., edit. Venice, 1728, c. xcvii.)

XLIII.

"Et nos ipsi corpus ejus effecti, sacramento et re sacramenti capiti nostro connectimur" (Ibid., c. civ.)

XLIV.

"Per mysteria autem significatur Ecclesia, quæ est Corpus Christi, et membra ex parte, quæ et tunc accepit Spiritum Sanctum et postquam Christus in cœlos assumptus est etiam nunc accepit donum Spiritus, susceptis donis in altari supercœlesti." (Nic. Cabasilas, Lit. Expos., cap. xxxvii., In Bibliotheca Max. Patr., Lugd. 1677, tom. xxvi. p. 191.)

XLV.

"Ita etiam Christi Ecclesiam si quis videre potuerit, eo ipso quod ei unita est, et est ejus carnis particeps, nihil aliud videbit quam ipsum Corpus Domini. Propter hanc rationem, Vos estis Corpus Christi, inquit Paulus, et membra ex parte." (Ibid., Lit. Expos., cap. xxxviii., In Bibliotheca Max. Patr., Lugd. 1677, tom. xxviii. p. 191.)*

* In the following passage a doubt may be felt as to the nominative case of *est*:
"Ista esca quam accipis, iste panis vivus qui descendit de cœlo, vitæ, æternæ sub-

So, also, it may be observed that Christ's representative presence in the poor is often spoken of in words which may illustrate the language of the Fathers concerning the Lord's Supper. Not only so, but it is sometimes set side by side with the Eucharistic Presence, and that in terms which show that the Presence in the Eucharist was certainly not considered as more real than that in the person of a needy, suffering Christian.

Indeed, some of the following extracts will be found to go far to justify the assertion that the Fathers taught Christians to regard Christ's Presence in His poor and suffering members more highly than His Body in the Eucharist:—

I.

'Η δὲ Βλανδίνα ἐπὶ ξύλου κρεμασθεῖσα . . . διὰ τῆς εὐτόνου προσευχῆς, πολλὴν προθυμίαν τοῖς ἀγωνιζομένοις ἐνεποίει, βλεπόντων αὐτῶν ἐν τῷ ἀγῶνι καὶ τοῖς ἔξωθεν ὀφθαλμοῖς διὰ τῆς ἀδελφῆς τὸν ὑπὲρ αὐτῶν ἐσταυρωμένον. (Eccles. Vien. et Lugd. in Eusebius, Hist. Eccles., lib. v. cap. i., Oxford, 1845, p. 143.)

II.

" Cum paupere domum una ingreditur Christus. . . . Qui pauperem suas in ædes induxerit, Christum ipsum secum adduxit, qui ait: Beati misericordes. . . . Qui peregrinum suo sub tecto excipit, Christum ipsum suscipit." (Sermo, " De Amore Pauperum," among the works not found in Syriac, attributed to Ephrem Syrus, Opera, edit. Venice, 1755, tom. i. p. 331.)

III.

Εἴ τι οὖν ἐμοὶ πείθεσθε, δοῦλοι Χριστοῦ, καὶ ἀδελφοὶ, καὶ συγκληρονόμοι, ἕως ἐστὶ καιρὸς, Χριστὸν ἐπισκεψώμεθα, Χριστὸν θεραπεύσωμεν, Χριστὸν θρέψωμεν, Χριστὸν ἐνδύσωμεν, Χριστὸν συναγάγωμεν, Χριστὸν τιμήσωμεν, μὴ τραπέζῃ μόνον, ὥς τινες, μηδὲ μύροις, ὡς ἡ Μαρία, μηδὲ τάφῳ μόνον, ὥς Ἰωσήφ . . . ἀλλ' ἐπειδὴ ἔλεον θέλει καὶ οὐ θυσίαν ὁ πάντων δεσπότης, καὶ ὑπὲρ μυριάδας ἀρνῶν πιόνων ἡ εὐσπλαγχνία, ταύτην εἰσφέρωμεν αὐτῷ διὰ τῶν δεομένων. (Gregorius Nazianz., Oratio xiv. § xl., Opera, edit. Benedict, tom. i. p. 285.)

stantiam subministrat; et quicumque hunc manducaverit, non morietur in æternum: et est Corpus Christi. Considera nunc utrum præstantior sit panis Angelorum, an Caro Christi, quæ utique corpus est vitæ." (De Mysteriis, cap. viii. In Op. Ambrosii, ed. Bened., tom. ii. c. 337.)

In this chapter the author proves that the Sacraments of the Christian Church are older than those of the Jews, by relating how Melchisedek " protulit ea quæ Abraham veneratus accepit " (§ 45). But none will maintain that what Melchizedek brought forth was the Body and Blood of Christ, otherwise than by effectual signification. (See above, pp. 242, 254.) It is added (§ 46): " Non igitur humani, sed divini est muneris sacramentum quod accepisti, ab eo prolatum qui benedixit fidei patrem Abraham, illius cujus gratiam et gesta miraris." (See above, pp. 34—36.)

IV.

Ὁ δὲ χήραν καὶ ὀρφανὸν οὐκ ἠλέησεν, οὐδὲ μετέδωκεν ἄρτου καὶ τροφῆς ὀλίγης τῷ δεομένῳ, μᾶλλον δὲ Χριστῷ τῷ τρεφομένῳ διὰ τῶν καὶ μικρῶς τρεφομένων. (Gregorius Naz., Oratio xvi. § xviii. tom. i. p. 313.)

V.

Μὴ καταφρονήσῃς τῶν κειμένων ὡς οὐδενὸς ἀξίων. Λόγισαι, τίνες εἰσὶ, καὶ εὑρήσεις αὐτῶν τὸ ἀξίωμα· τοῦ Σωτῆρος ἡμῶν τὸ πρόσωπον ἐνεδύσαντο. (Gregorius Nyss., Orat. i. De Pauperibus Amandis, Opera, edit. Migne, tom. iii. c. 460.)

VI.

Ὁρῶντες αὐτὸν προσαιτοῦντα παρατρέχομεν ... ἀλλὰ καὶ νῦν ὁ αὐτός ἐστιν. αὐτὸς γὰρ εἶπεν, ὅτι ἐγώ εἰμι· τίνος οὖν ἕνεκεν οὐ πάντα κενοῖς; καὶ γὰρ καὶ νῦν ἀκούεις λέγοντος, ὅτι ἐμοὶ ποιεῖς· καὶ οὐδὲν τὸ μέσον ἄν τε τούτῳ, ἄν τε ἐκείνῳ δῷς ... τὰ ῥήματα αὐτοῦ τῆς ὄψεως ἡμῶν πιστότερα. ἐπειδὴ ἂν οὖν ἴδῃς πένητα, ἀναμνήσθητι τῶν ῥημάτων δι' ὧν ἐδήλου, ὅτι αὐτός ἐστιν ὁ τρεφόμενος. εἰ γὰρ καὶ τὸ φαινόμενον οὐκ ἔστι Χριστὸς, ἀλλ' ἐν τούτῳ τῷ σχήματι, αὐτὸς λαμβάνει καὶ προσαιτεῖ. (Chrysostom, In Matth., Hom. lxxxviii. al. lxxxix., § 3, Opera, edit. Montfaucon, tom. vii. p. 828.)

VII.

Ἐκεῖνοι εἶδον τὸν ἀστέρα καὶ ἐχάρησαν· σὺ δὲ αὐτὸν ὁρῶν τὸν Χριστὸν ξένον ὄντα καὶ γυμνὸν οὐκ ἐπικάμπτῃ. (Ibid., In Matth., Hom. vii. § 5, Op., tom. vii. p. 113.)

VIII.

Πῶς οὐκ αἰσχρὸν μαρμάροις μὲν περιβάλλειν τοὺς τοίχους εἰκῇ καὶ μάτην, τὸν δὲ Χριστὸν γυμνὸν περιερχόμενον περιορᾶν; (Ibid., Ad Pop. Antioch., Hom. ii. § 5, Op., tom. ii. p. 27.)

IX.

Ὅταν πένητα ὑποδέξῃ πεινῶντα καὶ γυμνὸν, ἐκεῖνον [τὸν Χριστὸν] καὶ ὑπεδέξω καὶ ἔθρεψας. (Ibid., In Matth., Hom. xxvii. § 1, Op., tom. vii. p. 314.)

X.

Τοῦτο τὸ θυσιαστήριον ἐξ αὐτῶν τοῦ Χριστοῦ σύγκειται μελῶν καὶ τὸ σῶμα τοῦ δεσπότου θυσιαστήριόν σοι γίνεται· αἰδέσθητι τοῦτο αὐτό· ἐν τῇ σαρκὶ θύεις τοῦ δεσπότου τὸ ἱερεῖον. τοῦτο τὸ θυσιαστήριον, καὶ τούτου τοῦ νῦν φρικωδέστερον, οὐχὶ τοῦ παλαιοῦ μόνον· ἀλλὰ μὴ θορυβηθῆτε. τοῦτο μὲν γὰρ θαυμαστὸν, διὰ τὴν ἐπιτιθεμένην ἐν αὐτῷ θυσίαν· ἐκεῖνο δὲ τὸ τῆς ἐλεήμονος, οὐ διὰ τοῦτο μόνον, ἀλλὰ καὶ ὅτι καὶ ἐξ αὐτῆς σύγκειται τῆς θυσίας τῆς τοῦτο ποιούσης. θαυμαστὸν τοῦτο πάλιν, ὅτι λίθος μέν ἐστι τὴν φύσιν, ἅγιον δὲ γίνεται, ἐπείδη σῶμα δέχεται Χριστοῦ· ἐκεῖνο δε, ἐπειδὴ αὐτὸ σῶμα ἔστι Χριστοῦ. (Chrysostom, In 2 Cor., Hom. xx. § 3, Op., tom. x. p. 581.)

XI.

Σὺ δὲ τὸ μὲν θυσιαστήριον τοῦτο τιμᾷς, ὅτι δέχεται τοῦ Χριστοῦ σῶμα· τὸν δὲ αὐτὸ τὸ σῶμα τοῦ Χριστοῦ ὄντα καθυβρίζεις, καὶ περιορᾷς ἀπολλύμενον. (Ibid., In 2 Cor., Hom. xx. § 3, Op., tom. x. p. 581.)

XII.·

Βούλει τιμῆσαι τοῦ Χριστοῦ τὸ σῶμα; μὴ περιίδῃς αὐτὸν γυμνὸν. μηδὲ ἐνταῦθα μὲν αὐτὸν σηρικοῖς ἱματίοις τιμήσῃς, ἔξω δὲ ὑπὸ κρυμνοῦ καὶ γυμνότητος διαφθειρόμενον περιίδῃς, ὁ γὰρ εἰπὼν, τοῦτό μου ἐστὶ τὸ σῶμα, καὶ τῷ λόγῳ τὸ πρᾶγμα βεβαιώσας, οὗτος εἶπε· πεινῶντά με ἴδετε, καὶ οὐκ ἐθρέψατε. (Ibid., In Matth., Hom. l. al. li., § 3, Op., tom. vii. p. 518.)

XIII.

"Nec tu deficias, quia non potes quod Martha, suscipere Christum in domum tuam cum Apostolis suis: Facit te esse securum, quando uni ex minimis meis fecistis, mihi fecistis."* (Augustine, Serm. clxxix. § 3, Opera, edit. Benedict. 1683, tom. v. par. i. c. 855.)

* This and the following extract should be carefully considered in their bearing on the question of the Real Objective Presence. They could hardly have been written in the atmosphere of ideas cognate with that doctrine. Albertinus writes: " Quamobrem enim negaret Zacchæi et Marthæ beatitudinem nobis contingere posse, si in sacramento suo Dominus substantialiter ac personaliter in domos nostras intraret? Qua rursum de causa negationis hujus rationem arcesseret ab ascensione Domini ad dexteram Patris, ipsiusque in cœlis sessione, nisi ipsum supponeret in cœlo et in terra substantialiter simul esse non posse? Cur denique ad temperandam illam præsentiæ Dominicæ negationem ad membrorum ejus mysticorum præsentiam tanquam vicariam recurreret, si illum in sacramento substantialiter ac realiter residentem haberemus? Illum enim, licet invisibiliter, in sacramento habere, semper habere est, et quidem gloriosius quam illum aut Zacchæus olim, aut Martha receperint, cum ipsum ii tunc passibilem, nos jam (si ita est) gloriosum et impassibilem et immortalem habeamus. Ejusmodique præsentia, utpote substantialis et personalis longe est pretiosior repræsentativa illa per pauperes et egenos, ad quam tamen solam, consolationis causa, velut quodammodo compensativam refugit." (De Eucharistia p. 646.)

XIV.

"Dominus intravit in domum illius [Zacchæi]. O beatum! Numquid nobis potest ita contingere? Jam Christus in cœlo est. Recita mihi Christe, testamentum novum. Fac beatum de lege tua. Recita, ut scias te non fraudari Christi præsentia. Audi judicaturum: Quando uni ex minimis meis fecistis, mihi fecistis. Expectat unusquisque vestrum suscipere Christum sedentem in cœlo, attendite eum jacentem sub porticu, attendite esurientem, attendite frigus patientem, attendite egenum, attendite peregrinum." (Augustine, De Scrip., Serm. xxv. § 8, Opera, tom. v. par. i. c. 136.)

XV.

"Videbis eum in omni paupere, et tanges eum in omni egeno, recipies eum in omni hospite." (Paulinus Nol., Epist. xiii. ad Severum, In Biblioth. Max. Patr., Lugd. 1677, tom. vi. p. 194.)

XVI.

"Sic sacræ mensæ communicare debetis, ut nihil prorsus de veritate Corporis Christi et sanguinis ambigatis. Hoc enim ore sumitur, quod fide creditur : et frustra ab illis Amen respondetur, a quibus contra id quod accipitur, disputatur. Dicente autem Propheta *Beatus qui intelligit super egenum et pauperem*, ille circa pauperes vestimentorum et ciborum laudabilis distributor est, qui se Christum in indigentibus et vestire novit et pascere; quoniam ut ipse ait, *Quamdiu fecistis uni de fratribus meis, mihi fecistis.* Verus itaque Deus et Verus homo unus est Christus, dives in suis, pauper in nostris, dona accipiens et dona diffundens." (Leo Magn., De jejunio Sept. Men., Serm. vi., In Bibliotheca Max. Patr., Lugd. 1677, tom. vii. p. 1058.)

XVII.

"Hos enim ego omnes non aliter quam imitatores Christi honoro, non aliter quam Christi imagines colo, non aliter quam Christi membra suscipio." (Salvianus Massil., sub nomine Timothei, Ad Eccles. Cath., lib. ii., In Bibliotheca Max. Patr., Lugd. 1677, tom. viii. p. 387.)

So also Fulgentius says : "Putas jam non tibi licere suscipere Christum. Unde, inquis, licet?" And his answer says nothing of any Real Presence in the Eucharist: "Ille dives egens est . . . in membris suis. . . . Obsequamur Christo, et nobiscum est in suis, nobiscum est in nobis." (Homil. xxxvii., De tertio die Paschæ, In Bibliotheca Max. Patr., Lugd. 1677, tom. ix. p. 135.)

Such an answer, with such an omission, could scarcely have come from a mind which had ever apprehended the conception of the Romish doctrine of the Eucharistic Presence.

XVIII.

"Quare ergo dubitet aliquis indigentem pascere, cum videat so ista Christo nostro in pauperis refectione conferre?" (Valerianus, Hom. ix., In Bibliotheca Max. Patr., Lugd. 1677, tom. viii. p. 509.)

XIX.

"Intelliges ibi esse Christum nostrum, ubi abundantiam videris lachrymarum. Nec enim longe tibi quærendus est Dominus, si non tis avarus. Expectat nos ecce foris. . . . Ipsum scias esse Christum nostrum, quem videris nudum, quem aspexeris cæcum, quem offenderis claudicantem, quem pannis involutum, quem videris sordida veste contectum. In hac denique veste, cum a Magis quæreretur inventus est: et cum in præsepi positus jaceret, sub hoc habitu apertis thesauris munera oblata suscepit." (Ibid., Homil. vii. De Misericordia, In Bibliotheca Max. Patr., Lugd. 1677, tom. viii. p. 507.)

XX.

"Quando enim pauper esurit, Christus indiget. . . . Esurit modo Christus fratres in omnibus pauperibus : ipse esurire et sitire dignatur, et quod in terra accipit, in cœlo reddit." (Cæsarius Arelat., Homilia xxii., In Bibliotheca Max. Patr., Lugd. 1677, tom. viii. p. 842.)

XXI.

"Omnis qui jam eleemosynas facit, qui jam in bonis operibus studet, quasi Christum in convivium recipit, Christum pascit, quia eum in membris suis sustentare non desinit." (Angelomi Stromata, In Cant. Cant., cap. i., In Bibliotheca Max. Patr., Lugd. 1677, tom. xv. p. 419.)

NOTE H. (p. 181).

On the Teaching of the Fathers as to the Res Sacramenti of the Eucharist being the object of Spiritual Senses.

IT should be observed how, in the teaching of the Fathers, man is to be regarded as having spiritual needs and spiritual senses corresponding to those of his body; and while the *sacramentum* is the object of the touch, sight, taste of the outer man, the *res sacramenti* is the object of the spiritual senses—the touch, sight, taste of the inner man.

Thus the real eating and drinking of the Body and Blood of Christ is regarded as the spiritual act of the soul, which has a spiritual mouth for this purpose.

In accordance with this view, the receiving, eating, and drinking of the Spiritual Food signified and conveyed by the outward signs of bread and wine is the office of faith. It is by faith's operation that the soul is fed. Eating is by believing.* The eating of the flesh of the Son of Man is by believing that He died and gave Himself for our sins.

In accordance with this view also, Christ's Body is said to be eaten and Christ's Blood to be drunk in the Scriptures,† as well as in the Sacraments; and the Gospel itself is accordingly sometimes spoken of as the Body of Christ : ‡ and the remission of sins as the living bread, and the feeding on it as the feeding on eternal life.

* In the Confession of the Waldenses (1542) we seem to have a witness that this faith lived on in Alpine valleys through ages of superstition and in spite of cruel persecution : "Errant qui affirmant in Cœna Christi corpus comedi corporaliter: caro enim nihil prodest: Spiritus est, qui vivificat. Fideles igitur vere Jesu Christi carnem edunt, et sanguinem bibunt spiritualiter in ipsorum cordibus." (Confess. Vald. in Crispin, Act. Mart., lib. iii. p. 108.)

Again : "Quisquis credit Jesus Christum, tradidisse corpus suum, et profudisse sanguinem, ad remissionem peccatorum, ille comedit carnem, et bibit sanguinem Domini." (Ibid.)

See Faber's "Ancient Vallenses and Albigenses," pp. 441, 442.

† Special attention should be directed to the way in which the Fathers *speak alike* of the eating of Christ's Body in the Scriptures and in the sacrament. There is not the slightest appearance of an intention or desire to draw a clear distinction between the *eating* in the one case and the other.

Dean Goode (who in his valuable work on the Eucharist has quoted several of the passages given below, i. pp. 323—326) says very well : "The force of these passages lies more especially in the way in which the two modes of eating the Flesh and drinking the Blood of Christ are *coupled together*. We cannot suppose that the writers considered them to be so dissimilar in their nature as the authors under review would have them to be. The latter admit, as of course they are compelled to do, that the Fathers say we eat the Flesh of Christ and drink His Blood in reading the Scriptures ; but they contend that the Fathers give this only as a metaphorical application of our Lord's words, and confine the proper sense of His words to our participation of the Eucharist. But the passages just quoted are entirely opposed to this view. They *connect together* the acts in which it is said that we eat the Flesh and drink the Blood of Christ in a way that is inconsistent with such a notion, and at least implies a similarity in the mode in which such communion takes place in those acts." (P. 326.)

I think it might have been added, that so far as these sayings of the Fathers make any distinction of *propriety* in the two means of eating, they seem to give the highest place to the Scriptures.

‡ It is not pretended that each of the following extracts by itself would suffice to give evidence against the Real Objective Presence. Some will be found to go much further than others in witness against materialistic views of the Eucharist. But those which would separately be, perhaps, of little value, are capable of adding something to the sum of the testimony afforded by a general view of the whole.

It is also acknowledged that similar language may sometimes be found in the

I.

Φέρει ... οἶνον ἡ ἄμπελος, ὡς αἷμα ὁ Λόγος· ἄμφω δὲ ἀνθρώποις ποτὸν εἰς σωτηρίαν· ὁ μὲν οἶνος, τῷ σώματι· τὸ δὲ αἷμα, τῷ πνεύματι.

writings of some of those who adopted the views of Paschasius. With such writers the *materialistic* is, of course, subservient to that which is *spiritual* in their view of the Eucharist. And thus they seem to bear witness to the uselessness of a Presence, which only serves for a purpose for which *effectual symbols* would suffice. See above, p. 177.

Indeed the holding of these views, together with the doctrine of the Real Objective Presence, seems unavoidably to lead to something like the statement of contradictory doctrines ; as may be strikingly seen in the writings of the justly celebrated John Wessel of Gansfort, who, in addition to the cognomen of *Lux Mundi*, acquired also the appellation of "Magister Contradictionum." (See Ullmann's "Reformers before the Reformation," vol. ii. pp. 263, 331, ed. Clark.) In one place he writes : "Quisquis credit fide non ficta omnipotentiæ Dei, sub speciebus panis et vini veraciter sanctam illam carnem, sanctum illum sanguinem . . . præsentialiter contineri, nonnihil spiritalis vitæ experitur in se," &c. (De Sacr. Euch., cap. viii., Opera, p. 673, Gronin., 1614.)

In another place he writes : " Qui credunt in Eum, hi sunt qui manducant carnem Ejus. . . . Manducabat ergo Paulus primus Eremita, etiam temporibus illis, quibus mortalem nullum, ne dicam sacerdotem, communicantem videbat. Sed manducabat, quia credebat, et quod credebat, crebro commemorabat, quod commemorabat diligenter considerabat, quod desiderabat, esuriebat et sitiebat." (Ibid., cap. x. p. 678.) Again : " Quisquis visibiliter manducans, nisi spiritualiter manducet, non manducat.' (Ibid., cap. viii. p. 674.) Again : " Interior homo, quomodo manducat carnem, et sanguinem quomodo bibit, ubi non est nisi mens, intelligentia ? Ita circa Verbum carnem . . . . versetur interior homo, id est mens, intelligentia, voluntas, quemadmodum os, fauces, et stomachus exterior circa epulas negotiantur." (Ibid., cap. ix. p. 676.) And again : " Sacramentalis panis, quia sacramentalis est, et sacramentum significativum est, significatione nutrit et reficit." (Ibid., cap. xiii. p. 683. Compare pp. 656, 660, 664, 696, 697. See also Dorner's Hist. of Protestant Theol., vol. i. p. 78, ed. Clark ; and Ullmann, vol. ii. pp. 285, 503 *sqq*. Compare also Gabriel Biel, " S. Canonis Missæ Expos.," Lect. xl. and lxxxvi.)

There is a remarkable passage in the writings of Hildebertus Cenomanensis, in which he sets a saying of our Lord side by side with a saying of St. Augustine (which he regards as another saying of our Lord's) as teaching *apparently* contradictory doctrines. He says : " Inconstans verbo putabatur, dum contraria tradere videretur. Qui enim dixerat : *Nisi manducaveritis carnem meam, et biberitis sanguinem meum, non habebitis vitam in vobis*, ipse idem ait : *Non hoc corpus quod videtis, manducaturi estis ; nec bibituri illum sanguinem, quem fusuri sunt qui me crucifigent.*" (Sermo xii., De præclaris in nos Christi beneficiis, Opera, ed. Benedict. 1708, c. 719, 720.)

In his hands the reconciliation is effected by a method which seems virtually to involve the sacrifice of the Real Objective doctrine, and (notwithstanding the elaborate note of Beaugendre) can hardly—to ordinary minds at least—be made consistent with his own doctrine elsewhere : unless, indeed, his teaching of transubstantiation may be understood of a doctrine differing (in one essential particular, at least) from the doctrine subsequently known by that name.

The first saying he applies to spiritual manducation of spiritual flesh : "(De spirituali carne ait ; quam nemo sumit injuste, nemo sumit ad mortem, nemo manducat nisi bonus ") ; the second saying he understands of sacramental manducation ; and the sacramental Body which is its object is therefore *another* Body, distinct from the natural Body of Christ. (" *Non hoc corpus quod videtis*, &c. de sacramentali manducatione ait, quia boni et mali Corpus Christi sumunt :" p. 721.)

(Clem. Alex., Pædag. i. c. v., Opera, edit. Potter, Venice, 1757, tom. i. p. 107.)

II.

"Itaque sermonem constituens vivificatorem, quia spiritus et vita sermo, eumdem etiam Carnem suam dixit; quia et sermo caro erat factus; proinde in causam vitæ appetendus, et devorandus auditu, et ruminandus intellectu, et fide digerendus." (Tertullian, De Resurrectione Carnis, § xxxvii., Opera, edit. Rigaltius, 1689, p. 347.)

III.

Ὁ Σωτήρ φησιν· Ἐγώ εἰμί ὁ ἄρτος ὁ ἐκ τοῦ οὐρανοῦ καταβάς. Τοῦτον οὖν τὸν ἄρτον ἤσθιον μὲν πρότερον ἄγγελοι, νυνὶ δὲ καὶ ἄνθρωποι. Τὸ ἐσθίειν ἐνταῦθα τὸ γινώσκειν σημαίνει. Τοῦτο γὰρ ἐσθίει νοῦς ὃ καὶ γινώσκει, καὶ τοῦτο οὐκ ἐσθίει ὃ οὐ γινώσκει. (Origen, Selecta in Psalmos, Psal. lxxvii. v. 25, Opera, edit. Migne, tom. ii. c. 1541.)

IV.

"Evidenter ostenditur membrorum hæc nomina nequaquam corpori visibili aptari posse, sed ad invisibilis animæ partem virtutesque debere revocari: quoniam et vocabula quidem habent similia, aperte autem et sine ulla ambiguitate non exterioris, sed interioris hominis

Whatever, in this teaching, the Sacramental Body and Blood may be, it is clearly not the Body which was crucified, nor the Blood which was shed on the cross; and the oral manducation of this sacramental Body is not at all that which is meant by the saying, "Nisi manducaveritis," &c.

It is, perhaps, by mistake that Hildebert has been regarded as having been a pupil of Berengarius. (See Canon Robertson's History of Christian Church, vol. iv. p. 368, 1874.)

Let the reader be asked to mark also the incongruous connection of the material and the spiritual in such teachings as the following: "Christus de ore transit ad cor: melius est ut procedat in mentem quam descendat in ventrem. Cibus hic non carnis sed animæ venit ut comedatur, non ut consumatur; ut gustetur, non ut incorporetur; ore comeditur sed non in stomacho digeritur, reficit animum, non effluit in secessum. . . . Species quidem corroditur et maculatur, sed veritas numquam corrumpitur aut coinquinatur. Si quando tale quid videris, nihil time illi; sed esto sollicitus tibi, ne tu forte lædaris si male credideris." (Peter Damiani, Expositio Canonis Missæ, § 6, In Mai's Script. Vet. Nov. Coll., tom. vi. par. ii. p. 215.)

"Pascuntur corpore, sed animâ saginantur. Dentibus atterunt, sed quod ad mentem integrum perveniat." (Ven. Hildebertus Tur., In Euch. Sacr., Op., c. 497, ed. Beaugendre, 1708. See also c. 409.)

"Quis capiat intellectus qualiter caro Christi quotidie de coelis ad nos in altare, et ab altari in nos venit, nec tamen coelos deserit unde venit? . . . . Quid enim divinius, quam quod Christi Corpus, cum caro sit, et non spiritus, cibus tamen est non carnis et corporis, sed spiritus et mentis. Cibus quidem interioris hominis est, nec tamen humanus, sed divinus spiritualiter et divinè in spiritum vadens, non se in spiritum convertens, sed spiritum spiritualiter et divinè pascens, spiritualiter intrans, spiritualiter operans." (Ibid., c. 1103.)

significantias gerunt.* Est ergo materialis hujus hominis, qui et exterior appellatur, cibus potusque naturæ suæ cognatus, corporeus iste scilicet et terrenus. Similiter autem et spiritalis hominis ipsius qui et interior dicitur, est proprius cibus, ut panis ille vivus qui de cœlo descendit. Sed et potus ille est ex illa aqua quam promittit Jesus, dicens : Quicunque biberit ex hac aqua quam ego do ei, non sitiet in æternum. Sic ergo per omnia similitudo quidem vocabulorum secundum utrumque hominem ponitur : rerum vero proprietas unicuique

* So Gregory Nyss. : 'Αναλογία γὰρ τίς ἐστὶ τοῖς ψυχικοῖς κινήμασι καὶ ἐνεργήμασιν πρὸς τὰ τοῦ σώματος αἰσθητήρια. (In Cant. Cantic., Hom. i., Opera, edit. Migne, tom. i. c. 780.)
See also Basil Cæsar. as quoted below, p. 336.
So Vigilius Taps. : "Spiritualia Apostoli verba spiritualiter advertamus, quibus se, non oculis et manibus corporeis, sed interioris hominis membris vidisse et palpasse Verbum Dei testatur. Quia quibus naribus odor ejus hauritur, et quo ore suavitas ejus gustatur, ipsis oculis et auribus, et manibus contrectatur.... Credere ergo in Filium Dei, hoc est videre, hoc est audire, hoc est odorari, hoc est gustare, hoc est contrectare eum." (Contra Eutych., lib. iv. § xxii., Opera, edit. Chiffletii, Divione, 1664, p. 54.)
St. Chrysostom in a well-known passage declares that if we had been incorporeal, Christ would have delivered His gifts bare ; but because the soul is inclosed in the body, He gives us things, in sensible things, which are to be perceived by the mind— ἐν αἰσθήτοις τὰ νοήτα. (In Matt., Hom. lxxxii. al. lxxxiii., § 4, Opera, edit. Montfaucon, tom. vii. p. 787.)
Nicholas Cabasilas, maintaining a participation by disembodied spirits, argues that in the case of those in the flesh the organs of reception are those of the spirit, not of the body. Whether or not in this he is perfectly consistent with himself, he is herein doubtless bearing witness to a belief older than corruptions which may have overshadowed it. He says : "Consideremus causas sanctificationis, an non etiam animæ mortuorum se habent, sicut et viventium. Quænam sunt autem causæ sanctificationis? Numquid corpus habere, pedibus ad mensam currere, manibus sancta accipere, ore sumere, comedere, bibere? Nequaquam : Ad multos enim qui hæc fecerunt, et ita ad mysteria accesserunt, nulla rediit utilitas, et pluribus malis obnoxii recesserunt. Sed quænam sunt causæ sanctificationis iis qui sanctificantur, et quæ sunt quæ Christus a nobis exigit? animæ purgatio, in Deum dilectio, fideles, desiderium mysterii, alacritas ad participationem, fervens appetitio, sitientes currere. Hæc sunt quæ hanc sanctificationem attrahunt, et cum quibus necesse est eos qui accedunt esse Christi participes, et sine quibus fieri non potest. Sed hæc omnia non sunt corporalia, sed dependent a sola anima." (Liturgiæ Expositio, cap. xlii., In Biblioth. Max. Patr., Lugd. 1677, tom. xxvi. p. 192. See Claude's argument from this, " Cath. Doctr. of Euch.," London, 1684, par. i. pp. 146—151.)
Cabasilas argues further (cap. xliii.)—(1) That the gift is given only to worthy receivers, and that by Christ Himself. He says : "Non enim omnes quibus dat sacerdos, vere sumunt, sed illi omnino soli quibus dat ipse Christus. Sacerdos enim omnibus, ut semel dicam, qui accedunt. Christus autem dat iis solum qui participes esse digni sunt." (P. 193.) (2) Cabasilas also argues that the gift can affect the body only through the soul. He says : "Quoniam autem iis etiam qui adhuc vivunt corpore, datur quidam donum per corpus, sed primum pervadit in animæ substantiam, et per animam in corpus transmittitur. Et hoc significans beatus Paulus : Qui adhæret, inquit, Domino, unus est spiritus, utpote quod in anima primo et principaliter hæc unio et conjunctio consistat."

discreta servatur, et [corruptibili] corruptibilia præbentur, incorruptibili vero incorruptilia proponuntur." (Origen,* In Canticum Cantic., Prologus, interp. Rufino, Opera, edit. Migne, tom. iii. c. 66.)

V.

" Nobis et panis, verbum Dei est. Ipse enim panis vivus, qui de cœlo descendit, et vitam dat huic mundo. . . . Nec mireris quia verbum Dei et caro dicitur, et panis, et lac dicitur, et olera dicitur, et pro mensura credentium, vel possibilitate sumentium diverse nominatur." (Ibid., In Exod., Homil. vii. § 8, Opera, edit. Migne, tom. ii. c. 348.)

VI.

"Sed tu qui ad Christum venisti, pontificem verum, qui sanguine suo Deum tibi propitium fecit, et reconciliavit te Patri, non hæreas in sanguine carnis; sed disce potius sanguinem Verbi, et audi ipsum tibi dicentem, quia ' hic sanguis meus est, qui pro vobis effundetur in remissionem peccatorum.' Novit qui mysteriis imbutus est et carnem et sanguinem Verbi Dei." (Ibid., In Levit., Homil. ix. § 10, Opera, edit. Migne, tom. ii. c. 523.)

VII.

" Hic ergo sanguis qui nominatur uvæ, illius uvæ est quæ nascitur ex illa vite, de qua Salvator dicit : ' Ego sum vitis vera,' discipuli vero ' palmites, Pater autem agricola est,' qui purgat eos, ut fructum plurimum afferant. Tu ergo es verus populus Israel, qüi scis sanguinem bibere, et nosti carnem Verbi Dei comedere, et sanguinem bibere, et uvæ sanguinem illius quæ est ex vera vite et illis palmitibus quos Pater purgat, haurire. Quorum palmitum fructus, vulneratorum sanguis merito dicitur, quem ex verbis eorum et doctrina bibimus, si tamen simus ut catuli leonis exsurgentes, et ut leo exsultantes." (Ibid., In Num., Homil. xvi. § 9, Opera, edit. Migne, tom. ii. c. 702.)

VIII.

" Hoc quod modo loquimur, carnes sunt Verbi Dei; si tamen non quasi infirmis olera, aut quasi pueris lactis alimoniam proferamus. Si perfecta loquimur, si robusta, si fortiora, carnes vobis Verbi Dei apponimus comedendas." (Ibid., In Num., Hom. xxiii. § 6, Opera, edit. Migne, tom. ii. c. 752.)

IX.

" Jesus ergo quia totus ex toto mundus est, tota ejus caro cibus est, et totus sanguis ejus potus est ; quia omne opus ejus sanctum est, et omnis sermo ejus verus est. Propterea ergo et caro ejus verus est

---

* On the authorship see Albertinus, De Euch., p. 361.

cibus, et sanguis ejus verus et potus. Carnibus enim et sanguine verbi sui tanquam mundo cibo ac potu, potat et reficit omne hominum genus." (Origen, In Levit., Homil. vii. § 5, Opera, edit. Migne, tom. ii. c. 486, 487.)

X.

" Bibere autem dicimur sanguinem Christi, non solum sacramentorum ritu, sed et cum sermones ejus recipimus, in quibus vita consistit, sicut et ipse dicit: 'Verba quæ locutus sum, spiritus et vita est.' Est ergo ipse vulneratus, cujus nos sanguinem bibimus, id est, doctrinæ ejus verba suscipimus." (Ibid., In Num., Hom. xvi., Opera, edit. Migne, tom. ii. c. 701.)

XI.

"Non enim panem illum visibilem quem tenebat in manibus, corpus suam dicebat Deus Verbum, sed verbum in cujus mysterio fuerat panis ille frangendus. Nec potum illum visibilem sanguinem suum dicebat, sed verbum in cujus mysterio potus ille fuerat effundendus. Nam Corpus Dei Verbi, aut sanguis, quid aliud esse potest, nisi verbum quod nutrit, et verbum quod lætificat cor?"* (Ibid., In Matt. xxvi. 26 *sqq.*, Op., ed. Migne, tom. iii. c. 1734, 1735.)

XII.

Εὖ ἴστε, ὅτι τὰ ῥήματά μου ἃ λελάληκα ὑμῖν, πνεῦμά ἐστι καὶ ζωή ἐστι· ὥστε αὐτὰ εἶναι τὰ ῥήματα καὶ τοὺς λόγους αὐτοῦ, τὴν σάρκα καὶ τὸ αἷμα, ὧν ὁ μετέχων ἀεὶ, ὡσανεὶ ἄρτῳ οὐρανίῳ τρεφόμενος, τῆς οὐρανίου μεθέξει ζωῆς. (Eusebius Cæsar., Contra Marcell. de Eccles. Theol., lib. iii. c. xii., appended to Demonstr. Evangel., Paris, 1628, p. 180.)

XIII.

Διὰ τοῦτο τῆς εἰς οὐρανοὺς ἀναβάσεως ἐμνημόνευσε τοῦ υἱοῦ τοῦ ἀνθρώπου, ἵνα τῆς σωματικῆς ἐννοίας αὐτοὺς ἀφέλκυσῃ, καὶ λοιπὸν τὴν εἰρημένην σάρκα βρῶσιν ἄνωθεν οὐράνιον, καὶ πνευματικὴν τροφὴν παρ' αὐτοῦ διδομένην μάθωσιν. (Athanasius, Epist. iv. ad Serap., § 19, Opera, edit. Benedict., Patav. 1777, tom. i. par. ii. p. 568.)

XIV.

Ἴσον τῷ εἰπεῖν, τὸ μὲν δεικνύμενον καὶ διδόμενον ὑπὲρ τῆς τοῦ κόσμου σωτηρίας ἐστὶν ἡ σὰρξ ἣν ἐγὼ φορῶ. ἀλλ' αὕτη ὑμῖν καὶ τὸ ταύτης αἷμα παρ' ἐμοῦ πνευματικῶς δοθήσεται τροφὴ, ὥστε πνευματικῶς ἐν ἑκάστῳ ταύτην ἀναδίδασθαι, καὶ γίνεσθαι πᾶσι φυλακτήριον εἰς ἀνάστασιν ζωῆς αἰωνίου. (Ibid., p. 568.)

* See above, p. 101. The passage should be read in connexion with the other extracts here given from Origen.

XV.

Οι ειλικρινώς την ένσαρκον αυτού οικονομίαν παραδεξάμενοι, και τω της ψυχής λογισμώ δια της συγκαταθέσεως ώσπερ απογευσάμενοι του δόγματος, λογικώς εσθίουσι την άρκα και μεταλαμβάνουσι δια της πίστεως του αίματος. (Theodorus Heracleotes, In Cat. Patr. Græc. in S. Joann. ex antiquissimo Cod. MS., edit. Corderius, Antw. 1630, p. 193, cap. vi. vs. 55.)

XVI.

Γεύσασθε και ίδετε ότι χρηστός ο Κύριος· πολλαχού τετηρήκαμεν, ότι τοις έξωθεν μέλεσιν ομωνύμως αι της ψυχής προσαγορεύονται δυνάμεις, επεί δε άρτος εστίν αληθινός ο κύριος ημών, και η σαρξ αυτού αληθής εστι βρώσις, ανάγκη την ηδονήν της ευφροσύνης του άρτου, δια γεύσεως ημίν νοητής εγγίνεσθαι.* (Basil Cæsar., Hom. in Psalm. xxxiii. § 6, Opera, edit. Garnier, Paris, 1721, tom. i. pp. 148, 149.)

XVII.

Προς δη τούτο λέγομεν, ότι εστί μεν τι και νοητόν στόμα του ένδον ανθρώπου, ω τρέφεται μεταλαμβάνων του λόγου της ζωής, ός εστιν άρτος εκ του ουρανού καταβάς. (Ibid., § 1, p. 144.)

XVIII.

Ούτος ο άρτος ουκ εις κοιλίαν χωρεί και εις αφεδρώνα εκβάλλεται, αλλ' εις πάσαν σου την σύστασιν αναδίδοται, εις ωφέλειαν σώματος, και ψυχής. (Cat. Myst., In Op. Cyril. Hieros., lib. v. § 15, edit. Ben., p. 329.)

XIX.

Ώσπερ γαρ ο άρτος σώματι κατάλληλος, ούτω και Λόγος τη ψυχή αρμόδιος. (Ibid., Catech. xxii., Myst. iv. § v., Opera, edit. Ben., p. 321.)

XX.

Προκόπτει η ψυχή, λαβούσα ζωήν Πνεύματος αγίου, και απογευσαμένη του 'Αρνίου και χρισθείσα τω αίματι αυτού, και φαγούσα τον αληθινόν άρτον, τον ζώντα Λόγον. (Macarius, Ægypt., Hom. xlvii., § xi., Opera, edit. Migne, c. 804.)

* Compare Hesychius Hieros.: "Qui in nobis est divinus Spiritus, et sermo quem tradidit qui in nobis sunt, componit sensus, et non solum nostrum gustum producit ad mysterium, sed et auditum, et visum, et tactum, et odoratum, ita ut nil in eis minori rationi, et infirmæ menti proximum, de his videlicet, quæ valde superna sunt, suspicemur." (In Levit., lib. vi. cap. xxii., In Bibl. Max. Patr., Lugd. 1677, tom. xii. p. 148. See below, p. 344, No. lxiii.)

XXI.

Οἱ μεταλαμβάνοντες ἐκ τοῦ φαινομένου ἄρτου, πνευματικῶς τὴν σάρκα τοῦ Κυρίου ἐσθίουσι.* (Macarius, Hom. xxvii. § xvii. c. 706.)

XXII.

Σωματοποιεῖ γὰρ ἑαυτὸν καὶ εἰς βρῶσιν καὶ πόσιν ὁ Κύριος, καθὼς γέγραπται ἐν τῷ Εὐαγγελίῳ· Ὁ τρώγων τὸν ἄρτον τοῦτον, ζήσεται εἰς τὸν αἰῶνα, ἵνα ἀναπαύσῃ ἀνεκλαλήτως, καὶ ἐμπλήσῃ εὐφροσύνης πνευματικῆς τὴν ψυχήν· καὶ γὰρ φησιν· Ἐγώ εἰμι ὁ ἄρτος τῆς ζωῆς. Ὁμοίως καὶ εἰς πόσιν νάματος ἐπουρανίου, καθὼς φησιν, Ὁ πίνων ἐκ τοῦ ὕδατος οὗ ἐγὼ δώσω αὐτῷ, γενήσεται ἐν αὐτῷ πηγὴ ὕδατος ἁλλομένου εἰς ζωὴν αἰώνιον· καὶ πάντες, φησὶ, τὸ αὐτὸ πόμα ἐποτίσθημεν . . . καὶ ἐγὼ νομίζω, ὅτι Μωϋσῆς κατὰ πᾶσαν ὥραν ἐν τῷ ὄρει, ἐν τῇ τῶν τεσσεράκοντα ἡμερῶν νηστείᾳ εἰς ἐκείνην τὴν πνευματικὴν τράπεζαν εἰσερχόμενος ἐνετρύφα καὶ ἀπέλαυεν. (Ibid., Homil. iv. § 12, 13, Opera, edit. Migne, c. 481.)†

XXIII.

Ὥσπερ οὖν τῷ σώματι . . . ἡ ζωὴ οὐκ ἐξ ἑαυτοῦ ἐστὶν, ἀλλ᾽ ἔξωθεν αὐτοῦ . . . οὕτω καὶ ἡ ψυχή. . . . Ἔχει γὰρ ἡ θεία φύσις καὶ ἄρτον ζωῆς, τὸν εἰπόντα, Ἐγώ εἰμι ὁ ἄρτος τῆς ζωῆς· καὶ Ὕδωρ ζῶν· καὶ Οἶνον εὐφραίνοντα καρδίαν ἀνθρώπου. (Ibid., Homil. i. § xi., Opera, c. 461.)

XXIV.

Ζωῆς ἄρτος καταβαίνων ὁ τοῦ Θεοῦ θρεπτικὸς λόγος ἐστὶ, ὃν ἐσθίει ὁ πρὸς αὐτὸν ἐρχόμενος τῷ τὴν ἀρετὴν ἐνεργεῖν. ἐπειδὴ δε οὐ μόνον διὰ πράξεως ἰέναι δεῖ πρὸς αὐτὸν ἀλλὰ καὶ ἐπιστημονικῶς πιστεύοντα κατὰ θεωρίαν ἀληθῆ πίνει τις ἐξ αὐτοῦ, ἐκ πηγῆς ὕδωρ ζῶν, καὶ ἐξ ἀμπέλου οἶνον εὐφραίνοντα καρδίαν ἀνθρώπου λαμβάνων. (Didymus, In Catena Patr. Græc. in S. Joan. ex antiquissimo Cod. MS., edit. Corderius, Antw. 1630, p. 196, c. vi. vs. 59, 60.)

XXV.

"Dominus Jesus aquam de petra effudit, et omnes biberunt. Qui biberunt in typo, satiati sunt, qui biberunt in veritate inebriati sunt. . . . . . Utrumque ergo poculum bibe veteris et novi Testamenti, quia in utroque Christum bibis. Bibe Christum, quia vitis est: bibe Christum, quia fons vitæ est : . . . . bibe Christum, ut bibas sanguinem quo redemptus es: bibe Christum, ut bibas sermones

---

* See above, p. 289.
† Compare "De Elevatione Mentis," § vii., Op., c. 895.

ejus. . . . Bibitur scriptura divina, et devorantur Scripturæ divinæ, cum in venas mentis ac vires animæ succus verbi descendit æterni."* (Ambrosius, In Psalm. i. Enar. § 33, Opera, edit. Benedict., Paris, 1686, tom. i. c. 753, 754.)

XXVI.

" Hic est panis vitæ. Qui ergo vitam manducat, mori non potest. Quomodo enim morietur, cui cibus vita est?" (Ibid., In Ps. cxviii., Serm. xviii. § 28, Opera, tom. i. c. 1203.)

XXVII.

" *Ego sum panis vivus:* . . . . . si panem meum acceperit, vivet in æternum. Ille enim accipit, qui seipsum probat: qui autem accipit, non morietur peccatoris morte, quia panis hic remissio peccatorum est." (Ibid., De Benedic. Patriarch, cap. ix., Opera, Paris, 1686, tom. i. c. 525.)

XXVIII.

" Quisquis ergo verbo Christi pascitur, terrenum pabulum non requirit; nec enim potest sæculi panem cupere, qui pane reficitur Salvatoris. Habet enim Dominus suum panem, immo panis ipse Salvator est, sicut docuit dicens: *Ego sum panis,* &c. . . . . . . Negligit enim famem corporis, qui pabulo lectionis intendit: nec ventris curam habere poterit, qui alimentum verbi cœlestis adquirit. Ipsa est enim refectio, quæ saginat animam, quæ impinguat viscera; cum de divinis Scripturis cibum eloquii perennis accipimus. Ipsa est esca, quæ vitam æternam tribuit, et insidias a nobis diabolicæ tentationis excludit. Quod autem sacrarum literarum lectio vita sit, Dominus testatur dicens: *Verba quæ loquutus sum vobis, spiritus et vita sunt.*" (Sermo xxvii. De jejunio Dom., Quadrag. xi., In Op. Ambros., edit. Benedict., Paris, 1690, tom. ii. App. c. 429.)

XXIX.

Περὶ δογμάτων, ἄνω καὶ κάτω στρέφων τὴν πίστιν τὴν εἰς ἑαυτόν.† (Chrysostom, In Joan., Hom. xvii. al. xlvi. § 2, Opera, edit. Montfaucon, tom. viii. p. 277.)

XXX.

Ὅς ἂν φαγῇ ἐκ τοῦ ἄρτου τούτου, ζήσεται εἰς τὸν αἰῶνα. ἄρτον δὲ ἤτοι τὰ δόγματα λέγει ἐνταῦθα τὰ σωτηρία, καὶ τὴν πίστιν τὴν εἰς αὐτὸν, ἢ τὸ σῶμα τὸ ἑαυτοῦ. (Ibid., In Johan., Hom. xlvi. al. xlv. tom. viii. c. 270.)

---

* So Hesychius Hieros.: "Panes quidem primitiarum duos, *i.e.* legem et Evangelium: panes enim sunt cibi *animarum fidelium.*" (In Levit., lib. vi. cap. xxiii., In Bibl. Max. Patr., Lugd. 1677, tom. xii. p. 154*a*.)

† This is Chrysostom's account of the hard saying in John vi.

XXXI.

"Nos autem audiamus panem, quem fregit Dominus, deditque discipulis suis, esse Corpus Domini Salvatoris, ipso dicente ad eos, *Accipite, et comedite, hoc est Corpus meum:* et calicem illum esse, de quo iterum loquutus est: *Bibite ex hoc omnes: hic est enim Sanguis meus novi Testamenti, qui pro multis effundetur, &c.* Iste est calix de quo in Propheta legimus: *Calicem salutarem accipiam.* Et alibi: *Calix tuus inebrians quam præclarus est.* Si ergo panis, qui de cœlo descendit, Corpus est Domini; et vinum quod discipulis dedit, Sanguis illius est novi Testamenti qui pro multis effusus est in remissionem peccatorum, Judaicas fabulas repellamus, et ascendamus cum Domino cœnaculum magnum, stratum, atque mundatum, et accipiamus ab eo sursum calicem novi Testamenti; ibique cum eo Pascha celebrantes, inebriemur ab eo vino sobrietatis. *Non enim est regnum Dei cibus, et potus, sed justitia, et gaudium, et pax in Spiritu Sancto.* Ne Moyses dedit nobis panem verum; sed Dominus Jesus: ipse conviva et convivium, ipse comedens, et qui comeditur. Illius bibimus Sanguinem, et sine ipso potare non possumus, et quotidie in sacrificiis ejus de genimine vitis veræ, et vineæ *Soreo*, quæ interpretatur, *Electa*, rubentia musta calcamus, et novum ex his vinum bibimus de regno Patris, nequaquam in vetustate literæ, sed in novitate spiritus: cantantes canticum novum, quod nemo potest cantare, nisi in regno Ecclesiæ, quod regnum Patris est." (Hieronymus, Epistola cxx. ad Hedibiam, Qu. ii., Opera, edit. Vallarsius, tom. i. c. 824. See above, p. 73.)

XXXII.

"Hoc solum habemus in præsenti sæculo bonum, si vescamur carne ejus, et cruore potemur, non solum in mysterio, sed etiam in Scripturarum lectione. Verus enim cibus et potus, qui ex verbo Dei sumitur, scientia Scripturarum est." (Ibid., Comment. in Eccles., c. 3, Op., tom. iii. col. 413.)

XXXIII.

"*Et adipe frumenti satiat te.* Felix est qui in frumento isto adipem intelligit. Legimus sanctas Scripturas. Ego Corpus Jesu, Evangelium puto: sanctas Scripturas, puto doctrinam ejus."[*] (Breviar. in Psalm cxlvii., In Op. Hieronymi, edit. Vallarsius, tom. vii. Append. c. 580.)

XXXIV.

"Quando dicit, qui non comederit carnem meam, et biberit sanguinem meum, licet et in mysterio posset intelligi, tamen verius

---

[*] For "doctrinam," perhaps we should read "sanguinem." See Albertinus, De Euch., p. 725.

Corpus Christi et sanguis ejus sermo Scripturarum est, doctrina divina est." (Breviar. in Psalm. cxlvii., In Op. Hieronymi, edit. Vallarsius, tom. vii. Append. c. 530, 531.)

XXXV.

" Si quando audimus sermonem Dei, et sermo Dei, et caro Christi, et sanguis ejus in auribus nostris funditur, et nos aliud cogitamus, in quantum periculum incurrimus?" (Ibid., c. 531.)

XXXVI.

" In carne Christi, qui est sermo doctrinæ, hoc est Scripturarum sanctarum interpretatio, sicut volumus, ita et cibum accipimus." (Ibid., c. 531.)

XXXVII.

" Accepit Jesus panem, et benedicens fregit, transfigurans corpus suum in panem, quod est Ecclesia præsens, quæ accipitur in fide, benedicitur in numero, frangitur in passionibus, datur in exemplis, sumitur in doctrinis." (Comment. in Marc. cap. xiv., In Op. Hieronymi, edit. Vallarsius, tom. xi. par. iii. c. 118.)

XXXVIII.

" Comederunt enim in Sanctis Scripturis panem qui de cœlo descendit, et cum David dixerunt : *Incerta et occulta sapientiæ tuæ manifestasti mihi.*" (Comment. in Osee, lib. iii. cap. xiii. v. 5 & 6, In Op. Hieronymi, edit. Vallarsius, tom. vi. c. 148.)

XXXIX.

" Qui jejuni erant pabulo veritatis : qui esuriebant et sitiebant justitiam, modo pascuntur divinis scripturis : reficiuntur cœlestibus sacramentis : laudant qui requirunt eum : nam laus est domini, eructatio saturitatis illius. Inde vivunt corda eorum in æternum, quia cibus ille cordis et animæ est, de quo scriptum est, Qui manducaverit ex hoc pane, vivet in æternum." (Ruffinus, in Psalm. xxi. Comment., Opera, Paris, 1580, tom. ii. fo. 47, 48.)

XL.

" Has igitur immaculati Agni carnes, id est doctrinæ ejus viscera, neque cruda sine interpretatione sumi oportet, neque cocta in aqua, id est eorum dissertione dissoluta, atque decocta, qui velut aqua deorsum sunt, nihil supernum sentientes; sed assata, inquit, igni, id est Spiritu Divino solidata, atque tosta." (Gaudentius Brix., Sermo ii., Opera, edit. Galeardus, 1757, pp. 34, 35.)

XLI.

" Membra Agni Dei Scripturas ejus diximus." (Ibid., p. 35.)

XLII.

"Hujus carnem tam fideles in mysterio, quam simul universi credentes in fide, ita debemus edere, nostrique cordis interioribus commendare, ut non solum præcinctos habeamus castitate lumbos, verum etiam *calciati simus*, ut ait Apostolus, *in præparatione Evangelii pacis*." (Gaudentius Brix., Serm. v., Opera, edit. Galeardus, p. 54.)

XLIII.

"Credere in eum, hoc est manducare panem vivum. Qui credit, manducat." (August., In Johan., Tract. xxvi. § 1, Opera, edit. Benedict., 1680, tom. iii. par. ii. c. 358.)

XLIV.

"Ut quid paras dentes et ventrem? Crede et manducasti." (Ib., Tract. xxv. § 12, c. 354.)

XLV.

"Quis est panis de regno Dei, nisi qui dicit, Ego sum panis vivus qui de cœlo descendi? Noli pararo fauces, sed cor. Inde commendata est illa cœna, Ecce credimus in Christum, cum * fide accipimus. In accipiendo novimus quid cogitemus. Modicum accipimus, et in corde saginamur. Non ergo quod videtur, sed quod creditur, pascit." (Ibid., Sermo. cxii. De Verb. Ev., Luc. 14, Opera, tom. v. par. i. c. 566.)

XLVI.

"Erant ibi quibus plus Christus in corde, quam manna in ore sapiebat. . . . Eumdem ergo potum quam nos sed spiritualem; id est, qui fide capiatur, non qui corpore hauriebatur." (Ibid., Serm. ccclii., De Pœnitentia, Op., tom. v. par. ii. c. 1365.)

XLVII.

"Altera quidem illa petra, alter lapis quem sibi posuit ad caput Jacob; alter agnus occisus ut manducaretur Pascha, alter aries hærens in vepribus immolandus, quando filio suo pepercit Abraham jussus, quem jussus obtulerat; altera ovis et altera ovis; alter lapis et alter lapis, idem tamen Christus; ideo eumdem cibum, ideo eumdem potum. . . . Eumdem ergo cibum, eumdem potum, sed *intelligentibus et credentibus*. Non intelligentibus autem illud solum manna, illa sola aqua; ille cibus esurienti, potus iste sitienti; nec ille, nec iste credenti: credenti autem idem qui nunc. Tunc enim Christus venturus, modo Christus venit. Venturus et venit, diversa verba sunt, sed idem Christus." (Ibid., c. 1366.)

* Perhaps "quem." See Goode on Euch., i. p. 331.

XLVIII.

"Tunc vita unicuique erit Corpus et Sanguis Christi, si quod in Sacramento visibiliter sumitur, in ipsa veritate spiritualiter manducetur, spiritualiter manducetur, spiritualiter bibatur." (August., Serm. cxxxi. Op., tom. vi. par. i. c. 641.)

XLIX.

"Non hoc corpus, quod videtis, manducaturi estis, et bibituri illum sanguinem, quem fusuri sunt, qui crucifigent me. Sacramentum aliquod vobis commendavi. Spiritualiter intellectum vivificabit vos. Etsi necesse est illud visibiliter celebrari: oportet tamen invisibiliter intelligi." (Ibid., In Psalm xcviii., Op., tom. iv. par. ii. c. 1066.)

L.

"Misso enim de super Spiritu Sancto post Domini passionem et resurrectionem et adscensionem, cum miracula fierent in ejus nomine, quem tamquam mortuum persequentes Judæi contemserant, compuncti sunt corde, et qui sævientes occiderunt, mutati crediderunt; et quem sanguinem sæviendo fuderunt, credendo biberunt." (Ibid., In Johan. Evang., cap. 8, Tract. xl. § 2, Op., tom. iii. par. ii. c. 565.)

LI.

"Panis ille visibilis stomachum confirmat, ventrem confirmat: est alius panis qui cor confirmat, quia panis est cordis." (Ibid., Enarr. in Psalm. ciii., Serm. iii. § 14, Opera, tom. iv. par. ii. c. 1160.)

LII.

"Panis ille interioris hominis quærit esuriem: unde alio loco dicit: Beati qui esuriunt et sitiunt justitiam, quoniam ipsi saturabuntur, Justitiam vero nobis esse Christum Paulus Apostolus dicit." (Ibid., In Joan. Evang., Tract. xxvi. § 1, Op., tom iii. par. ii. c. 494.)

LIII.

"Inebriamini, sed videte unde. Si vos inebriat calix Domini præclarus, videbitur ista inebrietas in operibus vestris, videbitur in sancto amore justitiæ, videbitur postremo in alienatione mentis vestræ, sed a terrenis in cœlum. . . . Est ergo vinum quod vere lætificat cor, et non novit aliud nisi lætificare cor. Sed ne putes hoc quidem de spiritali vino debere accipi, de illo pane autem non; quod et ipse spiritalis sit, exposuit et ipsum: *Et panis*, inquit, *cor hominis confirmat*. Ergo sit accipe de pane, quomodo accipis de vino: intus esuri, intus siti. Beati enim qui esuriunt et sitiunt justitiam, quia ipsi saturabuntur. Panis ille justitia est, vinum illud justitia est: veritas est, veritas Christus est. Ego sum, inquit, panis vivus, qui de cœlo descendi, et Ego sum vitis, vos sarmenta." (Ibid., In Psalm. ciii. Enarr. Serm. iii. § 13, 14, Op., tom. iv. par. ii. c. 1159, 1160.)

LIV.

"Cum videritis filium hominis adscendentem ubi erat prius, certe vel tunc videbitis, quia non eo modo quo putatis erogat corpus suum; certe vel tunc intelligetis, quia gratia ejus non consumitur morsibus." (Aug., In Johan. Evang., Tract. xxvii. § 3, Op., tom. iii. par. ii. c. 502.)

LV.

"Credere in Eum, hoc est manducare panem vivum. Qui credit, manducat." (Ibid., In Johan., Tract. xxvi. § 1, Op., tom. iii. par. ii. c. 494.)

LVI.

"*Hic est* ergo *panis de cœlo descendens, ut si quis manducaverit ex ipso, non moriatur.* Sed quod pertinet ad virtutem sacramenti, non quod pertinet ad visibile sacramentum;* qui manducat intus, non foris: qui manducat in corde, non qui premit dente." (Ibid., In Johan. Evang. cap. vi., Tract. xxvi. § 12, Op., tom. iii. par. ii. c. 499.)

LVII.

"Verbum Domini cibus tuus est, et non solum cibus, sed et potus. Audi eum per Prophetam dicentem veteri populo, qui edunt me adhuc esurient; et qui bibunt me, adhuc sitient. Item per semetipsum, Caro mea, inquit, vere est cibus, et sanguis meus vere est potus." (Sermo ccclxvi., De Psalm. xxii., In Op. Aug., tom. v. par. ii. c. 1449.)

LVIII.

"Et verbum Dei quod quotidie prædicatur, panis est. Non enim quia non est panis ventris, ideo non est panis mentis." (Aug., Serm. lix. In Matt. vi., De Orat. Dom. ad Competentes, Op., tom. v. par. i. c. 344.)

LIX.

"De his [*i.e.* Augustini libris] cibum capio, non illum qui perit, sed qui operatur vitæ æternæ substantiam per fidem nostram, quâ adcorporamur † in Christo Jesu Domino nostro." (Paulinus, Ep. ad August., In Op. August., Ep. 25, § i. tom. ii. c. 36.)

LX.

"Pomarium salutare, ipsius *nex* sive *passio* pro salute humani generis potest intelligi, et cœlestis illa manna, Eucharistia scilicet, quæ si sancte meditetur, tantum dulcedinis cœlestis alimoniæ affert et suavitatis fructum, ut recte cum David dicere queat, Gustate et videte quam suavis est Dominus. . . . . . Patriarchæ et Prophetæ tanquam propinqui et amici, longius enim abfuere de verbo vitæ, et

---

* It may be observed here that there is no recognition of any real objective presence of an invisible "res sacramenti" as distinct from the "virtus sacramenti."
† See Goode on Eucharist, I. pp. 374—377.

passione Domini et Spiritus Sancti fluvio *comederunt biberuntque*. Apostoli vero et Discipuli illius omnes et Martyres qui illud videre et contrectare et divina gratia meruerunt, adeo inebriati sunt ad summum usque torrente Spiritus Sancti cœlitus diffuso, ut musto pleni putarentur dum magnalia Dei prædicarent. Mysticam ergo Paschatis comestionem, et cœlitus demissum Spiritus Sancti imbrem intelligit, de quo dixit, *Accipite et comedite:* et, *Accipite et bibite:* et, *Accipite Spiritum Sanctum.*" (Com. in Cant. Cant., sub nom. Philonis Carpath., In Bibliotheca Max. Patr., Lugd. 1677, tom. v. p. 679. See Cave, Hist. Lit., p. 203.)

LXI.

Γεύσασθε, καὶ ἴδετε, ὡς ἀληθέστατος ἐν ἅπασιν ἐγὼ ὁ Κύριος . . . φάγετέ με τὴν ζωὴν, καὶ ζήσεσθε . . . φάγετε τὸν ἐμὸν ἄρτον· ἐγὼ γὰρ εἰμι ὁ ζωοποιὸς κόκκος τοῦ σίτου. καὶ ἐγώ εἰμι ὁ ἄρτος τῆς ζωῆς. Πίετε οἶνον, ὃν κεκέρακα ὑμῖν· ἐγὼ γάρ εἰμι τὸ πόμα τῆς ἀθανασίας. . . . Ἐγώ εἰμι ἡ ἄμπελος ἡ ἀληθινή. Πίετε τὴν ἐμὴν εὐφροσύνην, οἶνον ὃν ἐκέρασα ὑμῖν. . . . Ἀλλ' οὐχ ὡς ἐκεῖνοι φαγόντες τὸ μάννα ἐν τῇ ἐρήμῳ ἀπέθανον, οὕτως ἐγὼ ὑμῖν παρέχω τὸ σῶμα μοῦ. Ὁ γὰρ τρώγων τοῦτον τὸν ἄρτον ζήσεται εἰς τὸν αἰῶνα. (Cyrillus* Alex., Homil. Div. x., "In Mysticam Cœnam," Opera, edit. Migne, tom. x. c. 1020, 1021.)

LXII.

"Credere in Filium Dei, hoc est videre, hoc est audire, hoc est odorari, hoc est gustare, hoc est contrectare eum." (Vigil. Taps., Contra Eutych., lib. iv. § xxii., Opera, edit. Chiffletius, p. 54)

LXIII.

"Quum reverendum altare cœlestibus cibis satiandus ascendis, sacrum Dei tui corpus et sanguinem fide respice, honora, mirare,

* "Adversus istos [Nestorianos] sic scribit Cyrillus [Ep. ad Euoptium, Appen. iii. ad tom. v., Act.Conc. Eph. c. ii.]: *Num hominis comestionem nostrum esse Sacramentum pronuncias? Et irreligiose ad crassas eorum cogitationes, qui sic crediderunt mentem nostram urges? Et attentas humanis cogitationibus* (corporeo nempe tactu, gustu, csu) *tractare illa* (carnem et sanguinem Christi) *quæ sola, pura, et inexquisita fide accipiuntur?* Ecce, carnem et Corpus Christi corporaliter in mysteriis comedi, tractari, accipi negat; fide, et *fide sola*, non manu, non ore, non ventriculo, sed *fide sola* tractari, et accipi declarat. Neque mens hæc Cyrilli solius. Consensu suo firmavit, et approbavit epistolas Cyrilli in causa Nestorii scriptas (earum hæc una est, eaque certe cum præcipuis numeranda) Concilium Chalcedonense [Art. 5], Concilium Generale Quintum [Collat. 8] itemque Sextum [Art. 18]. Horum fides eadem sine dubio quæ fuit Nicæni, Constantinopolitani Primi, et Ephesini Concilii; quare istorum omnium sex Generalium Conciliorum judicio, non *corporaliter*, non manibus, non dentibus, non ventriculo, sed *fide sola* tractatur in Eucharistia, et accipitur caro Christi." (Crakanthorp, Defensio Eccles. Anglicanæ, A. C. L., p. 516. See also Goode on Eucharist, i. pp. 375, 376, and Cyrilli Alex., Op., ed. Migne, tom. ix. c. 374, 375; Mansi, tom. v. c. 137.)

mente continge, cordis manu suscipe, et maxime haustu interioie assume." (Eusebius Emissenus? *)

LXIV.

"*Gustate et videte quam suavis est Dominus:* . . . Gustate non pertinet ad palatum, sed ad animæ suavissimum sensum qui divinâ contemplatione saginatur. Nam ut ipsum gustum intelligeres, sequitur *videte,* quod utique non ad os pertinet, sed ad inspectivam sine dubio qualitatem, ut cum tale corpus accipimus, vitæ nobis concedi gratiam confidamus. Et ut ipsam communicationem non ad corpus commune traberes, Dominum dicit esse suavem, qui in eâ salutem hominis pro sua pietate concedit. Vita enim nostra quæ revera Deus est, qui carnem sumptam ex Virgine Maria sibi univit, eamque propriam fecit, vivificatricem eam esse professus est, sicut ait in Evangelio: Amen, Amen, dico vobis, nisi manducaveritis carnem filii hominis, et biberitis sanguinem ejus, non habebitis vitam in vobis." (Cassiodorus, In Ps. xxxiii. v. 8, Opera, edit. Garetius, Rotom. 1679, tom. ii. p. 111.)

LXV.

"Litigantibus Judæis, et dicentibus ad invicem: *Quomodo potest hic nobis carnem suam dare ad manducandum?* Multi etiam ex

* "This passage from Eusebius of Emessa, a writer of the fourth century, is also often cited by the controversalists of the Reformation period. It is quoted in the 'Homily on the Sacrament,' immediately after the passage from the Council of Nicæa. . . .

"But there is considerable doubt about its authenticity. It is always quoted from the decretal of Gratian, where it occurs at the end of a long passage which Gratian introduces with 'Eusebius of Emessa says.' But the extract thus introduced is manifestly of late Roman doctrine, and it is stated by the editors of Migne's 'Patrologiæ Cursus,' in their edition of Gratian, that it is certainly not the work of Eusebius, but of some later writer, probably Rabanus or Beda. The concluding passage, however, which alone is quoted in this controversy, is so different in structure and sentiment from the rest of the extract, that it is probable that the author introduced this passage from some earlier writer, to conclude his Homily with authority, and may have given the name of that writer to the whole argument. Such enlargement of an author, with the preservation of his name, was not uncommon, as in the case of Ambrose, Augustine, &c.

"In the fourth century, the words 'quum ascendis ad reverendum altare,' would not mean a bodily ascent to a high altar, for of such ascent on the part of the communicants there is no trace in the ancient liturgies, but it alluded to the ascending by faith to the 'supercelestial altar,' where, according to the 'rationale' of the ancient liturgies, the whole transaction was really carried on; thither the elements were carried up (spiritually) by angelic ministries as an acceptable oblation; and there the participation of the Body and Blood of Christ was given to the faithful by 'the mighty hand' of Christ Himself." (Milton's Eucharist Illustrated, pp. 81, 82.)

The Homily is printed in Vallarsius's edition of the works of Jerome, tom. xi. par. ii. c. 349 *sqq.,* with the notice: "Hanc [homiliam] e primis statim verbis agnoscit Oudinus esse Fausti Rhegiensis Episcopi, qui sub nomine Eusebii Emisseni hactenus latuit. Habetur etiam inter hujus homilias impressa."

discipulis ejus audientes dixerunt: *Durus est hic sermo, quis potest eum audire?* ...... Interroganti Domino respondit et Petrus, ut non ideo se diceret nolle abire, quod mysterium intellexerit, sed quia illud ipsum quod a tali magistro diceretur, ad vitam æternam proculdubio pertineret. Ait enim: *Domine, ad quem ibimus? verba vitæ æternæ habes: et nos credidimus, et cognovimus quia tu es Christus Filius Dei vivi.* Quod si mysterium intellexisset, hæc potius dixisset: Domine, cur abeamus non est, cum credamus nos corporis et sanguinis tui fide salvandos." (Facundus Hermianensis, Pro Defens. Trium Capitat., lib. xii. cap. i. edit. Migne, c. 830, 831.)

LXVI.

"Sic comedite carnes corporis Sacræ Scripturæ, O fratres, eas esurientes: et absconsum in carne Scripturæ spirituali mysteriorum sanguinem sic bibete: Qui est enim sic ejus particeps, habet vitam æternam." (Anastasius Sinait., Anag. Contempl. In Hexaem., lib. viii., In Bibliotheca Max. Patr., Lugd. 1677, tom. ix. p. 900.)

LXVII.

"In hac ergo nube, Deus tam in Dominica carne, quam in Evangelica prædicatione insinuatur, et nihil amplius quæramus nos qui aliquid de Deo scrutari volumus, sed quantum nobis Evangelicus sermo tradit, quanta ex Dominica carne percipimus: neque enim frustra uno nomine carnem Domini, et Evangelium legislator significavit, sed quia Evangelio et carne Dominica, occasio atque subsistentia est." (Hesychius Hieros., In Lev., lib. v. cap. xvi., In Bibliotheca Max. Patr., Lugd. 1677, tom. xii. p. 119.)

LXVIII.

"Quis namque sit sanguis agni, non jam audiendo, sed bibendo didicistis. Qui sanguis super utrumque postem ponitur,* quando non solum ore corporis, sed etiam ore cordis hauritur." (Gregorius Magnus, In Evangel., lib. ii., Homil. xxii. § 7, Opera, edit. Benedict., Venice, 1744, tom. i. c. 1533.)

LXIX.

"Vobis adhuc parvulis incarnationis ejus tantummodo lambendum sanguinem trado. Nam qui prædicationem suam tacita divinitatis celsitudine, infirmos auditores de solo cruore crucis edocet, quid aliud quam sanguinem pullis præbet?" (Ibid., Moral. lib. xxxi. cap. lii. § 104, In Job, cap. xxxix., Opera, 1744, tom. i. c. 1043.)

---

* See Albertinus, De Euch., p. 316, where several parallel passages may be seen.

LXX.

"Cibum semetipsum mentibus mortalium præbuit, dicens: Qui comedit carnem meam, et bibit sanguinem meum, in me manet, et Ego in Eo." (Greg. Magn., Moral., lib. vii. c. vii., Op., tom i. c. 215.)

LXXI.

"Sicut visibilis panis et vini substantia exteriorem nutrit et inebriat hominem : ita verbum Dei, qui est panis vivus, participatione sui fidelium recreat mentes." (Isidorus Hisp., Etymol., quoted by Bertram,* De Corp. et Sang. Dom. § xliii. ed. Migne, c. 145, 146.)

LXXII.

"*Caro mea est,* inquit, *pro mundi vita.* Norunt fideles corpus Christi, si corpus Christi esse non negligunt, fiant corpus Christi, si volunt vivere de Spiritu Christi. . . . Quisquis vivere vult, credat in Christum, manducet spiritualiter spiritualem cibum." (Ven. Beda, In Evangel. Joan., cap. vi., Opera, Cologne, 1688, tom. v. c. 509.)

LXXIII.

"Ego quidem reddam vota, de quibus votis *edent pauperes*, id est mundi contemptores edent quidem realiter, si ad sacramenta referatur: et *saturabuntur* æternaliter, quia intelligent in pane et vino visibiliter sibi proposito aliud invisibile, scilicet corpus verum et sanguinem verum Domini, quæ verus cibus et verus potus sunt, quo non venter distenditur, sed mens saginatur." (Ibid., Comm. in Ps. xxi., Opera, edit. Cologne, 1612, tom. viii. c. 419.)

LXXIV.

"Bonum est itaque veros cibos et veram sumere potionem, quos de agni carne et sanguine in divinis voluminibus invenimus." (Alcuinus, Comment. Super Eccles., cap. ii., Op., edit. Paris, 1617, c. 323.)

LXXV.

"Legamus sanctas Scripturas. Quid est aliud nisi corpus? . . . . . Quid est hoc litera, quam in Evangelio legis vel in cæteris Scripturis sanctis, nisi corpus Christi, nisi caro Christi, quæ ab omnibus Christianis comeditur? Et tunc comeditur, quando legitur, et quando auditur." (Etherius et Beatus Contra Elipandum, lib. i., In Bibliotheca Max. Patr., Lugd. 1677, tom. xiii. p. 369.)

LXXVI.

"Audi ipsum panem nostrum quotidianum : Pete : Accipe. Manduca quotidie. Legamus sanctas Scripturas, et inveniemus hunc

* This is not now found in the printed copies of the works of Isidore. "The emendatory care of the Roman priesthood" is said to have "carefully excluded it." See Cosin, Hist. Trans., cap. v. § 26, Works, A. C. L., vol. iv. p. 78 ; Faber's "Difficulties of Romanism," p. 399, 2nd edit.

panem. Ego Corpus Jesu Evangelium esse* puto. Scripturas puto doctrinam ejus: et quoniam dicit Jesus. Qui non comederit carnem meam, et sanguinem meum non biberit: licet spiritualiter, et mysterio possit intelligi; tamen corporaliter panem, quem petimus quotidianum, vere corpus Christi, et sanguis ejus, sermo Scripturarum est, doctrina divina est. Et cum legimus eam, carnem Christi manducamus, et sanguinem ejus bibimus." (Etherius et Beatus Contra Elipandum, lib. i., In Bibliotheca Max. Patr., Lugd. 1677, tom. xiii. p. 376.)

LXXVII.

"Non iste panis est, qui vadit in corpus; sed ille panis vitæ æternæ, qui animæ nostræ substantiam fulcit." (De Sacramentis, lib. v. c. 4, § 24, In Op. Ambrosii, edit. Benedict., tom. ii. par. i. c. 378.)

LXXVIII.

" Panis et vinum, efficitur spiritualiter corpus Christi, &c. Mentis ergo est cibus iste, non ventris: nec corrumpitur, sed permanet in vitam æternam." (Synod. Carisiac., † MS. apud N. Ranchinum.)

LXXIX.

" Mentis ergo est cibus iste, non ventris; non corrumpitur, sed permanet in vitam æternam, quoniam pie sumentibus confert vitam æternam. Pie autem sumit qui, spiritu fidei illuminatus, in illo cibo et potu visibili virtutem intelligibilis gratiæ esurit ac sitit." (Florus Magister, Advers. Amalar., cap. i. § 9, Op., edit. Migne, c. 73.)

LXXX.

"Sacramentum ore percipitur, virtute sacramenti interior homo satiatur." (Rabanus Maurus, De Cleric. Institu., lib. i. c. xxxi., Opera, edit. Migne, tom. i. c. 317.)

LXXXI.

" Qui agnus licet ab omni populo totus, et a singulis totus sumatur, tamen totus et integer in cœlo permanere non dubitatur, sacramentum namque, quod ore percipitur, in alimentum corporis redigitur. Virtus autem sacramenti, qua interior homo satiatur, per hanc vita æterna adipiscitur." (Honorius Augustodunensis, Gemma Animæ, cap. cxi., in Bibliotheca Max. Patr., Lugd. 1677, tom. xx. p. 1062.)

LXXXII.

" In faith do I taste of Thy holy, lifegiving, and saving Body, O Christ my God and Jesus, for the forgiveness of my sins. In faith do I drink Thy sanctifying [purifying] and cleansing Blood, O Christ my

---

* See above, pp. 339, 340. † See Ussher's works, edit. Elrington, tom. iii. p. 82.

God and Jesus, for the forgiveness of my sins." (Armenian Liturgy, Malan's translation, D. Nutt, p. 50.)

LXXXIII.

" Demum in cœna corpus suum sub forma panis et vini discipulis dedit ad comedendum, et de cætero ad conficiendum, dicens, Accipite et comedite : Hoc est corpus meum. Et item : Hoc facite in meam commemorationem. Fuit Christus nobis in cruce pretium, in via viaticum, in patria erit præmium, existens cibus grandium, id est, perfectorum. Hunc cibum* Elias accepit, et in ejus fortitudine

* Elsewhere Petrus Blessensis calls the Eucharist "Panis Angelorum " (Serm. xliv. p. 1455. So also in his Tract. De Euch., cap. xvii. p. 1275.)

The passage above is cited as evidence of the teaching that the *res sacramenti* can be received without transubstantiation ; and that the Real Objective Presence is needless to give to the soul the true food of man. See above, p. 177. See also "Romish Mass and English Church," pp. 89, 90.

What Elijah received could only have been the Body of Christ in figure, and he could only have fed on the Thing signified by faith. See above, p. 387, No. xxii.

Peter of Blois flourished in the latter half of the twelfth century, when the doctrine introduced by Lanfranc had become dominant in the English Church. Yet there is something in his words which seems to tell that an echo of the doctrine of Elfric was still heard in the land, that something of the old teaching had survived the inroads of the new.

In Epist. cxl. (p. 1053) he uses the words "pane et vino transubstantiatis . . . . in corpus et sanguinem Christi" (see note, p. 1293), which has sometimes been regarded as the first example of the use of such an expression.

In this, however, there appears to be a mistake.

The noun " *Transubstantiatio*" is said to have been used by Peter Damiani, about the middle of the eleventh century. The following extract is from an Exposition which bears his name. " *Hoc est corpus meum.* Quæritur quid demonstret sacerdos per hoc pronomen *hoc?* Si panem, pani numquam congruit esse corpus Christi. Sed demonstrat corpus Christi ; sed quando profertur ipsum pronomen, nondum est *transubstantiatio.* Respondetur, quod sacerdos non demonstrat, cum illis verbis non utatur enunciative sed recitative ; quemadmodum cum ait, ego sum vitis vera, ego lux mundi, et multa alia." (Expositio Canonis Missæ, § 7.)

It should, however, be observed that this treatise will not be found in the collected works of Peter Damiani, as edited by Cajetan. Nor is it mentioned by Trithemius, or other bibliographers ; but it has been printed from a Vatican MS. in Mai's "Scriptorum Veterum Nova Collectio," where it will be found in tom. vi. par. ii. p. 211 *sqq*. It is entitled " Expositio Canonis Missæ *secundum* Petrum Damiani," and is supposed by some to have been written after his death. See Canon Robertson's Hist. of Christian Ch., vol. iv. p. 566, 1874.

Mai says of it : " Præter nomen auctoris bis inscriptum, ipsa sua dignitate genuinam se probat." (Tom. vi. Præf., p. xxxiii. See also par. ii. p. 211. The passage quoted will be found in Mai, par. ii. p. 215.)

About the year 1100, the term " transubstantiatio " appears again in the writings of Hildebert, Bishop of Le Mans, and afterwards Archbishop of Tours.

The following is an extract from one of his *sermones:* " Si fuero vas incontinentiæ et libidinis, in altari juxta filium Virginis statuo filium Veneris. Cum profero verba Canonis, et verbum *transubstantiationis*, et meum plenum est contradictione, et amaritudine, et dolo, quamvis eum honorem labiis, tamen spuo in faciem Salvatoris. Cum præsumo sumere Dominum meum, et panem in os meum sic pollutum, levius

quadraginta diebus ambulavit, donec ad Montem Dei Oreb pervenit."
(Petrus Blessensis, Sermo xvii., in Bibliotheca Max. Patr., Lugd.
1677, tom. xxiv. p. 1410.)

It is a matter of great difficulty, in making many quotations, to give just sufficient for the purpose—enough to avoid misrepresenting the author's meaning, yet not more than the occasion requires.

It is quite possible that in this Appendix I may sometimes have given too much and sometimes too little; but I hope I have never intentionally withheld anything. I entirely disclaim any purpose of supporting a cause by garbled quotations.

Those who are desirous of examining carefully the Patristic evidence on the subject of the Eucharistic Presence, should be strongly advised not to satisfy themselves with any catena of citations, but, as far as possible, to verify references, and to study the subject in the pages of the writers themselves.

It should also be ever borne in mind that the value of Patristic writings consists not so much in their making known to us the opinions of individual Fathers, as in their bearing on a consentient testimony to the unchanging faith once for all delivered to the Saints. And it must never be forgotten that, after all, our best witness to this faith is to be found in the INSPIRED WORD OF GOD.

---

esset si projicerem eum in lutum platearum." (Ven. Hildebertus Turonensis, Sermo vi. Synodicus ad Sacerdotes, Opera, ed. Beaugendre, Paris, 1708, c. 608. See also c. 442 and 1106, in which a doctrine of Transubstantiation is clearly stated. See above, pp. 331, 332.)

As to the use of the verb *transubstantio*, see "Romish Mass and English Church," p. 70. See also Waterland's Works, vol. iv. p. 599, edit. 1843; Gieseler, Eccles. Hist., vol. iii. p. 315, edit. Clark; Vogan's "True Doctrine," p. 51, and Blunt's "Dict. of Doct. and Hist. Theol.," p. 759 *sqq*.

INDEX OF AUTHORS AND WORKS

QUOTED AND REFERRED TO.

Acta Sanctorum, p. 3.
Adamantus, p. 61, 268, 292.
Ægidius, p. 3.
Ælfric : see Elfric.
Agellius, p. 64.
Agobardus, p. 219, 220, 323.
Alanus Magnus, p. 134.
Alanus: see Allen, Cardinal.
A Lasco, p. 184.
Albertinus, De Eucharistia, p. 59, 264, 267, 268 ; quoted—
    as to doctrine of Eutychians, p. 63.
    as to doctrine of Nestorius, p. 64.
    as to De Villiers' interpolation, p. 86, 87.
    as to language of Procopius, p. 91.
    as to language of Tertullian, p. 93, 94.
    as to language of Augustine, p. 76, 78.
    as to language of Chrysostom, p. 113, 114.
    as to invisibility of a body, p. 146, 147.
    as to language of Theodoret, p. 208.
    as to language of Gregory Naz., p. 212.
    as to sacraments of Old and New Testament, p. 223.
    as to sense of *symbola*, p. 283.
    as to language of Theodotus Antiochenus, p. 290.
    as to language of Pseudo-Andreas, p. 315.
    as to Christ's presence in the poor, p. 327.
    referred to, p. 1.
Albinus: see Alcuinus.
Alcuinus and Pseudo-Alcuinus, p. 235, 280, 347.
Aldrich, Dean, p. 15, 22, 40, 143, 161, 177, 181, 192, 201.
Allatius, p. 267.

Allen, Cardinal, p. 12, 13, 215.
Allix, Præf. Hist. in Determinatis Jo. Parisiensis, p. 19, 134, 158.
　Dissertatio de Sanguine Christi, p. 90.
　on the Albigenses, p. 221, 282.
Alstedius, p. 184, 223.
Alvarez, p. 241.
Amalarius, p. 236, 255, 310.
Ambrose (and Pseudo-Ambrose), quoted—
　as to Presence, p. 33, 34, 264.
　as to truth of Christ's Flesh, p. 60.
　as to sense of words of Institution, p. 74.
　as to Adoration, p. 203.
　as to use of terms *umbra* and *imago*, p. 271, 272.
　as to use of term *similitudo*, p. 272.
　as to *signification* in Eucharist, p. 276.
　as to use of *figura*, p. 280.
　as to Death the condition of the *res sacramenti*, p. 306.
　as to Christ's Body being eaten in the Scriptures, p. 338.
　as to remission of sins being the living bread, p. 338.
　as to the Bread of Life not going into the body, p. 348.
Anaphora of St. Basil's Liturgy, p. 275.
Anastatius the Presbyter, p. 108.
Anastasius Sinaita, p. 242, 346.
Andreas, Pseudo-Apostolus, p. 314.
Andrewes, Bishop, quoted as to Presence, p. 34, 186, 187, 304.
Angelomus, p. 329.
Angelus, p. 250.
Anselm, p. 55, 130.
Antirrheticon adv. Kohlium, in the Venice edition of Ephrem Syrus, p. 70.
Antonelli, p. 306.
Aphraates, p. 305, 306.
Apostolic Constitutions, p. 33, 34, 229, 261.
Apuleius, p. 8.
Aquinas, Thomas, p. 24, 220.
Arcudius, p. 53, 71, 240, 241.
Arevalus, p. 243.
Armenian Liturgy: see Liturgy.
Arnauld, p. 46, 47.
Arnobius, quoted, p. 153, 154.
　referred to, p. 196.
Arnoldus Bonævallensis, p. 315, 324.

Assemani, J. A., p. 212, 267, 299.
Athanasius (and Pseudo-Athanasius), quoted—
   as to reality of Christ's Body, p. 62.
   as to interpretation of John vi., p. 67, 79.
   as to sense of words of Institution, p. 74.
   as to being in two places at once, p. 143.
   as to the unity of the king and his picture, p. 290.
   as to Death the condition of the *res sacramenti*, p. 314.
   as to the Church being the Body of Christ, p. 323.
   as to Christ's Flesh being spiritual food, p. 335.
Aubertin : see Albertinus.
Augustine, quoted—
   as to Presence, p. 36, 48, 132, 138, 139.
   as to Figure in words of Institution, p. 76, 78, 80, 81, 275, 277.
   as to *facinus* in literal interpretation, p. 81, 82.
   as to caution in hearing God's Word, p. 90.
   as to sense of " Sacramentum," p. 120, 121, 253, 276.
   as to being in two places at once, p. 144.
   as to local circumscription of human body, p. 145, 149.
   as to invisibility of a body, p. 148.
   as to " Crede et Manducasti," p. 177.
   as to " sursum corda," p. 195.
   as to Adoration, p. 205, 206, 212.
   as to sacraments of Old and New Testament, p. 222, 254, 255.
   as to worship of Sun and Rock, p. 224.
   as to signs bearing the names of things signified, p. 253 *sqq*.
   as to nature of sacraments, p. 257 *sqq.*, 262, 264.
   as to many grains in one bread, p. 278.
   as to use of *memoria*, p. 293.
   as to sense of *signum*, p. 301.
   as to Death the condition of the *res sacramenti*, p. 308.
   as to the Giver of sacramental grace, p. 317.
   as to the Church being Christ's Body as truly as the Eucharist, p. 319.
   as to Christ's Presence in the poor, p. 327, 328.
   as to Christ's Body being spiritually eaten by faith, p. 341, 342, 3 3.
Auxerre, Council of, p. 53.
Averroes, p. 159.

Bale, p. 2.
Baluzius, on Agobard, p. 221.
Baronius, p. 88.
Basilius Magnus, p. 275, 289, 290, 393, 336 : see Liturgies.
Basnage, p. 106, 212.
Beatus, p. 75, 152, 314, 322, 347, 348.
Beaugendre, p. 331.
Beda, Ven., quoted—
    as to Presence, p. 132.
    as to "*figura*," p. 78, 278, 279.
    as to local circumscription of body, p. 151, 152.
    as to Sacraments of the Old and New Law, p. 221, 222.
    as to signs being the names of things signified, p. 259.
    as to *reference* of the *sacramentum* to the *res sacramenti*, p. 263.
    as to use of *pignus*, p. 296.
    as to spiritual eating of spiritual food, p. 347.
Belgian Confession, p. 184.
Bellarmine, Cardinal, p. 13, 15, 16, 28, 71, 143, 153, 177, 208.
Benedict XIV.: see Lambertinus.
Benedictine Editors, p. 144, 271.
Berengarius, p. 144, 221.
Berkeley, Bishop, p. 169.
Bertram, p. 83, 130, 131, 221, 224, 271, 297, 302, 310, 323.
Beza, p. 140, 141, 161, 184.
Bibliotheca Maxima Patrum, Lugd. 1677, p. 222, 243, 264, 274, &c.
Biel, Gabriel, p. 331.
Bigotius, p. 106.
Bilson, Bishop, p. 56, 57, 211, 260.
Bingham, p. 53 ; quoted on Adoration, p. 204.
Blærus, J. Diesthemius, p. 3.
Blondel, p. 47.
Blunt's " Early Fathers," p. 261.
Blunt, Rev. J. H., Dict. of Theol., p. 350.
Bohemia, Confession of, p. 184.
Boileau, p. 199, 203, 227.
Bollandists, p. 3.
Bona, Cardinal, p. 215, 239, 246.
Bosanquet, Rev. Claude, p. 171, 172.
Bossius, p. 7.
Bracara, Council of, p. 263.
Bramhall, Archbishop, p. 47.

Brevint, p. 154, 155, 198, 201.
Bulenger, Julius Cæsar, p. 287, 289, 290.
Bull, Bishop, p. 32, 199.
Bullinger, p. 184.

Cabasilas, Nicolas, p. 244, 264, 324, 333.
Cæsarius Arelat., p, 329.
Callixtus, Nicephorus, p. 9.
Canon Law, p. 129.
Carisiacum Synodon, p. 348.
Carolus Magnus, p. 270, 279, 280.
Carranza, Summa Conciliorum, p. 53, 263.
Carthage, Council of, p. 30, 230.
Casaubon, Bulenger's answer to, p. 287, 290.
Cassander, on Circumgestation, p. 179.
Cassiodorus, p. 300, 345.
Catalanus, p. 246.
Catena in Joannem, edited by Corderius, p. 67, 74, 336, 337.
Catharine de Medicis, on Corpus Christi, p. 179.
Cave, Historia Literaria, p. 87, 122, 235, 282.
Celsus, p. 158.
Chamier, Panstratia Catholica, p. 52, 210, 211, 216, 223, 240.
Charlemagne: see Carolus Magnus.
Chemnitz, p. 28.
Christian Druthmar: see Druthmar.
Chronicon Alexandrinum, p. 242.
Chronicon Belgicum, p. 3.
Chrysostom (and Pseudo-Chrysostom) : quoted—
    as to Presence, p. 35, 36, 48, 113, 114, 132.
    as to sense of words of Institution, p. 105, 106.
    as to comparison with Baptism, p. 119.
    as to invisibility of a body, p. 147.
    as to Adoration, p. 204, 209, 216.
    on $\tau \grave{a}\ \ddot{a} \gamma \iota a\ \tau o\tilde{\iota}\varsigma\ \dot{a}\gamma \acute{\iota}o\iota\varsigma$, p. 243.
    as to drawing the veil, p. 244.
    as to the mysteries being *called* Christ's Body, p. 256.
    as to the nature of mysteries, p. 257, 264.
    as to Christ's drinking His own Blood, p. 265.
    as to sense of $\dot{a}\nu\tau \acute{\iota}\tau \nu \pi o\nu$, p. 268.
    as to sense of $\sigma \kappa \iota \acute{a}$, p. 127.
    as to use of $\sigma \acute{\upsilon} \mu \beta o \lambda o \nu$, p. 283, 284.

Chrysostom (and Pseudo-Chrysostom): quoted—
 as to use of μνημόσυνον, p. 293.
 as to sense of σύμβολον, p. 302.
 as to death the condition of the *res sacramenti*, p. 306, 312, 313.
 as to sense of *spiritually*, p. 314.
 as to the Giver of Sacramental grace, p. 317.
 as to the Church being Christ's Body as truly as the Eucharist, p. 319.
 as to Christ's Presence in the poor, p. 326, 327.
 as to the use of sensible things in God's gifts, p. 333.
 as to interpretation of John vi., p. 338.
Church and the world, p. 225.
Cicero, De Nat. Deorum, p. 207.
Claude, p. 46, 47, 94, 256, 264, 315.
Claudianus Mamertus, p. 299.
Clemens Alexandrinus: quoted—
 as to change, p. 50.
 as to sense of words of Institution, p. 72, 92, 283.
 as to interpretation of John vi., p. 79.
 as to use of σύμβολον, p. 282.
 as to Christ's Blood being drink for the spirit, p. 331.
 referred to, p. 196.
Clemens Romanus (Pseudo-), p. 288.
Clementinæ, p. 240.
Coffetel, p. 91, 268.
Confession of the Belgian Church, p. 184.
Confession of the Waldenses, p. 330.
Confutatio Cavillationum (Gardiner), p. 93, 94.
Consensus Orthodoxus, p. 28, 30, 184.
Constantinople, Council of, p. 53, 217, 218.
Constantius, Marcus Antonius (*i.e.* Gardiner), p. 93.
Constitutiones Apostolicæ, p. 282, 283, 288.
Corderius, p. 133.
 Catena in Joannem, p. 67, 74, 336, 337.
Cosin, Bishop, p. 38, 39, 47, 48, 49, 50, 59, 68, 93, 177, 178, 182, 266, 347.
Coster, p. 115, 199.
Cotelerius, p. 261, 283, 288.
Councils of Carthage, p. 53.
 of Auxerre, p. 53.
 in Trullo, p. 53.

Councils of Constantinople (869) p. 53, (754) 217, 218, 269, 270, 274, 275, 296.
   of Nice (Second), p. 91, 152, 209, 217, 218, 259, 291.
   of Vercelli, p. 131.
   of Trent, p. 133, 192.
   of Carthage (Third), p. 230.
   of Mayence (1261), p. 247.
   of Bracara (675), p. 263.
   of Nicæa (First), p. 313.
Covel, Account of Greek Church, p. 7, 216, 227, 241, 242, 251, 252, 316.
Crakanthorp, p. 162, 214, 344.
Cranmer, Archbishop: quoted—
   as to Real Presence, p. 43.
   as to sense of words of Institution, p. 177.
  referred to, p. 205.
Cyprian and Pseudo-Cyprian, p. 72, 103, 104, 195, 261, 262, 278, 292, 305, 312, 315, 318, 324.
Cyrillus Alexandrinus : quoted—
   as to Presence, p. 35.
   as to change, p. 50.
   as to reality of Christ's Body, p. 62.
   as to language of Nestorius, p. 64.
   as to Ethiopian Eunuch, p. 82, 83, 265.
   as to local circumscription of body, p. 150.
   as to folly of confounding signs with things signified, p. 258.
   as to type in Eucharist, 274.
   as to use of ἀντίτυπον, p. 288.
   as to unity of the king and his picture, p. 290.
   as to death the condition of the *res sacramenti*, p. 313.
   as to spiritual feeding and tasting, p. 344.
Cyrillus Hierosolymitanus: quoted—
   as to interpretation of John vi., p. 67.
   as to sense of words of Institution, p. 74.
   as to sense of 1 Cor. x. 18—22, p. 164.
   as to Adoration, p. 213.
   as to the change of Consecration, p. 229.
   as to the use of τὰ ἅγια τοῖς ἁγίοις, p. 243.
   as to νοητὴ τράπεζα, p. 264.
   as to type in Eucharist, p. 273.
   as to being σύσσωμοι τοῦ Χριστοῦ, p. 318.
   as to analogies of bodily and spiritual food, p. 336.

D'Achery, Spicelegium, p. 84.
Dallæus, quoted, p. 156, 238, 239.
  referred to, p. 1, 24.
Damascenus, Joannes, p. 36, 55, 147, 209.
Damiani, Peter, p. 332, 350.
Decretum of Gratian: see Gratian.
De Medicis, Catharine, p. 179.
De Mysteriis: see Ambrose.
De Sacramentis: see Ambrose.
Desmarets: see Maresius.
D'Espence: see Espencæus.
De Spina, Alphonso, p. 167, 168, 173, 174.
Deylingius, p. 47, 105, 203, 247, 288.
Diatyposis of Gelasius Cyz., p. 313.
Didymus Alexandrinus, p. 74, 147, 337.
Diesthemius, p. 3, 7.
Dionysius Areop. (Pseudo-), p. 133, 215, 267, 286, 287.
Dionysius Bar Salib, p. 252.
Dorner, p. 331.
Dositheus Hieros, p. 288.
Drelincourt, p. 106.
Druthmar, Christian, p. 152, 281.
Du Cange, p. 272.
Du Moulin, p. 161, 184.
Du Perron, Cardinal, p. 98, 105, 281.
Du Pin, p. 88, 217, 219, 236.
Durandus, Rationale Div. Off., p. 245.
Durantus, p. 204.
Durel, p. 47.
Dux Viæ of Anastasius Sin., p. 242.

Edgar, Variations of Popery, p. 104.
Elfric, p. 122, 123, 224, 297.
Elias Cretensis, p. 267.
Elliott, Horæ Apocalypticæ, p. 7, 9.
Ephesus, Council of, p. 30.
Ephrem Syrus (and Pseudo-Ephrem), p. 61, 70, 270, 271, 273, 277, 325.
Epiphanius, p. 98, 290.
Epiphanius the Deacon, p. 288.
Erigena, p. 130.
Espencæus, p. 40.

Essays on the Reformation, p. 44, 187.
Estius, p. 80.
Etherius and Beatus, p. 75, 152, 314, 325, 347, 348.
Eusebius of Emessa (Pseudo-), p. 214, 263, 295, 321, 344, 345.
Eusebius Cæsar., p. 9, 91, 290 : quoted—
    as to interpretation of John vi., p. 67.
    as to sense of words of Institution, p. 69, 70, 268, 283.
    as to use of σύμβολον, p. 283, 315.
    as to Christ's words being His Flesh, p. 335.
Eustathius Antiochenus, p. 146, 147, 288.
Eustochium, p. 254.
Euthymius Zigabenus, p. 271.
Exeter, Synod of (1287), p. 247.

Faber, Rev. G. S., Difficulties of Romanism, p. 157, 213, 347.
    Ancient Vallenses and Albigenses, p. 330.
Facundus Hermianensis, quoted as to Presence, p. 117, 118, 121, 132, 259, 346.
Fancheur, Mich. le, p. 209.
Faustus Rhegiensis, p. 295, 345.
Felix Minucius, p. 156.
Field, Bishop, p. 183.
Fisen, Barth, p. 3.
Fisher against Œcolampadius, p. 199.
Flaviàcensis, p. 301.
Florus Magister, quoted, p. 33, 280, 281, 293, 296, 297, 348.
    referred to, p. 236.
Forbes, Bishop W., p. 192.
Forbes of Corse, p. 162, 210.
Fortalitium Fidei, p. 167, 173, 174.
Fortescue's Armenian Church, p. 240, 242.
Foxe, Acts and Monuments, p. 124, 128.
Freeman, Archdeacon, Principles of Divine Service, p. 16, 197, 226, 227, 228, 230, 234, 243, 248.
Frudegard, p. 83.
Fulbertus Carnotensis, p. 83, 294, 297, 298.
Fulgentius, quoted—
    as to sense of John vi., p. 82.
    as to local circumscription of human body, p. 145, 150, 151.
    as to sacrament of oil, p. 215.
    as to Sacraments of the Old Testament and the New, p. 221, 222.

Fulgentius, quoted—
    as to death the condition of the *res sacramenti*, p. 309.
    as to the Church being Christ's Body as truly as the Eucharist, p. 321, 322, 327.

Gabriel, Patriarch, p. 250.
Galeardus, p. 277, 294.
Gardiner, Bishop of Winchester, p. 93, 105.
Gaudentius, p. 75, 262, 277, 278, 294, 301, 307, 308, 313, 340, 341.
Geddes, Dr., p. 242.
Gelasius, Pope, p. 272.
Gelasius Cyz., p. 312.
Gemma Animæ of Honorius, p. 314, 324, 348.
Genebrard, p. 7.
Germanus, Theoria Rer. Eccles., p. 235, 237, 243, 292, 311.
Gibson's Preservative against Popery, p. 9, 192.
Gieseler, p. 2, 3, 9, 297.
Glosses on the Decretum of Gratian, p. 129, 276, 281.
Goar, Euchologion, p. 240, 241, 243, 245, 246, 249, 251, 291, 316.
Goldast, p. 279.
Goode, Dean, on Eucharist, p. 54, 102, 107, 129, 283, 330.
Gratian, p. 129, 263, 275, 276, 281, 308.
Gregory De Valentia: see Valentia.
Gregorius Magnus, p. 53, 148, 239, 291, 346.
Gregorius Nazianzenus, quoted—
    as to invisibility of a body, p. 147.
    as to Adoration, p. 209, 211.
    as to the Passover being a type of a type, p. 222, 273.
    as to the Eucharist being a shadow, 273.
    as to use of ἀντίτυπον, p. 289.
    as to Christ's Presence in the poor, p. 325.
Gregorius, Bishop of Neocæsarea, p. 272.
Gregorius Nyssenus, quoted, p. 48, 49, 50, 147, 264, 298, 306, 326, 333.
Grindal, p. 186.
Guido, p. 247.

Hagenbach, p. 58.
Hall's Harmony, p. 184.
Hammond, p. 184, 185, 201.

Harding, p. 93, 203, 206.
Harduin, p. 106, 218.
Harmonia Confessionum, p. 184.
Harrison, Dr., p. 48, 53, 54, 195, 223, 224, 244, 268.
Haymo, p. 294.
Henriquez, p. 15.
Heptas Præsulum, edit. Raynaudus, p. 222.
Herdesian : see Consensus Orthodoxus.
Hereford Missal, p. 212.
Hesychius (or Isychius) of Jerusalem, p. 75, 265, 301, 309, 310, 338, 346.
Heurtley, Professor, p. 229, 283.
Hickes, p. 126.
Hieronymus (and Pseudo-Hieronymus), quoted —
    as to Presence, p. 36, 114.
    as to interpretation of John vi., p. 67.
    as to phrase "making the Body of Christ," p. 68, 69.
    as to sense of words of Institution, p. 70.
    as to Adoration, p. 114, 204.
    as to type in Eucharist, p. 273
    as to the Church being Christ's Body, p. 320.
    as to feeding on Christ's Body in the Scriptures, p. 339.
Hilarius Papa ? p. 281.
Hildebertus Cenom. (rather Turonensis), p. 331, 332, 350.
Hincmar, quoted, p. 36, 108, 206, 310, 311.
    referred to, p. 221.
Hittorpius, p. 236, 310, 324.
Hoesemius, Joannes, p. 3.
Homilies of Elfric, p. 125.
Homilies of the Church of England, p. 345.
Honoratus, St. Augustine's Letter to, p. 206.
Honorius III., Pope, p. 247.
Honorius Augustodunensis, p. 314, 324, 348.
Hook, Dean, p. 126.
Hooker, p. 31, 171, 172, 182, 186.
    quoted, p. 52, 149 *seq.*, 177, 318.
Hospinian, quoted, p. 131, 243.
    referred to, p. 2, 4, 7, 11, 28, 184.
Huetius, p. 287.
Hugo de Sancto Victore, p. 237.
Hugo Lingonensis, p. 264. 266.
Hugo, as quoted by Waldenses, p. 300, 301.

Ignatius, p. 59.
Innocentius I., Pope, p. 275.
Irenæus, p. 32, 59, 60, 65, 213, 287.
Isidorus Hispalensis, p. 75, 78, 120, 151, 222, 235, 259, 263, 278, 310, 347.
Isidorus Pelusiot., p. 209.
Isychius : see Hesychius.
Ivo of Chartres, p. 245, 324.

James, St. : see Liturgies.
James, Corruptions of Scripture, Councils, and Fathers, p. 89, 110 124, 239.
James of Edessa, p. 252.
James of Nisibis, p. 306.
James the Lord's brother, Liturgy bearing his name, p. 196, 311.
Jerome : see Hieronymus.
Jewel, on Adoration as taught by St. Ambrose, p. 203.
  ,, ,, St. Augustine, p. 205, 206.
  ,, ,, Theodoret, p. 210, 211.
  ,, ,, Pseudo-Origen, p. 212.
 on Elevation, p. 244, 245.
Joannes Hierosolymitanus (Pseudo-), p. 256.
Jocelyn, p. 124.
Johai, Rabbi, p. 245.
John of Constantinople, p. 105.
Jovinianus, p. 116, 274.
Julian the Apostate, p. 157.
Julius, Pope, p. 263.
Justin Martyr, p. 32, 238, 292.

Keble, Rev. J., p. 205, 206, 213, 214, 225.
Ken, Bishop, p. 188.
Kettlewell, p. 188.
Kimmel, Monumenta Fid. Ec. Or., p. 227.
Kohlius, p. 70.
Krantz, p. 179.

Labbe, p. 282.
Labbæus, Concil., p. 91, 152, 218, 259.
Lactantius, p. 196.
Lambertinus, p. 5, 7, 236, 247,
La Milletière, p. 47.

Lanfranc, p. 94.
L'Aroque, History of Eucharist, p. 1, 7, 84, 179, 214, 240, 245.
Laski : see A Lasco.
Laud, Archbishop, p. 141.
Laudian Theology, Real Presence of, p. 305.
Le Brun, p. 193, 236, 244, 247, 250.
Le Comte, p. 221.
Lee, Rev. F. G., quoted, p. 38.
Leibnitz, p. 168, 169.
Le Moyne, p. 106.
Leo Magnus, p. 320, 321, 328.
Leontius Byzant., p. 274.
Leo Tuscus, p. 240.
Libri Carolini : see Carolus Magnus.
Lightfoot, Professor, p. 287.
Lingard, p. 125.
Linwood, p. 245.
L'Isle, p. 297.
Litany of Sacred Heart, p. 26.
Liturgy of Apostolical Constitutions, p. 34, 229, 261.
Liturgy, Mozarabic, p. 51, 230, 231, 316.
Liturgy, Syriac, of Pope Xystus, p. 196, 157.
    Syriac, of St. James the Lord's brother, p. 196, 311.
    of St. Mark, p. 225, 226.
    of Chrysostom, p. 228, 229, 240, 250, 316.
    of James Baradæus, p. 228.
    of John Bassora, p. 228.
    of Abyssinia, p. 230.
    Coptic (St. Gregory), p, 230, 231.
    Alexandrian (St. Gregory), p. 230.
    Gallician, p. 230.
    of St. James, p. 229, 231, 232, 315, 316.
    Armenian, p. 243, 251, 252, 348, 349.
    of St. Basil, p. 229, 275, 289.
Llandaff, Bishop of, p. 143.
Lorichius, p. 245.
Lyons and Vienne, Church of, p. 325.
Lyranus, p. 158.

Mabillon, Museum Ital., p. 236, 246.
Macarius Ægypt., p. 289, 336, 337.

Mai, Script. Vet. Nova Collectio, p. 332, 350.
Mahusius, p. 112.
Maitland, p. 9, 143, 282.
Malan, Rev. S. C., p. 226.
Mamertus, Claudianus, p. 299.
Mansi, Concil., p. 91, 152, 209, 218.
Marcellus Ancyranus, p. 298.
Maresius, p. 186.
Martene, De Ant. Eccl. Rit., p. 248.
Martyr, Justin, p. 32, 238, 292.
Martyr, Peter, p. 161.
Masius, Andr., p. 275, 289.
Mason, Vindicæ Eccles. Angl., p. 180.
Maurus: see Rabanus.
Maxentius, p. 322.
Maximus the Scholiast on Pseudo-Dionysius, p. 133, 235, 244, 269, 286, 287, 302.
Mayence, Council of, p. 247.
Menardus, p. 237, 246.
Mendham, p. 107.
Methodius, p. 146, 147.
Meynard: see Menardus.
Micrologus, p. 246.
Micronius, p. 137.
Middleton, Letter from Rome, p. 207.
Migne, p. 345.
Milman, Latin Christianity, p. 131.
Milton, Rev. W., p. 77, 195, 314, 345.
Missal, p. 26, 193.
     of Hereford, p. 212.
Moehler, p. 213.
Montfaucon, p. 108, 109.
Morinus, p. 235.
Morley, Bishop, p. 25.
Morton, Bishop, on Eucharist, p. 5, 51, 52, 148, 206, 215, 240, 295.
Mosheim, p. 2.
Moulin, Du, p. 161, 184.
Moyne, Le, p. 106.
Mozarabic L.: see Liturgies.
Muratori, p. 6, 7, 67, 93, 115, 117, 118, 216, 236.
Museum Italicum: see Mabillon.

Neale, Dr., p. 44, 46, 225, 226, 231, 232, 241, 242, 251, 315.
Neander, p. 217, 264.
Nestorius, p. 64.
Newman, Dr., p. 142.
Nicæa, or Nice : see Councils.
Nice : see Councils.
Nicephorus Constantinopolitanus, p. 91, 108, 290.
Nicholson, Bishop, p. 184.
Nicolas : see Cabasilas.
Nicole, p. 46, 47.
Nisibis, James of, p. 305, 306.

Oakley, p. 211, 237.
Odo of Paris, p. 247.
Œcumenius, p. 164, 324.
Onuphrius Panvinius, p. 4, 5.
Optatus, p. 215, 318.
Opus Imperfectum in Matt. in Op. Chrys., p. 35, 109, 110.
Ordo Communis Liturg. Syr., p. 197, 228.
Ordo Romanus, p. 235, 246.
Origen and Pseudo-Origen, p. 96, 97, 266.
 as to interpretation of John vi., p. 66, 100, 101.
 as to sense of words of Institution, p. 72, 73, 97, 98, 132.
 as to local circumscription of body, p. 149.
 as to Adoration, p. 212.
 as to use of ἀντίτυπα, p. 287.
 as to sense of *signum*, p. 301.
 as to Christ's Body being spiritually eaten in the Scriptures, p. 332—335.
Oudin, p. 280.

Pachymeres, p. 215, 243, 269, 287.
Palladius, p. 106, 284.
Panstratia Catholica : see Chamier.
Panvinius, p. 4, 5.
Papers on the Doctrine of the Church of England concerning the Eucharistic Presence, p. 26.
Parasceve Paschæ, p. 183.
Parisiensis, Joannes, p. 19.
Parker, Archbishop, p. 124.
Paschasius, p. 56, 57, 131, 281.
Patrick, p. 89, 103, 133, 233.

Paula, p. 254.
Paulinus of Nola, 328, 343.
Payne, Prebendary, p. 7, 9, 10, 15, 21, 29, 30, 185, 193, 194, 199, 200, 201, 216, 227, 228, 234, 235, 238.
Pelagius (?), Commentary on 1 Cor. xi., p. 293.
Perkins, p. 182, 186.
Perpetuity of the Faith, p. 46, 47.
Perrone, J., p. 22.
Perronius: see Du Perron.
Petrus Benedictus, p. 277.
Petrus Blessensis, p. 349.
Petrus de Vincis, p. 270.
Petrus Damiani: see Damiani.
Pfaffian Fragments of Irenæus, p. 261, 287.
Philadelph., Gabriel, p. 241, 242.
Philo Carpath., p. 344.
Picherellus, p. 77.
Porphyry, p. 153.
Primasius, p. 164, 295, 296.
Proclus, quoted, as to Presence, p. 35.
Procopius of Gaza, p. 69, 91, 268, 272, 274.
Prosper, p. 129, 308.
Pusey, Dr., p. 19, 44, 49, 94, 205, 266, 277, 280, 284.

Rabanus Maurus, p. 75, 83, 164, 224, 236, 263, 275, 323, 348.
Radulphus Flaviacensis, p. 301.
Ranchinus, p. 348.
Ratramnus: see Bertram.
Raulin, p. 242.
Raynaldus, Theoph., p. 221.
Reformation, Essays on, p. 44.
Remigius of Auxerre, p. 294, 296, 323, 324.
Renaudot, p. 195, 215, 216, 226, 243, 248, 249.
Rhemigius: see Remigius.
Rhenanus, p. 93.
Ricaut's Present State of the Greek and Armenian Churches, p. 227, 241, 244.
Ridley, p. 186.
Riva, p. 3.
Robbe, p. 101.
Robertson, Canon, p. 2, 5, 87.
Robertson's translation of Moehler's Symbolism, p. 213.

Rock, Dr., Church of our Fathers, p. 127, 128.
    Hierurgia, p. 225.
Romanoff's Liturgy of St. Chrysostom, p. 240, 242.
Romish Mass and English Church, p. 89, 177, 178, 232.
Routh, Dr., p. 124, 126, 127.
Ruffinus Aquil., p. 340.
Rupertus Tuitiensis, p. 84, 127, 255, 311.

Sacramentarium Gelasianum, p. 227.
    Gregorianum, p. 237, 238.
Sacraments, the Doctrine of, in relation to the Doctrines of Grace, p. 31.
Sadeel, p. 161, 184.
Sadler, Rev. M. F., p. 10, 226.
Salisbury Manual, p. 229.
Salvianus Massil., p. 328.
Samona, p. 268.
Schröekh, p. 87.
Scotus, Johannes, p. 130.
Scrivener, p. 285.
Scudamore, Notitia Eucharistica, p. 9, 11, 230, 241, 243, 247, 252, 280.
Sedulius Scotus, p. 164.
Severus, Episcopus Aschmonin, p. 250.
Shuttleworth, Bishop, p. 44.
Sixtus Senensis, p. 111, 281.
Smith's Account of the Greek Church, p. 226, 240, 241, 244.
Soames, Rev. H., Latin Church in Anglo-Saxon Times, p. 57, 126, 131.
    Anglo-Saxon Church, p. 125, 128.
    Bampton Lectures, p. 125, 237, 238, 279.
Spina, Alphonso de, p. 168, 173, 174.
Spinkes, p. 180, 188, 189.
Stephanus Junior, p. 272, 279, 291.
Stephens, Dr., p. 189, 192.
Stillingfleet, Bishop, p. 16, 39, 40, 41, 42.
Strabo, Walafrid, p. 297.
Suarez, p. 15.
Suicer, p. 64, 267.
Surius, p. 272, 279, 291.
Symeon of Thessalonica, p. 242, 252.
Synesius, p. 64.

Synod of Exeter, p. 247.
Synodon Carisiacum, p. 348.

Tatian, p. 156.
Taylor, Bishop Jeremy, quoted—
    as to local Presence, p. 160.
    as to Adoration, p. 188, 209.
Taylor, Rev. J., True Doctrine of Eucharist, p. 53, 212.
Tennison, Archbishop, p. 42.
Tertullian, quoted—
    as to evidence of senses, p. 24.
    as to Mysteries, p. 53, 54.
    as to doctrine of Marcion, p. 58, 59.
    as to reality of Christ's Body, p. 61.
    as to sense of words of Institution, p. 66, 67, 72, 92, 94, 273, 276, 277.
    as to interpretation of John vi., p. 66.
    as to phrase, "making the Body of Christ," p. 68.
    as to invisibility of a body, p. 146.
    as to the waters of Baptism, p. 229.
    as to representation of Christ's Body, p. 94, 262.
    as to interpretation of Jerem. xi. 19, p. 273.
    as to figure in Eucharist, p. 276, 277.
    as to use of *memoria*, p. 292.
    as to Christ's Word being His flesh, p. 332.
Tetralogia Liturgica : see Neale.
Theodoret, quoted—
    as to reality of Christ's Body, p. 62.
    as to local limitations of Christ's Body, p. 270.
    as to sense of words of Institution, p. 71, 74, 102, 103, 104, 132, 268, 284.
    as to Adoration, p. 207, 208, 209, 210.
    as to use of term εἰκών, p. 268, 298.
    as to interpretation of Jerem. xi. 19, p. 273.
    as to type in Eucharist, p. 274, 301.
    as to use of σύμβολον, p. 284, 285, 286.
    as to use of ἀντίτυπον, p. 291.
    as to death the condition of the *res sacramenti*, p. 309.
Theodorus Heracleotes, p. 67, 336.
Theodotus Antiochenus, p. 290.
Theodotus the Heretic, p. 318.

Theophilus of Alexandria, p. 98, 99, 262.
Theophylact, p. 267.
Theoria Rerum Eccles. : see Germanus.
Thesaurus Eccles. of Suicer, p. 267, 268.
Thomas Waldensis : see Waldensis.
Thompson's Edition of the " Testimonie of Antiquitie," p. 124.
Thorndike, Herbert, p. 140.
Thorp, p. 126.
Thrasybulus, p. 272.
Thuanus, p. 179.
Tillotson, p. 217.
Times, Correspondent of, from Rome, p. 36, 37.
Titus Bostrensis, p. 146, 147.
Toutte'e, p. 173, 267, 288.
Tracts for the Day, p. 18, 135.
Trent, Council of, p. 192.
Trevor, Canon, p. 205.
Trithemius, Joannes, p. 131.
Trullo, Council in, p. 53.
Turretin, p. 29, 30, 160, 161, 184, 201, 208.
Turrian, p. 105, 267.
Turton, Bishop, p. 25, 80, 166, 168, 170.

Ullmann, p. 331.
Ultramosanus, p. 3.
Ursinus, p. 161, 184.
Ussher, Archbishop, p. 4, 5, 86, 124, 127, 132, 218.
Utenovius, p. 137, 172, 173, 176.

Valckenier, p. 201.
Valentia, Gregory de, p. 15, 20, 115, 192, 193.
Valerianus, p. 328, 329.
Vallarsius ; *Admonitio* on the Epistle to Paula and Eustochium, p. 204.
Varia Sacra of Le Moyne, p. 106.
Vasquez, p. 105, 212, 267.
Vercelli, Council of, 131.
Vergil, Polydore, p. 7.
Victor Antiochenus, p. 103, 284.
Vienne and Lyons, Church of, p. 325.

Vigilius Tapsensis, p. 333; quoted—
  as to local circumscription of human body, p. 145, 151.
  as to spiritual touching and tasting by faith, p. 344.
Villiers, De, p. 85, 86.
Vogan, Prebendary, True Doctrine of the Eucharist, p. 9, 16, 29, 185, 189, 190, 214, 300, 303, 304, 305.
Vossius, G. I., p. 184.

Wake, Archbishop, p. 16, 39, 47, 48, 105, 106, 107, 187, 202.
Walafrid Strabo : see Strabo.
Walchius, p. 46, 47, 168.
Waldenses, Confession of, p. 330.
Waldensis, Thomas, p. 300, 301.
Warnantius, p. 3.
Wastelius, p. 256.
  referred to, p. 59, 164.
Waterland, quoted, p. 52, 288, 289.
Weismann, p. 217.
Wessel of Gansfort, p. 331.
White, Bishop, Reply to Fisher, p. 182.
Wimpheling, p. 282.
Wiseman, Cardinal, p. 80.
Woodhead, p. 22.
Wordsworth, Bishop, p. 3, 7.
Wright, p. 306.

Zuingle, p. 25, 31, 36.
Zurich Ministers, p. 29.

INDEX OF SUBJECTS.

Abraham, p. 243, 254.
Adoption of the Elements, Theory of, p. 54, 316.
Adoration: see Host.
    lower sense of, p. 236, 242, 243.
    not the purpose of the Eucharistic Presence, p. 178.
    as taught by English Divines, p. 185—190.
    as taught by the Fathers, p. 203 *sqq*.
    as taught by the Liturgies, p. 225 *sqq*.
Ælfric : see Elfric.
Aer, p. 251.
Agobard, his reforming tendency, p. 221, 223.
Alacoque, Marie, the Nun, p. 37.
Albigenses, the, p. 330.
Alcuin, p. 235, 294.
Ambrose of Cahors, p. 280.
'Ανάδειξις, p. 215, 216.
Analogy between the senses of the outer and the inner man, p. 329,
    sqq.
'Αναμνήσις, use of, p. 292 *sqq*.
'Αναφορά, p. 195.
Andrewes, Bishop, his views, p. 186, 187.
Anglo-Saxon Church, Faith of, p. 122, 125.
'Αντίτυπον, sense of, p. 64, 211, 212, 266, 267, 268, 274, 286, 289,
    290, 291.
    examples of, p. 287 *sqq*.
Aphraates, the author of the Sermons attributed to James of Nisibis,
    p. 306.
Apologists, their ridicule of that in Heathen idolatry which has its
    counterpart in the Mass, p. 153 *sqq*.
Apostles, sense in which they understood the words of Institution,
    p. 166 *sqq*.
Ark (or tabout?), adoration of, in Ethiopia, p. 242.

Armenian Church, Faith of, p. 276, 277.
Ascension of Christ, its bearing on the doctrine of the Eucharist,
p. 139, 140.
Aubertin unjustly accused of bad faith, p. 282.
Augmentation, theory of, p. 54, 218, 294, 295, 316.

Baptism, p. 54, 83, 118, 120, 177, 204, 229, 284, 321.
Basil, St., desired a part of the Eucharist to be buried with him,
p. 53.
Basil's Liturgy, p. 289.
Beguardi, p. 240, 244.
Beguinæ, p. 240, 244.
Bell, sacring, p. 11.
Benedict XII., Report made to him as to the faith of the Armenians,
p. 276, 277.
Berberini MS., p. 230.
Berengarius, Confession of, p. 56.
 misunderstood by Hugo Lingonensis, p. 264.
Blandina, her confession concerning the Eucharist, p. 65.
 her martyrdom, p. 325.
Blood, question concerning Christ's having blood after Resurrection,
p. 89, 90.
Body of Christ, as crucified, not as glorified, the *res sacramenti* in the
Eucharist, p. 136, 137, 232, 233, 304, 305 *sqq*.
Bolsena, miracle of, p. 4.
Bulenger, Julius Cæsar, p. 287, 290.

Cabasilas, his views on the Eucharist, p. 333.
Canterbury, Dean of, p. 277, 306.
Carthusians, p. 247.
Ceres, worship of, p. 216.
Chalices, veneration of, p. 114, 209 : see Vessels.
Chancel, p. 251.
Change effected by consecration, p. 32, 229.
Charlemagne, his objection to the word *imago*, p. 279.
Chrism, p. 54.
Church, the, as truly the Body of Christ as the Eucharist, p. 317 *sqq*.
 of England in relation to Elevation and Adoration, p. 224,
 248.
Clement V., Pope, p. 2.

Communion of Christ's Body, a phrase interpretative of the words of Institution, p. 177.
of Devils and of the Lord's Table, p. 164, 295.
of Saints, supposed to comprehend the Real Presence, p. 134.
Conficere Corpus Christi, and similar expressions, p. 68, 69.
Consubstantiation needless for Communion, p. 177.
Contradictions, p. 181.
Contradictory doctrines, p. 331.
Controversy, p. 202.
Corinthian Christians, their faith as to the Eucharist, p. 165.
Corporal : see Presence.
Corpus Christi, Festival of, p. 2, 5, 6.
some Romanists almost ashamed of it, p. 179.
Corruptions of Patristic testimonies, p. 84, 102, 106, 124, 144, 145, 239, 347.
Creeds, ancient, contain no article on the Real Presence, p. 133.
Cross, language of Augustine and Damascenus concerning, p. 35.
worship of, p. 157, 209, 237.
Cyprian, observations on his language, p. 261, 262.

David's words concerning the Well of Bethlehem, p. 174.
Dead, the, their participation in the Eucharist according to Cabasilas, p. 333.
Dean of Canterbury, p. 277, 306.
Death the condition of the *res sacramenti* in the Eucharist, p. 136, 137, 232, 303 *sqq*.
De Sacramentis, probably the work of Ambrose of Cahors, p. 280.
Development of doctrine, p. 36, 179.
De Villiers, his interpolated edition of Fulbertus Carnotensis, p. 83 *sqq*.
Diana, festival of, p. 7, 8.
Docetæ, p. 58.
Donation effectual in Eucharist, p. 180.
Druthmar, Christian, Protestants accused of falsifying his testimony, p. 281, 282.
curious edition of his comment on St. Matthew, p. 282.
Du Perron, Cardinal, his Confession concerning Transubstantiation, p. 105, 106.
Durandus, the first to connect Elevation with Adoration, p. 245.

Eastward position, p. 37.

Ebionites, p. 59.
Ecloga of Amalarius, p. 236.
Εἰκών, p. 91, 218, 259, 260, 268 *sqq.*, 298.
Ἐκκλησις, p. 213.
Elements, consecrated, given to school-children, p. 9.
    sent by a boy, p. 9.
    the "worship" due to them, p. 32, 33.
Elevation : see Host.
Elfric, p. 123 *sqq.*, 224.
English Church in relation to Elevation and Adoration, p. 224, 248.
Entrance, the greater, p. 242, 316.
Ἐν τυπῷ, p. 214, 254.
Ἐπίκλησις, p. 213.
Ethiopian Eunuch, p. 265.
Ethiopians, their customs as to the Eucharist, &c., p. 242.
Eusebius of Emessa, Homily falsely attributed to him, p. 345.
Eustochium, p. 204.
Eutychians, p. 61, 63.
Eva, p. 2.
Extension of the Incarnation, p. 17.

Faith that which receives and eats, p. 330 *sqq.*
Fathers, the, their teaching as to Eucharistic worship, p. 203 *sqq.*
Figura, sense of, p. 301.
    as applied to Eucharist, p. 276 *sqq.*
    new sense given to, p. 280.
    distinguished from *Imago*, p. 279, 280.
Figure, p. 180.
Freeman, Archdeacon, his peculiar interpretation of τὰ ἅγια τοῖς ἁγίοις, p. 243.
Friday, Good, ritual of, p. 237.
Fulbert of Chartres, his views, p. 294, 297.

Gelasius Cyz., his account of the Nicene Council, p. 313, 314.
God, not man, the Giver of the *res sacramenti*, p. 317, 318.
Good Friday, ritual of, p. 237.
Gorgonia, p. 211.
Gospel, spoken of as the Body of Christ, p. 330 *sqq.*
    elevation of, p. 239, 240, 244.
Greeks, their tokens of excessive reverence, p. 241.
    their customs as to Elevation, &c., p. 251.
Guidó, p. 247.

Heart, the Sacred, p. 36, 37.
Heathens, their ridicule of Christians, p. 157.
       ridiculed by Christians, p. 153, 154, 156.
Heb. xiii. 10, sense of, p. 266, 267.
Hildebert and his teaching, p. 331, 332.
Hincmar, his views, p. 310.
Honorius III., Pope, p. 40, 247.
Host, adoration of, p. 40.
     elevation of, p. 11, 237, 239 *sqq*.
Hypostatical union, p. 20 *sqq*.

Idolatry in the adoration of the Host, p. 199 *sqq*.
     not excused by mistake, p. 201.
Image and pledge applied to Eucharist, p. 237.
Image-worship, p. 239, 291.
Images, claim made for them to rank with the Eucharist, p. 280.
Imaginarius, p. 272
Imago, p. 91, 237, 270, 271, 272, 279, 280, 299, 300.
Impanation, p. 22.
Incarnation in relation to Eucharist, p. 136.
Inclination during the Canon, p. 236.
Incognito of a Prince, p. 29.
Infallibility of the Pope, p. 141.
Ink, consecrated wine mixed with, p. 53.
Innocent III., p. 11.
Institution, words of, p. 72 *sqq*., 76, 77, 168 *sqq*., 177.
Intelligibilis, and similar terms, p. 264.
Intense adoration, prayer of, p. 225.
Interpretative Dicta of the Fathers, p. 48, 253 *sqq*., 260 *sqq*.
     modes of expression, p. 261 *sqq*.
Invisibility as applied to a body, p. 146, 147.
Isidorus Hispalensis, p. 235, 347.
Ivo of Chartres, p. 245.

James of Nisibis, Homilies falsely attributed to him, p. 306.
Jeremiah xi. 19, interpretation of, p. 273.
Jesuit intrigues, p. 246, 238, 239.
Jews, their view of the words of Institution, p. 167.
     their derision of adoration of the host, p. 158.
Jocelyn, p. 124.

John vi., interpretation of, p. 65, 66, 67, 79, 80, 82, 314, 318, 321,
334, 335, 337, 338.
John of Constantinople, p. 105.
Juliana, p. 1.
Julian the Apostate, p. 157.
Justin Martyr, his account of the Eucharist, p. 238.

Kneeling at reception, p. 40, 227.

Labbe, Father, his accusation of Aubertin, p. 292.
Lambeth Library, p. 90, 107, 282.
Lanfranc, p. 125.
Light borne before host, p. 11.
Liturgical writers, p. 235 *sqq*.
Liturgies, p. 11, 12, 225 *sqq*.
 their general structure, p. 229.
Liturgy of St. Basil, its doubtful character, p. 289.
Local circumscription of human body, p. 144 *sqq*., 268, 270.
 Presence, p. 160, 161, 162, 192.
Lutheran doctrine of Eucharist, p. 28, 177.
 divines, p. 173.
Lux Mundi, p. 331.
Lyons, Church of, p. 40, 248, 281.

Magister contradictionum, p. 331.
Manichæan heretics, p. 144, 198, 201.
Martha, p. 327, 328.
Materialistic notions of Eucharist, p. 51, 52, 56, 57, 330, 331.
Matter, the question of its existence, p. 169.
Marcus the Magician, p. 213.
Martyr: see Justin.
Maximus, p. 235.
Melchizedec, p. 242, 254, 267, 289.
Memoria, &c., applied to Eucharist, p. 292 *sqq*., 302.
Metaphysicians, p. 169.
Μεταβάλλειν, p. 50.
Μεταρυθμίζειν, p. 50.
Μετασκευάζειν, p. 50.
Μεταστοιχειοῦν, p. 50.
Μεταποιεῖσθαι, p. 49.
Messalians, p. 59.

Micrologus, p 246.
Miracles, p. 24, 25.
Μνημόσυνον, use of, p. 292 *sqq*.
Moon obscured in Juliana's vision, p. 1.
Mouth of the soul, p. 330, 336.
Mystery, ambiguity of the term, p. 181.
Mysteries, p. 53.
    Christ adored in, p. 204.
Mysterium, p. 70, 108, 120, 257.

Nestorius, Doctrine of, p. 64.
New Testament : see Testament.
Nicholas, Pope, p. 56.
Nisibis, James of, p. 305, 306.
Νοήτος, and similar terms, p. 264.

Oblation, its position in ancient Liturgies, p. 229, 283.
Odo of Paris, p. 247.
Oil, sacrament of, addressed, p. 215.
    the effect of the invocation upon it, p. 229, 267.
Old Testament, Sacraments of, p. 221.
Ὁμοίωσις, p. 300.
Opus Imperfectum in Matthæum, MSS. of, p. 111.
Oral manducation, p. 81.
Ordo Romanus, p. 235.
Orvieto, Cathedral of, p. 4.
Outlined sketch, p. 223.

Partaking of devils compared with partaking of Eucharist, p. 164, 295.
Paschasian doctrine, p. 55.
Past things present to faith, p. 311.
Paul, St., explains the words of Institution, p. 177.
Paula, p. 204.
Penitent thief, prayer of, p. 250, 251.
Persians, sacred fire of, p. 8.
Person of Christ not present in the elements, p. 225.
Petavius, MS. of Fulbert's writings belonging to, p. 85.
Pfaffian fragments of Irenæus, p. 261, 287.
Phantasiasts, p. 60.

Pictures, adoration of, p. 242.
    in their relation to sacramental symbols, p. 256, 268, 269, 286, 290, 291.
Pignus, memoria, &c., applied to Eucharist, p. 292 *sqq.*, 302.
Pledge applied to Eucharist, p. 237, 302.
Πνευματικῶς, sense of, p. 67, 289, 314, 335, 336.
Polemon, p. 219.
Poor, the, Christ's representative Presence in them in its bearing on the Eucharist, p. 325 *sqq.*
Pope, the, receives sitting, p. 40.
Prayers of ancient Liturgies, not addressed to Christ as present in the host, p. 225, 228, 230, 231, 250, 251.
Presence, lax language concerning, p. 35, 209.
    of things past to faith, p. 311.
    of Christ, distinctions as to, p. 15, 16, 161, 162; patristic conception of, p. 33, 34, 35, 36, 231, 250, 251, 313;
    patristic distinction between corporal and spiritual, p. 149.
    of Christ in the poor, p. 325 *sqq.*
    Real, a new term, p. 33.
    Real, the definition of its mode, p. 186, 187.
Priest related to Christ as the Sacrament to Christ's Body, p. 255.
Procession of Corpus Christi, p. 7.
Προσκύνησις, p. 157, 208, 209, 241, 242, 249.
Prostration, p. 233, 240, 241.
Prothesis, p. 241, 316.
Πρωτότυπον, p. 91.
Proxy, deliverance of a gift by a, p. 180, 181.

Rabanus Maurus, p. 236, 237.
Real Objective Presence needless for purposes of Communion, p. 177.
Red Sea, a type of Baptism, p. 223.
Relics, p. 128.
Remission of sins—the living bread, p. 330, 338.
Renaudot, his note on Elevation, p. 248 *sqq.*
Repræsento, sense of, p. 94.
Res sacramenti, the, given by God, p. 317, 318, 333.
    in state of death, p. 136, 137, 232, 303 *sqq.*
    the object of spiritual senses, p. 329 *sqq.*
Rhemigius of Auxerre, his views, p. 294.
Rock in the wilderness, p. 77, 78, 224.

Rubric, Black, p. 42, 43.
  of the Mass, p. 193.
  of the English Church before the Reformation, p. 248.
Rupert of Deutz, his views, p. 311.

Sacrament, including the species, adored in the Church of Rome, p. 192 *sqq*.
Sacraments, p. 253 *sqq.*, 257 *sqq.*
  of the Old and New Law, p. 220 *sqq.*, 254, 255.
Sacramental union, p. 182 *sqq.*, 270.
Sacred Heart, p. 36, 37.
Sacrifice, p. 178, 230, 232, 233.
"quasi sacrum factum," p. 259.
School-children, remains of Eucharist given to, p. 8.
Scriptures, Christ's Body said to be eaten in them, p. 330 *sqq*.
Senses, evidence of, p. 24.
  spiritual, p. 329 *sqq*.
Sepulchre, worshipped, p. 209.
Sigeric, Archbishop of Canterbury, p. 125.
Signs, p. 257 *sqq*.
Signum, examples of its use, p. 275 *sqq*.
  its sense, p. 301.
Similitudo, p. 270 *sqq.*, 272, 300.
Sketched outline, compared with Sacraments of the Old Testament, p. 223.
Σκιά, p. 271, 273, 284.
Sorbonne, Doctors of, p. 106.
Species, sense of, p. 262, 276.
Spiritual senses, which have for their object the *res sacramenti*, p. 329 *sqq*.
Spodicon, p. 249.
Stall, Christ worshipped in, p. 204, 209.
Σύμβολον, used as equivalent to τύπος, p. 274.
  used as equivalent to ἀντίτυπον, p. 286.
  examples of its use, p. 282 *sqq*.
  its sense, p. 302.
Sun, worship of, p. 223, 224.
Superstitions, with reference to monuments of martyrs, p. 143.
Superstitious additions to the faith of the Eucharist, p. 53, 213.
Suppositum, one, p. 21, 22, 194.
Supra-local Presence, plea of, p. 160 *sqq*.

Supremacy of the Pope, p. 142.
Sursum corda, p. 195, 199.
Symbolical Body, p. 96, 97.

Τὰ ἅγια τοῖς ἁγίοις, p. 243, 249, 252.
Tabout, p. 242.
Testament, the New, in the Eucharistic cup, p. 307, 309, 339.
Theoria Rerum Eccles., p. 235.
Transfigurans, use of the term, p. 320.
Transubstantiation needless for Communion, p. 177.
  early history of the term, p. 349, 350.
Τύπος, and ἐν τύπῳ, p. 214, 273 *sqq.*, 300, 301.
  used as equivalent to ἀντίτυπον and σύμβολον, p. 274.

Union, hypostatical, p. 20, 22.
  sacramental, p. 182 *sqq*.
Urban IV., Pope, p. 2.

Veil of Chancel, p. 244.
Vessels of Eucharist, p. 116, 117, 291 : see Chalices.
Vestments, Eucharistic, p. 38.
Vienne, Council of, p. 2.
  Church of, p. 325.
Villiers, De, p. 85 *sqq*.
Vine, its relation to Christ, as wine to His Blood, p. 72 *sqq*. 261, 307, 314, 331, 334, 336, 339, 342, 344.
Visions of Juliana, p. 1 *sqq*.
  of Maria Alacoque, p. 37.

Waldenses, the, p. 330.
Water, addressed as a person, p. 215.
  representing the people, p. 262, 263.
Wessel of Gansfort, called " Magister Contradictionum," p. 331.
Wimpheling's edition of Christian Druthmar in Matt., p. 281, 282.
Wine, consecrated, mixed with ink, p. 53.
Worship of that which is eaten, p. 156, 207.
Wulfsine, p. 123.
Wulstan, p. 123.

Zacchæus, p. 327, 328.

CORRIGENDA.

In *Papers on the Eucharistic Presence*, p. 228, line 11, for "of the misery of Mankind" read "of charity."

Ibid., p. 245, line 19, for "of St. Augustine" read "as of St. Augustine."*

Ibid., p. 261, omit lines 7, 8, 9.

Ibid., p. 480, lines 12, 13, for "written during the last revision, and published a few years after it," read "published in 1659, shortly before the last revision."

In *Real Objective Presence*, p. 41, foot-note, omit "L'Estrange."

In *Romish Mass and English Church*, p. 91, line 34, for "So *e.g.* St. Augustine says," &c. read "See *e.g.* St. Chrysostom, as quoted above, p. 85, note."

In *Eucharistic Worship*, p. 152, line 5, for "ever" read "even."

Ibid., p. 168, line 17, for "first appeared in 1487," read "was first printed in 1485 (?), having been written (it is said) in 1459."†

Ibid., p. 174, line 7, for "Nam" read "Unum."

Ibid., p. 213, line 29, for "corruptabilia" read "corruptibilia."

Ibid., p. 213, line 35, for "unquentum" read "unguentum"

Ibid., p. 216, line 15, for "baptismati" read "baptismate."

Ibid., p. 224, line 1, for "Adorara" read "Adora."

---

* The words quoted by Harding and others (after Gratian) as from St. Augustine, are found in Lanfranc, not in St. Augustine. (See Albertinus, De Eucharistia, pp. 471, 659.)

† I have in my possession a copy of an edition of 1485 (Nuremberg, A. Koberger). Fol. 1 commences thus: "Incipit prohemium fortalicii fidei: conscripti per quendam doctorem eximium ordinis minorum, Anno Domini MCCCCLIX in partibus occidentis."

BY THE SAME AUTHOR.

THE ROMISH MASS
AND
THE ENGLISH CHURCH.
WITH NOTES AND APPENDIX.

Price 2s. 6d.; in cloth, 3s. 6d.

POPULAR EDITION, 3d.

BY THE SAME AUTHOR.

THE DOCTRINE OF THE SACRAMENTS,

IN RELATION TO THE DOCTRINES OF GRACE, AS CONTAINED IN THE SCRIPTURES, TAUGHT IN OUR FORMULARIES, AND UPHELD BY OUR REFORMERS. 5s. 6d.

"This volume is from the same pen as the valuable series of papers on the Eucharistic Presence, of which we have had occasion more than once to speak in terms of high commendation. It is a short treatise, a *concio ad clerum*, prepared for a clerical meeting, enlarged. But it is very thoughtful, and comes from one who has both read for himself, and learned to think for himself. The work is the expression of that fuller appreciation of the nature and meaning of the sacraments, which we fully believe that God is working in the minds of Evangelical men through the means of controversy. We can remember the time when it was thought a suspicious thing to recognise the sacraments as means of grace: we fancy that in the present year (1872) very few men could be found to deny it. Of this we will not say higher—but of this more adequate view of the sacraments, an English Presbyter is a warm as well as an able advocate. . . . The subject is treated with equal accuracy and learning."—*Christian Advocate*, Feb. 1872.

BY THE SAME AUTHOR.

POPULAR EDITION of EUCHARISTIC WORSHIP IN THE CHURCH OF ENGLAND. 6d.

London: HAUGHTON & Co., 10, Paternoster Row.

BY THE SAME AUTHOR.

Now Ready. Cheap Edition (Abridged) of

Papers on the Doctrine of the English Church
CONCERNING THE
EUCHARISTIC PRESENCE.

Price 2s., or in ornamental cloth, 3s. 6d.; each No. separately, price 2d.

The original Edition can still be had, as under:

I.—*Views of our Reformers—Archbishops of Canterbury.*
II.—*Views of our Reformers—Reformers of the Reigns of Henry VIII. and Edward VI.*
III.—*Views of our Reformers—Reforming Divines of the Reign of Queen Elizabeth.*
IV.—*Books of Sanction.*
V.—*The Homilies.*

(PRICE SIXPENCE EACH.)

VI.—*The Catechism.*
VII.—*The Order of the Administration of the Lord's Supper.*
VIII.—*The Thirty-nine Articles.*

(PRICE ONE SHILLING EACH.)

Index: (1) *Of Authors quoted*, (2) *Of Subjects*. (Price 6d.)
Supplement, containing—

I.—*The Real Objective Presence: Questions suggested by the Judgment of the Arches Court in the Bennett Case.*
II.—*Postscript on "The Real Presence" of Laudian Theology.*

(PRICE SIXPENCE EACH.)

The whole Series bound in Two Volumes, ornamental cloth, 4s. each.
The Series without the Supplement, in One Vol., 6s.
The Doctrine of the Sacraments in Relation to the Doctrine of Grace. 5s. 6d.
A Word for Warning and Defence of the Church of England against Ritualism and Romanism. 6d.

London: WILLIAM MACINTOSH, 10, Paternoster Row.

The Principles of the Reformation. 3d.
Our Present Duty to the Church of England. 2d.
Maidstone: W. S. VIVISH.

www.ingramcontent.com/pod-product-compliance
Lightning Source LLC
Chambersburg PA
CBHW032012220426
43664CB00006B/219